Introductory Accounting

Introductory Accounting adopts a measurement approach to teaching graduate students the basics of accounting. Integrating both financial and managerial principles from the U.S. and around the globe, it links accounting to other areas of business (such as finance, operations, and management).

Providing students with the context to understand how and why accounting is a valuable part of business, readers will gain an understanding of accounting's role in financial analysis and managerial decision-making. Tinkelman discusses accounting as an imperfect measurement system, offering guidance on how quantitative data can benefit analysts and managers when used with an understanding of its limitations. The book is strongly grounded in research, and draws on plenty of examples and cases to bring these issues to life.

The conversational style of *Introductory Accounting* will appeal to MBA students, while key terms and illustrative problems make assignments easy for instructors. Additional materials for students and instructors are available on the book's companion website.

Daniel P. Tinkelman is Professor of Accounting, Taxation, and Legal Studies in Business at Hofstra University, USA. He teaches courses in financial accounting, financial statement analysis, and auditing.

"*Introductory Accounting* is a breath of fresh air in the accounting library. It dares to depart from the well-trodden path of introductory accounting texts by presenting accounting as a solution to a societal problem, beyond a set of rules. Tinkelman's problem-solving approach to accounting measurement, carefully embedded in research, will appeal to instructors and students, alike."

Shyam Sunder, Yale School of Management, USA

"In this innovative accounting text, Tinkelman combines financial accounting with managerial, introduces relevant research, and organizes topics better than other books. *Introductory Accounting* should be seriously considered for adoption by any accounting instructor."

**Baruch Lev, Leonard N. Stern School of Business,
New York University, USA**

"Tinkelman's *Introductory Accounting* is thoughtful and lucidly written, an admirable synthesis of the accounting profession's longstanding concerns with accounting measurement and modern social science. It provides an intellectually broadminded yet practical foundation in financial and managerial accounting for managers."

**Stephen G. Ryan, Leonard N. Stern School of Business,
New York University, USA**

 A range of further resources for this book is available at www.routledge.com/cw/Tinkelman

Introductory Accounting

A Measurement Approach for Managers

Daniel P. Tinkelman

*For Dave & Sam,
with love =

Dan*

Routledge
Taylor & Francis Group

NEW YORK AND LONDON

First published 2016
by Routledge
711 Third Avenue, New York, NY 10017

and by Routledge
2 Park Square, Milton Park, Abingdon, Oxon, OX14 4RN

Routledge is an imprint of the Taylor & Francis Group, an informa business

© 2016 Taylor & Francis

Library of Congress Cataloging in Publication Data
Tinkelman, Daniel P., author.
   Introductory accounting : a measurement approach for managers/Daniel Tinkelman.
      pages cm
   1. Managerial accounting. I. Title.
   HF5657.4.T56 2016
   658.15'11–dc23   2015024630

ISBN 978-1-138-95620-9 (hbk)
ISBN 978-1-138-95621-6 (pbk)
ISBN 978-1-315-66580-1 (ebk)

Typeset in Times New Roman
by Sunrise Setting Ltd, Paignton, UK

Printed and bound in the United States of America by
Edwards Brothers Malloy on sustainably sourced paper

Dedication

To my parents

Contents

Preface

General

For many years I have wanted to write a new introduction to accounting that truly advocates for the worth, complexity, and value of accounting as its own discipline. As I taught financial accounting using conventional texts, I noted that they typically placed the spotlight on decision-making, rather than accounting. If I were a student using one of those texts, I would want to become a decision-maker, not the person who simply follows some rules and puts some numbers together. This text, in contrast, focuses on the importance and difficulty of creating and communicating measurements about business. Both people who plan to become accountants, and those who plan to use the measurements, need to understand how the accounting measurement system works. They also need to understand its imperfections.

   Three quotations inspired me in writing this text:

> No science attains maturity until it acquires methods of measurement.
>
> *Logan Clendening*[1]

I passionately believe that measurement is important. The social sciences of economics and business, as empirical disciplines, rely heavily upon accounting measurements. Economists and business people need to understand the sources, benefits, and limitations of accounting data. It is equally important for accountants to understand the models used by economists and business managers, so that appropriate data can be generated.

> Accounting courses should present accounting as an information development and communication process. The central theme should be how information is identified, measured, communicated and used.
>
> *Accounting Education Change Commission*[2]

Too often, accounting is taught as a collection of rules dealing with isolated topics, such as inventory or stock dividends. Such an approach tends to be both complex and confusing, since there are few unifying themes. This text treats all forms of accounting as growing from the central concepts of measuring, communicating and using information.

> [G]iving economic accounts is a ubiquitous human practice; something that all of us do in diverse cultural, social, political, and economic settings.
>
> *C. Edward Arrington, and Jere R. Francis*[3]

Arrington and Francis remind us that, while a major function of accounting is to provide inputs to various decision models, a second function is to fulfill ethical and legal requirements to "account for" our performance while in a position of trust. Clear and honest accounting is a moral imperative. Within this book, ethical issues are discussed in every chapter in either the text or in problems, or both.

Why is Accounting a Core Course in Most Business Programs?

In modern business, accounting is used in two major tasks. First, it is a measurement system that generates data to support business decisions. In order to succeed, all graduate students of business need to understand how to obtain, communicate, and use data for decision-making. Second, accounting tracks (or "accounts for") the way managers have handled the duties and assets entrusted to them. Clearly, in the wake of the various business scandals of recent years, all managers need to understand how accounting fits into businesses' internal control systems.

My Approach

This text addresses the field of accounting broadly, as a measurement system that changes and adapts as necessary. The breadth of discussion shows itself in several ways.

First, the text integrates topics that traditionally have been studied in separate "financial accounting" and "management accounting" courses. Bringing these topics together within one framework helps demonstrate that the "best" accounting for an event always depends on the accounting's purpose.

Second, the text places the current U.S. and international accounting rules into both historical and international perspective. The history of how rules came to be adopted is discussed. It quickly becomes clear that neither current U.S. generally accepted accounting principles nor International Financial Reporting Standards are indisputable or immutable.

Third, the discussion includes insights from a variety of disciplines, such as linguistics, philosophy of science, behavioral science, information theory, and economics, to demonstrate that accounting does not exist in a vacuum. Each chapter includes a brief listing of some areas of research that may yield insights to improve accounting.

This course is aimed at graduate students.

A first course in accounting should serve two groups of students:

First, business students who are planning to major in fields other than accounting should emerge with an understanding of the potential value and limitations of accounting data. They should understand that what is the "right" piece of information depends upon the decision at hand. They should obtain general skills in understanding, controlling, and reporting quantitative data. They should learn enough about the accounting process to allow them to intelligently interact with accounting professionals.

Second, students intending to become accountants need to learn more than a collection of rules. The AICPA Core Competency Framework listed the following core competencies of accountants: decision modeling; risk analysis; measurement; reporting; research; and leveraging technology to develop and enhance functional competencies. While no one course can teach all these competencies, they are all addressed to varying degrees in this text.

Organization of the Text

After an introductory chapter, I spend four chapters discussing how accounting *should* function as a measurement system. By the end of Chapter 5, the student should realize that accounting can provide interesting, decision-useful data for a variety of purposes. Both internal decision-making and external analysis of financial statements are explained.

Once the student understands how things are supposed to work, it is time to indicate the various factors that in the real world complicate or limit the accountant's ability to create useful measurements. Chapters 6 through 11 deal with such issues as allocation, valuation, uncertainty, internal control, human reactions to being measured, and fraud. The discussion in these chapters is organized by measurement issue, not by account. The organization of this text is very different from conventional texts, which tend to discuss topics in the order they appear on the balance sheet and income statement. Here, bad debt reserves, contingencies, and the expensing of research and development are all related to the discussion of uncertainty, whereas they are typically treated in separate chapters in financial accounting textbooks. As a second example, the discount rate for capital budgeting is also sensitive to uncertainty, but would typically be treated in a managerial accounting text separately from issues of uncertainty in financial accounting.

To allow students the time needed to understand the major issues of measurement, I defer the introduction of debits and credits and the bookkeeping process until Chapter 11. Since the accounting equation is introduced in Chapter 2, by Chapter 11 students should be very familiar with analyzing transactions using the accounting equation. Chapter 12 employs standard journal entry notation, providing adequate practice for students to obtain mastery of the debit and credit system.

The problem of ensuring the reliability of accounting data is a critical one. The Sarbanes–Oxley Act of 2002 has highlighted the importance now being placed on internal controls over financial data. Chapter 11 discusses the COSO Framework for analyzing internal controls, and discusses a variety of traditional control techniques.

To conclude the course, the final chapter provides a case study of two people forming a publishing business. The case study builds on the topics in the first 11 chapters, showing how a business is accounted for, and how various accounting issues apply to even a simple business. The case study also introduces three new topics: forms of doing business; rules for distinguishing employees and contractors; and different ways businesses obtain financing.

A variety of chapter-end problems are provided to support a variety of instructional approaches. Each chapter includes the following types of problems or exercises:

- Comprehension questions. These basically test recall and comprehension of key terms and numerical ideas.
- Application questions. These questions require the student to use concepts in the chapter to solve problems. They might involve numbers (e.g. given a trial balance, compute equity and net income) or the verbal application of concepts to a new situation.
- Discussion questions. These questions highlight the ambiguities and frontiers of accounting.

Some chapters also include questions requiring research or the use of spreadsheet or graphing techniques.

Conclusion

This preface began with two quotations. It ends with two more.

> In general, the first course in accounting should be an introduction to accounting rather than introductory accounting. It should be a rigorous course focusing on the relevance of accounting information to decision-making (use) as well as its source (preparation).[4]
>
> *Accounting Education Change Commission*

In this spirit, this text presents serious material, on an advanced conceptual level, not material "dumbed down" to be "introductory accounting." Since no one text can present all aspects of a complex discipline, the presentation throughout indicates areas where the interested student (or professor) can go beyond the "introduction to accounting" to a better acquaintance with the field.

The second quotation, from a 1924 address by noted accounting scholar Henry Rand Hatfield, puts my hopes for this text eloquently (although in the gender-biased language of his time):

> I have tried to remove the stigma attached to accounting by showing that in its origin it is respectable, even academic; that despite its present disrepute it has from time to time attracted the attention of men of unquestioned intellectual attainment; that it justifies itself in that it has arisen to meet a social need, for its function is to place responsibility, to prevent fraud, to guide industry, to determine equities, to solve the all essential conundrum of business: "What are my profits?", to facilitate the government in its fiscal operations, to guide the business manager in the attempt to secure efficiency. Are not these efforts worthy of any man's attention?[5]

Notes

1 as cited by Neil deGrasse Tyson (1999), p. ix. Tyson, N. D. (1999). Measure for Pleasure. Foreword. In K. Ferguson, *Measuring the Universe: Our Historic Quest to Chart the Horizons of Space and Time* (pp. ix–xiii). New York: Walker & Company.

2 Accounting Education Change Commission (1990), p. 309. Accounting Education Change Commission. (1990). Objectives of Education for Accountants: Position Statement Number 1. *Issues in Accounting Education*, 5(2), 307–12.

3 C. Edward Arrington & Jere R. Francis (1993), p. 107. Arrington, C. E., & Francis, J. R. (1993). Giving Economic Accounts: Accounting as Cultural Practice. Accounting, Organizations, and Society, 18(2/3), 107–24.

4 Accounting Education Change Commission (1992), p. 250. Accounting Education Change Commission (1992). The First Course in Accounting: Position Statement Number 2. *Issues in Accounting Education*, 7(2), 249–51.

5 Henry Rand Hatfield (1924), p. 253. Hatfield, H. R. (1924). An Historical Defense of Bookkeeping. *The Journal of Accountancy*, 37(4), 241–53. In Hatfield's day very few women were accountants. That situation has changed dramatically over the past 30 years. A majority of accounting students in the U.S. today are women.

Acknowledgments

I wish to acknowledge the assistance and support of numerous people. First, I wish to thank my wife and family for their support and for encouraging me to become a professor. Second, I wish to thank Pace University and Hofstra University and my colleagues and assistants who have provided comments and support over the course of this endeavor, including: Miao Miao, Rudy Jacob, Lewis Schier, Mary Ellen Oliverio, Alan Rabinowitz, Bernard Newman, Nikhil Agrawanal, Ralph Polimeni, Cheryl Lehman and Nathan Slavin. And, of course, I wish to thank my students, who have helped me learn how to teach accounting.

Part 1
Introduction

1 Introduction to Accounting as a Measurement System

Outline

- Preliminary Thoughts
- Learning Objectives
- Why Approach Accounting as a Measurement System?
- Measurements and Measurement Systems
- Accounting is a Measurement System
- Areas of Knowledge Related to Accounting Measurement
- What Different Fields of Accounting Measure
- How Society Shapes Accounting
- How External Accounting Measurement Affects Society
- Measuring Shapes the Measurers

Preliminary Thoughts

Counting is the most fundamental quantitative procedure of science.

Yuji Ijiri (1967, p. 78, note 11)

There is no task so simple, yet so profound in its consequences, as the act of taking a measurement. The scientific and technological foundations of modern society depend upon it. Without it, that which we call knowledge would have little objective meaning and our understanding of the natural world would reduce to mythological proclamations.

Neil deGrasse Tyson (1999, p. ix)

When astrophysicists are at work, chances are we are trying to measure something about the universe. How tall? How far? How luminous? How massive? How hot? How big? How fast? How energetic?

Neil deGrasse Tyson (1999, p. xii)

Does accounting measure anything? Should accounting measure anything? Can accounting measure anything? If the answers to these questions are affirmative, what does, what should, or what can accounting measure? If the answers are negative, of what other use is accounting? And why are accountants so concerned with definitions of terms and discussions of ways of quantifying things?

R. J. Chambers (1965, p. 33)

Only with accounting . . . have economic concepts become coherent, comprehensive, axiomatic, codified, comparable, reportable, demonstrable, controllable and altogether account-able to the extent that we now know them.

Tomo Suzuki (2003, p. 69)

Learning Objectives

After studying this chapter, you should understand:

1   The nature of measurement systems
2   The different parts of accounting measurement systems
3   The criteria used to judge measurement systems' quality
4   That many academic fields are related to accounting measurement
5   The key objectives, objects and attributes of the financial and management accounting measurement systems
6   That accounting is shaped by the surrounding social system
7   That accounting systems affect the societies around them
8   Different perspectives on how accounting rules should be set
9   That managerial accounting changes as business needs change
10 That the role and image of accountants has changed over time.

Why Approach Accounting as a Measurement System?

There are various ways to approach the role of accounting. Accounting has been described as: a historical record; a branch of economics; an information system; a language; a form of rhetoric; a political activity; mythology (to justify decisions); magic;[1] a form of discipline and control; a method of domination and exploitation; ideology; and a commodity (Morgan 1988). While some of these descriptions may seem crazy, as one learns more about accounting each has some merit.

This book teaches accounting as a measurement system for several reasons:

1   Measurement is an essential characteristic of accounting. Accounting is used to measure and report on economic activities.
2   This approach highlights similarities of accounting issues with measurement issues in other fields. All social and natural sciences measure things. The text discusses broad, generally applicable concepts rather than the details of particular business transactions.[2]
3   Considering the measurement issues that arise in business helps us understand that accounting rules have evolved as imperfect solutions to measurement issues. Accounting is not just a collection of rules.
4   A measurement focus requires understanding how people use accounting reports. There are many types of users, who make many different decisions. Accounting is not a "one-size-fits-all" discipline. Instead, accounting must adapt to users' needs. Discussing how this adaptation process has worked in the past, and in different countries, provides insight into the differences in accounting in different times, in different countries, and in different aspects of business. Accounting is not immutable. As economic activities and the needs of users change, accounting changes. That process has occurred for millennia, and will continue to occur.
5   Finally, a measurement system, like a language, shapes our conceptions of reality. Language affects our thinking in two ways. First, it provides definitions, which limit what can be spoken of. Second, it defines relations between objects.[3] As Tomo Suzuki (2003, p. 69) notes, our thoughts about the economy are shaped by the way in which we learn about it:

We do not observe it with our direct senses. We observe the data of the economy, and a number of economic data take the form of statistics. An important question is whether statistics of numerical data best present the entity of economic society. There is no obvious logical reason why economic society has to take statistics as its form of presentation. Moreover, there is no apparent rationale why economic statistics have to take the form of accounting.

Measurements and Measurement Systems

Measurement in General: Definitions and Rules

A *measurement* is formally defined as a way of assigning numbers to objects. It is a special type of language. The purpose of measurement is to allow us to represent relations between objects by the relation between the numbers (Ijiri 1967).

For example, if we know the measured heights of two students, we can conclude, *even without looking at the students or knowing anything else about them*, that the student with the height of 6 feet is taller than the student with the height of 5 feet, because "6" is greater than "5." The height measurements summarize one characteristic of these two students in a way that can be easily communicated. Mathematics allows us to compare the two measures, even though we know nothing else about these students.

There are some fundamental rules for measurements.

1   Quantities are always defined *within* some class of objects. For example, the 5 foot *height* of one student and the 130 pound *weight* of another are measurements from different classes.
2   Quantities must be *additive*. If the 5-foot-tall student grows by six inches, his or her height will now be 5½ feet. The two students have a combined height of 11 feet.
3   The user must be *indifferent* between two items in the same class with the same measurement. Thus, the user must be willing to say two 5-foot-tall students are the same height (Ijiri 1967).
4   The measures must be *objective*, in the sense that different measurers should, within limits of error, come up with the same measurement (Micheli and Mari 2014).
5   The measures should come from *observations* of real world things (Micheli and Mari 2014).

Parts of a Measurement System

A *measurement system* is an organized way of creating, communicating and verifying useful measurements. A measurement system generally has the following components:

- *Objects* to be measured
- *Rules* for measuring *attributes* of the objects, and methods of forming *secondary measures*. The existence of rules implies the existence of *standard-setters* that create the rules
- *Measurers*
- *Verifiers*
- *Users* and their *decision models*
- *Communication or reporting* of measurements to users

For example, consider the measurement system needed to determine the total numbers of students of various heights in the United States.

- "Students in the United States" would be the *objects* of measure. But, what is a "student"? Do we mean children? Are university students, graduate students, or enrollees in adult education courses included? Are we planning to include students living in overseas possessions of the United States?

- Height would be the key *attribute*. *Secondary measures* might include totals of the students with various heights who meet other criteria, for example who are 8 years old.
- *Rules* for measurement and a measuring device must be chosen. Units of measure, such as inches or centimeters, must be determined, along with rules about what fraction of a measurement is to be reported. Procedures need to be uniform. For example, there need to be rules about how to deal with the effect of hair styles on measurements.
- *Standard-setters* are needed to create and publicize the measurement rules.
- *Measurers*, such as school nurses or doctors, would measure the students.
- Someone needs to *verify* that the measurements were collected properly and were transmitted and summarized properly.
- The entire measurement exercise only has a purpose if there is a *user*, for whom this information is input into some thought process or mental model.
- The measurements must be *reported* to the intended user. In some cases, it may also be important *not to communicate the data to unintended users*.

Relation of Measurement and Theory

Measurement systems and theories are always developed together. As a committee of the American Accounting Association wrote, in 1971:

> Theory construction and measurement development are inseparable. The theory specifies, in a conceptual sense, what is to be measured, how the measurements are to be manipulated, and what measurable outcomes one can expect. This implies that the theory is constrained by what can be measured. It also implies that the measurements interact with the theory in that the predicted occurrences will either be verified or falsified by separate measurements.
>
> *(American Accounting Association 1971b, p. 62)*

The student height example indicates the need for measurements and theory to proceed together. Without underlying theory, we don't know whether "students" should include both kindergarten children and graduate students. We don't know what subclassifications are appropriate. If the information is to be used to test hypotheses about children's growth rates from birth through age 10, then we would only include children of the appropriate age. If the hypothesis is about a subtle effect of environment on growth, we need exact measurements. If the information is being used by a manufacturer of school uniforms to determine how many of what size garments to produce, both the definition of the object of measure, and the degree of precision, would be different. However, once measurements of heights are performed, the scientists studying children's growth can form new hypotheses, requiring new types of measures.

Relations Between Parts of Measurement Systems

Different parts of the measurement system are *not* independent of each other. In particular, there is a critical relationship between the types of rules and the qualities required of the measurers. As Ijiri (1967) notes:

> If the measurement rules in the system are specified in detail, we expect the results to show little deviation from measurer to measurer. On the other hand, if the measurement rules are vague or poorly stated, then the implementation of the measurement system will require

judgment on the part of the measurer; hence the output of the measurement system is more likely to show wider deviation from measurer to measurer.

(p. 135)

In some fields, professionals are expected to use a great deal of discretion, and rules are either nonexistent or broadly specified. In the student height example, measurers are probably trusted to get the students to stand up straight, and to make rational decisions concerning the impact of unusual hairstyles. In other fields, the use of discretion is not desired, and rules tend to be quite specific. Where no discretion at all is required, the measurement can be computerized.

Theodore Porter (1995) suggests that quantitative measurements and precise standards for measurement arise when society does not trust the professionals to use their discretion wisely. One reason why U.S. accounting has developed so many rules is that tax authorities and investors do not trust companies to report objectively.

What Makes a Measurement System Good or Bad?

Certain criteria can help judge how good a measurement system is. Some criteria that have been suggested are:

- the theoretical fruitfulness of the qualities measured
- the power of the system to measure many things
- the ability to assign numbers to all objects we wish to measure
- clarity
- simplicity (Rudner 1966)
- relatively low cost.

Thus, a system that produces data that are directly usable for the intended purpose, can be applied in many circumstances, is simple to use, gives clear results, and is relatively low cost is a high-quality measurement system.

One final point needs to be made about measurement systems in general, and that is that a measurement of an object is never either totally accurate nor a complete description of the object. People often make the mistake of thinking a measurement is a complete description. As Richard Rudner (1966, p. 69) writes:

[T]he mistake involved consists in assuming that it is the function of science to *reproduce* "reality" and concluding that science is defective from the fact that it accomplishes no such thing. Basically, this error rests on a confusion between a description and what is described. Albert Einstein once remarked, it is not the function of science "to *give* the taste of the soup." To be a description of the taste of the soup is clearly not to *be* the taste of the soup. . . . Of course, if we are intelligent and lucky, and employ sensibly the information conveyed by the statements of science, we may be able to put ourselves into the position of tasting soup. But this is, of course, quite different from expecting that the statements of science (the ones *about* the taste of soup) are defective, or somehow fail, because *they* don't taste like soup.

Accounting is a Measurement System

Defining Accounting

One widely used definition of accounting was provided by the Accounting Principles Board, which stated that accounting is a system for providing "quantitative information, primarily financial in nature, about economic entities that is intended to be useful in making economic decisions" (APB 1970, para. 9). This definition is compatible with the concepts underlying a measurement system, but some of the components of a measurement system are assumed, not explicitly mentioned. For example, the information must obviously be provided by people, but the existence of measurers is not explicitly specified in the definition.

Components of the Accounting Measurement System

Accounting systems contain the various components of a measurement system. There are objects of measure, rules for measuring key attributes, standard-setters, measurers, verifiers, and users with decision models. However, a number of theoretical and practical issues make it hard for accounting to give clear and unambiguous measurements. (See Chapters 6 to 11.) The accounting measurement system's components are briefly described below.

The *objects* of accounting measurement can be companies, groups of companies, subdivisions of companies, governmental units, nonprofit organizations, other legal entities such as trusts, products, production activities, or people. We usually refer to the object of accounting measurement as an "*accounting entity*," or simply an "entity." The key point is that the user believes a separate measurement of the activities of that entity is useful. The objects and attributes of different fields of accounting are discussed below.

The "useful information" referred to by the APB corresponds to the *attributes* of a measurement system. Accounting *rules* for creating externally reported measurements are called "accounting standards." There are standard classifications of attributes of entities, such as their assets, liabilities, and cash flows. There are rules for when these attributes are considered to exist, how to quantify them, and how particular measures can be used to form additional, *secondary measures*, such as "net income" or "equity." In accounting, measures such as "income" and "equity" are always formed from the "bottom up," by adding up more basic measures to find totals. This is in contrast to some other fields where totals are independently calculated. Chapter 2 discusses how the basic accounting measurement rules function in principle.

There are a variety of accounting rule-makers (or "*standard-setters*"). Tax rules are set by Congress, the Internal Revenue Service ("IRS"), and the courts. Financial accountants in the United States follow what are called "generally accepted accounting principles" ("GAAP"). Some of these principles owe their authority to long practice, but others are actually promulgated by key organizations. In the United States, a private body called the Financial Accounting Standards Board ("FASB") has set standards for companies and nonprofit organizations since 1972. A similar body, the Governmental Accounting Standards Board ("GASB") sets standards for state and local governmental bodies. The Securities and Exchange Commission ("SEC") has authority to set rules for companies that sell securities on public exchanges. Internationally, companies in most countries follow standards set by the International Accounting Standards Board ("IASB"). Where these authoritative bodies have not set rules, accountants seek guidance from other sources, such as textbooks, publications of the American Institute of Certified Public Accountants ("AICPA"), or industry practices.

Clearly, financial accounting existed for many years before the founding of the APB or the FASB in the 20th century. Research shows that many accounting practices arose over time on the basis of the experience of accountants and practical necessity.[4] Common management accounting techniques spread through professional journals, training, and standardized accounting courses. Professional associations also helped educate accountants about best practices. For example, the IMA (formerly the Institute of Management Accountants) publishes guidelines for management accountants to follow.

The APB definition does not explicitly mention *measurers*, but the existence of measurers is assumed. Clearly someone must be doing the accounting. Traditionally, this was done by bookkeepers and accountants, but over time the amount of work performed by computers has increased tremendously. A large amount of sales and purchase information is now recorded by barcode scanners. The vast majority of processing of initial data into summary form is now performed electronically.

As noted above, the idea of verification is implicit in the APB definition. Accounting measures are *verified* by a variety of people. These include supervisors, internal auditors, external auditors, and tax authorities. Under U.S. law, external audits can only be performed by Certified Public Accountants, or CPAs. CPAs must be licensed. Generally, states require attainment of certain levels of education and experience, as well as passing the Uniform CPA Examination. Many other countries have similar rules. Auditors of public companies must also register with the Public Company Accounting Oversight Board, a federal body. Internal auditors do not need to meet any special legal requirements, but many have obtained certification as Certified Internal Auditors.

There is a great variety of *users* of accounting measurers, who have different *decision models*. This is discussed in more detail later in this chapter.

More About Objects and Attributes in Accounting

General Points

The most basic question here is: "*What* is being measured?" Measurement is always of some characteristic, or "*attribute*" of some *object*. For example, when an astronomer measures the brightness of a star, the star is the object of measure, and brightness is the relevant attribute. In accounting, we are concerned with attributes like wealth, solvency, and profitability of such objects as corporations or divisions. In managerial accounting, we are often interested in the attributes of cost and efficiency of a production process, or the profitability of a product or customer or potential investment.

What objects and attributes we measure depend upon *why* we are measuring. Typically, the choices of both the objects of measure and the relevant attributes are determined by the user's interests. Financial accounting and managerial accounting serve different uses, and measure different objects and attributes.

Financial Accounting Objectives, Objects and Attributes

According to the FASB (2010), "The objective of general purpose financial reporting is to provide financial information about the reporting entity that is useful to existing and potential investors, lenders, and other creditors in making decisions about providing resources to the entity" (para. OB2). The FASB (2010) also believes that financial reporting helps shareholders determine "how efficiently and effectively the entity's management and governing board have discharged their responsibilities to use the entity's resources" (para. OB4)[5]

What types of information do these users need? The FASB's Concepts Statements indicate that users need information about:

- the timing, amounts, and uncertainty of flows of resources into and out of the business
- the resources of the entity
- claims against the entity, and
- how efficiently and effectively the management and governing board have discharged their responsibilities to use the entity's resources.

The objects of financial reporting tend to be either legal entities or controlled groups of legal entities. For legal and tax purposes, it is common in the U.S. for operations to be split into more than one entity. Creditors, whose loans may be secured by the assets of a particular company, may focus on legal entities. Investors often look at the ability of the entire controlled group of companies to generate returns on shareholders' investments. Also, shareholders try to evaluate the efficiency and effectiveness of management by considering all the resources available to the managers.

It is important to note that usually accountants treat a business as separate from its owners. This is sometimes referred to as the "*entity principle.*"

The key attributes of entities depend on the user's interest. Investors are of course interested in the *value* of their investment, and its likely future changes in value. Thus, investors are concerned with the value of resources and liabilities of the entity, and in changes in these values over time. Both the *amounts* of the changes in net resources, and the *uncertainties* and risks related to the company's ability to generate wealth, are relevant attributes.

Lenders are concerned with these factors, as well as the timing of the company's future receipts and scheduled payments of cash, which affect the company's ability to repay loans. Thus, lenders are concerned, not just with the values, but also with the likely *timing* of future receipts and obligations.

Both investors and creditors are also interested in holding managers accountable for efficient and honest use of company resources. They are concerned with the *propriety* and *efficiency* of recorded expenditures.

Finally, it is important to properly characterize the claims of various parties to the company's resources, and the changes in those claims. For example, a company needs to be able to say what portion of its resources is available for dividends to shareholders, or what funds must by law or contract be set aside to service particular obligations. Thus, investors, creditors, and managers care about *legal restrictions* on particular assets or net resources.

Managerial Accounting Objectives, Objects, and Attributes

Managerial accounting "is designed to assist management decision making, planning, and control at the various administrative levels of an enterprise" (FASB 1978, para. 27). This different focus affects both the objects and attributes of managerial accounting. In general, information for managerial purposes must be more detailed and timely than information for external use. Managerial decisions require such information as the cost of a product and the likely costs and returns on a particular investment. Just as financial accounting should allow users to evaluate the efficiency and effectiveness of management on an overall basis, managerial accounting should allow this evaluation of particular parts of the business, and even for particular employees. Managerial accounting tracks managers' compliance with corporate plans. Thus, variances from planned budgets, or from the expected ("standard") costs, are measured and reported.

One important branch of managerial accounting is managerial costing. The IMA (2014) states that: "The objective of managerial costing is to provide a monetary reflection of the utilization of business resources and related cause and effect insights into past, present, or future enterprise economic activities. Managerial costing aids managers in their analysis and decision making and supports optimizing the achievement of an enterprise's strategic objectives." (p. 5)

While managerial accountants sometimes deal with the company as a whole, much of the time they are dealing with smaller objects such as a product, a process, a potential investment, a department or even an employee.

Because of the wide variety of decisions that managers make, a wide variety of attributes are sometimes measured. The cost incurred in a process, or in making a product, is often the attribute of interest. Key concerns include how costs vary with the volume of production, and which costs are relevant to particular managerial decisions.

Likely revenues or profits from a product or investment are sometimes attributes of interest. If judging efficiency, quantities produced may be the relevant attributes.

How Good is the Accounting Measurement System?

An important question is how well accounting meets the criteria of a good measurement system as described above:

- Power to explain many things;
- Theoretical fruitfulness;
- Simplicity;
- Clarity; and
- Reasonable cost.

A short answer is that accounting is useful but is far from perfect. Millions of U.S. businesses use accounting measurements for decision-making. Accounting has the potential to be an excellent measurement system for many purposes, but there are situations in which current accounting practices violate the criteria of a good measurement system.

Financial statement analysts who look at a company's financial statements consider what is called the "*quality of earnings*" for the company. In general, high-quality earnings are those that are likely to occur year after year. Another way of saying this is that the earnings are *persistent*. The earnings are not due to manipulation, or to one-time events.[6]

Mary Barth, a former member of the IASB, noted in a 2013 article that at the time of writing, the standard-setters for the FASB and the IASB had not defined accounting measurement clearly in their Conceptual Framework:

> [T]he Framework does not specify the objective of measurement and provides neither a conceptual definition of accounting measurement nor a conceptual basis for standard setters to choose among alternative measurement bases when setting accounting standards. Thus, standard-setting measurement decisions have been necessarily ad hoc and based more on historical precedent and the combined judgment of individual FASB and IASB members derived from their experience, expertise, and intuition than on agreed upon measurement concepts. This lack of concepts relating to measurement is a glaring hole in the Framework that impedes progress on financial reporting standards involving measurement.
>
> *(Barth 2013, p. 332)*

There are two fundamental limits on how good any measurement system can be.

- An accounting description of a company will always be an incomplete description. It will focus on quantitative aspects. In Einstein's example, it may be a description of the soup, but it will never give the full flavor.
- Trade-offs must be made between different criteria for good measurement systems. The simplest measures may not be the most theoretically fruitful. The most powerful measures may not be the clearest or the least costly. Different users will weigh these trade-offs differently.

Theory and measurement are always interdependent. Accountants need to be aware of the applicable decision theories.

Areas of Knowledge Related to Accounting Measurement

A surprisingly wide range of fields of study are related to accounting questions. See Table 1.1 for examples.

Table 1.1 Some Accounting Questions and Related Fields of Study

Accounting question	Related fields of study
What entity should be measured?	Law; tax; management science; finance
What measures of company performance do investors need?	Finance, economics
What measures of company resources do creditors need?	Bankruptcy law; finance; economics
What data do shareholders need in order to hold top management accountable?	Corporate law; economics of information
How can values of assets and liabilities be estimated without current market values?	Finance; economics
What factors determine the cost of producing manufactured products?	Engineering
How can pension obligations be estimated?	Economics; probability; actuarial science; pension law
Who should receive financial reports? How frequent and detailed should reports be?	Corporate law; securities law; finance; economics of information; ethics
What type of reporting inside the company best ensures effective control?	Management science; psychology
How should reports be formatted to maximize clarity?	Perceptual science
How can errors in processing information be minimized?	Computer science; communications theory; behavioral science and process design
Who should set accounting rules?	Political science; economics; ethics
What qualifications do measurers need?	Theory of education; psychology

One question that accounting professors often get at parties is "but how can you do research in *accounting*?" The person asking the question always assumes that accounting is simply the process of recording transactions, and that bookkeeping has been largely unchanged for 500 years. Both assumptions are incorrect.

In fact, because accounting is a measurement system for business and economics, the list of unsolved questions which researchers can address is long. Each chapter of this book lists some questions. Here are some general questions:

- Related to economics: What information do decision-makers need for particular decisions? What would be the impact of additional information? Will the marketplace provide adequate information, or is government regulation necessary or desirable?
- Related to finance: How do securities markets process information? Do stock price reactions to information releases indicate whether the market "understands" accounting information, and reacts to it efficiently? Does the format of information affect its use in the marketplace?
- Related to psychology: Should limits in the human ability to process information affect the design of reporting systems? For example, can people handle many details, or is it better to provide summary data?
- Related to sociology: Do cultural differences impact choices of accounting measures?[7] Does the designation of people as "professionals" affect their ability to give legitimacy to concepts?
- Related to information technology: How can systems of collecting data be made faster, cheaper, and more reliable?
- Related to philosophy of science: To what degree is an accounting system something that is testable?
- Related to ethics: What are the relative rights of company owners, workers, and outside parties to information? What is the "right" perspective to use in standard setting?

What Different Fields of Accounting Measure

Accounting data are always produced for users. Because users' needs vary widely, accounting is often divided into three major fields: *financial accounting, managerial accounting,* and *tax accounting.* Certain regulated industries also have to follow prescribed regulatory accounting.

Financial accounting provides information to people outside the organization, such as investors, lenders, vendors, customers, employees and the general public. Investors, for example, are concerned with valuing the company, and are interested in its resources and earnings ability. Lenders, vendors, customers and employees are all interested in evaluating the company's ability to fulfill its obligations. Shareholders also want to judge whether management is competent and honest.

Accounting standard-setters believe that government, management, and tax authorities already can require companies to account in particular ways. However, outside investors typically do not have this power, and also often want to compare reports from different companies. Therefore, the accounting standard-setters deliberately decided to focus their standards outside investors' needs. While financial accounting may sometimes meet needs of managers, government regulators, or tax authorities, that is not what financial accounting is designed for (Barth 2007).

The type of data that is useful to outsiders depends on their decision models. Accounting standard-setters must understand how investors and creditors make decisions in order to set appropriate rules. A major goal of financial accounting is "to help investors, creditors, and others assess the amounts, timing, and uncertainty of prospective net cash inflows to the related enterprise" according to the FASB (1978, para. 37), which believes this information is needed for their investing and credit decisions.

Financial accounting typically addresses some of the following key questions:

- What are the entity's resources and obligations at a point in time?
- How well has the entity performed over a period?
- Who has benefited from the entity's performance?
- What ownership interests do various parties have in the entity, and how have those interests changed over time?

Providing information to outsiders has both costs and benefits for the organization. Clearly, accounting reports showing high profits and a large amount of available assets may benefit the firm by encouraging investors to give it capital, encouraging vendors to offer it credit, encouraging customers to rely on it for long-term contracts, and so forth. However, accounting reports showing low profits might discourage lenders, vendors, and customers from offering the company good terms. Even when the firm is profitable, outsiders could use the information against the company. Competitors might move into profitable business areas, or try to hire key employees. Employees may request higher wages. A major issue in financial reporting is striking the right balance between disclosure of information that investors and other users need, and protecting proprietary information.

Because outsiders use accounting data for economic decisions, financial accountants put a premium on reliability and verifiability. Companies obviously have incentives to present a favorable picture to outsiders. Outsiders who rely on accounting reports, and then make unprofitable investment or credit decisions, are likely to claim they were misled by improper accounting, and to sue for damages. A major goal of financial accounting rules is to reduce the opportunity for management to unduly bias their reports, and to provide a framework to judge accusations of improper accounting.

Outsiders put a premium on the comparability of accounting across companies. Outside users want to be able to read company reports without investing time in learning a unique accounting system, and they also want to compare various companies' reports. Standard-setters face a tension between allowing companies flexibility to describe unique circumstances, and allowing so much flexibility that reports are not comparable. In the United States, financial accounting reports usually follow "generally accepted accounting principles" ("GAAP"). Internationally, most countries use International Financial Reporting Standards ("IFRS"). GAAP and IFRS somewhat restrict companies' ability to choose their own unique measurement rules, but they still allow some flexibility.

Managerial accounting is the field of accounting that produces information to help management understand, plan and control business operations. The primary users of the information are internal—the Board of Directors, top managers, lower level managers, and employees. The IMA's Statement of Management Accounting Number 1 defined management accounting:

> Management accounting is a profession that involves partnering in management decision-making, devising planning and performance management systems, and providing expertise in financial reporting and control to assist management in the formulation and implementation of an organization's strategy.
>
> *(IMA 2008, p. 1)*

Managerial accounting tries to provide inputs to the decision models that management uses to make key production, investment, and marketing decisions. Later chapters discuss such concepts as the "relevant costs" of a product. What is "relevant" depends upon the decision model.

Key questions that management accounting tries to answer include:

- What is the cost of producing an item?
- Would a new investment be cost-beneficial?
- How efficient is a process?
- How efficient is a manager?
- Why are there variances from managerial plans?
- How will planned activities affect future financing needs?

While the goals of management accounting are typically set to benefit managers, not workers, managerial accounting often serves as a two-way communication flow. Top managers review accounting reports to understand what has happened in the business. For example, they learn about unexpected changes from planned sales patterns. In addition, management can use the accounting system to communicate goals to lower level personnel. For example, by approving budgets and standard costs of production management can communicate its expectations for proper performance.

Managerial accounting tends to be more detailed, less standardized, and often more subjective, than financial reporting. Because the information is for internal use, and there is not the same concern that outsiders will use the data against the company's interests, management reports go into far more detail regarding costs and revenues than would external reports. Because the managers are only focused on one company, data need not be measured using the same standards that other companies use. Thus, there are no "generally accepted management accounting principles." Companies are free to design measures that they consider most beneficial. Similarly, since the management is presumably not trying to deceive itself, the information does not need to be subject to objective verification. Companies generally do not obtain external audits of managerial accounting data.[8]

Tax accounting measures income based on federal, foreign and state income tax laws and regulations. The key question is "How much tax is due?" The definition of taxable income under the U.S. income tax code has developed over 100 years through legislation and through court decisions.

Tax accounting and financial accounting both measure income during a period of time. However, several factors cause tax and financial accounting to measure income differently.

- In some cases, Congress excluded items from the definition of income to reward or penalize certain activities. For example, the payment of a parking ticket is not a deductible expense for tax purposes, because Congress did not want to allow a benefit for illegal behavior.
- Because taxes are often disputed, the tax code puts a higher stress on verifiability than financial accounting does. Estimates are more likely to be permitted in financial accounting than in tax accounting.
- Financial accounting tries to follow the economic substance of transactions, whereas the tax code generally follows their legal forms.
- Financial accounting rules are sometimes biased to understate income. Tax authorities tend to be biased towards collecting taxes, and thus to higher measurements of income.

This text will not treat tax accounting. It is a separate, and complex, field.

This text discusses both managerial and financial accounting. Both fields provide two different kinds of measures. The first is *information that is relevant for economic models used for future decision-making*. How this information is best measured depends upon economic theory and decision models. The second type of measure is *used to determine the actual outcome of some agreed-upon arrangement between two or more parties*. Another way to express this is *accountability*. The arrangement may be a contract, such as an employee compensation arrangement or royalty agreement. Often, accounting needs to track changes in the ownership interest of the entity. It may also be a more general arrangement, where the shareholders want to hold managers accountable for acting honestly and competently. Historically, the term "stewardship" was often used to describe the manager's obligation to serve the shareholders faithfully.[9] The measurement of the second type of information depends on the rules set by law, or agreed to by the parties. These two sets of criteria are very different.

An example may make this clear. Assume that we are watching a basketball game. If we want to determine which team has better athletes, than we will consider a whole host of factors, including players' speed, strength, coordination, agility, etc. If, instead, we want to know who won the game, we will only consider the final score. The final score is determined by an arbitrary set of rules which, for example, say that certain actions called "shots" count for one point, others count for two points, others for three points, and still others (the ones that "missed" the "basket") don't count at all. In order to know who "won," we don't have to agree that someone who makes a three-point shot is three times as good an athlete as someone who makes a one-point shot. We just need to know the scoring system that the basketball teams, the fans and the referee agreed on.

Financial accounting tries to serve both purposes—to provide useful information for decisions, and to "keep score" of how much income shareholders have "won" or "lost" during the year. The rules for the second purpose are often arbitrary, but as long as the company, its investors, and other interested parties agree upon them, they serve their purpose.[10]

Historically, accounting practices grew up primarily as a means of keeping score, or judging stewardship. However, the FASB has focused over the last 50 years its attention primarily on providing information that is useful for future decision-making.[11] Its first statement of Financial Accounting Concepts FASB (1978) stated: "The function of financial reporting is to provide information that is useful to those who make economic decisions about business enterprises and investments in or loans to business enterprises." (para. 16) This means that the current accounting system still has some features that come from the older objective of reporting on stewardship, but also other rules that are meant to serve the idea of decision-usefulness.

Attempting to serve more than one purpose with one set of measures creates difficulties that we discuss in later chapters. Information that is used to track ownership claims must be verifiable, comprehensible to all users, and above all compliant with the underlying agreements or rules. It need not actually represent economic reality. In contrast, information that is useful for decision-making may be subjective and hard to understand, as long as it is relevant to the decision at hand and accurately represents the underlying reality. Thus, the criteria to be used when choosing financial accounting measures to serve these two goals can conflict.

Summary of Different Fields of Accounting

Tax, financial, and managerial accounting have different goals. Tax accounting follows the law, and is primarily devoted to "score-keeping"—determining the amounts of money that tax rules allocate to the taxpayer and the government. Financial accounting balances the need to provide "score-keeping" data and the need to provide inputs to economic decision models. In general, managerial accounting does not have to conform to any outside standards. Managerial accountants are not bound to use any particular "score-keeping" system, and can develop whatever systems best serve their needs for understanding and controlling business processes.[12]

It is conceptually perfectly appropriate for the same event to be measured differently for tax, financial accounting, and managerial accounting purposes.

How Society Shapes Accounting

The FASB (1978) stated:

> Financial reporting is not an end in itself but is intended to provide information that is useful in making business and economic decisions. . . . Thus, the objectives set forth stem largely from the needs of those for whom the information is intended, which in turn depend significantly on the nature of the economic activities and decisions with which the users are involved. Accordingly, the objectives . . . are affected by the economic, legal, political, and social environment in the United States. The objectives are also affected by characteristics and limitations of the information that financial reporting can provide.
>
> (para. 9)

Historical Perspective

Because accounting developed to serve user needs, it is affected by all the factors that affect users. Users had different needs in different times and in different places. Accounting in different time periods, or different countries, has been different.

Table 1.2 shows how, historically, accounting developed and changed over human history. Accounting has been affected by technological, social, legal and economic factors. Technological influences have ranged from the inventions of coinage and paper to the introduction of "Arabic" numerals to the invention of computers and barcode scanning. Social factors included the formation of societies with stable governments and widespread education. Legal factors included the definition of individual property rights, the introduction of income taxes, and the creation of the corporate form of business with tradable stock. Economic factors included increases in the scope of trade, from small enterprises to multinational enterprises, and increases in the time and complexity of production systems.[13] Accounting rules have also changed as a result of financial crises.[14]

Table 1.2 Some Key Developments in the History of Accounting

Period	Stimulus	Accounting response
4000–1200 (BC)	Private property Governments formed Writing developed	Systematic recording Controls over data reliability
900–500 (BC)	Early trade Development of coined money	Recording using monetary accounts
100–1200 (AD)	Manors often run by stewards rather than owners	Accounting for entrusted resources; early forms of auditing taught at the University of Oxford
1100–1500	Arabic numerals reach Europe Algebra reaches Europe	Double-entry bookkeeping from 1300 or earlier
1200–1500	Ephemeral trade (Short-term mercantile ventures)	Venture accounting; tracking flow of capital
1400	Early factories in Italy	Earliest cost accounting
1600–1750	Continuous trade begins with such companies as Muscovy Company (1555) and British East India Company (1600); separation of ownership and management Entrepreneurial capitalism	Model of capital developed; periodic accounting and reporting; use of estimated amounts
1750–1850	Industrial Revolution and railroad building require more capital	Cost accounting more necessary; diversity of accounting practices increases; conservatism begins to be common; depreciation first recorded
1840–1860	Britain passes early Company Acts; rights of creditors need to be distinguished from those of owners; capital becomes more mobile	Theory of capital maintenance needed to define "income"; periodic reporting more common; disclosure rules
1800–1850	Early laws relate accounting and company profits 1799 Britain introduced an income tax 1830s some states regulate railroad rates	Measurements chosen based in part on tax and regulatory impacts First professional accounting society founded in 1853

(Continued)

Table 1.2 (Continued)

Period	Stimulus	Accounting response
1851–1870	Shareholders allocate funds based on expected return on investment	Matching of expenses to revenue; costing of products
1871–1900	Stability of investments Falling prices	Concentration on objectivity Going concern concept introduced Conservatism is more common
1880–1920	Production more complex	Development of cost accounting, budgeting, and other management accounting tools; research and development costs first disclosed
1901–1920	Corporations retain most of earnings; income taxes	Accurate measurement of profits; verifiability becomes more important; financial analysis tools develop
1921–1970	Increased corporate retention of profits; stock market failures; increased investor focus on appreciation and income	Increased focus on disclosure; more standard accounting rules, and stock market regulation; growth of auditing profession; materiality concept; concentration on income statement rather than balance sheet
1971–	Greater social awareness	Attempts to develop social or environmental accounts
1970–	Increasingly complex production processes; increased computerization	More complex cost accounting becomes more feasible and needed
1970–	Multinational corporations; international cooperation increases	Efforts to reduce international differences in accounting standards
1980–	Complexity of business transactions and financial instruments; stock markets more sensitive to earnings shortfalls; stock compensation of managers	FASB conceptual framework; more specific rules; renewed emphasis on balance sheet; increased attention to internal controls and fraud; increased use of fair value accounting

Features Shaping U.S. Accounting

The FASB (1978) cites five important factors that shape our accounting needs. These factors, together with my interpretation of them, are as follows:

- The United States has a highly developed system of markets, and most goods and services have prices in terms of money. This is an essential prerequisite to certain methods of valuing a company's resources and obligations.
- There is often a long process of producing and marketing goods. This raises the issue of when, during this process, costs and revenues should be considered to have occurred. The complexity of the process, and the variety of industries in our economy, suggests that no one system can meet all needs.
- People can trade both stocks and debt instruments. This means that accounting needs to track the rights various parties have at various times. The need of investors for timely information is a factor calling for transparency, rather than secrecy, in reporting. The need to treat both buyers and sellers in stock markets fairly is a factor influencing the FASB to favor neutral reporting, rather than conservative reporting.
- Ownership and management of modern corporations is usually separate. As a result, share-holders are not able to order managers to produce specific reports. Shareholders must rely on standardized sets of accounts to provide adequate disclosure of what has happened to the company. Again, this factor would call for transparency, rather than secrecy.
- The United States is a free-enterprise (or capitalist) society, where businesses are generally privately owned. This has numerous consequences.

  o Reporting tends to be from the perspective of owners, not from workers or creditors.
  o Companies try to keep certain facts secret for competitive reasons.
  o Companies do not generally try to measure the social value of their operations.
  o The rights of owners, creditors, and other claimants to the company's income must be established by measurement.
  o Because businesses have different owners, they can make different accounting decisions. If all enterprises were under common control, a uniform system of accounts would be more appropriate.

In the United States, which generally has had low inflation, the dollar has been treated as having a stable value.

In addition to economic and legal factors, improvements in economic theory and technology have caused changes in accounting. For example, modern finance theory lets us value stock options, and modern computer systems let us track production costs in ways that would have been impractical 50 years ago. As the FASB (1980) stated, in discussing desirable characteristics of accounting, "Although those characteristics are expected to be stable, they are not immutable. They are affected by the economic, legal, political, and social environment in which financial reporting takes place and they may also change as new insights and new research results are obtained." (para. 2)

International Differences

Because accounting reflects social influences, different societies have had different means of accounting.

The degree to which U.S. standards depend on their environment can be seen clearly by contrasting them with the accounting standards of the 1980s Soviet Union. The goal of Soviet enterprises was not to produce profits (there were no owners) but to meet production plans.

Production, not income, was the focus. Since the state needed to be able to control the entire economy, all companies used the same accounting classifications and methods. Since the state owned all enterprises in the economy, there was no concern about disclosing proprietary information to competitors. Equity in the enterprise was not tradable, so the complex types of debt and equity instruments common in the U.S. did not exist. Since the creditor banks, and vendors and industrial customers, were also owned by the state, there were fewer issues of collectibility of receivables. Prices were set by the state, not the market, so measurements of earnings and of the values of assets were artificial. All property was owned by the state, and the laws against misuse of state property were strict, so the accounting system put a premium on tracking the use of assets (Ash and Strittmatter 1992).

Researchers have tried to relate international differences in accounting rules and practices to underlying cultural factors. Salter and Niswander (1995) found some association between certain cultural values, and the degree of development of capital markets, and tax rates, with accounting practices. The types of accounting values that varied across countries included preferences for:

- *Professional judgment* vs. *statutory control.* A preference for professional judgment lets individual accountants decide how to categorize something, and how to account for it. A preference for statutory control means that the law rigidly specifies how things are accounted for.
- *Uniformity* vs. *flexibility.* Uniform systems require each company to treat a particular event the same way, while flexible systems allow companies in different situations to account for these transactions differently.
- *Conservatism* vs. *optimism.* Companies with conservative accounting are slow to assume that good things have happened, and quick to assume that bad things have happened. They show lower income and assets than companies with more optimistic accounting.
- *Secrecy* vs. *transparency.* (See Salter and Niswander 1995.) Transparency refers to the degree to which the company makes information about itself visible to outsiders. Companies typically want to keep certain information secret. For example, they may be afraid that their workers will ask for higher pay if they know the business can afford it, or that competitors will offer special deals to the company's best customers and employees. If the business is doing poorly, the company may fear that its suppliers and banks will stop dealing with it. On the other hand, shareholders will not buy the company's stock, and suppliers and lenders won't deal with it, unless the company discloses enough information to make these outside parties comfortable.

Inflation varies across countries. Many countries that have high inflation use methods of accounting that adjust for inflation. Countries with low inflation, such as the U.S., tend to assume the value of their currency is stable.

The way the U.S. has set accounting standards is not the only way they could have been set. Other countries have, for example, placed far more weight on achieving uniformity of accounting, at the cost of flexibility. France and the former Soviet Union had standard sets of accounts that all companies had to use. The result was a greater ability to combine individual company reports into nationwide aggregate totals, at the cost of less flexibility at the individual company level. International standards sometimes also strike different balances between judgment and statutory control, and between conservatism and optimism, than do U.S. standards.

Since 1990, as the economies of the countries of the world have become more interdependent, there have been increasing efforts to agree on one set of worldwide standards. Over the last 10 years, various countries, the FASB and the IASB have taken various steps to eliminate unnecessary differences in accounting rules. As of 2005, the European Economic Community adopted International Accounting Standards. The SEC has proposed allowing these international accounting standards to be used in the United States within a few years, based on progress in bringing about convergence between those standards and American standards (Norris 2005).

However, even when countries adopt IFRS, there is not uniform accounting. IFRS allows companies certain choices, and companies in different places tend to make different choices. There still tend to be differences between countries in how these standards are applied. It is likely that over time differences in accounting across countries will become smaller, but not disappear entirely. See Nobes (2011).

Clearly, no one set of accounting rules can cover such different accounting systems as the U.S. and the 1980s Soviet Union. As Robert Jensen (1971, p. 38) wrote: "At present there is no universal system of accounting theory, nor will there likely be such a system during our lifetime."

Pressures to Distort Measurements

There are many incentives to distort reported measures. For example, companies face temptations to under-report income to tax authorities. Regulated companies face incentives to report expenses in a way that will justify rate increases. Managers of publicly owned companies face temptations to over-report income, to boost stock prices.

Temptations to distort measurements for personal gain are not new, nor are attempts by society to ensure measures are trustworthy. The Bible forbids cheating others with unfair measures.[15] Centuries later, one of the complaints fueling peasant anger in the French Revolution was unfairness in how the grain they had to pay to the nobles as rent was measured. Porter (1995) notes that the demand for better measures led, indirectly, to the development of the metric system.

In the face of these temptations, it has been hard for the accounting profession to maintain public trust. As a result, we have seen two major developments. The first is the growth of a body of professional accountants, as a means of assuring the public that accounting was being done by qualified, independent practitioners. The second is the growth of rules to curb the exercise of discretion in measurement by managers and accountants.

Crises and Changes in Accounting

Table 1.3 lists some key events that led to greater regulation of accounting.

Over time, many rules were created to reduce managers' and accountants' ability to distort measurements of corporate performance. As recently as the early 1930s, there were no standard accounting rules for financial reporting. However, as a reaction to a variety of abuses that occurred during the 1920s, the SEC pressed the accounting profession to create accounting rules. Concepts that are now accepted unquestioningly were introduced during the 1930s, such as the need for conservatism and objectivity, recognition of revenue at time of sale, and the use of historical cost to value assets. These topics are all discussed in more detail in Chapter 2, and in later chapters.[16]

In addition, companies and their accountants realized they were more likely to be criticized by outsiders when they overstated their assets and income than when they understated them. For example, if a lender was told a company had adequate collateral, when it did not, the lender could sue for his or her loss. If, on the other hand, the company had more collateral than the lender believed, the lender was unlikely to complain. This caused accountants to tend to bias their measures of income and assets downwards. This downward bias is referred to as "*conservatism*."

Table 1.3 Business Crises and Their Impact on Accounting

Crisis	Impact
Britain—Early 1700s Excessive speculation in shares of the South Sea Company causes massive losses.	Britain passes the Bubble Act, limiting formation of new corporations.
Britain—1830s and 1840s After Britain repealed the Bubble Act and made incorporation easy, there were numerous bankruptcies and company failures.	Britain—Companies Acts of 1840s and 1850s require publication of certain information, including balance sheets. They also require that bankruptcies be administered by accountants.
Britain—Mid-1800s Many people administering bankruptcies, calling themselves accountants, were poorly trained or unethical.	Establishment of standards for Chartered Accountants in Scotland (1854) and England (1880).
U.S.—1870s Railroads failed during Credit Mobilier scandal and 1870s depression.	European creditors chartered accountants to monitor their investments in the U.S.
U.S.—Panic of 1907 Many banks failed.	Formation of Federal Reserve Bank and Federal Trade Commission. Beginning of pressure for standardized accounting.
U.S.—1929 Stock market crash and Great Depression of 1930s.	Formation of SEC in 1933, which presses the accounting profession to establish accounting and auditing standards.
U.S.—late 1960s, early 1970s Economic recession, and criticism of accounting practices during 1960s merger wave.	Replacement of APB with FASB. Increased pace of standard setting.
Worldwide—1970s Increased inflation, and unstable currencies.	Experimentation with inflation accounting.
U.S.—1980s Savings and loan crisis.	Increased focus on fair value of bank assets, and on bank internal controls.
East Asia—1990s Fiscal crisis.	Increased use of International Accounting and auditing standards.
U.S.—2001 and 2002 End of stock market boom. Exposure of Enron, WorldCom, and other accounting frauds.	Passage of Sarbanes–Oxley Act; increased regulation of the auditing profession. Changed accounting for stock options.
U.S.—2008 Fiscal crisis arising from bad home mortgage lending.	Increased attention to fair value accounting and accounting for derivatives.

How External Accounting Measurement Affects Society

> Accounting is a member of a battery of belief-forming institutions, including the law, education, the media, religion, and the family.
>
> *Tony Tinker (1985, p. 82)*

Types of Impacts

The previous section noted that accounting rules are partly determined by the needs of the surrounding society. This section explores a related question: how accounting affects the larger society. Accounting influences society in several ways. First, accounting definitions create the concepts people use to approach problems. Second, standard accounting practices make certain types of action seem normal and legitimate. Third, people react to accounting measurements in predictable ways. Fourth, accounting is used to help control operations and businesses.[17]

Accounting Concepts Shape Thinking

Accounting definitions and ideas are basic to our thinking about economic events and business activity.

In some cases external reality is independent of language, while in other cases language creates a form of "social reality." A rock exists, whatever we choose to call it. However, a "touchdown" in an American football game is something that only exists because people have agreed on what a "touchdown" is.[18] Similarly, key accounting measures only exist because people have agreed on the rules for defining them. Tom Mouck (2004) wrote:

> Take away the rules of football and things such as "first downs", "touchdowns", and "extra points" disappear. Take away the rules of double-entry accounting and things such as the monetary amount of total assets, owners' equity, net income, or earnings per share disappear." . . .
> Within the rules of football, it is possible to watch a television replay of a game and objectively verify that "touchdowns" did occur. Similarly, within the context of a given set of accounting rules, "total assets", "owners' equity", and "net income" may be considered to be objectively verifiable even though there is no objective basis in nature for the rules themselves.
>
> (p. 536)

Some concepts that come from accounting are "assets," "liabilities," "owners' equity," "income," "costs," and "rate of return on equity." These concepts underlie how people think about business and economic life, and have very pervasive effects.

See Box 1.1 for an extreme example of how some scholars suggest that accounting concepts affected society.

Box 1.1 Did Double-Entry Bookkeeping Inspire Capitalism?

One extreme suggestion regarding the impact of accounting thought on society was raised by Werner Sombart. Sombart claimed the development of double-entry bookkeeping in the 1300s was essential to the development of a capitalist economy. As explained by Most (1979), Sombart wrote that:

> The concept of "capital" could be formulated only under these conditions; prior to double-entry bookkeeping there was no "capital"; thus, capital could be defined as the property of wealth represented in a double-entry system of accounts. Double-entry bookkeeping also led to the principle of economic rationality. . . . Economic rationality went hand in hand with planning and control; the accounting system permitted the analysis of business operations and the establishment of plans for their progressive and systematic improvement. The invention of double-entry bookkeeping in this way created the necessary conditions for the essential principles of capitalism to develop.
>
> (pp. 246–7)

Was he correct? Probably not. Various comparisons of business practices to the use of double-entry bookkeeping tend to show that capitalist business practices were not dependent on the development of double-entry bookkeeping.*

However, Eve Chiapello (2007) found that accounting terms, and especially the way the accounting system defines owners' equity and income, were important to Karl Marx and other 19th century thinkers who defined what "capitalism" means.

*For a summary of related research, see Chiapello 2007.

Accounting Ideas Help Make Certain Actions Legitimate

When people become used to certain measurements, they use those measurements to decide what is normal and legitimate. High school grades are an example. Because students are used to the idea of tests and grades, they accept it is appropriate that students who get higher grades are more likely to get into colleges.

There are many examples of accounting helping companies to justify actions. For example:

- Companies with high profits pay their CEOs more.
- Companies with low profits close facilities, or fire employees, or cut wages.
- Electric utilities justify charging higher prices to their customers, claiming that the companies are entitled to earn a "fair rate of return."
- Managers who are unable to meet budget targets are fired while managers who exceed budget targets get bonuses.

The fact that people share common ideas about how certain things are measured helps them agree on economic transactions and thus helps our economy function.[19]

The advantage of accounting rules as a means of reconciling different economic interests is that they appear objective, and thus "fair." They create social norms.[20] Theodore Porter (1995) noted that the desire for apparent fairness has been a factor behind the rise of standard and quantitative decision rules in a number of areas over the last 200 years.

> The appeal of numbers is especially compelling to bureaucratic officials who lack the mandate of a popular election, or divine right. Arbitrariness and bias are the most usual grounds upon which such officials are criticized. A decision made by the numbers (or by explicit rules of some other sort) has at least the appearance of being fair and impersonal. Scientific objectivity thus provides an answer to a moral demand for impartiality and fairness. Quantification is a way of making decisions without seeming to decide. Objectivity lends authority to officials who have very little of their own.
>
> (p. 8)

Because accounting concepts can have important effects, the process of creating them can be very political. Different interest groups try hard to get favorable rules. For example, where taxes are based on income, companies tried to have rules that resulted in low measured income. Ross Watts and Jerold Zimmerman wrote that "Understanding why accounting theories are as they are requires a theory of the political process." (p. 275) They argue that different interest groups demand different theories, each trying to help their own interests. Since the interest groups have different interests, they propose different accounting theories, and will never finally agree. Watts and Zimmerman (1979) suggest that "it is this diversity of interests which prevents general agreement on accounting theory" (p. 275).

People React to Accounting Measurements

This topic is covered in Chapter 6.

People who know they are being measured usually try to act in a way that makes them look good. (So, for example, students who think that Chapter 1 will be covered in the test read it more carefully.)

Businesses use accounting information to guide their future actions. If something appears to be more profitable, they do more of it. If something looks unprofitable, they do less. Similarly, employees try hard to meet targets that will get them bonuses and promotions, and spend less time on things that their employers do not measure.

Box 1.2 Did Accounting Contribute to the 2008 Financial Crisis?

The global financial crisis of 2008 sparked a major recession in the U.S., Europe, and other economies around the world. It began when investments in various types of securities based on home mortgages (such as collateral mortgage obligations) lost value rapidly. The U.S. investment bank Bear Stearns was forced to merge, then Lehman Brothers failed, and the major insurance company AIG was forced to get U.S. government help. People rapidly stopped wanting to buy collateral mortgage obligations and other related investments, and the market for them froze up. Other banks and financial institutions around the world also found themselves in need of government support, and some closed.

Under accounting rules at the time, financial institutions generally recorded the value of their investments in the collateral mortgage obligations at their estimated market value. When the market values rapidly decreased, the institutions' holdings had to be written down, and this reduced their net worth. Under bank regulations, when banks have less net worth, they cannot make as many loans, and may need to sell assets. The banks reduced their lending, which affected many businesses that relied on obtaining loans. Banks also tried to sell some of these assets, increasing the downward pressure on the market.

Some people claim that the use of market values to record these assets contributed to the crisis. In years leading up to 2007, the market for these assets was strong, so banks' holding appeared very valuable. This allowed banks to buy a lot of the assets. Then, when the market for collateral mortgage obligations collapsed, banks were all forced to sell them at the same time, even though it was likely that the market for these assets was only temporarily depressed. This is called "contagion" in the financial markets. Thus, the argument is that the accounting made the effects of the economic cycle stronger—it encouraged the boom in these securities while markets were rising, and increased the problems when the values fell. This is called a "pro-cyclical" effect.

A second factor that helped to make the crisis possible is that banks that made risky loans were able to find ways to keep control over the loans, but account for the loans as if they had been sold by transferring the loans to specially formed companies. The accounting rules are beyond the scope of this textbook, but using these methods allowed banks to increase their lending beyond what regulations would normally allow, which also increased their risks. During the crisis, it turned out that the banks actually still had responsibility for the losses in these specially formed companies.

See: Arnold (2009), Laux and Leuz (2009) and De Jager (2014).

There are many examples of how accounting measurements can affect society. For example, for many years companies did not have to measure a liability for the promises they had made to pay pensions or medical insurance premiums to employees after retirement. After the FASB required companies to record such liabilities, many companies stopped offering these benefits.

A controversial issue is whether the methods of accounting for financial assets helped cause the worldwide financial crisis starting in 2008. See Box 1.2 for a summary of the arguments. There is additional discussion of this topic in Chapter 7.

Accounting is Used to Help Control Actions

Accounting has always been used by people in authority to exert control over other people. Tax authorities use information in order to assess taxes. Owners use knowledge of what money is coming in and out of their businesses, and what goods are being produced, to run the business and to control their employees' actions.

Accounting data in the form of budgets and targets helps managers to control activities in advance. Using accounting reports about what has been produced or sold and what labor and other costs have been incurred helps managers control employee actions.

How Should Accounting Rules be Set?

The accounting standard-setters face a key ethical question: How should they use this power to measure and to define?

Brian Shapiro (1997) summarizes the arguments made on this point into three opposing perspectives on the objectives of financial reporting.

* The *"critical–interpretive"* perspective suggests that accounting should be used as an instrument of social change.
* The *economic consequences* perspective suggests that when rules are designed or accounting choices are made, they should be made in a way that benefits the preparers of financial statements.
* The *decision-usefulness* school holds that information should be relevant and reliable to the user, even if the preparer or society is hurt.

To illustrate these three perspectives, consider the debate over whether stock options granted to employees should be treated as an expense. For simplicity, assume that prior to 2004 companies generally did not record any expense when they gave their employees stock options.[21]

The FASB, taking a decision-usefulness view, wanted companies to record expenses for stock options. It believed that granting such options involves a real cost to shareholders, and measuring income without such costs leads to poor economic decisions.

The FASB proposal inspired loud opposition from managers, particularly in the software industry. Most opponents took the economic consequences view. They argued that stock options are often granted by new, innovative companies to hold key employees. If these companies were required to expense stock options, they would not offer as many, which would keep them from recruiting talented employees. The chain of causation would lead to fewer new innovative firms being started, and a loss of competitiveness in the American economy.[22]

Someone taking a critical–interpretive perspective might believe that the rules should encourage companies to share ownership broadly, with the whole workforce, but discourage stock options that are simply a giveaway to top management. Thus, a critical–interpretive perspective might lead to the suggestion that large grants of options to top management be treated differently (and less favorably) than grants to lower level employees. One proposal in Congress took this position.

Over the last several decades, the accounting profession and the FASB have argued that accounting should be decision-useful. The FASB (1978) stated that "The role of financial reporting in the economy is to provide information that is useful in making business and economic decisions, not to determine what those decisions should be" (para. 33). It explicitly rejected the critical–interpretive perspective, saying it did not want to produce "information that is directed toward a particular goal, such as encouraging the reallocation of resources in favor of a particular segment of the economy" (para. 33). However, the FASB and IASB face pressure from governments and other parties to consider the economic consequences of their acts, and this pressure is sometimes very strong.[23]

Measuring Shapes the Measurers

Accounting measurement is done by accountants. How have the requirements of the measurement process, and of society, affected the measurers themselves?

For centuries, accounting was primarily an exercise in bookkeeping. Recording and summarizing transactions involved a great deal of copying and adding of numbers. Because owners were close to their business operations, there was relatively little need to explain financial results to the owners. Bookkeepers needed to be careful and accurate. They did not need to be good communicators. In fact, because they saw much confidential information, it was better if they did not communicate too much.

Until the mid-1800s, no special qualifications were needed to be an accountant. The need for qualifications came about because of scandals. The British Companies Acts in the mid-1800s required that companies in bankruptcy be supervised by accountants, without specifying what that term meant. Numerous untrained or unscrupulous people began claiming to be accountants, and a variety of scandals threatened to make accountants disreputable (Bougen 1994).

The Scottish and English accountants of the 19th century sought to create a professional image to increase public trust in their work. The first societies of chartered accountants were formed in Scotland in 1854 and England in 1880. Later, in 1896, New York State established the designation of "Certified Public Accountant," and created requirements for holding that designation. The idea of professional certification, with special education and training, grew rapidly in the U.S. in the early 1900s.

One publication of the New York State Society of CPAs is titled "The Trusted Professional." This title is revealing. Accountants must be seen as "professionals," abiding by standards of competence and ethics. Accountants, to function, must be trusted by their clients and the public. Clients must trust them to keep corporate secrets, and to give competent and objective advice. The public must trust auditors' opinions to be independent and competent, or the opinions will be worthless.

Over the last century and a half, technical and economic changes have greatly changed accountants' work. Computerization has eliminated the vast majority of the computational work that accountants once performed—companies no longer need rooms full of people to add and copy

---

Box 1.3 The Accountant as a Stereotype

The stereotype of accountants as dull goes back a long time. Sir Walter Scott, writing to his brother in 1820, advised him that if Scott's nephew "is high spirited and impatient of long and dry labour . . . you will never make him an accountant" (Bougen 1994, p. 326).

The British comedy group Monty Python had several sketches making fun of accountants. In one, a vocational guidance counselor tells a client that "in your report here it says that you are an extremely dull person. Our experts describe you as an appallingly dull fellow, unimaginative, timid, lacking in initiative, spineless, easily dominated. . . . Whereas in most professions these would be considerable drawbacks, in Accountancy they are a positive boon" (quoted in Bougen 1994, p. 320).

More recently, the image of accountants has been changing. Accounting firms, in their recruiting literature, show young, trendy accountants (Jeacle 2008). A study (Dimnik and Felton 2006) of the representation of CPAs and chartered accountants in 121 North American movies found that while in earlier movies accountants were usually white males, in the late 20th century, more women and minorities were being portrayed. Also, over time, they looked at whether the accountants were shown as "Dreamers, Plodders, Eccentrics, Heroes or Villains." They found that CPAs were more likely to be shown as heroes than any other stereotypes.

The stereotype of accountants as dull made sense when much accounting work was simple copying and addition. Bougen (1994) says it may even have been helpful, because while accountants were considered boring, that was better than reckless or dishonest. The British magazine *The Economist* (1990) once claimed that accountants were "best when boring."

numbers. However, the growth of companies, and the separation of management from owner-ship, means that owners and top managers now need help understanding the operations of their businesses. The accountant's work has changed from adding and copying to analyzing and inter-preting data, and then communicating the results. Consistently, accounting firm recruiters indi-cate they are looking for new recruits with strong communication and leadership skills. Box 1.3 discusses the changing image of accountants.

Accounting is a challenging field. It requires people who are creative, and able to not only arrive at solutions to complex problems, but to communicate the solutions effectively to a variety of users. Accountants must understand both the underlying economic issues affecting a business and the relevant measurement and reporting issues.

Key Terms

Attributes—The characteristics of something that we are interested in measuring. Some attributes of a person might be their height and age.

Conservatism—FASB (2008)[24] defined conservatism as "A prudent reaction to uncertainty to try to ensure that uncertainty and risks inherent in business situations are adequately considered" (para. 95). In accounting, this means that where there is a choice of acceptable accounting methods, one would use the method that shows lower income or net assets.

FASB—See Financial Accounting Standards Board.

Financial Accounting—The branch of accounting that focuses on preparation of financial state-ments and other reports to owners, investors, and others outside the company.

Financial Accounting Standards Board (FASB)—A private organization that was established in 1973 and makes accounting standards in the United States. The Securities and Exchange Commission (SEC) and the American Institute of Certified Public Accountants generally require accountants and companies to follow the standards set by the FASB. These standards are often referred to as GAAP, or "generally accepted accounting principles."

Flexibility—A flexible set of standards gives accountants and companies choices of how they wish to account for certain things.

GAAP (generally accepted accounting principles)—At one time, this term simply meant the methods that most practicing accountants used. In the U.S., this term's meaning has changed. For businesses, it now means the set of rules that have been set by the FASB. Companies that sell their stocks and bonds to the public, and that are registered with the SEC, must also follow additional rules set by the SEC. For state and local governments, GAAP refers to standards set by the Governmental Accounting Standards Board. See FASB (2009).

International Accounting Standards Board (IASB)—A private organization, established in 1971, that sets International Financial Reporting Standards (IFRS).

International Financial Reporting Standards—These are rules set by the IASB that are followed by companies in many countries around the world. At the time this text is being written, the United States allows foreign companies to use IFRS in their reports in the United States, but does not yet allow United States public companies to follow IFRS.

Managerial Accounting—This branch of accounting provides information that is useful to managers in planning and controlling the operations of a business, and in making a variety of managerial decisions.

Measurement—This involves assigning a number value to some attribute of an object. For example, one way to measure a bag full of beans is to assign a weight of 1.2 kilograms.

Measurement system—This includes all the components discussed in the chapter:

- Objects to be measured
- Particular attributes to be measured for each object

- Rules for measurement
- Makers of the rules
- Measurers (people or machines to do the measuring)
- Verifiers of the measurement
- Reports by the measurers to the users
- Users of the measurements
- Decision models that the users employ to make decisions based on the measurements

Objects of measurement—The things or processes or business entities that are being measured. For financial reporting, a company or a group of companies is usually the object of measurement. For managerial accounting, the object of measurement is usually something that managers need to make a decision about. Examples of objects of measurement would include a product or a division of the company.

Secondary measurements—The result of combining more than one measure together. For example, accountants separately measure the amounts of various assets. When they add the totals together, to compute "total assets," total assets is a secondary measure.

Transparency—The idea of transparency is that a business discloses enough information that people outside the company can understand fully its operations and accounting. Transparency is the opposite of secrecy.

Uniformity—In accounting, uniformity would exist if all companies had to account for the same transaction the same way. The opposite of uniformity is flexibility.

Verifiers—To be general, this text uses the term verifiers to refer to people who check that measurements and reports are prepared correctly. In actual business practice, you are unlikely to see anyone have a job title of "verifier." Internal auditors and independent public accounting firms serve this function. Much of the job of a supervisor also involves checking other people's work.

Questions and Problems

Comprehension Questions

C1. (General measurement) Define the term "measurement."

C2. (General measurement) Name the various components of a measurement system.

C3. (General measurement) Assume you are going to cook spaghetti and tomato sauce for six people for dinner, and you are going shopping for the ingredients. You have everything you need, except tomatoes and pasta.

    A. What objects are you are shopping for?

    B. What is the most important attribute that you need to consider in order to make sure you have enough spaghetti?

    C. With regard to the tomatoes, why would you be more interested in the total weight of the tomatoes than in the number of tomatoes?

    D. How would you measure the weight of the tomatoes?

C4. (General measurement) When you buy a box of cookies in the store, the box usually has information on it containing many different types of measurements about the nutritional content of a "serving" of cookies.

    A. What is the object of measurement?

    B. Name at least two attributes that are typically measured about the nutritional content of the food.

    C. What are likely the kinds of rules that are set about how these attributes are measured?

    D. Who do you think sets the rules for measuring?

    E. Who does the measuring?

    F. Who is likely to be the one who verifies the measurements?

    G. Who are the users of the measurements?

    H. What kinds of decisions are the users trying to make?

    I. How are the measurements reported to the users?

C5. (General measurement) What criteria have been suggested to judge whether a measurement system is good or bad?

C6. (General measurement) The United States government measures many different things. For each of the following, indicate whether the measurement meets the normal goals of a measurement system:

    A. The Weather Service reports the high temperature for the day in many cities. Is this measurement:

        a. Powerful (capable of being used for many situations)?

        b. Capable of assigning numbers to every day?

        c. Theoretically fruitful (useful in making decisions and doing analysis)?

        d. Clear?

        e. Simple?

    B. The United States Commerce Department reports the rate of unemployment in various locations. Is this measurement:

        a. Powerful (capable of being used for many situations)?

        b. Capable of assigning numbers to every day?

        c. Theoretically fruitful (useful in making decisions and doing analysis)?

        d. Clear?

        e. Simple?

    C. The United States Commerce Department reports the number of Americans who are in poverty. Is this measurement:

        a. Powerful (capable of being used for many situations)?

        b. Capable of assigning numbers to every day?

        c. Theoretically fruitful (useful in making decisions and doing analysis)?

        d. Clear?

        e. Simple?

C7. (General measurement) A local magazine makes a listing every year of the places that sell the best pizza in your city. Do you think that a valid measurement system is used to make this list? Why or why not?

C8. (Objects of measurement) What are the typical objects of financial accounting?

C9. (Objects of measurement) What are some examples of the objects of managerial accounting?

C10. (Accounting measurement) In the accounting measurement system, give an example of:

    A. An object of measurement

    B. An attribute that accountants measure

    C. Rule-makers

    D. Measurers

    E. Verifiers

    F. Users and a decision that a user might make

C11. (Related fields to accounting) The chapter indicates that there are a variety of other fields that can provide insights to help accountants deal with certain measurement issues. What fields might be relevant to the following issues?

    A. Deciding what information investors want from financial statements?

    B. Deciding what factors need to be considered when determining the cost that a beer company incurs to brew beer out of grain?

    C. Deciding how to estimate the future costs that will be needed to pay pensions to employees when they retire in 30 years?

    D. Deciding how to process large amounts of accounting information in a way that will be quick and low on errors?

    E. Deciding who should set accounting standards?

    F. Deciding whether the language of accounting reports is clear and understandable?

C12. (Different fields of accounting) Explain the different purposes of financial accounting, managerial accounting, and tax accounting.

C13. (Different fields of accounting) Who are main users of financial accounting reports, managerial accounting reports, and tax returns?

C14. (Standard-setters) Who sets standards for:

    A. Financial accounting rules in the United States?

    B. Financial accounting rules in most other countries?

C15. (Standard-setters) Why is there no one standard-setter for managerial accounting rules?

C16. (Society affecting accounting) Match the four types of differences in accounting values mentioned in the text to the examples below:

    A. Professional judgment versus statutory control

    B. Uniformity versus flexibility

    C. Conservatism versus optimism

    D. Secrecy versus transparency

_____ In the former Soviet Union, all companies had to use the same accounts and accounting methods. In the United States, companies have a choice of accounting methods, and their accountants can use the method that they think best describes their companies. (This could fit more than one of the differences in values.)

_____ You and your friend are both unsure what grade you will get in a course. It could be an A, but it could also be a B. You tell your parents you are likely to get a B, but your friend tells her parents she expects an A.

_____ For financial reporting purposes, companies estimate an expense each period for the losses they expect to have on obsolete inventory. For tax accounting, companies are not allowed to estimate this expense. Instead, they can only record an expense when they actually discard the obsolete inventory.

_____ The Hershey Company, makers of chocolate bars, is a public company and each year reports its financial results to the public. Mars, Inc. is another large maker of candy and other products. It is not a public company, and it does not publish its financial statements.

C17. (Society affecting accounting) The chapter lists a number of features of the U.S. economy that the FASB says shape the accounting system. Indicate whether it is true or false that the following items are among those that shape the U.S. financial accounting system:

_____ The U.S. is a private enterprise economy, with privately owned businesses

_____ The U.S. government wants to encourage research by U.S. companies

_____ In the U.S. economy, most goods and services have prices in terms of money

_____ In the U.S., there are markets to trade stocks and bonds

_____ The U.S. Commerce Department tries to collect total data for the economy, so all companies must use the same accounting methods

_____ There is often a long period of time involved in producing and marketing goods.

_____ The managers and owners of U.S. companies are always the same people.

C18. (Society affecting accounting) Give three examples of changes in accounting that have followed business crises.

C19. (Accounting affecting society and business) Explain what is meant by each of the following views on the proper objectives of accounting:

A. The decision-usefulness view
B. The economic consequences view
C. The critical–interpretive view

C20. (Accounting affecting society and business) What is the FASB's view of what the purpose of financial accounting should be?

C21. (Accounting affecting society) The chapter says that a measurement system can affect society in several ways. As an example, consider the use of GMAT scores in the United States.

A. Do they shape how people think about the ability of applicants to business schools to succeed in the schools?
B. Do they help make business school admission decisions more legitimate?
C. Do they affect the actions of people, especially those applying to business schools?
D. Are they ways that someone is exerting control over the schools, or the applicants, or both? Explain your answers.

C22. (Accounting affecting society) The chapter says that a measurement system can affect society in several ways. As an example, consider a European-owned company that mines gold in Africa.[25] The company is worried that the African people and government will believe it is making too much money, and not sharing enough with the local people. The company uses accounting methods that show it has low profits. Explain whether this decision affects the company's reactions with the African people and government in any of the four ways listed in the chapter:

A. Does the report of low profits shape how people think about whether the company is treating the local society fairly?
B. Do the low reported profits make the company's actions seem legitimate?
C. Do the low reported profits affect the actions of:

a. The local government?
b. The company's own owners and investors?
c. The workers?

D. Are the choices of types of reports ways that the company's owners exert control over their managers?
Explain your answers.

C23. (Accounting affecting business) The chapter says that a measurement system can affect a business in several ways. As an example, consider a worldwide company with headquarters in New York City and divisions in many different locations. The company has an annual budget, and every month every part of the company has to report and compare its actual operating results to the results in the budget. Discuss how this reporting system affects the actions of the division managers in any of the four ways listed in the chapter:

A. Does the reporting system shape how the division managers think about their responsibilities?
B. Does the reporting system make certain actions by the company headquarters more legitimate?
C. Does the reporting system likely affect the actions of the division managers?
D. Does the reporting system affect the ability of the headquarters to control the actions of the division managers?
    Explain your answers.

Discussion Questions

D1. (General measurement—college education) Consider a college transcript as the output of a measurement system.

A. Identify the:

    a. "Object" being measured
    b. "Attribute" of the object being measured
    c. "Rules" for measurement
    d. "Standard-setters"
    e. "Measurers"
    f. "Verifiers"
    g. "Users" and their decisions
    h. Process of communicating or reporting the measures.

B. To what extent do you think this measurement system meets the needs of the key users?
C. How does this measurement system affect the actions of the "objects" being measured?
D. How does this measurement system affect the measurers?
E. To what extent do the grades on the transcript serve to legitimize actions by the school with regard to students and faculty?
F. To what extent does the measurement process add to the control exerted by the college administration on students and faculty?

D2. (General measurement—elementary school education) Under the No Child Left Behind Act, passed in 2001, every public elementary school that receives some federal funding is required to give its students certain tests of reading and math every year. Schools whose students do poorly on these tests for several years are labelled "failing schools," and face various types of penalties, which could include replacing principals and teachers or even closing the school.

A. Identify the:

    a. "Object" being measured
    b. "Attribute" of the object being measured
    c. "Rules" for measurement
    d. "Standard-setters"
    e. "Measurers"
    f. "Verifiers"
    g. "Users" and their decisions.

      B.   To what extent do you think this measurement system meets the needs of the key users?

      C.   How does this measurement system affect the actions of the "objects" being measured?

      D.   How does this measurement system affect the measurers?

      E.   To what extent does this measurement system create a new concept, a "failing school"?

      F.   To what extent does this measurement process serve to make certain actions by people who run school systems legitimate?

      G.   To what extent does the measurement process add to the control exerted by the federal government on local schools?

D3. (General measurement—crime)[26] In the U.S. the Federal Bureau of Investigation ("FBI") uses a Uniform Crime Reporting ("UCR") system to track violent crimes (like murder) and property crimes (such as theft of motor vehicles or burglary). Local police departments report certain data to the FBI, who create reports. From 1979 to 2004, the FBI reported "indexes" of crime by adding together the totals of eight different types of crime: murder and non-negligent manslaughter; forcible rape; robbery; aggravated assault; burglary, larceny-theft, motor vehicle theft, and arson. The FBI stopped publishing these indexes in 2004 because they "were not true indicators of the degrees of criminality because they were always driven upward by the offense with the highest number, typically larceny-theft. The sheer volume of those offenses overshadowed more serious but less frequently committed offenses, creating a bias against a jurisdiction with a high number of larceny-thefts but a low number of other serious crimes such as murder and forcible rape."[27] The FBI now publishes separate statistics for various types of crimes, without creating overall indexes.

In this situation, the objects being measured were local cities and towns. The relevant attributes were the rates of certain types of crimes.

The FBI was the rule-maker, because it published certain definitions of crimes that were included on the index, and others that were not included. For example, "aggravated assault" was on the index, but less serious types of assault were not.

Local police departments were the measurers. There was not a strong process of verifying the reports.

Users included local police departments, city governments, state governments, and voters.

      A.   To what extent do you think the "crime index" measurement system met the needs of the key users?

      B.   How does this measurement system affect the actions of the local police departments to actually reduce crime?

      C.   How might this system affect the actions of the local police, not to fight crime, but in how they collect data on crime?

      D.   To what extent does this measurement system create a new concept, a "crime rate"?

      E.   To what extent does this measurement process serve to make certain actions by police departments legitimate?

      F.   To what extent does the measurement process add to the control exerted by the federal government on police departments?

      G.   How does this measurement system affect the measurers?

D4. (Accounting measurement) Assume that you own and manage a small clothing store.

      A.   What kinds of financial information would you want to run your business?

      B.   What kinds of nonfinancial information would you want (for example, about customers, employees or suppliers)?

      C.   What information would you want to keep private from competitors?

D5. (Accounting measurement) One of the first U.S. major industries to be regulated was the railroads. Farmers and manufacturers depended on railroads to get their products to market, and often there was only one railroad serving an area. Farmers and manufacturers had very little bargaining power, and they believed that the railroads were charging excessive fees. Various states made laws that said railroad prices had to be at a level that gave them a reasonable rate of profit.

In this case, the objects being measured were railroad companies, and the relevant attributes were "profits." The measurers were the railroads' accountants. The users were regulators who used the measurements to set rates. The accounting rules to measure profits were initially unclear. For example, no one knew how long a locomotive or a train track would last.

A. What do you think were likely pressures on the state regulators?
B. How would these pressures affect the rules on what was a profit?
C. What do you think the likely pressures were on the railroad accountants in defining what they considered to be profits?

D6. (Accounting measurement) The chapter indicates that two very different objectives of accounting are to provide useful information for making decisions about the future, and to provide accountability for what happened in the past.

A. Assume you are an investor, trying to predict a company's future profits. Indicate whether you would consider each of the following things that happened either very relevant to your decision, or not very relevant:

a. The company learned this year (2016) that it had won a lawsuit with the Internal Revenue Service about its 2005 tax return. The lawsuit related to some activities that the company no longer does.
b. The part of the company that it sold in June had made profits of $200 million before its date of sale.
c. The sales of its major product increased 4% during this year.
d. The prices of one of the major raw materials it uses had increased 2% during the year.
e. The company had received $15 million dollars as a gain from a piece of land that it had held for 30 years. The company has no other such investments in land.
f. The company is very large, with sales in the billions of dollars. The CEO has been taking $500,000 per year from the company without permission. The CEO otherwise does a good job.

B. For any of the items in Part A that you considered "not very relevant," do you think they should still be reported to shareholders? Why, or why not?

D7. (Accounting measurement) In many companies, the top management receives bonuses based upon the profits measured by the accounting system. Also, many companies believe that the stock market reacts strongly to reported profits.

For accounting purposes, at the time the money is spent, expenditures on training employees, advertising products, and doing research on new products are all expenses that reduce reported profits. However, training, advertising, and research are all likely to be vital for the long-term success of companies.

A. Explain how the way training, research, and advertising are measured could cause managers to behave in ways that hurt the company.
B. Can you suggest any ways in which a company could avoid these problems?

D8. (Accounting measurement) An early accounting scholar wrote, in 1933, "The central accounting issue in a corporation concerns the amount of profit available for dividends." (Littleton 1933, p. 206)

A. What user group would see this as the central issue in accounting for corporations?
B. What might each of these other parties see as the "central accounting issue" for a corporation?

    a. Its workers
    b. Its suppliers
    c. Its customers
    d. Its bankers
    e. The local government in which it operates

D9. (Accounting measurement and society) Joni Young (2006) criticized the Financial Accounting Standards Board's (FASB's) focus on providing information to investors and creditors. She wrote:

From the perspective of a rational, economic decision-maker, sweatshop labor is significant or meaningful only to the extent it reduces cash outflows (and increases profits) by reducing labor costs. Likewise, the elimination of health care benefits . . . can be considered meaningful or significant only to the extent that these actions may reduce an entity's future obligations. . . . Indeed, the impact of corporate actions and choices upon the lives of current and former employees, the environment, communities and almost anyone or anything other than investors and creditors is likely to be regarded as irrelevant, insignificant, meaningless and inappropriate for inclusion in accounting reports.

(pp. 596–7)

A. Should companies try to measure their effects on the environment?
B. Should they try to measure their effects on their employees?
C. Do you agree that a focus on measuring profits, but not measuring other impacts of the corporation, can have bad effects on society?

D10. (Accounting measurement and society) In the 1980s and early 1990s, the "savings and loan" banks in the United States ran into great financial difficulty because of mismanagement, changes in regulations, and changes in interest rates. Over 1,000 were closed by the U.S. government. Because the U.S. government insured the deposits in these banks, the cost to the U.S. government was very large—about $160 billion.
During the "Savings and Loan Crisis," regulators had to decide whether to declare that particular banks were "insolvent." If the bank was declared insolvent, the government would incur costs of closing it. If the bank was not declared insolvent, it would stay in business, and might earn enough money to get out of trouble. Of course, it might also lose more money, and the later cost of closing it would be higher.
Whether a bank was "insolvent" depended on the accounting rules used to measure the value of its assets.
The chapter discussed three different views of how accounting rules should be set: a critical–interpretive view; an economic consequences view; and a decision-usefulness view. Consider how each of these views might be used to decide on either valuing the bank's assets optimistically, or conservatively.

D11. (Standard-setters) In the 1930s, when the SEC was created, it was not clear whether the SEC would simply set all accounting standards, or whether it would let the private sector, and private bodies of accountants, take the lead on setting standards. The decision by the SEC to allow private standard-setting bodies to take the lead on accounting principles came on a 3–2 vote in 1938 (Davidson and Anderson 1987). As noted in the text, U.S. and international standards are set by private organizations, the FASB and the IASB, and not mainly by governments.

A. What are reasons that the standards should have been set by governments instead of private bodies?
B. What are reasons that private bodies would do a better job of setting standards than governments?

Research Questions

R1. (SEC) The SEC website contains a great deal of information about accounting rules and particular companies. The home page is at www.sec.gov.

A. Go to the SEC home page, and click "About" and then "What We Do." What does the SEC see as its goals?
B. From the SEC home page, click "Divisions" and then "Corporate Finance" and then "Accounting and Financial Reporting Guidance." What types of activities does the SEC perform in this area?
C. From the SEC home page, click "Enforcement" and then "How Investigations Work." What are some common types of violations of the law that the SEC investigates?

R2. (FASB) The FASB website contains copies of standards it has set, and information about its activities. Parts of this website require you to pay for access, but other parts are publicly available. Many universities have purchased academic access codes, so your instructor may be able to give you an access code. The website is www.fasb.org.

A. Go to the FASB home page, and then click "about us" and then "Facts About FASB."

    a. What is the mission of the FASB?
    b. Is it part of the government?

B. From the home page, go to the tab marked "About Us" and then "Standard-Setting Process." Read this information.

    a. Do you think this process for setting standards works quickly, or slowly? Why?
    b. Why do you think that the FASB uses this process of setting standards after getting input from various stakeholders?

R3. (FASB Concepts) Go the FASB's website at www.fasb.org. Click the tab for "Standards," and then "Concepts Statements."

A. What does the FASB say is the purpose of the Concepts Statements?
B. Are these Concepts Statements binding rules?
C. On the same page, scroll down until you find "Concepts Statement Number 8, as issued." Click on this and accept the FASB's terms of use. You should now see the Concepts Statement.

    a. Look at paragraph OB2. What are the main objectives of financial reporting?
    b. Look at paragraphs OB9 and OB10. Who are some other potential users of financial statements? Does the FASB intend financial statements to be useful for these other users?

R4. (IASB) The IASB website, www.iasb.org, contains much information about this organization.

  A. Go to the home page, and then click on the tab "About us." What kind of organization is the IASB? Is it a governmental or private organization?
  B. From the "About us" tab, click on "Who we are and what we do." What is the IASB's goal?
  C. On the "Who we are and what we do" page, there is a list of members of the International Accounting Standards Board. How many countries do they come from?
  D. From the same "Who we are and what we do" page, find out about how many countries either permit or require the use of International Financial Reporting Standards (IFRS).
  E. From the IASB home page, click "Standards development," and then "Standard-setting process."

  a. Do you think this process for setting standards works quickly, or slowly? Why?
  b. Why do you think that the IASB uses this process of setting standards after getting input from various stakeholders?

Notes

 1 Arthur C. Clarke's 1968 comment that "Any sufficiently advanced technology is indistinguishable from magic" (cited in Shapiro (2006), p. 157) can apply to how accounting reports are viewed by non-accountants.
 2 Detailed knowledge of particular accounting issues is important, but discussing it too early will get in the way of understanding more general concepts. Part 4 deals with detailed recording of particular business events. The discussions of general principles and problems in Parts 2 and 3 provide the necessary context.
 3 See Stevens, Dillard, and Dennis 1985.
 4 See for example Biondi et al. (2012). See also Waymire and Basu (2008), who write that "By 1900, elements of modern principles were grounded in longstanding conventions characterizing practice in both Britain and the United States. These conventions included the entity concept, going concern, periodicity, revenue realization, historical cost, and conservatism, all of which had been fostered by the combined forces of corporate expansion, legal precedents, and economic crises" (p. 125).
 5 Note that this is the idea of "stewardship," although that term is not used. The FASB noted that "The Board decided not to use the term *stewardship* in this chapter because there would be difficulties in translating it into other languages. Instead, the Board described what stewardship encapsulates" (para. BC128).
 6 This view of earnings quality is widespread. See, for example, American Accounting Association (2009).
 7 A literature review of studies trying to relate differences in both financial accounting practices and management control systems to cultural values across countries is Chanchani and MacGregor (1999).
 8 Of course, companies do guard against accidental or intentional distortions of internal information. Employees, for example, might be tempted to distort sales in order to meet bonus targets. Chapters 9 and 10 discuss these issues.
 9 This term goes back to the practices of owners of land in England of hiring people called "stewards" to run their land. The stewards then had to account for the earnings and expenses of the farms.
10 A committee of the American Accounting Association (1971a) stated that "The . . . accounting system does not have to reflect economic reality as long as it is accepted by the parties involved, although it will generally be less controversial if it does mirror economic reality".
11 Stephen Zeff (2005) cites a 1973 report as the first authoritative adoption of a "decision-usefulness" approach to accounting standards. The traditional emphasis was on stewardship reporting. McKernan (2007) notes that Zeff, in 1978, had suggested that a decision-usefulness approach "served to lessen the inclination of accountants to argue over the inherent 'truth' of different accounting incomes, and instead to focus on the use of information by those who receive accounting reports" (p. 174). The shift from an emphasis on accountability for past actions to focusing on usefulness for future decisions was controversial. Young (2006) notes that most people responding to a 1974 FASB discussion memorandum opposed the decision-usefulness view. Young also notes that the focus on the presumed needs of rational

investors and creditors simplified the process of rule-making, since the FASB did not have to consider other users' needs.

12   There are situations where there is a "score-keeping" aspect to managerial accounting. For example, an employee may be entitled to a bonus computed using the amount by which measured results exceed budgeted results. In this case, the fact that the rules defining budgeted and actual measurements are agreed-upon is more important to the accounting than exactly how well the rules comply with economic theory.

13   Table 1.2 represents my synthesis of ideas from a number of sources, including: Littleton (1933); Most (1982); Fesmire (1967); Inoue (1978/1979); Bougen (1994); Waymire and Basu (2008) and Salvary (1979).

14   See Englund, Gerdin, and Burns (2011). They also list changes in ownership structure and general social conditions as sources of accounting changes.

15   There are several biblical references to proper measurement. For example, "A false balance is an abomination to the Lord; but a perfect weight is his delight." (Proverbs 11:1) and "Ye shall do no unrighteousness in judgment, in mete-yard, in weight, or in measure. Just balances, just weights, a just ephah, and a just hin, shall ye have." (Leviticus 19:35–36) The Jewish Publication Society of America 1955.

16   Objectivity requires that values be based on independently verifiable evidence, rather than subjective estimates. Revenue recognition at time of sale means that a firm is considered to earn revenues when it delivers goods to customers. Finally, historical cost accounting requires companies to value at assets at their cost, not at their current value. All these concepts helped to increase the SEC's ability to check companies accounting, but they also reduced the ability of ethical managers to communicate changes in the values of their businesses.

17   Englund, Gerdin, and Burns (2011) discuss research on the "constituting power" of accounting, its role in legitimation and its roles in "facilitating the exercise of power" (p. 500).

18   See Searle 1965.

19   See Tinker 1985.

20   "Numbers create and can be compared with norms, which are among the gentlest and yet most pervasive forms of power in modern democracies" (Porter 1995, p. 45).

21   A stock option gives the holder the right to buy stock at a specified "exercise price" for some period of time. If the stock's market price is higher than the exercise price, the holder of the option can exercise the option, and sell the stock for a profit. If the market price of the stock stays under the exercise price, the holder of the option will not exercise it. In that case, the holder has neither gain nor loss.

22   Another reason cited by the opposition is the difficulty of accurately valuing options.

23   For example, after the 2008 financial crisis, European Union countries pressured the IASB to change rules measuring the solvency of banks. See Bengtsson (2011).

24   This statement restates ideas in FASB (1980).

25   This example is loosely based on a situation reported by Tony Tinker (1985).

26   See the FBI website, www.fbi.gov/stats-services/crimestats (last accessed August 14, 2015).

27   www2.fbi.gov/ucr/cius2006/about/about_ucr.html (last accessed August 14, 2015).

References

American Accounting Association. (1971a). Report of the Committee on Foundations of Accounting Measurement [Supplement]. *Accounting Review, 46*(4), 1–48.

American Accounting Association. (1971b). Report of the Committee on Accounting Theory Construction and Verification [Supplement]. *Accounting Review, 46*(4), 51–79.

American Accounting Association. (2009). The impact of academic accounting research on professional practice: An analysis by the AAA Research Impact Task Force. *Accounting Horizons, 23*(4), 411–56.

APB. (1970). *Statement of the Accounting Principles Board No. 4, Basic Concepts and Accounting Principles Underlying Financial Statements of Business Enterprises.* New York: AICPA.

Arnold, P. J. (2009). Global financial crisis: the challenge to accounting research. *Accounting, Organizations and Society, 34*(6), 803–9.

Ash, E., & Strittmatter, R. (1992). *Accounting in the Soviet Union.* New York: Praeger.

Barth, M. E. (2007). Standard-setting measurement issues and the relevance of research [Supplement]. *Accounting and Business Research, 37,* 7–15.

Barth, M. E. (2013). Measurement in financial reporting: The need for concepts. *Accounting Horizons, 28*(2), 331–52.

Bengtsson, E. (2011). Repoliticalization of accounting standard setting—The IASB, the EU and the global financial crisis. *Critical Perspectives on Accounting, 22*(6), 567–80.

Biondi, Y., Glover, J., Jamal, K., Ohlson, J. A., Penman, S. H., Sunder, S., & Tsujiyama, E. (2012). Some conceptual tensions in financial reporting. *Accounting Horizons, 26*(1), 125–33. (American Accounting Association's Financial Accounting Standards Committee)

Bougen, P. D. (1994). Joking apart: The serious side to the accountant stereotype. *Accounting, Organizations and Society, 19*(3), 319–35.

Chambers, R. J. (1965). Measurement in accounting. *Journal of Accounting Research, 3*(1), 32–62.

Chanchani, S., & MacGregor, A. (1999). A synthesis of cultural studies in accounting. *Journal of Accounting Literature, 18*, 1–30.

Chiapello, E. (2007). Accounting and the birth of the notion of capitalism. *Critical Perspectives on Accounting, 18*(3), 263–96.

Davidson, S., & Anderson, G. D. (1987). The development of accounting and auditing standards. *The Journal of Accountancy* (May), 110–27.

De Jager, P. (2014). Fair value accounting, fragile bank balance sheets and crisis: A model. *Accounting, Organizations and Society, 39*(2), 97–116.

Dimnik, T., & Felton, S. (2006). Accountant stereotypes in movies distributed in North America in the twentieth century. *Accounting, Organizations and Society, 31*(2), 129–55.

The Economist. (1990, December 22). Blowing the Whistle on Accountancy. *The Economist*, p. 15.

Englund, H., Gerdin, J., & Burns, J. (2011). 25 years of Giddens in accounting research: achievements, limitations and the future. *Accounting, Organizations and Society, 36*(8), 494–513.

FASB. (1978). Statement of Financial Accounting Concepts No. 1, *Objectives of Financial Reporting by Business Enterprises*. Stamford, CT: FASB.

FASB. (1980). Statement of Financial Accounting Concepts No. 2, *Qualitative Characteristics of Accounting Information*. Stamford, CT: FASB.

FASB. (2008). Statement of Financial Accounting Concepts No. 2 (as amended), *Qualitative Characteristics of Accounting Information*. Norwalk, CT: FASB.

FASB. (2009). Statement No. 168 (Superseded). *The FASB Accounting Standards Codification® and the Hierarchy of Generally Accepted Accounting Principles—a replacement of FASB Statement No. 162*. Norwalk, CT: FASB.

FASB. (2010). Concepts Statement No. 8, *Conceptual Framework for Financial Reporting*—Chapter 1, *The Objective of General Purpose Financial Reporting*, and Chapter 3, *Qualitative Characteristics of Useful Financial Information* (a replacement of FASB Concepts Statements No. 1 and No. 2) (pp. 1–14, 16–22). Norwalk, CT: FASB.

Fesmire, W. (1967). A peripatetic history of accounting. *Cost and Management* (July–August), 33–8.

Ijiri, Y. (1967). *The Foundations of Accounting Measurement: A Mathematical, Economic, and Behavioral Inquiry*. Englewood Cliffs, NJ: Prentice-Hall, Inc.

IMA. (2008). *Statement on Management Accounting No. 1. Definition of Management Accounting*. Montvale, NJ: Institute of Management Accountants.

IMA. (2014). *Conceptual Framework for Managerial Costing. Report of the IMA Managerial Costing Conceptual Framework Task Force*. Montvale, NJ: Institute of Management Accountants.

Inoue, K. (1978/1979). The oldest book of double entry bookkeeping in Germany. Working Paper No. 24. In E. N. Coffman (Ed.), *The Academy of Accounting Historians Working Paper Series, Vol. 2 (Working Papers 21–40)*. Richmond, VA: Virginia Commonwealth University. (Original work published 1978.)

Jeacle, I. (2008). Beyond the boring grey: The construction of the colourful accountant. *Critical Perspectives on Accounting, 19*(8), 1296–1320.

Jensen, R. E. (1971). Logic and Sanctions in Accounting: Critique. In R. R. Sterling & W. F. Bentz (Eds.), *Accounting in Perspective: Contributions to Accounting Thought by Other Disciplines*. Papers and Discussions from an Accounting Colloquium by the University of Kansas School of Business and the Arthur Young Foundation. Houston, Texas: Scholars Book Co.

Jewish Publication Society of America. (1955). *The Holy Scriptures According to the Masoretic Text: A New Translation*. Philadelphia: The Jewish Publication Society of America.

Laux, C., & Leuz, C. (2009). The crisis of fair-value accounting: Making sense of the recent debate. *Accounting, organizations and society, 34*(6), 826–34.

Littleton, A. C. 1933. *Accounting Evolution to 1900*. New York: American Institute Publishing Company.

McKernan, J. F. (2007). Objectivity in accounting. *Accounting, Organizations and Society*, *32*(1), 155–80.

Micheli, P., & Mari, L. (2014). The theory and practice of performance measurement. *Management Accounting Research*, *25*(2), 147–56.

Morgan, G. (1988). Accounting as reality construction: Towards a new epistemology for accounting practice. *Accounting, Organizations and Society, 13*(5), 477–85.

Most, K. S. (1979). Sombart on accounting history. Working Paper No. 35. In E. N. Coffman (Ed.), *The Academy of Accounting Historians Working Paper Series, Vol. 2 (Working Papers 21–40)*. Richmond, VA: Virginia Commonwealth University.

Most, K. S. (1982). *Accounting Theory* (2nd ed). Columbus, Ohio: Grid Publishing, Inc.

Mouck, T. (2004). Institutional reality, financial reporting, and the rules of the game. *Accounting, Organizations, and Society, 29,* 525–41.

Nobes, C. (2011). IFRS practices and the persistence of accounting system classification. *Abacus, 47*(3), 267–83.

Norris, F. (2005, April 28). Accounting rules in U.S. a bit lacking, Europe says. *New York Times*, p. C4.

Porter, T. M. (1995). *Trust in Numbers: The Pursuit of Objectivity in Science and Public Life*. Princeton, NJ: Princeton University Press.

Rudner, R. S. (1966). *Philosophy of Social Science*. Englewood Cliffs, NJ: Prentice-Hall, Inc.

Salter, S. B., & Niswander, F. (1995). Cultural influence on the development of accounting systems internationally: A test of Gray's [1988] theory. *Journal of International Business Studies, 26*(2) 379–97.

Salvary, S. C. W. (1979). Tracing the development of a conceptual framework of Accounting—A Western European and North American linkage: A partial examination. Working Paper no. 40. In E. N. Coffman (Ed.), *The Academy of Accounting Historians Working Paper Series, Vol. 2 (Working Papers 21–40)*. Richmond, VA: Virginia Commonwealth University.

Searle, J. R. (1965). What is a Speech Act? In M. Black (Ed.), *Philosophy in America* (pp. 221–39). London: George Allen & Unwin Ltd.

Shapiro, B. P. (1997). Objectivity, relativism, and truth in external financial reporting: What's really at stake in the disputes? *Accounting, Organizations and Society, 22*(2), 165–85.

Shapiro, F. R. (Ed.). (2006). *The Yale Book of Quotations*. New Haven: Yale University Press.

Stevens, R. G., Dillard, J. F., & Dennis, D. K. (1985). Implications of formal grammars for accounting policy development. *Journal of Accounting and Public Policy, 4,* 123–48.

Suzuki, T. (2003). The accounting figuration of business statistics as a foundation for the spread of economic ideas. *Accounting, Organizations and Society, 28,* 65–95.

Tinker, T. (1985). *Paper Prophets: A Social Critique of Accounting*. New York: Praeger Publishers.

Tyson, N. D. (1999). Measure for Pleasure. Foreword. In K. Ferguson, *Measuring the Universe: Our Historic Quest to Chart the Horizons of Space and Time* (pp. ix–xiii). New York: Walker & Company.

Watts, R. L., & Zimmerman, J. L. (1979). The Demand for and Supply of Accounting Theories: The Market for Excuses. *The Accounting Review, 54*(2), 273–305.

Waymire, G. B., & Basu, S. (2008). *Accounting is an Evolved Economic Institution*. Hanover, MA: Now Publishers Inc.

Young, J. J. (2006). Making up users. *Accounting, Organizations and Society, 31*(6), 579–600.

Zeff, S. A. (2005). The evolution of U.S. GAAP: The political forces behind professional standards—Part 2: 1973–2004. *The CPA Journal, 75*(2), 18–29.

Part 2

Measurement Under Ideal Conditions

The next four chapters discuss how accounting is supposed to work as a measurement system. Chapter 2 explains the rules accountants use to recognize and classify economic events. Chapter 3 discusses how accounting measurements are reported. Chapters 4 and 5 explain the usefulness of financial and managerial accounting information in making a variety of decisions.

Readers interested in understanding the bookkeeping process may also wish to refer to Appendix A.

2   Classifying and Measuring Activities

Outline

- Preliminary Thoughts
- Learning Objectives
- Desirable Characteristics of Accounting Measurements
- Classification of Accounting Data into Elements
- Fundamental Rules of Accounting
- Special Rules of U.S. Financial Accounting
- Illustration of Concepts—Smith's Clothing Store
- Usefulness of the Accounting Elements and Rules
- Issues of Accounting Measurement
- Role of Standard-Setters
- Research and Accounting Classification and Measurement Rules

Preliminary Thoughts

Accounting does not wait to be found or discovered, like an atomic particle or a pulsar; subjects like accounting must be invented or created.

Tony Tinker (1985, p. 206)

What's in a name? That which we call a rose
By any other name would smell as sweet

William Shakespeare (1595)[1]

Accounting has a complicated set of rules on how one may express economic events of an entity. These rules are aimed at serving people; but, on the other hand, people are constrained by them. Unless people sacrifice their freedom and observe the rules, accounting cannot serve them.

Yuji Ijiri (1971, p. 3)

Accounting standard-setting is a process . . . which constructs . . . accounting facts by including and excluding particular matters, transactions and objects within the financial statements. Through inclusion by measurement and disclosure, importance and relevance are assigned to some matters and objects; and through exclusion, immateriality and insignificance are ascribed to others. This assignment into categories of importance and unimportance is a crucial aspect of standard-setting in which reality is both ordered and constructed. This construction is controversial as items are not easily assigned to accounting categories but must instead be prodded, probed, snipped, and made to fit into these categories. Furthermore, the categories themselves are neither fixed nor immutable but are instead ambiguous and highly adaptable. With each issuance of a new standard, new items are called expense or revenue or asset or liability; new things are measured; and new things are disclosed. As these things are fitted into the old categories, the categories are stretched and perhaps twisted and are themselves altered—subtly at times and not so subtly at other times.

Joni J. Young (2003, p. 621)

"When I use a word," Humpty Dumpty said, in rather a scornful tone, "it means just what I choose it to mean — neither more nor less."
"The question is," said Alice, "whether you can make words mean so many different things."
"The question is," said Humpty Dumpty, "which is to be master—that's all."

Lewis Carroll (1871)[2]

These five quotations together outline some things to keep in mind as you encounter the basic concepts of accounting. There is some human-created world of business transactions and events. We use names and measurement systems to comprehend aspects of that world, but then our thoughts become limited by the way we measure them. How we see the world affects our freedom to act, and the decisions we make. The standards that are set make some things seem important, and other things unimportant. Who gets to set the names and measures? In Humpty Dumpty's words: "Which is to be master?"

This chapter begins by discussing general criteria for deciding what makes a measure good or bad. Next, the chapter outlines the specific vocabulary, classification system, and rules for using and combining elements that together form the basis of financial accounting. The particular rules that govern U.S. "generally accepted accounting principles" (GAAP) are briefly outlined. IFRS rules are generally similar. The remainder of the chapter expands upon these ideas: a long example illustrates the concepts; the usefulness and limitations of the system are explored; and the role of standard-setters is described. Finally, the chapter outlines areas of ongoing accounting-related research in the field of accounting classification and measurement rules.

Learning Objectives

After studying this chapter, you should understand:

1   The key qualitative factors that information should possess for:

    a.   Financial accounting, according to the FASB
    b.   Managerial accounting, according to the IMA

2   The key classifications used for accounting information:

    a.   For financial accounting purposes, the elements of accounting set by the FASB (assets, liabilities, equity, revenues, gains, expenses, losses, distributions to owners, investments by owners, and comprehensive income)
    b.   Cash flow classifications
    c.   For managerial purposes, types of costs

3   The fundamental rules of U.S. accounting

    a.   The fundamental equation (assets = liabilities + equity)
    b.   The general rules for revenue and expense recognition
    c.   GAAP accounting uses different values for different items, including historical cost for some items
    d.   The entity principle
    e.   Companies have choices of accounting policies in certain areas

4   The roles of various accounting standard-setters
5   That accounting rules, while useful, have limitations.

Desirable Characteristics of Accounting Measurements

General

What makes one measure better than another? How do we judge the effectiveness of a measurement system? In Chapter 1, some generally desirable characteristics of measurement were listed:

*   Theoretical fruitfulness
*   Power
*   Simplicity
*   Clarity
*   Relatively low cost

Those criteria are quite general, and could be applied to measures of weather as well as to accounting. The FASB has devoted considerable energy to outlining specific criteria for desirable characteristics of financial accounting information. The IMA has also established some criteria for managerial accounting measurements. The relationship of the FASB and IMA criteria to the more general criteria is the subject of this section.

IASB and FASB Criteria for Financial Accounting Measures

Primary Characteristics

The IASB and FASB have very similar conceptual frameworks. While this section mainly cites the FASB, you should assume the IASB rules are similar (IASB 2010).
   The FASB (2010) says that:

> If financial information is to be useful, it must be relevant and faithfully represent what it purports to represent. The usefulness of financial information is enhanced if it is comparable, verifiable, timely, and understandable.
>
> (para. QC4)

This short statement summarizes a lot of information. To the FASB, the two *primary characteristics* that information should have are "*relevance*" and "*faithful representation*." The other characteristics listed above are nice, but not as important. They are *enhancing qualitative characteristics*.
   Information is *relevant* if it is capable of making a difference in a user decision. One way a piece of information might be useful is if it has "*predictive value*"; that is, if it helps the user predict future results for the business. A second way information might be useful is if it has "*confirmatory value*," which helps the user decide if previous reports or decisions came out the way the user thinks they did. For example, a company might announce in January that it expects to sell some asset for $100 million. When the company later says what it actually sold the asset for, that information will either confirm the figure in the earlier announcement, or will indicate that the previous announcement was not correct.
   Some information that might be relevant to a decision becomes unimportant if the amounts involved are very small. The term that describes whether something is big enough to affect a decision is "*materiality*." *Material* items are big enough to be important, and *immaterial* items are

not. Deciding if something is material requires judgment, and materiality depends on the nature of the item, its size, the size of other financial aspects of the entity, and the needs of the user. See FASB (2010).

To summarize: to be relevant, information must have either predictive or confirmatory value (or both) and must also be large enough to be material.

Information is *representationally faithful* if it actually shows what is supposed to be the underlying concept. Thus, most people would agree that a student's height, in inches or centimeters, is representationally faithful to the commonly accepted idea of "tallness." However, it is far less clear that a GMAT score represents "intelligence."

The FASB (2010) says that for an accounting measurement to be a *"faithful representation"* of some economic transaction or event, the measurement should be as *complete, neutral,* and *free from error* as possible. *"Completeness"* means that the measurement and any extra explanatory material the accountant provides includes all the information the user needs to understand the item. A *neutral* description is unbiased. "A neutral depiction is not slanted, weighted, emphasized, deemphasized, or otherwise manipulated to increase the probability that financial information will be received favorably or unfavorably by users" (FASB 2010, para. QC14). Producing information that is *free from error* is clearly the right goal, because obviously erroneously recorded information cannot be a faithful representation of actual events. However, the FASB realizes that perfection is not always possible, and that estimates are often needed.

This emphasis on neutrality has long historical roots. Accountants have believed for a long time that public trust in the integrity of their advice and reports was essential to the survival of the accounting profession. According to Lambert and Lambert (1979, p. 40), a speaker at a 1906 convention of the American Association of Public Accountants said:

> The underlying reason for our employment is the belief of our clients that they will obtain from us a faithful representation of the true state of affairs; that we cannot be influenced to swerve from the strict line of our professional duty. . . . Our professional integrity, I repeat, is our most precious possession.

Enhancing Qualitative Characteristics

The FASB (2010) states *"comparability, verifiability, timeliness,* and *understandability* are qualitative characteristics that enhance the usefulness of information that is relevant and faithfully represented" (para. QC19, emphasis in the original). When the FASB considers two different approaches to measuring to be equally relevant, and to be equally faithful representations, it considers these secondary characteristics in choosing between the alternatives.

"Comparability" means that readers are able to properly compare two items – readers should understand the extent to which two items are similar, or different. Things that are truly similar should look similar, and things that are different should look different. When two companies report their inventory using the same accounting method, it is more likely that users can make valid comparisons of the amounts of inventories on hand than if the companies use two different accounting methods. If a company changes its accounting method, it makes it harder to compare measurements over time.

"Consistency" within one company is helpful in making numbers comparable. The FASB (2010) says: "Consistency refers to the use of the same methods for the same items, either from period to period within a reporting entity or in a single period across entities. Comparability is the goal; consistency helps to achieve that goal." (para. QC22)

"Verifiability" means that a group of competent and neutral accountants who look at the measurement would likely reach a consensus and agree that it was a faithful representation. Verifiability could relate to a point estimate, or a range, or a set of probabilities. People could verify

some measurements by directly observing something, such as by counting items of inventory, or by repeating a computation. The claim that a pizza weighs 2 pounds is verifiable because people agree on how to weigh things, but the claim that the pizza is the "best in town" may not be verifiable without agreement on what it means for pizza to be the "best."

"*Timeliness*" means that the information is given to users fast enough to be used in their decisions.

"*Understandability*" means that information is presented clearly and concisely. A limiting factor here is that accounting sometimes deals with complicated events or transactions. The FASB (2010) assumes that the users are smart, and read carefully. "Financial reports are prepared for users who have a reasonable knowledge of business and economic activities and who review and analyze the information diligently." (para. QC32)

Constraints

The FASB realized that in the real world, it is not possible to always produce information that has all of the desired characteristics.

A major constraint is *cost*. It takes time and effort to produce measurements, and sometimes it simply is not worth it to produce very exact measurements.

Uncertainty about the future means that certain measurements need to be estimated. This makes it harder to achieve verifiability.

In some cases, the various criteria conflict. For example, what value should a company place on its investment in research for a new product? What is most relevant is what the company thinks it can earn from this research. However, the company is not neutral about its own product, and it is not clear that the company's own estimate would therefore be a faithful representation of value.

IMA criteria for desirable managerial cost information

The IMA (formerly the Institute for Management Accountants) has also tried to define what makes information about product costs useful. As noted below, there are many similarities between the two sets of criteria. It has defined the two basic desirable characteristics as "*causality*" and "*analogy*."[3]

Information about costs of a product meets the idea of "*causality*" if there is a clear "cause and effect" relation between the computation of the product cost and the inputs into that cost. The strength of the causal relation may vary from strong to weak. For example, a manufacturer of shirts would see a clear causal relation between the amount of cloth that goes into a shirt and the cost of the shirt. The relation between the cost of any one shirt and the cost of heating the factory that makes many different kinds of clothes is less clear.[4] While the IMA does not discuss this, its concept of "causality" is in some ways similar to the FASB's idea of "faithful representation"—information that clearly represents a cause and effect relation can be seen as a faithful representation of how the process of producing a product works.

The IMA defines "analogy" as "The use of causal insights to infer past or future causes or effects." (p. 35) Using this criterion, information is judged on how useful it is in making future decisions. This idea is similar to the FASB's idea of *predictive value* as a component of relevance.

The IMA notes five constraints that apply when coming up with modeling the way costs behave: objectivity, accuracy, verifiability, measurability, and materiality. It also notes two constraints in how the information should be used. Managers using the information should be impartial, and managers must also try to make sure that their actions fit in with the company's overall objectives.

The constraints on modeling costs are:

- *Objectivity*: "A characteristic of a cost model that shows it to be free of any biases" (p. 69). This is similar to the FASB's concept of neutrality.

- *Accuracy*: "The degree to which managerial costing information reflects the concepts you intended to model" (p. 73). This is similar to the FASB's concept of representational faithfulness.
- *Verifiability*: "A characteristic of modeling information that leads independent reviewers to arrive at similar conclusions" (p. 75). This is the same as the FASB's view of verifiability.
- *Measurability*: "A characteristic of a causal relationship enabling it to be quantified with a reasonable amount of effort" (p. 78). This is similar to the FASB's cost constraint.
- *Materiality*: "A characteristic of cost modeling that would allow for simplification without compromising managers' decision-making needs" (p. 78). This view of materiality has a similar effect to that used by the FASB, which focused on how small the size of an item has to be before it is OK to ignore it. The IMA's view is that something is immaterial if leaving it out of a model doesn't change the model's recommendations for decisions.

The constraints on how managers should use cost information are:

- *Impartiality*: "The unbiased consideration of all resource application alternatives" (p. 78). The FASB's conceptual framework has no corresponding item, since the FASB does not suggest how users should use financial data. The FASB assumes users will be rational.
- *Congruence*: "The interdependence of individual managerial actions to attempt to achieve both individual and enterprise objectives in an optimal manner" (p. 78). The idea of congruence requires managers to recognize how their decisions affect the overall organization. Again, there is no corresponding FASB concept. The FASB is trying to help outside investors, and individual investors make their decisions separately. The IMA is dealing with managers within an organization, and decisions by some managers affect other parts of the organization.

Comparing the General Criteria for Measurements With the Sets of Criteria for Managerial and Financial Accounting

The five general criteria for measurement systems are: theoretical fruitfulness; power; simplicity; clarity; and relatively low cost. Table 2.1 compares how the FASB and IMA's systems relate to these general criteria.

Theoretical fruitfulness is important in both the FASB's and the IMA's systems, although they use other terms. Both organizations want information to be useful in decision-making. The FASB says "predictive value" is part of the *relevance* of information, and the IMA speaks of the *"analogy"* characteristic as describing the usefulness of the information for predicting the future.

Neither organization explicitly discusses the power of their systems, but both state that their systems are meant to help certain types of decisions, and other uses would need other measurements. For example, financial accounting is not meant to meet the needs of the tax authorities. The FASB assumes that its rules will be helpful to investors and creditors of all U.S. businesses and nonprofit organizations. The IMA assumes its cost principles will be useful for managerial decisions in all businesses. However, both organizations realize that there will be situations where it will be hard to perform measurements. The FASB has at various times considered whether certain rules should apply to both large and small businesses.

Simplicity and clarity are not primary goals for either the FASB or the IMA. The FASB lists understandability as an enhancing characteristic, not a primary one, and the IMA does not refer to either simplicity or clarity.

The fifth general criterion is cost. Both the FASB and IMA note the issue of cost. The FASB sees cost as a constraint on the process of providing information. The IMA uses the term "measurability" to describe the same issue.

Table 2.1 Summary of Characteristics of High-Quality Information Systems

General criteria	FASB/IASB conceptual frameworks	IMA conceptual framework for managerial costing
Theoretical fruitfulness	*Relevance* (predictive value)	*Analogy*—future decisions *Causation*—understanding past relations
	Freedom from errors is assumed to be needed for fruitfulness *Timeliness* and *completeness* are needed for fruitfulness	*Accuracy* is assumed to be needed for usefulness
	Materiality is part of relevance	*Materiality* relates to what information is needed
Power	Limited to the needs of investors and creditors	Limited to managerial decision-making
Simplicity	*Understandability* is a related but different concept. FASB will not over-simplify complex items	Not mentioned
Clarity	*Understandability* to educated and diligent users	Not mentioned
Relatively low cost	*Cost* is listed as a constraint	*Measurability* concept involves low costs
Not mentioned	*Verifiability*	*Verifiability*
Not mentioned	*Neutrality*	*Objectivity*
Not mentioned	Not mentioned	Criteria for proper use of measurements— *congruence* and *impartiality*
Not mentioned	*Consistency* and *comparability*	Not mentioned

Both the IMA and the FASB go beyond the general criteria by adding ideas related to objectivity or verifiability. The IMA also adds criteria on how measurements should be used.

Classification of Accounting Data into Elements

The next step in designing a measurement system, after deciding upon the objects and attributes, is designing a system to classify information about the objects and attributes. Businesses are complex, and many transactions and events occur every day. We need ways to mentally sort and simplify the flow of activity into a form that we can understand and use in our models and decisions.

We need a *classification system. Classification* lets us group observations into a limited number of categories, and make generalizations about the observations in each category. (See Chambers 1965.) As an example from biology, the human eye can discriminate approximately 7.5 million different colors. Obviously, we don't have 7.5 million different names for colors. Categorization of these 7.5 million different types of perception into a relatively small number of color names serves several mental functions. It reduces the need for detail descriptions. It enhances the ability to respond to stimulus. It eases mental manipulations. (See Bornstein 1979.) While all shades of red are slightly different, they are enough alike that the category "red" is useful to us.

As a general matter, the number of categories we need will depend on the decisions we need to make. There is no one theoretically correct way of categorizing accounting data. Since different users make different decisions, they need data categorized differently. Outside investors have relatively few decisions to make: for example, should they buy or sell the company's stock. Managers need much more detailed information in order to make decisions about products and operations.

Table 2.2 Accounting Classifications Used for Accrual Accounting,
         Cash Flows, and Costs

Accrual accounting	Cash flows	Costs
Assets	Operating	Variable
Liabilities	Investing	Fixed
Equity	Financing	Semi-variable
Revenues*†		
Expenses*†		Period
Gains*†		Product
Losses*†		
Investments by owners†		
Distributions to owners†		

* These four categories are the components of "comprehensive income".
† These six categories increase or decrease equity over time.

Another issue is that the users don't always know the future, and later discover they need to make decisions that they did not expect at the time the accounting system was set up.

It is hard to overstate how important classification is in accounting. In fact, one meaning of "*account*" is a category. A large part of the accounting process is devoted to deciding which "accounts" particular transactions affect.

The major categories used in accounting are listed in Table 2.2. We use three major categorization systems: *accrual accounting* for determining the company's resources, its obligations, and the changes in its position over time; *cash flows* for understanding what underlies the movements of cash into and out of the company; and *cost categories* for understanding the behavior of costs of production. Each category will be discussed separately.

Accrual Accounting Classifications

The FASB, in its Statement of Accounting Concepts Number 6 (1986), defined 10 elements of financial statements for business enterprises.[5] These serve as the fundamental categories of *accrual accounting*. They are:

• Assets
• Liabilities
• Equity (also called "net worth" or "owner's capital")
• Revenues
• Gains
• Expenses
• Losses
• Comprehensive income
• Investments by owners
• Distributions to owners.

Each of these terms is discussed below. The definitions build on each other.

Accrual Accounting

The idea of the accrual accounting system is to record the effects of events on a company at the time the events make the company better or worse off. This time is often different from the time the company receives or pays cash. For example, assume that you went out to dinner with friends, and you paid for your dinner with a credit card. You might not pay the credit card bill until much later. Under the accrual system, the idea is that the cost of the dinner should be recorded on the date of the dinner, not when the payment is made. The FASB (1978) believes that: "Information about enterprise earnings and its components measured by accrual accounting generally provides a better indication of enterprise performance than information about current cash receipts and payments" (para. 44).

Assets

Most people have an intuitive idea of what an asset is. It is something good that you own. An individual's assets might include cash, jewelry, a home, furniture, savings bonds, stocks, and so on. Luca Paciolo, in 1494, advised people to count their clothing and silverware as well (Brown and Johnston 1963). The word "asset" comes from the French for "enough" or "much" (Baladouni 1984).

Formally, FASB (2008) defines "assets" as "probable future economic benefits obtained or controlled by a particular entity as a result of past transactions or events" (para. 25).

There are a number of key aspects to this definition.

- We measure assets as of a particular date, such as at the end of business on December 31.
- The definition is future-oriented. An asset is something that will have an economic benefit in the future. Cash will have a benefit in the future, since it can be used to buy things we need or want. A building has a future economic benefit, since we can sell it, and get cash, or we can use it to earn income. Similarly, most things we think of as assets meet this definition.
- Because the future is unknown, certainty is not required. It is enough that the item will *probably* be useful in the future. Cash might be lost or stolen before it gets used, but probably will not. A building might burn down before we get any benefit from it, but that is improbable. Cash and buildings both qualify as assets. Other situations are less clear. An idea for a new product might work, but it also might not. Is it an asset?
- The definition includes the phrase "obtained or controlled by the entity." Whether a business calls something its asset is not dependent on legal ownership. It is possible for a business to have the full use of something, such as a car, without actually having legal title.[6] Accounting tries to focus on economic substance, not legal form.
- The definition limits assets to things that were acquired in *past* transactions. The things we listed as assets previously all meet this standard. Cash in the bank today was received in the past. "*Accounts receivable*," which are amounts that customers owe for items they bought on credit, exist today because the customers bought things in the past. A building is an asset now because it was bought in the past.

Some of a business's resources do not meet the definition, because they do not result from past events. For example, a sports team may announce today that it has signed a contract with some star player, who agrees to play for the team in future years in return for $50 million. Is this contract an asset? Economically, it certainly represents something that the team believes is a probable future economic benefit—the presence of this player will help the team's ticket sales and television revenues for years to come. However, it fails the accounting definition because all the events in the contract will take place in the future. The player will play in the future, and the team will pay the player in the future.

A contract which has not yet been performed by either party is called an *executory contract*. Executory contracts do not meet the accounting definition of an asset. Other examples of executory contracts include orders for goods and services that have not yet been delivered and leases of office space for future periods.

Table 2.3 Typical Assets

Cash	Accounts receivable
Marketable securities	Accrued interest receivable
Buildings	Cars
Prepaid rent	Supplies
Prepaid insurance	Land
Copyrights	Furniture and office equipment

Table 2.3 lists a number of common types of assets. Most of the terms are probably familiar. Some things that are worth noting about these terms are:

- The term *cash* usually includes both money in bank accounts and actual paper money and coins.
- *Inventory* consists of products the company expects to sell to customers as part of its ordinary business.
- *Accounts receivable* is the money that a company expects to receive from customers who have bought products in the past on credit.
- *Prepaid rent* or *prepaid insurance* or other *prepaid expenses* are recorded when a company has paid for something in the past, and expects to get a future benefit. For example, a company may pay for a full year's insurance at once, and at that time it expects to enjoy the benefits of insurance coverage in the future.
- *Accrued receivables* arise when the company has earned something, but has not yet been paid. For example, a company may have loaned money to another company, and interest has been earned, but not yet collected.

Liabilities

In common speech, liabilities are obligations to pay something. For example, car loans, home mortgage loans, credit card debt, bills received from suppliers for merchandise shipped, and unpaid income taxes are all liabilities.

The FASB (2008) defines liabilities as "probable future sacrifices of economic benefits arising from present obligations of a particular entity to transfer assets or provide services to other entities in the future as a result of past transactions or events" (para. 35).

This definition is parallel to the definition of an asset. Like assets, liabilities are measured at a point in time. Again, we are dealing with probable future events affecting an accounting entity. Assets relate to future economic benefits; liabilities involve giving up ("sacrificing") economic benefits in the future. A business might give up economic benefits by paying cash, but it might also give up other assets, or deliver services, to satisfy its creditors.[7] A bank loan is a liability now because a future payment is required. Once there are no more future payments, there is no more liability.

Just as the definition of an asset does not rest on legal title, a liability need not be an enforceable legal obligation at the current time. For example, businesses generally recognize liabilities for pensions earned by their employees when the employees earn the pensions, because that is when a future obligation is created, even if the pension laws do not make these pensions immediately legally enforceable.

Like assets, liabilities exist *now* because of *past* events, and must be measured as of a particular instant in time. A bank loan is a liability now because the business borrowed the cash at some past time. An "*account payable*" is the money due to a supplier for goods that have been delivered in the past, on credit. It is a liability now because of the shipment in the past.

Box 2.1 Typical Liabilities

Accounts payable	Accrued wages payable to employees
Loans payable to banks	Payroll taxes withheld from employees
Accrued income taxes payable	Accrued rent payable
Accrued interest payable on loans	Unearned income (also called "deferred revenue")
Long-term debt	Notes payable
Loans payable to shareholders	Accrued accounting fees payable

---

Accrued income taxes payable is a liability now because of income the business has had up until now.

We do not recognize as liabilities the entity's obligations that may occur in the future under executory contracts, or other future events. For example, a business may have a five-year employment contract with a key employee. The five years of future pay is not a liability, since the employee has not yet done the work needed to earn it.

The definitions of assets and liabilities both involve *past* events, *present* conditions, and *future* benefits or sacrifices.

Box 2.1 lists some typical liabilities. Most are probably familiar to you. A few points should be noted:

- Accounts payable are amounts the company owes to suppliers because it bought inventory on credit. What is an account payable to the buyer is an account receivable to the seller.
- Certain liabilities arise because some obligation has built up, or "accrued," but has not yet been paid. Examples are accrued wages payable, accrued rent payable, and accrued interest payable.
- "Unearned income" arises when a company has received cash, but has not yet delivered the related service. The term "deferred revenue" means the same thing. For example, an insurance company that receives a car insurance premium for the next 12 months has not yet earned all 12 months of this payment. It will only earn the money over time, as it provides the insurance coverage. The payment of the insurance premium for 12 months in advance causes the company paying the premium to record a prepaid insurance asset, and the insurance company to record an unearned income liability.

Equity

The *equity* (sometimes called "net worth" or "net assets") of an entity is the difference between the total of its assets and the total of its liabilities. Algebraically, equity is defined by the following identity:

assets – liabilities ≡ equity.

If there are more assets than liabilities, equity is a positive number. If there are more liabilities than assets, equity is negative. The FASB's (2008) definition is "Equity or net assets is the residual interest in the assets of an entity that remains after deducting its liabilities." (para. 49) Like assets and liabilities, equity is measured at a point in time. The terminology used for equity varies somewhat depending on the type of business. Table 2.4 lists some common terms.

Table 2.4 Typical Equity Accounts

For a one-person business	John Doe, capital
For a partnership	John Doe, capital
	Mary Roe, capital
For a corporation	Common stock, at par value
	Contributed capital in excess of par
	Retained earnings
For a nonprofit organization	Fund balance or equity or net assets

The definition of equity can be rearranged as

assets ≡ liabilities + equity.

This equation is the *fundamental accounting equation.* It is the basis of financial accounting. There are several important points to make about it.

First, the left side (the asset side) lists the company's resources. The right side lists the various claims against those resources. Someone must have a claim to every resource, because any resources left unclaimed by creditors belong to the owners by definition. Therefore, the total resources must equal the total claims on the assets.

Second, the right side lists the financing that was provided to the business, by owners or investors. Liabilities occur when creditors advance funds or other assets to the business. Equity arises when owners either advance new funds, or allow the company's income to stay in the business. The left side shows the company's investments in assets at the present time. Again, the relationship must balance. All investments must have been financed somehow, and all financing must either have been left in cash, or invested in some other asset that exists now.

Third, an accountant can never make a change in just one item, because the accounting equation must always be kept in balance. Because we must always change at least two categories, the accounting system based on this equation is called "*double-entry bookkeeping.*" (Appendix A discusses how this system works in detail, including how every transaction is recorded using "debits" and "credits.")

The requirement to keep the equation in balance enforces discipline on the accounting process. As Yuji Ijiri (1967) has noted:

> An accountant who has been trained in double-entry does not and cannot look at an increase in inventories [by] itself since he has no means to express such an isolated change in assets. In order to express the change he must search for . . . [another] account and in doing so he is unconsciously looking for the cause or the effect of the change in inventories. This puts tremendous pressure on his thinking processes, considering that he has to make a judgment on causality every time he records business operations . . . Thus the real significance of the bookkeeping system involving double entry . . . lies in the fact that the double-entry bookkeeping system compels us to look into the causal relationships among changes in assets.
>
> (p. 109)

The net worth of a company is normally affected by four different types of transactions: revenues (and gains); expenses (and losses); investments from owners; and distributions to owners. Therefore, the relationship between the equity of a business at the beginning of a year and its equity at the end of the year can be expressed as:

ending equity = beginning equity + revenues + gains − expenses − losses
+ investments by owners − distributions to owners.

Revenues and Gains

The FASB (2008) says that revenues and gains are transactions or events, other than those with owners, which increase equity. Formally, "revenues are inflows or other enhancements of assets of an entity or settlements of its liabilities ... from delivering or producing goods, rendering services, or other activities that constitute the entity's ongoing major or central operations" (para. 78). Gains arise from peripheral or incidental activities, such as an occasional sale of a factory or other investment.

Some examples of revenues and gains are given in Table 2.5.

The distinction between revenues and gains is useful because managers and analysts use financial data to try to predict the future success of the company. Revenues such as rentals and sales are likely to recur in the future; gains are often one-time events.

Four points about revenues should be kept in mind:

1   In accrual accounting, revenues do not need to be in the form of cash. Inflows of many types of assets can be revenues. An inflow of accounts receivable would meet this definition.

2   The inflow must be "earned." All of the examples given in Table 2.6 meet these definitions— sales of products, fees for treating patients, insurance premiums, rent, and so on are all earned by the company providing the goods or services. A key issue in accounting is determining when revenue is earned.[8]

3   Unlike assets, liabilities, and equity, which are measured at a *point in time*, revenues and gains are measured *over a period* of time. Knowing a company's sales becomes far more meaningful when we know whether this is a yearly, quarterly, monthly, weekly, daily, or hourly figure. For example, knowing that sales for *Harry Potter and the Half-Blood Prince* were over six million copies becomes more impressive when we learn those were the first *day's* sales. See Box 2.2 below for a fuller discussion of the difference between measurements at a point in time and those for a period of time.

4   Both revenues and gains are net inflows of assets. Since assets increase more than liabilities, by the fundamental accounting equation equity must increase. When revenues and gains occur, their effect on the fundamental accounting equation is to increase equity on the right side of the equation. Usually, the revenue is in the form of an inflow of assets, which increases the left side of the equation, keeping it in balance. Sometimes, the revenue is in the form of a reduction in liabilities. Schematically, the effect of revenue that results in an inflow of cash (an asset) on the fundamental accounting equation is:

assets   =   **liabilities**   +   **equity**

$\uparrow$ =   (unchanged)   + $\uparrow$

Table 2.5 Some Examples of Revenues and Gains

Revenues	Gains
Sales of food by restaurant	*Sale* of factory by manufacturer
Premiums earned by insurance company	*Sales* of stock by retailer
Rents earned by a landlord	*Settlement* of patent infringement lawsuit
Interest earned by a lending company	*Insurance benefit* received on death of executive
Fees earned by a doctor	
Commissions earned by a broker	

Table 2.6 Examples of Expenses and Losses

Expenses	Losses
Salaries	Damage due to storm
Rent	Fall in value of investment
Insurance	Reduced value of foreign currency holdings due to changes in currency values
Income taxes	Unfavorable settlement of lawsuit
Cost of goods sold	Sale of factory at low price

Box 2.2 Stocks and Flows

A quantity that exists at a point of time is a "stock." A change in a stock over time is a "flow." Flows affect stocks, but are not stocks. Here is an example. Assume that your bank balance at the end of last December was $12,000. That is a stock of cash. It was affected by how much salary and interest you earned last year, and what you spent on bills. The salary was an inflow, and the payments of bills were outflows. The ending $12,000 balance is the result of some beginning balance, plus all the inflows, minus all the outflows. Similarly, a company's end of year equity is a stock, which results from the effect of various flows on the beginning balance. The flows are revenues, expenses, investments by owners, and distributions to owners.

Revenue that results in a reduction of a liability can be viewed as:

assets	=	**liabilities**	+	**equity**
(unchanged)	=	↓	+	↑

Expenses and Losses

FASB (2008) defines these terms in a fashion parallel to revenues and gains. "Expenses are outflows or other using up of assets or incurrences of liabilities . . . from delivering or producing goods, rendering services, or carrying out other activities that constitute the entity's ongoing major or central operations." (para. 80) Losses are outflows or other net reductions of assets that arise from peripheral or incidental activities or events. The distinction between losses and expenses helps us judge the underlying cost of running the entity's operations under normal conditions. Some examples of typical expenses and losses are shown in Table 2.6.

The points to note about expenses and losses are parallel to the discussion of revenues, but there are important differences.

1   In accrual accounting, expenses need not be in the form of cash. Often accountants recognize the existence of an expense before cash has to be paid, if a liability has been incurred. Other times, the outflow of assets that creates the expense is of non-cash assets. For example, when a store sells shoes, the outflow of shoes to customers is an expense.

2   The definition of expenses is not as restrictive as that of revenues. Revenues must be "earned." The question of exactly when expenses are deemed to have been "incurred" is discussed later in this chapter, and in Chapters 8 and 9. At this point, it is worth noting that in some

situations accountants require more evidence to conclude a firm has earned revenues than that it has incurred expenses.

3   Expenses and losses are measured *over a period* of time.

4   Both expenses and losses are net outflows of assets. Since assets decrease more than liabilities, by the fundamental accounting equation equity must decrease. For example, assume a company has salary expense, and uses cash to pay its employees. Schematically, the effect of the expense on the fundamental accounting equation is:

$$\textbf{assets} \quad = \quad \textbf{liabilities} \quad + \quad \textbf{equity}$$
$$\downarrow \quad = \quad (\text{unchanged}) \quad + \quad \downarrow$$

What would happen if the company had incurred salary expense, but had not yet paid its employees? In that case, it would owe the employees money, meaning a liability existed. This situation would affect the fundamental equation as follows:

$$\textbf{assets} \quad = \quad \textbf{liabilities} \quad + \quad \textbf{equity}$$
$$(\text{unchanged}) \quad = \quad \uparrow \quad + \quad \downarrow$$

Comprehensive Income

FASB (2008) says: "Comprehensive income is the change in equity of a business enterprise during a period from transactions and other events and circumstances from nonowner sources. It includes all changes in equity during a period except those resulting from investments by owners and distributions to owners." (para. 70)[9]

To put it another way,

comprehensive income = (total revenues + gains) – (total expenses + losses).

For simplicity, we usually assume the term "revenues" includes "gains," and "expenses" includes "losses." Then the equation reduces to:

comprehensive income = revenues – expenses.

Of course, it is possible for income to be negative. Then, we would refer to a comprehensive loss.

In analyzing the value of a business, it is very important to separate the nonreciprocal transactions with the owners from the business's performance in dealing with third-party customers and suppliers. The long-term economic worth of a business depends on whether it can deliver goods and services that people want at a cost less than its selling prices. Revenues, gains, losses and expenses measure this ability. Investments and distributions are not relevant to measuring earnings capacity, and could easily be manipulated by the owners. That is why investments and distributions are not part of comprehensive income.

Since comprehensive income = revenues + gains – expenses – losses, we can express the change in equity during any period as:

ending equity = beginning equity + comprehensive income
+ investments – distributions.

Comprehensive income measures the net inflow of assets into the business during some period of time due to the business's central operations and whatever miscellaneous events caused gains or losses. It measures the economic viability of the business. Managers can improve a company's income both by increasing revenues and by decreasing expenses.

This definition of income differs from how people normally speak of their own personal finances. In common speech, "income" is sometimes used to mean what accountants mean by "revenues." Someone who says she has an income of $120,000 per year is probably referring to her salary, bank interest, and any other inflows of money. These would all be "revenues" in the accounting classification system. She is probably not trying to say that she keeps $120,000 of her salary after paying taxes, insurance, food, and all of her other expenses. When accountants use the term "income," we mean to consider not just revenues but also expenses. By this definition, most people's income would be far smaller than their salaries.

The term "comprehensive income" is relatively recent. There are some older and related terms that are still used in accounting.

- *"Earnings"* is similar to comprehensive income, but the computation of "earnings" does not include certain special items. One of these items is adjustments in the current year for the way certain things were accounted for in previous years. Also, the FASB and IASB have said that certain other gains and losses should not count in "earnings."
- *"Net income"* is similar to "earnings." Again, the FASB (1984) and IASB have said that certain gains and losses should not count in "net income."

Why is comprehensive income different from net income and earnings? We discuss some of the differences in later chapters, but they arise partly because different financial statement users have different needs. Over time, many contracts came to depend on net income, as it was traditionally defined. For example, loan agreements and managers' bonus agreements often referred to net income. At certain points in time the FASB and the IASB changed the rules on accounting for certain items that could have had major impacts on the reported quarterly measures of net income. These include the effects of stock market or foreign exchange market fluctuations on the values of marketable securities and investments in overseas subsidiaries. Many users felt that fluctuations in the values of these items were not useful in judging managers' performance, and therefore wanted them kept out of the definition of net income.

Investments by Owners and Distributions to Owners

Businesses interact with their owners differently than they do with their customers or suppliers. "Third parties," such as customers and suppliers, do not control the business.[10] The transactions with third parties are *"reciprocal"* transactions because each side expects to benefit. For example, a customer buys a business's products because the customer wants them, and the customer considers the price fair. The business sells to that customer because the price the customer will pay is high enough to cover the costs of the product. In reciprocal transactions, both sides expect to be better off.

Owners' dealings with the business are different. Owners can simply order the managers to do certain things, whether or not those actions benefit the company. Two important categories of *"non-reciprocal"* transactions are *"investments by owners"* and *"distributions to owners."*

Investments by owners are transfers of assets to the business by its owners, not in return for goods or services. For example, when a business is first started, the owner may contribute cash or land or a patent to the business. An investment of cash by an owner can be represented as:

$$\textbf{assets} \quad = \quad \textbf{liabilities} \quad + \quad \textbf{equity}$$
$$\uparrow \qquad = \quad \text{(unchanged)} \quad + \qquad \uparrow$$

Distributions to owners occur when the business gives assets to its owners, not in return for any service the owners have done for the business. Many American companies pay regular cash dividends to their stockholders. These dividends are a way of giving the shareholders some of the company's profits.

Investments and distributions change the equity of the *business*, but they don't make the *owners* as a group any better or worse off. For example, when a business pays a cash dividend, cash has moved from the business's bank account to the bank accounts of the owners. The company clearly has less equity. It has less cash; liabilities are not affected; therefore net assets are smaller. Schematically, a cash dividend payment can be represented as:

assets = **liabilities** + **equity**

$\downarrow$ = (unchanged) + $\downarrow$

However, the owners as a group are not worse off. Every dollar of reduced equity on the company's part is offset by an increase in the personal bank accounts of the owners. Similarly, when owners invest money in businesses, the increased worth of the business compensates for the reduction in their personal cash.

It is possible for investments and distributions to make certain owners better off than others. Accounting statements normally don't try to measure this. For example, sometimes a company will pay a high price to buy out a particular shareholder. Certain types of transactions that favor particular shareholders over others may be illegal.

Cash Flow Classifications

The previous pages dealt with classifications used in accrual accounting. This section explains the three categories used to describe cash movements (or "flows").

Financing cash flows include inflows of cash from investors and lenders when the company sells stock and borrows money. This category also includes outflows of cash to lenders for repayment of the principal of loans, and outflows of cash to shareholders for dividends or for repurchases of stock.

Investing cash flows are related to either the purchase or sale of the company's investments. For this purpose, investments include not only stocks and bonds the company owns, but factories, land, patents, and other long-lived productive assets.

Operating cash flows are cash movements that do not qualify for the other two categories. This is a residual category. Generally, operating cash flows relate to the basic operations of the company. They include cash collections from customers, receipts of interest income, payments to suppliers and employees, and so forth.

When the FASB first required companies to report cash flow information, it wanted the operating cash flows to mirror net income as closely as possible. Therefore, it defined certain types of items as operating cash flows, even though logically they might be better classified in other areas, or allocated between more than one category. Tax payments are operating cash flows. Interest payments are operating cash flows.

For certain items, the IASB allows some items to either follow the same categories as the FASB uses, or to use more logical categories. For example:

- The FASB considers interest and dividends earned on investments to be operating cash inflows. The IASB allows companies to consider these as either operating or investing cash inflows.
- The FASB requires that the interest that companies pay on their borrowings be recorded as operating cash outflows. The IASB allows companies to treat these payments as either operating or financing cash outflows.

Cost Classifications

Managerial accounting is often concerned with the behaviors of *costs*. The cost of an item represents the sacrifice incurred to obtain it. There are different ways of classifying costs, depending on the purpose of analysis.

Accountants distinguish between *product costs* and *period costs*. Product costs can be directly traced to the cost of having that a particular product. For example, when a clothing store sells a coat, the cost of the coat is a product cost. Other costs of running the store, such as the cost of heating the store, don't relate directly to any specific item sold, and they are considered costs of the time period in which they occur.

Another way that accountants classify costs, especially manufacturing costs, is based upon their relationship to the volume of production (or sales). Costs that vary directly with volume are *"variable costs."* Costs that do not vary with volume over the short term are *"fixed costs."* Costs that vary somewhat with volume are *"semi-variable costs."* For example, a retailer's variable costs include the costs of the product itself, since every sale involves a sacrifice of an item of inventory, and perhaps sales commissions that vary directly with the amount sold. The monthly rent might represent a fixed cost, if it does not vary based on sales.

A third way to classify costs is based on their relationship with the activity we are concerned with. Thus, we distinguish between the *direct costs* of producing a product, the *indirect costs* of producing the product, *selling costs* (incurred not in production but in distribution and sales), *administrative or general costs* (incurred in administering the overall enterprise), and *other costs*.

How Good is the Accounting Classification System?

A good classification system should meet certain general criteria. Some criteria that have been cited are:

1   Consistency. Similar items are always classified the same way
2   Exhaustibility, meaning we can classify all the items that we need to account for
3   Mutual exclusivity, meaning no item is classified into two different categories
4   Hierarchical integrity, meaning that subcategories can be put together in a sensible way
5   Simplicity
6   Usefulness (see Grojer 2001).[11]

Later sections of this text consider a number of issues in accounting. For right now, we can say that the classification system meets most of these criteria fairly well. Because different companies can choose different accounting methods, consistency is sometimes an issue. Also, in practice the definitions of the categories can be hard to apply. For example, an asset is something with "probable" future economic benefits. In practice, the question of how likely benefits need to be to meet this definition can be hard to apply.

Fundamental Rules of Accounting

Any formal measurement system needs a set of rules. The previous section dealt with the basic classifications used in accounting. This section deals with several pervasive types of rules for recording and measuring accounting elements.

1   *Recognition rules*—The FASB (1984) said: "Recognition is the process of formally incorporating an item into the financial statements of an entity as an asset, liability, revenue, expense, or the like. A recognized item is depicted in both words and numbers, with the amount included in the statement totals." (para. 143)

a. The rules vary among accounting systems, but every accounting system has rules to decide *when* events worth recording have occurred. For example, *cash-basis accounting* recognizes revenues when cash is received and recognizes expenses when cash is paid. Recognition under accrual accounting in the U.S. is discussed in more detail later in this chapter.

b. Accounting systems must also decide what is important enough to be worth measuring and recording. Importance in accounting is called "*materiality*." Items too small to be recorded are "immaterial."[12]

2   *Numbers*—Accounting measurements must be expressed in numbers.

3   *Consistency of usage*—Similar events, occurring at different times or to different entities, should be treated reasonably consistently.

4   *Mutually exclusive categories*—When some set of events is divided into categories, an item should not fall into two different categories. For example, a cash flow should be either operating or financing or investing, but not all three.

5   *Rules for obtaining secondary measures*—"Primary" accounting measures are measured directly. They include counts of inflows, outflows, and balances of cash or inventory or amounts owed. "Secondary" measures are obtained by transforming primary measures. For example, "total assets" is a secondary measure, created by summing all the individual assets. Proper accounting requires these transformations to be done correctly. The total must always equal the sum of its parts. (See American Accounting Association 1971.)

6   *Time*–Accounting measurements all have a time dimension. They are either measured at a point of time, or relate to a particular period. As Ijiri (1989) notes: "While each observation in the time series may contain useful information in itself, an increment or decrement, relative to its predecessor or successor, may reveal additional, potentially useful information." (p. 2)

7   *Stock/flow relationship*—The quantity on hand of some item at a point of time is sometimes referred to as the *stock* of the item. The movements of the item in and out of the organization are referred to as *flows*. A pervasive assumption in accounting is that the stock at any period of time always equals the beginning stock plus or minus the sum of all the flows during the period.

8   *Algebraic identities must be maintained*—The primary example of this rule is that accountants record transactions in a way that keeps the fundamental equation of accounting in balance. An accountant cannot record a transaction that increases the left side of the equation more than the right side without violating this rule.

Some of these ideas seem trivial, but they are all necessary.

Special Rules of U.S. Financial Accounting

General

The prior section outlined some very general rules that apply to all types of accounting. This section focuses on special rules in financial accounting as it is currently practiced in the U.S. The special aspects of U.S. accounting mainly pertain to the general rules relating to recognition, to assigning number to events, and to consistency. Where IFRS has different rules, I note these differences.

Entity Principle

This idea means that the business is the object of the accounting process. Accounting is done for particular entities. They are accounted for separately than their owners. So, for example, if you own stock in a corporation, the corporation's accounts will reflect the corporation's assets, and not the other assets and liabilities you, its stockholder, own.

Recognition Rules

Recognition in financial accounting is the process of deciding that an item or event should be recorded in the company's accounting records.

The rules for recognizing transactions and events under U.S. accounting have followed *accrual accounting* since the early 1900s.[13] Accrual accounting tries to record the effects of events on an entity when the effects build up ("accrue").

The FASB (1984) stated that, in concept, an item should be recognized if, and only if, the following four criteria are met:

- The item meets the definition of an element of financial statements.
- It can be measured with sufficient reliability.
- The information is relevant; that is, capable of making a difference in user decisions.
- The information is reliable. It is representationally faithful, verifiable, and neutral.

Revenues and gains are recognized in accordance with what is sometimes called the *realization principle*, or the *revenue recognition principle*. The word "realization" in this context means that something has "become real" by being converted into cash. This principle holds that revenues can only be recognized once they have been earned *and* they have either been realized in cash or the entity has received some other benefit that is realizable in cash. Table 2.7 shows some examples of when some kinds of revenue are considered to meet the recognition criteria.

Recently, the FASB (2014) and IASB have issued a revised principle for deciding if revenues should be recognized, which is effective for annual reporting periods starting after December 15, 2017. Under this standard, the key for whether a company can recognize revenues from dealings with customers is whether the company has fulfilled its performance obligations. For most common revenue transactions, the revised principle will result in similar treatment to the current principles.

Expenses and losses are recognized when it is clear that the entity has lost or consumed some economic benefits, whether in operations or otherwise. See FASB (1984).

What does "lost or consumed" mean? In some case, the entity simply *loses* value without getting anything in return. An example might be storm damage, which would be recognized when

Table 2.7 When Some Common Revenues are Recognized

Revenue type	When recognized
Sales of product by retailer	Upon delivery to customer who either paid or promised to pay. The revenue was earned by providing the product. The receipt of the promise to pay is considered a benefit that is realizable in cash.
Increase in value of stock held by a stockbroker	Upon change in value of the stock. The broker earned the revenue by deciding to hold, not sell, the stock. The stock is realizable in cash.
Rent revenue by a landlord	Recognized as the tenant occupies the space, regardless of the timing of payment of rent. Providing the space is the activity that earns the revenue.
Insurance premium revenue by a car insurance company	Recognized monthly as insurance coverage is provided. Usually, premiums were received in cash at the start of the policy, but they are not earned until the company provides coverage.

it occurs. In other cases, the entity spends money or incurs a liability in one period in order to be in a position to earn revenue in another period. For example, a company must buy inventory before it can sell it. For accounting purposes, the purchase of the inventory is not an expense; the consumption of the inventory at the time of sale to the customer is the expense.

In some cases, the timing of exactly how much of the asset's value was consumed in a year is difficult to figure out. For example, a company may use a factory for 30 years, and it may use a patent for 10 years. Over the lives of the building and the patent, clearly value is being consumed, but the company may have no good way to estimate how much value is consumed each month or each year. In these situations, accountants apportion or *"allocate"* the value to time periods when these assets are being used in some systematic and rational way. Terms used in accounting to describe allocation of values to time periods include depreciation (for physical assets like buildings) and amortization (for non-tangible items like patents). Chapters 9 and 10 deal with allocation issues.

U.S. accounting historically had a conscious bias towards *"conservatism"* or *"prudence."* When there was doubt as to whether to recognize an item, or the amount at which to recognize it, it was considered "conservative" to be reluctant to recognize revenues and assets, and to be more willing to recognize expenses and liabilities. Waiting to recognize revenues until the company has realized cash from a transaction is a conservative approach to revenue recognition.[14] The FASB and IASB's conceptual frameworks now reject the idea of conservatism as a violation of their principle that measurements should be neutral and unbiased.[15]

In most cases, following the accounting rules will mean the expenses of earning revenue will be recognized at the same time as the revenue. This is called *"matching."* It is easier to analyze the profitability of a business when all related revenues and expenses are properly matched. However, there are situations where the FASB and IASB rules will not result in good matching.[16]

An assumption that underlies the expense and recognition rules is that the company is going to continue to operate in the future much as it does now. This is called *the going concern assumption*, or *going concern principle*. It allows us to assume that the business has a future, and that some costs incurred today can appropriately be allocated over future periods. If the company is clearly going out of business, different accounting rules will be used.

The revenue and expense recognition rules make accrual accounting very different from cash-basis accounting. Under the accrual basis, revenues and expenses are often recognized in different time periods than the periods in which cash is received or spent.[17] The differences in timing between the cash movements and the recognition of revenues and expenses require us to define four new concepts, summarized in Table 2.8.

- A *"deferred"* or *"unearned"* revenue is a liability that arises when the business receives cash from a customer before it earns it. The business has an obligation to either finish the work of earning the money, or to refund the money. The business records both an increase in cash and a liability called deferred or unearned revenue.
- A *"prepaid expense"* is an asset that is recorded when the business pays cash for a service it has not yet consumed. For example, businesses often pay insurance in advance. The money that has been spent on future insurance is not yet an expense, according to the matching principle, since it relates to future months' operations. When companies pay for these services, they record a decrease in cash, and an increase in "prepaid assets." The term "deferred charges" is also sometimes used in these situations.
- *"Accrued liabilities"* are liabilities that occur when the business obtains goods and services, or incurs a liability, but has not yet paid cash. For example, each month interest builds up, or "accrues" on outstanding loans.
- *"Accrued revenues"* are assets recorded when a business earns money, but the customer has not yet paid. For example, a bank earns ("accrues") interest on money it has loaned to borrowers each month.

Table 2.8 When are Deferred and Accrued Assets and Liabilities Recorded?[18]

	Did cash move before or after goods and services were provided?	
	Before	*After*
Buyer records—at time of cash payment	Prepaid asset	Accrued liability/accounts payable
Seller records—at time cash is received	Unearned/deferred revenue	Accrued revenues/accounts receivable

Values in U.S. Accounting

A second distinguishing feature of U.S. accounting is the number values it assigns to items. What numerical values should be assigned to items like buildings or inventory or loans payable? Chapter 7 will deal with this topic in more depth.

The U.S. system of accounting was historically considered to use the "*historical cost*" basis, because we generally measured such items as inventory and buildings based on what the items actually *cost* when the company bought them. Historical cost has the great advantage of being easy to verify, so it is a reliable basis of accounting. In addition, in periods of inflation, the cost of assets was often lower than their current value, so historical accounting produced "conservative" measurements of assets' income and equity.

There are times when other bases of accounting than historical cost are more relevant, and sufficiently reliable to be used. There are times when U.S. accounting uses such other measures as the current cost of replacing an item, the current market value of the item, and the present dis-counted value of the future cash flows from the item. See FASB (1984) and FASB (2000). IFRS allows companies the option of using fair market values for some items that the U.S. accounts for under historical cost. For example, companies can account for buildings using either historical cost or fair value under IFRS. Chapter 7 will deal with different types of measures that are in use in the U.S. and under IFRS.

U.S. accounting in the 20th century placed great stress on data being objectively verifiable.[19] Clearly, having objectively verifiable rules for computing income simplified administering both the income tax laws (adopted in 1912) and laws on proper disclosure of company information (adopted in the 1930s). The wide use of both the principle for recognizing revenue and the histor-ical cost basis of accounting help ensure accounting is objectively verifiable. However, this also means that sometimes the accounting rules for measuring income differ from the definitions used by economists. Table 2.9 summarizes the history of various U.S. accounting principles.[20]

Variations in Methods

A third area that distinguishes U.S. accounting relates to the variation of accounting methods across companies. In some countries, the choice of accounting methods, and the system of cat-egorizing data, is highly regulated. In the U.S. and under IFRS, companies are allowed a fair amount of choice in how they categorize transactions, and when they recognize them. The FASB and IASB deal with the issue of ensuring that users can understand and compare financial state-ments of different companies in three ways:

- Choice of accounting methods is limited to methods deemed acceptable by standard-setters. Certain methods are not allowed.

Table 2.9 Timing and Reasons for Wide Adoption of Selected Accounting Principles in the U.S.

Principle	Dates	Reasons
Conservatism	1700s to early 1900s	The main external users of financial statements were lenders. Their concern was the adequacy of their collateral. Conservatism is not now a part of the IASB or FASB conceptual framework as revised in 2010.
Going concern	Late 1800s, Early 1900s	First popularized by Lawrence Dicksee in 1892. Large companies with expensive equipment and factories became common. Cost allocation required assuming the business would continue.
Objectivity	1912, and again in 1930s	Income tax enacted in 1912. In the 1920s, many companies overestimated asset values. SEC formed in 1933.
Realization principle	Mid-1800s	Corporate form became common. Needed to determine funds available for dividends.
Realization principle, again	1920, and again in 1930s	1920—U.S. Supreme Court said income, for tax purposes, had to be realized. 1930s—SEC wanted an objective way of determining income.
Historical cost	1930s	Favored by the SEC for similar reasons as the realization principle and objectivity.
Consistency/disclosure of principles	1930s	The SEC pressed the accounting profession to adopt standard accounting principles. Firms wanted to retain some choice of principles. A compromise allows choice, as long as methods are disclosed and used consistently.
Matching	1912, then 1940s	1912—adoption of the income tax. 1940s—monograph by Paton and Littleton argued that the measurement of recurring income was what mattered to investors in stock. Since 1980s this has *not* been a principle used by the FASB in its conceptual framework.
Materiality	Unclear	The idea dates back to at least Luca Pacioli in 1494. As U.S. accountants began adopting uniform principles in the 1930s, materiality was cited as a justification for limiting the application of rules.

The information in this table relies on a variety of sources, including: Bierman et al. (1965), Brown (1975), Carey (1979), Chatfield (1977), Flamholtz (1979), Porter (1995) and Waymire and Basu (2008).

- Companies must disclose what methods they use. (Some accountants speak of a "*full disclosure principle*.")
- Companies, once they choose a method, should use it *consistently* to allow comparability of data over time. If they have a good reason to change methods, they should disclose the fact they are changing methods, as well as the effect of changing methods. This is sometimes referred to as the "consistency principle."

Illustration of Concepts—Smith's Clothing Store

This section is an extended example of how accrual accounting concepts apply to a relatively simple business situation.

Assume that, on January 1, Year 1, John Smith decides to open a clothing store. He thinks it will take three months to get the business started. For the next three months, he does all the things necessary to get the business organized. He rents a store, he buys an inventory of clothing, he finds employees, he buys $500,000 worth of shelves, cash registers, and other equipment, and he does all the other work essential to opening the store.

On April 1, Year 1, he opens the store. He sets selling prices at three times the price that he pays his suppliers for the inventory of clothing. The difference between selling and purchase prices is used to pay other bills, such as electricity, salaries, and taxes, and to earn a profit.

The store stays open until December 31, Year 5, when Mr. Smith decides to retire. In December, Year 5, Mr. Smith sells off all his remaining inventory and furniture, and pays off all the bills. He then keeps whatever money is left.

Assume he originally invested $1,000,000 in his business, and he has not had to invest any more money in the business since then. Between January 1, Year 1, and the end of the business on December 31, Year 5, he took $3,000,000 out of the business for himself.

This was obviously a profitable business. Over five years, Mr. Smith got back $2,000,000 more than he put in. His decision to keep the business running for five years looks like a good decision.

We know that his store was profitable, because we know how everything turned out at the end of five years. However, Mr. Smith had to make decisions at various times without the luxury of knowing the future. He needed reasonably timely, reliable information about how his business is doing economically.

Let's consider the type of information that he would get from an accrual accounting system at different times over the five years, and how that information would cause him to make different decisions than he would have made if he looked only at his net cash flows.

1. March, Year 1—At this point, the business is paying bills, but is not yet open for business. Rent needs to be paid, expensive furniture is being bought, inventory is being bought, and other costs are being incurred. His insurance broker insists that he pay the whole year's premium at once. Clearly March, Year 1, is a time when more money is being spent than is being earned. On a cash basis, the business is losing money.

A decision he faces is whether to keep pouring money into the business, or to give up now. If he only looks at cash, the last two months were terrible.

Under accrual accounting he probably would think he has lost money, but not that much. His business has not yet had any revenue, since he has not yet delivered goods to customers.

Under accrual accounting, not all costs are expenses. Some costs are incurred to buy other assets. Some of the bills he has paid may be considered expenses, if he can't relate them to future revenues. For example, the heating bill paid in January is not directly related to any future revenues. However, most of his outflows of cash are not expenses under accrual accounting: they are conversions of cash into other assets. The payments for furniture, inventory, and a year's worth of insurance are not yet recognized as expenses. The costs of the inventory will be recorded as assets until the inventory is sold to customers. The costs of the furniture will be allocated a little bit each month to expenses until the furniture is no longer usable. The costs of the insurance policy will be shown as expenses a little bit each month that the policy lasts. He does have less cash, but he is not economically worse off for buying inventory and furniture. Indeed, assuming he is a rational businessman, he bought each of these items expecting to be better off. However, due to the way that accounting recognizes revenues, we do not assume that he will have gains on the inventory until he actually sells it to customers.

2. April, Year 1—Customers are starting to come, and he has "earned" more than enough from clothing sales to cover his labor, rent, and other cash expenses. However, he gave 30-day credit to many customers, and he actually will not collect a large part of the money until May. Based on his cash receipts alone, he did not cover his cash costs. Should he stay open? If he does stay open, should he stop granting 30-day credit, since this caused his cash-basis loss in April?

Under accrual accounting rules, he should include both cash sales and sales on credit in his April revenues. He earned the revenues by providing goods to customers, and he received either cash or accounts receivable at the time of sale, so the revenue recognition principle is satisfied. His store made enough sales to justify staying open. If he stops giving credit, he may lose customers.

3. June, Year 1—Smith is selling clothes for an average price equal to three times what he pays his suppliers. Even after paying for labor, rent and other cash costs, his cash increased in June. All his furniture was bought in March, so there are no more furniture bills to pay, and the insurance was also prepaid in March. He was a little worried about whether he could afford high salaries, so he hired people with the promise of only moderate salaries, and a promise of bonuses in January if the year's sales were good. Cash flow for June looks really good.

A decision he faces is whether he should cut prices, to make his store a better competitor. After all, his prices seem more than high enough to cover costs.

If he bases his prices solely upon June cash flow he will underprice his product: he needs to consider all applicable costs of the business in setting prices. Accrual accounting, and a reasonable way of allocating the costs of furniture and insurance to time periods, will give him this information. June cash flow only includes a month's spending on labor and rent and other monthly cash costs. Other costs, which were either incurred in advance or incurred in future months, are not in the June cash flow computation. Prices based on June cash flow would not allow Smith to recover all the money he spent in March on furniture and inventory. Accrual basis accounting would allocate some of the costs of the furniture, the insurance, and other similar items to June. Accrual accounting would also record the cost of the items sold in June to the month of June, even though it was paid for at a different time. Mr. Smith needs to know the full costs of providing goods in order to set adequate prices.

A second problem with using cash flow information to set prices is that cash movements are volatile. If he tried to make each month's prices reflect each month's cash payments, his prices would fluctuate wildly. For example, he would have to raise prices each year in the month he paid the annual insurance bill. Given a normal competitive market, he would not always be able to sell his products in the months when he sets the higher prices.

4. December, Year 1—Sales are high, as shoppers buy their Christmas gifts. Cash flow looks great. Most of the suppliers have agreed to sell to Smith on credit, and he doesn't have to pay them until January. However, most customers pay in cash this month.

A decision he has to make is how much money he can take out of the business. As the owner, he is entitled to take some or all of the business's profits out for his own use. There's a lot of money in the bank, and he wants to enjoy his own Christmas holiday. How much of the money in the bank can he take?

Accrual basis data can help prevent him from taking too much money out of the business. Even though he does not have to pay his suppliers until Year 2, the liabilities to them are recognized when goods are received. Expenses of making sales are recorded, even if cash is not yet paid. As a result, Smith would know that enough cash must be left in the business to cover all liabilities that were incurred.

5. January, Year 2—This month, Mr. Smith wrote checks for far more money than the business received. First of all, the employees got their bonuses for Year 1. Second, the suppliers had to be paid for the big shipments they made in December. Third, about 10% of the Christmas gifts people had bought in December were returned, and he had to issue refund checks.

A decision he has to make is whether to stay in business, or "cut his losses" and stop the business.

On a cash basis, the business looks unprofitable, but on an accrual basis January was not bad. The cash-basis information for January is misleading because it counts payments that relate to prior months as expenses. January looks bad largely because Year 1 was so good—the bills to suppliers, the employee bonuses, and the sales returns are all related to money earned in December. December was not as good as it looked on a cash basis, which failed to consider the various bills that would come due in January. January was not as bad as it looks on a cash basis—many of the bills relate not to that month's operations, but to December's.

Using accrual accounting, the cost of goods sold in December, and the employee bonuses, would have already been recorded as Year 1 expenses. The sales returns also would have been considered Year 1 expenses, because they should be "matched" with the related sales.[21] Therefore, the January, Year 2 income would not be burdened by them.

Usefulness of the Accounting Elements and Rules

The example illustrates a number of ways in which the accrual accounting system provides more decision-useful information than a cash basis. A summary of its advantages includes the following:

- The system gives us tools—The concepts of assets, liabilities, equity, revenues, expenses, income, and transactions with owners. These concepts give us a framework for thinking about such transactions as the company's purchase of furniture early in the year, or the gradual build-up of bonuses due to employees.
- It forces us to think about causes—The need to keep the accounting equation in balance makes us consider the causes of all changes to accounts. For example, when the bonus obligation increases during the year, the system forces us to recognize that the company is incurring an expense.
- It focuses on earnings power—Accrual accounting focuses on the business's ability to earn more from operations than it spends, on an ongoing basis. Revenues are recognized when earned, and in most cases related expenses are recognized in the same time period. The recognition and allocation processes keep accrual-basis income from being distorted by small changes in the timing of payments and receipts.
- It realizes not all cash disbursements are expenses—Accrual accounting gives us the criteria to distinguish between "good" expenditures (those expected to bring in future benefits) and "bad" expenditures (which will not bring in future benefits). Expenditures expected to bring in future benefits are treated as assets; other expenditures are expensed. This process forces us to be forward-thinking; we must consider the impact of future events on the assets we record.
- It realizes not all cash receipts are revenues—Accrual accounting distinguishes between cash receipts which represent real net improvements of the company's position (e.g. revenues) and cash receipts which do not, such as receipts of the proceeds from borrowing. Money received now for services we have to deliver in the future creates a liability now (unearned revenues) and will not be a revenue until the company delivers the services to the customer.
- It focuses on the economic situation—Accrual accounting focuses on the economic substance of events, rather than their legal form.

Chapter 4 will be largely devoted to showing how analysts can fruitfully use accrual-basis financial reports.

Issues of Accounting Measurement

While accrual accounting provides a wealth of useful information, it is imperfect. Some of the imperfections will be discussed in detail in Part 3 of this book. However, some general issues of the accounting classification system and measurement rules should be noted here.

1. The right degree of detail in classification—There is no clear general answer as to how simple or complex the accounting classification system should be. It is not clear how summarized or detailed the categories should be. The more summarized (or "aggregated") the system, the easier it is to comprehend and the lower the cost of teaching and maintaining it. However, more

summarized systems will combine, or aggregate, more items into a single category.[22] The aggregation causes a loss of information, which is generally seen as a bad effect.

Researchers have tried to determine an optimal level of aggregation, using concepts from information theory, but have not yet been successful.[23] One issue is that accounting serves many users, who need different data inputs for their decision models. Until we know all the users, and all their decision models, we can't know precisely how best to categorize data.[24]

An American Accounting Association (1971) committee noted we need enough categories to support our decisions, and cited information theory to support the idea that a fairly complex set of categories is likely to be necessary. "[A]ccounting measurement must provide at least as many varieties as there are alternatives in a decision. . . . As the number of decisions increases, the requisite variety of accounting measurement must necessarily increase" (p. 18).

2. Ambiguity or vagueness in categories—Ideally, the accounting classifications should be mutually exclusive. We should be able to tell without any ambiguity which category to place a given item in. Unfortunately the inherent vagueness of language creates border classes. For example, the definition of assets includes the idea of "probable future benefits." Exactly how is "probable" defined? Also, some objects may strain the boundaries of our categories. For example, a convertible bond gives its owner the right to get interest income, and to be repaid when the bond becomes due. These are rights that creditors normally have. However, the owner of the bond can, at any time, convert it into stock, and become an owner. Should the holder of a convertible bond be treated as an owner, or as a creditor?[25] The difference between a revenue and a gain relates to whether the item is part of normal operations, or if it is "peripheral" to normal operations. The boundary between normal and peripheral may not be obvious.

By exploiting ambiguities in categories, companies can try to make themselves look more profitable, or more efficient, or less heavily indebted. They also can try to avoid tax payments. Many accounting standards, and much of tax law, are devoted to trying to keep people from abusing the basic principles of accounting. This ends up making accounting rules far more complicated than they would otherwise be. Theodore Porter (1995) has remarked, "Especially in law, philosophy, and finance, where clever people make a business of exploiting ambiguities, much of what would otherwise go without saying ends up having to be said." (p. 5)

3. Effect on perceptions—Like any model, or language, the accounting system shapes the way people approach the world. According to Gareth Morgan (1988),

> The idea that accountants represent reality "as is" through the means of numbers that are objective and value free, has clouded the much more important insight that accountants are always engaged in *interpreting* a complex reality, partially, and in a way heavily weighted in favour of what the accountant is *able* to measure and *chooses* to measure, through the particular schemes of accounting to be adopted.
>
> (p. 480, emphasis in the original)

Accrual accounting focuses on the measurement of income and shareholder wealth. One predictable effect of this focus would be to concentrate business people on maximizing wealth. Werner Sombart (1919) suggested this would lead people towards extremes:

> The idea of creation of wealth is developed in double-entry bookkeeping to the point where the . . . amount invested for the purpose of obtaining profits is separated from all natural objectives of human welfare. In double-entry bookkeeping there is only one objective: the increase of a sum of money, expressed in purely quantitative terms. He who buries himself in double-entry bookkeeping forgets all quantities of goods and work, forgets all the organic limitations of the necessity to satisfy human wants, and satisfies himself solely with the idea

of wealth: he cannot do otherwise if he is to understand this system: he may not see shoes or ships, corn or cotton, but only sums of money which grow bigger or smaller.

(p. 252)

At the firm level, some important organizational attributes are not directly measured by the accounting system. For example, the accounting system does not directly measure the skills, training, or motivation of the workforce. This can lead to dysfunctional behavior. For example, cutting expenditures on training will improve profits in the short term, since the expenditures on training are counted as expenses but the resulting improved employee skills are not counted by the accounting system.[26] As a second example, the accounting system is focused solely on the effect of events upon the firm. It is simply not meant to look at the impact of the firm upon society.[27]

Role of Standard-Setters

The classifications and rules of accounting are not natural phenomena. They are man-made. They derive from three major sources. In part, they have been created by an evolution of historical practices of tracking economic information. These practices arose in response to changes in business practices, and in response to taxation and other government regulations. In part, they are due to published ideas that achieved widespread voluntary adoption; for example the publication of the basic concepts of double-entry bookkeeping in Italy in 1494 shaped much subsequent development.[28] In the last century, a major source of new rules and terms has been formal bodies who are given the authority to set accounting standards.

Table 2.10 lists the major standard-setting bodies. They are a mix of government and private bodies. Internationally, standards are also set by a mix of government and private bodies. The International Accounting Standards Board is the primary private body. Most countries,

Table 2.10 Major Accounting Standard-Setting Bodies

Name	Type	Role
Securities and Exchange Commission (SEC)	Government	Can establish accounting rules for companies selling securities to the public.
Financial Accounting Standards Board (FASB)	Private	Establishes standards for for-profit and nonprofit organizations.
Governmental Accounting Standards Board (GASB)	Private	Similar to FASB, but for state and local governments.
American Institute of Certified Public Accountants (AICPA)	Private	Gives advice in areas where the FASB and SEC have not set rules. Until 1959, it also issued "Accounting Research Bulletins," some of which were adopted by the FASB.
Emerging Issues Task Force (EITF)	Private	Deals with narrow issues related to for-profit organizations.
International Accounting Standards Board (IASB)	Private	Similar to FASB, but deals with countries beyond the U.S. as well.
Accounting Principles Board (APB)	Private	This was a predecessor to the FASB. It no longer exists, but most of its "opinions" were adopted by the FASB.
Public Company Accounting Oversight Board (PCAOB)	Government	Does not set accounting rules, but sets rules auditors must follow in audits of public companies.
Government Regulatory Agencies	Government	Agencies regulating banks, railroads, utilities, and certain other industries can set rules for making regulatory reports.

including those in the European Economic Community, have adopted International Financial Reporting Standards (IFRS) for use by their public companies. The United States currently allows foreign companies to file their reports with the Securities and Exchange Commission (SEC) using either IFRS or U.S. rules, but U.S. companies must follow U.S. rules in their filings with the SEC.

The most important U.S. governmental standard-setting body is the Securities and Exchange Commission. By law, all "public companies" (those that sell stocks and bonds to a broad public) in the U.S. must comply with the SEC's rules. The SEC was created in the 1930s, to help restore public trust in the securities markets after the 1929 stock market crash. At the time, there was no such term as "generally accepted accounting principles," nor was there even any general agreement that uniform accounting standards were needed. Beginning in the 1930s, the SEC pressed the accounting profession, and the stock exchanges, to codify accounting rules.

Historically, the SEC has relied upon private bodies created by the accounting profession to create rules, and then has generally adopted those rules as its own. At first, rules were set by a committee of the AICPA. Around 1959, a new Accounting Principles Board (APB) took over the standard-setting job. The Financial Accounting Standards Board (FASB) replaced the APB in 1973. Later, the Governmental Accounting Standards Board (GASB) was established to deal with the special rules applicable to state and local governments.

The most important U.S. private bodies are the Financial Accounting Standards Board, which sets rules for both U.S. for-profit and nonprofit organizations, and the Governmental Accounting Standards Board, which sets rules for state and local government reporting. Their importance comes from two sources. First, the SEC usually requires public companies to follow FASB or GASB standards. Secondly, the ethical codes of both the American Institute of Certified Public Accountants and most state accounting licensing authorities require accountants to consider FASB and GASB statements as authoritative.

The International Accounting Standards Board is a private organization which sets International Financial Reporting Standards. Over 100 countries now allow or require their companies to use IFRS.

Standard-setting bodies can be seen as having three broad roles: a role of stimulating *research and discussion* regarding measurement tools; a *maintenance* role of preserving the usefulness of the measurement system in the face of both natural changes in the business environment and deliberate attempts to abuse the system; and a role of *balancing competing interests*.

The research role is an important one. Issues develop over time that need careful study before deciding on the proper accounting. An example is the development of accounting for companies' obligations to pay pensions to their employees. How should this obligation be measured? There are many actuarial techniques. Are all of them equally valid? What would be the effect of adopting a new rule suddenly? What would companies' financial statements look like? Would the change in their recorded liabilities cause some companies to default on bank loans? The standard-setters generally invite public comment and research as they consider new standards. They also sometimes sponsor research studies on issues.

If there were no standard-setters, the accounting measurement rules would tend to become more vague over time. In part, the drift is due to economic changes. New forms of business events arise, and in the absence of standard-setters, accountants might come up with several different ways of dealing with them. These different approaches would create ambiguity. If different accountants can measure the same thing in many different ways, the users of financial reports would be so confused that the reports would become useless.

In addition to the natural pressures on any set of rules as the economy changes, the accounting system is also under deliberate pressure from people who could gain money by changing the accounting rules. When money is at stake, people push the rules as far as they can. As Porter (1995) notes:

> Fortunes have been made and lost through the reinterpretation of financial categories; heroic entrepreneurship and criminal embezzlement may be distinguished by no more than a subtle point enunciated a few years back by the regulatory agencies. Income taxes mean nothing if definitions of investment income, depreciation, necessary business expenses, and capital gains are not defensible in courts of law.
>
> (p. 97)

In this situation, it's hard to trust people to use their judgment neutrally. Instead, there is a tendency to impose rules to ensure accounting is unbiased. In both the accounting and tax fields, a great deal of regulatory effort is needed to plug "loopholes" so existing rules will be enforced as they were originally intended to be. Unfortunately, clever people then find new loopholes, leading to still more regulation.[29]

The third key role of standard-setters is to balance competing interests. This chapter listed many different criteria for judging accounting measurements. These criteria are often in conflict. It is the role of standard-setters to make judgments. Here are some examples of choices that have to be made.

- Between relevance and faithful representation—The most relevant value is often not objectively verifiable. For example, for many decisions a manager might consider the current market value of land and buildings to be more relevant than their historical cost. However, market value is not objectively determinable in a way that is totally free from error (unless the property is actually sold), but historical cost can be easily and reliably determined.
- Between freedom from error and timeliness or cost—Some information can either be estimated quickly, or determined precisely after a considerable period of time and at considerable expense. Should quick and cheap estimates be allowed?
- Between disclosures and the interests of the owners—Disclosure can be harmful to the company. Some information can be used by competitors to hurt the company, or may cause its vendors and creditors to ask for better terms. On the other hand, outside investors and lenders need information.
- Between providing information and affecting company behavior—The FASB has been repeatedly warned that certain accounting rules, meant to provide information to investors, might make companies take actions that are not in the best interests of society. For example, in the 1970s it was warned that if it required companies to treat their expenditures on research as expenses, and not as assets, U.S. companies would do less research, and the country would become less economically productive. In the 1980s it was warned that if it required companies to report their pension obligations as liabilities, companies would stop offering generous pension benefits to employees.
- Between relevance and comparability—Requiring all companies to use the same accounting rules would improve the comparability of company performance. However, companies face different conditions, and the same rules may not be equally relevant to measuring their performance.

The three roles of standard-setters are generally more applicable to financial than to managerial accounting. For example, since managerial accounting is for internal use, there is less pressure to distort the accounting terms. Also, each management would want to make its own trade-offs between desirable features of the accounting system. Accordingly, there is less formal standardization of managerial accounting. What standardization there is tends to arise through managers choosing to use "best practices" suggested by industry associations or business schools.

Research and Accounting Classification and Measurement Rules

Here are some questions about the accounting measuring system that need better answers.

- What level of aggregation of accounting information is optimal? This requires both a better understanding of human cognition and processing of perceptions, and an economic analysis of the usefulness of different levels of information.
- What magnitude of information is immaterial? This would help auditors and regulators avoid spending time on unimportant matters. This requires understanding the decision models of users.
- How can disaggregated data be made cheaply available? This is a technical question, having to do with information coding and processing. There is a system used to encode financial accounting data in a common language ("XBRL") to make it easily shareable and comparable across companies.
- To what extent are specific rules being abused? Research is ongoing on the extent of fraud or "earnings management."
- What can be done to measure aspects of performance that are currently unmeasured? Some writers have suggested measuring companies on a "triple bottom line" that incorporates environmental, social, and financial performance. Others have suggested designing "balanced scorecards" to incorporate such factors as customer satisfaction and innovation. Government and nonprofit regulators are trying to find ways to measure the service accomplishments of these entities, not just the costs of providing services.
- How should particular transactions or events be classified? New financial instruments have been developed that do not fit neatly into the categories of liabilities and equity.
- Are there other attributes of economic activity that accounting can measure? Yuji Ijiri, for example, has proposed a variety of extensions to the traditional framework of measuring equity and income.[30] In his system, accountants would try to measure not just equity and income, but the rate at which income is changing, and the factors causing it to change.

Key Terms

Accrual accounting—This tries to record revenues, gains, expenses and losses at the time events make the company better or worse off, rather than the time that cash is received or paid. Both IFRS and GAAP follow accrual accounting.

Accrued assets or liabilities—Assets or liabilities that have built up ("accrued") over time but where the cash has not yet moved. For example, interest that has built up on a loan is an accrued asset for the lender and an accrued liability for the borrower.

Accuracy (IMA framework)—The accuracy of cost information is the extent to which it reflects the concepts the accounting is trying to measure. This is very similar to the FASB's concept of faithful representation.

Allocation—The process of splitting up some amount and assigning parts of it to various time periods, or to various products. Depreciation and amortization are allocations of costs to fixed assets and to intangible assets.

Analogy (IMA framework)—This term indicates the usefulness of some cost concept for making predictions and decisions about the future. It is similar to the FASB's concept of predictive value.

Assets—Probable future economic benefits obtained or controlled by a particular entity as a result of past transactions or events.

Attributes—See Chapter 1's key terms.

Causality (IMA framework)—This is the relation between some quantitative output of a product or process and the quantities of inputs needed to achieve this.

Comparability (FASB framework)—Comparability relates to the ability of users to understand the extent to which two items are similar or different.

Completeness (FASB framework)—A measurement (and related explanatory material) that has all the information the user needs to understand it is complete.

Comprehensive income—This is the change in equity during a period for all reasons except transactions with the owners.

Confirmatory value (FASB framework)—Information has confirmatory value when it helps verify whether information provided in the past was accurate.

Congruence (IMA framework)—This means that managers should use managerial costing information in a way that fits with other goals of the business.

Conservatism—See Chapter 1's key terms.

Consistency (FASB framework)—The same accounting methods should be used for the same items. This refers both to an entity using the same methods over time, and to different entities using the same method.

Cost—Something sacrificed to obtain another thing. Some costs give rise to assets, and others are expenses.

Cost constraint (FASB framework)—The FASB considers both costs and benefits of accounting rules. In some cases, the benefits of better quality accounting measures are not justified by their costs.

Distributions to owners—These are net outflows of assets to the business's owners, when the business receives nothing in return. For corporations, distributions include dividends and stock buybacks.

Double-entry bookkeeping—This is the process of accounting which keeps the fundamental equation in balance. See Appendix A for a detailed description.

Earnings—Similar to comprehensive income, but it does not contain certain gains and losses that are included in comprehensive income.

Enhancing characteristic (FASB framework)—Usefulness of financial information is enhanced (improved) if the information has the characteristics of "comparability," "verifiability," "timeliness," and "understandability." See the definitions of these terms.

Entity principle—Accounting focuses on some object to account for. In financial accounting, the entity is usually a company, or a group of related companies, and not its owners.

Equity—This is the company's "net worth" or "net assets" as reflected in the accounting records. Equity is defined algebraically as total assets minus total liabilities.

Expenditures—Expenditures are payments of cash. They can be used to buy assets, repay liabilities, pay distributions, and pay for expenses.

Expenses—Expenses are reductions in net assets that occur because of carrying out the business's major or central operations.

Faithful representation (FASB framework)—Information that accurately shows some underlying reality. Faithful representation requires that the information be as *complete*, *neutral*, and *free from error* as possible.

Financing cash flows—These are cash movements related to either obtaining financing through loans or stock, or repaying this financing.

Fixed cost—Fixed costs do not vary with volume of production (or with some other cost driver) in the short run.

Flows—In accounting, flows are things that change an account over time. They are added to or subtracted from an account over a time period.

Freedom from errors – This is information that was recorded and computed without mistakes. The FASB recognizes that estimates are often necessary, and perfect precision is rarely possible.

Full disclosure principle—This principle requires companies to provide enough information for financial statement users to understand events during the period and the accounting methods used.

Fundamental equation of accounting—Assets = Liabilities + Equity

GAAP—See Chapter 1's key terms.

Gains—These are increases in net assets arising from peripheral or incidental activities.

Going concern assumption—We assume the business will continue to operate in the future in a similar fashion to the past. The business is not expected to be shut or sold in the near future.

Historical cost —This is the cost at which an item was originally purchased.

IFRS—See Chapter 1's key terms.

Immaterial—An item is not material when it is not large or important enough to make a difference in a user decision. See materiality.

Impartiality (IMA framework)—When managers use managerial accounting information, they should consider all ways of using resources in an objective, unbiased way.

Investing cash flows—Investing cash flows involves either buying or selling investments. Investments include stocks in other companies, bonds, long-term physical assets such as land and equipment, and intangible assets.

Liabilities—FASB (2008) defines liabilities as "probable future sacrifices of economic benefits arising from present obligations of a particular entity to transfer assets or provide services to other entities in the future as a result of past transactions or events" (para. 35).

Losses—Reductions of net assets that arise from peripheral or incidental activities or events.

Managerial costing—This branch of managerial accounting focuses on understanding cost and benefit relations between inputs and outputs, and seeks to aid managerial decision-making in areas where the costs of products or activities is relevant.

Materiality (FASB and IMA frameworks)—This is something that is large enough or otherwise important enough to make a difference in a user's decision.

Measurability (IMA framework)—Measurability is the characteristic of a cause and effect relation between inputs and products produced that allows it to be measured with a reasonable amount of effort.

Net income—Similar to comprehensive income, but net income excludes certain gains and losses that are included in comprehensive income.

Neutral (FASB framework)—Neutral information is unbiased.

Objectivity (IMA framework)—An objective cost model is free from biases. [Note – older versions of the FASB framework also used the term "objectivity" in a similar manner. They now use the term "neutral."]

Objects of measurement—See Chapter 1's key terms.

Operating cash flows—Operating movements of cash are related to the operations of the business, not to investing and financing activities.

Period costs—Costs that are related to a period of time, and are not directly traceable to the sale or production of a particular item or service.

Predictive value (FASB framework)—Information with predictive value is useful in making judgments about the future.

Prepaid expenses—An asset called "prepaid expenses" arises when a company pays for some service in advance.

Primary characteristics (FASB framework)—The FASB defined *relevance* and *faithful representation* as primary characteristics.

Product costs—Product costs are directly traceable to particular items produced or sold.

Realization—"Unrealized gains or losses" are changes in market value for items you have not yet sold. When you sell them, and convert them to cash, the gains or losses are "realized."

Receipts—Inflows of cash. They may represent revenues, but may also be collections of amounts previously recorded as revenues. They also occur when the company borrows money or sells stock to shareholders.

Recognition—This is the process of reporting an item as part of the financial statements as an asset, liability, or some other element of financial reporting.

Relevance (FASB framework)—Information is *relevant* if it is capable of making a difference in a user decision. To be relevant, the information must have *predictive value* or *confirmatory value*, or both. It must also be *timely* and large enough to be *material*.

Revenues—Increases in net assets arising from the entity's major or central operations.

Semi-variable costs—These costs have both a fixed and a variable component.

Stocks—These are quantities at a particular time. For example, the cash in the bank at the end of business on December 31 is the "stock" of cash on hand that day. Receipts and expenditures the next month are "flows."

Timeliness (FASB framework)—An enhancing characteristic of information. Information should be reported to users fast enough to be used in decisions.

Understandability (FASB framework)—An enhancing characteristic of information. Information should be presented clearly and concisely.

Unearned revenues (also called deferred revenues) —These are liabilities that arise when the company has received a customer payment but has not yet provided services to the customer.

Variable costs—These costs change proportionally to volume of production, or to some other cost driver.

Verifiability (FASB and IASB frameworks)—Information is verifiable when competent and neutral accountants would likely agree on the measurement.

Questions and Problems

Comprehension Questions

C1. (User needs for information—from Chapter 1) What are some of the attributes of a company that the FASB thinks are important to potential investors?

C2. (FASB primary criteria for information) What does the FASB consider the two most important criteria for information to have in order to be useful to potential investors and creditors?

C3. (FASB enhancing characteristics) What does the FASB consider to be "enhancing characteristics" of accounting information?

C4. (FASB primary criteria for information) Explain what the FASB means by "relevance" and "faithful representation."

C5. (FASB criteria—materiality) Explain what the FASB means by "materiality."

C6. (Elements of financial statements) What is "equity"? How is it defined?

C7. (Elements of financial statements) Equity at the beginning of one period is a "stock." What are the flows that explain the change in equity from the beginning of one period to the end of the period?

C8. (Elements of financial statements) What is the difference between a revenue and a gain?

C9. (Elements of financial statements) What is the difference between an expense and a loss?

C10. (Asset definition) Why does prepaid insurance meet the FASB's definition of an asset?

C11. (Liability definition) Why do bonuses that employees have earned, but that the company has not yet paid, meet the FASB's definition of a liability?

C12. (Types of costs) What is the difference between a product cost and a period cost?

C13. (Types of costs) What is the difference between fixed costs, variable costs, and semi-variable costs?

C14. (Expense definition) Is a cost the same as an expense? Explain.

C15. (Expense definition) Is an expense the same as an expenditure? Explain.

C16. (Revenue recognition) What is required, under FASB rules, for a revenue to be recognized?

C17. (Expense recognition) Under FASB rules, when do expenses have to be recognized?

C18. (Accrual accounting) What is accrual accounting?

C19. (Standard-setters) Which standard-setter would do each of the following:

    A. Set accounting rules used by U.S. public companies?

    B. Set accounting rules generally followed in the U.S. by private companies?

    C. Set accounting standards followed in most countries around the world?

Application Questions

A1. (Financial statement elements) The FASB defined the following elements of financial statements: assets, liabilities, equity, revenues, gains, expenses, losses, investments by owners and distributions to owners. For each of the items below, indicate which element best describes it:

    A. _____ Cash

    B. _____ Sales to customers during a period

    C. _____ Cost of the goods sold to customers during a period

    D. _____ Note payable to a bank

    E. _____ Salaries earned by employees during a period

    F. _____ Interest earned by a bank on loans it made during a period

    G. _____ Dividends paid by a company to its shareholders during a period

    H. _____ Accounts receivable

    I. _____ Money received by the company from selling its stock to the public

A2. (Financial statement elements) The FASB defined the following elements of financial statements: assets, liabilities, equity, revenues, gains, expenses, losses, investments by owners and distributions to owners. For each of the items below, indicate which element best describes it:

    A. _____ Land owned by the company

    B. _____ Electricity costs incurred by a business during a period

    C. _____ Unearned revenues

    D. _____ Sales of products to customers during a period

    E. _____ Interest incurred in a month related to money the company has borrowed

    F. _____ Dividends paid by a company to its shareholders during a period

    G. _____ Accounts payable

    H. _____ Money paid by the company to buy back its stock from the public

    I. _____ Rent received by a landlord for renting space during a period

A3. (Fundamental equation) Use the data given to find the missing figure:

	Assets	Liabilities	Equity
A.	$20,000	$17,000	?
B.	$3,000,000	?	$2,500,000
C.	?	$1,900,000	$100,000

A4. (Changes in equity—equity as stock and comprehensive income, investments, and distributions as flows) Use the data given to find the missing figures:

	Beginning Equity	Comprehensive Income (loss)	Distributions to Owners	Investments by Owners	Ending Equity
A.	$0	$3,000,000	$200,000	$1,000,000	?
B.	$2,000,000	$1,000,000	$500,000	?	$2,750,000
C.	$4,000,000	$1,500,000	?	$1,000,000	$4,500,000
D.	$7,000,000	?	$0	$2,000,000	$4,000,000
E.	?	$3,000,000	$2,000,000	$3,000,000	$9,000,000

A5. (Comprehensive net income) Use the data given to find the missing figures:

	Revenues	Gains	Expenses	Losses	Comprehensive Income (Loss)
A.	$10,000,000	$500,000	$5,000,000	$300,000	?
B.	$8,000,000	$100,000	$7,000,000	?	$900,000
C.	$4,000,000	$1,500,000	?	$1,000,000	$100,000
D.	$6,000,000	?	$4,000,000	$1,000,000	$1,000,000
E.	?	$300,000	$6,000,000	$2,000,000	$10,000,000

A6. (Cost types—fixed, variable, step, semi-variable) Assume a university is trying to analyze its costs for a possible new program. For each of the following situations, indicate if the cost is fixed, variable, step or semi-variable with regard to the number of students:

A. The university prints an ID card for each student. There is a cost for each card made.
B. The university has a library building. The library building is depreciated over a life of 40 years.
C. The university believes it needs to hire one faculty member for every 15 students it admits.
D. The university pays its president $1,000,000 per year under a long-term contract.

A7. (Cost types—fixed, variable, step, semi-variable) A company is being created that will tutor high school students who are studying for college entrance exams. It could be set up in different ways. It expects to teach 100 classes a year. Explain whether each decision would result in a fixed cost, a variable cost, step, or a semi-variable cost with regard to the number of classes it offers. (Assume that it will only offer a class if it gets 10 students for that class.)

A. It hires 20 teachers as full-time employees, and agrees to pay them a certain amount per year. The teachers will teach up to six classes each. If they teach less, they still get the same pay.
B. It makes agreements with 30 different people, and agrees to teach them a certain amount for each class they teach during the year. They are not full-time employees, and only get paid if they teach a course. The company does not promise them how many courses they will teach.
C. It hires five teachers as full-time employees, and agrees to pay them a certain amount per year. The teachers will teach up to six classes each. If they teach less, they still get the same pay. Because the company expects to have more classes than these five teachers can handle, it also makes agreements with additional people, who will be paid only when they teach courses. These other people are not promised any particular number of classes to teach.
D. It buys a photocopier to make copies of materials for the classes, and records depreciation on the copier based on an expected useful life of five years.

    E.   It buys paper for the photocopier.

    F.   It provides textbooks to the students as part of the service. It buys the textbooks from an outside publisher as it needs them.

A8. (Cost types—product, period) A company makes kitchen pans. It has various costs. Which are costs that relate directly to the products made, and which are costs of the period?

    A.   Metal bought that is made into the pans
    B.   Wages paid to the people who make the pans
    C.   Wages paid to the company chief financial officer
    D.   Electricity used to heat the factory
    E.   Advertising used to help sell the products
    F.   Income taxes paid
    G.   Property taxes paid on the factory

A9. (Accounting equation and transactions) For each of the following situations, indicate how it affects: total assets; total liabilities; and equity. For example, when a company borrows money from a bank, it has more cash and it also has a liability. Therefore, assets increase, liabilities increase, but equity is unchanged.

    A.   The company sells its stock to the public.
    B.   A landlord receives cash in payment for the current month's rent on an apartment.
    C.   A landlord receives rent now that relates to the next period. The customer has paid in advance.
    D.   A company repays its bank loan.
    E.   A company buys land in return for cash.
    F.   A company uses cash to buy back stock held by a shareholder.
    G.   A company pays an accounts payable.
    H.   During the last week of the year, the company's employees earn six days' wages. The company will pay these wages in the first week of the next year.
    I.   A company buys insurance today, for cash, that will be useful for the next three years.

A10. (Accounting equation and transactions) For each of the following situations, indicate how it affects: total assets; total liabilities; and equity. For example, when a company borrows money from a bank, it has more cash and it also has a liability. Therefore, assets increase, liabilities increase, but equity is unchanged.

    A.   A company pays money to its shareholders as dividends.
    B.   An accounting firm provides services to a client, and receives cash as payment.
    C.   An accounting firm provides services to a client, and the client promises to pay cash in the next accounting period.
    D.   A manufacturer buys raw materials "on credit," meaning it will pay for them later.
    E.   A company buys stock in Microsoft for cash.
    F.   A company had previously made a sale to a customer on credit in the last accounting period. This period, it receives the customer's cash payment.
    G.   A clothing store sells a shirt to a customer for cash. The price is greater than the amount the store had to pay to buy the shirt.
    H.   New investors buy stock in the company.
    I.   The company receives money in advance from customers for services that the company will provide next year.

A11. (What affects comprehensive income) For each of the transactions in A9, indicate if they affect comprehensive income.

A12. (What affects comprehensive income) For each of the transactions in A10, indicate if they affect comprehensive income.

A13. (Other events that need to be recorded/adjustments) Accountants need to record some things that happen that are not transactions with other companies. For each of the items listed below, indicate how you think they should affect the accounting equation. For example, assume that a company had paid its rent before the month started, and recorded the asset "prepaid rent." Then a month goes by, and the rent is no longer prepaid. The effect of a month going by is that the asset is now decreased to zero. An expense has been incurred. The result of this expense is that equity is also decreased.

    A.   The company owns a machine that it depreciates over five years. What is the effect of another year of time going by?

    B.   The company had recorded prepaid insurance because it bought six months of car insurance at one time. Now one month has passed.

    C.   The company had recorded an asset for office supplies, when it spent $10,000 to buy a large supply of them. It does not bother to account for them as they are used. At the end of the year, it looks at the supplies, and realizes that only $2,000 worth of supplies are left. However, its accounting records still show a balance of $10,000.

    D.   The company only records salaries when it pays them. Pay day is every Friday. This year ends on Wednesday, and the company wants to recognize that employees have earned three days' pay even though they have not received the cash.

    E.   The company did services for a client, and has earned $20,000.

    F.   The company believes that the income tax for this year is $30,000, which it expects to pay early next year.

A14. (Other events that need to be recorded/adjustments) Accountants need to record some things that happen that are not transactions with other companies. For each of the items listed below, indicate how you think they should affect the accounting equation. For example, assume that a real estate company had received some rent from a tenant before the month started, and recorded the liability "unearned rent." Then a month goes by, and the rent has now been earned. The effect of a month going by is that the liability is now decreased to zero. A revenue has been earned. The result of this revenue is that equity is also increased.

    A.   The company has loaned money to another company. Interest on the loan is due early next year. What is the effect of more interest becoming due, even though it has not yet been collected?

    B.   The company had recorded prepaid rent because it paid three months of rent to its landlord in advance. Now one month has passed.

    C.   The company sells a large number of different products. It records an asset for inventory when it buys the products. It does not bother to account for the costs of each items it sells at the time of the sale. It started the year with $2,000,000 of inventory. During the year, it paid $10,000,000 for all its new purchases of inventory. At the end of the year, it counts all the remaining inventory, and realizes that only $2,100,000 worth of inventory is left. However, its accounting records show a balance of $2,000,000 plus $10,000,000 = $12,000,000.

    D.   The company has promised its employees bonuses equal to 4% of the company's profits for the year. Bonuses will be paid in the first month of the next year.

E.   The company owns stock in a public company. The investment has been incredibly successful, and the value of the investment has increased by $3,000,000 this year.

F.   The company owns a truck, which it depreciates over a life of eight years. What is the effect of one year going by?

G.   The company owns a patent that it amortizes over 10 years. What is the effect of another year going by?

A15. (Revenue recognition) The general criteria for revenue recognition are explained in the chapter. For each of the following, say if you believe if these criteria have been met.

A.   A grocery store sells three cans of tuna fish to a customer for cash.

B.   A grocery store sells $70 worth of groceries to a customer, who uses a credit card to pay. The credit card company will pay the grocery store in three days.

C.   A landlord has rented office space to a tenant this month. The tenant has promised to pay in two months.

D.   A company owns beef cattle. It bought some young cattle at the beginning of the year, and this year they have grown larger and gained weight. It will not sell them until next year.

E.   An accounting firm does bookkeeping services for a client this month, and is paid in cash.

F.   A shoe manufacturer makes winter boots during July. It expects to ship them out to customers in August.

A16. (Expense recognition) For each of the following situations, indicate whether you think an expense should be recognized during the current period.

A.   A law firm pays its employees for work they did during the period.

B.   A law firm buys new office furniture that it expects to last for five years. Should the amount paid for the furniture be an expense?

C.   At the end of the period, a company has earned income, and it expects to owe income tax on that income. Is there an expense in this year, or in the year when the tax is paid?

D.   In a previous year, the company bought some inventory. This year, the inventory was sold. Is the cost of the inventory an expense this year, or in the prior year?

E.   In a previous year, the company incurred telephone bills related to the telephones for its administrative offices. This year, it paid the bills. Should the telephone expense be recorded in the previous year, or in the year the bill is paid?

A17. (FASB qualitative concepts) For each of the situations below, indicate which of the qualitative characteristics listed by the FASB are being violated. The characteristics are: relevance; faithful representation; timeliness; verifiability; understandability; and comparability.

A.   A company's investors need to file their tax returns in April, but the company does not report its income until May.

B.   The company uses an unusual method of recording revenue, but the company does not tell readers what it actually does.

C.   A major asset for a company is an investment that is not publicly traded. The company measures this asset using its own methods, which have several assumptions that people outside the company might not agree with.

D.   When the company computed its income tax expense, it accidentally multiplied wrong, and the expense it reported was much too big.

E. The company wanted to show low income, so it deliberately overestimated some expenses.
F. When the company computed its expenses, it left out one type of expense.
G. The company included in its report a great deal of information about a very small matter that investors usually do not care about.
H. The company chose to measure certain items in a way that is not helpful to investors who are trying to use information to project future performance.

A18. (Cash flow classifications) Indicate whether each of the following is either an inflow or an outflow of cash, and indicate if the item should be classified as operating, investing, or financing.

a. Receipt of cash from customers for goods sold.
b. Payment of cash to suppliers for inventory purchased.
c. Receipt of cash from a bank as a loan.
d. Payment of cash in return for buying a U.S. Treasury bond.
e. Payment of cash for buying a building.
f. Receipt of cash from selling a U.S. Treasury bond that had been held as an investment.
g. Payment of cash to employees for wages.
h. Receipt of cash for interest on a U.S. Treasury bond the company owns.
i. Payment of income taxes.
j. Receipt of cash for issuing stock to new shareholders.
k. Payments of dividends to shareholders.

A19. (Stocks and flows—inventory) The chapter makes a distinction between stocks and flows. In this example, the "stock" is the amount of inventory on hand at any one time. The "flows" are the purchases of inventory and the costs of the inventory sold to customers. Use the information shown to find the missing items.

	Beginning Inventory	Purchases	Cost of Goods Sold	Ending Inventory
a.	20	200	185	?
b.	100	500	?	120
c.	0	?	175	10
d.	?	350	425	100

A20. (Stocks and flows—accounts receivable) The chapter makes a distinction between stocks and flows. In this example, the "stock" is the amount of accounts receivable at any one time. The "flows" are new sales on credit and amounts collected from customers related to sales made in the past. Use the information shown to find the missing items.

	Beginning Accounts Receivable	Sales on Credit credit sales	Collections from prior Receivable	Ending Accounts
a.	2,000	10,000	9,000	?
b.	8,000	50,000	?	7,000
c.	9,000	?	80,000	2,000
d.	?	100,000	90,000	13,000

A21. (Stocks and flows—cash) The chapter makes a distinction between stocks and flows. In this example, the "stock" is the amount of cash at any one time. The "flows" are the operating, investing, and financing cash flows during the year. Use the information shown to find the missing items.

	Beginning Cash	Operating Cash Flows	Investing Cash Flows	Financing Cash Flows	Ending Cash
a.	5,000	+10,000	–8,000	+20,000	?
b.	10,000	–4,000	–8,000	?	6,000
c.	20,000	–2,000	?	–3,000	6,000
d.	30,000	?	–20,000	–25,000	50,000
e.	?	+30,000	–14,000	+30,000	80,000

Discussion Questions

D1. (FASB concepts) The FASB lists a number of desirable characteristics of information. In practice, a choice of one way of measuring things may make one of these characteristics better, but might make another worse. Explain what factors are made better or worse in each of these choices:

A. The FASB had to choose between having companies record their inventory at historic cost, or what the companies think they can sell the inventories for.

B. The FASB had to decide whether to have companies record an expense in the current year for the amount of their accounts receivable that the companies think they will not collect.

C. The SEC decided to require all public companies to report their annual results within 60 days after year end, even though the companies might be more accurate if they had more time.

D. The FASB requires companies to disclose very complicated information about their trading in certain financial instruments, even though many users are confused by how financial instruments work.

E. The FASB allows companies to choose the method of accounting for inventory that the company's management feels best reflects its performance, even though other companies in the industry use other methods.

D2. (Other concepts) The chapter discusses the characteristics of information that the FASB and the IMA consider desirable. In many cases, their ideas are similar. However, one place in which they differ is that the IMA has two criteria for how information should be used. The IMA say managers should use information in a way *congruent* to the goals of their organizations, and in an *impartial* manner. Why doesn't the FASB have similar criteria?

D3. (Concepts—classification issues) The FASB has made definitions of various financial statement elements. However, in practice, it is sometimes not obvious whether something meets the definition of an element or not. For each of the following, comment on how the item should be classified.

A. A company has sold a special kind of stock for $1,000 per share to some shareholders. Unlike most stock, this "Class X" stock has certain special rights. If the company goes out of business, the Class X shareholders are entitled to $1,000 each before other shareholders get paid. The Class X shareholders are also entitled to dividends of $50 per share every year. Also, in 20 years, the company has promised to buy back the Class X shares at $1,000 each. Are these shares equity, or liabilities?

B. A company sold bonds to the public, promising to pay interest of 4% every year, and to buy back the bonds in 1,000 years. Is this a liability, or a sale of equity?

C. A company's normal business is selling clothing. It also, from time to time, buys and sells stock. Over the last 10 years, the income from sale of stock has amounted to 10% of total income. Should the income from sales of stock be considered a gain, or a revenue? At what level of activity would your answer change?

D.   A company's normal business is selling food in restaurants. It has hundreds of restaurants around the world. It has made a decision to restructure its business, and change its way of operating. This will involve substantial costs. Are these costs expenses, or losses?

E.   A company spends money on research to be used to make a new product. The company thinks there is a 10% chance the new product will be successful. Should the research expenditures be considered assets, or expenses? At what level of probability might your answer change?

D4. (Desirable characteristics of accounting information) The FASB has designed an accounting system that is meant to serve the needs of outside investors and creditors. However, there are other parties that are interested in a company's performance, and they may have other needs. Consider each of the following:

A.   The FASB often requires companies to estimate certain liabilities, in order to present relevant information. For example, companies that expect to pay bonuses in January of Year 2, based on earnings in Year 1, must recognize the estimated bonus expense and liability in Year 1. Do you think that tax authorities would follow the same rule? Why or why not?

B.   Lenders typically have the rights to get interest on the loan, and to be repaid at the end of the loan, but they usually don't share in the company's profits. Would lenders prefer neutral accounting, or conservative accounting? Why?

D5. (Cash and accrual methods) The cash method of accounting basically recognizes expenses when cash is spent, and revenues when cash is received. The accrual method uses the revenue and expense recognition methods described in this chapter. For each of the following, indicate whether it would be recognized under the accrual method, the cash method, or both, on the date of the event listed.

Revenues:

A.   Cash received by a grocery store at the time the customer buys food.

B.   On December 29, a company ships a product to a customer on credit, giving the customer 30 days to pay.

C.   This question follows part B. In January, the customer pays for the product.

D.   A company has invested in land. During the year, the value of the land goes up by $200,000. The company does not sell the land during the year.

E.   On December 29, the company receives a payment in advance from a customer. The company will provide the service to the customer in January. Is there revenue on December 29?

F.   This question follows part E. Is there revenue in January, when the company provides the service to the customer who had paid in December?

Expenses:

G.   A grocery store buys (for cash) an inventory of food that it plans to sell.

H.   A grocery store buys (on credit) an inventory of food that it plans to sell. It does not pay for these items until a later period.

I.   This question follows part H. Is there an expense in a later period, when the store pays its supplier the amount it owes?

J.   Is there an expense at the time a store sells some inventory, if the store paid for the inventory in a previous period?

K.   Is there an expense in December when a company prepays January's rent?

L.   This question follows part K. Is there an expense in January when the company uses its store without making a further rent payment?

D6. (Cash and accrual methods) Assume that you own an accounting business, and that you account for this business on a cash basis. Also assume that you are trying to show a low income for the year for your tax return.

A. Which of these possible actions in December would help you report lower income on your tax return?

    a. Asking clients who owe you money to wait until January before paying you.

    b. Making sure you pay for all your bills in December, instead of waiting until January, when they become due.

    c. Prepaying various expenses that will need to be paid in January and February.

B. Would those actions reduce your income if you were using the accrual basis? Explain.

D7. (Cash flow classifications) The text indicates that the FASB's rules for classifying cash flows differ in some cases from the IASB's rules. Indicate in each case which rule you think is more appropriate.

A. The IASB allows a company to classify interest it pays on its loans as a financing cash flow. The FASB does not, and requires them to be classified as operating cash flows. (The IASB also allows the interest to be called operating.)

B. The IASB allows companies that receive dividends from stock in other companies to classify these inflows as investing cash flows. The FASB requires these receipts to be shown as operating cash flows. (The IASB also allows the dividends received to be called operating.)

D8. (Standard setting) The United States is considering adopting IFRS for public companies. One issue is that this would transfer the authority to set standards from the SEC (part of the U.S. government) to the IASB, a foreign non-governmental organization. Do you feel comfortable with this change in who sets rules? Why or why not?

D9. (Illustration of accounting rules)[31] A number of the principles of accrual accounting can be illustrated with a simple example. An 11-year-old girl, Mary, decides to make a little bit of money by setting up a lemonade stand. She plans to sell lemonade every Saturday for 10 weekends. The following events take place on the first weekend:

Friday:

A. She takes $25 from her drawer, and puts it in a box that she will use for the lemonade stand business.

B. She gives her mother the money to buy some lemonade and cups. The lemonade and cups cost $10.

C. She asks her father to make a little tent for her to sell the lemonade under, which she expects to use for all 10 weekends. It cost $30. She promises to pay her father back after the weekend is over.

D. A neighbor gives her $4 as payment in advance for four cups of lemonade. The neighbor will come by on Saturday and get the four cups.

Friday cash summary: Cash into the business = $25 + $4 = $29
                            Cash out of the business = $10
                            Net cash movement = +$19

Saturday:

A. She sells so many cups of lemonade she has to ask her mother to buy another $20 worth of lemonade.

B. She collects $60 from people who buy lemonade. She actually gives out 65 cups of lemonade, since the neighbor who paid in advance comes by and she also gives a cup to a friend who promises to give her a dollar the next day.

C. She is so busy she asks a little boy next door to help her. She promises to give him $10 on Sunday.

D. At the end of the day, she realizes she has ingredients left that cost $4.

E. She takes $2 out of the box, and buys candy for a treat. She has worked hard.

Saturday cash summary: Cash into the business: $60
Cash out of the business: $20 + $2 = $22
Net cash movement = +$38

Sunday:

A. She pays her father $30 for the tent.

B. She pays the boy next door $10 for helping her on Saturday.

C. She receives the $1 owed her for the lemonade from the day before.

Sunday cash activity: Cash into business: $1
Cash out of business: $10 + $30 = $40
Net cash movement = −$39
Weekend cash summary = +$19 + $38 − $39 = +$18.

Questions:

1. If Mary just used cash-basis accounting, would she consider her business profitable or unprofitable on

   a. Friday?
   b. Saturday?
   c. Sunday?

2. Under accrual accounting:

   a. Which of the events represent buying an asset?
   b. Which of the events involve creating a liability?
   c. Which of the events represent earning revenue? And when is revenue earned?
   d. Which of the events represent incurring an expense?
   e. Over what period of time should the cost of the lemonade stand be allocated to an expense?
   f. How should the initial movement of $25 to the business be treated? Should it be considered part of the business's income?
   g. How should the movement out of $2 for a treat for Mary be treated? Is it an expense?

3. Using the data in the problem, compute what you think the income under the accrual basis would be for:

   a. Friday
   b. Saturday
   c. Sunday.

4. Using the data in the problem, compute what you think the assets, liabilities, and equity of this business are on Saturday evening.

5. For each of the events, indicate how you think it affects the fundamental accounting equation on that day.

D10. (Rule-making—rules versus principles) Historically, the FASB has tended to issue very precise rules on how businesses must account for particular transactions. The IASB has instead tended to decide on general principles to be followed, and has expected accountants and businesses to use their judgment in applying the principles. This difference has been referred to as the debate over rules versus principles. Explain whether you think that, in general, the use of specific rules that all companies must follow would be better, or worse, than setting general principles with regard to the following criteria of information:

A. Predictive value
B. Neutrality
C. Comparability across companies
D. Low cost of producing information
E. Understandability
F. Verifiability

D11. (Classifications and measurement—social impact) The choices by the FASB and the IASB of what to measure also mean that some things are not typically measured or recognized in accounting. Consider what you think the effects of the following may be:

A. Companies do not record an asset for the skills of their workers.
B. Companies typically do not record an asset for their reputation for good customer service.
C. Companies do not typically record an expense for actions that adversely affect other people, unless the other people have the right to get cash. For example, a bar may be noisy, which bothers neighbors, but those neighbors are not entitled to any payments from the bar for this inconvenience.

D12. (Balancing interests) In the early 20th century, lenders were the most important users of company financial statements. Over time, shareholders and potential buyers of stock became more important. Historically, lenders were believed to have favored "conservative" accounting, and U.S. accounting used to have a conservative bias. Now, the FASB and IASB say they want accounting to be neutral.

A. Why would lenders have favored conservative accounting?
B. Would current shareholders want accounting to be conservative? Why or why not?
C. Would potential shareholders want accounting to be conservative? Why or why not?
D. Would tax authorities want companies to use conservative accounting?
E. Would labor unions want employers to use conservative accounting?

D13. (Role of accountants in society) Tony Tinker (1985) wrote that one theme that runs through the history of accounting is:

[A] concern to present an image of objectivity, independence, and neutrality by shunning "subjective" questions of value and confining accounting data to "objective" market prices (historical and current). This image is often extended to portray the accountant as a disinterested, innocuous historian. The need for the imagery stems from a desire to deny responsibility for shaping subjective expectations which . . . affect decisions about resource allocation and income distribution between and within social classes.

(p. 107)[32]

Consider how accounting rules on when to recognize income and expenses might affect:

A. The relative rights of shareholders and tax authorities.
B. The relative rights of executives with contractually specified bonuses, and shareholders.
C. Decisions on how much customers of electric utilities and other regulated businesses should be charged.
D. The ability of shareholders to take out dividends, leaving less money in a company to repay lenders.

Research

R1. (IASB) Go to the IASB website (www.iasb.org) and find out:

A. How many members are there of the IASB?
B. What countries have representatives on the organization that oversees the IASB?

R2. (FASB) Go to the FASB website (www.fasb.org) and find out:

A. How many members are there of the FASB?
B. How are they selected?

R3. (Real company) Go to the website of a public company that interests you, and find its latest financial statements. (Usually you can find a company's financial statements in a section called "investor relations." Often, the company provides SEC filings, and the annual financial statements are in the Form 10-K.) In the financial statements:

A. Look at the company's balance sheet, and find out what its largest assets and liabilities are.
B. Look at the company's income statement.

    a. What are its major expenses?
    b. Does the company show any losses or gains? What are they?

C. Typically, the first footnote lists major accounting policies. From this footnote, identify:

    a. What entity is covered? Is it just one company, or a consolidated group of companies?
    b. What does the company say is its policy for recognizing income?

Notes

1 Romeo and Juliet, Act II, scene ii, lines 43–44. Cited in Shapiro (2006), p. 682.
2 From *Through the Looking Glass, and What Alice Found There*. Cited in Shapiro (2006), p. 136.
3 All references to the IMA criteria in this section are from IMA (2014).
4 More formally, "Causality" is "the relation between a managerial objective's quantitative output and the input quantities consumed if the output is to be achieved" (IMA 2014, p. 33).
5 For nonprofit enterprises, another element is "contributions" from donors, who do not expect anything back in return for their contributions. See FASB (1986).
6 A lender or lessor might technically have legal title, which would be meaningful if the business is unable to pay its debts, but otherwise doesn't affect the day-to-day operations of the business.
7 A "creditor" is someone to whom a business or individual owes a debt.
8 The FASB and IASB made new standards regarding revenues in 2014, but these rules do not go into effect until 2017. See FASB (2014). Chapter 9 discusses the new rules.
9 Mary Barth (2007) says the FASB and IASB have tried to follow the concept first described by Hicks of economic income as being the change in wealth during a period. "Defining financial position elements is the only way standard setters have been able to determine how to measure revenues and expenses,

which comprise profit or loss. To date, attempts to define revenues and expenses without reference to assets and liabilities have been unsuccessful." (p. 10)

10 The term "third party" here means someone other than the business and its owners.

11 See also Report of the American Accounting Association Committee on International Accounting Operations and Education 1975–76, published in *The Accounting Review*, 1977, Volume 22, Supplement (American Accounting Association 1976)

12 The earliest explanation of double-entry accounting, published over 500 years ago by Luca Paciolo, quotes a maxim ("The magistrate does not busy himself with unimportant matters") to explain why some things were not worth accounting for. See Littleton (1933, p. 85).

13 According to Littleton (1933) accrual accounting was not well developed in the 19th century. Only about 10% of 50 bookkeeping texts published between 1788 and 1899 attempted to reflect accruals.

14 "Aggressive" accounting is the opposite of "conservative" accounting. Recognizing revenues early, and expenses late, is considered "aggressive."

15 See also Barth (2007).

16 See Barth (2007, p. 10): "[M]atching is not a separate concept in the *Framework*. This is because matching is not an objective of accounting recognition or measurement, per se. . . . The *Framework* is based on the notion that if assets and liabilities are appropriately recognised and measured, profit or loss will be too, which obviates the need for a separate concept of matching. . . . The existing *Framework* ends by stating 'However, the application of the matching concept under this *Framework* does not allow the recognition of items in the balance sheet which do not meet the definition of assets or liabilities.' Thus, matching . . . cannot be used to justify income or expense recognition that is inconsistent with the definitions of assets and liabilities."

17 A *receipt* occurs when a business receives cash. A *disbursement* is an expenditure of cash.

18 I thank Professor Alan Rabinowitz for suggesting this chart.

19 This was sometimes referred to as the *objectivity principle*. FASB (2010) lists faithful representation of some underlying economic reality as a primary qualitative characteristic of information. Neutral measurement is needed to achieve faithful representation. Verifiability is an enhancing characteristic of information.

20 See Chatfield (1977). He noted that "many if not most of the rules used today by accountants in determining business income emerged from tax cases decided between 1913 and 1920" (p. 258). Economists are not as vulnerable to lawsuits, and need less objectivity in measurement. "The greatest difference between the accounting and economic approaches to income finding is the economist's willingness to recognize the effects of inflation, holding gains, increments to goodwill, and other value changes as they accrue. He would insist that a man is 'better off' at the moment when his asset increases in value, not at the time when it is sold." (p. 264)

21 Some estimation would be necessary in Year 1 to accrue the right amount of sales returns. See Chapter 8.

22 The Civil War general, and later president, Ulysses S. Grant, supposedly said he could only recognize two tunes: one was Dixie (the Confederate battle anthem), and the other wasn't. For some purposes, such as distinguishing the enemy on the battlefield, this classification system might be adequate, even though grouping all tunes other than Dixie into one category represents an enormous loss of information.

23 See Lev (1968) and Ronen and Falk (1973). Ronen and Falk argue that disaggregated information can have greater uncertainty, and can cause "information overload." Also, Dye and Sridhar (2004) argue that disaggregated data may actually be less useful, when the manager has an ability and incentive to bias some (but not all) of the data. In those cases, the reduced incentive to manipulate created by aggregation may outweigh the information loss.

24 See Bernhardt and Copeland (1970) and American Accounting Association (1971). The AAA committee recommended less aggregation of data when the objective was to formulate a future action.

25 For a discussion of these issues, see Grojer (2001) and Penno (2008).

26 See Rosen and Schneck (1967).

27 The same problem of unmeasured items occurs at the national level. Measurements of Gross Domestic Product are flawed by what is not counted. For example, GDP places no value on leisure. It does not take into account damage done by production to the environment. It does not assign any value to unpaid work done in the home. See Baumol and Blinder (1997).

28 See Waymire and Basu (2008). "By 1900, elements of modern principles were grounded in longstanding conventions characterizing practice in both Britain and the United States. These conventions included the entity concept, going concern, periodicity, revenue realization, historical cost, and conservatism, all of which had been fostered by the combined forces of corporate expansion, legal precedents, and economic crises." (p. 125)

29   Porter (1995) pessimistically concludes that "the presuppositions of accounting rules must themselves be codified and published and so on until the whole Malthusian cascade presses up against the supply of paper and patience" (p. 97).

30   Ijiri (1982) makes an extended analogy between concepts in physics and accounting. Physics has ideas of location, distance between locations, velocity, acceleration, momentum, forces, impulses, and so on. These all involve relations of location and time. In accounting, analogous concepts relate a company's wealth and changes in wealth to time. Ijiri's concept of income momentum measures the company's ability to generate recurring earnings. Momentum changes when "forces" are applied. Forces might include price changes, new product introductions, a natural "friction" causing decay in customer demand, and so on.

31   This example is based on Cushing (1997), but it has been substantially modified.

32   See also Tinker, Merino and Neimark (1982) for similar remarks.

References

American Accounting Association. (1971). Report of the Committee on Foundations of Accounting Measurement [Supplement]. *Accounting Review, 46*(4), 1–48.

American Accounting Association. (1976). American Accounting Association Committee on International Accounting Operations and Education Report 1975–76 [Supplement]. In *The Accounting Review* (1977), *22*.

Baladouni, V. (1984). Etymological Observations on Some Accounting Terms. *The Accounting Historians Journal, 11*(2), 101–9.

Barth, M. E. (2007). Standard-setting measurement issues and the relevance of research [Supplement]. *Accounting and Business Research, 37*, 7–15.

Baumol, W. J., & Blinder, A. S. (1997). *Economics—Principles and Policy* (7th ed). Fort Worth: Dryden Press.

Bernhardt, I., & Copeland, R. M. (1970). Some problems in applying an information theory approach to accounting aggregation. *Journal of Accounting Research* (Spring), 95–8.

Bierman Jr., H., Black, M. A., Gray, J., Sapienza, S. R., & Davidson, S. (1965). The Realization Concept: 1964 Concepts and Standards Research Study Committee of the AAA. *The Realization Concept, 40*(2), 312–22.

Bornstein, M. H. (1979). Perceptual development, stability, and change in feature perception. In M. H. Bornstein & W. Kessen (Eds.), *Psychological Development From Infancy: Image to Intention*. NY: John Wiley & Sons.

Brown, C. D. (1975). The emergence of income reporting. *International Journal of Accounting* (Spring), 85–107.

Brown, G. R. & Johnston, K. S. (1963). *Paciolo on Accounting*, McGraw-Hill Book Company, Inc., New York, 1963.

Carey, J. L. (1979). The CPA's professional heritage, part II. Working Paper No. 5. In E. N. Coffman (Ed.), *The Academy of Accounting Historians Working Paper Series, Vol. 1*. Richmond, VA: Virginia Commonwealth University.

Chambers, R. J. (1965). Measurement in Accounting. *Journal of Accounting Research, 3*(1), 32–62.

Chatfield, M. (1977). *A History of Accounting Thought* (Revised Edition). New York: Robert E. Krieger Publishing Company.

Cushing, B. E. (1997). Instructional case: Christy's lemonade stand: An introduction to accrual accounting. *Issues in Accounting Education, 12*, 161–70.

Dye, R., & Sridhar, S. (2004). Reliability-relevance trade-offs and the efficiency of aggregation. *Journal of Accounting Research, 42*(1), 51–89.

FASB. (1978). Statement of Financial Accounting Concepts No. 1, *Objectives of Financial Reporting by Business Enterprises*. Stamford, CT: FASB

FASB. (1984). Statement of Financial Accounting Concepts No. 5, *Recognition and Measurement in Financial Statements of Business Enterprises*. Stamford, CT: FASB.

FASB. (1986). Statement of Financial Accounting Concepts No. 6, *Elements of Financial Statements*. Stamford, CT: FASB.

FASB. (2000). Statement of Financial Accounting Concepts No. 7, *Using Cash Flow and Present Value in Accounting Measurements*. Stamford, CT: FASB.

FASB. (2008). Statement of Financial Accounting Concepts No. 6 (as amended), *Elements of Financial Statements: a replacement of FASB Concepts Statement No. 3 (incorporating an amendment of FASB Concepts Statement No. 2)*. Norwalk, CT: FASB.

FASB. (2010). Concepts Statement No. 8. Conceptual Framework for Financial Reporting—Chapter 1, *The Objective of General Purpose Financial Reporting,* and Chapter 3, *Qualitative Characteristics of Useful Financial Information* (a replacement of FASB Concepts Statements No. 1 and No. 2) (pp. 1–14, 16–22). Norwalk, CT: FASB.

FASB. (2014). Financial Accounting Standards Update No. 2014-09. *Revenue from Contracts with Customers*. Norwalk, CT: FASB.

Flamholtz, D. (1979). The Role of Academic Accounting Research: An Historical Perspective. Working Paper No. 26. In E. N. Coffman (Ed.), *The Academy of Accounting Historians Working Paper Series, Vol. 2 (Working Papers 21–40)*. Richmond, VA: Virginia Commonwealth University.

Grojer, J.-E. (2001). Intangibles and accounting classifications: In search of a classification strategy. *Accounting, Organizations and Society, 26,* 695–713.

IASB. (2010). *The Conceptual Framework for Financial Reporting*. London: International Accounting Standards Board.

Ijiri, Y. (1967). *The Foundations of Accounting Measurement: A Mathematical, Economic, and Behavioral Inquiry*. Englewood Cliffs, N. J: Prentice-Hall, Inc.

Ijiri, Y. (1971). Logic and Sanctions in Accounting. In R. R. Sterling & W. F. Bentz (Eds.), *Accounting in Perspective: Contributions to Accounting Thought by Other Disciplines.* Papers and Discussions from an Accounting Colloquium by the University of Kansas School of Business and the Arthur Young Foundation. Houston, Texas: Scholars Book Co.

Ijiri, Y. (1982). *Triple-Entry Bookkeeping and Income Momentum*. Studies in Accounting Research # 18. Sarasota, FL: American Accounting Association.

Ijiri, Y. (1989). *Momentum Accounting and Triple-Entry Bookkeeping: Exploring the Dynamic Structure of Accounting Measurements*. Studies in Accounting Research # 31. Sarasota, FL: American Accounting Association.

IMA. (2014). *Conceptual Framework for Managerial Costing. Report of the IMA Managerial Costing Conceptual Framework Task Force*. Montvale, NJ: Institute of Management Accountants.

Lambert, J. C., & Lambert III, S. J. (1979). Working Paper No. 23. In E. N. Coffman (Ed.), *The Academy of Accounting Historians Working Paper Series, Vol. 2 (Working Papers 21–40)*. Richmond, VA: Virginia Commonwealth University.

Lev, B. (1968). The aggregation problem in financial statements: An informational approach. *Journal of Accounting Research, 6*(Autumn), 247–61.

Littleton, A. C. (1933). *Accounting Evolution to 1900*. New York: American Institute Publishing Company.

Morgan, G. (1988). Accounting as reality construction: Towards a new epistemology for accounting practice. *Accounting, Organizations and Society, 13*(5), 477–85.

Penno, M. C. (2008). Rules and accounting: vagueness in conceptual frameworks. *Accounting Horizons, 22*(3), 339–51.

Porter, T. M. (1995). *Trust in Numbers: The Pursuit of Objectivity in Science and Public Life*. Princeton, NJ: Princeton University Press.

Ronen, J., & Falk, G. (1973). Accounting aggregation and the entropy measure: An experimental approach. *The Accounting Review* (October), 696–717.

Rosen, L. S. & Schneck, R. E. (1967). Some Behavioral Consequences of Accounting Measurement Systems. *Cost and Management, 41*(9), 6–16.

Shapiro, F. R. (Ed.). (2006). *The Yale Book of Quotations*. New Haven: Yale University Press.

Sombart, W. (1919). *Moderne Kapitalismus*, on double entry. Trans. in Most, K. S. (1979). Sombart on Accounting History. Working Paper No. 35. In E. N. Coffman (Ed.), *The Academy of Accounting Historians Working Paper Series, Vol. 2 (Working Papers 21–40)*. Richmond, VA: Virginia Commonwealth University.

Tinker, T. (1985). *Paper Prophets: A Social Critique of Accounting*. New York: Praeger Publishers.

Tinker, A. M., Merino, B. D., & Neimark, M. D. (1982). The normative origins of positive theories: Ideology and accounting thought. *Accounting, Organizations, and Society*, *7*(2), 167–200.

Waymire, G. B. & Basu, S. (2008). *Accounting is an Evolved Economic Institution*. Hanover, MA: Now Publishers Inc.

Young, J. J. (2003). Constructing, persuading and silencing: The rhetoric of accounting standards. *Accounting, Organizations and Society*, *28*(6), 621–38.

3 Reporting Measurements

Outline

- Preliminary Thoughts
- Learning Objectives
- General Guidance on Reporting
- Information Overload
- General methods of Reporting Quantitative Information

  - Raw (Unsummarized) Data
  - Oral Reports
  - Prose Reports
  - Tables
  - Graphs

- General Accounting Reports
- Basic Financial Statements and External Financial Reporting
- Limitations of External Financial Statements
- Basic Internal Reports
- Unresolved Issues and Areas for Future Research

Preliminary Thoughts

To say that someone should be accountable for particular events or actions is to hold certain expectations about what this person or organization should be able and obliged to explain, justify and take responsibility for.

Martin Messner (2009, p. 173)

Adequate and reliable information is the only sound basis for business decisions or for corrective actions; accounting should therefore be understood as a service by which reliable information is supplied to business executives on problems which confront them.

R. J. Chambers (1948/1969, p. 3)

The decision maker will seldom see firsthand the situation which represents the problem environment. . . . A decision maker's choice is largely the result of the information related to him. . . . There are three media which are extremely useful in describing or representing reality: words, pictures, and quantitative models. The three media are quite interdependent.

American Accounting Association (1971a, p. 216)

Information is the reply to a question.

Jacques Bertin (1981, p. 11)

> Data, by itself, has little value. To take on value, data must be turned into information by being organized, modeled, formatted, edited, verified, placed in context, and delivered in a timely manner to decision makers.
>
> *Richard Due (1997, p. 36)*

> [Reports] are printed to convey results in a familiar, standardized form. . . .They conveniently summarize a multitude of complex events and transactions. . . .Quantification is a technology of distance. . . .Since the rules for collecting and manipulating numbers are widely shared, they can easily be transported across oceans and continents and used to coordinate activities or settle disputes. Perhaps most crucially, reliance on numbers and quantitative manipulation minimizes the need for intimate knowledge and personal trust. Quantification is well suited for communication that goes beyond the boundaries of locality and community.
>
> *Theodore M. Porter (1995, p. ix)*

This chapter deals with a variety of ways of reporting quantitative data. The quotations above help set the framework for the discussion.

The first two quotations identify two reasons for reports.

- Managers are *accountable* to other people for what they have done with the company during the year. They have a duty to explain what has happened, because they are responsible for operating the company properly.
- Managers need to provide users with *information for decision-making*.

The next quotations indicate that very often decision-makers do not actually see the company's operations themselves. They need to get reports. The reports are only useful when they contain information that users care about. To paraphrase Jacques Bertin, a report only has information when it answers users' questions. Richard Due notes that data only becomes valuable when it is processed into a form that users can understand, and is delivered to them in a timely manner. When reports work well, they provide what Theodore Porter calls "a technology of distance." The users are able to make decisions even though they are far from the company, and are not acquainted with all the details that went into preparing the reports. In the modern economy, where businesses operate on a global scale, with shareholders and customers throughout the world, this ability to communicate information over great distances is vitally important.

Learning Objectives

This chapter has two major purposes:

- To provide guidance on reporting that will be useful whenever you need to communicate quantitative information. The ability to summarize and communicate quantitative data is becoming increasingly important in business.
- To introduce you to the most common types of financial and managerial accounting reports. These reports are discussed further in Chapters 4 and 5.

More specific learning objectives are:

1   To familiarize you with the various ways of reporting quantitative data and to provide guidance on using each method
2   To help you understand the general types of accounting reports: lists of items; computations; and reconciliations are common examples

3   To introduce you to the most common financial accounting reports:

    a.   Balance sheets
    b.   Income statements
    c.   Statements of comprehensive income
    d.   Statements of cash flows
    e.   Statements of shareholders' equity

4   To introduce some common types of managerial accounting reports
5   To introduce certain limitations of financial accounting reports.

General Guidance on Reporting

Assume the Reader Cares About Content, not Decoration

Accounting reports exist because someone wants the information.

If no one thinks the information is important, then you probably should not waste your time and your company's money reporting it. Remember from Chapter 2 that the FASB indicates that information that is not "material" is not needed for reports to be considered relevant. The IMA had a similar idea—items that don't affect decision models are not material. The FASB and IMA both recognize the need to balance costs of obtaining information and measurements against the benefits that users derive from them.

So, if the information is important enough to be reported, then the user wants it, and isn't bored. You do not have to "dress up" a report with special effects to make it interesting. To quote Edward Tufte (1990, p. 34, with emphasis added):

> Cosmetic decoration, which frequently distorts the data, will never salvage an underlying lack of content. . . . *If the numbers are boring, then you've got the wrong numbers.*

Accountants should always assume that the user is intelligent, and wants honest and clear information. Tufte (1990) wrote that "no matter what, the operating moral premise of information design should be that our readers are alert and caring; they may be busy, eager to get on with it, but they are not stupid" (p. 34).

Some General Criteria

All of the following criteria should be considered when designing and preparing reports. You should always start by considering who the intended users are, and what their needs are.

The report should:

*   *Be relevant*: Provide information that the user actually wants.
*   *Be complete*: Include *all* relevant information.
*   *Be clear and easy to understand*: It is almost always possible to design a report to present information clearly. Tufte (1990, p. 51) wrote: "Clutter and confusion are failures of design, not attributes of information."
*   *Be honest*: The report should not include information that is known to be incorrect. It should also not be designed to cause a user to come to incorrect conclusions or to overlook certain information.
*   *Be succinct*: Avoid giving extra and unnecessary information. It is always costly for companies to provide information, so giving unwanted information is a waste of money for the preparers of reports. It also makes the report longer and makes it harder for users to concentrate

on important information. Shakespeare wrote (in *Hamlet*), "Brevity is the soul of wit, and tediousness the limbs and outward flourishes thereof."[1] Accounting researchers have found that financial statement users tend to underreact to long disclosures, and have trouble processing long or complex notes.[2]

- *Allow comparisons*: Normally, accounting information needs to be compared either to reports from other companies, or to information from the same company in other time periods. Reports should make comparisons easy. Readers should be able to focus on differences in data, and not be distracted or confused by differences in the format of the reports.
- *Be timely*: Reports should be available fast enough to be useful. However, note that if reports are given too frequently, several problems can arise. One is that frequent reports will be more variable than longer term reports, which may mislead users. Second, managers may be pressured into acting to show short-term results at the expense of longer term results. Finally, the frequent reports may simply put a burden on the users of needing to look at them frequently, and may end up being ignored.
- *Be distributed to the intended users, and not to others*: Accountants must carefully avoid giving reports or information to people who do not have a right to the information. Confidential data needs to be protected from competitors or malicious hackers.
- *Have clear boundaries*: It should be clear where the report begins and ends. This is rarely a problem with paper reports, but it is sometimes unclear on websites where one "document" ends and another begins.
- *Be worth the cost*.

The goals set by the IMA and FASB match up well with these general criteria. Both the FASB and IMA criteria speak of predictive value or relevance. Completeness is part of the FASB's criteria of faithful representation. The FASB's criteria of neutrality and freedom from errors are similar to the idea of honest reporting listed above. The FASB's enhancing characteristics include timeliness, comparability, and understandability. Both the IMA and the FASB's conceptual frameworks have a concept that the cost of a measurement should be reasonable. The FASB does not address the issue of confidentiality, but the AICPA's (2013) Code of Professional Conduct forbids accountants from disclosing client information without permission.

Ideally, users will tell the accountant what information they want, so the accountant can design reports that meet the users' needs. This is usually possible in management accounting situations, since management employs the accountants. However, in external reporting situations, the issue is more complicated. There are many different users, who do not all want the same information. Also, public companies worry that releasing certain information could actually damage the company by allowing competitors to compete better. Competitors who know detailed product cost data/employee salary data, might be able to take actions that hurt the company's sales, or cause the loss of key employees. For external reporting, accountants use standard types of reports designed by the SEC or the FASB that are meant to satisfy most needs of outside investors and creditors without forcing companies to give away confidential information that could help competitors.

Information Overload

There has been extensive research on how well human beings are able to encode information into memory, retrieve it from memory, and process it.[3]

Humans can only mentally process a fairly small number of things at the same time. A famous paper in psychology by George A. Miller (1955) indicated that most people could only work with around seven things at once in their active memory. There is much research in psychology indicating that when people are given too much information at once, they are not able to use it well in making decisions. This is called *information overload.*

When decision-makers receive more information than they can adequately handle, a number of bad things can occur. People may simply omit to process some information. They may make errors by processing some information incorrectly. They may delay processing information or making decisions, in hopes of catching up later. They may try to reduce their workload by "filtering," meaning they decide not to look at certain types of information. They may simply try to escape from dealing with the task altogether.[4]

Information overload should be considered when designing accounting reports. Many companies have a huge number of transactions during a year, far more than any human being can keep track of mentally. For example, Federal Express delivers hundreds of thousands of packages each day, and has thousands of employees. There is simply no way that its CEOs can mentally handle information about hundreds of thousands of events, one at a time. A recent report by two professional groups (Accountancy Futures Academy 2013) identified the ability to help deal with "big data" as one of the major opportunities for the accounting profession over the next decade.[5]

There are three ways that have been suggested to help reduce information overload:

1   *Leave out unimportant data.* As John Tukey (1977, p. 128) wrote, "We must play down or eliminate anything that might get in the way of our seeing what appears to go on." In accounting, we refer to things that are large enough to be important as "material" items, and we speak of the concept of "materiality." Accountants often do not report, and may not even record, items that they consider "immaterial." For example, most companies do not keep track of daily usage of paper clips because these items are so inexpensive. Instead, the company will track total usage of office supplies for a month.

2   *Aggregate information into summary totals.* As an example, instead of reporting each package delivery for the month, Federal Express could aggregate this data into daily or weekly totals. This process of putting data from many events together into a briefer form of information is "aggregation." There are both advantages and disadvantages of aggregating information.

   a.   The aggregated presentation is *shorter and simpler*, which is an advantage.
   b.   Mathematically, summarized information tends to be *less variable* than the individual items that go into it. For example, think about the packages that Federal Express delivers in a single day. The deliveries to any one building are likely to vary more on a percentage basis than Federal Express's worldwide deliveries. Why? Because on days when that one building has unusually low deliveries, some other buildings around the world may offset the effect by having unusually high deliveries.
   c.   Unfortunately, the summarized total always has *less information* than the "disaggregated" information. Accounting researchers have tried to quantify this loss of information, but have not reached definite conclusions on ways to measure it.[6]
   d.   The total also blends together results of different kinds. This may make it *hard to see patterns in the groups* that have been combined. G. A. Feltham (1977) wrote that "Aggregation is a garbling of information." (p. 48) For example, the total sales of a company might stay constant when sales of Product A increase at the same time as sales of Product B decrease.

3   *Better report design.* Research shows that presentation methods can impact user behavior.[7] The next section gives guidance on properly using different reporting techniques. Humans process images differently than we process words or numbers. Thus, presentations in graphic form may be helpful in allowing people to see patterns, trends, and anomalies in data. The Accounting Futures Academy (2013) report on the impact of "big data" on the accounting profession says that accountants need to create a "visual language of data 'art'" to help convey data (p. 7).

General Methods of Reporting Quantitative Information

This section discusses five ways of communicating information to users: providing them with raw, unsummarized data; oral reports; prose reports; tables; and graphs. The emphasis is on tables and graphs. Accounting research has shown that in many cases the ability of readers to understand and use accounting data is affected by the "cognitive fit" between the format of the reports and the task at hand.[8]

These communication methods can all help users find what they need. Shneiderman (1996) has created what he called an "information-seeking mantra." The presenter of information should give the users an overview first. Then, the users should be able to filter the information, and zoom in on the areas of interest. Details should be available on demand.

Unsummarized (Disaggregated) Data

When there are many users, with different decision needs, it may make sense to simply give the users all the data, and let them summarize it themselves.[9] With computerization, this approach has become practical.

XBRL is a computer reporting language that facilitates the sharing of financial data. A company using XBRL must encode its information in a standard format: all companies would use the same code for, for example, sales to customers. If companies used this format for all their original transactions, then anyone who understands XBRL could take an XBRL database, perform their own analysis, and produce their own reports.

The use of XBRL has not reached that stage of detail for most companies. However, large U.S. public companies are required to report summarized financial data to the SEC using this computer language. People are able to access the information from the SEC directly. The advantages of XBRL are that information goes into the SEC system directly, without human copying of data, and thus avoiding data copying errors. Also, because companies must report in a standardized form, it is possible to search SEC databases for particular items and to compare these items across companies.[10]

Within companies, top management must decide which information should be available to which people. Certain people may need full access to databases, and the ability to tailor their own reports, while others do not.

Oral Reports

Accountants frequently report information orally. Within a business, this happens often. An accountant or a CFO will present data at a meeting or in response to a phone call.

Many public companies have quarterly conference calls with securities analysts and investors. These conference calls generally include a prepared presentation of information about quarterly financial results and perhaps forecasts of the future, followed by responses to questions. Companies use these conference calls as a way of fairly giving out information to all interested investors at the same time. (It would be potentially illegal for a public company to give out information to only one or a few investors.)

Advantages of oral communication include speed and adaptability to user requests. The user gets to ask exactly what he or she wants, and gets a response right away. No one has to write up and proofread long reports.

Oral reports have several disadvantages, which mainly relate to speed and limited information content:

- Listening is *slower* for users than scanning written materials. You have all listened to people read PowerPoint slides, and you usually finished reading them well before the presenter stops talking. Consider how long it would take you to describe a map of the United States to someone.

- Far *less information* fits in a speech than into a written report.
- Oral presentations are *not well designed to serve different needs of different users at the same time*. Each listener must wait patiently until the presenter gets to the interesting part for that user. In contrast, with written reports, each user can focus immediately on the parts that interest him or her.

When presenting information orally at meetings, it is now common to use PowerPoint or other presentation software to help organize and present the materials. Usually, if there is very detailed quantitative information to be conveyed, this is better done through handouts of tables than with slides.[11]

Prose Reports (Sentences and Paragraphs)

Many accounting reports are prose. Examples include: internal memos; the "Management's Discussion and Analysis" (MD&A) section of public company SEC filings; press releases; auditors' reports; and footnotes to financial statements.

Good accounting reports should be clear and objective.

SEC rules require public companies to discuss the financial results each quarter in a "Management's Discussion and Analysis" section. These "MD&A" sections of the Form 10-Q or Form 10-K reports discuss such matters as: changes in sales compared to prior years; changes in expenses; changes in borrowings or investments; and special items that affected the company's results, such as acquisitions of other companies.

The footnotes to financial statements include a wide variety of information. Their purpose is to explain information in the basic financial statements, and also to include other information that is important for users to know. Public company footnotes are often many pages long. Typical company footnotes include the following.

1   Significant accounting policies. Companies often have choices of how to account for inventory, fixed assets, revenues, and other important items. The company must explain to users what methods it is using.

2   Discussion of important changes to the company, such as:

    a.   Acquisitions of other companies
    b.   Disposal of major parts of the company
    c.   Major new borrowings or sales of stock.

3   Details on the components of certain accounts. Footnotes might indicate:

    a.   How much of the inventory represents raw materials, work in process, and finished goods
    b.   How much of "fixed assets" represents different types of equipment, buildings, and so on
    c.   The details of when loans payable are due, and their interest rates
    d.   What items have been combined in a caption like "other expenses"
    e.   Details about the tax expense and liability items
    f.   Important rights of shareholders or lenders.

4   Information about potential risks:

    a.   A company will typically describe such "contingent liabilities" as lawsuits that have been filed against the company.
    b.   A company may describe the risks of holding certain types of investments.

Box 3.1 Some Guidance for Clear Prose Communication*

Some guidance from the great American writer, Mark Twain: An author should:

"Say what he is proposing to say, not merely come near it."
"Use the right word, not its second cousin."
"Eschew surplusage."
"Not omit necessary details."
"Avoid slovenliness of form."
"Use good grammar."
"Employ a simple and straightforward style."

(Twain 1895/1992, p. 182)

Other guidance for business writing

Use short, simple words instead of long ones. Use "do" instead of "accomplish."
Use fewer words. Eliminate deadwood and redundancy
Break long sentences (over 20 words) into short ones
Use active, not passive voice. Say "We sold the car," not "The car was sold."

*See Twain (1895/1992) and McKay and Rosa (2000).

The basic advantage of the prose form of reporting is its flexibility. It can describe any type of events using sentences and paragraphs. However, it is slow for users to read. Key ideas may be buried inside long pages and paragraphs of prose.

To help readers, it is important to organize prose reports clearly. The following techniques help users find information quickly, without reading non-relevant sections:

- A table of contents or index.
- Section headings that can be seen clearly.
- Being brief.
- Using tables or graphs where helpful.
- Using the same format consistently from report to report. This means that once users become familiar with any particular report, they do not need to spend time learning the format each time the report is issued.

Various studies have looked at what makes business writing hard or easy to understand. Some suggestions based on these studies are listed in Box 3.1, along with advice from the great American writer, Mark Twain, over a century ago. Studies of the readability of financial statements have shown that users have a high degree of difficulty in reading them. While some of this is unavoidable, much of the problem could have been reduced by following the practices listed in Box 3.1. In particular, short words and simple sentence structures can often be used, and technical jargon can often be avoided or at least explained.[12]

Tables

A table presents information in an organized form. Typically, there are row and column labels, and data in the "cells" of the table. Some examples of tables that are commonly used to report accounting information include balance sheets, income statements, and comparisons of performance relative to budget. A later section of this chapter describes these reports in detail. Other tables include listings of data related to a particular account. For example, an organization often produces for management use a tabular listing of the various customers who owe it money at any particular date.

The basic advantages of a table over prose are *speed of use and clarity*. Readers who are familiar with how a table is organized can immediately spot the information they are interested in. There is no need to read full sentences or paragraphs—the information is presented in a way that the eye can find quickly. Tables are very effective for:

- *Presenting exact values.* As an example, the Manhattan telephone book is one very large table with many exact values for telephone numbers and street addresses.
- Presenting data of different types near each other, to *make comparisons easy.*

Tables are less effective in helping users find trends or patterns in data.

Box 3.2 summarizes some guidance on presenting information effectively in tables, based on works by A. S. C. Ehrenberg (1977) and Stephen Few (2004).

Ehrenberg says that the minimum criterion for a good table is that "the patterns and exceptions should be immediately obvious at a glance, at least once one knows what they are" (p. 277). With an even better table, the patterns and exceptions are immediately obvious even if one does not know in advance what they are. However, he notes that most tables do not meet this criterion.

Spacing and methods of giving emphasis (color, fonts, etc.) should be used to highlight key information and help the reader. However, use of bright colors is often distracting, and extraneous ink or data is confusing and impedes understanding. It is usually possible to omit gridlines.

Normally, data should be rounded to two or three significant digits unless there are strong reasons to present exact data. It is easier for humans to understand and compare shorter numbers. Thus, normally it is clearer to report 2.1 than 2.07894563.

Box 3.2 General Guidance for Producing Useful Tables

1   Make the purpose of the table clear in headings and organization.
2   Organize the rows and columns intelligently:

   a.   Group data by categories.
   b.   Put the rows and columns into an intelligent order. This may be alphabetical, or by size, or by some other effect of interest.
   c.   Put numbers meant to be compared in close proximity to each other.
   d.   It is easier to compare numbers looking down columns than across rows.

3   Eliminate unnecessary detail:

   a.   Generally, round figures to two digits.
   b.   Minimize "non-data ink." Use white space or subtle fill effects, not heavy lines, to separate rows and columns.

4   Use consistent table structures when preparing multiple tables.
5   Help the user by providing summary data, such as column totals or averages. These data summaries should be presented in distinct ways, so they are not confused with the individual data points.

It is often helpful to present summary column and row data. This might be totals, but might also be averages or minimums or maximums. This saves the reader from computing the data themselves. It also gives the reader a point of comparison for any particular item.

Often, you wish your table to make a point. If you have already discovered some interesting pattern in the data, you should organize the table to show that pattern. This means data might sometimes be organized by the size of one particular variable, or by grouping together items of a particular category.

It is easier to compare figures looking down a column, rather than looking across. For example, compare: 6,237   4,967   76,856   9,326.

Then compare:

6,237
4,967
76,856
9,326

Information should be spaced close together, to minimize eye movement. Studies of human perception and memory indicate that people's ability to compare data is much greater when the eye can move between them quickly—items on the different pages are much harder to compare than items close to each other on the same page.[13]

An example can help make these points clear. Table 3.1 is an example of poor table design. It presents some information for nine different companies. See if you can see patterns in the relative revenue per employee and the relative income per employee in this table. I suggest it will be hard for several reasons. First of all, the companies are listed in alphabetical order, which is not related to any underlying patterns. Second, there are too many digits being presented. The digits are not even separated with commas.

Now look at Table 3.2.

It should be very quickly obvious from Table 3.2 that the revenue per employee and income per employee are smallest in the fast food companies and highest in the computer companies from Table 3.2. That point was much harder to see in Table 3.1. Why is Table 3.2 clearer? It sorts the nine companies into three industries. Within each group, the companies are listed in increasing order by revenue per employee. Most numbers are rounded, without digits after the decimal point. Where long numbers are used, comma separators help make them readable. The column captions are shortened. For example, there was no need to say the data came from 2012 in every column— that can be said once, in the table's title. Table 3.2 could still be improved. For example, summary data by category of company could be inserted.

Table 3.1

Company	Revenue per employee—2012	Net 2012 income per employee	Number of employees in 2012	Total 2012 revenues	Total net income—2012
Apple	2056609.724	548396.846	76100	156508000000	41733000000
Coca Cola	318204.109	59768.058	150900	48017000000	9019000000
Dr. Pepper Snapple Group	315526.316	33105.263	19000	5995000000	629000000
Google	931564.583	199346.466	53861	50175000000	10737000000
McDonalds	62652.273	12420.455	440000	27567000000	5465000000
Microsoft	786353.535	220838.384	99000	77849000000	21863000000
Pepsico	235582.734	22223.022	278000	65492000000	6178000000
Starbucks	83121.875	8643.75	160000	13299500000	1383000000
Wendy's	56931.818	161.364	44000	2505000000	7100000

Table 3.2 2012 Data for Nine Companies

All figures in thousands

Company	Revenue per employee	Net income per employee	Number of employees	Total revenues	Total net income
Fast food					
Wendy's	57	0	44	2,505,000	7,100
McDonald's	63	12	440	27,567,000	5,465,000
Starbucks	83	9	160	13,299,500	1,383,000
Beverages					
Pepsico	236	22	278	65,492,000	6,178,000
Dr. Pepper Snapple					
Group	316	33	19	5,995,000	629,000
Coca cola	318	60	151	48,017,000	9,019,000
Computer					
Microsoft	786	221	99	77,849,000	21,863,000
Google	932	199	54	50,175,000	10,737,000
Apple	2.057	548	76	156,508,000	41,733,000

Graphs

"Tables usually outperform graphics in reporting on small data sets of 20 numbers or less. The special power of graphics comes in the display of large data sets."

Edward Tufte (1983, p. 56)

Graphs are excellent at presenting large amounts of data visually. People are good at seeing visual representations of trends, patterns and exceptions. Graphs can portray very large data sets. Maps, for example, contain huge amounts of information. Graphs are widely used in science to display data. They also appear in many corporate annual reports. Graphs are not as good as tables at reporting exact values.

Graphs are likely to be used increasingly to present accounting data. Historically, financial reports used the form of tables. Before computerization, it was difficult to compile information rapidly, and producing graphs was also time-consuming. With computerization, it is easier for companies to produce information quickly and to graph it. Many companies now use "*dashboard*" displays of information, containing both tables and graphs, to report key information quickly to management.[14] Companies often include graphs as supplemental information in their annual reports.

Used properly, graphs can quickly portray important trends and relationships in accounting data. Unfortunately, there are many badly prepared graphs that either intentionally or unintentionally mislead users. Box 3.3 presents guidance on what to do, and what not to do, when presenting financial information in graphs.[15]

Sometimes you will see companies that clutter up a graph with unnecessary and distracting elements. Tufte refers to such elements as "chartjunk."

Tufte (1983, p. 51) described certain rules of graphical excellence. They can be summarized as follows:

- "Graphical excellence is the well-designed presentation of interesting data—a matter of *substance*, of *statistics*, and of *design*." (Emphasis in the original.)
- "Graphical excellence consists of complex ideas communicated with clarity, precision, and efficiency."

Box 3.3 General Criteria for Good Graphs

Above all else show the data.

> The physical representation must be proportional to numerical values.
> Show data variation, not design variation.
> Graphs should serve a clear purpose (description? exploration? tabulation?).
> Time series of money often should be adjusted for inflation.
> Maximize the ratio of data to ink.
> Provide context.

Revise and edit.
Avoid the following:

> Inconsistent axes. Usually the vertical axis should start at zero.
> Data distortion (such as failure to label partial years, or not starting axis at zero).
> Selectivity.
> Selective enhancements.
> Confusing design variation hiding data variation.
> "Chartjunk"—cosmetic features that get in the way of seeing the data.
> Distracting uses of color.

The material in this exhibit is largely quoted from the writings of Edward Tufte, especially Tufte (1983), p. 92.

- "Graphical excellence is that which gives to the viewer the greatest number of ideas in the shortest time with the least ink in the smallest space."
- "Graphical excellence is nearly always multivariate." Usually one is using a graph to compare one thing to another, or to show a trend over time.
- "And graphical excellence requires telling the truth about the data."
- "*Above all else show the data.*" (p. 92, emphasis in the original.)
- Use the same design techniques consistently for different graphs, so a user who compares graphs can focus on differences in the data, not in the designs.
- Graphs should place information in a proper context. Thus, rather than simply showing a graph with two figures, which indicates that sales are up this year from last year, it is more meaningful to include more years of data, so the reader can see if these two years are unusual. It would also be helpful to add data for the whole industry, or for competitors, to give more context.

Achieving an excellent graph usually requires several drafts. You need to think clearly about what you want to show, and then revise and refine your graph to be as clear as possible. After you design the first draft, look carefully at it for ways to minimize the amount of extraneous "ink" in the graph, so the reader can see your data clearly. Consider deleting unneeded grid lines, duplicated labels, and other unnecessary elements.

An honest graph must show the size of the data element in a graph in accurate mathematical proportion to its quantity. Thus, in a bar graph, if one item is 3 and the other is 6, the second item should *look* twice as big as the first—no more, no less.

You should avoid using two- or three-dimensional graphic techniques for one-dimensional data, because the human eye tends to interpret images as if they are three-dimensional. Consider two data points, one of size 4 and one of size 5. The bigger one is 25% larger than the smaller one. This will be properly shown by two lines, of different lengths. However, if we graph them as cubes, one with a side of length 4 and one of a side of length 5, the two cubes will have volumes of 125 and 64. Our minds will compare the two volumes, and the larger one will seem almost twice as big as the smaller one.

The vertical axis should normally start at zero.

The scales used in the graphs must be clearly shown.

The importance of these rules can be best demonstrated by showing what happens when the rules are broken. Consider the following four numbers.

   203   204   206   212

They are all within 4.5% of each other. Now let's look at five graphs of these figures, presented as Figure 3.1.

Two show what we expect, which is not much change. Three others exaggerate the change by starting the vertical axis at a point other than zero, by changing the dimensions of the table, and by using three-dimensional effects. The three exaggerated graphs, with axes that do not start at zero, were all produced using default settings in Microsoft Excel. To obtain an axis starting at zero, in Excel, you must reset the settings for the vertical axis to start at zero.

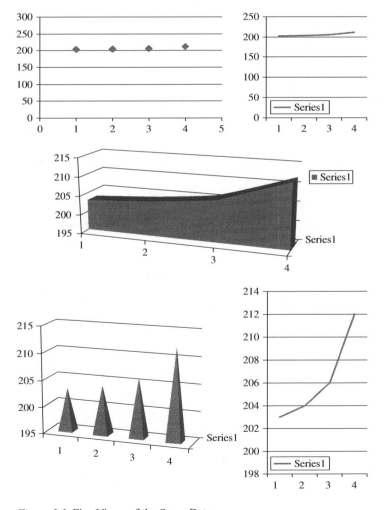

Figure 3.1 Five Views of the Same Data.

Unfortunately, studies have shown that many graphs in company reports are misleading. Companies selectively present graphs when they want to draw attention to good news, and omit graphs for bad trends. They also add color or other enhancements to "good news" graphs. Altered vertical scales sometimes depict a more positive picture than is warranted. In some cases, users were fooled into believing data were volatile, when they weren't, or believing data were more stable than they were.[16]

General Accounting Reports

Basic Types of Common Reports

Accountants prepare many different reports. Most reports fall into the following basic types:

1   *Lists of items that exist at the current time.* The lists generally have a summary total. Examples include:

    a.   A list of items in inventory
    b.   A list of all the accounts in the general ledger, and their balances. This a "*trial balance*"
    c.   A list of customers that owe the business money, and how much they owe. This is an "*accounts receivable trial balance*"
    d.   A list of vendors that the business owes money to. This is an "*accounts payable trial balance.*"

2   *Lists of transactions or events that happened over time.* Examples include:

    a.   A list of sales that occurred during the year. Companies usually keep a "*sales journal*" that records all sales as they occur
    b.   A *cash receipts journal*—a listing of cash received
    c.   A *cash disbursements journal*—a listing of amounts paid in cash
    d.   A *payroll journal*—a listing of amounts paid to employees as wages.

3   "*Reconciliations*" of two different numbers. A reconciliation is an explanation of why one number differs from another number.

    a.   A "*bank reconciliation*" explains why the figure the company has in its books for the amount of money in a bank account differs from the bank statement. See Chapter 11.
    b.   An "*account analysis*" generally explains the changes between the beginning balance and the ending balance in some account. For example, a "*statement of owners' equity*" explains why the equity at the end of the year is different from the equity at the start of the year. Reasons normally include: income during the year; dividends paid; and new sales of company stock. Similarly, a "*statement of cash flows*" explains why the company has a different amount of cash at the beginning and end of the year.

4   *Side by side comparisons* of two different sets of figures. For example, a budget comparison report typically has columns for the budgeted figures and the actual figures to let users compare data.

5   *Organized computations.* These reports show how some figures were computed. Examples include:

    a.   *Income statements* show how net income was computed
    b.   *Tax returns* show how the tax due was computed.

Usually, these reports are in the form of tables.

Basic Financial Statements and External Financial Reporting

Financial reporting is broader than financial statements. The FASB (1978) said: "Financial reporting includes not only financial statements but also other means of communicating information that relates, directly or indirectly, to . . . an enterprise's resources, obligations, earnings, etc." (para. 7)

Financial statements have evolved over centuries since they were first recommended by Angelo Pietra in 1586 (Gamble 1979). Britain began requiring corporations to distribute annual audited balance sheets to their shareholders in 1844, and a few years later income statements were also required (Chatfield 1977). Cash flow statements evolved later, but some form of these statements was used by some U.S. companies from at least 1903 (Chatfield 1977). The FASB began requiring cash flow statements in their current form in 1987. The statement of comprehensive income was first required by a FASB statement issued in 1997.

U.S. public companies must file certain information with the SEC every year. Box 3.4 contains a summary of the required reports. Public companies must report certain annual financial data within 60 days after the end of their fiscal year, and they also must report a smaller amount of information on a quarterly basis for their first three quarters. The annual filing is on Form 10-K. Some companies also publish separate annual reports to shareholders. The quarterly SEC filings are on Form 10-Q. Depending on the size of the companies, 10-Q forms are due either 40 or 45 days after the end of the quarter. Financial information in SEC filings includes financial statements, explanatory footnotes, and management's discussion and analysis of the financial results. The financial statements and a few of the footnotes are tables, and the other footnotes and management discussion are prose narratives.

Box 3.4 Required SEC Filings for U.S. Public Companies

Required filings for companies first issuing securities to the public:

Form S-1—Contains audited financial statements for several prior years, a management discussion and analysis section, and extensive narrative disclosures about the company and its officers.

Required filings for companies already registered with the SEC:

Form 10-Q—A quarterly form containing summarized financial statements that receive a lesser degree of scrutiny from auditors than a full audit. There is a management discussion and analysis section, but fewer disclosures than in an annual filing. Due from 40 to 45 business days after year end, depending on the company's size.

    Form 10-K—An annual form containing audited financial statements for three years, management discussion and analysis of the financial results, and extensive narrative disclosures about the company and its officers. Large U.S. firms and their auditors must also give an opinion as to whether the company's internal controls over financial reporting were operating effectively. Typically due 60 days after the end of the fiscal year. Foreign firms use the 20-F instead.

    Form 8-K—This form is filed whenever some important event occurs, such as a merger, issuance of new types of stock, or resignation of the auditors or the resignation of important corporate officers. Companies typically have four business days to file an 8-K.

    Form 20-F—This is a form that non-U.S. firms that are registered with the SEC use instead of a 10-K. It has similar information to the 10-K.

A complete set of financial statements includes the following statements:

- A statement of financial position, also called a balance sheet
- An income statement
- A statement of comprehensive income
- A statement of changes in owners' equity
- A cash flow statement

The statement of comprehensive income may be a separate statement. Companies can also choose to combine it with either the income statement or the statement of changes in owners' equity.

The five basic statements provide information about the company's assets, liabilities and equity at different points in time, and about changes in two key areas: equity and cash. The FASB strongly urges users to consider all the information in these statements, and not to overly focus on any one statement or any one number. The FASB (2008) stated: "No one financial statement is likely to provide all the financial statement information that is useful for a particular kind of decision" (p. Con5-1), and added that "the Board believes that it is important to avoid focusing attention almost exclusively on 'the bottom line,' earnings per share, or other highly simplified condensations" (para. 22).

Descriptions of these statements follow. Financial statements from The Gap, Inc. SEC filings, with minor formatting changes for clarity, are used to illustrate the points.

Balance Sheet (Statement of Financial Position)

A balance sheet is a table that contains a list. The *balance sheet* has this name for two reasons. It lists the running totals (or "balances") of all the ledger asset, liability, and equity accounts at a moment in time. Also, because this statement is based on the accounting equation, the total assets must always equal (or balance) the total of the equity plus liabilities. Another name is the *Statement of Financial Position*, because the statement indicates where the company stands at a point in time.

U.S. public companies must report *comparative balance sheets*, showing two years of information. This allows readers to compare the levels of assets and liabilities over time, and provides context for the data.

Most U.S. companies prepare what are called *"classified balance sheets."* They list assets in the order with which they can be turned into cash, and liabilities in the order in which they are due to be paid. The ability to turn an asset into cash is referred to as "liquidity", and assets which can be converted quickly to cash are called "liquid assets." Thus, cash is typically first, then such assets as accounts receivable and inventory, that are expected to be turned into cash within a year. These are referred to as *"current assets."* Such assets as land, buildings, and intangible assets are listed as "noncurrent assets." Similarly, liabilities are separated between *current liabilities*, expected to be paid within a year, and noncurrent liabilities.[17]

Comparative balance sheets for The Gap, Inc. appear in Table 3.3. Note that headings, indentation, and spacing have been used to help make the table easier to use. Accountants typically use underlines to indicate when figures are being totaled, and to indicate a total or subtotal. So, in the example, the last of the current assets in the list is underlined, to let you know a total is coming, and then the total current assets is underlined. When a total is a final total, double underlines are used. In this case, double underlines are used for the total assets, and for the total of the liabilities plus the equity.

These balance sheets are "consolidated" for The Gap and its subsidiaries. Often, public companies are organized in a complicated way, with many companies involved. *Consolidated financial statements* present information for the whole group of legal corporations that are under common control, not just the parent corporation.

Table 3.3 The Gap Inc. Consolidated Balance Sheets

In millions, unless otherwise specified	Feb. 1, 2014	Feb. 2, 2013
Current assets:		
Cash and cash equivalents	$1,510	$1,460
Short-term investments	0	50
Merchandise inventory	1,928	1,758
Other current assets	992	864
Total current assets	4,430	4,132
Property and equipment, net	2,758	2,619
Other long-term assets	661	719
Total assets	7,849	7,470
Current liabilities:		
Current maturities of debt	25	0
Accounts payable	1,242	1,144
Accrued expenses and other current liabilities	1,142	1,092
Income taxes payable	36	108
Total current liabilities	2,445	2,344
Long-term liabilities:		
Long-term debt	1,369	1,246
Lease incentives and other long-term liabilities	973	986
Total long-term liabilities	2,342	2,232
Stockholders' equity:		
Common stock $0.05 par value	55	55
Additional paid-in capital	2,899	2,864
Retained earnings	14,218	13,259
Accumulated other comprehensive income	135	181
Treasury stock at cost (660 and 643 shares)	−14,245	−13,465
Total stockholders' equity	3,062	2,894
Total liabilities and stockholders' equity	$7,849	$7,470

Some of the accounts in the balance sheet are probably unfamiliar to you at this point. They will be explained later. The key to understand at this point is how the balance sheet is set up. Assets and liabilities that exist as of a particular date are listed, and totaled. The total of the assets must always equal the total of the liabilities and equity.

Income Statement

The income statement is a table containing a computation. It shows the company's revenues and gains, and the various expenses and losses that must be subtracted in order to compute what is called net income.[18] The computation is always for a period of time—for example, three months or a year. It can be combined with other items that make up comprehensive income, or it can be a separate statement.

U.S. public companies typically show three years of information in an income statement, in three columns.

A "multi-step income statement" includes not just a listing of revenues and expenses, but also various useful subtotals. Frequently, you will see the following captions. I have shown the subtotals and totals in italics:

Sales
Cost of sales
   Gross profit (the difference between sales and cost of sales)

Various "operating expenses," such as "selling" or "administrative" expenses
Total operating expenses
Operating income (This subtotal equals gross profit minus operating expenses.)

Various "other income and expense items." These include interest income and expenses for most commercial companies
Earnings (or net income) before income taxes

Income taxes
Net income

Public companies would then show earnings per share of stock. Typically, they report earnings per share computed two different ways—one using more optimistic assumptions and one using less optimistic assumptions. This will be discussed later.

The Gap income statement in Table 3.4 follows the general format discussed above. The Gap was profitable in all three years. Both sales and net income increased each year.

Like most U.S. companies, The Gap groups its expenses in what are called *functional categories*. The caption "cost of goods sold" totals all the various expenses that relate to the inventory that was sold to customers. The caption "operating expenses" includes various expenses that relate to general administration and selling the products. Many companies would use the functional categories "selling expenses" and "administrative expenses" as categories of "operating expenses." What this method of presentation does not tell the reader is the amounts of expenses by what are called *natural categories*," such as salaries, depreciation expense, or heating costs. Some companies do choose to report in these natural categories. For example, most airlines will report labor and fuel costs.

Statement of Comprehensive Income

This is a relatively new statement, which did not exist decades ago. As noted above, it can be a separate statement, or it can be part of either the income statement, or the statement of owners' equity. When the FASB defined the various elements of financial accounting, it said that "comprehensive income" included all changes to the owners' equity except transactions with owners. "Earnings" and "net income" were terms that did not include certain items that are in

Table 3.4 The Gap, Inc. Consolidated Statements of Income for the 12 Months Ended

In millions, except per share data, unless otherwise specified	Feb. 1, 2014	Feb. 2, 2013	Jan. 28, 2012
Net sales	$16,148	$15,651	$14,549
Cost of goods sold and occupancy expenses	9,855	9,480	9,275
Gross profit	6,293	6,171	5,274
Operating expenses	4,144	4,229	3,836
Operating income	2,149	1,942	1,438
Interest expense	61	87	74
Interest income	–5	–6	–5
Income before income taxes	2,093	1,861	1,369
Income taxes	813	726	536
Net income	$1,280	$1,135	$833
Earnings per share—basic ($ per share)	2.78	2.35	1.57
Earnings per share—diluted ($ per share)	2.74	2.33	1.56

"comprehensive income." "Net income" is often used to judge managers' performance. Statements of comprehensive income start with net income, and add or subtract other components of comprehensive income as required by FASB or IASB rules.

Here are some of the things that the FASB has decided should be in comprehensive income, but not net income:

- Changes in the value of stocks and bonds that a company holds in a long-term investment portfolio. The idea is that markets go up and down, and any changes are likely to reverse themselves over time. Therefore, it would be unfair to judge managers by short-term fluctuations in the value of something being held as part of a long-term strategy.
- Changes in the book value of an international subsidiary caused by changes in currency exchange rates. Again, the idea is that rates go up and down, so these changes may reverse themselves over time. The decision to have an overseas subsidiary is a long-term strategy, and it is unfair to judge managers by short-term exchange fluctuations.
- Changes in the assumptions of pension plans. Pension plans often have very large estimated liabilities. The pension payments will be paid out over many years. Minor changes in assumptions can cause the large changes in recorded balances. Again, it seems unfair to judge managers this quarter based on changes of estimates of something that will take place over many years.
- Certain gains and losses involving derivative securities. Some companies use derivative securities to offset, or "hedge," risks in their business. The theory is the derivative securities will have gains at a time when these other risks create losses. There are special IASB and FASB rules to ensure that gains and losses on derivatives are only shown as part of net income at the same time as the company recognizes the effects of whatever created the underlying risk. If the values of the derivatives change before the company recognizes the effect of the underlying risk, the derivative gains and losses are shown as part of comprehensive income, not net income. Rules for this subject are complex, and beyond the scope of this course.

Table 3.5 shows The Gap, Inc.'s statements of comprehensive income for three years. The statements begin with the net income figures. These are the same figures as appear in the income statement, Table 3.4. Then The Gap, Inc. adds or subtracts items relating to: foreign exchange effects on its subsidiaries; derivatives; and other items.

Statement of Shareholders' Equity

This statement is a table containing a reconciliation. It shows the reasons that the beginning and ending equity accounts are different. U.S. public companies must show data for three years. Typical items shown in this statement are:

- Beginning balances for the various equity accounts
- Net comprehensive income or loss, as computed on the statement of comprehensive income
- Dividends paid
- Reductions of equity resulting from buybacks of company stock
- New sales (issuances) of company stock
- Ending balances for the various equity accounts.

Table 3.6 presents a statement of changes in equity for The Gap, Inc. Only one year is shown here for brevity.

Table 3.5 The Gap, Inc. Consolidated Statements of Comprehensive Income

In millions, unless otherwise specified	*12 months ended*		
	Feb. 1, 2014	*Feb. 2, 2013*	*Jan. 28, 2012*
Net income	$1,280	$1,135	$833
Other comprehensive income (loss), net of tax:			
Foreign currency translation, net of tax (tax benefits)	−51	−71	24
Change in value of derivative financial instruments, net of tax (tax benefits)	48	28	−11
Adjustment for realized (gains) losses on derivative financial instruments, net of (tax) tax benefits	−43	−5	31
Other comprehensive income (loss), net of tax	−46	−48	44
Comprehensive income	$1,234	$1,087	$877

Statement of Cash Flows

This statement is a table containing a reconciliation of the cash account. It explains the change in cash between the end of the previous year and the end of this year. U.S. public companies must report data for three years.

Cash movements are grouped into three categories: operating, investing, and financing cash flows. Chapter 2 discussed these three categories.

While the other four basic financial statements are prepared on the accrual basis of accounting, the cash flow statement is not. It simply measures and reports cash movements.

Table 3.7 contains cash flow statements for The Gap, Inc., for three years.

The Gap reported total positive cash provided from operating activities for 2012, 2013, and 2014 of $1,363, $1,936, and $1,705, respectively. This is good—it means that its basic operations provide cash that can be used for investing activities and to repay sources of financing. This is a common pattern for profitable companies in a mature stage of their corporate life cycle. The investing section of the cash flow statement shows that The Gap used some cash each year to buy property and equipment. It also used a small amount of cash to buy another business in 2013. The financing section of the cash flow shows that The Gap had negative financing cash flows in each year. In 2012, it borrowed $1,646, but used $2,092 to buy back common stock and $236 to pay dividends. In 2013 and 2014, it did not borrow large amounts, and used cash to repurchase common stock and to pay dividends.

The Gap, like most U.S. companies, uses what is called the "*indirect method*" of presenting the operating cash flow section. If you look at the operating cash flow section of the statement, it starts with net income, and then adds or subtracts items that affect income differently than they affect operating cash flow. Some of these items affect income, but do not affect cash at all in this year. Depreciation and amortization are examples. Another example is giving employees stock, rather than cash, as compensation. The other items that are shown in this section relate to changes in operating assets and liabilities. These need to be included in this computation because they are all accounted for on the accrual basis when computing income, not the cash basis. For example, a sale to a customer on credit increases net income, but does not affect operating cash flow until the customer actually pays.

For The Gap, the operating cash flow each year is larger than the net income. This is common for companies that have sizable amounts of depreciation expense.

An alternative way of showing the operating cash flow section is called the "direct method." In this method, the company shows such captions as cash received from customers and cash paid for interest, taxes, salaries, and so forth.

Table 3.6 The Gap, Inc. Consolidated Statements of Shareholders' Equity

In millions	Total	Common stock	Additional paid-in capital	Retained earnings	Accumulated other comprehensive income (loss)	Treasury stock
Balance at Feb. 2, 2013	$2,894	$55	$2,864	$13,259	$181	($13,465)
Balance (in shares) at Feb. 2, 2013	1,106	1,106				–643
Net income	1,280			1,280		
Other comprehensive (loss), net of tax	–46				–46	
Repurchases of common stock	–1,009					–1,009
Repurchases of common stock (in shares)	–26					–26
Reissuance of treasury stock under share-based compensation plans	97		–132			238
Tax benefit from exercise of stock options and vesting of stock units	50		50			
Share-based compensation, net of estimated forfeitures	117		117			
Common stock cash dividends	–321			–321		
Balance at Feb. 1, 2014	$3,062	$55	$2,899	$14,218	$135	($14,245)
Balance (in shares) at Feb. 1, 2014	1,106	1,106				–660

[Author's note—for brevity, only the last year is shown. The Gap, Inc. reported three years' data.]

Table 3.7 The Gap, Inc. Consolidated Statements of Cash Flows

In millions, unless otherwise specified	*12 months ended*		
	Feb. 1, 2014	*Feb. 2, 2013*	*Jan. 28, 2012*
Cash flows from operating activities:			
Net income	$1,280	$1,135	$833
Adjustments to reconcile net income to net cash provided by operating activities:			
Depreciation and amortization	536	559	592
Amortization of lease incentives	−66	−76	−86
Share-based compensation	116	113	58
Non-cash and other items (condensed by author)	3	27	60
Changes in operating assets and liabilities:			
Merchandise inventory	−193	−143	4
Other current assets and other long-term assets	−44	−44	−101
Accounts payable	105	91	11
Accrued expenses and other current liabilities	−5	68	−45
Income taxes payable, net of prepaid and other items	−74	146	−91
Lease incentives and other long-term liabilities	47	114	128
Net cash provided by operating activities	1,705	1,936	1,363
Cash flows from investing activities:			
Purchases of property and equipment	−670	−659	−548
Purchases of short-term investments	0	−200	−50
Maturities of short-term investments	50	150	150
Acquisition of business and other	−4	−135	−6
Net cash used for investing activities	−624	−844	−454
Cash flows from financing activities:			
Proceeds from issuance of short-term debt	0	0	16
Payments of short-term debt	0	−19	0
Proceeds from issuance of long-term debt	144	0	1,646
Payments of long-term debt and issuance costs	0	−400	−11
Proceeds from issuances under stock	97	174	62
Repurchases of common stock	−980	−1,030	−2,092
Tax benefit from exercise of stock options	56	34	13
Cash dividends paid	−321	−240	−236
Net cash used for financing activities	−1,004	−1,481	−602
Effect of foreign exchange rate fluctuations on cash	−27	−36	17
Net increase (decrease) in cash and cash equivalents	50	−425	324
Cash and cash equivalents at beginning of period	1,460	1,885	1,561
Cash and cash equivalents at end of period	$1,510	$1,460	$1,885

Relations Between the Five Statements

The information on these statements fits together, or "*articulates*." Here are some key relations:

- The net income from the income statement is used in the computation of comprehensive income and in the computation of operating cash flows.
- Comprehensive income is used in the statement of shareholders' equity.
- The equity balances from the previous and current years' balance sheets are the starting and ending values in the statement of shareholders' equity.
- The statement of cash flows uses the cash balances from the previous and current years' balance sheets as the starting and ending cash balances.

Are These Well-Designed Reports?

Let's consider whether these basic accounting reports compare favorably to the FASB's objectives and to the ideas listed earlier for good tables.

The FASB (1978) says: "Financial reporting should provide information to help investors, creditors, and others assess the amounts, timing, and uncertainty of prospective net cash inflows to the related enterprise." (para. 37) This is a goal of assessing the future. The five financial statements do *not* show the future—they show historical data. The FASB's hope is that the information provided about assets, liabilities and equity today, measured on the accrual basis, and changes in equity and cash over the year, can help users predict the future amounts of inflows to the firm. The use of classified balance sheets can help users predict the timing of certain cash receipts and payments. The FASB also hopes that by providing information for more than one year, the statements can provide information to help users judge the uncertainty or variability of inflows to the company. Also, the separation of revenues from gains, and expenses from losses, can help users decide what items were central to the company's operations, and therefore likely to be repeated.

How do the financial statements measure up to the general criteria for reports discussed early in the chapter? In my opinion, they measure up well.

- The tables are standardized, making it easy for users to compare the financial statements of different companies, or the same company over time.
- The tables contain few words, making them easy to read.
- Immaterial items are omitted, to reduce information overload and clutter.
- The tables are generally rounded to the millions or billions.
- Due to the accounting equation, the balance sheet has to contain a complete list of assets, liabilities and equity in order to balance. Similarly, the other statements must contain complete data in order to articulate properly.
- Footnotes present necessary explanations of the tables and additional supplemental information needed for the completeness of the presentation.
- The tables contain information that is relevant to user needs.
- Public companies report their annual data within 60 days after year end, and quarterly data within around 45 days of the end of the quarter. This is reasonably timely.
- Most companies prepare their statements honestly. The task of auditors is to provide an extra level of assurance on the honesty of the presentation.

Limitations of External Financial Statements

Different users have different needs, and no one set of financial reports can meet every need. The standard financial statements are meant to focus on information of interest to the owners and potential owners (FASB 1978). The key computation on the income statement is income, which is an increase of the owners' wealth. The balance sheet shows clearly the amount of owners' equity. The financial statements are *not* meant to highlight information that is of use to other interested parties. For example, the total salaries paid by the company are usually not shown.

Statements could be prepared differently, and different economic systems have prepared statements differently. For example, when the former Soviet Union was a centrally planned economy, industrial income statements focused on how much value was produced, and how that value was shared among workers, suppliers, and other parties (Ash and Strittmatter 1992).[19] There were, of course, no owners.[20]

As another example, the level of summarization of data on the financial statements is a balance between trying to provide enough data, and trying to avoid information overload. Different users will want different levels of detail.

Financial statements are historical. They provide information about the past, and not the future. For companies that are early in their life cycles or are in rapidly changing environments, past information may be of very little usefulness.

While financial statements come out reasonably soon after the end of the period, there are usually more timely sources of information about important aspects of company operations. For example, some companies report weekly sales figures, and news of major corporate actions is released the day these events happen.

Another limitation is that financial statements as currently prepared are *not* meant to report the market value of the company (FASB 2008). We will discuss this more in Chapter 7, which deals with the values used in accounting measurement. However, it can be noted here that the market value of a company depends on many different factors, and the financial statements do not try to include such relevant factors as future plans; competition; and management talent.

Also, the reporting rules have tried to strike a balance between costs and benefits of disclosure. The FASB (1978) noted that the cost of providing information "includes not only the resources directly expended to provide the information but may also include adverse effects on an enterprise or its stockholders from disclosing it. For example, comments about a pending lawsuit may jeopardize a successful defense, or comments about future plans may jeopardize a competitive advantage." Therefore, some important information is not disclosed.

Basic Internal Reports

Accounting reports are used within a business both to educate workers and lower level managers about what top management wants, and to keep management informed about, and to control, the operations. Chapter 5 discusses internal reports in more detail. This section briefly introduces budgets and variance reports. Some general principles for writing management reports are presented in Box 3.5.

Budgets

Budgets are financial presentations of the company's plans for future periods. For companies, they are private documents, and are not released to the public.

Box 3.5   Some General Principles for Internal Accounting Reports

From Lehmann and Heagy (2014)

1   *Provide only relevant information, in a concise manner.*
2   *Provide both physical (or nonfinancial) and monetary information*—e.g., information such as number of hours of overtime for a payroll period.
3   *Determine how often the information should be reported*—Reports relating to higher risk data should be issued more frequently.
4   *Report by function (to higher levels).*
5   *Report by area of responsibility*—in reports to managers, include only information relevant to their responsibilities and over which they have control.
6   *Comparative reporting*—allows managers to compare performance from one period to the next, or to budgets.
7   *Exception reporting*—contains information with regard to variances or deviations from some norm or expected level.

See Lehmann and Heagy (2014), p. 131.

A company's master budget package typically contains many individual budgets, which all have to fit together. For example, in order to arrive at company-wide budgeted financial statements, the company may first have to make budgets for each major operating unit. The overall budgeted financial statements would often include separate budgets (by unit) for:

- Sales
- Purchases of inventory or raw materials
- Necessary manpower
- Production timing and amounts (for manufacturers)
- Selling expenses (fixed and variable)
- General and administrative expenses
- Cash needs
- Expected investments in equipment and other production facilities

Each of these reports is typically presented in the form of a table, with headings, captions and numbers. Typically, the budget also contains explanations of key goals and assumptions.

Budgets list accounts and the management's goals of what level of performance it wants to meet. Often, a budget will list not just the goals for the coming year, but other figures to give context. Thus, columns in a budget for 2015 that was prepared in September 2014 might include:

- 2013's budget number
- 2013's actual performance
- 2014's budget for the full year
- The forecast as of today of what the 2014 performance will be
- The budget for 2015
- Columns showing the difference between the 2015 budget and some of the other columns.

By telling lower level managers what the budget is, top management is performing a key control and communication task. It is informing employees of what they must produce.

Performance (or Variance) Reports

Performance reports, tracking whether the company is meeting its budget goals, are another key part of the control system. They allow top management to stay informed, and to take timely corrective action when needed.

A performance report for 2014 through the end of August might be in the form of a table, with rows for each item of interest, and columns showing:

- The budget for the period through August
- The actual performance through August
- The difference ("*variance*") between the budget and actual performance.

The report would also have prose footnotes indicating reasons for the variances.

Unresolved Issues and Areas for Future Research

There are many unresolved issues related to reporting accounting data. Here are some of them:

1   How do we balance the need of the public to know about a company's operations with costs, including the cost to the company caused by competitors or other parties who use the information against the company?

2   Does the preparer of a report have any ethical responsibility for how information is used? For example, a company might be able to keep going as long as its lenders and customers had faith in it, but a report showing that a company is losing money might actually cause these people to stop doing business with it, and thus cause the company to go bankrupt.

3   What is the best level of detail to report? Technology allows companies to quickly prepare information in great levels of detail. Should this be made available to users? Will it cause information overload?

4   How frequently should information be reported? While more frequent reports would let users react faster, they also have disadvantages. They may come so frequently as to produce information overload. They may cause short-term fluctuations to receive excess attention. There is also a cost to more frequent production of reports.

5   What size of transaction is material?

6   Are there ways to expand the reporting system to include reports on the company's environmental impact? What about its impact on society more generally?

7   How do users process information in accounting reports? What ways of disclosing information are most effectively processed?

   a.   Do users react the same way to information that is "recognized", and shown numerically on the balance sheet, as they do to a number in the financial statement's footnotes? Different studies have had different findings. For example, see Bratten, Choudhary, and Schipper (2013).

   b.   Do users react the same way when something is called "extraordinary" and when the same item is not called extraordinary?[21]

   c.   Are people able to compare two pieces of information as well when they are presented on the same page, or in different places, in a report?[22]

8   How common is it for company "insiders" to use their special information to trade stocks before the information is revealed to the public?

Key Terms

Aggregation/Aggregated information—This is information that has been summarized. For example, instead of listing every single sale made in day, a company might "aggregate" the total dollars into a single figure.

Balance sheet—This financial statement lists the company's assets, liabilities, and equity at a single point in time. It is also called a statement of financial position.

Budget—An internal company document that represents management's plan for the period, expressed in financial terms. Companies often budget such items as sales, production, the intended net income, inventory levels, cash balances, and new capital expenditures on factories and equipment.

Classified balance sheet—A balance sheet with separate sections for current and noncurrent assets, and for current and noncurrent liabilities.

Consolidated financial statements—Many businesses operate in a complicated legal structure. The business's shareholders own shares in a company, called the "parent company," which in turn owns shares in various other legally distinct companies, called "subsidiaries." Consolidated financial statements show the results of the parent and the subsidiaries together, as if they were a single company.

Current assets—Assets that are either cash, or are expected to be turned into cash, within one operating cycle of the business, or one year, whichever is greater. For simplicity, in this course we assume that they will be collected within one year. The term *short-term assets* is also used for these items.

Current liabilities—These liabilities will either be paid in cash, or with other current assets, within one year or one operating cycle of the business, whichever is longer. For simplicity, in this course we assume they will be paid within a year. The term *short-term liabilities* is a synonym.

Income statement—This financial statement shows revenues, gains, expenses and losses, and uses them to compute "net income." Certain types of gains and losses are not included in the computation of net income, but are part of the computation of comprehensive income. The income statement may be combined with the statement of comprehensive income.

Information overload—Information overload occurs when people receive more information than they can readily process.

Long-term assets and **long-term liabilities**—See noncurrent assets and noncurrent liabilities.

Management's Discussion and Analysis ("MD&A") —A section of an SEC filing in which management comments on the financial results, including matters related to profitability and the business's capital resources.

Materiality—Something large enough or otherwise important enough to make a difference in a user's decision.

Noncurrent assets—Assets that do not meet the definition of current assets, because they will take longer to be converted into cash. "Long-term assets" means the same thing.

Noncurrent liabilities—Liabilities that do not meet the definition of current liabilities, because they will be paid later. "Long-term liabilities" means the same thing.

Reconciliation—A report or analysis explaining why two numbers are different. For example, "bank reconciliations" compare the balance in a bank account according to bank statements with the company's own records of what should be in the account.

Statement of cash flows—A statement that reconciles the beginning and ending cash balances of the company. The various cash movements ("flows") are divided into the categories of operating, investing, and financing. See Chapter 2 for definitions of these categories.

Statement of changes in owners' equity (or statement of changes in shareholders' equity)—A statement that reconciles the beginning and ending balances of each of the accounts used to track parts of the owner's equity in a company.

Statement of comprehensive income—This statement shows the computation of comprehensive income. Comprehensive income includes certain types of gains and losses that are not included in an income statement. This statement may be combined with either the income statement or the statement of changes in shareholders' equity.

Statement of financial position—See **balance sheet**.

Variance—This term is usually used in management accounting to mean the difference between the predicted amount of something and the actual amount.

XBRL—A computer language used by companies to encode data, and report it, in a standard manner. It allows information from different companies to be combined and analyzed without the need to be re-keyed. Large U.S. companies report financial data to the SEC using XBRL as well as in word filings.

Questions and Problems

Comprehension Questions

C1. (Reasons for reporting) What are the two basic reasons managers report financial results to shareholders?

C2. (General guidance) What is the relationship between the idea of "materiality" from Chapter 2 and the guidance on design of reports in this chapter?

C3. (General criteria) Why is it important for reports to be:

    A. Succinct?
    B. Comparable in design?
    C. Distributed only to intended users?
    D. Timely?

C4. (Information overload) What is meant by information overload?

C5. (Information overload) What are some of the bad effects that occur when decision-makers are overloaded with information?

C6. (Information overload) What are the three methods suggested in the chapter for reducing information overload?

C7. (Information overload/aggregation) What are benefits and disadvantages of reporting aggregated data?

C8. (Providing disaggregated data) What are advantages and disadvantages of providing disaggregated data to users?

C9. (Oral communication) What are advantages and disadvantages of providing information orally?

C10. (Prose reports) What are advantages and disadvantages of reporting accounting data in prose narratives, e.g. sentences and paragraphs?

C11. (Prose reports) What are some examples of accounting reports in prose form?

C12. (Prose reports) What are some techniques suggested in the chapters to help organize prose reports, so readers can find information quickly?

C13. (Prose reports) List three guidelines given in the chapter for ways to make business writing more clear and understandable for readers.

C14. (Tables) What are advantages and disadvantages of using tables to report data?

C15. (Tables) What are some examples of accounting reports that are in the form of tables?

C16. (Tables) List three guidelines given in the chapter for ways to make tables clearer.

C17. (Graphs) What are some advantages and disadvantages of using graphs to report financial data?

C18. (Graphs) What are three guidelines the chapter cites for creating good graphs?

C19. (Graphs) What are three things the chapter indicates should be avoided when preparing graphs?

C20. (Graphs) Why should graphs usually not use three-dimensional formats?

C21. (General accounting reports) What is a reconciliation?

C22. (Basic financial statements) Explain what you would normally see on a:

    A. Balance sheet
    B. Income statement
    C. Statement of comprehensive income
    D. Statement of shareholders' equity
    E. Statement of cash flows.

C23. (Basic financial statements) Which, if any, of the five basic financial statements is:

    A. A list of things at one point in time?
    B. A computation?
    C. A reconciliation?

C24. (Classified balance sheet) What does it mean for a balance sheet to be "classified?"

C25. (Classified balance sheet) What is the difference between a "current asset" and a "noncurrent asset"?

C26. (Income statement) What is a "multi-step" income statement?

C27. (Comprehensive income) What is the difference between a statement of comprehensive income and an income statement?

C28. (Limits of external statements) What are two limitations of the usefulness of financial statements?

C29. (Internal reports—budgets) What are some separate budgets that might be part of a company's overall master budget package?

C30. (Internal reports—performance reports) What is meant by a variance in a performance report?

Application Questions

A1. (General criteria) Match the following general criteria of good reports with definitions:

A.	Timeliness	___ 1.	including all relevant information
B.	Succinctness/brevity	___ 2.	having value worth more than the cost
C.	Proper distribution	___ 3.	Reaches decision-makers when they need it
D.	Completeness	___ 4.	Allows users to see differences in data between firms
E.	Cost-beneficial	___ 5.	Contains no unneeded material
F.	Comparability	___ 6.	Reaches only the intended users

A2. (General Criteria) The chapter indicates certain general criteria for reports. For each of the examples below, explain what criteria you believe have been violated:

A. A boss asked a research assistant to find out what the longest river in the world was. The assistant gave the boss a book that contained a list of longest rivers.

B. Information that was needed for a Board of Directors meeting on Monday was not ready until three days later.

C. An executive wanted to know which of five products had been most profitable during the month of February. She received a report showing the profitability of four of the five products for the first two weeks of February.

D. A report contained a table of information that contained numerous figures like 106835425.1224, in six-point font.

E. A report contained good news that was prominently displayed, with some big graphs to highlight it, but the bad news was only briefly mentioned in the last pages, with no graphs to highlight it.

A3. (General methods of reporting information) The chapter lists five different ways of reporting raw data: providing unsummarized data; oral reports; prose; tables, and graphs. For each of the following situations, indicate which method you feel would be most appropriate:

A. Your boss is about to go into a meeting, and wants to know the approximate total sales for the month.

B. Your boss wants to know the monthly sales, by department, for the last two years. Your company has three departments. The boss needs exact figures to make certain bonus computations.

C. Your boss wants to know what factors kept a department from achieving its budget.

D. Your boss wants to compare general trends in production over the last 104 weeks for two departments.

E. Your boss wants to perform her own analysis of employee data. She is not sure exactly what she wants, but is very capable of analyzing data herself.

A4. (Prose reports) The chapter cited various guidelines about clear business writing. For each of the following examples, suggest a clearer way to say the same thing.[23]

    A. A management letter comment was generated by our firm in prior periods regarding the collection of these types of accounts.

    B. Management must be provided with information by the accounting department to assist in the evaluation of operating results and the facilitation of appropriate decision-making.

    C. It is my understanding that this information will be utilized in connection with your evaluation of the company's operations.

A5. (Prose reports) For each of the terms or phrases below, suggest a simpler word or phrase with the same meaning.

    A. Endeavor
    B. Optimum
    C. Subsequent to
    D. Communicate
    E. Modification

A6. (Tables) Table 3.8 violates several of the rules listed in the chapter for preparing clear tables. Briefly explain the problems with this table.

A7. (Tables) Prepare a better version of Table 3.8. Your purpose is to better understand what factors result in tenure being granted. What trends do you see in this revised table? What makes it clearer?

A8. (Tables) Table 3.9 presents data from six public companies from 2013, slightly modified for teaching purposes. Briefly explain the things that are wrong with this table, using the guidance in the chapter.

A9. (Tables) Prepare a better version of Table 3.9. Assume your purpose is to clearly show patterns in the relative income and revenue per employee in the drug and soft drink industries.

A10. (Tables) Table 3.10 is a table of balance sheet data for eight companies.

    A. Suggest ways to make this table clearer.
    B. What patterns do you see in this data?

Table 3.8

Professor name	Teaching ratings	Number of publications	Tenure decision
Alexander	Excellent	7	Granted
Baker	Poor	4	Not Granted
Chen	Good	3	Not Granted
Diamond	Poor	8	Granted
Early	Good	22	Granted
Feng	Excellent	5	Not Granted
Galway	Excellent	16	Granted
Harris	Good	7	Granted
Isaacs	Excellent	4	Not Granted
Jones	Good	8	Granted
Kelly	Poor	9	Granted
Lenox	Poor	5	Not Granted
Mason	Good	9	Granted

Table 3.9 Some Statistics on Six Companies

	2013 revenues	2013 net income	2013 employees	2013 net income per employee	2013 revenue per employee	2013 total assets
Coca Cola Co.	46854213423	8584348921	130600	65730.08	358761.20538	90,055,384,735
Dr. Pepper	5997378211	624000145	19,017	32812.75	315369.312	8201421389
Eli Lilly	23113100769	4684800216	37,925	123528	609442.34065	35,248,701,899
Merck	44032988768	4516877980	76,114	59343.59	578513.66067	105645365826
Pepsico	66,415,000,000	6,787,000,000	273689	24798.22	242665.94565	77478423110
Pfizer	51584091374	22,003,034,934	77714	283128.3	663768.32198	172101000000

Table 3.10 Balance Sheet Data for Eight Companies

	Total assets	Total liabilities	Equity in 2013	Equity/assets	Type
	In 2013 in millions	In 2013 in millions	In millions		
Bank of America	2,102,273.00	1,869,588.00	232,685.00	11.07%	Bank
Chevron Corp	253,753.00	103,326.00	150,427	59.2809%	Oil
Citigroup Inc.	1,880,382.00	1,674,249.00	206,133	10.9623%	Bank
ExxonMobil	346,808.00	166,313.00	180,495	52.04465%	Oil
Hess Corp.	42,754.00	17,970.00	24,784	57.9688%	Oil
JP Morgan Chase	$2,415,689	2,204,511.00	211,178	8.7419%	Bank
Occidental Petroleum	69,443.00	26,071.00	43,372	62.4570%	Oil
Wells Fargo & Co	1,527,015.00	1,356,007.00	171,008	11.1988%	Bank

A11. (Tables) Make your own version of Table 3.10. Assume the point of the table is to compare the relative sizes and the relative ratio of equity to assets of leading banks with those of leading oil companies.

A12. (Graphs) The graph in Figure 3.2 is a reconstruction of one that was shown on television, in a 2012 story about the effects on personal income tax rates if the "Bush tax cuts" were allowed to expire. The top personal income tax rate would rise from 35% to 39.6%.[24]

   A. In what way do you think this graph violates the rules set forth in the chapter?
   B. Using Excel, produce a graph with a vertical axis that starts at zero.
   C. Compare your graph with Figure 3.2. Comment on whether you believe the graph in Figure 3.2 was likely drawn by someone favoring, or opposing the expiration of the tax cuts.

A13. (Graphs using Excel) The data in Table 3.11 are the closing prices for the Dow Jones average for a week in November, 2014.

   A. Input this information into two columns in an Excel spreadsheet. Then, create a line graph using the first column to label the horizontal axis, and the second column as the data to plot. Excel's automatic setting does not start the vertical axis at zero. Print or save this graph.

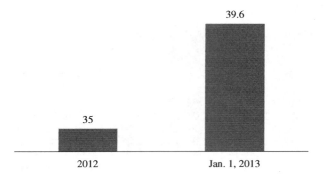

39.6

35

2012   Jan. 1, 2013

Figure 3.2

Table 3.11 Various Closing Stock Prices

Date	Close
11/14/2014	17,635
11/13/2014	17,653
11/12/2014	17,612
11/11/2014	17,615
11/10/2014	17,614

B.   Copy the first graph into another part of your spreadsheet, and then modify the graph by moving the cursor to a number on the vertical axis, and then clicking "format axis." Then, reset the minimum figure from "automatic" to zero. Save or print this graph.

C.   Copy the first graph (with a vertical axis that does *not* start at zero) into another part of your spreadsheet. If you move the cursor over this graph, and right click, the borders of the graph should change from a straight line to a thick one. If you move the cursor to the middle of a side, Excel should give you the ability to move the sides of the graph in or out by using the cursor. Move the top down by about one-third of the original height, and move the right side outward by about half the original width. You should have a shorter, wider graph. Print it or save it.

D.   Copy the first graph to a new part of the spreadsheet. Place the cursor on the graph, and right click. When Excel gives you option, select "change chart type." Change it to an "area" shape. Save it or print it.

E.   Compare the graphs you have made.

   a.   Do some seem to exaggerate the actual changes in the Dow Jones index during the week?

   b.   On the other hand, is the graph that shows the index almost unchanged useful to stock traders?

A14. (Graphs) Shown below are values for five months for an item from a company's income statement.

Item	Value
1	15
2	20
3	14
4	15
5	16

A. Input this information into two columns in an Excel spreadsheet. Then, create a line graph using the first column to label the horizontal axis, and the second column as the data to plot. Excel's automatic setting should start the vertical axis at zero. Print or save this graph.

B. Copy the original graph. Now, change the vertical axis so it starts at 12, not zero. To do this, move the cursor over one of the values on the vertical axis, and right click. Select "format vertical axis." Then change the minimum value for the vertical axis from automatic to a fixed value of zero. Print or save this graph. Which of the two graphs do you feel better shows the data?

C. Copy the original graph (with a vertical axis starting at zero) into a new location. Now change the method of displaying data from a line graph to a pie graph. Print or save this graph. Do you feel a pie graph is useful in showing the trend in the data?

D. Copy the original graph into a new location. Change the method of displaying data to a scatter plot. Save or print this graph. Compare the display of data in this graph with the display in the original line graph.

E. Copy the original graph into a new location, and change the method of displaying data to a column graph. Print the graph. Now compare this to the original graph. Which does a better job of displaying the data?

F. Look back at the graphs you have made. Which graphs do you think accurately and clearly show the trends in the data, and which are either unclear or misleading?

A16. (Accounts and financial statements) Listed below are various account titles or financial statement totals. For each one, indicate which financial statement (balance sheet, income statement, statement of comprehensive income, statement of cash flows, and statement of owner's equity) you would expect to see it on. Note—some items may appear on more than one statement.

A. Selling and administrative expense
B. Issuance of new share of stock by the company
C. Cash balance, end of year
D. Accounts payable balance
E. Sales revenues
F. Dividends declared and paid to shareholders
G. Total equity, end of year
H. Total operating cash flows
I. Short-term loans payable
J. Income tax expense

A17. (Accounts and financial statements) Listed below are various account titles or financial statement totals. For each one, indicate which financial statement (balance sheet, income statement, statement of comprehensive income, statement of cash flows, and statement of owner's equity) you would expect to see it on. Note—some items may appear on more than one statement.

A.   Net investing cash flows
B.   Retained earnings
C.   Accounts receivable
D.   Interest expense
E.   Net income
F.   Comprehensive income
G.   Land
H.   Cash received from new borrowings
I.   Total current assets
J.   New increase/decrease in cash

A18. (Accounts and financial statements) The following information all pertains to the Able Company.

Cash	57,200
Accounts receivable	10,000
General expenses	9,400
Sales	69,000
Accounts payable	5,400
Interest payable	5,000
Cost of goods sold	26,800
Prepaid assets	3,300
Ending contributed capital	10,000 (part of equity)
Beginning contributed capital	9,000
Retained earnings	14,000, end of year
Notes payable	72,800
Selling expenses	18,000
Inventory	6,500
Equipment	30,200
Tax expense	5,000
Beginning Retained earnings	10,200
Dividends	6,000
Sales of company stock	1,000 (investments by owners)

There were no items affecting comprehensive income except the ones that are reported in the income statement.

A.   Prepare a multi-step income statement.
B.   Prepare a statement of changes in shareholders' equity.
C.   Prepare an ending classified balance sheet.

A19. (Accounts and financial statements) The following information all pertains to the Baker Company

Accounts receivable	68,000
Accounts Payable	1,000
Bank loans payable (current)	30,000
Buybacks of company stock	4,000
Cash	82,600
Ending contributed capital	10,000
Beginning contributed capital	14,000

Cost of goods sold	310,000
Equipment, net of depreciation	124,200
Income tax expense	40,000
Interest and other expense	11,000
Interest payable	6,000
Inventory	61,000
Notes payable (long term)	100,000
Other current assets	8,200
Ending retained earnings	195,000
Beginning retained earnings	151,000
Sales	500,000
Selling and administrative expenses	80,000
Taxes payable in 6 months	2,000
Dividends	15,000

There were no items affecting comprehensive income except the ones that are reported in the income statement.

A. Prepare a multi-step income statement.
B. Prepare a statement of changes in shareholders' equity.
C. Prepare an ending classified balance sheet.

A20. (Cash flow statements) In which section (operating, investing, or financing) of a cash flow statement would you expect to see each of the following items? The cash flow statement is prepared under the indirect method, like the example in the chapter.

A. Net income
B. Dividends paid
C. Depreciation and other non-cash expenses included in net income
D. Proceeds from new borrowings
E. Proceeds from sales of land
F. Amounts paid to buy back stock
G. Capital expenditures made
H. Changes in accounts receivable during the year
I. Purchases of marketable securities

A21. (Cash flow—indirect method) Listed below are items taken from the cash flow statement of the Chowder Company.

Net income	40,000
Depreciation	20,000
Dividends paid to shareholders	10,000
Cash received from selling equipment	10,000
Capital stock repurchased	30,000
Decrease in inventory	2,000 (increases cash)
Capital expenditures paid in cash	270,000
Cash received from issuing stock	90,000
Increase in accounts receivable	27,000 (decreases cash)
Increase in accounts payable	35,000 (increases cash)
Cash borrowed with note payable	120,000
Beginning cash	42,000
Ending cash	22,000

Use the information shown to create a cash flow statement for the company, with separate totals for operating, investing, and financing cash flows. Hint—the net change in cash for the year should equal a decrease of $20,000.

A22. (Cash flow—direct method) Listed below are items taken from the cash flow statement of the Bisque company. This company is just like the company in the previous problem, except that it uses the direct method of reporting operating cash flows.

Cash received from customers	240,000
Income taxes paid	20,000
Dividends paid to shareholders	10,000
Cash received from selling equipment	10,000
Capital stock repurchased	30,000
Cash paid to vendors for inventory	110,000
Capital expenditures paid in cash	270,000
Cash received from issuing stock	90,000
Salaries paid	30,000
Interest expense paid	10,000
Cash borrowed with note payable	120,000
Beginning cash	42,000
Ending cash	22,000

Use the information shown to create a cash flow statement for the company, using the direct method of reporting cash flows. Show separate totals for the operating, investing, and financing cash flows.

Discussion Questions

D1. The FASB and IASB have stated that the purpose of financial reporting is to meet the needs of current and potential investors and creditors. Look at the income statement for The Gap, Inc., presented in the chapter as Table 3.4.

A. What needs of current shareholders does this statement seem to meet?
B. Does this kind of format contain the information that would be most of interest to:

    a. A labor union of the company?
    b. The state in which The Gap has its headquarters?

Explain your answers.

D2. (Alternative presentations) At one time, railroads used a different income presentation to try to convince workers that the shareholders were not getting an excessive share of the company's earnings.
A graph like Figure 3.3 below was produced by the Southern Pacific Railroad in 1950 (Feeney 2004).
Do you think this was a persuasive way to make this point? Why or why not?

D3. (Graphs) Find the current day's *Wall Street Journal*, and look at the graphs. Can you find any that violate the guidelines given in this chapter?

A. For example, do you see any with "chartjunk", or any graphs where the vertical scales do not start at zero?
B. Are there reasons why the *Wall Street Journal* may have chosen not to follow the guidelines for these graphs?

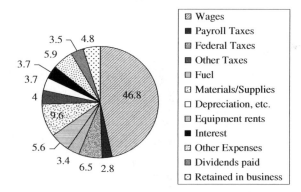

Figure 3.3 The 1950 Railroad Dollar: How it was used.

D4. (Income statement formats) Most U.S. companies report their expenses in functional categories such as "cost of goods sold" or "selling expenses" instead of using such "natural categories" as salaries, rents, property taxes, and depreciation.

A. Do you have an opinion as to which method is more helpful to investors? Why?
B. Which method would be more useful labor unions? Why?
C. Which method would be more useful to local governments where the companies are located? Why?

D5. (Ways of presenting data) In an article, Agnes Herzberg (1977) cited a saying that "Words are for those who cannot understand tables, and graphs are for those who cannot read." Do you agree that the main purpose of graphs should be to provide information to people too dumb to study tables? Why or why not?

D6. (Financial reporting versus news reporting) This chapter has been largely devoted to discussing financial reports. Every day, most people listen to, or read, news reports on radio, television, the internet, or in newspapers. Do you see financial reporting as similar to, or different from, regular news reports with regard to:

A. Whether the reader is expected to use the information to make a decision?
B. Whether the reader is expected to need to be entertained, or whether the reader is already paying attention?
C. Whether the reader is able to understand complex ideas?

D7. (Materiality, beyond financial statements) The FASB (1980) defined "materiality" as "The magnitude of an omission or misstatement of accounting information that, in the light of surrounding circumstances, makes it probable that the judgment of a reasonable person relying on the information would have been changed or influenced by the omission or misstatement." (p. 2–6) Basically, material things are considered likely to affect decisions, and immaterial things are not.

During the war in Iraq that started in 2003, the U.S. and its allies kept count of the dead and wounded U.S. and allied citizens, but made a point of *not* counting Iraqi military or civilian casualties. As the leading U.S. general, Tommy Frank, said, "We don't do body counts." (Epstein 2003)[25] Do you think it would be fair to say that the military's failure to count civilian deaths indicates that civilian deaths are not considered important for decision-making? Or, are there other reasons that they would not be counted?

Notes

1 Cited in Shapiro (2006), p. 688.
2 See literature review by Libby and Emett (2014).
3 See Libby, Bloomfield, and Nelson (2002).
4 See Rosen and Schneck 1967.
5 This report was sponsored by the Association of Certified Chartered Accountants, a U.K. organization, and the IMA, an organization of management accountants.
6 See Lev (1968), Ronen and Falk (1973), and Dye and Sridhar (2004).
7 See Libby and Emett (2014) for a literature survey.
8 See Vessey (1991). For a more recent literature summary, see Kelton, Pennington and Tuttle (2010).
9 An American Accounting Association (1971b) committee recognized this possibility in 1971. "The need to report simultaneously to many users of an accounting system will require output consisting largely of primary measures, with aggregation occurring mostly at the time of decision making. Ideally, aggregation of information must not deprive any decision maker of the information he needs to deal correctly with each state he may face. Organizationally, this implies decentralization of accounting systems and a need for multiple, simultaneous capabilities to aggregate information as a basis for decision." (p. 19)
10 See Kernan (2009).
11 For a critical discussion of using PowerPoint to present complex materials, see Tufte (2003).
12 See Riahi-Belkaoui (1995).
13 See Wickens and Carswell (1995). For an accounting application, see Hodge, Hopkins and Wood (2010).
14 See Yigitbasioglu and Velcu (2012).
15 Some of the guidance in this section comes from Jarett and Babad (1988).
16 See Burgess (2002). See also Beattie and Jones (2008).
17 More advanced accounting courses define current assets as those that turn into cash within the greater of 12 months or one operating cycle.
18 For many years, the last item on the income statement was net income, so one term for net income was "the bottom line." Also, because the income statement showed whether the company had a profit or a loss, the statement was sometimes called the "P and L."
19 The required information provided included, among other matters, the amount spent by enterprises on child care centers for employees.
20 As a second example, Islamic enterprises might have special needs. See Baydoun and Willett (2000) for discussion. "The power of the income statement to corrupt Islamic values (and indeed the ethical codes of other non-materialist belief systems) through its solitary focus on one dimension of firm performance and an emphasis on the self at the expense of the community seems to leave no other course of action than to replace it with a report which focuses on the benefit to the community. Nothing less than this would seem to be consistent with Islamic values." (p. 86)
21 See Bartov and Mohanram (2014). In 2010, of 500 companies studied by the AICPA, only 24 reported "extraordinary items. Of these, 11 extraordinary items were due to early retirement of debt (AICPA 2011).
22 See Hodge, Hopkins, and Wood (2010).
23 These examples are from McKay and Rosa (2000).
24 Based on an example shown on the "Statistics How To" website: www.statisticshowto.com/misleading-graphs/, last accessed June 9, 2015.
25 Similarly, a December 8, 2004 article by Rory McCarthy in *The Guardian* quoted Brigadier General Vince Brooks, deputy director of operations at U.S. Central Command, "It is just not worth trying to characterise by numbers." The article went on to say "Over the past 20 months the military has made no effort to record the thousands of Iraqi civilians who have been killed." See "Blair rejects call for count of Iraqi deaths" at www.theguardian.com/world/2004/dec/09/iraq.iraq (last accessed 15 August 2015).

References

Accountancy Futures Academy. (2013). *Big data: Its powers and pitfalls.* London: IMA & ACCA.

American Accounting Association. (1971a). Report of the Committee on the Measurement Methods Content of the Accounting Curriculum [Supplement]. *The Accounting Review,* 46(4) 212–45.

American Accounting Association, (1971b). Report of the Committee on Foundations of Accounting Measurement [Supplement]. *The Accounting Review,* 46(4) 1–48.

AICPA. (2011). *Accounting Trends and Techniques.* New York: AICPA.

AICPA. (2013). *Professional Standards as of June 1, 2013, Code of Professional Conduct*, New York, NY: AICPA.

Ash, E., & Strittmatter, R. (1992). *Accounting in the Soviet Union*. New York: Preager.

Bartov, E., & Mohanram, P. S. (2014). Does income statement placement matter to investors? The case of gains/losses from early debt extinguishment. *The Accounting Review, 89*(6), 2021–56.

Baydoun, N., & Willett, R. (2000). Islamic corporate reports. *Abacus, 36*(1), 71–90.

Beattie, V., & Jones, M. J. (2008). Corporate reporting using graphs: a review and synthesis. *Journal of Accounting Literature, 27*, 71–110.

Bertin, J. (1981). *Graphics and Graphic Information Processing* (W. J. Berg and P. Scott, Trans). Berlin: Walter de Gruyter & Co.

Bratten, B., Choudhary, P., & Schipper, K. (2013). Evidence that market participants assess recognized and disclosed items similarly when reliability is not an issue. *The Accounting Review, 88*(4), 1179–210.

Burgess, D. O. (2002). Graphical Sleight of Hand. *Journal of Accountancy* (February), 45–51.

Chambers, R. J. (1969). *Accounting Finance and Management*. Sydney, Australia: Hogbin, Poole (Printers) Pty. Ltd. (Reprint of Accounting and Management. Original work published 1948)

Chatfield, M. (1977). *A History of Accounting Thought* (revised edition). New York: Robert E. Krieger Publishing Company.

Due, R. T. (1997). "The Value of Information" Information Strategy. *The Executive's Journal* (Winter), 36–41.

Dye, R. A. & Sridhar, S. S. (2004). Reliability-relevance trade-offs and the efficiency of aggregation. *Journal of Accounting Research, 42*(1), 51–89.

Ehrenberg, A. S. C. (1977). Rudiments of numeracy. *Journal of the Royal Statistical Society, 140*(3), 277–97.

Epstein, E. (2003, May 3). News Analysis: How many Iraqis died? We may never know. *San Francisco Chronicle*. Retrieved from www.sfgate.com/news/article/NEWS-ANALYSIS-How-many-Iraqis-died-We-may-2650855.php (last accessed 15 August 2015).

FASB. (1978). Statement of Financial Accounting Concepts No. 1, *Objectives of Financial Reporting by Business Enterprises*. Stamford, CT: FASB.

FASB. (1980). Statement of Financial Accounting Concepts No. 2, *Qualitative Characteristics of Accounting Information*. Stamford, CT: FASB.

FASB. (2008). Statement of Financial Accounting Concepts No. 5, *Recognition and Measurement in Financial Statements of Business Enterprises (as amended)*. Norwalk, CT: FASB.

Feeney, K. (2004). *Railroad Annual Reports in the Post World War II Era (1946–1975): A Study in Voluntary Compliance*. Doctoral Dissertation. New York: Pace University.

Feltham, G. A. (1977). Cost aggregation: An information economic analysis. *Journal of Accounting Research* (Spring), 42–70.

Few, S. (2004). *Show Me the Numbers*. Oakland, CA: Analytics Press.

Gamble, F. E. (1979) [name of paper and paper number needed] In E. N. Coffman (Ed.), *The Academy of Accounting Historians Working Paper Series, Vol. 2 (Working Papers 21–40)*. Richmond, VA: Virginia Commonwealth University.

Herzberg, A. M. (1977). In comment on Ehrenberg, Rudiments of Numeracy. *Journal of the Royal Statistical Society, 140*(3), 307–14.

Hodge, F. D., Hopkins, P.E., & Wood, D. A. (2010). The effects of financial statement information proximity and feedback on cash flow forecasts. *Contemporary Accounting Research 27*(1), 101–33.

Jarett, I. M., & Babad, Y. (1988). Guidelines and standards for accounting graphics. *Journal of Accounting and EDP* (Summer), 4–14.

Kelton, A. S., Pennington, R. R., & Tuttle, B. M. (2010). The effects of information presentation format on judgment and decision making: A review of the information systems research. *Journal of Information Systems, 24*(2), 79–105.

Kernan, K. (2009). *The story of our new language: Personalities, cultures, and politics combine to create a common, global language for business*. New York: AICPA.

Lehmann, C. M., & Heagy, C. D. (2014). Organizing information into useful management reports: Short cases to illustrate reporting principles and coding. *Journal of Accounting Education, 32*(2), 130–45.

Lev, B. (1968). The Aggregation Problem in Financial Statements: An Informational Approach. *Journal of Accounting Research, 6*(Autumn), 247–61.

Libby, R., Bloomfield, R., & Nelson, M. W. (2002). Experimental research in financial accounting. *Accounting, Organizations and Society, 27*(8), 775–810.

Libby, R., & Emett, S. A. (2014). Earnings presentation effects on manager reporting choices and investor decisions. *Accounting and Business Research, 44*(4), 410–38.

McKay, M., & Rosa, E. (2000). *The Accountant's Guide to Professional Communication: Writing and Speaking the Language of Business.* Fort Worth: The Dryden Press.

Messner, M. (2009). The limits of accountability. *Accounting, Organizations and Society, 34*(8), 918–38.

Miller, G. A. (1955). The magic number seven, plus or minus two: Some limits on our capacity for processing information. *Psychological Review, 63*, 81–97.

Porter, T. M. (1995). *Trust in Numbers: The Pursuit of Objectivity in Science and Public Life.* Princeton, NJ: Princeton University Press.

Riahi-Belkaoui, A. (1995). *The Linguistic Shaping of Accounting.* Westport, Connecticut: Quorum Books.

Ronen, J., & Falk, G. (1973). Accounting aggregation and the entropy measure: An experimental approach. *The Accounting Review, 48*(October), 696–717.

Rosen, L. S., & Schneck, R. E. (1967). Some Behavioral Consequences of Accounting Measurement Systems. *Cost and Management, 41*(9), 6–16.

Shapiro, F. R. (Ed.). (2006). *The Yale Book of Quotations.* New Haven: Yale University Press.

Shneiderman, B. (1996). The eyes have it: A task by data type taxonomy for information visualizations. In *Proceedings of 1996 IEEE Symposium on Visual Languages* (pp. 336–43). Washington, DC: IEEE Press.

Tufte, E. R. (1983). *The Visual Display of Quantitative Information.* Cheshire, Connecticut: Graphics Press.

Tufte, E. R. (1990). *Envisioning Information.* Cheshire, Connecticut: Graphics Press.

Tufte, E. R. (2003). *The cognitive style of PowerPoint: pitching out corrupts within* Cheshire, Connecticut: Graphic Press.

Tukey, J. W. (1977). *Exploratory Data Analysis.* Reading, Mass: Addison-Wesley Publishing Company, Inc.

Twain, M. (1895/1992). "Fenimore Cooper's Literary Offences" Reprinted in L. J. Budd (Ed.) (1992), *Mark Twain, Collected Tales, Sketches, Speeches, & Essays,* 1891–1910 (p. 182). New York: The Library of America.

Vessey, I. (1991). Cognitive fit: A theory-based analysis of the graphs versus tables literature. *Decision Sciences, 22*(2), 219–40.

Wickens, C. D., & Carswell, C. M. (1995). The proximity compatibility principle: Its psychological foundation and relevance to display design. *Human Factors: The Journal of the Human Factors and Ergonomics Society, 37*(3): 473–94.

Yigitbasioglu, O. M., & Velcu, O. (2012). A review of dashboards in performance management: Implications for design and research. *International Journal of Accounting Information Systems, 13*(1), 41–59.

4 Using Financial Accounting Measurements

Outline

- Preliminary Thoughts
- Learning Objectives
- General Comments on Financial Statement Analysis
- Practice Reading Basic Financial Statements—Panera Bread Company
- Judging Company Profitability
- Judging Leverage
- Judging Solvency, Liquidity and Risk
- Judging Stewardship and Accountability
- Limitations of Financial Statement Analysis
- Unresolved Issues and Areas for Future Research

Preliminary Thoughts

Financial reporting should provide information to help investors, creditors, and others assess the amounts, timing, and uncertainty of prospective net cash inflows to the related enterprise.

FASB (1978, para. 37)

General purpose financial reports are not designed to show the value of a reporting entity; but they provide information to help existing and potential investors, lenders and other creditors to estimate the value of the reporting entity.

FASB (2010, para. OB7)

We report. You decide.

Slogan – Fox News

The separation of those who measure and those who analyze the relations based on the measures is efficient, but it can also lead to confusion since the underlying relation can be understood only by comprehending the integration of measurement and functional expressions. This is not necessarily a serious problem in physics or engineering since physicists and engineers have complete control over both measurement and functional expressions, and if existing measures are not satisfactory in expressing observed relations among objects, a physicist can devise new measures and with such new measures he can revise his functional expressions. However, this is a serious problem in accounting where the measurers (the accountants) are separated from the users of the measures. The measurers must clearly understand what the users want and the users must clearly understand how the measurement system works.

Yuji Ijiri (1967, p. 31)

This chapter discusses using financial reports. The reports are designed by the FASB with the goal of helping current and potential investors and creditors. As the first two quotes show, the reports are meant to provide information to help users assess the likely future cash inflow to the company. Hopefully, the information will let users predict the amounts of the future inflows, their timing, and the level of uncertainty surrounding this prediction.

The FASB does not, however, try to tell users how to make these assessments. To paraphrase the Fox News slogan, the accountants report, and the users decide what to do with the reports. As Yuji Ijiri notes, this separation between the accountants and the readers can cause problems, unless the users know how the accountants prepared the reports, and the accountants keep the interests of the users in mind. This chapter is meant to help prospective accountants and users bridge that gap.

Learning Objectives

After studying this chapter, you should:

1   Understand which companies prepare financial statements
2   Have gained practice in reading typical financial statements
3   Understand the concept of leverage, and its potential effect on profitability and risk
4   Be familiar with typical financial statement tools used to judge:

    a.   Company profitability
    b.   Company solvency and liquidity
    c.   Management stewardship

5   Understand some of the limitations of typical financial statement analysis tools.

General Comments on Financial Statement Analysis

What Companies Prepare Financial Statements?

The United States has millions of businesses. IRS (2014) statistics for 2008 indicated that about 32 million organizations filed returns. Of these, about 23 million were from sole proprietorships, 6 million from corporations, and 3 million from partnerships. Very few of these companies are publicly traded. A *Wall Street Journal* article in 2014 (Strumf 2014) cited a figure of 5,008 public companies that are listed on major U.S. stock exchanges. While these public companies are much larger, on average, than the nonpublic companies, it is important to realize that a huge part of the work of accountants and users of financial statements involves nonpublic companies.

Public companies prepare financial statements in connection with their required filings with the SEC. They file audited annual financial statements, and three quarterly sets of unaudited, condensed financial statements. The expected readers are financial analysts and current and potential shareholders and bondholders. The filings must conform to SEC standards. U.S. companies must follow GAAP, while foreign filers may use either GAAP or IFRS.

Nonpublic companies do not file financial statements with the SEC. There is no general legal requirement for nonpublic companies to prepare financial statements, or for these statements to be audited. However, many companies do prepare regular annual statements. Some reasons that companies may choose to prepare financial statements include:

- The company has several owners, who want to know how their investment is doing
- The company has outside lenders who require regular financial statements. Lenders often request statements to keep aware of changes in the credit-worthiness of companies they have

loaned to. In some cases, failure to meet certain financial targets can cause a loan to be in default

- The company plans to obtain new financing. The company expects that potential new shareholders or lenders will want to see financial information, so the company prepares them in advance
- The company has contracts with payments that depend on financial results. For example, it may have bonus or profit-sharing plans with employees, and it may have contracts with outside parties that depend on other financial targets. As another example, a store's lease might include a provision that part of the rent depends on the level of sales.

What Do Users Look for When Reading Financial Statements?

On a basic level, for something to be informative, it has to tell you something you didn't already know. One basic role of financial statements is to *provide new information* to users. In many cases, especially for private companies, the users are first learning key details about the company's sales, expenses, assets, and liabilities by reading the financial statements. Financial reporting also has a second, important function of *confirming that prior reports were correct.* By providing regular, periodic reports that confirm each other, the financial reporting system gives the users information about the credibility of the management's reporting process. This is why the FASB's Conceptual Framework (FASB 2010) indicates that to be relevant, information can have either predictive or confirmatory value, or both.

As an example, assume that in its 2012 financial statements, a company said it had $20 million of loans receivable. If this information is correct, then the 2013 cash flows will include the cash collected from these accounts, and the 2013 financial statements will not show any bad debt expense. If, on the other hand, the loans receivable were not collectible, then the 2013 cash flows and income statement will have to reflect this unfavorable news. Thus, the 2013 financial statements will either confirm that the 2012 loans were properly reported, or indicate that they were wrongly stated. This regular process of reporting helps to discourage improper reporting, since the true state of affairs will eventually need to be reported.

In this chapter, we will assume users are looking for information in three areas:

- profitability and cash flows;
- the liquidity, solvency and riskiness of the business; and
- the performance of management in operating the company.

Much academic research has focused on the ability of people to use financial reports of public companies to predict future income or stock prices. While this is an important topic, it is by no means the only use of financial data. As noted above, the vast majority of American businesses are not publicly traded. Ray Ball (2013) has stated that:

> Both theory and evidence lead to the conclusion that the social value of accounting does not arise largely from its relation with revisions in equity prices, as evident for example in regressions of stock returns on earnings. In my view, this is a minor part of the social value of accounting: a metaphorical "tip of the iceberg."
>
> (p. 849)

Comparability and Context

Assume that Company A had 2013 net income of $274 million dollars. Is this a lot, or a little? It all depends on the context. Accounting measures, to be understood, almost always need to be compared against something to be meaningful. Often, the comparison is over time, but comparisons to other facets of the company's own operations, or to other companies' results, are often useful.[1]

If this $274 million of net income is compared against my teaching salary as a professor, it is enormous and wonderful. However, this was not anyone's salary—it was the reported 2013 net income of Amazon.com. $274 million is still a big number by ordinary standards, but Amazon is a very big company. If we relate the net income to some of Amazon's other data, we find that the net income was about 0.36% of revenues, about 2.8% of the ending shareholder's equity, and about 0.7% of year-end assets. As a percentage of revenues, or as a return on equity or on assets, the $274 million of income no longer looks enormous. On the other hand, in the prior year Amazon reported a loss of $39 million, so maybe the $274 million income should be seen as a big improvement.

A company's reported income, revenues, and other operating statistics are often compared against one or more of the following:

- prior performance
- competitor performance
- budget or forecast
- analyst or other expectations formed based on the company's plans and strategies.

A company's solvency and liquidity are often compared against one or more of:

- actual needs of the business
- industry norms
- contractual or legal minimum standards.

A company's degree of riskiness is measured against:

- the user's risk preference
- industry/market norms
- the company's past risk profile

Management's performance in fulfilling its duties is partly judged by the company's profitability performance. Shareholders will also consider the company's ability to report on a timely and accurate basis, the company's reports on its internal controls, and indications of losses caused by poor leadership. They will judge managers against both legal standards and normal business expectations of effective and honest leadership.

Horizontal and vertical analysis

Two tools for helping give accounting reports comparability are called horizontal and vertical analysis.

Horizontal analysis involves comparing the same accounts, over time. In the standard formats used for financial statements, the different years are in columns, so when you compare data across a row, you are looking horizontally. Typically, in horizontal analysis, people compute the percentage change in an item from year to year. Thus, an analyst doing horizontal analysis of Amazon.com might note that its revenues increased 22% in 2013 from the previous year.

Vertical analysis involves comparing different figures for the same year. In this case, the analyst looks down the columns. Typically, to make this analysis easy to perform, an analyst would express everything on the income statement in terms of a percent of total revenues, and everything on the balance sheet as a percent of total assets. For Amazon in 2013, its cost of sales was 72.8% of total revenues, and its marketing costs were 4.2% of sales.

Note that by expressing items as a percentage of sales, this method allows the reader to compare statistics for companies of different sizes, and also companies that use different currencies.

Ratio Analysis

A ratio is the result of the division of one number by another. Since it always involves at least two numbers, it helps analysts understand relationships involving more than one account. For many years, analysts have used a variety of ratios to judge company performance and solvency. An early study comparing companies based on financial statements was published in 1919. Companies have also long used ratios internally to judge performance. The Du Pont Company had developed a ratio-based system for judging management performance by 1919 (Horrigan 1968).

Ratio analysis has several benefits. The first is that it allows the user to look at one item in relation to another one. As noted above, it is hard to judge whether $274 million is a good income figure for Amazon. Expressing the figure as a ratio of total revenues, or of equity, or of assets, helps put it in perspective. A second benefit is that ratios are simple to compute. A third is that the ratios allow the reader to compare companies of different sizes and of different currencies. The ratio of $240 million to $480 million is the same as the ratio of €1 to €2.

One limitation of ratio analysis is that it is often hard to know what the "best" value for a ratio is. The value may depend on the company's industry and its strategy. As an example, consider whether it is good news or bad news if a company's selling expenses are increasing as a percentage of sales. The answer, according to one empirical academic study, is that it depends on the reason for the increase. If the reason was poor cost controls, then this is a signal of further earnings problems to come. If, on the other hand, management intentionally increased selling efforts to spur future revenues, this is a signal of future improved earnings. The figures on their own could mean either good or bad news: an analyst must get other information to give them context.[2]

Some Relevant Academic Findings

As you would expect, accounting scholars have spent a lot of time trying to find out if accounting information is in fact useful, and what factors make it more or less useful to readers. Here are some key findings.

1   Even though the way accountants measure income differs in various ways from the methods recommended by economists, stock markets do in fact react to the information in public company financial statements. This means that the information is in fact considered useful by the key users.[3]
2   However, financial reports are not the major source of information to these users. Most movement of stock prices is related to other, more timely, information that becomes known to the markets before financial reports are published. Also, the strength of the relation of reported earnings to stock prices has declined over time (Hail 2013).
3   Income statement information has a stronger relation to movement in stock prices than information from other statements, but some stock price movements are related to the cash flow statement and balance sheet. (Nichols and Wahlen 2004).
4   Movement in stock prices is greater for income statement items that are expected to recur than for those that are not expected to be "persistent."[4]
5   Financial information can be used to create models to help predict company bankruptcy (American Accounting Association 2009). Of course, the models are not perfect predictors.

6   Financial information can also be used to create models to identify companies that are reporting information improperly. This can be either fraud or using legal techniques to "manage earnings."[5] Again, the models are not perfect detectors of problems.

Practice Reading Basic Financial Statements—Panera Bread Company

Background on Panera Bread Company

Panera was chosen as an example because it is in a familiar type of business, and its financial statements are relatively simple. The information in this section is all drawn from the company's Form 10-K report for 2013, filed with the SEC in early 2014.

Panera is known as a chain of combinations of bakery-cafes. In 2013, there were 1,777 locations in the U.S. and Canada. It competes with such other chains as Starbucks and Dunkin' Donuts, as well as many other types of restaurants.

Panera does not own all the bakery-cafes. It owns about half of the locations, but the rest are operated under franchise agreements. For the bakery-cafes that Panera owns, it has sales revenues, and the typical expenses you would expect for running restaurants – food, rent, labor, and so on. For the locations that are operated under franchise agreements, however, the economics are different. The person or company that operates the restaurants (the "franchisee") is the one who reports these sales and expenses. Panera is entitled to various types of fees from the franchisee. There is an initial franchise fee for each location. There is typically a royalty of 5% of net sales. Franchisees must generally buy certain raw materials from Panera. There are also other fees charged for information technology services to some franchisees.

Balance sheet

Panera's balance sheet is shown in Table 4.1. It follows the format set by the SEC, and shows comparative information for the two latest years. Panera's fiscal years were set to end on the last Tuesday in December. The 2013 year contains 53 weeks and the other years contain 52. The statements are rounded – the figures are in thousands.

The balance sheets are classified balance sheets, because they separate items into current and noncurrent categories. Recall from Chapter 3 that current assets are, generally, those expected to turn into cash within a year. The balance sheets show the company's assets, liabilities, and equity at the end of the two latest fiscal years.

Let's look first at the current assets. In the latest year, Panera reported having current assets of $302,716,000. (Remember that the figures shown by Panera are in thousands.) The items considered "current" by Panera are the following:

- Cash and cash equivalents. Cash includes actual currency on hand, in cash registers and safes, as well as money in checking and savings accounts at banks. Cash equivalents are very safe, short-term investments, whose value is highly unlikely to fluctuate. Major companies typically seek to try to earn interest on temporarily idle funds, and therefore don't leave anything more than they have to in non-interest-bearing bank accounts.
- Trade accounts receivable, net. This is a common caption for companies, and represents the money that is due for sales to customers on credit, "net" of (reduced by) amounts that are not expected to be collected. For Panera, most customers at its stores pay in cash or by credit cards, so this account does not represent customer purchases of coffee. Instead, it mostly represents money due to the company from franchisees for purchases of bread dough and other items.

Table 4.1 Panera Bread Company Consolidated Balance Sheets (in thousands, except share and per share information)

	December 31, 2013	December 25, 2012
Assets		
Current assets:		
Cash and cash equivalents	$ 125,245	$ 297,141
Trade accounts receivable, net	32,965	43,843
Other accounts receivable	51,637	42,419
Inventories	21,916	19,714
Prepaid expenses and other	43,064	42,223
Deferred income taxes	27,889	33,502
Total current assets.	302,716	478,842
Property and equipment, net.	669,409	571,754
Other assets:		
Goodwill	123,013	121,903
Other intangible assets, net	79,768	88,073
Deposits and other	5,956	7,591
Total other assets	208,737	217,567
Total assets	$1,180,862	$1,268,163
Liabilities		
Current liabilities:		
Accounts payable	$17,533	$9,371
Accrued expenses.	285,792	268,169
Total current liabilities	303,325	277,540
Deferred rent	65,974	59,822
Deferred income taxes	65,398	60,655
Other long-term liabilities	46,273	48,227
Total liabilities	480,970	446,244
Commitments and contingencies (Note 13)		
Stockholders' equity		
Common stock, $.0001 par value per share:		
Class A, 112,500,000 shares authorized; 30,573,851 shares issued and 26,290,446 shares outstanding at December 31, 2013 and 30,458,238 shares issued and 28,208,684 shares outstanding at December 25, 2012	3	3
Class B, 10,000,000 shares authorized; 1,382,393 shares issued and outstanding at December 31, 2013 and 1,383,687 shares issued and outstanding at December 25, 2012	—	—
Treasury stock, carried at cost; 4,283,405 shares at December 31, 2013 and 2,249,554 shares at December 25, 2012	(546,570)	(207,161)
Preferred stock, $.0001 par value per share; 2,000,000 shares authorized and no sharesissued or outstanding at December 31, 2013 and December 25, 2012	—	—
Additional paid-in capital	196,908	174,690
Accumulated other comprehensive (loss) income	(333)	672
Retained earnings.	1,049,884	853,715
Total stockholders' equity.	699,892	821,919
Total liabilities and stockholders' equity	$ 1,180,862	$ 1,268,163

The accompanying notes are an integral part of the consolidated financial statements.

- Other accounts receivable. These are amounts due to the company for reasons other than sales to customers. The notes to the financial statements indicate that part of the balance is a tax refund receivable.
- Inventories. The amount shown here is the cost of the materials that Panera has bought for resale to franchisees or to retail customers. Presumably, this is a lot of coffee beans, bread dough, and other food items, as well as packaging. Because food can spoil quickly, one would not expect the company to have a huge inventory at any one time. The balance of about $22 million is a relatively small part of the overall total assets.
- Prepaid expenses. This is an asset that arises when Panera pays for something, such as rent or insurance, before the time period in which it uses the related benefit. Usually this is a relatively small item for U.S. companies.
- Deferred taxes. We will see both deferred tax assets and liabilities on company financial statements. They arise because the financial statements use the accrual basis of accounting, and the tax system in the U.S. sometimes uses other rules. In general, a deferred tax asset indicates that either the company expects to receive an actual tax refund in some future year because of these accounting differences, or that it expects that it will have some benefit that will reduce its future taxes from what they otherwise would be. We will talk more about deferred taxes in Chapter 9.
- There are some other typical current assets that Panera does not list. For example, it does not list any short-term investments. If something is not listed, you can assume it is either zero or immaterial.

Panera lists four noncurrent asset captions.

- Property and equipment, net. This would include the cost of land, buildings, restaurant equipment, vehicles, and other types of physical equipment the company owns, reduced by ("net of") depreciation that has been charged to date. For Panera, this was the largest single asset, making up more than half of the total assets. This makes sense, since the company has so many locations.
- Goodwill. *Goodwill* is an intangible asset that is only recorded under GAAP and IFRS after one company buys another. The goodwill value is meant to represent that part of the purchase price that is *not* identified to any particular other asset. For example, if you consider a local bar, it has furniture, some liquor, and not much else in the way of assets. However, it may be a valuable business because of the fact that customers love it. That "goodwill" of the customers results in the business having future earnings prospects far better than you would know if all you did was add up the value of the furniture and liquor inventory. In the case of Panera, it has recorded goodwill when it bought out the operations of some of its franchisees.
- Other intangible assets. Panera indicates that this caption largely includes rights to set up bakery-cafes in certain locations that it has bought back from franchisees, favorable leases it acquired when it bought other companies, and trademarks it acquired. Where these items have a definite economic life, Panera has been reducing the net value by amortizing them.
- Deposits and other. Deposits are amounts that Panera has paid as deposits with landlords, and does not expect to receive back within a year. "Other" are long-term assets too small to merit a separate caption by the company.

The company lists two current liabilities, and three noncurrent ones.

- Accounts payable. The $17 million of accounts payable represents amounts the company owes to its suppliers, for inventory it has purchased. It is typical for vendors to give their customers 30 days to pay, although this varies by industry. As noted above, since Panera sells food items, one would expect it to keep the inventory pretty small, to ensure freshness. This means that one would expect both inventory and accounts payable to be kept relatively small.

- Accrued expenses. These are other expenses that have been built up, but have not been paid. For Panera, this includes a number of different items, including its obligations under customer loyalty programs and for gift cards.
- Deferred rent. Some landlords gave Panera various breaks, benefiting the company in the early years after signing leases. The accounting rules require Panera to record as a liability the expected higher costs in the later years of the leases.
- Deferred income taxes. See the discussion above about the deferred tax asset. Deferred tax liabilities typically arise when the differences between tax accounting and GAAP mean that the company has been able in the past to put off (defer) paying taxes related to events that have happened. The deferred tax liability is the amount that has been deferred, but will have to be paid at some future date.
- Other long-term liabilities. This caption can contain a variety of obligations that do not have to be paid within a year.
- Panera does not list various other common liabilities. For example, it lists no bank loans payable, and no bonds payable.

The equity section has typical captions for a U.S. company.

- Common stock and additional paid-in capital. In the U.S., for legal reasons, companies often have what is called a "par value" of common stock. When the companies sell stock to investors, they divide the amount of money they receive between the "par value" and the amount of "additional paid-in capital." Most U.S. companies have extremely low values for par value, and Panera is no exception. Its par value is $0.0001 per share. As a result, the value shown for "common stock" in the balance sheet is only $3,000, while the value of additional paid-in capital is $196,908,000.[6]
- Treasury stock. This represents the money the company has spent to buy back stock from shareholders. It holds these shares in its treasury. Legally, shares held by the company have no voting rights and do not get dividends. The amount shown of $546,570,000 is negative – it is a reduction of shareholders equity. This makes sense in terms of the fundamental equation – when the company spent cash to buy back shares, the company used an asset (cash), did not change its liabilities, and did not get any other asset of value. Therefore, its equity must have been reduced.
- The company has two classes of common stock, and also has some preferred stock outstanding. Preferred stock usually has different voting and dividend rights than common stock. Panera's footnotes explain the relative rights of these types of stock.
- "Retained earnings" represent the money Panera has earned in its operations since its inception, reduced by the money it has given back to shareholders in the form of dividends. The caption is literally accurate: These are the earnings that the company has retained. If the company had losses instead of profits, the caption would be "accumulated deficit."
- Accumulated other comprehensive loss or income is the cumulative effect of the various items that affect comprehensive income but that do not affect net income. In the case of Panera, this seems to be mainly due to foreign exchange translation adjustments related to its Canadian operations. For Panera, the total figure at the end of 2013 was a net accumulated loss of $333,000, which was relatively small compared to the total equity of $699,892,000.

Shown in Table 4.2 are common size and percentage change balance sheets. These are used for vertical and horizontal analysis. I prepared them using the company's reported figures.

The *common size balance sheets* present all the items as a percentage of total assets for the year. You can clearly identify the relative size of the assets. Property and equipment was the

Table 4.2 Panera Bread Company

Consolidated Balance Sheets ($thousands)	Dec. 31, 2013	Dec. 25, 2012	Common size		% change
			2013	2012	2013
Current assets:					
Cash and cash equivalents	$125,245	$297,141	11%	23%	−58%
Trade accounts receivable, net	32,965	43,843	3%	3%	−25%
Other accounts receivable	51,637	42,419	4%	3%	22%
Inventories	21,916	19,714	2%	2%	11%
Prepaid expenses and other	43,064	42,223	4%	3%	2%
Deferred income taxes	27,889	33,502	2%	3%	−17%
Total current assets	302,716	478,842	26%	38%	−37%
Property and equipment, net	669,409	571,754	57%	45%	17%
Other assets:					
Goodwill	123,013	121,903	10%	10%	1%
Other intangible assets, net	79,768	88,073	7%	7%	−9%
Deposits and other	5,956	7,591	1%	1%	−22%
Total other assets	208,737	217,567	18%	17%	−4%
Total assets	$1,180,862	$1,268,163	100%	100%	−7%
Current liabilities:					
Accounts payable	17,533	9,371	1%	1%	87%
Accrued expenses	285,792	268,169	24%	21%	7%
Total current liabilities	303,325	277,540	26%	22%	9%
Deferred rent	65,974	59,822	6%	5%	10%
Deferred income taxes	65,398	60,655	6%	5%	8%
Other long-term liabilities	46,273	48,227	4%	4%	−4%
Total liabilities	480,970	446,244	41%	35%	8%
Common stock, $.0001 par value:	0	0			
Treasury stock, carried at cost	−546,570	−207,161	−46%	−16%	164%
Preferred stock	0	0	0%	0%	
Additional paid-in capital	196,908	174,690	17%	14%	13%
Accumulated other comprehensive income	−333	672	0%	0%	−150%
Retained earnings	1,049,884	853,715	89%	67%	23%
Stockholders' equity attributable to parent	699,892	821,919	59%	65%	−15%
Total liabilities and stockholders' equity	$1,180,862	$1,268,163	100%	100%	−7%

largest account in both years. In 2013, it was 57% of total assets. Inventories were only 2% of 2013 assets. You can also clearly see the relative size of the equity and liability sections of the balance sheet. For 2013, the total liabilities were 41% of total assets, while the shareholders' equity was 59%.

The percentage change column shows the percentage difference between the 2012 and 2013 items. For example, cash decreased 58% during the year, while inventories grew 11%. You can use both the percentage change column and the common size columns to understand the reasons for changes in key totals and subtotals. For example, the current assets had a 37% decline in 2013, according to the percentage change column. If you look at the common size columns, you will see the major reason for the change is the decrease in cash from 23% of total assets to 11%.

Income Statement and Statement of Comprehensive Income

Panera has chosen to combine the statement of comprehensive income with the income statement. Panera's statement is shown in Table 4.3. Like most U.S. public companies, it presents information for the latest three years.

Table 4.3 Panera Bread Company Consolidated Statements of Comprehensive Income (in thousands)

	December 31, 2013	December 25, 2012	December 27, 2011
Revenues:			
Bakery-cafe sales, net............................	$ 2,108,908	$ 1,879,280	$ 1,592,951
Franchise royalties and fees........................	112,641	102,076	92,793
Fresh dough and other product sales to franchisees......	163,453	148,701	136,288
Total revenues...................................	$ 2,385,002	$ 2,130,057	$ 1,822,032
Costs and expenses:			
Bakery-cafe expenses:			
Cost of food and paper products	$ 625,622	$ 552,580	$ 470,398
Labor......................................	625,457	559,446	484,014
Occupancy...................................	148,816	130,793	115,290
Other operating expenses.........................	295,539	256,029	216,237
Total bakery-cafe expenses.......................	1,695,434	1,498,848	1,285,939
Fresh dough and other product cost of sales to franchisees ..	142,160	131,006	116,267
Depreciation and amortization......................	106,523	90,939	79,899
General and administrative expenses..................	123,335	117,932	113,083
Pre-opening expenses.............................	7,794	8,462	6,585
Total costs and expenses..........................	2,075,246	1,847,187	1,601,773
Operating profit.................................	309,756	282,870	220,259
Interest expense.................................	1,053	1,082	822
Other (income) expense, net........................	(4,017)	(1,208)	(466)
Income before income taxes........................	312,720	282,996	219,903
Income taxes...................................	116,551	109,548	83,951
Net income....................................	$ 196,169	$ 173,448	$ 135,952
Earnings per common share:			
Basic..	$ 6.85	$ 5.94	$ 4.59
Diluted......................................	$ 6.81	$ 5.89	$ 4.55
Weighted average shares of common and common equivalent shares outstanding:			
Basic..	28,629	29,217	29,601
Diluted	28,794	29,455	29,903
Other comprehensive income (loss) net of tax:			
Foreign currency translation adjustment	$ (1,005)	$ 364	$ 33
Other comprehensive (loss) income..................	$ (1,005)	$ 364	$ 33
Comprehensive income............................	$ 195,164	$ 173,812	$ 135,985

Panera shows three basic types of revenues: sales from its own bakery-cafes, sales of dough to franchisees, and franchise royalties and fees. It also shows enough details on its expenses so the reader can understand which expenses relate to the bakery-cafes and which to the sales of dough. The bakery-cafes that it owns account for about $2,108 million in sales, but also have associated expenses of $1,695 million, so the "gross margin" of that part of the business is about $413 million, or about 20% of the related revenue. Panera has costs of $142 million related to its sales of $163 million in dough to franchisees. Its gross margin on the sales of dough is $21 million, or about 13%. It also receives franchise fees and royalties of $113 million. There are no specific expenses identified as relating to these revenues.

Panera gives more descriptions of its expenses than many companies. Panera not only shows the total expenses that fit the functional category of "bakery-café expenses," but it also describes the major "natural" expenses that comprise this total, such as the cost of food, labor, and occupancy. A reader can use the information to see, for example, that the cost of food was about 30% of the sales revenues from the cafes.

The income statement contains a number of useful subtotals and categories. The major ongoing revenues and expenses related to the business are all parts of the computation of "operating profit." The interest cost of financing the business and certain non-operating revenues are shown below this subtotal, as other income and expense items. Income before taxes is shown, so that the reader can quickly see the company's average effective tax rate. In 2013, income taxes were $116,551,000 or about 37% of the income before taxes of $312,720,000. Since the normal statutory tax rate for corporations in the U.S. is 35%, it seems that Panera is not only incurring the normal statutory U.S. taxes but also some state and local taxes as well.

Panera does not identify any items as being one-time or special items. Many companies do report items such as large gains on selling some investment, restructuring charges, losses from lawsuits, or other unusual items.

Panera then shows the net income on a per share basis. The "basic" earnings per share uses the result of dividing actual net income by the actual number of shares outstanding during the period. (Shares in the treasury are not outstanding.) The diluted earnings per share is computed using certain assumptions that are less favorable to the company, and results in somewhat lower earnings per share.

Finally, Panera shows items that are part of comprehensive income, but not part of net income. For Panera, there is only one item – the effect of translating the operations of foreign subsidiaries into U.S. dollars for reporting purposes. The 2013 figure of $1,005,000 is quite small compared to the net comprehensive income of $195,164,000.

Table 4.4 shows common size and percentage change income statements for Panera, prepared by the author based on the company's reported figures. In some cases, captions were shortened to help the formatting.

Table 4.4 Panera Bread Regular, Common Size, and Percent Change Statements of Operations

$ in thousands	Regular statements			Common size (%)			Percent change	
	2013	2012	2011	2013	2012	2011	2013	2012
Revenue, net	$2,385,002	$2,130,057	$1,822,032	100	100	100	12	17
Bakery-cafe expenses:								
Food and paper	625,622	552,580	470,398	26	26	26	13	17
Labor	625,457	559,446	484,014	26	26	27	12	16
Occupancy	148,816	130,793	115,290	6	6	6	14	13
Other bakery	295,539	256,029	216,237	12	12	12	15	18
Bakery expenses	1,695,434	1,498,848	1,285,939	71	70	71	13	17
Cost—dough sales	142,160	131,006	116,267	6	6	6	9	13
Depreciation	106,523	90,939	79,899	4	4	4	17	14
Administrative	123,335	117,932	113,083	5	6	6	5	4
Pre-opening costs	7,794	8,462	6,585	0	0	0	–8	29
Total expenses	2,075,246	1,847,187	1,601,773	87	87	88	12	15
Operating profit	309,756	282,870	220,259	13	13	12	10	28
Interest expense	1,053	1,082	822	0	0	0	–3	32
Other (income) expense, net	(4,017)	(1,208)	(466)	0	0	0	233	159
Pre-tax income	312,720	282,996	219,903	13	13	12	11	29
Income taxes	116,551	109,548	83,951	5	5	5	6	30
Net income	196,169	173,448	135,952	8	8	7	13	28
Other comprehensive income (loss), net of tax:								
Foreign currency translation adjustment	(1,005)	364	33	0	0	0	–376	1003
Comprehensive income	$195,164	$173,812	$135,985	8	8	7	12	28

The common size financial statements show that net income has been fairly stable as a percentage of revenues. It was 7% in 2011 and 8% the next two years. The figures for comprehensive income as a percentage of sales are the same, since the foreign currency adjustments were always almost zero as a percentage of sales.

The percentage change statements show the company has been growing. Revenues rose 17% in 2012 and another 12% in 2013. Bakery expenses kept pace – the bakery expenses rose at the same rates as the overall revenues. In 2012, certain expenses did not rise as fast as revenues, so net income as a percentage of sales rose from 7% to 8%. In 2013, overall expenses rose at about the same pace as sales, so comprehensive income rose by 12%, which is the same rate of increase as for the revenues.

I noted before that the income statement does not list any one-time or nonrecurring expenses. The stability of the numbers in the common size income statements tends to confirm that Panera was not hiding any one-time items in other captions. If it had, then there would have been more variation in the common size figures. The overall consistency of the figures from year to year suggests that Panera is using a fairly consistent strategy, and has not experienced any major shocks to its business.

Statement of Changes in Shareholders' Equity

Table 4.5 is the company's statement of changes in equity for the three years. It is a complicated statement that shows, in each column, the changes in that item over the three years.

The first four columns deal with factors that affected the number of Class A and Class B common shares of the company, and the related amounts recorded for their par value. The types of items in these columns relate to new issuances of stock, conversion of stock from one class to another, and repurchases of stock when the shares were retired. Note that normally the items related to issuing and buying back stock are not considered part of comprehensive income. Remember from Chapter 2, comprehensive income does not include changes in equity due to the company's transactions with owners. There are special rules related to issuing stock as compensation to employees.

The next two columns deal with treasury share transactions. Again, these items do not affect net income or comprehensive income, since they are dealings with owners.

The additional paid-in capital column is mainly affected by the proceeds of new shares of stock and by the value of shares given to employees in option and stock compensation plans.

The changes in the accumulated other comprehensive income account are explained on the statement of comprehensive income.

The only changes in retained earnings shown are the net incomes for the three years. Apparently, Panera paid no dividends during this period. If it had, the dividends would have been subtracted from retained earnings.

Cash Flows

Panera's cash flow statement is shown in Table 4.6. It follows the SEC format of providing information for the last three fiscal years. Unlike the other statements, this is prepared on the cash basis. All the others are on the accrual basis.

The operating section is presented using the indirect method. Each year, the operating section starts with the company's net income, which has been computed on the accrual basis. Then, figures are shown that differ between the net income and the operating cash flows. Panera shows positive total operating cash flows every year. Each year, the operating cash flows are greater than the net income.

In general, there are three types of reconciling items.

Table 4.5 Panera Bread Company Consolidated Statements of Changes in Equity (in thousands)

| | Common stock | | | | Treasury stock | | Additional paid-in capital | Retained earnings | Accumulated other comprehensive income (loss) | Total |
| | Class A | | Class B | | | | | | | |
	Shares	Amount	Shares	Amount	Shares	Amount				
Balance, December 28, 2010	29,007	3	1,392	$ —	1,119	$ (78,990)	$ 130,005	$ 544,315	$ 275	$ 595,608
Comprehensive income:										
Net income	—	—	—	—	—	—	—	135,952	—	135,952
Other comprehensive income	—	—	—	—	—	—	—	—	33	33
Comprehensive income										135,985
Issuance of common stock	21	—	—	—	—	—	2,040	—	—	2,040
Issuance of restricted stock (net of forfeitures)	93	—	—	—	—	—	—	—	—	—
Exercise of employee stock options	65	—	—	—	—	—	3,193	—	—	3,193
Stock-based compensation expense	—	—	—	—	—	—	9,861	—	—	9,861
Conversion of Class B to Class A	8	—	(8)	—	—	—	—	—	—	—
Exercise of SSARs	1	—	—	—	—	—	—	—	—	—
Repurchase of common stock	(929)	—	—	—	929	(96,605)	—	—	—	(96,605)
Tax benefit from exercise of stock options	—	—	—	—	—	—	4,994	—	—	4,994
Balance, December 27, 2011	28,266	$ 3	1,384	$ —	2,048	$ (175,595)	$ 150,093	$ 680,267	$ 308	$ 655,076
Comprehensive income:										
Net income	—	—	—	—	—	—	—	173,448	—	173,448
Other comprehensive income	—	—	—	—	—	—	—	—	364	364
Comprehensive income										173,812
Issuance of common stock	20	—	—	—	—	—	2,462	—	—	2,462
Issuance of restricted stock (net of forfeitures)	28	—	—	—	—	—	—	—	—	—
Exercise of employee stock options	96	—	—	—	—	—	4,455	—	—	4,455

Table 4.5 (Continued)

| | Common stock | | | | Treasury stock | | Additional paid-in capital | Retained earnings | Accumulated other comprehensive income (loss) | Total |
| | Class A | | Class B | | | | | | | |
	Shares	Amount	Shares	Amount	Shares	Amount				
Stock-based compensation expense . . .	—	—	—	—	—	—	9,094	—	—	9,094
Exercise of SSARs	1	—	—	—	—	—	(1)	—	—	(1)
Repurchase of common stock	(202)	—	—	—	202	(31,566)	—	—	—	(31,566)
Tax benefit from exercise of stock options	—	—	—	—	—	—	8,587	—	—	8,587
Balance, December 25, 2012	28,209	$ 3	1,384	$ —	2,250	$ (207,161)	$ 174,690	$ 853,715	$ 672	$ 821,919
Comprehensive income:										
Net income	—	—	—	—	—	—	—	196,169	—	196,169
Other comprehensive income	—	—	—	—	—	—	—	—	(1,005)	(1,005)
Comprehensive income										195,164
Issuance of common stock	20	—	—	—	—	—	2,841	—	—	2,841
Issuance of restricted stock (net of forfeitures)	78	—	—	—	—	—	—	—	—	—
Exercise of employee stock options . . .	12	—	—	—	—	—	575	—	—	575
Stock-based compensation expense . . .	—	—	—	—	—	—	10,703	—	—	10,703
Conversion of Class B to Class A	2	—	(2)	—	—	—	—	—	—	—
Exercise of SSARs	2	—	—	—	—	—	(1)	—	—	(1)
Repurchase of common stock	(2,033)	—	—	—	2,033	(339,409)	—	—	—	(339,409)
Tax benefit from exercise of stock options	—	—	—	—	—	—	8,100	—	—	8,100
Balance, December 31, 2013	26,290	$ 3	1,382	$ —	4,283	$ (546,570)	$ 196,908	$ 1,049,884	$ (333)	$ 699,892

The accompanying notes are an integral part of the consolidated financial statements.

Table 4.6 Panera Bread Company Consolidated Statements of Cash Flows (in thousands)

	For the fiscal year ended		
	December 31, 2013	December 25, 2012	December 27, 2011
Cash flows from operations:			
Net income	$ 196,169	$ 173,448	$ 135,952
Adjustments to reconcile net income to net cash provided by operating activities:			
Depreciation and amortization.	106,523	90,939	79,899
Stock-based compensation expense.	10,703	9,094	9,861
Tax benefit from exercise of stock options	(8,100)	(8,587)	(4,994)
Deferred income taxes	10,356	20,334	1,351
Loss on disposals of property and equipment . . .	5,764	3,995	1,789
Other	589	475	634
Changes in operating assets and liabilities, excluding the effect of acquisitions and dispositions:			
Trade and other accounts receivable, net	3,021	(31,414)	(16,369)
Inventories	(2,186)	(2,440)	(2,183)
Prepaid expenses and other	(841)	(10,995)	(7,323)
Deposits and other	1,449	161	117
Accounts payable	8,162	(6,513)	8,538
Accrued expenses.	13,372	49,246	19,630
Deferred rent	5,868	5,718	6,081
Other long-term liabilities	(2,432)	(4,005)	3,906
Net cash provided by operating activities	348,417	289,456	236,889
Cash flows from investing activities:			
Additions to property and equipment	(192,010)	(152,328)	(107,932)
Acquisitions, net of cash acquired	(2,446)	(47,951)	(44,377)
Purchase of investments	(97,919)	—	—
Proceeds from sale of investments	97,936	—	—
Proceeds from sale of property and equipment . . .	—	—	115
Proceeds from sale-leaseback transactions.	6,132	4,538	—
Net cash used in investing activities	(188,307)	(195,741)	(152,194)
Cash flows from financing activities:			
Repurchase of common stock	(339,409)	(31,566)	(96,605)
Exercise of employee stock options	573	4,455	3,193
Tax benefit from exercise of stock options.	8,100	8,587	4,994
Proceeds from issuance of common stock under employee benefit plans . .	2,842	2,462	2,040
Capitalized debt issuance costs.	—	(1,097)	—
Payment of deferred acquisition holdback	(4,112)	(2,055)	(4,976)
Net cash used in financing activities.	(332,006)	(19,214)	(91,354)
Net (decrease) increase in cash and cash equivalents	(171,896)	74,501	(6,659)
Cash and cash equivalents at beginning of period	297,141	222,640	229,299
Cash and cash equivalents at end of period	$ 125,245	$ 297,141	$ 222,640

- Non-cash items in the income statement. For Panera, depreciation, deferred taxes, and stock-based compensation were expenses used in computing net income, but none involves cash. Therefore, their impact on the computation of net income has to be reversed. Because they were subtracted in computing net income, they need to be added here to bring their net impact to zero. Panera, like many companies, has large depreciation expense. This accounts for most of the difference between operating cash flows and net income.

- Non-operating items included in income. The computation of net income often involves items that relate to financing and investing activities, rather than to operating activities. These need to be removed from the computation of operating cash flows. In the case of Panera, a loss on sale of investments was part of the computation of net income, but it should not be part of the computation of operating cash flows. Therefore, it is added back in order to reverse the effect.

- Changes in operating assets and liabilities. These changes correct for the fact that there are numerous differences in timing of the recognition of revenues and expenses in accrual-based net income and the timing of cash movements. Net income is computed on the accrual basis, not the cash basis. For example, making a credit sale to a customer is recorded as a revenue, even though cash has not yet been received. The difference between revenues and cash receipts for this event will equal the amount of the change in accounts receivable. As a second example, if a company buys inventory that is not sold by the end of the year, there is no effect on its net income, but the company had to use cash to buy the inventory. The change in inventory in this case equals the difference between expenses and cash outflows. When you examine the statement of cash flows, you will see that:

  - Increases in current assets on the balance sheet appear on the cash flow statements as negative cash flows. You can think of this as the company using cash to buy these assets
  - Decreases in current assets appear as positive cash flows. Think of this as the company selling its assets to gain cash
  - Increases in current liabilities on the balance sheet result in positive figures in the operating cash flows. Think of it as the company getting money by borrowing
  - Decreases in current liabilities appear on the cash flow statement as negative cash flows. Think of this as the company using cash to pay off liabilities.

Box 4.1 summarizes how these items affect the computation of operating cash flows.

The investing section of Panera's cash flow statement shows three types of activity. Each year, it bought some new property and equipment. Also, in the latest year, it seems to have bought and sold a nearly equal amount of investments. Companies must show both the amounts paid for short-term investments and the amounts received from selling them. Finally, in the two previous years, it made some acquisitions of other businesses.

The financing section of a cash flow statement would normally show new borrowings, repayments of loans, new sales of stock, buybacks of stock, and dividends paid. Apparently, Panera has very little borrowing activity, because no new borrowings or loan repayments are shown. This is consistent with the lack of loans payable on the balance sheet. In addition, there are no cash dividends shown. This is consistent with the absence of dividends on the statement of changes in equity. Panera does show the cash effect of various dealings in its own stock. The largest item is repurchases of common stock.

A fast summary of Panera's cash flow statement might be the following:

1 Panera earned positive income every year, and had operating cash flows greater than its net income. Operating cash flow ranged from around $237 million in 2011 to $348 million in 2013. It totaled $874 million over the three years.

2 Panera used some of this operating cash flow to pay for investing activities. These were mainly additions to property and equipment, although there were also acquisitions of other companies totaling around $100 million. Total investing cash outflows for the three years were about $536 million.

3 Panera used the remainder of the operating cash flows (874 − 536 = 338), and also about $104 million of cash it had on hand at the start of 2011, for financing activities. These principally related to about $467 million of stock buybacks.

Box 4.1 A Typical Computation of Operating Cash Flows—Indirect Method

Start with: net income or loss

Add back: non-cash expenses

+ depreciation expense
+ amortization expense
+ compensation in the form of stock or options
+ deferred income taxes

Remove: gains or losses related to investing or financing

– gains on sales of assets
+ losses on sales of assets
– gains on refinancing bonds
+ losses on refinancing bonds

Adjust for: changes in current assets and liabilities

– increases in current assets
+ decreases in current assets
– decreases in current liabilities (other than borrowings)
+ increases in current liabilities (other than borrowings)

End with: net cash flows from operations

The general pattern is typical for a company that has passed its early growth stage, and is now profitable. Such companies earn enough cash from operating activities to finance continued expansion, and also to repay financing and to give shareholders a return on their investments.

Judging Company Profitability

Table 4.7 lists some of the tools commonly used to judge and compare profitability. There are many tools in widespread use, and in some cases people use differing formulas. For example, "return on assets" is defined differently in two textbooks I teach from each year. Be cautious when using ratios from on-line data sources – they also vary in their definitions.

The most obvious way to judge a company's profitability is by looking at the net income on the income statement. Panera, as we saw, had net income every year. While this is useful to know, it does not give us enough context to know if management is doing a good or bad job with the resources on hand. At the start of this chapter, I noted that the 2013 income for Amazon was $274 million. While this is a big number in some ways, it is very small compared to Amazon's overall total revenues.

Another factor to consider in judging profitability is that some items in the current year's income statement may not be recurring. Analysts try to separate out items that are expected to continue, or "persist," from items that lack persistence. Research shows that special items on the income statement have less effect on stock prices than items expected to recur (Libby and Emett 2014).

Another way that people judge profitability is by looking at the reported earnings per share. While this is a widely followed number, it is hard to compare across companies because companies have the freedom to adjust the number of shares of stock they have outstanding. A company

Table 4.7 Tools Used to Judge Profitability

Name	Formula	Comment
Net income	Revenues − total expenses	Commonly used. Not good for comparisons of different size companies
Earnings per share	Net income for common shares ÷ average common shares outstanding	Commonly used. Affected by arbitrary decisions on numbers of shares. Not comparable across companies
Return on assets (ROA)	Numerator: Net income + (1 − t) × interest expense + noncontrolling interest in income Denominator: Average total assets	Allows comparison of companies, of different sizes and different financing structures
Profit margin for ROA	Numerator: same as for return on assets Denominator: total revenues	Measures ability to get income from sales
Total asset turnover	Numerator: total revenues Denominator: Average total assets	Measures ability to use assets to generate revenues
Return on assets = (profit margin for return on assets) × (asset turnover)		
Return on common equity (ROCE)	Numerator: Net income − preferred stock dividends Denominator: Average common shareholders' equity	Focuses on the return earned for the common shareholders
Profit margin for ROCE	Numerator: Net income − preferred stock dividends Denominator: total revenues	This differs from the profit margin for ROA because the costs of interest and noncontrolling interests are not added back here
Capital structure leverage	Average total assets ÷ average common shareholders' equity	A measure of the use of liabilities to obtain assets
ROCE = profit margin for ROCE × asset turnover × capital structure leverage		
Gross margin percentage	(Revenues − cost of goods sold) ÷ total revenues	A measure of the profit per dollar sold before considering general expenses
SG and A percentage	Selling, general and administrative expenses ÷ total revenues	
Effective tax rate	Income tax expense ÷ pretax income	

is free to choose whether they issue 1,000 shares, each with a one-thousandth ownership percentage, or 1 million shares, each with a one-millionth interest in the company.

The focus in this chapter is on ratio analysis, because it gives us better tools to compare performance. In particular, the chapter follows a method of analysis that was first developed in the Du Pont Powder Company by 1919.[7] In this system, we look at two key indicators of profitability, and then look more closely at factors that affect them.

Return on assets (ROA) is a measure of the ability of management to generate positive income from the assets they have, without considering how those assets were financed. As Table 4.7 shows, the denominator is the average total assets on hand during the year. The numerator measures all the returns that were earned *before* parts of these returns were allocated to lenders in the form of interest and to noncontrolling shareholders. That is why these items are added back in the numerator. One complication is that interest is tax-deductible. Net income is not reduced by $1,000 if a company has an interest expense of $1,000 and the company has a 30% tax rate—net income is reduced by $1,000 × (1 − 30%), or $700. Therefore, the numerator of the ROA formula has a factor of "t" where "t" is the tax rate.

The ROA can be computed directly, or it can be computed as the product of multiplying together a profit margin for ROA and total asset turnover. (We talk about "decomposing" ROA into two other ratios.) If you look at the formulas, you can see that the algebra works. The denominator of profit margin is total revenues, and the numerator of asset turnover is total revenues, so total revenues "drops out" when you multiply profit margin by the asset turnover.

Expressing the ROA as the product of the profit margin and the asset turnover gives us extra insight. A company can achieve a ROA of 0.10 in a variety of ways. It could have a low profit margin of 0.001, and an asset turnover of 100. It could have a high profit margin of 0.10, but a very low asset turnover of 1. In practice, it is clear that companies follow widely different strategies. Walmart's "everyday low prices" strategy is meant to achieve a high asset turnover, but the low prices mean it will have low profit margins. Tiffany does not try to achieve the same asset turnover that Walmart does, but Tiffany aims for a much higher profit margin on each necklace and other piece of fine jewelry sold.

Return on common equity (ROCE) is a measure of the returns earned for common shareholders on the money the shareholders as a group have invested in the company. The numerator is the net income, reduced by any dividends that will be paid from the income to the preferred shareholders. The denominator is the average common shareholders' equity during the period. The average common shareholders' equity equals total equity minus anything that is specifically designated for the preferred shareholders. [*Caution*—The "common stock at par" account is only a small part of the total common shareholders' equity.]

ROCE can be decomposed into three ratios: profit margin for ROCE, asset turnover, and capital structure leverage. The formulas are listed in Box 4.1. If you look closely at the formulas for these three ratios, you will see that when they are multiplied together, the total revenues and average total asset parts of the ratios "drop out," and the result is ROCE.

By breaking the ROCE into three parts, we gain insight into how a company tries to get returns for shareholders. One method is to seek high profits per dollar sold. A second is to seek to use many sales for each dollar of assets. A third is to seek financing in order to have more for each dollar that the shareholders themselves invested. Each strategy may involve trade-offs. For example, in order to get a high profit margin, you may need to raise prices, which normally will hurt sales. As a second example, using leverage can increase profits in good times, but it also exposes the company to greater losses in bad years. This is discussed in the next section.

Judging Leverage

Leverage is an important concept in business. Leverage is something that increases the effect of changes in revenues on net income. When companies have increases in demand, being leveraged can allow them to become extremely profitable. However, in bad times, the impact of leverage is to increase the likelihood of financial distress.

Operating leverage results from the existence of fixed operating costs that do not vary with revenues. Some industries with high fixed costs include oil refineries, airlines and hotels. For example, whether an airplane is full or only half full the cost of flying it is almost unchanged.

Financial leverage results from the existence of fixed financing costs. From the point of view of common shareholders, financial leverage results either from borrowing at fixed interest rates or issuing preferred stock with fixed dividend rates.

Box 4.2 illustrates the effect of leverage on profits. In Case 1, when there are no fixed operating or interest costs, changes in net income are proportional to changes in sales. When the sales increase 50% (from 100 to 150), the net income also increases 50% (from 80 to 120). In Cases 2 and 3, there is some fixed cost. In Case 2, it is an operating cost, and in Case 3, it is an interest expense. In either of these two cases, the net income now moves disproportionately to sales. When sales increase by 50%, to 150, then the net income increases by 185%, from 20 to 55.

When sales fall to 60, which is a decline of 40% from the original 100 level, the profits of 20 turn into a loss of 8, which is a decline of 140%.

In general, using financial leverage to expand a business can help a company as long as it expects to earn more from the assets than its interest cost. Similarly, increasing operating leverage by buying fixed assets would help profitability as long as the expected returns from the assets exceed the fixed costs of owning and operating them. The risk comes because the future returns are uncertain.

Box 4.2 Illustrations of Financial and Operating Leverage

Case 1. No financial or operating leverage.

Assume a company has no fixed costs, and its variable costs = 80% of sales. Look at what happens to profits as a percentage of sales as sales vary:

Year	Sales	Expenses	Operating income	Net income
1	$100	$80	$20	$20
2	$150	$120	$30	$30
3	$60	$48	$12	$12

Profits are proportional to sales. They move proportionately the same—when sales move up 50%, so does net income.

Case 2. Operating leverage due to fixed operating costs.

Assume a company has $50 of fixed costs, and variable costs = 30% of sales. The fixed cost might, for example, be rent on a store, or it might be contractual salaries, or it might be equipment depreciation. Look at what happens to profits as a percentage of sales as sales vary.

Year	Sales	Fixed costs	Variable costs	Operating income	Net income
1	$100	50	30	$20	$20
2	$150	50	45	$55	$55
3	$60	50	18	$(8) loss	$(8) loss

Profits are *not* proportional to sales. Increases or decreases in sales create more than proportional movement in net income.

Case 3. Financial leverage due to fixed interest costs.

This is exactly the same as Case 2, but instead of a fixed operating cost of $50, there is a fixed interest cost on loans of $50. Look at what happens to profits as a percentage of sales as sales vary.

Year	Sales	Fixed interest	Variable costs	Operating income	Net income
1	$100	50	30	$70	$20
2	$150	50	45	$105	$55
3	$60	50	18	$42	$(8) loss

Profits are *not* proportional to sales. Increases or decreases in sales create more than proportional movement in net income.

Table 4.8 Some Tools for Measuring Leverage

Operating leverage effect	(Revenues – variable costs) ÷ operating income
× Financial leverage effect	Operating income ÷ net income
= Total leverage	(Revenues – variable costs) ÷ net income
Capital structure leverage	Average total assets ÷ average common equity

Table 4.8 presents some tools used in measuring leverage. The "total leverage" is found by dividing (revenues – variable costs) by net income. If a company has zero costs other than its variable costs, then revenues – net costs will equal net income, and the ratio will equal 1. For example, in Case 1 in Box 4.2, the company had revenues of 100, variable costs of 80, and net income = 20. The total leverage = $(100 – 80) ÷ 20$, which = 1. In Cases 2 and 3, with revenues of 100, but some fixed costs, the total leverage is higher than 1. Sales = 100, variable costs = 30, and net income = 20. Now, the total leverage is computed as $(100 – 30) ÷ 20$, which = 3.5.

In Table 4.8, two different ratios are shown which, if multiplied together, equal the *total leverage ratio*.

- The *operating leverage effect* = (revenues – variable costs) ÷ operating income. If you refer back to the Panera income statement earlier in this chapter, you will see that operating income is computed before subtracting interest expenses. For the example in Box 4.2, we get the following results, showing there is only operating leverage in Case 2:

  - Case 1: $(100 – 80) ÷ 20 = 1$
  - Case 2: $(100 – 30) ÷ 20 = 3.5$
  - Case 3: $20 ÷ 20 = 1$

- The *financial leverage* effect = operating income ÷ net income. For the three cases in Box 4.2, we find that only Case 3 has financial leverage:

  - Case 1: $20 ÷ 20 = 1$
  - Case 2: $20 ÷ 20 = 1$
  - Case 3: $70 ÷ 20 = 3.5$

- The combined effect (which is the total leverage ratio) can be found by multiplying the operating leverage effect by the financial leverage effect. When we do this for the three cases in Box 4.2, we find that both Cases 2 and 3 have the same leverage. Whether it comes from operating factors or financing, the total effect is the same.

  - Case 1: $1 × 1 = 1$
  - Case 2: $3.5 × 1 = 3.5$
  - Case 3: $1 × 3.5 = 3.5$

This framework of ratios is theoretically clear, but in some cases it is hard to use. Companies do not clearly indicate in their financial statements which costs are fixed, and which are variable. Analysts tend to use their judgment, and to make certain assumptions. For example, they often assume that rents and depreciation are fixed. Chapter 5 will also suggest a technique for identifying the fixed cost part of a company's cost structure.[8]

The last ratio in Table 4.8 is the capital structure leverage ratio. This compares the average total assets on the balance sheet to the total average common shareholders' equity. The higher the ratio, the higher the leverage.

Judging Solvency, Liquidity and Risk

Introduction

This section deals with the basics of using financial statement information to assess a company's liquidity and solvency. *Liquidity* is the company's ability to pay obligations as they become due. It is a short-term measure. Solvency refers to the company's medium- or long-term ability to service its debts and stay in operations. They are different concepts. Two examples may help illustrate this:

- Classically, banks had to worry about short-term liquidity risks. A typical bank loans out most of the money it gets from depositors—very little is kept on hand, because on a normal day the bank does not need much to service the depositors. However, if, all at once, customers lost confidence in the bank, they could all ask for their money at once. This is called a "run on the bank." Even if a bank had more assets than liabilities, it could easily be forced to close by a bank run, because it could not sell off its assets fast enough to pay the depositors.
- It is also possible for a company to have less assets than liabilities, but to have no liquidity risk. For example, assume a company has $100 million in liabilities, of which $95 million is a bond due in 30 years. Even if the company only has $80 million in assets today, it would not be in any danger of failing to pay this year's bills. The $80 million of assets are far bigger than the $5 million liabilities other than the bond, and the company doesn't have to pay the bond for another 30 years.

There has been a great deal of research over a long period of time to try to identify signals in company financial statements of financial problems. One accounting historian (Horrigan 1968) notes that banks began routinely asking for company financial statements in the 1890s, and it was common for them to compare current assets with current liabilities. By 1919, Horrigan (1968) says there was widespread belief that a healthy company should have a ratio of current assets to current liabilities of at least 2. Over the last 50 years, people have analyzed large databases of company data, and found a variety of measurements that are associated with financial distress. The discussion in this section reflects the general findings of this line of research.[9] People have also developed multivariate models to try to predict bankruptcy. These models are beyond the scope of this course.[10]

Asset-related factors

1   A company has less risk if its assets are relatively liquid. How does one judge this? The most obvious factor is the amount of cash and short-term investments a company has on hand. Second, you can look at the other current assets in the balance sheet. Typically, accounts receivable is collected quickly.
2   A company has less risk if it has high "turnover" from its assets. "Turnover" measures the rate at which a company uses its assets to make sales.

Table 4.9 describes a number of tools used to measure liquidity and turnover.

The *current ratio* and the *quick ratio* both compare some groups of assets to the amount of current liabilities. The major difference between these two ratios is that the quick ratio does not assume that inventories or prepaid assets get turned into cash quick enough to pay the current liabilities. The higher these ratios are, the less risk the company has of suffering liquidity

Table 4.9 Tools Used to Measure Liquidity of Assets and Turnover of Assets

Current ratio	(Current assets) ÷ (current liabilities)
Quick ratio	(Cash + accounts receivable + marketable securities) ÷ (current liabilities)
Total asset turnover	Total revenues ÷ average total assets
Inventory turnover	Total cost of goods sold ÷ average inventory
Average days of inventory on hand	365 ÷ inventory turnover
Accounts receivable turnover	Total revenues ÷ average accounts receivable
Average days of accounts receivable outstanding during period	365 ÷ accounts receivable turnover

problems. If the company, on the other hand, has very few current assets on hand, relative to bills that need to be paid soon, it is at high risk. So, clearly, companies do not want very low current ratios. However, usually holding current assets is not the best way for a company to make money for its shareholders, so a very high current ratio may be a signal that the management is not being smart in maximizing income. For Panera, the current ratio in 2012 was 1.73 (478,842/277,540) and the current ratio in 2013 was 1.00 (302,716/303,325). Comparing the 2012 and 2013 balance sheets shows the company had less cash in 2013. Whether this decrease in cash is a cause for concern is not clear. An analyst would want to know if the decrease in cash was part of a strategy, or the result of problems. An analyst would also want to compare the 2013 ratio with those of other companies. In fact, many U.S. companies have current ratios of around or slightly under 1.0.

Accounts receivable turnover measures how many times a year a company collects its average receivable balance. For a company that normally sells to customers on credit, and gives them 30 days to pay, one would normally expect the receivables turnover to be about 12 times per year. Another way to get at the same concept is to look at the average number of days' sales that are waiting to be collected in accounts receivable. If the company normally sells to customers and grants them 30 days to pay, one would expect the days of sales in receivables to be about 30.

For Panera, the accounts receivable turnover is hard to interpret. The total 2013 revenues were $2,385,002,000 and the average of the beginning and ending receivables was $38,404,000 (= one half of $32,965,000 + $43,843,000). This would make the accounts receivable turnover 62, and the average days of receivables on hand equal to just under six days. That sounds pretty good. However, the receivables are mainly related to sales of dough to franchisees. Those sales were $163,453,000. If all the receivables relate to these sales, the accounts receivable turnover would be about 4.3, and the days of receivables on hand would be almost 86.

Inventory turnover compares the cost of goods sold to the average inventory on hand. Note that both the numerator and the denominator use cost figures, not selling prices. In general, the faster the inventory can be sold, the less liquidity risk the company has. For Panera, the cost of goods sold in 2013 has two parts: a bakery part of $625,622,000 and a dough cost of $142,160,000, so the total cost of goods sold = $767,782,000. The average inventory on hand = 0.5 × ($21,916,000 + $19,714,000) = $20,815,000. The inventory turnover = almost 37. This means that, on average, there is less than 10 days' worth of inventory is on hand. Since food is perishable, this makes sense.

The total asset turnover is an indicator of the company's ability to use its assets to generate cash. For Panera, 2013 revenues were $2,385,002,000. The average total assets were = 0.5 × ($1,180,862,000 + $1,268,163,000) = $1,224,512,500. The asset turnover = about 1.9.

Why is the total asset turnover only about 1.9, when Panera turns over total receivables 62 times a year and inventory 37 times per year? The answer is that Panera has some assets that are not obvious immediate sources of cash. Recall from our discussion of its balance sheet that it has large amounts of property and equipment, goodwill, and intangible assets. These assets are part of the denominator of the total asset turnover ratio.

Liability-Related Factors

A previous section has discussed the idea of financial leverage, and indicated that leverage increases risk. Research has confirmed the following two fairly obvious points.

1 A company has higher risk if it has a higher proportion of short-term liabilities in its capital structure.
2 A company has higher risk if it has a higher proportion of debt to total assets in its capital structure.

Since companies go bankrupt when they are unable to pay their debts, it makes sense that the higher the level of debt, the greater the risk. Also, it is fairly obvious that debt that is due soon is more of a potential problem than debt that is not due until future years.

Table 4.10 shows how to compute some of the commonly used tools to assess these factors related to liabilities.

The ratio of current liabilities to total assets is a simple way of judging how important current liabilities are in the company's financing structure. Lower ratios would be associated with lower liquidity risk.

The next two ratios are the *ratio of liabilities to assets* and *ratio of liabilities to equity*, both measured at the end of the year. These are indicators of the company's long-term solvency. One compares liabilities and equity, and the other compares liabilities and assets. Since for any company liabilities + equity = assets, the two measures tell the same basic story. Companies are less risky when they have lower ratios of liabilities to either assets or to equity.

The *capital structure leverage* ratio is computed using the average total assets and the average total common shareholders' equity during the period. The equity related to preferred stock is not counted here. The higher the ratio, the greater the amount of liabilities that the company has used in its operations. A higher value means greater solvency risk.

The *interest coverage ratio* compares the company's income before it has to pay interest or taxes to the annual interest payment. The idea here is to get an idea of how close a company is to being unable to cover its interest. Since we want to know the money available to pay interest, we look at income before the interest has already been paid. Also, since income tax is only payable on income after all expenses, taxes would not have to be paid if the company could not cover its interest. For Panera, in 2013, net income was $196,169,000. If we add back income taxes of $116,551,000 and interest of $1,053, 000, we get a numerator of $313,773,000. When we divide

Table 4.10 Tools to Judge Risk Related to Total Liabilities and Current Liabilities

Current liabilities to assets ratio	Current liabilities ÷ total assets
Liabilities to assets ratio	Total liabilities ÷ total assets
Liabilities to equity ratio	Total liabilities ÷ total equity
Long-term debt to equity ratio	Long-term debt ÷ total equity
Capital structure leverage ratio	Average total assets ÷ Average common equity
Interest coverage ratio	Numerator: Net income + interest expense + tax expense Denominator: Interest expense
Operating cash flow to total liabilities ratio	Operating cash flow ÷ total liabilities
Operating cash flow to current liabilities ratio	(Cash flow from operations) ÷ (average current liabilities)

this by interest expense, we get an interest coverage ratio of almost 298. Clearly, Panera is easily able to cover its interest payments out of current income.

The *ratio of operating cash flows to total liabilities* gives some insight on the company's ability to service its liabilities out of its operating cash flows.

The *ratio of operating cash flows to current liabilities* is a way of comparing the ability of the company to generate cash during a period with the liabilities that need to be paid within a year. The higher this ratio is, the less likely it is that the company will have liquidity issues. On the other hand, accounts payable may be a relatively cheap source of financing, so companies should probably not try to bring this ratio to zero.

For both these last two ratios, it is unclear what the "right" level of the ratio is. A study cited by Wahlen, Baginski and Bradshaw (2015) cites a figure of 0.40 for the ratio of operating cash flows to current liabilities as typical of healthy manufacturing and retail companies, and 0.20 as a typical ratio of operating cash flows to total liabilities. Unfortunately these figures are based on 1980s data. For Panera, the 2013 operating cash flows were $348,417,000, and the year-end current liabilities were $303,325,000 so the ratio as of year end would be 1.15. The ratio of operating cash flows to average total liabilities equals about 0.75.

Operating Factors

Research has also found that two operating factors are related to solvency risk. Both seem fairly intuitive.

1   Relative profitability. The more profitable companies are, the less risk there is of insolvency.
2   Variability of operations. Companies whose operations are subject to wide swings in customer demand or to availability of materials are more risky.

Tools to judge profitability are discussed elsewhere in this chapter.

There are several factors an analyst might consider in judging the variability of operations.

An important factor is the nature of the company's industry. Is it, like fashion and movies, subject to wide swings in consumer taste? Is it, like technology, subject to major changes as competitors invent new and better products? Is it an industry that depends on making major bets, some of which will prove to be right and others that will be wrong, like investment banking?

We have already discussed operating leverage. Greater operating leverage, which is created by having fixed operating costs, will increase the variability of income as customers demand changes. The operating leverage effect ratio was described earlier.

An analyst should also look at the pattern of earnings and sales over a five- or 10-year period. The "selected financial data" section of a 10-K report typically contains this data. Table 4.11 shows the selected financial data for Panera Bread, with data for five years. The pattern is of steady growth in revenues and net income.

Another factor is whether the company's financial statements indicate swings due to nonrecurring or special items. These might include special gains or losses related to restructuring of operations, sales of divisions, or write-offs of assets. Panera's income statement shows none of these items.

Other Factors Affecting Solvency and Liquidity Risk

In general, larger companies are less likely to face sudden liquidity or solvency problems than smaller companies (Wahlen, Baginski and Bradshaw 2015). One reason for this is large companies often find it easier to get bank loans. Also, they often have multiple products, so that problems with a single product can be offset by continued sales of the others.

Table 4.11 Panera Bread – Item 6. Selected Financial Data from Form 10-K

The following selected financial data has been derived from our consolidated financial statements. The data set forth below should be read in conjunction with "Management's Discussion and Analysis of Consolidated Financial Condition and Results of Operations" and our consolidated financial statements and notes thereto.

	For the fiscal year ended (1) (in thousands, except per share and percentage information)				
	December 31, 2013	December 25, 2012	December 27, 2011	December 28, 2010	December 29, 2009
Revenues:					
Bakery-cafe sales, net	$ 2,108,908	$ 1,879,280	$ 1,592,951	$ 1,321,162	$ 1,153,255
Franchise royalties and fees	112,641	102,076	92,793	86,195	78,367
Fresh dough and other product sales to franchisees	163,453	148,701	136,288	135,132	121,872
Total revenues	2,385,002	2,130,057	1,822,032	1,542,489	1,353,494
Costs and expenses:					
Bakery-cafe expenses:					
Cost of food and paper products	$ 625,622	$ 552,580	$ 470,398	$ 374,816	$ 337,599
Labor	625,457	559,446	484,014	419,140	370,595
Occupancy	148,816	130,793	115,290	100,970	95,996
Other operating expenses	295,539	256,029	216,237	177,059	155,396
Total bakery-cafe expenses	1,695,434	1,498,848	1,285,939	1,071,985	959,586
Fresh dough and other product cost of sales to franchisees	142,160	131,006	116,267	110,986	100,229
Depreciation and amortization	106,523	90,939	79,899	68,673	67,162
General and administrative expenses	123,335	117,932	113,083	101,494	83,169
Pre-opening expenses	7,794	8,462	6,585	4,282	2,451
Total costs and expenses	2,075,246	1,847,187	1,601,773	1,357,420	1,212,597
Operating profit	309,756	282,870	220,259	185,069	140,897
Interest expense	1,053	1,082	822	675	700
Other (income) expense, net	(4,017)	(1,208)	(466)	4,232	273
Income before income taxes	312,720	282,996	219,903	180,162	139,924
Income taxes	116,551	109,548	83,951	68,563	53,073
Net income	196,169	173,448	135,952	111,599	86,851
Less: net (loss) income attributable to noncontrolling interest	—	—	—	(267)	801
Net income attributable to Panera Bread Company	$ 196,169	$ 173,448	$ 135,952	$ 111,866	$ 86,050
Earnings per common share attributable to Panera Bread Company:					
Basic	$ 6.85	$ 5.94	$ 4.59	3.65	$ 2.81
Diluted	$ 6.81	$ 5.89	$ 4.55	$ 3.62	$ 2.78
Weighted average shares of common and common equivalent shares outstanding:					
Basic	28,629	29,217	29,601	30,614	30,667
Diluted	28,794	29,455	29,903	30,922	30,979

There are a variety of other financial disclosures that can indicate that a company is facing problems. One important thing to check is the auditor's opinion. The auditing rules require that if auditors have significant doubt about a company's ability to continue as a going concern for at least 12 months, the auditors are supposed to include a comment about this in their report. Auditors do not make these comments lightly. They would only make them if they see signs of problems, and after considering plans the company management has to fix the problems.

Another indicator of problems would be a disclosure by the company that it has violated some of the terms of its loans. Many loans have provisions (called "debt covenants") that require the company to meet various financial targets. If a company fails to meet these targets, the lender can ask for immediate repayment. Such defaults on debt can quickly cause a company to enter bankruptcy.

Judging Stewardship and Accountability

Financial statements can help investors judge how well management is doing its job. This section will discuss some factors managers can consider.

Investors will often look to whether a company is profitable in order to judge the performance of management. Previous sections discussed profitability measures. Also, unexpected losses or unusual items may indicate problems with management's method of running the company. However, as the FASB (1978) noted, companies are complex, and some events are recognized in financial statements in different periods than when management initiated them, so the results of operations in any one period may or may not be directly related to management's actions during the period.

> What happens to a business enterprise is usually so much a joint result of a complex inter-action of many factors that neither accounting nor other statistical analysis can discern with reasonable accuracy the degree to which management, or any other factor, affected the joint result. Actions of past managements affect current periods' earnings, and actions of current management affect future periods' earnings. . . . The information is there-fore limited for purposes of assessing management performance apart from enterprise performance.
>
> (para. 53)

Part of the responsibility of management is to report honestly. The reports of the independent public accountants on the financial statements provide some assurance to the readers that the financial statements are prepared fairly. It is important to realize that auditors do not check every transaction, and do not guarantee the accuracy of the financial statements. Instead, they perform enough tests, often on a sample basis, to achieve reasonable assurance that there are no material errors or omissions in the financial statements. All annual financial statements in filings to the SEC must be accompanied by an auditor's report that states that the auditors have done enough work to reach such a conclusion, and that they believe the financial statements to conform to GAAP or IFRS. Such an opinion is called an *"unqualified report."* Sometimes, for private companies, auditors will give an opinion that reports exceptions, or "qualifications," about either their ability to do enough work or about items in the financial statements that were improperly stated.

There have been various attempts to devise models that will help financial statement readers detect if earnings are being manipulated. These are beyond the scope of this course.[11] These models typically look for firms that have unusual relations of financial data that would be possible indicators of intentional misstatement. The models developed so far are imperfect. They sometimes do not identify manipulation when it is occurring, and also sometimes incorrectly cite a company for manipulating earnings when it is simply having an unusual year.

It is also part of management's duties to maintain effective control systems. Investors can gain some insight on whether management is fulfilling this duty by examining the SEC filings of large companies. The Sarbanes–Oxley Act required large public companies to report in their 10-K filings with the SEC whether their internal controls over financial reporting were operating effectively at the end of the year. Section 404 of the Sarbanes–Oxley Act requires auditors to comment on the effectiveness of these controls.

Limitations of Financial Statement Analysis

Not Intended to Give the Value of the Company

Financial statements prepared under GAAP or IFRS are not designed to measure the company's current market value. They contain information that users will hopefully find helpful in valuation, but the statements themselves do not present the value of the firm. In fact, there are typically large differences between the market valuation of public companies and their total recorded shareholders' equity.

Different Companies use Different Accounting Methods

Under both GAAP and IFRS, companies are allowed to make certain choices of accounting methods. This means that the ability of analysts to compare different companies' performance is sometimes limited. It also means that company financial reports cannot be easily added together to get economy-wide totals.

Timeliness

Traditional financial statements are prepared after the period ends. Public companies report their annual results to the SEC within 60 days, and their quarterly reports after around 40 days. Often, important information becomes publicly known well before these reporting dates. As Ball and Shivakumar (2008) wrote:

> By its nature, accounting earnings is low frequency (quarterly), not discretionary (announced every quarter, independent of whether there is substantial new information to report), and primarily backward-looking. Other information, and hence revision in share price, is comparatively high frequency, frequently discretionary (released only when there is substantial information to report), and both forward-looking and backward-looking. . . . Consistent with this thesis, there is abundant evidence that accounting reports in fact do not provide a relatively large proportion of the new information used by the equity market.
>
> (pp. 979–80)

Vagueness of Reports

There are certain things that users want to know that are often either not reported, or reported imprecisely in financial statements.

One example is that financial statements do not typically separately discuss whether expenses are fixed, variable, or mixed. As we noted, some measures of leverage require this information.

A second example is that analysts wish to separate income statement items into those that are recurring, and those that are not. The income statements partially achieve this goal by listing some items separately as one-time events. However, there are other events that may be one-time but are not clearly identified. For example, Scholastic Publishing had very high sales on the date on which it released the last of the Harry Potter series of novels. These sales were not shown separately in its financial statements, but instead were simply included in the total sales figures.

Inflation

U.S. financial statements are prepared without any corrections for the changing value of the dollar. Over long periods, or if inflation becomes rapid, this may impair the comparability and meaningfulness of the information in financial statements. For example, in times of rapid inflation, for a company that moves its inventory slowly, profits will tend to be overstated. Sales will be reported as a big number, in inflated dollars, but the depreciation on equipment bought in prior years looks small, and the prices paid to buy the inventory months ago also look small.

Not Including Nonfinancial Measures

Financial measures are only part of the factors that affect a company's long-term health. In fact, if you focus too much on short-term measures, like this quarter's ROA, a company may take actions that hurt in the long term. For example, it might skimp on training, or on research, or on advertising to build its brand recognition in the future. Various suggestions have been made to augment the information in financial statements with other measures. One widely cited idea is the "*balanced scorecard*" as described by Kaplan and Norton (1992). The scorecard requires a company to specify objectives and to measure outcomes in four different areas: financial; dealings with customers; internal business processes; and learning and growth activities.

Honesty of Reports

Financial reports are not always prepared honestly and objectively. Chapter 6 will discuss this issue in more detail. Managers are under pressure to ensure that financial results meet targets, and there are steps that they sometimes take that make financial statements inaccurate measures of company performance.

Unresolved Issues and Areas for Future Research

In its introduction, I indicated that one purpose of this chapter is to help bridge the gap between the accountants who prepare financial statements and the investors and other people who use the statements. The chapter discussed some ways in which people try to use financial statements to judge company solvency, leverage, and profitability, as well as the performance of management. It should be clear from the materials in the chapter that financial statements as now prepared can be helpful on these tasks, but that they are far from perfect. Questions for future research are many, and include the following:

1   Among the existing types of accounting rules, which are most helpful to users? This would involve comparing IFRS and GAAP, and also some of the accounting alternatives that are allowed by both systems. The results could help the FASB and IASB design better accounting rules. For example, a 2013 paper (Choi, Peasnell and Toniato 2013) sought to measure whether the adoption of IFRS in the U.K. made reporting more useful for predicting future earnings.

2   What are the best models for helping financial statement users predict future company profitability, or solvency? Answering these questions could help investors use existing accounting reports better.

3   Can ways be found to better detect dishonest reporting? If such methods can be found, and used, they would help investors avoid being fooled by management. The fact that such models exist would also deter management from reporting dishonestly in the first place.

4   Can reporting be expanded in ways that better serves investors' needs? Currently, financial reporting is done on a periodic basis, and focuses on past information. Can it be extended in ways that make it more timely, and more future-oriented?

Key Terms

Accounts payable—Obligations that a company has to pay to suppliers of inventory.

Accounts receivable turnover—See Table 4.9.

Accrued expenses—Liabilities a company has for various obligations it has incurred and not yet paid. Common examples are accrued rent, accrued interest expense, accrued salaries, and accrued taxes.

Accumulated comprehensive income (or loss)—The component of shareholders' equity that includes the net effects, from the company's start until the current date, of items that affect comprehensive income but are excluded from the computation of net income.

Additional paid-in capital—An equity account that records the amounts that shareholders paid the company for common stock in excess of the stock's stated "par value." For most U.S. companies, this account is much larger than the "common stock at par" account.

Asset turnover (also called total asset turnover)—See Table 4.9.

Basic earnings per share—A measure of how much of the company's income relates to a single share of common stock. It is found by dividing the net income by the average number of outstanding shares of common stock. See Table 4.7.

Capital structure leverage—See Table 4.7 or 4.8.

Common size balance sheets—These balance sheets express each item as a percentage of total assets.

Common size income statements—These income statements express each item as a percentage of total revenues.

Common stock at par value—The part of the equity section that shows the amount of "par value" the company received when it issued stock to shareholders. For many U.S. companies, par value of common shares is tiny, so this account typically has a small value. Most of the value received when companies issue shares is recorded as additional paid-in capital.

Current liabilities to assets ratio—See Table 4.10.

Current ratio – See Table 4.9.

Days of accounts receivable outstanding during the period. Also referred to as the number of **days' sales in accounts receivable**. See Table 4.9.

Days of inventory on hand (average)—See Table 4.9. Note—some analysts compute the ending days of inventory on hand, instead of the average during the period.

Diluted earnings per share—This is a measure of the net income that might have been applicable to a single share of common stock during the period, if certain events had happened that would have increased the number of shareholders. For example, the computation may assume that owners of convertible bonds had actually converted their bonds during the period. Diluted earnings per share are always lower than basic earnings per share.

Effective tax rate—This is the income tax expenses ÷ income before taxes. This shows, on average, how much of the pre-tax income had to be used for taxes. This will often differ from the statutory rate of tax, because of certain legal benefits the company may have.

Financial leverage—This measures how the company's financing methods affect the sensitivity of its income to changes in revenues.

Financial leverage effect—See Table 4.8.

Goodwill—This intangible asset is recognized when a company buys another company, and pays more than the total fair values that can be identified for the identifiable assets acquired.

Gross margin = total revenues − cost of goods sold.

Gross margin percentage = gross margin ÷ total revenues

Horizontal analysis—This method of analyzing financial statements compares levels of a given account over time. Both common size and percentage change statements are often helpful in horizontal analysis.

Interest coverage ratio—See Table 4.10.

Inventory turnover—See Table 4.9.

Leverage—Leverage increases the effect of changes in revenues on profits. See "operating leverage" and "financial leverage." For related measures, see: capital structure leverage; financial leverage effect; operating leverage effect; and total leverage.

Liabilities to assets ratio—See Table 4.10.

Liabilities to equity ratio—See Table 4.10.

Liquidity—A company's ability to pay its obligations in the near future as they become due.

Long-term debt to equity ratio—See Table 4.10.

Operating cash flow to current liabilities ratio—See Table 4.10.

Operating cash flow to liabilities ratio—See Table 4.10.

Operating leverage—This measures how the company's method of operations affects the relation that changes in revenues have on net income. Operating leverage is caused by fixed operating costs, such as rentals, depreciation, or guaranteed employment contracts.

Operating leverage effect—See Table 4.8.

Persistence of income statement items—This relates to the likelihood that the items will recur in similar amounts in future years.

Qualified auditor's report—The auditor reports some "exception" that causes them to amend, or "qualify" an otherwise favorable report. They may not have been able to do sufficient testing, or may think some parts of the financial statements are not properly stated. If the problems are very severe, they would give an "adverse" report, saying that the financial statements were not fairly stated. Such "adverse" opinions are rare.

Quick ratio—See Table 4.9.

Retained earnings—This is the part of the equity section of the balance sheet that shows the total net income that the company has accumulated since it began, reduced by dividends and certain other distributions to shareholders. If a company has had losses, and this figure is negative, it is usually called "accumulated deficit."

Solvency—A company's long-term ability to service its debts and remain in operations.

Total leverage—See Table 4.8.

Treasury stock—This negative figure in the equity section of a company's balance sheet represents the amount the company has paid to buy back shares of stock that it is holding temporarily. Treasury shares are non-voting and do not receive dividends. They are not considered outstanding shares when computing earnings per share.

Unqualified auditors' report—The auditors' report includes no exceptions, or qualifications. The auditors say they have done adequate work to form an opinion, and that in their opinion the financial statements are presented fairly in accordance with GAAP, or with IFRS.

Vertical analysis—This is a method of analyzing financial statements by looking at relations among accounts in a single year. For example, an analyst might look at selling expenses as a percentage of sales, or fixed assets as a percentage of total assets.

Questions and Problems

Comprehension Questions

C1. (General) About how many public companies are there in the U.S.? Why do they prepare financial statements?

C2. (General) About how many businesses are there in the U.S., including nonpublic companies? Why would they prepare financial statements?

C3. (Purpose) Explain how financial reports can:

    A. Provide new information

    B. Confirm prior information.

C4. (Context) If you were looking at a company's reported profits and revenues, what are some things you might compare the reported results to, in order to judge whether performance was good or bad?

C5. (Context) If you were looking at a company's ratios related to liquidity and solvency, what are some things you might compare the reported results to, in order to judge whether these measures were good or bad?

C6. (Vertical and horizontal analysis) Explain what is meant by both vertical analysis and horizontal analysis.

C7. (Ratio analysis) What are some benefits of using ratios in financial analysis?

C8. (Ratio analysis) What is a limitation of using ratio analysis?

C9. (Research findings) Do movements in stock prices of public companies seem most related to information in the balance sheet, the income statement, or the statement of cash flows?

C10. (Research findings) Do movements in stock prices of public companies seem most related to persistent, recurring items in the income statement, or to one-time items?

C11. (Reading basic financial statements) What does the caption "cash and cash equivalents" mean in the Panera financial statements?

C12. (Reading basic financial statements) What is "goodwill" in the Panera financial statements?

C13. (Reading basic financial statements) In the Panera balance sheet, the equity section contains a caption for "common stock." Many students incorrectly think this represents all the equity that relates to the common shareholders. Explain why they are wrong, and why this caption does *not* contain all of the equity attributable to common shareholders.

C14. (Reading basic financial statements) Explain how you can tell that Panera has a classified balance sheet.

C15. (Common size financial statements) Explain what is meant by:

    A. A common size balance sheet

    B. A common size income statement

    C. A percentage change income statement.

C16. (Earnings per share) Explain what is meant by "basic" earnings per share.

C17. (Statement of changes in equity) List some of the types of things that you would expect to see on a statement of changes in equity.

C18. (Statement of changes in equity) What is meant by retained earnings? What might change its balance during the year?

C19. (Statement of changes in equity) What is meant by accumulated comprehensive income? What might change its balance during the year?

C20. (Statement of changes in equity) What is meant by additional paid-in capital? What might change its balance during the year?

C21. (Statement of cash flows) When a company uses the indirect method of showing operating cash flows, it starts with net income, and then shows items that explain why net income is different from operating cash flows. In general, what are the three types of items listed in the chapter that explain the difference?

C22. (Profitability ratios) Explain the difference between return on assets (ROA) and return on common equity (ROCE).

C23. (Profitability ratios) Explain how "decomposing" ROCE into three ratios can provide an analyst with more insight into a company's basic strategy.

C24. (Leverage) Explain what is meant by:

    A. Leverage
    B. Operating leverage
    C. Financial leverage.

C25. (Solvency and liquidity) Explain what is meant by the terms "solvency" and "liquidity."

C26. (Solvency and liquidity) How can a company stay in business if it has more liabilities than assets, and therefore has negative equity?

C27. (Solvency and liquidity) How can a company go bankrupt if its balance sheet shows more assets than liabilities?

C28. (Solvency and liquidity) Explain what is meant by each of the following:

    A. Current ratio
    B. Accounts receivable turnover
    C. Inventory turnover
    D. Days' sales in receivables
    E. Interest coverage ratio

C29. (Auditors' role) For public companies, what clues to management's stewardship might you find in reports by auditors?

C30. (Limitations of reporting) The chapter mentions some limitations of financial statements. Explain why each of the following statements is not correct:

    A. The market value of any company can be found by looking at its balance sheet. The total shareholders' equity is the company's market value.
    B. The first indication anyone ever has to a company's performance during the year is when the financial statements are published.
    C. It is easy to compare the performance of different companies because they all use the same accounting methods.
    D. Financial statements include all the important information about a company's activities during the year.

Application Questions

Problems A1 to A4 all use Tables 4.12 and 4.13. These are financial statements for The Gap, Inc.

A1. (Common size financial balance sheets) Refer to Table 4.12. Express each of the following as a percentage of total assets in both 2012 and 2013. Indicate if you believe the percentages have changed substantially.

    A. Cash
    B. Inventory
    C. Property and equipment

Table 4.12 The Gap, Inc.

CONSOLIDATED BALANCE SHEETS (USD $)

In millions, unless otherwise specified	Feb. 1, 2014	Feb. 2, 2013
Current assets:		
Cash and cash equivalents	$1,510	$1,460
Short-term investments	0	50
Merchandise inventory	1,928	1,758
Other current assets	992	864
Total current assets	4,430	4,132
Property and equipment, net	2,758	2,619
Other long-term assets	661	719
Total assets	7,849	7,470
Current liabilities:		
Current maturities of debt	25	0
Accounts payable	1,242	1,144
Accrued expenses and other current liabilities	1,142	1,092
Income taxes payable	36	108
Total current liabilities	2,445	2,344
Long-term liabilities:		
Long-term debt	1,369	1,246
Lease incentives and other long-term liabilities	973	986
Total long-term liabilities	2,342	2,232
Stockholders' equity:		
Common stock $0.05 par value, authorized 2,300 shares and Issued 1,106 shares for all periods presented; outstanding 446 and 463 shares	55	55
Additional paid-in capital	2,899	2,864
Retained earnings	14,218	13,259
Accumulated other comprehensive income	135	181
Treasury stock at cost (660 and 643 shares)	−14,245	−13,465
Total stockholders' equity	3,062	2,894
Total liabilities and stockholders' equity	$7,849	$7,470

Table 4.13 The Gap, Inc. CONSOLIDATED STATEMENTS OF INCOME

($ and shares in millions except per share amounts)	Fiscal year		
	2014	2013	2012
Net sales	$16,148	$15,651	$14,549
Cost of goods sold and occupancy expenses	9,855	9,480	9,275
Gross profit	6,293	6,171	5,274
Operating expenses	4,144	4,229	3,836
Operating income	2,149	1,942	1,438
Interest expense	61	87	74
Interest income	(5)	(6)	(5)
Income before income taxes	2,093	1,861	1,369
Income taxes	813	726	536
Net income	1,280	1,135	$833
Weighted-average number of shares—basic	461	482	529
Weighted-average number of shares—diluted	467	488	533
Earnings per share—basic	$2.78	$2.35	$1.57
Earnings per share—diluted	$2.74	$2.33	$1.56

D.   Total liabilities
E.   Total shareholders' equity

A2. (Common size income statements) Express each of the following as a percentage of total revenues for 2013 and 2014. Indicate if you believe the percentages have changed substantially.

A.   Gross profit
B.   Operating expenses
C.   Operating income
D.   Income before taxes
E.   Income taxes
F.   Net income

A3. (Leverage ratios) For Gap, assume that all cost of goods sold and operating expenses are variable expenses. Compute the following ratios for 2014:

A.   Operating leverage effect
B.   Financial leverage effect
C.   Total leverage
D.   Capital structure leverage

A4. (Profitability ratios) For Gap, compute the following profitability ratios for 2014. Assume a tax rate of 35%.

A.   Profit margin for ROA
B.   Asset turnover
C.   ROA
D.   Profit margin for ROCE
E.   Capital structure leverage
F.   ROCE

Questions A5 to A8 use Tables 4.14 and 4.15. These questions all deal with Occidental Petroleum, a major oil company. You will notice that Occidental Petroleum has discontinued some operations. The effect of these operations is shown on each year's financial statements in a single line, so that you can do ratio analysis using data for the continuing operations.

A5. (Common size financial balance sheets) Refer to Table 4.14. Express each of the following as a percentage of total assets in both 2013 and 2014. Indicate if you believe the percentages have changed substantially.

A.   Cash
B.   Receivables
C.   Inventory
D.   Property and equipment
E.   Long-term debt
F.   Total liabilities
G.   Total shareholders' equity

A6. (Common size income statements) Express each of the following as a percentage of total revenues for 2013 and 2014. Indicate if you believe the percentages have changed substantially.

A. Cost of sales
B. Depreciation, depletion and amortization expenses
C. Income before taxes
D. Income taxes
E. Net income from continuing operations

A7. (Leverage ratios) For Occidental Petroleum, assume that all cost of goods sold and all the operating expenses except depreciation, depletion, and amortization are variable expenses. Assume that *half* the depreciation, amortization, and depletion expenses are *fixed*. Compute the following ratios for 2014:

Table 4.14 Occidental Petroleum

Consolidated Balance Sheets (USD $)

In millions, unless otherwise specified	Dec. 31, 2013	Dec. 31, 2012
CURRENT ASSETS		
Cash and cash equivalents	$3,393	$1,592
Trade receivables, net of reserves	5,674	4,916
Inventories	1,200	1,344
Other current assets	1,056	1,640
Total current assets	11,323	9,492
INVESTMENTS IN UNCONSOLIDATED ENTITIES	1,459	1,894
PROPERTY, PLANT AND EQUIPMENT		
Oil and gas segment	72,367	65,417
Chemical segment	6,446	6,054
Midstream, marketing and other segment	8,684	7,191
Corporate	1,555	1,434
GROSS PROPERTY, PLANT AND EQUIPMENT	89,052	80,096
Accumulated depreciation, depletion and amortization	−33,231	−28,032
TOTAL PROPERTY, PLANT AND EQUIPMENT	55,821	52,064
LONG-TERM RECEIVABLES AND OTHER ASSETS, NET	840	760
TOTAL ASSETS	69,443	64,210
CURRENT LIABILITIES		
Current maturities of long-term debt	0	600
Accounts payable	5,520	4,708
Accrued liabilities	2,556	1,966
Domestic and foreign income taxes	358	16
Total current liabilities	8,434	7,290
LONG-TERM DEBT, NET	6,939	7,023
DEFERRED CREDITS AND OTHER LIABILITIES		
Deferred domestic and foreign income taxes	7,197	6,039
Other	3,501	3,810
Total deferred credits and other liabilities	10,698	9,849
STOCKHOLDERS' EQUITY		
Common stock, $0.20 par value, authorized shares: 1.1 billion, outstanding shares: 2013—889,919,058 and 2012—888,801,436	178	178
Treasury stock: 2013—93,928,179 shares and 2012—83,287,187	−6,095	−5,091
Additional paid-in capital	7,515	7,441
Retained earnings	41,831	37,990
Accumulated other comprehensive loss	−303	−502
Total equity attributable to common stock	43,126	40,016
Noncontrolling interest	246	32
Total equity	43,372	40,048
TOTAL LIABILITIES AND STOCKHOLDERS' EQUITY	$69,443	$64,210

Table 4.15 Occidental Petroleum

Consolidated Statements of Income (USD $)

In millions, except per share data	12 months ended		
	Dec. 31, 2013	Dec. 31, 2012	Dec. 31, 2011
REVENUES AND OTHER INCOME			
Net sales	$24,455	$24,172	$23,939
Interest, dividends and other income	106	81	180
Gain on sale of equity investments	1,175	0	0
TOTAL REVENUES AND OTHER INCOME	25,736	24,253	24,119
COSTS AND OTHER DEDUCTIONS			
Cost of sales (excludes depreciation, depletion and amortization of $5,341 in 2013, $4,504 in 2012 and $3,584 in 2011)	7,562	7,844	7,385
Selling, general and administrative and other operating expenses	1,801	1,602	1,523
Depreciation, depletion and amortization	5,347	4,511	3,591
Asset impairments and related items	621	1,751	0
Taxes other than on income	749	680	605
Exploration expense	256	345	258
Interest and debt expense, net	118	130	298
TOTAL COSTS AND OTHER DEDUCTIONS	16,454	16,863	13,660
INCOME BEFORE INCOME TAXES AND OTHER ITEMS	9,282	7,390	10,459
Provision for domestic and foreign income taxes	−3,755	−3,118	−4,201
Income from equity investments	395	363	382
INCOME FROM CONTINUING OPERATIONS	5,922	4,635	6,640
Discontinued operations, net	−19	−37	131
NET INCOME	$5,903	$4,598	$6,771
BASIC EARNINGS PER COMMON SHARE			
Income from continuing operations (in $ per share)	$7.35	$5.72	$8.16
Discontinued operations, net (in $ per share)	($0.02)	($0.05)	$0.16
BASIC EARNINGS PER COMMON SHARE ($ per share)	$7.33	$5.67	$8.32
DILUTED EARNINGS PER COMMON SHARE			
Income from continuing operations ($ per share)	$7.34	$5.71	$8.16
Discontinued operations, net ($ per share)	($0.02)	($0.04)	$0.16
DILUTED EARNINGS PER COMMON SHARE ($ per share)	$7.32	$5.67	$8.32

    A. Operating leverage effect
    B. Financial leverage effect
    C. Total leverage
    D. Capital structure leverage

A8. (Profitability ratios) For Occidental Petroleum, compute the following profitability ratios for 2014. For the purposes of this question, ignore the fact that some of the income is from discontinued operations. Assume a tax rate of 30%.

    A. Profit margin for ROA
    B. Asset turnover
    C. ROA
    D. Profit margin for ROCE
    E. Capital structure leverage
    F. ROCE

Questions A9 to A12

The next several questions deal with Starbucks and Dunkin' Brands. These are two major companies, with many locations selling coffee and snacks. Dunkin' Brands also owns Baskin-Robbins ice cream stores.

The two companies are structured differently. As of September, 2014, Starbucks owned and operated 59% of the Starbucks locations. The rest were operated under license or franchise agreements. When Starbucks owns a location, they record the sales, cost of sales, and related operating expenses. When a location is operated under a franchise agreement, Starbucks does not record the sales and related operating expenses. Instead, Starbucks records the fees it is entitled to, including a percentage of store revenues, but does not record the costs of coffee and food sold. Dunkin' Brands owns almost none of the Dunkin' Donuts and Baskin-Robbins locations. Instead, these locations are franchises. Therefore, its income statement shows fees related to this franchise activity, but does not show the costs of sales or operations of the various locations.

Another difference between the companies is their history. Starbucks was started in 1985, and it has never been acquired by other companies. It has made some minor acquisitions of other companies over its history. Its balance sheet shows some goodwill and some intangible assets related to these acquisitions, but, the balance sheet does *not* show the value of the Starbucks trademark or of the goodwill of the Starbucks business itself. The brands that make up Dunkin' Brands have been the subject of more than one acquisition over their history, including an acquisition in 2005. In the process of these transactions, values were assigned to the Dunkin' and Baskin-Robbins trademarks and to goodwill.

A9. (Common size financial balance sheets) Refer to Tables 4.16 and 4.18. Express each of the following as a percentage of total assets in 2013 for both Dunkin' and Starbucks:

    A. Cash
    B. Receivables
    C. Inventory
    D. Property and equipment
    E. Goodwill
    F. Other intangible assets
    G. Long term debt
    H. Total shareholders' equity

A10. (Common size income statements) Refer to Tables 4.17 and 4.19. Express each of the following as a percentage of total revenues for the latest year shown:

    A. Cost of sales (includes occupancy for Starbucks; ice cream costs and costs of company restaurants for Dunkin')
    B. Depreciation, and amortization expenses
    C. General and administrative expenses
    D. Operating income
    E. Interest expenses
    F. Income before taxes
    G. Income taxes

A11. (Financial leverage ratios) Compute the following ratios for both Dunkin' and Starbucks for the latest year shown.

    A. Financial leverage effect
    B. Capital structure leverage

Which company is more leveraged? Explain.

A12. (Profitability ratios) For both Dunkin' and Starbucks, compute the following profitability ratios for the latest year. Assume a tax rate of 30%.

    A. Profit margin for ROA
    B. Asset turnover
    C. ROA
    D. Profit margin for ROCE
    E. Capital structure leverage
    F. ROCE

Table 4.16 Dunkin' Brands

Consolidated Balance Sheets (USD $) In thousands	Dec. 28, 2013	Dec. 29, 2012
Current assets:		
Cash and cash equivalents	$256,933	$252,618
Accounts receivable, net	47,162	32,407
Notes and other receivables, net	32,603	20,649
Assets held for sale	1,663	2,400
Deferred income taxes, net	46,461	47,263
Restricted assets of advertising funds	31,493	31,849
Prepaid income taxes	25,699	10,825
Prepaid expenses and other current assets	19,746	21,769
Total current assets	461,760	419,780
Property and equipment, net	182,858	181,172
Equity method investments	170,644	174,823
Goodwill	891,598	891,900
Other intangible assets, net	1,452,205	1,479,784
Restricted cash	305	367
Other assets	75,320	69,687
Total assets	3,234,690	3,217,513
Current liabilities:		
Current portion of long-term debt	5,000	26,680
Capital lease obligations	432	371
Accounts payable	12,445	16,256
Liabilities of advertising funds	49,077	45,594
Deferred income	28,426	24,683
Other current liabilities	248,918	239,931
Total current liabilities	344,298	353,515
Long-term debt, net	1,818,609	1,823,278
Capital lease obligations	6,996	7,251
Unfavorable operating leases acquired	16,834	19,061
Deferred income	11,135	15,720
Deferred income taxes, net	561,714	569,126
Other long-term liabilities	62,816	79,587
Total long-term liabilities	2,478,104	2,514,023
Redeemable noncontrolling interests	4,930	0
Stockholders' equity:		
Preferred stock, $0.001 par value	0	0
Common stock, $0.001 par value	107	106
Additional paid-in capital	1,196,426	1,251,498
Treasury stock, at cost	−10,773	0
Accumulated deficit	−779,741	−914,094
Accumulated other comprehensive income	1,339	9,141
Total stockholders' equity of Dunkin' Brands	407,358	346,651
Noncontrolling interests	0	3,324
Total stockholders' equity	407,358	349,975
Total	$3,234,690	$3,217,513

Table 4.17 Dunkin' Brands

Consolidated Statements of Operations (USD $)

In thousands, except per share data, unless otherwise specified	12 months ended		
	Dec. 28, 2013	Dec. 29, 2012	Dec. 31, 2011
Revenues:			
Franchise fees and royalty income	$453,976	$418,940	$398,474
Rental income	96,082	96,816	92,145
Sales of ice cream products	112,276	94,659	100,068
Sales at company-owned restaurants	24,976	22,922	12,154
Other revenues	26,530	24,844	25,357
Total revenues	713,840	658,181	628,198
Operating costs and expenses:			
Occupancy expenses—franchised restaurants	52,097	52,072	51,878
Cost of ice cream products	79,278	69,019	72,329
Company-owned restaurant expenses	24,480	23,133	12,854
General and administrative expenses, net	228,010	239,574	227,771
Depreciation	22,423	29,084	24,497
Amortization of other intangible assets	26,943	26,943	28,025
Long-lived asset impairment charges	563	1,278	2,060
Total operating costs and expenses	433,794	441,103	419,414
Total net income (loss) of equity method investments	18,370	22,351	–3,475
Other operating income, net	6,320	0	0
Operating income	304,736	239,429	205,309
Other income (expense):			
Interest income	404	543	623
Interest expense	–80,235	–74,031	–105,072
Loss on debt extinguishment and refinancing transactions	–5,018	–3,963	–34,222
Other gains (losses), net	–1,799	23	175
Total other expense	–86,648	–77,428	–138,496
Income before income taxes	218,088	162,001	66,813
Provision for income taxes	71,784	54,377	32,371
Net income including noncontrolling interests	146,304	107,624	34,442
Net loss attributable to noncontrolling interests	–599	–684	0
Net income attributable to Dunkin' Brands	$146,903	$108,308	$34,442
Earnings (loss) per share:			
Common-basic (in dollars per share)	$1.38	$0.94	($1.41)
Common-diluted (in dollars per share)	$1.36	$0.93	($1.41)

- Comment on how the difference in the relative proportion of company-owned stores has on the profit margin ratios.
- Comment on how the fact that Dunkin' Brands shows large values for intangible assets affects its asset turnover ratios.
- Comment on the difference in capital structure leverage ratios between the two companies.

A13. (Impact of payments on current ratio) Assume a company has current assets of 150, and current liabilities of 100.

   A. Compute the current ratio.
   B. Assume that, just before the end of the year, the company uses 75 of its cash to pay off current liabilities of 75. Compute the current ratio after this payment.
   C. Do you believe this payment would be legal?
   D. Do you believe it is unethical for a company to improve its current ratio using this strategy? Why or why not?

Table 4.18 Starbucks Balance Sheets

Consolidated Balance Sheets (USD $)

In millions, unless otherwise specified	Sep. 28, 2014	Sep. 29, 2013
Current assets:		
Cash and cash equivalents	$1,708.40	$2,575.70
Short-term investments	135.4	658.1
Accounts receivable, net	631	561.4
Inventories	1,090.90	1,111.20
Prepaid expenses and other current assets	285.6	287.7
Deferred income taxes, net	317.4	277.3
Total current assets	4,168.70	5,471.40
Long-term investments	318.4	58.3
Equity and cost investments	514.9	496.5
Property, plant and equipment, net	3,519	3,200.50
Deferred income taxes, net	903.3	967
Other assets	198.9	185.3
Other intangible assets	273.5	274.8
Goodwill	856.2	862.9
TOTAL ASSETS	10,752.90	11,516.70
Current liabilities:		
Accounts payable	533.7	491.7
Accrued litigation charge	0	2,784.10
Accrued liabilities	1,514.40	1,269.30
Insurance reserves	196.1	178.5
Deferred revenue	794.5	653.7
Total current liabilities	3,038.70	5,377.30
Long-term debt	2,048.30	1,299.40
Other long-term liabilities	392.2	357.7
Total liabilities	5,479.20	7,034.40
Shareholders' equity:		
Common stock ($0.001 par value)—authorized, 1,200.0 shares; issued and outstanding, 749.5 and 753.2 shares, respectively	0.7	0.8
Additional paid-in capital	39.4	282.1
Retained earnings	5,206.60	4,130.30
Accumulated other comprehensive income	25.3	67
Total shareholders' equity	5,272	4,480.20
Noncontrolling interest	1.7	2.1
Total equity	5,273.70	4,482.30
TOTAL LIABILITIES AND EQUITY	$10,752.90	$11,516.70

A14. (Impact of sale of accounts receivables) A company has had sales of $10 million during the year. At the beginning of the year, it had $3 million of receivables. On December 30 of this year, it has $3 million of receivables.

    A. Compute the accounts receivable turnover ratio.

    B. The company has the opportunity to sell $2 million of its accounts receivable to a financial institution for $1.9 million. The financial institution will take the risk of non-collection. Compute the accounts receivable ratio if the company makes this deal. Note—the transaction does not affect total sales. Total sales are only sales of products to customers.

    C. Do you believe this transaction would be legal?

    D. Do you believe it is ethical for a company to improve its reported accounts receivable turnover using this strategy? Why, or why not?

Table 4.19 Starbucks Income Statements

Consolidated Statements of Earnings (USD $) In millions, except per share data, unless otherwise specified	12 months ended		
	Sep. 28, 2014	Sep. 29, 2013	Sep. 30, 2012
Net revenues:			
Total net revenues	$16,447.80	$14,866.80	$13,276.80
Cost of sales including occupancy costs	6,858.80	6,382.30	5,813.30
Store operating expenses	4,638.20	4,286.10	3,918.10
Other operating expenses	457.3	431.8	407.2
Depreciation and amortization expenses	709.6	621.4	550.3
General and administrative expenses	991.3	937.9	801.2
Litigation charge/(credit)	–20.2	2,784.10	0
Total operating expenses	13,635	15,443.60	11,490.10
Income from equity investees	268.3	251.4	210.7
Operating income/(loss)	3,081.10	–325.4	1,997.40
Interest income and other, net	142.7	123.6	94.4
Interest expense	–64.1	–28.1	–32.7
Earnings/(loss) before income taxes	3,159.70	–229.9	2,059.10
Income tax expense/(benefit)	1,092	–238.7	674.4
Net earnings/(loss) including noncontrolling interests	2,067.70	8.8	1,384.70
Net earnings/(loss) attributable to noncontrolling interests	–0.4	0.5	0.9
Net earnings/(loss) attributable to Starbucks	2,068.10	8.3	1,383.80
Earnings per share—basic	$2.75	$0.01	$1.83
Earnings per share—diluted	$2.71	$0.01	$1.79

A15. (Du Pont ratios—ROA) For each of the cases below, compute the ROA.

	Asset Turnover	Profit Margin for ROA	ROA
A.	2	5%	?
B.	1	10%	?
C.	15	2%	?
D.	0.5	20%	?

Which of these is the strategy with the highest ROA?

A16. (Du Pont ratios—ROCE) For each of the cases below, compute the ROCE.

	Asset Turnover	Profit Margin for ROCE	Capital Structure Leverage	ROCE
A.	2	5%	1	?
B.	3	2%	1.3	?
C.	1	5%	3	?
D.	5	0.5%	6	?

Which is the case that gives the highest ROCE?

Discussion Questions

D1. (Thinking about ratios) Assume that a company is in a fast-changing industry. You notice at the end of the latest year that the number of days' sales in inventory has increased compared to prior years.

A. What might be a valid business reason that the company might have chosen to increase inventory?

B. What types of problems in the business might an increase in inventory indicate if the increase was not planned by management?

C. Auditors worry that an increase in days' sales in inventory could be a sign of fraudulent financial reporting. Why might a company committing fraud overstate inventory?

D2. (Thinking about ratios) Assume that a company normally gives credit to customers, and has substantial accounts receivable. You notice that in the latest year the accounts receivable turnover ratio has gone down. Even though sales have increased by 10%, receivables have grown proportionally faster.

A. What might be valid business reasons that would cause a company to allow its accounts receivable to increase faster than sales?

B. What might be business problems that are indicated by a decrease in the accounts receivable turnover?

C. Auditors worry that increases in accounts receivable could be a sign of fraudulent financial reporting. Why might a company committing fraud overstate its accounts receivable?

D3. (Thinking about ratios) Assume that a new executive at Walmart decides that he has come up with a sure-fire way to increase the company's ROA. They will keep their same planned asset turnover ratio, but they will change their pricing on all their products to get the same profit margin that Tiffany gets on jewelry. What's wrong with this plan?

D4. (Thinking about ratios) Assume a company now has the following financial figures:

Accounts receivable	100
Inventory	50
Total current assets	300
Total assets	1,000
Accounts payable	30
Total current liabilities	80
Total liabilities	400
Total equity	600
Total revenues	5,000
Total expenses	4,800
Net income	200

Assume there are no taxes.

Indicate whether the following transactions would increase, decrease, or leave unchanged the ratios indicated:

A. Pay 20 of accounts payable with cash:

    a. Current ratio
    b. Capital structure leverage
    c. Profit margin for ROA

B. Borrow 500 of cash using a long-term loan:

    a. Current ratio
    b. Capital structure leverage
    c. Profit margin for ROA
    d. Assuming income is unchanged, ROA

C. Take out a long-term loan and use it to buy machinery, leaving cash unchanged. Assume sales and income are unchanged:

    a. Current ratio
    b. Capital structure ratio
    c. Asset turnover
    d. ROA

D. Lease machinery, without either recording the machinery as an asset (since you don't own it) or recording the remaining lease payments as a liability. Again, assume income is unchanged:

    a. Current ratio
    b. Capital structure ratio
    c. Asset turnover
    d. ROA

D5. (Thinking about ratios) Assume Company A acquires Company B for a lot of money, and records the value of Company B's brand names as intangible assets. Company B had never recorded these values. In future years, when Company A looks at the profitability of its acquisition, what will the effect of recognizing these values be on:

- Profit margin for ROA?
- Asset turnover?
- ROA?
- Capital structure leverage?
- ROCE?

D6. (Thinking about ratios) Many new companies have tried to follow an "asset light" strategy. Instead of having their own factories or equipment, they obtain the goods and services they need from other companies. What would you expect the impact of this strategy of trying to own few assets to be on the company's ratios of:

- Profit margin for ROA?
- Asset turnover?
- ROA?
- Capital structure leverage?

D7. (Persistence) Research has indicated that stock prices are affected more by reported items that are "persistent," meaning they are likely to recur.

A. Explain why the market would react this way.

    a. Is there any value at all to one-time items, like winning or losing a lawsuit?
    b. Why would recurring items have more impact on stock price than one-time items?

B. If you were managing a company, would you be more likely to classify something as "one time" if it were good news, or bad news? Why?

Research Questions

R1. (Using SEC data and Excel skills) This question is designed to give you practice in accessing the SEC website, obtaining data in Excel form, and using that data. Follow the steps below:

A. Go to the SEC website, and get an Excel version of the financial statements on Form 10-K for Dunkin' Brands for the year ended December 28, 2013. To do this:

    a. Go to www.sec.gov.
    b. Click on "Filings" and then "Search for Company Filings."

    c.   When asked for search tools, click on "Company or fund name, ticker symbol. . ."

    d.   For company name, insert Dunkin Brands and click Search.

    e.   There is more than one company listed starting with "dunkin." You should click on the one whose name includes Dunkin Brands.

    f.   On the EDGAR search screen, for filing type, type in 10-K.

    g.   You will see that one of the forms was filed in early 2014. This is the form that contains data for the year ended December, 2013. If you wanted the whole text, you would click on "Documents" but for this exercise, click on "Interactive Data."

    h.   Now, click on "View Excel Document." You should be able to download an Excel workbook with various tabs.

    i.   Open that workbook. It is protected from editing, but you should click on the "Enable Editing" tab.

B.   Go to the tab that has the balance sheet. Your task is to create common size balance sheets for the two years shown. This means that every item in the balance sheet for any one year must be shown as a percentage of total assets for that year. You should be able to do this relatively quickly, using the copy command. (Note—when using Excel, you are going to want Excel to look at the figure for 2013 total assets a lot. If you want Excel to always look at the same cell for this item when you copy formulas, then you need to use an "absolute" cell address. If, for example, total assets was in cell b19, to tell Excel you want to use an absolute address you would type in b19.)

C.   Go to the tab that has the income statement. Create common size income statements for the three years by expressing all the items as a percentage of total revenues.

R2. (Different ratios) The purpose of this question is to let you see that different definitions of certain ratios exist in the world. Look up how ROA is defined by:

A.   Yahoo Finance (go to their website, pick a stock to look at, then look at key statistics. You should be able to find "Key Statistics Help")

B.   Morningstar

C.   Investopedia

D.   NASDAQ

Notes

1 Ijiri (1989) wrote that "One common property of accounting measurements is that they are all functions of time. . .This allows a comparison of each observation with its predecessors and successors. While each observation in the time series may contain useful information in itself, an increment or decrement, relative to its predecessor or successor, may reveal additional, potentially useful information." (p. 2)

2 See Baumgarten, Bonenkamp, and Homburg (2010).

3 The seminal paper in this stream of research is Ball and Brown (1968).

4 Kormendi and Lipe (1987). See also Nichols and Wahlen (2004). For mention of later papers, see American Accounting Association (2009).

5 Beneish (1997). See also American Accounting Association (2009).

6 In the 1800s there were some scandals where owners of companies gave shares to their friends for nothing, and paid such big dividends that the companies went bankrupt, leaving no money for creditors. As a result, laws were passed requiring that anyone who got their stock for less than par value should pay back the difference if the company went bankrupt. This was a well-meaning law, but was easily evaded by companies that set par values very low. In the case of Panera, anyone who got the stock for free would only have to pay back $0.0001 per share.

7 According to Johnson and Kaplan (1987) "The idea for the formula is attributed to F. Donaldson Brown, the CFO, who had no formal accounting background." (p. 86) See also Horrigan (1968).

8 One technique that can be used is to assume that the change between two years is representative, and that fixed costs did not change during the year. So, if we look at Case 2 in Box 4.2, sales change by 50 from

Year 1 to Year 2, and total costs changed by 15, from 80 to 95. If we divide the change in costs of 15 by the change in sales of 50, we get 30%. If we assume that this is representative, it means that variable costs are 30% of revenues. If we apply this to the Year 1 data, we would compute that variable costs would = 30% of 100, or $30, and that fixed costs would be the remainder of the total costs. We would compute the fixed costs as 80 – 30 = $50. These computations agree with the facts given in the case.

9 The organization of this section follows the research synthesis in Wahlen, Baginski and Bradshaw (2015).
10 An early model was by Edward Altman (1968). A later, widely cited model was developed by James Ohlson (1980).
11 For one such model, see Beneish (1997). For a discussion of several other models, see Dechow, Sloan, and Sweeney (1995).

References

Altman, E. (1968). Financial ratios, discriminant analysis, and the prediction of corporate bankruptcy. *Journal of Finance, 23*(4), 589–609.

American Accounting Association. (2009). The impact of academic accounting research on professional practice: An analysis by the AAA Research Impact Task Force. *Accounting Horizons, 23*(4), 411–56.

Ball, R. (2013). Accounting informs investors and earnings management is rife: Two questionable beliefs. *Accounting Horizons, 27*(4), 847–53.

Ball, R., & Brown, P. (1968). An empirical evaluation of accounting income numbers. *Journal of Accounting Research, 6*(2), 159–78.

Ball, R., & Shivakumar (2008). How much new information is there in earnings? *Journal of Accounting Research, 46,* 975–1016.

Baumgarten, D., Bonenkamp, U., & Homburg, C. (2010). The information content of the SG&A ratio. *Journal of Management Accounting Research, 22*(1), 1–22.

Beneish, M. D. (1997). Detecting GAAP violation: Implications for assessing earnings management among firms with extreme financial performance. *Journal of Accounting and Public Policy, 16*(3), 271–309.

Choi, Y. S., Peasnell, K., & Toniato, J. (2013). Has the IASB been successful in making accounting earnings more useful for prediction and valuation? UK evidence. *Journal of Business Finance & Accounting, 40*(7–8), 741–68.

Dechow, P. M., Sloan, R. G., & Sweeney, A. P. (1995). Detecting earnings management. *The Accounting Review, 70*(2), 193–225.

FASB. (1978). Statement of Financial Accounting Concepts No. 1, *Objectives of Financial Reporting by Business Enterprises.* Stamford, CT: FASB.

FASB. (2010). Concepts Statement No. 8. Conceptual Framework for Financial Reporting—Chapter 1, *The Objective of General Purpose Financial Reporting,* and Chapter 3, *Qualitative Characteristics of Useful Financial Information* (a replacement of FASB Concepts Statements No. 1 and No. 2) (pp. 1–14, 16–22). Norwalk, CT: FASB.

Hail, L. (2013). Financial reporting and firm valuation: relevance lost or relevance regained? *Accounting and Business Research, 43*(4), 329–58.

Horrigan, J. O. (1968). A short history of financial ratio analysis. *The Accounting Review, 43*(2), 284–94.

Ijiri, Y. (1967). *The Foundations of Accounting Measurement: A Mathematical, Economic, and Behavioral Inquiry.* Englewood Cliffs, NJ: Prentice-Hall, Inc.

Ijiri, Y. (1989). *Momentum Accounting and Triple-Entry Bookkeeping: Exploring the Dynamic Structure of Accounting Measurements.* Studies in Accounting Research # 31. Sarasota, FL: American Accounting Association.

IRS. (2014). SOI Tax Stats—Integrated Business Data, Table 1: Selected financial data on businesses. Retrieved from www.irs.gov/uac/SOI-Tax-Stats-Integrated-Business-Data (last accessed August 16, 2015).

Johnson, H. T., & Kaplan, R. S. (1987). *Relevance Lost: The Rise and Fall of Management Accounting.* Boston, MA: Harvard Business School Press.

Kaplan, R. S., & Norton, D. P. (1992). The Balanced Scorecard—Measures That Drive Performance, *Harvard Business Review* (January–February), 7–79.

Kormendi, R., & Lipe, R. (1987). Earnings innovations, earnings persistence, and stock returns. *Journal of Business, 60,* 323–45.

Libby, R., & Emett, S. A. (2014). Earnings presentation effects on manager reporting choices and investor decisions. *Accounting and Business Research, 44*(4), 410–38.

Nichols, D. C., & Wahlen J. M. (2004). How do earnings numbers relate to stock returns? A review of classic accounting research with updated evidence. *Accounting Horizons, 18*(4), 263–86.

Ohlson, J. A. (1980). Financial ratios and the probabilistic prediction of bankruptcy. *Journal of Accounting Research, 18,* 109–31.

Strumf, D. (2014, February 5). U.S. public companies rise again. *Wall Street Journal.* Retrieved from http://online.wsj.com/articles/SB10001424052702304851104579363272107177430 (last accessed August 16, 2015).

Wahlen, J. M., Baginski, S. P., & Bradshaw, M. T. (2015). *Financial Reporting, Financial Statement Analysis and Valuation: A Strategic Perspective* (8th ed). United States: Cengage Learning.

5 Using Managerial Accounting Measurements

Outline

- Preliminary Thoughts
- Learning Objectives
- Providing Cost models That Link Inputs and Outputs

  - Cost Drivers
  - Cost–Volume–Profit Analysis

- Incremental Effects of Alternative Decisions

  - Short-Term Operating Decisions
  - Long-Term Capital Investments

- Budgeting and Planning
- Evaluating Performance

  - Key Performance Indicators
  - Standard Costs
  - Variance Analysis

- Unresolved Issues and Areas for Further Research

Preliminary Thoughts

The mass of accounting data is accumulated voluntarily by the individual firm. . . . The bulk of accounting data is never made available to people outside the business firm itself. Thus it seems safe to conclude that accounting information must principally serve the functions of management.

Edgar O. Edwards and Philip W. Bell (1961, p. 4)

The following eight tenets capture the scope of managerial costing for internal use.

A. Provide managers and employees with an accurate, objective cost model of the organization and cost information that reflects the use of the organization's resources. . . .
B. Present decision-support information in a flexible manner that caters to the timeline for insights needed by internal decision makers. . . .
C. Provide decision makers with insight into the marginal/incremental aspects of the alternatives they are considering. . . .
D. Model quantitative cause and effect linkages between outputs and the inputs required to produce and deliver final outputs. . . .

E.   Accurately value all operations (support and production) of an organization (i.e., the supply and consumption of resources) in monetary terms. . . .

F.   Provide information that aids in both immediate and forward-looking decision making for optimization, growth, and attainment of enterprise strategic objectives. . . .

G.   Provide information to evaluate performance and learn from results. . . .

H.   Provide the basis and baseline factors for exploratory and predictive managerial activities. . . .

IMA Managerial Costing Conceptual Framework
Task Force (2014, pp. 22–24)

Complex accounting systems can reduce or camouflage the very uncertainties that managers need to be aware of and can eliminate the ability to detect and correct error.

Matthew Hall (2010, p. 304)

The use of subjective decision making instead of or in addition to the use of quantitative techniques remains widespread, as indicated by surveys of practice over time and around the world.

Joan Luft and Michael D. Shields (2009)

Managers primarily use accounting information to develop knowledge of their work environment rather than as an input into specific decision-making scenarios. In this role, accounting information can help managers to develop knowledge to prepare for unknown future decisions and activities. Second, as accounting information is just one part of the wider information set that managers use to perform their work, it is imperative to consider its strengths and weaknesses not in isolation but relative to other sources of information at a manager's disposal. Third, as managers interact with information and other managers utilising primarily verbal forms of communication, it is through talk rather than through written reports that accounting information becomes implicated in managerial work.

Matthew Hall (2010, p. 302)

The first quotation points out that it is managerial accounting, not financial accounting, that uses most of the data that companies gather. This raises the question: what is all this data being used for? The next quotation helps answer that question. It is a list, prepared by an IMA task force, of the uses of managerial cost accounting information. This chapter introduces you to some of the management accounting concepts and tools that are used to serve the purposes on the IMA's list.

The next quotations suggest the limits on these tools' usefulness. Matthew Hall cautions that when accounting aggregates information, it can hide important details and variations that a manager needs to know. You will see that managerial information is reported on a much more detailed level than the company-wide data we discussed in Chapter 4, and often focuses on one product or one investment decision. Even so, the summarization may hide important details. Luft and Shields note that many business decisions are not made using precise models, but, instead, are subjective decisions. This occurs because companies must consider nonfinancial factors, such as the impact on company morale, of many decisions.

The last quotation, from Matthew Hall, points to uses of managerial accounting that go beyond specific decision-making. Accounting data helps managers form a general understanding of operations, and it provides managers a language for discussing issues.

You will see that the chapter presents a number of tools and concepts that can be used to help think about managerial decisions. However, the accounting tools only answer some of the questions that arise in making decisions.

Learning Objectives

After studying this chapter, you should understand:

1   Key concepts and terms describing the behavior of costs
2   The cost–volume–profit relation with linear costs
3   How avoidable costs affect decision-making
4   Several methods of evaluating capital budgeting decisions
5   How accounting information is used in the planning and budgeting process
6   How accounting information is used to evaluate performance. This includes understanding variance analysis at a basic level.

Providing Cost Models That Link Inputs and Outputs

Introduction

This section discusses various ways of modeling cost behavior. It addresses points "A" and "D" on the IMA's list of ways that accounting information should be used. Point "A" was: "Provide managers and employees with an accurate, objective cost model of the organization and cost information that reflects the use of the organization's resources." Point D was: "Model quantitative cause and effect linkages between outputs and the inputs required to produce and deliver final outputs".

Some Concepts and Definitions for Cost Modeling

We need to learn a specialized vocabulary for discussing cost behavior. An American Accounting Association committee on measurement (1971) wrote:

> A decision maker's choice is largely the result of the information related to him. Likewise, he is limited by his ability to understand and interpret the communication which he receives. One way of developing an individual's ability to communicate effectively is to increase his vocabulary.
>
> (p. 216)

The IMA's (2014) conceptual framework is the basis of the definitions used in this section, unless otherwise noted. The IMA defines "*cost*" as: "A monetary measure of consuming a resource or its output to achieve a specific managerial objective or making a resource or its output available and not using it." (p. 77)

Cost Drivers

A "*cost driver*" is something that "drives" (causes or influences) costs. Often, it is the volume produced, but it could be other factors. For example, if one is producing shirts, clearly the number of shirts produced "drives" the amount of cloth used to produce them.

Some costs would not exist if a particular product was not being produced. The IMA uses "*avoidability*" to identify inputs that could be eliminated as a result of a decision.

The IMA (2014) defines "*responsiveness*" as "the correlation between a particular managerial objective's output quantity and the input quantities required to produce that output" (p. 77). This concept is applied to individual inputs to specific products. The idea of responsiveness is applicable to quantities of inputs used. It is not primarily concerned with the dollar cost of those inputs.

Some resources come in large fixed amounts, while others come in quantities that vary more directly with outputs. The IMA (2014) defines "*divisibility*" as a characteristic that allows a resource to be associated in its entirety with the change in an output resulting from a decision. For example, assume an airline decides to lower prices in order to sell the last 10 seats on a flight from New York to Los Angeles. The cost of having a pilot on that flight is not divisible in a way that relates to the last 10 passengers, but the number of meals served is divisible.

"*Variability*," according to the IMA, implies a straight-line relation between the *total* volumes of product produced and *total* costs. Note that this is different than responsiveness, which refers to quantities of particular inputs, not total dollar costs of producing the product.

In some cases, it is possible to clearly see that an input is used specifically to obtain a particular objective. This is called "*traceability*." A traceable input can be matched completely with a specific output, in a way that can be verified.

The IMA (2014) uses another term where there are not strong cause and effect relations between use of a resource and a managerial objective. That term is "*attributability*." Attributability is defined as: "The responsiveness of inputs to decisions that change the provision and/or consumption of resources." (p. 77) "*Attributable costs* are the costs of an output that could be eliminated in time if the output was discontinued and resource consumption and/or provision were reduced accordingly." (p. 72, emphasis mine.) The IMA notes that often companies have fixed costs common to several outputs, and there is no clear way to associate them with specific outputs in a causal way in the short term. However, for longer term business decision-making, they may need to be considered.

Often, in a complex business, decisions with regard to one production process have effects on others. For example, if a company puts its best workers on a new product, labor productivity on its other products is likely to fall. The concept of "*interdependence*" is a relation between managerial objectives that occurs because a decision to use resources for one objective affects the amount or quality of the resources needed to meet other objectives.

"*Capacity*" is defined as "the potential for a resource to do work" (p. 77). Typically, there are two different types of inputs that need to be considered with the capacity of a resource. Consider, for example, a furnace in a steel factory. There were inputs needed to buy the furnace and make it ready for operation. This includes costs of buying machinery, transporting it to the factory, and installing it. A second set of inputs is needed to continue to use the capacity. For example, electricity is needed to heat the furnace each time the company makes steel.

"*Idle capacity*" (or "*excess capacity*") is capacity that is not currently scheduled for use. This may be because of a strategic management decision, market factors, or technical factors that make the capacity temporarily unavailable. (The term "*nonproductive capacity*" refers to capacity that is not in a productive state. This term includes setups, and facilities undergoing maintenance or scheduled down times.)

Companies use many inputs. For example, Federal Express uses many planes each day, and thousands of drivers. Can they be treated similarly, or should each plane and person be treated individually? The IMA (2014) defines the term "*homogeneity*" as: "A characteristic of one or more resources or inputs. . . .that allow for their costs to be governed by the same set of determinants and in an identical manner" (p. 77). This term is connected with the concept of "*interchangeability*." This relates to different resources that can be substituted for each other without affecting the costs of other resources needed to produce the product. For example, if a company makes shirts, 100% cotton cloth might be interchangeable with a cotton-polyester blend, if changing the fabric does not affect the costs of cutting the cloth and sewing the shirts.

The IMA's terms are summarized in Table 5.1.

Table 5.1 Some Key Terms Used by the IMA (2014) Conceptual Framework

Some modeling concepts	
Resource	A definitive component of an enterprise acquired to generate future benefits.
Cost	A monetary measure of (1) consuming a resource or its output to achieve a specific managerial objective or (2) making a resource or its output available and not using it.
Responsiveness	The correlation between a particular managerial objective's output quantity and the input quantities required to produce that output.
Traceability	A characteristic of an input unit that permits it to be identified in its entirety with a specific managerial objective on the basis of verifiable transaction records.
Capacity	The potential for a resource to do work.
Attributability	The responsiveness of inputs to decisions that change the provision and/or consumption of resources.
Homogeneity	A characteristic of one or more resources or inputs of similar technology or skill that allow for their costs to be governed by the same set of determinants and in an identical manner.
Primarily related to analysis	
Avoidability	A characteristic of an input that allows for the input (and its costs) to be eliminated as a result of a decision.
Divisibility	A characteristic of a resource that allows it to be associated in its entirety with the change in a managerial objective's output resulting from a decision.
Primarily related to decisions	
Interdependence	A relation between managerial objectives that occurs because of a decision to use resources to achieve one objective that affects the amount or quality of resources required to achieve other objectives.
Interchangeability	An attribute of any two or more resources or . . . outputs that can be substituted . . . without affecting the costs of the other resources that are required to carry out the activities to which the interchangeable resources are devoted.

Some Models of Relations Between Inputs and Outputs

Clearly, there are many ways that costs could relate to cost drivers. A typical economics text will show "cost curves" that are not linear, and that in fact show decreasing marginal costs until production reaches certain levels, and then increasing marginal costs after other levels of volume. For the purposes of this text, we assume that over the "*relevant range*" of outputs that are actually likely to be considered, the relationships are linear. We limit discussion to four types of cost behavior:

- A "*fixed responsiveness relationship*" where the same amount of the input is used regardless of the level of the cost driver. This is also called a "fixed cost." A graph of input on the vertical axis versus output would show a straight horizontal line.
- A "*proportional responsiveness relationship*" where the amount of the input varies in a straight-line relation with the cost driver. A graph of the relation of input to output would show a straight line that passes through zero on the X and Y axis at the origin.
- A "*mixed cost*" or "*semi-variable cost*" relation where the total costs include both a fixed portion and a variable portion.
- A "*step cost*" relation where the costs are constant for certain levels of output, and then jump to a higher level at some increased level of output. An example would be the number of buses needed to transport students on a trip. The first 40 students would all fit on one bus. There is no difference in the number of buses needed between four students and 39 students.

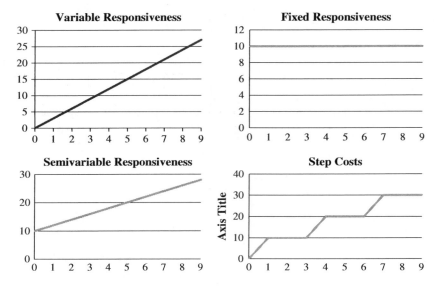

Figure 5.1 Graphs of Various Relations of Costs to Inputs.

However, as soon as we go over the 40-seat capacity, a second bus is needed. A graph of a step cost relation would show straight horizontal lines, moving up like steps on a staircase. Figure 5.1 shows these four cost relations.

How Does a Company Learn How its Costs Behave?

In the previous section, we listed some ways that costs might relate to inputs. How can a company learn how its costs actually behave?

This can be a complex problem, especially where a company produces a number of different products. Some costs are common to various products. Some inputs are interchangeable, while others are not. The efficiency of people and machines varies.

In some cases, where costs are traceable, management can study cost behavior on the basis of the process used to produce the products, For example, Ford Motor Company can easily trace the costs of the tires it puts onto every new car it sells. Clearly, the usage of tires is proportionally responsive to the number of cars made.

In more complicated cases, managers sometimes use past data on costs and outputs to infer what the underlying cost patterns are. Some techniques that are suggested in textbooks to model this behavior are scatter diagrams, regression analysis, and high–low estimation.

A manager using *"scatter diagrams"* plots past data for inputs and outputs in a graph, and looks to see if a pattern is evident, or if any particular observations appear to be highly unusual. Extreme observations can distort overall cost statistics, and should be examined carefully.

"Regression analysis" is a statistical procedure designed to find the best mathematical relation between a dependent variable (such as cost) and one or more independent variables. "Ordinary least squares" regression is used to find a linear relation that relates one or more independent variables to cost in a way that optimizes the fit of the line to the data.[1]

Microsoft Excel can perform regression analysis and provide graphs showing equations and what is called the R^2 statistic. The R^2 statistic indicates how well the regression line fits the data. A value of 1 is a perfect fit, and a value of 0 shows no relation between the line and the data.

Figures 5.2 and 5.3 show two scatter plots of nine data points, with regression lines. The data for all nine data points in Figure 5.2 is based on the following straight-line equation, with some random variation added in.

$$Y = 100 + 3 \times X$$

In Figure 5.3, eight of the data points are also based on this equation, with some random variation, but the ninth data point is much larger than the others, and has a bigger variance from the equation.

In Figure 5.2, the regression procedure worked well. The regression line has an intercept of 108, and a slope of 2.87. This is fairly close to the equation used to generate the data, which had an intercept of 100 and a slope of 3. The R^2 statistic of 0.93 indicates the line fits the data very well.

However, in Figure 5.3 one extreme observation has skewed the results. The estimated regression line has a negative intercept = –62, and a slope of 6.08. A manager using this result would think variable costs per unit are over \$6, when the true figure for eight of the data points is \$3.

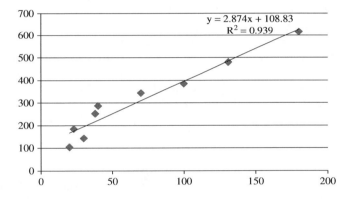

Figure 5.2 Sample Regression.

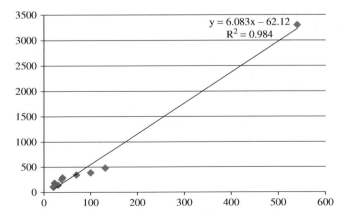

Figure 5.3 A Sample Regression with one extreme Data Point.

Box 5.1 Example of Using the High–Low Method to Understand Cost Behavior

Assume that a manager sees the following observations of costs and outputs:

Cost	Output
35	15
45	20
21	8
33	14

A manager using the high–low method to study costs would notice that the highest output was 20, with a cost of 45, and the lowest output was 8, with a cost of 21.

The difference in costs = 45 – 21 = 24.

The difference in outputs = 20 – 8 = 12.

By definition, costs that vary are responding proportionally.

The ratio of the change in costs to the change in output is 24 to 12, meaning costs increase by 2 for every extra item of output.

This means that in the case of the highest level of output, when output was 20 and total costs were 45, the total variable costs equaled 2 × 20 = 40. That means that the total costs must include 45 – 40 = 5 of fixed costs.

Notice that we could have found the fixed costs by using the data for the low level of production. With 8 items produced, total variable costs must = 8 × 2 = 16. This means that fixed costs = 21 – 16, or 5.

In this example, we could have used any two observations to find the cost relation. All the observations were created based on the equation Cost = 5 + (2 × output).

The R^2 statistic of 0.98 does not give any clue that there is a problem, since it indicates the line fits the data well. The point is: be careful of extreme observations when using regression analysis!

High–low estimation is a method of separating out fixed and variable costs. It assumes that costs really contain fixed and variable parts. Therefore, the difference between any two observations must be due to variable costs. The reason for using the highest and lowest observations is that, if there are minor random fluctuations, they will tend to cancel out over the range between the top and bottom observations. Box 5.1 uses the high–low method. One caution when using the high–low method is to avoid observations that have been affected by non-typical events. For example, don't use a "low" observation that occurred when a major snowstorm disrupted activity.

Analysts sometimes use the same techniques to understand the overall cost structure of a company. Table 5.2 is an example of using published data on revenues, operating expenses, and operating income to compare the cost structure of Hertz rental car company.

Cost–Volume–Profit Analysis

Key Equations of CVP

The cost patterns described in the previous section can help managers model how their profits will respond to changes in output. This modeling of the relation of costs, output level, and

Table 5.2 Using Published Data to Understand Cost Structures of Hertz Based on Data From Form 10-K

	2012	*2013*	*Change*
Hertz (millions)			
Revenues	9,025	10,772	1,747
Operating expenses	7,933	9,354	1,421
Operating Profits	1,092	1,418	326

Changes in operating expenses ÷ change in revenues = 1,421/1,747 = 0.81
2013 variable cost = 0.81 × 2013 revenues of 10,772 = 8,725
2013 fixed costs = total operating expenses − variable costs = 9,354 − 8,725 = 629.
2013 operating leverage effect = (revenues − variable costs) ÷ operating profits =(10,772 − 8,725)/1,418 = 1.44
It is not surprising that Hertz has an operating leverage effect greater than one. Hertz has considerable fixed costs in maintaining offices and in the depreciation of its cars.

Form 10-K filings can be reviewed on the SEC website: www.sec.gov/edgar/searchedgar/companysearch.html (last accessed August 14, 2015).

profits is typically called "*cost–volume–profit analysis*" (CVP analysis). We will go through a mathematical derivation of key equations, and then will discuss some examples.

Let profit = π (the Greek letter pi)
Let total costs = TC, and total revenues = TR.

Then,

$\pi = TR - TC$ This simply says that revenues minus costs = profits.

If we are selling one product, then:

Let price = P
Let quantity sold = Q.

Then total revenue = TR = P × Q. This says revenues depend on the number sold and the price.

Let total fixed costs = TFC Let variable costs = TVC.

Let the variable cost per unit = VC.

Then TVC = VC × Q. This says total variable cost depends on unit variable cost and the number of units.

TC = TFC + TVC Total costs equals the fixed part plus the variable part.

When we put the equations together, we get:

$\pi = TR - TC = P \times Q - VC \times Q - TFC$

Or if we rearrange terms slightly we get:

$\pi = Q \times (P - VC) - TFC$ The term in parentheses is called the *unit contribution margin.*

The term "*contribution margin*" is used in two different ways. One way is the contribution margin per unit, which equals the selling price for one unit minus the variable costs for one unit. The other way is the contribution margin for the company as a whole, which equals total sales revenue for the company minus the variable costs of producing all those items.

The last equation above is a key to the CVP analysis. It says that profits equal the per unit contribution margin, times the quantity produced, minus any fixed costs.

CVP Examples

Let's consider some implications, through examples.

Example 1. Assume a company sells its items for $10 each, and the per unit variable cost = $4. It has fixed costs of $60. Let's look at profits at various levels of production:

Production	Profits
No units	−60
5 units	−30
10 units	0
15 units	30
100 units	540

Each item in the table above fits the profit equation $\pi = Q \times (10 - 4) - 60$. Notice that the profits do *not* change proportionately with output. Between 15 units and 100, production went up about sevenfold, but profits grew by a factor of 18.

At zero production, there are no revenues and no variable costs, so total profits are a net loss equal to the fixed costs.

In this method of analysis, the level of production at which costs exactly equal revenues is the "*break-even point*." We could find this point by solving the profit equation for Q while setting the profit to 0. We would find that the break-even quantity = fixed costs divided by contribution margin.

Break-even quantity $q = TFC \div (P - VC)$

In this example, that means that:

$Q = 60 \div (10 - 4)$ which $= 10$ units.

We could also figure out the level of production that is needed for any given target level of profits. Assume that fixed costs are $60, as in the original example, and that the company wants profits of $100. How many units are needed? To solve this, we need to solve the equation for q with π set to $100. The equation would be:

$100 = Q \times (10 - 4) - 60$

Solving it would give us:

$160 = Q \times 6$

$Q = 160 \div 6 = 26.67.$

Example 2. Assume the same facts as in Example 1, except this company has fixed costs = 0. This makes life simpler in a couple of ways. First, the profit equation simplifies to $\pi = Q \times (10 - 4)$. Second, the break-even point is now zero. With no production, the company has neither a profit nor a loss. Third, profits will change proportionately with volume.

Some implications from these examples are the following:

1   Unless a company has zero fixed costs, there will be some level of production below which it has losses. Any company with fixed costs will lose money at very low production levels.
2   Unless a company has zero fixed costs, as long as price is greater than variable costs, there will be some break-even level of production. Above that level, the company will make profits.
3   Unless a company has zero fixed costs, profits will *not* change proportionately with output.
4   All other things being equal, the greater a company's contribution margin (price – variable unit cost), the lower will be its break-even point.
5   All other things being equal, the lower the total fixed costs, the lower will be the break-even point.

These are important concepts, and can be very helpful to managers in deciding on the capacity and cost structures they need to create in order to have successful products.

Relating CVP to the Concept of Operating Leverage

Chapter 4 discussed the concept of leverage, where changes in volume of sales can have an expanded effect on profits. In particular, the "operating leverage effect" as defined as:

Operating leverage effect = (revenues – variable costs) ÷ operating income.

The concepts we have been using in CVP analysis can help a company understand the leverage implications of different ways of structuring its production processes.

Table 5.3 presents a company with a choice of two production methods. Method A has $100 of fixed costs, and a variable cost of $3 per unit. Method B has $600 of fixed costs, and a variable cost of $1 per unit. So, Method B has much higher fixed costs, and it also has a higher per unit contribution margin. This could happen, for example, if Method B involved buying expensive machinery that allowed it to make its products with less labor. The company can sell its products for $4 each, regardless of which production method it chooses.

Method A, with lower fixed costs, has a lower break-even point. Its break-even point is 100, compared to 200 for Method B.

The two methods result in the same operating profits at a volume of 250 units. Both methods yield a profit of $150.

Above the 250 unit level, Method B is consistently more profitable. Below that level, it is less profitable. If we look at the lowest and highest quantities shown in Table 5.3, the operating profit for Method A ranges from a loss of $100 at zero production to a profit of $900 at the 1,000 unit level. The change in profits is $1,000. Now look at Method B. The operating profits go from a loss of $600 at zero production to a profit of $2,400 at a volume of 1,000. The range in profits is $3,000, triple that of Method A. Method B is clearly more leveraged.

Table 5.3 shows the computation of the operating leverage effect at a level of 250 units. The values of this ratio are 1.4 for Method A and 5.0 for Method B.

Do companies actually use this type of cost and leverage analysis? Research indicates they use it for planning. See, for example, the study of public manufacturing company data by Banker, Byzalov and Plehn-Dujowich (2013).

CVP Limitations

Some limitations of this analysis need to be kept in mind.

First, the profit equation we used is only valid where costs and revenues behave linearly. If, for example, it were necessary to cut prices to achieve higher sales volumes, or if costs grew

Table 5.3 Example of Impact of Two Different Cost Patterns on Profits

The company has a choice of two production methods. In each case, selling price = $
per unit. The cost patterns for the two methods are:

	Fixed costs	Variable costs per unit
Method A	$100	$3
Method B	$600	$1

Quantity	Revenues	Method A		Method B	
		Costs	Operating Profits	Costs	Operating Profits
0	0	100	−100	600	−600
50	200	250	−50	650	−450
100	400	400	0	700	−300
150	600	550	50	750	−150
200	800	700	100	800	0
250	1,000	850	150	850	150
300	1,200	1,000	200	900	300
500	2,000	1,600	400	1,100	900
1,000	4,000	3,100	900	1,600	2,400

The operating leverage effect for the two methods at a quantity of 250 units, where the
operating profits are the same, is:
Method A   1.4 = (1,000 revenues − 750 variable costs) ÷ 150 operating profits
Method B   5.0 = (1,000 revenues − 250 variable costs) ÷ 150 operating profits

more than proportionately with higher sales volumes, we would need a more complicated profit equation.

Second, it assumes we accurately separate fixed and variable costs.

Third, this analysis assumed a single product, with no interdependencies in production with other products. The same analysis works if there is a standard mix of products being produced, but will run into problems if, at different levels of total output, the mix of products changes.

Incremental Effects of Alternative Decisions

This section of the chapter deals with item "C" on the IMA's list of uses of managerial costing. The IMA says managerial accounting should "Provide decision makers insight into the marginal/incremental aspects of the alternatives they are considering. . . ." This section describes various decisions involving the incremental effects of particular short-term operating decisions, and capital budgeting decisions.

Short-Term Operating Decisions

Types of Decisions Discussed

In this section we deal with questions like the following:

- Should the company accept a special order for its products?
- Should the company continue to make a component of its product, or buy it from someone else?
- Should the company stop making a particular product, or servicing a particular customer?

Relevant Revenues and Relevant or Avoidable costs

In each decision, we need to look at the incremental effect of the decision on the company. To make these decisions efficiently, managers need to focus on those revenues and expenses that will change based on this decision. These are called the *"relevant costs"* and *"relevant revenues"* in most textbooks, although the term *"differential cost"* is also used. The IMA uses *"avoidable costs"* to identify costs that will be eliminated if the need for a particular managerial objective is eliminated. The avoidable costs may be eliminated at once, or after some period of time.

The relevant revenues related to a decision are those that will change. These may be obvious, or they may be hard to determine. For example, assume that Levi's decides to stop selling shirts. Clearly, they will lose the revenues they now get from shirts. But will sales of other types of Levi's products be affected? This is harder to predict. It depends on the interdependence of the various products.

Avoidable costs are those that will be affected by the decision. An analysis of avoidable costs would normally include:

- *Outlay costs.* These are future direct cash outlays related to the decision. In the short run, they are variable costs.
- *Salvage value.* If the decision involves disposing of some assets, the money that can be received from selling them is relevant.
- *Opportunity costs* of the decision. Opportunity costs occur when the company loses the opportunity to do something valuable. For example, a landlord who decides not to rent an apartment for two months to paint it has an opportunity cost – the landlord could have received two months' rent on that apartment.

Past costs are not avoidable. Money that was spent in the past to buy facilities, for example, is not an avoidable cost. "Sunk costs" is a term used to describe costs related to past decisions that cannot be changed. Sunk costs are always irrelevant costs – they do not change based on the effects of the decision.

However, managers often have difficulty ignoring sunk costs. A sports analogy may help make this clear. Assume a basketball team has two players who are performing badly. It makes sense in each case to admit these players are terrible, and get new players. However, the team had signed one of these players only six months ago and has given that player a one-time bonus of $40 million. That bonus is a sunk cost, and should be irrelevant to the decision, but the team manager may not want to admit that the bonus was an enormous mistake. A study of NBA players (Staw and Hoang 1995) found that sunk costs seemed to be an explanation of why some poorly performing players, who had been high draft choices, were kept on their teams. In industries where bad performance is less obvious than it is in the NBA, a manager may also try to avoid admitting sunk costs no longer have value, in order to help maintain the manager's own reputation.[2] There is extensive research in the psychology literature, and the economics literature, on the "sunk cost effect."

Some costs are theoretically avoidable, but may be difficult to avoid in the short term if the inputs are not *divisible*. For example, assume a company has fixed employment contracts with its workers, and the workers are guaranteed fixed annual salaries. Even if the company finds a way to change a process to reduce the need for labor hours, it might not be able to avoid paying the workers their full yearly salaries. As another example, assume a retail company finds a way to rearrange its stores so that each store could sell the same amount of products using 5% less selling space. If the store facilities are on fixed lease arrangements, it might not be able to avoid paying the full rental costs. Note that in the long run, the company might be able to reduce its costs. It could slowly shrink its workforce by hiring fewer new workers, and could rent smaller stores in the future. Whether costs are avoidable often depends on the time period for our decision.

The analysis in this section is limited because it only discusses financial effects on the company. Nonfinancial considerations, or externalities, can be very important. A decision to drop a product and fire the workers who make it may have a variety of effects not considered in the company's books. It may affect workers' livelihoods and the loyalty of the remaining workers. It may affect customer loyalty. It may affect the tax base and economic vitality of the local community. It may affect consumers.

Operating Decision Example—Special Order Decisions

Assume a company makes textbooks for the U.S. market. Key facts regarding this product are in Table 5.4.

At the moment, the company is clearly making a profit from this book. The costs per item total $130 and the selling price is $150. On a *full-cost basis*, including both fixed and variable costs, the company is making $150 – 130 = $20 per book.

The company now receives an inquiry from a college in Liberia about buying 1,000 books for $90 each, instead of the normal price of $150. Should the company take this offer? Assume it would not need any new equipment to make these extra copies – it has idle capacity.

The first question is to identify avoidable (or relevant) revenues and costs.

The revenues from the special offer would be 1,000 copies at $90 = $90,000.

The avoidable outlay costs are the variable costs of $70 per copy. These include variable labor costs, variable materials costs, shipping costs, and authors' royalties. These will all increase when the company makes and ships an extra 1,000 copies. The total of these costs = 1,000 copies at $70 = $70,000.

The fixed costs of $60 per copy are not avoidable. They are sunk costs. They relate to depreciation on equipment that was bought in prior years. Since no new equipment is needed, there is no new outlay for equipment.

So, at this point, accepting the order would result in $90,000 of incremental revenues, and $70,000 of incremental costs, netting the company $20,000 in incremental profits. This implies that the offer should be accepted.

However, some other factors normally should be considered.

We have only considered outlay costs, not opportunity costs. Could the company have used its facilities for something more profitable? In this example, because of the idle capacity, we assumed the answer was "no." However, the company might consider seeking out other ways to use that idle capacity that would be more profitable.

We have also assumed there is no interdependency between taking this order and sales to existing customers. Will U.S. customers find out that the company is selling its books for $90, instead of $150, in Liberia? Will some U.S. customers start buying their books in Liberia?

Table 5.4 Example of Special Order Decision

Normal selling price	$150	
Raw materials per book	$30	
Variable labor cost per book	$20	
Author royalties per book	$15	
Variable shipping costs per book	$5	
Total variable costs per book	$70	
Normal sales per year	100,000 copies	
Total fixed costs attributable	$6,000,000	(depreciation of equipment)
Total fixed cost per item	$60	($6 million ÷ 100,000 copies)
Total costs per item	$130	($70 + $60)

(Some U.S. students buy "international editions" of textbooks to save money.) Will some U.S. customers either demand lower U.S. prices, or be offended and switch to the company's competitors?

Operating Decision Example 2—Outsourcing ("Make or Buy") Decisions

Manufacturers often buy some parts of their products from other companies, and make some parts of their products themselves. For example, a car company might make motors itself, but might buy ignition switches from another company. Buying from another company is called "outsourcing." Some companies in fact outsource the majority of their production. For example, the Nike Form 10-K for the year ended May 31, 2014 says: "Virtually all of our products are manufactured by independent contractors."

Outsourcing goes well beyond the manufacturing environment. For example, companies often outsource telephone marketing to companies that operate call centers. Professional services, including computer programming and tax preparation services, are sometimes outsourced to less expensive overseas locations. Consumer products companies need to consider how much marketing expertise they need to have in their own company, as opposed to the expertise of their outside advertising and marketing consultants. Large corporations need to decide how large a legal staff they want, and how much legal work they wish to outsource to outside law firms.

Let's first consider an example to illustrate the direct financial factors involved in a typical decision, and then we will consider some nonfinancial factors.

Assume a car company currently makes an ignition switch for its trucks. It uses 100,000 of these switches each year. It is considering the offer of a supplier to sell the company the switches for $80 each. If it stops making its own switches, it will be able to avoid incurring certain costs that would otherwise be fixed costs. Summary facts regarding this decision and the current cost structure are shown in Table 5.5.

The relevant factors are what the company will have to spend to buy the outsourced switches, and what avoidable costs are now incurred in making the switches internally. In this example, the avoidable costs include direct labor, direct materials, variable overhead costs, and some avoidable fixed costs. Certain other fixed costs will not be avoided by this decision, and therefore are irrelevant.

In this example, the company could save a net of $500,000 by continuing to make the switches itself. However, this analysis is incomplete. We should consider opportunity costs and nonfinancial factors.

What are the opportunity costs of continuing to produce the switches? Can the facilities or workers that are freed up by stopping producing switches be used to make other products? Could the management time devoted to making this product be better used on other areas?

Table 5.5 Example of Make or Buy Decision—Ignition Switches

	Cost to make	Cost to buy	Difference (effect on income of buying)
Cost to buy (100,000 at $80)		$8,000,000	($8,000,000)
Cost to make			
Direct variable materials	$5,000,000		5,000,000
Direct labor	1,000,000		1,000,000
Variable overhead	1,000,000		1,000,000
Avoidable fixed costs	500,000		500,000
Unavoidable fixed costs	Not relevant		
Totals	$7,500,000	$8,000,000	($500,000)

What nonfinancial factors should be considered? Are there quality differences between production internally and outsourcing? Some outside suppliers may have the abilities to produce at higher quality than the company itself, while others do not. Could problems in product quality affect the company's reputation, or legal liabilities? I write this section in a year when major car companies have been reporting major safety problems due to ignition switches and to components of air bags. Will outsourcing production of a component affect relations with the remaining workers? Would outsourcing to a company with low environmental or labor standards affect the company's reputation? Will the supplier meet delivery schedules, or will delivery problems affect other parts of the company's production?

One model of the "make or buy" decision (Padillo and Diaby 1999) argues that financial factors are only one of four relevant criteria. The others are strategic competitive performance, managerial focus and performance, and minimization of the risks involved in sourcing the production.

Operating Decision Example 3—Exiting a Market or Dropping a Product

Let's assume a company operates 100 stores. It is considering closing 10 stores, which are the worst performing. What factors would be relevant to this decision?

The directly relevant costs and revenues are the following:

1   Lost sales from the closed stores.
2   Savings of labor costs related to the closed stores.
3   Any extra costs related to shutting the stores—these might include employee severance or costs of moving remaining inventory or penalty costs in building leases.
4   Savings of costs of goods sold related to the closed stores.
5   Avoidable occupancy costs on the closed stores. These might be all the occupancy costs. But some occupancy costs might not be avoidable in the short term. For example, the company may have rental commitments to a landlord. If it owns the property, it might still have continuing real estate taxes and other costs.
6   Other avoidable costs directly related to the closed stores.

Certain costs would be sunk costs, and are irrelevant. For example, special costs involved in remodeling and decorating the unprofitable stores years ago, when they opened, are now sunk costs.

Companies need to be very careful in analyzing their costs. For example, there are probably some costs of running the entire business that have been allocated to individual stores. In this example, we have assumed the company has correctly determined whether these costs are avoidable if the 10 unprofitable stores are closed.

The decision is complex, and needs to consider more than just the differential costs and revenues considered above.

Are there opportunity costs? Could something else be done with the space, or these stores, that would be more profitable than simply closing them? On the other hand, does closing these stores let management focus better on the remaining 90 stores?

Are there interdependencies with the remaining stores? Perhaps you expect most people who shopped at these stores to shift over to your remaining 90 stores. In that case, not all of the sales at the 10 closed stores will be lost. This might be the case, for example, when two banks merge, and they have numerous branch offices near each other. In this case, most customers will stay within the banking system even if some branches close. However, if the 90 branches are in distant locations, then almost all the customers of the 10 closed branches will be lost.

Will closing these stores affect the company's reputation, and therefore sales at the remaining stores? Will customers and suppliers worry about the company's soundness? Or, on the other hand, were these particular stores hurting the company's reputation? For example, if a company wants to project an exclusive image, dingy and old stores may hurt these branding efforts, and closing the bad stores may help the remaining ones.

Are there externalities that the company should consider? What will be the effects of store closures on workers and communities? For example, assume one of the stores is the only super-market or pharmacy in a small town.

Accounting research finds that in practice, managers often base their product pricing decisions and decisions to keep or drop products on the "full costs" of products, including the sunk costs. See Balakrishnan and Sivaramakrishnan (2002). Why would managerial practice ignore the con-cept of basing decisions on only relevant, avoidable costs? Some researchers suggest that the full cost, which includes depreciation of long-term fixed assets, provides a better view of the long-run consequences of decisions than does the total short-term avoidable cost. In this view, considering full costs is necessary to understand the implications of the decision for long-term capacity plan-ning (Balakrishnan and Sivaramakrishnan 2002).

Long-Term Capital Investments

General Points

This section deals with long-term capital investment decisions. Such decisions might include building a new factory, or changing a computer system.

Several characteristics of these decisions are different from the decisions in the prior section:

1   Capital investments typically require large initial cash outlays.
2   The expected returns from the investments are spread over long future periods. This requires considering the time value of money in the decision-making. In the previous section, we ignored the timing of returns.
3   Fewer costs should be considered as fixed. Because we are dealing with a longer period of time, the manager can assume that more costs will change over this long time horizon.
4   Capital investments often have pervasive effects on a company. For example, a decision on where to place a factory, and how large it should be, affects the company's use of labor, its closeness to suppliers and markets, and many other aspects of its business. A wide range of information may be needed to predict the full effects of the decision.[3]

The tools discussed in this section cannot determine the final decision on a project, because they do not incorporate nonfinancial impacts. However, they are helpful in screening and ranking choices. They also give managers a set of common terms to use in discussing projects.

Time Value of Money

Capital investment decisions need to compare the initial costs of projects with the returns that the projects will generate over some future period of years. This requires using the mathematical concept of present value. In this chapter, I assume that you are familiar with this concept. *If you are not familiar with present value concepts, you should read Appendix B before continuing.*

Appendix B includes tables that can be used to find:

•   The present value of a sum of money to be received in the future
•   The present value of an annuity. An annuity is a series of payments of the same amount that occur regularly over future periods.

Four Ways of Measuring the Value of a Potential Investment

This section describes four methods used to judge potential investments. Each method compares future expected net cash inflows from an investment with the initial cash outlays.

Note that, because no one knows the future, the measurement of the future inflows is uncertain. Long-term investments are inherently riskier than short-term ones, because the uncertainty is greater for more distant future years.

The four methods are:

Net present discounted value of the future cash flows (NPV). This method uses the standard present value formula, and computes the value today of the expected future cash flows.[4] The standard present value formula is:

$$PV_0 = \sum_{t=0}^{t=\infty} \frac{FV_t}{(1+i)^t}$$

In this formula, PV_0 is the present value at the time of the investment. The numerator contains the various expected future inflows, shown as "FV", for future values, with subscript t indicating the time period in which they will be received. The denominator contains 1 plus the interest rate i, raised to the t power. The interest rate is also referred to as the discount rate.

The net present value of any investment equals the difference between the investment and the present value of the expected cash flows. This method results in a dollar figure. For example, the net present value may be $3 million. If the net present value is positive, then the investment is expected to be profitable.

Internal rate of return (IRR). This method is similar in concept to the net present value method, and uses the same basic formula. The internal rate of return is the discount rate that makes the present value of the future benefits exactly equal to the initial investment.

Mathematically, you use the formula above, insert the future values, and solve for an interest rate that makes the future value equal to the amount of the investment. In practice, since the equation gets very complex for large numbers of time periods, people may use a trial and error process to estimate the rate of return.

This method gives a rate of return. As long as the total (undiscounted) future returns are higher than the investment, the internal rate of return will be positive. The higher the internal rate of return is, the more profitable the project is. Typically companies set some target rate of return, called the "*hurdle rate*," and only accept projects with IRR above the hurdle rate.

Accounting rate of return, also known as unadjusted rate of return (AROR). This method does not consider the time value of money. It expresses the average future increased profits as a percentage of the initial investment. The formula is:

Accounting rate of return = (average future increased profit) ÷ (initial outlay)

Like the IRR, this method gives a rate of return. The higher the return, the more desirable is the project.

Payback period. This method indicates the number of years it will take for a project to "pay back" the initial investment. For example, assume that company needs to spend $4 million on new machinery, and the new machinery will improve profits by $1 million a year. In this case, the payback period is four years. If the machinery improved profits by $2 million per year, the payback period would be two years.

The shorter the payback period, the better the project.

Comparing the Four Methods of Evaluating Projects

Each of the four methods has benefits and drawbacks. In fact, many companies use more than one method. A longitudinal study of 100 British firms, ending in 1992 (Pike 1996), indicated that 96 of the firms used at least two methods to judge the projects. For some years, studies of the methods actually used had indicated the payback method and the IRR were the most popular. However, Ryan and Ryan's (2002) survey of Fortune 1000 Chief Financial Officers, with around 200 responses, indicated that their most favored method was the NPV method. Internal rate of return was a close second.[5]

The payback period's main advantage is its simplicity. It does not require choosing a discount rate, and it only requires forecasting future inflows until the investment is "paid back." It is a quick way of seeing if a project is likely to provide benefits in the short term. When companies are in rapidly changing environments, this may be critical. For example, in some fields it does not make sense to assume that technology and consumer demands will be the same for more than two or three years, so a firm would want to screen out projects that do not pay back the investments quickly.

The payback period method has important disadvantages. One is that it ignores some information—it does not consider anything about what happens after the payback period. If two investments have the same payback period, but one has much higher cash inflows in the following years, this method ignores that information. The payback period also ignores the time value of money. If two projects both have four-year payback periods, this method ranks them the same. If one project returns money faster within the four years, the payback period method will ignore that fact.

The accounting rate of return is also a simple method. It does not require the company to decide on a discount rate. Its advantage over the payback period is that it does consider the amounts of all the future inflows, not just the ones up until the payback period. It also has the advantage of comparing the future inflows to the initial investment, in the form of a percentage return. Like the payback period method, it has the disadvantage of not considering the time value of money. This method does not use the information on *the timing of* future inflows. The accounting rate of return is based on the average return during the life of the investment. This method will not distinguish between projects that return funds quickly, and those that return funds slowly.

The net present value method does consider the time value of money. It has the advantage of being consistent with finance and economic theory. Also, all the information is considered in this method. The amounts of each future inflow, and the timing of each inflow, are considered.

The NPV method has two disadvantages. The first is that a discount rate must be determined. This is a complex decision. Theoretically, the appropriate discount rate depends on the riskiness of the investment, expectations of inflation, market rates of interest, the time period of the investment, and other factors. In this text, we assume that the proper rate is the company's average cost of capital, and that this rate is known.[6] A second disadvantage is that this method does not relate the NPV to the size of the investment. For example, two investments with an NPV of $10 million are ranked equally, even though one requires a $5 million investment and the other requires a $500 million investment.

The internal rate of return method shares the key advantages of the NPV method. It is based on the theoretically justified present value equation, and it uses all future information about both the amounts and the timing of inflows. In addition, the company does *not* have to assume any specific discount rate in making the computation. Instead, the IRR method computes what the return is expected to be on the proposed investment, and the manager can then decide if that return is high enough to make the investment. The disadvantage of using the IRR to rank projects is that it gives rates of return, not absolute amounts. Thus, a project with an IRR of 14% looks much better than a project with an IRR of 6%, but it is possible that the first project is quite small in size, and the absolute dollars earned by the second project might be much higher.

One theoretical difference between the IRR and NPV values is how the methods mathematically treat reinvested money over the relevant time period. IRR assumes these funds are discounted at the internal rate of return, while NPV uses the discount rate, which is usually the cost of capital.

Box 5.2 Example of Use of Four Capital Budgeting Measures

Assume that a company is considering two different capital budgeting decisions. One involves its car business, and one involves the truck business. The required investments, and expected cash inflows, are presented below, in billions. Assume the company's cost of capital is 5%.

	Cars	Trucks
Investment	15	30
Inflows by year		
1	3	10
2	3	8
3	4	6
4	5	6
5	4	20
6	6	0
Total inflows	25	50
Net cash profit	**$10**	**$20**
Payback period computation	4 years	4 years
	(3 + 3 + 4 + 5) = 15	(10 + 8 + 6 + 6) =
	investment	30 investment

Accounting rate of return computation:

Average annual income	25/6 = 4.17	50/5 = 10
Investment	15	30
Accounting rate of return	**28%**	**33%**

NPV computation	(5% cost of capital)	
Value of inflows by year		
1	2.86	9.52
2	2.72	7.26
3	3.46	5.18
4	4.11	4.94
5	3.13	15.67
6	4.48	0
Total PV of inflows	20.76	42.57
NPV (net of investment)	**$5.76**	**$12.57**
IRR computation	14.88%	17.61%

The internal rates of return shown bring the present value of the future payments = the investments.

Box 5.2 provides an example of the use of all four methods to evaluate an investment. In this case, a company is considering between investing in its car and truck divisions. The car investment would be $15 billion, and the truck investment would be $30 billion. How do these potential investments compare? The example was chosen so the truck example has twice the cost of the car example, and exactly double the cash inflows, but the pattern of the timing of the inflows differs somewhat. The truck inflows come somewhat faster.

According to the data in Box 5.2, both projects would have payback periods of exactly four years. On this criterion, they are equal. However, you should notice that after the fourth year, the remaining cash from the truck project is received faster. The payback computation does not consider this factor.

The two projects differ in their accounting rate of return. In each case, the return is quite high. The car project shows an accounting rate of return of 28% for six years, while the truck project's rate of return is 33% for five years. In this case, the fact that all the inflows from the truck project would come in over five years, as opposed to six for the car project, makes the truck project look better. If the 50 of truck inflows had been averaged over six years, instead of five, then the two projects would have had exactly the same accounting rate of return.

However, the accounting rate of return would not change at all if the returns for Years 4 and 5 were switched. This method does not consider the timing of the inflows within the investment period – just the average inflows.

A net present value computation with a cost of capital of 5% is shown. The NPV of the truck project is $412.57 billion, or 2.18 times the $5.76 billion NPV of the car project. Why isn't it exactly twice the size, since the total investment and the total returns are double? The answer is that the timing of the returns of the truck project is quicker than the returns for the car project, and that affects the NPV.

Finally, the internal rate of return for the two projects is 14.88% for cars, and 17.61% for trucks. These are the discount rates that make the present value of the inflows equal to the investments. The truck project has a higher IRR.

Should the company do both projects? Both have positive NPV, and both have IRR well above the company's assumed cost of capital of 5%. That would indicate they are both worthwhile projects. However, in the real world, most companies don't have enough financing to do every possible project. In this example, these are projects that together would require $45 billion in financing. Where capital is rationed, companies have to make choices.

Another factor that companies consider is how major decisions affect how analysts view the company. Companies often consider how decisions affect the profitability and risk measures in Chapter 4, such as: return on equity; return on assets; earnings per share; asset turnover; and leverage ratios.

Budgeting and Planning

General

The preceding section dealt with using managerial accounting measures to help make specific decisions. This section deals with more general issues of planning and budgeting. The IMA's (2014) list of uses of managerial accounting included:

> Provide information that aids in both immediate and forward-looking decision making for optimization, growth, and attainment of enterprise strategic objectives

and

> Provide the basis and baseline factors for exploratory and predictive managerial activities.

This section briefly describes how accounting is used in corporate long-term planning and budgeting processes.

Definition, Types and Purposes of Budgets

Budgets are formal plans of action, expressed in quantitative or money terms.

Budgets can be made at many levels of an organization – products, departments, groups of departments, subsidiaries, or the entire consolidated group of companies. A company may have a variety of budgets for various activities. For example, a company might have a sales budget, an inventory purchases budget, a selling expenses budget, a cash collections budget, and other budgets.

Budgets help in planning, communicating, setting benchmarks, coordinating operations, assessing risk, and controlling the business.[7] Let's consider each of these purposes.

Planning. Managers need plans in order to make decisions. Should they be planning for more sales next month, or fewer, should they be hiring employees, or firing them? Should the treasury department of the company find places to invest cash, or should the treasurer be looking for ways to borrow? A budget is a plan that provides guidance to these and other questions.

The budget is not simply a passive prediction of things that may happen. Instead, it includes the expected impacts of decisions that management is making—new product introductions, changes in staffing, pricing decisions, and so on.

Communicating. The budgeting process can serve as a two-way channel of communication.

Top management uses the budget process to tell workers and managers what is expected of them.

Lower level managers, by commenting on proposed budgets, can provide information to top management about opportunities in the business, and the feasibility of management plans, before the budget is finalized. Thus, top management can use the process to gather information from those personnel who are close to the customers and the production processes.

Setting specific benchmarks. Particular departments or product managers or supervisors will be given very specific targets that they are expected to meet. For example, an auto dealership might have a target of 1,000 cars sold per month.

Coordination. Modern businesses are complex, and many different people and departments must coordinate their activities in order for the organization to succeed. If, for example, the company wants to increase its units sold by 10%, that will require actions by salespeople, the shipping department, warehouse personnel, production personnel, and the raw material purchasing department. It may require additional facilities, or more borrowing to finance the higher level of activity. A central purpose of the budgeting process is to ensure that all necessary activities are properly aligned so that objectives can be achieved.

Assessing risk. As part of the process of setting budgets, the company can evaluate the possible consequences of things not going according to plan. What would be the impact, for example, if the sales target is not met, or if raw material prices rise?

Controlling operations. The budget serves as an instruction to managers as to what they are supposed to do. Generally, managers try hard to meet or exceed the budget in profits, and to stay below the budgeted costs.

Budget figures also help top management monitor operations. Positive deviations from budget may indicate unexpected opportunities in the business. Negative deviations from budget indicate problem areas, which need attention.

Budgets work best for control when the budgets are prepared in a way that makes particular departments or people responsible for meeting particular targets. For example, it makes no sense to use budgets to try to induce salespeople to produce products more efficiently, since the salespeople have no control over the production process.

General Approaches to Budgeting

Budgeting is an incredibly complex task. It requires thinking about everything that is happening at all levels of the company, and considering what plans can be made to optimize the company's profitability. People use various ways of simplifying this problem.

One approach is the *incremental approach*. This focuses on what should change next year. It is simple, and assumes that past practices are reasonably good. One might simply assume that a 4% increase in sales volume would require a 4% increase in inputs, or perhaps a bit less if the company can become more efficient.

A second approach is to closely consider *inputs and outputs*. A manager using this approach would carefully consider the goal in terms of increased sales of particular products, and then would use his or her knowledge of the cost process to compute what types of inputs would be needed. In some cases, all the inputs might vary directly with output, but in other cases they would not.

A third approach is to force managers to justify all planned expenditures above a particular basic level that is understood by everyone to be necessary. This is called the "*minimum level approach.*" When the manager must justify all expenditures, this is called "*zero-based budgeting.*" Some companies have adopted this as an alternative to incremental budgeting, because they fear that over time, with incremental budgets, the company continues to fund operations that are no longer needed.

Who Should Participate in Budgeting?

Companies vary in the extent to which budgets are set in a "top-down" or "bottom-up" manner.

When companies use "top-down" or "imposed" budget, the top management sets the goals and prescribes the precise budget targets. The principal disadvantages of this method are:

- Top management may lack detail information about what is feasible, and that may lead to bad planning
- Top management may set unreachable targets, and this may affect the morale and job performance of lower level managers.

When companies use "participative" or "bottom-up" budgeting processes, managers at all levels are involved in the discussions and the process of setting budgets. The advantages of this method are that it allows the information known at all levels of management to be used, resulting in more realistic budgets, and that it obtains better acceptance of the budget targets by lower level managers. Principal disadvantages of participative budgeting include:

- It is very time-consuming
- There is an increased level of conflict between various departments with conflicting goals
- There is the risk that lower level managers will build "slack" into their budgets, deliberately setting targets that are easy to achieve. As a result, the company will fail to reach its full potential. Chapter 6 discusses in more detail the issue of the impact of budget targets on motivation and performance.

In Shastri and Stout's (2008) survey of 720 members of the IMA, 69% said that budgets in their organizations were developed in a negotiated process that blended the "top-down" and "bottom-up" styles.

Timing of Budget Preparation

The budget process can be quite time-consuming and intense. It typically needs to be finished before the start of the next year, but companies try to wait before starting the process until they have good information about current year operations.

Typically, the starting point in each division of the company is a sales budget. This should reflect not only past experiences, but everything the company can forecast about its own plans and new products, and the needs of its customers. It may make sense to budget the sales together with selling expenses and marketing campaigns, since these areas are so tightly related.

Once there is a forecast of sales, then the company is in a position to budget production. This involves budgeting the amounts of raw materials that will be needed, and when. It involves budgeting labor resources, and other services that are needed to make production happen efficiently. The company should also budget any desired changes to its equipment or other productive assets.

With sales and production budgeted, the company can now budget other selling and operating expenses.

At this point, the company can add together the operating budgets of all its decisions, and see what implications these budgets have for its cash planning and its investing and financing activities. Does it expect to have extra cash to invest? If so, it can budget interest income. Does it expect to need financing? Then it should budget interest expense.

With all items affecting pre-tax income budgeted, the company can budget its income taxes.

At this point, the company can budget future balance sheets, income statements, and cash flow statements.

This is an immense amount of work. What makes it even harder is that a typical budget goes through numerous revisions and drafts.

Adjusting the Plan/Flexible Budgets

Companies vary in how often they modify their budgets during the year. One procedure that is often used is a *"flexible budget,"* which makes the cost budget vary depending on the level of sales volume. The concept behind this is easy to see by an example. Let's say you were the manager of a pizzeria, and, based on the expected number of pizzas to be sold, you had a budget target of costs for ingredients (flour, cheese, etc.) equal to $100,000 for the month. Because your restaurant was making great pizza, it became more popular, and you sold triple the budgeted number of pizzas. It would be totally unfair for top management to blame you for using more than the original budgeted cost of $100,000 for ingredients. Instead, it would be reasonable for them to expect that, for triple the number of pizzas sold, you would use around triple the expected amount of ingredients.

A budget that is not "flexible" is called a "static" budget. The targets do not vary as volume changes.

Evaluating Performance

The IMA's (2014) list of uses of management accounting includes "Provide information to evaluate performance and learn from results". In this section, we discuss three tools that are used commonly in business: key performance indicators; standard costs; and variance analysis.

Key Performance Indicators

These are quantitative measures that companies use to judge whether they are succeeding at critical tasks. Key performance indicators vary by organization, and usually include both financial and nonfinancial measures. Examples of key indicators include:

- Sales and sales growth rates
- Profits
- Gross profit margin
- Customer turnover
- Number of employees
- Employee turnover
- Capacity utilization rates

- Production backlogs
- Customer complaints.

They are often reported on "executive dashboards," which may combine text, tables, and graphs. "Dashboards" present the same kind of summarized and select information to managers as car dashboards give to drivers.

Every organization will set different key performance indicators. The important point is that they should help management track and control the important facets of the business.

Standard Costs

Why Used?

Standard costs are what the management of the company says the costs should be. Companies use standard costs for several reasons:

- They set a standard for judging performance.
- They are useful in budgeting.
- They may serve as a benchmark for setting prices.
- They can be used to help simplify the accounting process.

People Involved in Setting Price and Quantity Standards

Typically, for a manufactured item, a company has both price and quantity standards for the inputs. Developing these standards requires careful consideration, and information from different people.

A company that makes chocolate bars, for example, expects a certain number of grams of cocoa beans and of sugar and of other ingredients to be used for each batch of 1,000 bars produced. The production staff's knowledge of the production process is used to set the quantity standard. The company's purchasing department has expectations about what sugar, cocoa beans and other ingredients should cost. This knowledge is used to set the price standard for the raw materials.

The company's engineers and production supervisors would have expectations about the amount of labor needed to produce 1,000 bars. The human resources department would have information about wages and fringe benefits. This knowledge is used to set labor efficiency and rate standards.

The production staff and engineering staff would have information about the amount of machine time, and of other "overhead" factors, that are needed in production. The purchasing department, or other departments, would have information about the costs of obtaining and servicing the machines.

Tight Versus Loose/Achievable Standards

Companies differ in their approach to setting standards.

"Tight" standards assume that production will occur under close to ideal conditions, and the company will operate at the optimal levels predicted by the engineering design of the processes. There will be little or no accidental spoilage of products, little or no inefficient labor, and little or no down time due to machine problems or supply interruptions.

"Achievable" standards assume normal conditions, and therefore assume that there will be certain normal levels of inefficiency. For example, there will always be some new workers, who are learning their jobs and not yet working at peak efficiency.

Each approach has its advantages and disadvantages. "Tight standards" indicate a goal to strive for, and they encourage peak effort. On the other hand, they may end up discouraging workers and managers. If managers and workers see the goals as unachievable, they may ignore the standards altogether. Achievable standards are less likely to discourage workers. On the other hand, if they are set too loosely, the result will be to reward managers and workers for a lower level of effort than they could have produced.

Variance Analysis

General

Variance analysis involves examining the difference between actual performance and budgeted (or standard) levels of performance. It is associated with "management by exception," where managers focus their attention on things that happened that were unexpected.

There are many different ways that companies do variance analysis. In this chapter, the focus is on variances in labor and raw materials due to unexpected differences in their prices and the quantities used. We also discuss variances in revenues. Overhead variances are not discussed in detail, but are set forth in Box 5.3.

Breaking Down Total Variance Into Parts

Assume that a printing department was expected to produce 10,000 books, at a cost of $10 per book, for a total cost of $100,000. It actually produced 10,000 books, and the total cost was $98,000. The total variance equals $100,000 – $98,000 = $2,000. Since costs were less than

---

Box 5.3 Conventional Variance Analysis Formulas

Raw materials:

- Materials price variance = actual quantity × (actual price – standard price)
- Materials usage variance = standard price × (actual quantity – standard quantity)

Direct labor:

- Direct labor rate variance = actual labor hours × (actual rate – standard rate)
- Direct labor efficiency variance = standard rate × (actual labor hours – standard labor hours)

Variable overhead:

- Variable overhead spending variance = actual labor hours × (actual price – standard price)
- Variable overhead efficiency variance = standard price × (actual labor hours – standard labor hours)

If overhead is allocated based on some other cost driver than labor hours, modify the formulas accordingly.
Fixed overhead:

- Fixed overhead spending variance = actual fixed overhead – budgeted fixed overhead
- Fixed overhead volume variance = budgeted fixed overhead – applied fixed overhead
  which = budgeted fixed overhead – (actual volume × standard overhead application rate)

expected, we will call this a favorable variance. If the costs were more than expected, it would be an unfavorable variance.

It may be that a manager says this is all the information that is needed, and the analysis can stop here. However, a manager may want more information about what was happening. How did the quantities of labor, paper, and machine time used compare with the budget? How did the price of paper, the wages of the workers, and the costs of machinery and electricity compare with the budget? To gain a better understanding of what was happening, accountants break down ("decompose") the total variance into pieces.

The following numeric example shows the basic ideas. Assume we are analyzing the raw materials cost. For the printing department, this would be the paper. Our first equation is:

Total variance = actual cost − standard cost

In symbols,

1 TV = TAC − TSC where
   TV = total variance, TAC = total actual cost, and TSC = total standard costs.
   We now want to break down this total variance. We need some new terms.
   Let AP = actual price per unit and SP = standard price per unit
   AQ = actual quantity and SQ = standard quantity.
   Then,
2 TV = AP × AQ − SC × SQ.
   We typically want to know how much of the total variance relates to problems with price, or with quantity. We therefore separate the total variance into two pieces.
   Usage variance measures the impact of using a different number of units than were planned, at the standard cost. It is also called an *efficiency variance*.
3 Usage variance = SP × (AQ − SQ)
   Price (or rate) variance deals with the impact of the different price on the actual number of units produced.
4 Price variance = AQ × (AP − SP)
   Adding the two variances together gives the total variance.
5 TV = quantity variance + price variance.[8]

Box 5.4 gives an example of computing variances in a simple case. In this situation, we are ignoring overhead costs. Also, in this case, the actual quantity produced equals the budgeted quantity.

Take a few minutes and read through the example in Box 5.4.

In this case, the company's costs were lower than expected. The budgeted costs for this level of production were $150,000, but the company only spent $141,180. The overall variance was favorable, of $8,820.

When the company looks more closely at its variances, it will see that there were three favorable variances. Less material needed to be used, the material cost was less than expected, and less labor was needed than the company had budgeted. There was one unfavorable variance. The average wages paid to workers were $0.25 per hour more than expected, causing an unfavorable labor rate variance of $700.

In real life, if the company considered these variances within normal levels of fluctuation, it might stop the analysis here. However, at this point we have not yet tried to understand three important things about these variances:

- What caused them?
- Will they continue?
- Will they affect other parts of the operations?

Box 5.4 Materials and Labor Variance Analysis Example—Budgeted Quantity Produced

Bremen Industries has the following standards for one of its products:

Direct materials–3 feet at $5 per foot = $15 per unit produced
Direct labor–(0.5 hours per unit, at $20 per hour)

Assume it is budgeted to produce 6,000 units. During the most recent period, it actually did produce 6,000 units. It used 17,600 of materials, at a unit cost of $4.80 per foot, and a total materials cost of $84,480. It used 2,800 hours of direct labor, at an average hourly wage of $20.25, and a total labor cost of $56,700. The actual total cost, including both materials and labor, was $141,180.

   Problem: Compute the total variance, the total materials and labor variances, and the quantity and rate variances for both materials and labor.

Step 1 Computing total budgeted cost of production

Budgeted materials = 6,000 units × 3 feet per unit × $5 per foot = 90,000
Budgeted direct labor = 6,000 units × 0.5 hours per unit × $20 =   60,000
The total budgeted cost = $150,000

We could also have found the total budgeted cost by multiplying 6,000 units times the budgeted total cost per unit of $25. However, we will also need the separate budget figures for materials and labor.

Step 2 Computing total budget variance

Total budget variance = total actual cost – total budget cost
So, total budget variance = 141,180 – 150,000 = $8,820 favorable.

Step 3 Computing materials variances

Total materials variance = total materials cost – total budgeted cost
                = 84,480 – 90,000 = 5,520 favorable
Materials usage (or quantity) variance = SP × (AQ – SQ)
So the materials usage variance = $5 × (17,600 – 18,000) = $2,000 favorable
Materials price (or rate) variance = AQ × (AP – SP)
                = 17,600 × ($4.80 – $5) = $3,520 favorable.
They add to the total materials variance we computed before = $5,520 favorable

Step 4 Computing labor variances

Total labor variance = total labor cost – total budgeted cost
                = 56,700 – 60,000 = 3,300 favorable
Labor efficiency (or quantity) variance = SP × (AQ – SQ)
So the labor efficiency variance= $20 × (2,800 – 3,000) = $4,000 favorable
Labor price (or rate) variance = AQ × (AP – SP)
                = 2,800 × ($20.25 – $20) = $700 unfavorable.
   They add to the total labor variance we computed before = $3,300 favorable

Step 5 Check the work—Total variance should = labor variance + materials variance
in this example. $5,520 F materials variance + $3,300 F labor variance = $8,820 F total variance.

For example, why were there price savings on raw materials? Was the company just fortunate, and, if so, will that good fortune continue? Or, were the price savings due to buying lower quality materials? Will this affect customer satisfaction, or warranty costs? Or, was the price savings due to buying unusually large quantities? If so, will the company have unexpected storage costs, or is it at risk of losses due to price changes?

As a second example, the average wages paid are higher than expectations. Why? If the company gave out higher raises than expected, this will affect profits for the rest of the year. If the management used a blend of more experienced workers than expected, where are the less experienced workers now? Should we expect difficulties on other products?

In this example, the total quantity produced was the same as the budgeted quantity produced. More complicated examples would include variances due to changes in total quantity produced. The problems at the end of this chapter include some examples.

The same variance analysis that we have used on costs is also applicable to revenues. For example, when a company reports an increase in total dollars of sales from the prior year, it could be because of increases in the number of units sold, the price per unit, or both. For sales, the quantity and pricing variances could be computed as:

Quantity variance = prior year price × (difference in number of units sold)
Pricing variance = actual units sold × (average price increase)

For example, assume a company sold 1,000 units last year, at an average price of $10, for total sales of $10,000. It decided to reduce its selling price by 5%, to $9.50, and this year it sold 1,300 units, for a total dollars sold = $12,350. So, total sales in dollar and units went up by $2,350. Variance analysis would indicate:

Sales volume variance = 10 × (1,300 − 1,000) = 3,000 favorable
Pricing variance = 1,300 × (9.50 − 10) = 650 unfavorable
Total variance = 3,000 favorable − 650 unfavorable = $2,350.

While the company reduced its revenues per unit by cutting prices, its total dollar sales increased by a greater amount.

As noted earlier in this section, different companies use different ways of looking at variances. The variances discussed in this section are conventional ones, typically discussed in textbooks. Other methods have been proposed. Box 5.5 gives an example of one of these other methods.

Closing Comment on Using Measurements to Control Performance

This section has discussed three different types of measures that managers can use to help monitor operations. They vary in complexity, from fairly simple counts for the outputs of a value stream to efficiency variances of particular inputs that can only be computed after establishing standard costs and tracking detailed data usage and price data. As noted earlier, proponents of "lean" manufacturing use simple, easily computed measures that can be posted on signs so that people on production teams can see how they are doing in real time. Textbooks, including this one, devote considerable space to complicated variance analyses. What measurements do companies actually use?

Matthew Hall (2010) suggested, based on his review of related research, that:

> Three factors influence the usefulness of accounting information for developing knowledge of the work environment: "closeness" to operational activities, time horizon, and diversity of operational factors under consideration. Managers who are close to operations use

---

Box 5.5 Another Way to Look at Variances

The method of looking at variances in profits taught in this chapter is similar to that normally taught in textbooks. To understand the variance in net profit, one would look at:

Revenue variance
Direct labor variance
Materials variance
Variable overhead variance
Fixed overhead variance
Selling expense variance.

Each of these variances in turn can be decomposed into quantity and rate variances.

An alternative way of looking at variances in profits, proposed by Banker, Datar, and Kaplan (1989), decomposes variances in profits into three parts:

- *Sales activity variance* (due to differences in output sold)
- *Productivity variance* (due to differences in efficiency in production)
- *Price recovery variance* (related to the company's ability to pass on, through output price increases, the increases in the rates it needs to pay for its labor and materials.)

  Sales activity variance = (actual units sold − budget units sold) × budget contribution margin where the contribution margin is a per unit margin.

Productivity variance = sum of the usage variances for materials, labor, variable overhead and fixed overhead. (This chapter has not discussed variances for fixed overhead.)

The usage variances follow the definitions we have used before, equal to the difference in quantity times the standard rate.

Price recovery variance = *the selling price variance − the sum of the various cost variances.*

---

observations of physical processes and informal reports from subordinates and peers as their primary means of developing knowledge of the work environment. . . . Managers with little contact with operations, however, devote considerable attention to accounting reports as they have limited opportunities for picking up information from actual observations of work being conducted. . . . For day-to-day concerns, developing knowledge is facilitated most efficiently by nonfinancial numbers as they relate more directly to operational activities, and, importantly, are usually available immediately without delay. . . . In contrast, events and transactions take too long to go through the formal accounting reporting system for the output to be actionable. For example, McKinnon and Bruns . . . found that financial numbers were not used in any of the 12 organisations they studied as a key daily production indicator: all managers used non-financial numbers. Furthermore, the aggregations required for the production of financial numbers can obscure details that are important for understanding day-to-day problems. For example, an injury to an employee becomes aggregated with other costs and is thus obscured from the manager's view. . . . As the time horizon lengthens, however, financial information becomes much more important in providing overall measures of effectiveness and in highlighting key problem areas that require further investigation. . . . When managers have only a few operational factors to consider, non-financial measures and direct observation of processes can provide adequate information. However, as managers consider a more diverse range of operational factors, financial information can operate to translate these factors into a single, financial dimension, which allows for an overall assessment of the net effect of all kinds of disturbances and actions that have taken place.

(p. 304)

Unresolved Issues and Areas for Further Research

This chapter has discussed a variety of tools used in managerial accounting to estimate costs, to aid in short-term decisions, and to budget and plan for the future. Issues that could benefit from additional research include:

1 Better ways of estimating the behavior of various types of costs, especially for organizations that produce multiple products
2 Understanding when managers consider nonfinancial costs in decision-making
3 Understanding which types of budget processes are the most appropriate in particular situations. Presumably, the speed of change in a company's industry, and its strategy, will affect the type of budget process that is appropriate
4 Understanding which types of performance measurement tools are most useful, given a company's environment and strategy
5 Understanding how increasing use of data analytics can affect performance management measures.

Key Terms

Accounting rate of return—A ratio used to evaluate capital investment projects, computed by dividing the average future increased profits by the initial investment. The formula is: Accounting rate of return = (average future increased profit) ÷ (initial outlay).

Attributability/attributable costs—The IMA uses these terms to describe a relation between physical inputs and outputs. See Table 5.1. The IMA (2014) says that "Attributable costs are the costs of an output that could be eliminated in time if that output were discontinued and resource consumption and/or provision were reduced accordingly." (p. 71)

Avoidability/avoidable costs—See Table 5.1. Inputs are avoidable if they can be eliminated as a result of a decision. "Relevant costs" is a similar concept.

Break-even point—The level of production at which the company's expenses exactly equal its revenues.

Capacity—The potential amount of work a resource can do. It is typically measured in the number of units per time period that can be processed.

Contribution margin—As used in cost–volume–profit analysis, "contribution margin" equals revenues from a product minus variable costs of producing and selling it. Contribution margin can be expressed per unit, or for the company as a whole.

Cost—According to the IMA (2014), "cost" is: "A monetary measure of consuming a resource or its output to achieve a specific managerial objective or making a resource or its output available and not using it." (p. 77)

Cost driver—A "cost driver" causes a cost to increase. Examples include: the total number of units being produced; the amount of human labor required to make a product; the amount of machine time required to manufacture it; or the amount of other special activities that are required, such as design changes.

Divisibility/divisible cost—See Table 5.1 for the IMA definitions. A cost is not divisible if it comes in "lumpy" amounts. An example is the cost of flying a passenger airplane. Certain inputs (like having a pilot) are "lumpy," and do not vary with the number of passengers on the plane.

Excess or idle capacity—Capacity that is not being used at present and is not currently planned to be used.

Fixed responsiveness relationship—This refers to an input that is used in fixed amounts, not varying with the output. It is a similar concept to "fixed cost," but the IMA uses fixed responsiveness to refer to physical inputs, and fixed costs for dollar amounts.

High–low method—This method of estimating the amount of variable costs and fixed costs in a company's cost structure uses the changes in volume (or other cost driver) and cost between the highest and lowest observations. See the example on p. 190 of this chapter.

Homogeneity—See Table 5.1 for the IMA definition. Homogeneous inputs behave the same way in a cost process. Two equally skilled workers might be homogeneous, while an experienced skilled worker is probably not homogeneous to a new and untrained worker.

Hurdle rate—The minimum internal rate of return that a company considers acceptable for potential new projects.

Incremental approach to budgeting—This budgeting method focuses on changes from existing levels in the new budget period, and does not typically re-examine the underlying cost structure or need for a program.

Interchangeability—See Table 5.1 for the IMA definition. Interchangeable inputs are not identical. However, changing one of these interchangeable inputs for another will not affect the amounts of other inputs needed in the production process. So, two machines might be different, but interchangeable, if they don't affect the amount of labor or raw materials needed.

Interdependence—See Table 5.1 for the IMA definition. Interdependence involves the relation of different managerial objectives to each other. If achieving one objective affects the inputs to another objective, then the two are interdependent.

Internal rate of return—This measure evaluates capital investment projects by computing the interest rate at which the present value of the expected future net inflows from the project exactly equals the initial outlays.

Key performance indicators—These are quantitative measures a company uses to track key aspects of its business. Some are financial, such as sales, while others may be nonfinancial measures, such as the number of customer complaints.

Minimum level approach to budgeting—This budgeting method requires managers to justify all budget requests over some minimum level. If that minimum level is zero, then it is called zero-based budgeting.

Mixed cost—This is a cost that is partly fixed and partly variable.

Net present value—See Appendix B for a full discussion of concepts related to the time value of money. The "present value" of expected future inflows from an investment is found by discounting each future payment. "Net present value" equals the sum of the present values of all future inflows, minus the initial outlay.

Opportunity costs—Opportunity costs represent the inflows the company is *not* receiving, but could have received if it had used a resource in some other way. For an example, the opportunity cost of getting an MBA as a full-time student is the salary you could have earned during that time period.

Outlay costs—Future cash payments or other uses of resources.

Participatory budgeting—This budgeting method encourages participation and input from all levels of management. It is sometimes called "bottom-up" budgeting. It is the opposite of "top-down" budgeting.

Payback period—This method of evaluating investments computes the number of years it will take for the future inflows to equal the initial investment amount. The time value of money is not considered.

Proportional responsiveness relationship—A relationship between inputs and outputs where the inputs vary at the same rate as the outputs.

Quantity (or usage) variance—This part of the total variance comes from differences in the amount of labor or machine time used (or items sold), not from differences in prices or cost rates. See the text for the related formulas.

Rate (or price) variance—This part of the total variance in results comes from changes in input prices or selling prices. See the text for related formulas.

Responsiveness—See Table 5.1 for the IMA definition. This term relates to the way quantities of an input change in response to changes in desired outputs.

Salvage value (also **residual value**)—This is the amount of money that can be received from selling an asset when a company is done using it.

Standard costs—These are the costs a company believes it should incur to produce a product, under efficient operating conditions. (Companies differ in what degree of efficiency they assume for computing standard costs.)

Step costs—Step costs remain the same for some level of production, as existing capacity (or non-divisible input) is used, and then they increase by a "step" as another non-divisible input is added.

Sunk costs—These are costs incurred in the past, due to past decisions, that cannot now be changed.

Top-down (imposed) budgeting—In this budgeting process, top management sets the budget, rather than inviting lower level managers to set the targets.

Traceability—See Table 5.1 for the IMA definition. Traceable inputs have a direct, verifiable causal relation to outputs.

Variability—See Table 5.1 for the IMA definition. Variability involves the way that input costs change in response to volume or to another cost driver. The IMA uses the concept of responsiveness to refer to changes in input quantities.

Variable costs—Costs that change proportionally with changes in volume of output, or of other cost drivers.

Variance—This is the difference between a budgeted or expected result, and the actual result.

Zero-based approach to budgeting—This budgeting method requires managers to justify why a program should exist at all, and why a budget over zero is appropriate.

Questions and Problems

Comprehension Questions

C1. (Basic terms) Define the terms "avoidability" and "divisibility." Is there a relation between these two concepts?

C2. (Basic terms) Define the terms "homogeneity" and "interchangeability." Are these related concepts?

C3. (Basic terms) Define the terms "variability" and "responsiveness." Are these related terms?

C4. (Basic terms) The IMA uses the terms "fixed responsiveness" and "proportional responsiveness."

    A. Define these terms.

    B. Give an example of inputs to a process that are likely to show fixed responsiveness.

    C. Give an example of inputs to a process that are likely to show proportional responsiveness.

C5. (Basic terms) What are "mixed costs"? Are they the same as "step costs"? Explain your answer.

C6. (Cost estimation) Name and briefly describe some of the methods described in the chapter that companies use to understand the patterns of their costs.

C7. (Cost estimation) Explain how the high–low method works.

C8. (Cost–volume–profit analysis) In the cost-volume–profit model:

    a.   What is meant by contribution margin per unit?
    b.   What is meant by break-even point?
    c.   What is the formula for the number of units to be produced at the break-even point?

C9. (Cost–volume–profit analysis.) What are some limitations to the usefulness of cost–volume–profit analysis? (This relates to the underlying assumptions of this method.)

C10. (Short-term operating decisions) What are sunk costs? Are they relevant to decisions about future actions? Why, or why not?

C11. (Short-term operating decisions) What costs are relevant to short-term decision-making?

C12. (Short-term operating decisions) Explain what is meant by:

    A.   Outlay costs
    B.   Opportunity costs
    C.   Sunk costs
    D.   Relevant costs.

C13. (Capital budgeting decisions) The chapter discussed four measures used to evaluate proposed investments. Briefly describe how each one works:

    A.   Payback period
    B.   Accounting rate of return
    C.   Internal rate of return
    D.   Net present value

C14. (Capital budgeting decisions) The chapter discussed four measures used to evaluate proposed investments. For each of the following, list one advantage and one disadvantage of the method:

    A.   Payback period
    B.   Accounting rate of return
    C.   Internal rate of return
    D.   Net present value

C15. (Budgeting) List and briefly explain three reasons that companies prepare budgets.

C16. (Budgeting) What is the difference between "imposed" budgets and "participative" budgets?

C17. (Budgeting) What is meant by a "flexible" budget? Why is it useful?

C18. (Budgeting) Explain what is meant by an incremental budget, and how it differs from a zero-based budget.

C19. (Standard costs) What is a standard cost? Why do companies use them?

C20. (Standard costs) What are the advantages of setting "tight" standards, rather than "achievable" standards? What are the disadvantages?

C21. (Key performance indicators) What is a key performance indicator? Does it have to be a financial measure? Explain.

C22. (Variances) Define the terms "usage" and "rate" variances. Give the formulas used to compute these variances for materials.

Application Questions

A1. (Concepts–matching question) For each of the examples A–F, indicate which of the terms apply. (Some terms may apply more than once—others might not apply at all.) The terms are:

Avoidability
Traceability of costs
Divisibility of costs
Homogeneity
Interchangeability
Interdependency

A. John Lee is trying to model the costs of producing a product. The factory has two different models of cutting machines that it uses. He needs to know if he can consider them the same for purposes of computing the labor needed to operate them.

B. The company pays its workers differently, depending on how long they have been employed. However, skill levels do not vary much. Lee wants to know if he can consider the different workers the same for purpose of the model, and just use an average wage cost.

C. The product has to be made in a factory that is kept at a constant temperature. However, John Lee is not sure how he can associate the heating and cooling costs with a particular unit of product.

D. Lee knows that each item produced requires 40 grams of a particular raw material.

E. If the product were discontinued, the company would stop incurring the cost of maintaining a special facility to inspect the incoming raw materials. No other product needs that particular facility.

F. Expanding production of this product to meet new increases in demand will pull good workers off other products, which will increase the costs of the other products.

A2. (Concepts–cost types) For each of the following examples, indicate which of these terms apply. (Some terms may apply more than once—others might not apply at all.) The terms are:

Fixed responsiveness of input
Proportional responsiveness of input
Variable cost
Fixed cost
Step cost
Mixed cost

A for-profit school provides classes of instruction. This requires it to have instructors, classrooms, and textbooks. It rents the classrooms. It also has a principal overseeing the school. Up to 25 students can be taught in a single room, but one instructor. Each student needs their own textbook. Which term applies to:

A. The number of textbooks?
B. The cost of the textbooks?
C. The number of teachers?
D. The cost of the teachers?
E. The number of principals?
F. The cost of the principal?
G. The overall cost of the school?

A3. (Cost concepts) Match the terms below to the IMA's (2014) definitions:

Avoidability
Capacity
Divisibility
Homogeneity
Interchangeability
Responsiveness
Traceability

A. "A characteristic of an input that allows for the input (and its costs) to be eliminated as a result of a decision." (p. 60)
B. "A characteristic of an input unit that permits it to be identified in its entirety with a specific managerial objective on the basis of verifiable transaction records." (p. 47)
C. "An attribute of any two or more resources or . . . outputs that can be substituted . . . without affecting the costs of the other resources that are required to carry out the activities to which the interchangeable resources are devoted." (p. 63)
D. "The correlation between a particular managerial objective's output quantity and the input quantities required to produce that output." (p. 42)
E. "A characteristic of one or more resources or inputs of similar technology or skill that allow for their costs to be governed by the same set of determinants." (p. 54)
F. "The potential for a resource to do work." (p. 48)

A4. (Cost behavior) Assume that a dairy sells milk by the gallon. For each gallon of milk, it has the following costs:

Container $ 0.40
Milk $2.00

Within the relevant range of activity, it has other costs that are fixed at $2 million per month.

A. Compute the total costs required for production of 500,000 gallons.
B. Compute the total costs required for production of 10,000,000 gallons.
C. Is this a fixed cost, variable cost, or mixed cost situation?
D. Compute the cost per gallon produced at the two levels of production. What is the reason for the difference in the cost per gallon?

A5. (Cost estimation—high–low method) You have been given the data on nine observations of volume and cost below.

Volume	Cost ($)
20	204
30	242.4
40	287.2
70	343.6
100	384.6
131	480.4
230	805.4
38	253.2
540	1850

Using the high–low method:

A. Identify the high and low observations
B. Compute the difference in volume between the high and low observations
C. Compute the difference in cost between the two observations
D. Compute the ratio of change in cost to change in volume
E. Compute the amount of variable cost at the high level of activity
F. Compute the fixed cost at the high level of activity
G. State the equation for the relation of costs to level of activity.

A6. (Cost estimation—high–low method.) You have been given the data on nine observations of volume and cost below. The data is the same as that in the previous problem except for one observation.

Volume	Cost ($)
20	204
30	242.4
40	287.2
70	343.6
100	384.6
131	480.4
230	805.4
38	253.2
540	3,096.2

Using the high–low method:

A. Identify the high and low observations
B. Compute the difference in volume between the high and low observations
C. Compute the difference in cost between the two observations
D. Compute the ratio of change in cost to change in volume
E. Compute the amount of variable cost at the high level of activity
F. Compute the fixed cost at the high level of activity
G. State the equation for the relation of costs to level of activity.

A7. (Cost estimation—high–low method) The data below, in millions of dollars, were taken from the 2013 Form 10-K of Zipcar. Zipcar is a very short-term car rental company, specializing in providing cars for periods that can be as short as an hour.

	2012	2013
Revenue	242	279
Operating expenses	244	273
Operating profits	–2	6

A. Compute the change in 2013 in:

    a. Revenues
    b. Operating expenses.

B. Compute the ratio of the change in operating expenses in 2013 to the change in revenues.
C. Using your results from part B, estimate the variable costs in the 2013 operating expenses.
D. Using your results from part C, estimate the fixed costs in the 2013 operating expenses.

    E. Compute the operating leverage effect for this company in 2013.

    F. This is a relatively new company. If its sales increase substantially in 2014, would you expect profits to increase proportionally to sales, or faster than sales? Explain.

    G. If sales grow substantially in 2014, would you expect operating leverage to stay the same, or go down? Explain your answer.

A8. (Cost estimation—scatter plot) Use the data in application question A5, and:

    A. Draw a scatter plot, using Excel

    B. Does the pattern seem generally linear?

    C. Do any of the observations seem out of line, or unusual?

    D. Does the pattern seem to indicate any fixed costs, at a volume of zero?

A9. (Cost estimation—scatter plot) use the data in application question A6, and

    A. Draw a scatter plot, using Excel.

    B. Does the pattern seem generally linear?

    C. Do any of the observations seem out of line, or unusual?

    D. Does the pattern seem to indicate any fixed costs, at a volume of zero?

A10. (Cost estimation—regression) Use a spreadsheet program, or special purpose statistical software, to do this problem. Use the data in application question A5, and:

    A. Compute the regression line that best fits the data

    B. What is the R^2 statistic for your regression line? Is this indicative of a good fit to the data?

    C. The data were actually generated using an equation that total cost = 200 of fixed costs plus variable costs of $3 per level of input, plus or minus a random variation. Do you feel the regression line gives a reasonable estimate of this relation? Explain.

A11. (Cost estimation—regression) Use a spreadsheet program, or special purpose statistical software to do this problem. Use the data in application question A6, and:

    A. First, use only the first eight observations. Compute the regression line that best fits the data. What is your estimate of:

        a. Fixed costs?

        b. Variable costs?

    B. What is the R^2 statistic for your regression line. Is this indicative of a good fit to the data?

    C. Now, use all nine observations. Compute the regression line that best fits the data. What is your estimate of:

        a. Fixed costs?

        b. Variable costs?

    D. Does your estimate of fixed costs seem economically realistic?

    E. The data for the first eight observations were actually generated using an equation that total cost = 200 of fixed costs plus variable costs of $3 per level of input, plus or minus a random variation. Do you feel the regression line for the first eight observations (part a) gives a reasonable estimate of this relation? Explain.

    F. The ninth observation was created to have a large upward cost variance. Comment on how this affected the regression line and your estimates of fixed and variable costs.

    G. What steps might you take to avoid distorted results from regression analyses?

A12. (Cost–volume–profit analysis) The Joffre Company has the following cost function for one of its products:

Fixed costs = $500,000
Variable cost per unit = $36
Selling price per unit = $41

A. Compute the operating profit or loss at the following levels of output:

    a.   0 units
    b.   50,000 units
    c.   150,000 units
    d.   1,000,000 units.

B. Compute the volume at the break-even point.
C. Compute the volume needed to achieve an operating profit = $2,000,000.
D. Compute the operating leverage effect at a volume of 1,000,000 units.

A13. (Cost–volume–profit—graphs) Using data in the previous problem for the Joffre Company, use Excel or another spreadsheet program, graph for each 100,000 level of production from zero to 600,000 units:

A. Total costs
B. Operating profits or losses

A14. (Cost–volume–profit) The Kitchener Company has the following cost function for one of its products:

Fixed costs = $2,700,000
Variable cost per unit = $91
Selling price per unit = $100

A. Compute the operating profit or loss at the following levels of output:

    a.   0 units
    b.   150,000 units
    c.   250,000 units
    d.   400,000 units
    e.   1,000,000 units.

B. Compute the volume at the break-even point.
C. Compute the volume needed to achieve an operating profit = $9,000,000.
D. Compute the operating leverage effect at a volume of 400,000 units.

A15. (Cost–volume–profit—graphs) Using data in the previous problem for the Kitchener Company, use Excel or another spreadsheet program to graph for each 100,000 level of production from zero to 500,000 units:

A. Total costs
B. Operating profits or losses

A16. (Cost–volume–profit) Assume that you are an analyst who is studying the Tirpitz Shipping Company. The company has a fleet of 40 large ships. Right now, about 40% of its operating costs are fixed costs related to depreciation and maintenance of the ships, and the other

60% vary with the amount of cargo it carries. It has idle capacity allowing it to carry up to 20% more cargo than it is now carrying. Using the ideas of cost-volume-profit analysis, explain how you expect Tirpitz's operating profits to respond to:

A.   A 10% increase in cargo, due to improving world economic conditions.
B.   A 10% decrease in cargo, due to a worldwide economic slowdown.

If the company said that a 5% decrease in the volume of the cargo carried would only reduce profits by 3%, would you believe them? Why, or why not?

A17. (Cost–volume–profit) The Ludendorf Company is an information company, which has begun operations this year. It has purchased the facilities it needs, and hired a great staff of people at fixed annual salaries. This year, it reported fixed costs of $100 million, sales of $30 million, and variable costs of $2 million. The operating loss was $68 million on sales of $30 million. The company has come to your bank for a loan, and you believe if they get the loan they can increase sales to $600 million. Should your bank encourage the Ludendorf to expand this money-losing business, or should you advise them to stop now and cut their losses? Explain your answer.

A18. (Short-term decisions—understanding terms) The Petain Company produces and sells 40,000 units each month. It has the capacity to produce 50,000 units. A large retailer has asked Petain if the company would make a special, one-time order of 14,000 units. If Petain accepts the order:

- There will be higher variable manufacturing costs
- It will have to increase its administrative and selling facilities, so the selling fixed costs will increase
- Administrative fixed costs will not change
- It will be unable to handle all its orders, so it will have to reduce its sales to regular customers by 4,000 units.

Note which of the terms below are applicable to the items A to I. More than one term may be applicable.

Avoidable revenues
Non-avoidable revenues
Non-avoidable variable costs
Non-avoidable fixed outlay cost
Sunk cost
Avoidable fixed outlay cost
Avoidable variable outlay cost
Opportunity cost

A.   Lost contribution margins from the 4,000 units it will not sell to regular customers.
B.   Revenues from the 14,000 special order.
C.   Variable costs of the 14,000 unit special order.
D.   Increase in selling fixed costs due to the order.
E.   Increase in administrative costs due to new government regulations enacted last year.
F.   Cost of the equipment, purchased in prior year, that is used to produce the special order.
G.   Salary paid to factory manager on an annual basis.
H.   Variable costs of making other kinds of products in the same factory.
I.   Increase in fixed production costs due to the need to replace the roof of the factory (now 70 years old).

A19. (Short-term decisions—special order—with excess capacity) Assume that Jellico Inc. normally sells its products for $12 each. Assume that a customer asks for a special order of 10,000 units at a price of $70,000, or $7 per unit. Jellico has excess capacity.

Currently, Jellico is producing 100,000 units.

Variable manufacturing costs	$640,000
Variable marketing and administrative costs	$20,000
Fixed manufacturing expenses	$100,000
Fixed marketing and administrative costs	$80,000

Given these facts:

A. Find the cost per unit before accepting the special order, considering all costs.
B. Compute the operating profits at the current level of production, with a selling price of $12 each.
C. Find the total costs that Jellico would have if it accepted the special order, and the cost per the new volume of 110,000 units.
D. Find the operating profit if Jellico accepts the special order.
E. Should Jellico accept the special order at a $7 per unit price? Explain.

A20. (Short term decisions—special order—limited excess capacity) Assume that Haig Inc. normally sells its products for $23 each. A customer asks for a special order of 5,000 units at a price of $80,000, or $16 per unit. Haig has excess capacity to make 4,000 units, and this means that if it accepts this order, it will not be able to sell 1,000 units to regular customers at regular prices.

Currently, Haig is producing 50,000 units.

Variable manufacturing costs	$650,000
Variable marketing and administrative costs	$200,000
Fixed manufacturing expenses	$100,000
Fixed marketing and administrative costs	$50,000

Given these facts:

A. Find the cost per unit before accepting the special order, considering all costs.
B. Compute the operating profits at the current level of production, with a selling price of $23 each.
C. Find the total costs that Haig would have if it accepted the special order, and the cost per the new volume of 55,000 units.
D. Find the operating profit if Haig accepts the special order.
E. Should Haig accept the special order at the $16 per unit price? Explain.

A21. (Short-term decisions—make or buy) Samsonov Corp. is trying to decide whether to make packaging for its products itself, or whether to outsource the materials to the Moltke Corp. Its current cost to produce 250,000 packages is:

Direct materials	$50,000
Direct labor	$30,000
Variable manufacturing overhead	$24,000
Fixed manufacturing overhead	$46,000
Total manufacturing cost	$150,000
Cost per package	$0.60

Moltke Corporation offers to sell packages to Samsonov for $0.50 each.

A. Based only on financial considerations, and assuming the fixed costs are not avoidable, should Samsonov buy from Moltke? Why, or why not?

B. Assume that Samsonov could avoid $30,000 of the fixed costs if it stopped producing its own packages. Based only on financial considerations, should Samsonov buy from Moltke? Why, or why not?

A22. (Short-term decisions—drop product line?) The Foch Corp. has two product lines: Somme and Verdun. Data for these two product lines is shown below:

	Total	Somme	Verdun
Sales revenue	$1,300,000	$1,200,000	$100,000
Variable expenses	$880,000	$790,000	$90,000
Fixed expenses, allocated based on revenue	$390,000	$360,000	$30,000
Operating income or loss	$30,000	$50,000	($20,000)

A. Assuming that all of the fixed costs allocated to Verdun are avoidable if the product line is dropped, should Foch drop this line? Explain.

B. If the fixed costs allocated to Verdun are *not* avoidable, should Foch drop this product line? Explain.

A23. (Capital budgeting—payback method) Allenby Corp. has $10 million to invest. Listed below are the expected future cash inflows to be received for four alternative investments, in millions of dollars.

	Investment A	Investment B	Investment C	Investment D
Year 1	7	1	0	7
Year 2	1	2	0	3
Year 3	2	7	3	0
Year 4	2	8	7	0
Year 5	2	9	10	0

A. Compare investments A and B.

    a. Compute the payback periods for Investments A and B.
    b. Which one would you pick, based only on payback period?
    c. Do you think one is a better investment?

B. Compare investments C and D.

    a. Compute the payback periods
    b. Which one would you pick, based on the payback periods?
    c. Do you think this is the better investment? Why, or why not?

A24. (Capital budgeting—accounting rate of return) The Liman Corp. has a choice among the following investments. Each requires an initial outlay of $10 million. Figures are shown in millions of dollars.

	Investment A	Investment B
Year 1	5	1
Year 2	5	3
Year 3	3	5
Year 4	3	7

A. Compute the accounting rate of return for both projects.
B. Using only the accounting rate of return, which project would you pick? Why?

A25. (Capital budgeting—net present value) Use the same data as question A23.

    A. Compute the net present value at an interest rate of 5% for the four alternative projects.
    B. Which one would you choose?
    C. Compute the net present value of the projects at an interest rate of 10%.
    D. Does your choice of which project is best change?

A26. (Capital budgeting—net present value) Use the same data as question A24. Compute the net present value of both projects at a discount rate of 8%, and decide which one you prefer.

A27. (Capital budgeting—NPV and IRR) The Pershing Company is considering an investment. The investment will cost $900,353. The projected net cash flows are

Year 1	$260,000
Year 2	$250,000
Year 3	$225,000
Year 4	$210,000
Year 5	$208,000
Year 6	$160,000

There will be no cash flows after Year 6.

    A. Compute the NPV of the project at a discount rate of 12%.
    B. Compute the IRR of the project.
    C. Assume the company has a "hurdle rate" of 11%. Should it do this project?

A28. (Capital budgeting—NPV and IRR) The Falkenhayn Company is considering an investment. The investment will cost $9,805. The projected net cash flows are

Year 1	$1,000
Year 2	$1,500
Year 3	$1,300
Year 4	$8,000
Year 5	$1,000

There will be no cash flows after Year 5.

    A. Compute the NPV of the project at a discount rate of 7%.
    B. Compute the IRR of the project.
    C. Assume the company has a "hurdle rate" of 9%. Should it do this project?

A29. (Capital budgeting—NPV) The Hindenberg Corp. is comparing the following two investment projects. Each requires an initial outlay of $8,000. The projected inflows are shown below.

Year	Project A	Project B
1	$8,000	$1,000
2	$1,500	$1,500
3	$1,300	$1,300
4	$1,000	$1,859
5	$1,055	$10,000

Inflows after Year 5 are zero.

    A. Compute the NPV of both projects at an interest rate of 9%.
    B. Which project would you prefer? Why?

A30. (Capital budgeting—NPV) The Fisher Corp. is comparing two investment projects. Information for the two projects is shown below. The company uses 8% as a discount rate. The initial outlays and estimated future cash inflows for the two projects are shown below.

	Project A	Project B
Initial outlay	$9,503,715	$90,005,298
Inflows:		
Year 1	$3,000,000	$30,000,000
Year 2	$3,000,000	$30,100,000
Year 3	$2,000,000	$20,100,000
Year 4	$3,000,000	$28,000,000
Year 5	$2,000,000	$1,300,000

A. At an 8% discount rate, compute the NPV of the two projects.
B. Which project would you prefer? Why?
C. If the discount rate were 9%, which project would you prefer? Why?
D. If the discount rate were 7%, which project would you prefer? Why?

A31. (Budgeting) Listed below are several terms related to budgeting.

Top-down budgets
Participatory budgets
Incremental budgets
Zero-based budgets
Flexible budget
Static budget

For each of the situations below, identify which budgeting term is involved:

A. In our company, we don't trust the department managers to set their own budgets. The CEO sets the budget targets for all departments.
B. When the new governor took office, he said he thought that over time the state government had become too big, and was filled with unnecessary programs. He made every department justify every penny of its spending, and each department had to explain what its role was and why it was needed.
C. In our company, we realize that cost budgets have to change when there is a change in customer demand.
D. In our company, we see it as too time-consuming to write up reasons every year for every project. Things just don't change that much, so we only ask departments to explain why this year's budget request is different from last year's.
E. Our CEO is a financial guy, and doesn't really know the nuts and bolts of the business. He asks the people who are close to production, and close to the customers, to take the first crack at the budget.

A32. (Budgeting—using Excel) The Ren Company had the following income statement for 2013:

Gross sales	800,000
Less: estimated uncollectible sales	(8,000) (1%)
Net sales	792,000
Cost of goods sold	(400,000)
Gross profit	392,000
Cash operating expenses	60,000

Depreciation	<u>75,000</u>
Income before taxes	257,000
Taxes	<u>90,000</u> (35%)
Net income	<u>$167,000</u>

Using a spreadsheet, make a budgeted income statement for 2014 using the following assumptions:

- Sales increase by 6%.
- The uncollectible sales are 1.1% of sales.
- Cost of goods sold in 2013 contained $40,000 of fixed costs that are not expected to change. The variable costs increase at the same 6% rate as sales.
- Cash operating expenses are 7.5% of gross sales.
- Depreciation increase to $78,000 due to capital additions.
- The tax rate for 2014 goes up to 36% of pre-tax income.

A33. (Budgeting—usefulness of Excel) Use the same spreadsheet you have just used to answer the previous problem. In this problem your boss asks you to change various assumptions, one at a time. In each case, your starting point is the spreadsheet you created for the previous problem. What will the budgeted net income for 2014 be if you make only the change listed in each of the following assumptions?

A. Uncollectible sales are 1.5% instead of 1.1%.
B. Cash operating expenses are 8% of gross sales.
C. Taxes decrease to 33%.
D. The cost of goods sold for 2013 contained $100,000 of fixed costs, not $40,000. The variable costs increase at the same 6% rate as sales.
E. While sales increase by 6%, and fixed costs in cost of goods sold are $40,000, efficiency savings in the variable cost of goods sold mean that these costs only increase by 3% in 2014.

A34. (Variances—static budgets) The Brusilov Company makes chairs. The budget and actual results for the month are shown below:

	Budget	Actual
Sales	1000 at $500 = <u>500,000</u>	980 at $490 = <u>480,200</u>
Variable costs		
Materials	3,000 kilos at $18 = $54,000	3,100 kilos at 17.80 = $55,180
Labor	10,000 hours at $9.10 = $91,000	9,700 at 9.30 = $90,210
Variable overhead, allocated based on kilos	3,000 at $10.00 $30,000	3,100 at $12.80 = $39,680
Fixed manufacturing overhead	<u>$60,000</u>	<u>$62,000</u>
Total cost of goods sold	<u>$235,000</u>	<u>$247,070</u>
Gross profit	<u>$265,000</u>	<u>$233,130</u>

A. Compute the following sales variances:
    a. Total sales variance
    b. Variance due to price changes
    c. Variance due to volume

    B.   Compute the following materials variances:

        a.   Total materials variance
        b.   Materials usage variance
        c.   Materials price variance

    C.   Compute the following labor variances:

        a.   Total labor variance
        b.   Labor efficiency variance
        c.   Labor rate variance

    D.   Compute the following overhead variances:

        a.   Total variable overhead variance
        b.   Variable overhead quantity variance
        c.   Variable overhead rate variance
        d.   Total fixed overhead variance

A35. (Variances—flexible budget) Use the facts for the Brusilov Company from the previous problem. Assume the company uses a flexible budget.

    A.   Compute the flexible budget target for sales.
    B.   Compute the sales variance from the flexible budget target (adjusted for the actual volume of sales).
    C.   Compute the materials usage and price variances from the flexible budget.
    D.   Compute the labor efficiency and rate variances from the flexible budget.
    E.   Compute the variable overhead quantity and rate variances from the flexible budget.

A36. (Variances—materials) The Scheer Corporation produces ship models. The company uses a standard cost system and has set the following standards for materials and labor.

Wood	2 pieces per unit, at $1 each	$2
Direct labor	2 hours per unit, at $14 per hour	$28
Total direct costs		$30

During this period, Scheer produced 10,000 ship models. The actual wood purchased and used was 22,000 pieces, at $0.90 per piece. There were no starting or ending inventories of wood. The actual direct labor used was 18,500 hours at $15 per hour.

    A.   Compute the standard cost of wood which should be incurred to produce 10,000 ship models.
    B.   Compute the actual total cost of the wood.
    C.   For the wood, compute:

        a.   The total variance
        b.   The materials usage variance
        c.   The materials rate variance.

A37. (Variances—labor) Use the same facts as the previous problem. For the Scheer Company:

    A.   Compute the standard cost of labor that should be incurred to produce 10,000 ship models.
    B.   Compute the actual total cost of direct labor.
    C.   For direct labor, compute:

        a.   Total labor variance
        b.   The labor quantity (efficiency) variance
        c.   The labor rate variance.

A38. (Variances—materials) The Conrad Company makes one product. The standard amount of material per unit is set at 2 kilograms, with a standard price per kilogram of €3. During the month, 6,000 units were produced. 11,800 kilograms of material were used, at an average cost per kilogram of €3.20.

    A. Compute the total standard cost of producing 6,000 units.
    B. Compute the actual cost of production.
    C. Compute the total materials variance.
    D. Compute the materials usage variance.
    E. Compute the materials price variance.

A39. (Variances—fixed overhead costs per unit) The French Corp. has budgeted fixed overhead costs for the year of $1,200,000. It budgeted that it would produce 200,000 units.

    A. What is the budgeted fixed cost per unit?
    B. Assume that it actually spends $1,200,000 on fixed costs, and produces 300,000 units because the sales force has found more customers than expected.

        a. What is the fixed cost per unit?
        b. Is the variance in fixed costs per unit favorable, or unfavorable?
        c. Who deserves the credit for the favorable variance in fixed costs per unit, the production staff or the sales staff?

    C. Assume that the production staff finds a way to reduce its machinery, and reduces the spending to fixed costs to $800,000. The amount of production is 200,000 units.

        a. What is the fixed cost per unit?
        b. Is the variance in fixed costs per unit favorable, or unfavorable?
        c. Who deserves the credit for the favorable variance in fixed costs per unit, the production staff or the sales staff?

A40. (Variances in revenues) The French Company had budgeted to sell 2 million units at $6 each. Actual sales were 2.1 million units at $6.30 each. Compute:

    A. The total variance in sales.
    B. The part of the variance due to a difference in units sold.
    C. The part of the variance due to a difference in average selling price.

Discussion Questions

  D1. (Short-term decisions—relevant costs) Accounting textbooks generally say that the decision to accept a special order should be based on the "relevant" or avoidable costs of filling the order, not the normally computed full costs of production. The full costs include some fixed costs per unit. Studies of managers typically show that they are very reluctant to price anything at a level below the full costs. To put it another way, the evidence is that most managers do not follow the textbook advice to ignore fixed costs in short-term pricing decisions. Can you suggest reasons why managers do not follow the textbook advice?

  D2. (Sunk costs—psychology) Theoretically, sunk costs should be irrelevant to short-term decision-making, since these are costs that do not vary between alternatives. However, some psychological studies show that people are very reluctant to give up on projects once costs have been incurred. Can you suggest reasons why managers might not want to ignore sunk costs?

  D3. (Outsourcing—nonfinancial decisions) The discussion in this chapter on whether to discontinue a product has focused on the avoidable financial costs. Assume that a company located in a small city in Ohio is deciding whether to buy the major components of its product from a supplier in Asia, rather than making the parts in its own factory in Ohio. If it buys the parts from Asia, it can close a factory employing 300 people.

The company has already gone through an analysis of the avoidable costs that would be saved by buying the parts from Asia, and it knows the amounts it would have to pay to the new Asian supplier.

A. What might be some effects of closing the plant and outsourcing production on the company that are not captured in a standard financial analysis?
B. What might be effects on the local city?
C. Should any effects on the local city be considered relevant to the company's decision?

D4. (Make or buy—interaction with financial ratios) Assume a company is trying to decide whether to manufacture products itself, or to outsource the production to foreign factories. Assume that, at anticipated levels of production, the cost of goods sold will be better by 2% of sales than if it makes the products itself. If it makes the products itself, the company needs more fixed assets, and will have more debt. The company expects that even after the interest cost, the net income will be slightly better as a percentage of sales if it manufactures the product itself.

Comment on how the decision to outsource the production, and reduce fixed assets and related debt, would affect the numerators and denominators of the following ratios:

A. Return on assets
B. Return on equity
C. Capital structure leverage ratio
D. Debt to equity ratio
E. Profit margin
F. Asset turnover
G. Operating leverage effect

D5. (Investigating variances) The Hamilton Corp. uses a standard cost system, and computes variances using the methods described in this chapter. Consider what impact each of the following actions might have on the company's labor and materials usage and rate variances, and on other company costs:

A. The purchasing department buys unusually cheap raw materials. The material is inexpensive because it is poor quality, and requires extra labor to process.
B. The purchasing department buys a very large quantity of material, of the standard level of quality, and gets a quantity discount. The large shipment will satisfy the needs of production for nine months. Normally the company keeps two weeks of inventory on hand.
C. The company decides to reduce its average payroll costs by firing all the older, more highly skilled workers. They are replaced by slower, but lower paid, employees.
D. The production supervisor orders employees not to take breaks, and to report working less time than they actually do.

D6. (Impacts of variances) You are investigating variances at the Hamilton Corp. You note that there is a favorable labor usage variance, which is good, since there had been unfavorable variances for the last year. However, you also notice the number of defective products produced has gone up. Could there be a relation between these two changes? Explain.

D7. (Performance evaluation.) Charities are often evaluated based on certain efficiency ratios. One ratio is the percentage of donated funds raised that is used for program expenses. Assume that a company is sponsoring a complicated, three-day charity walk to raise money for breast cancer. Each person who walks promises to raise $3,000 in donations. The cost structure of the event is as follows:

Not varying by number of walkers

Costs to advertise the event and attract walkers	$1,400,000
Costs to arrange the route, pay legal costs, and set up campsites	$500,000
Administrative fees, insurance, etc.	$200,000

Costs varying per walker

Food	$30 per walker
Other items (t-shirts, etc.)	$20 per walker

Any money that is not spent on these expenses is used for cancer research programs.

A. If the walk attracts 1,000 people who each raise $3,000 in donations:

    a.   Compute the total walk-related expenses

    b.   Compute the total money remaining to be used for cancer research programs

    c.   Compute the amount in "b" divided by the dollars raised by the walkers.

B. Repeat the steps in the previous question, assuming that 3,000 people walk, and raise $3,000 each in donations.

C. Comment on what is causing the difference in the ratio of program spending to dollars raised.

Notes

1   The procedure minimizes the sum of the squared deviations from the data and the line that is the "best fit."

2   See Kanodia, Bushman and Dickhaut (1989).

3   Harris and Raviv (1996) indicate that information-sharing problems in decentralized firms can adversely affect capital budgeting decisions.

4   The first published advice to compare options using discounted cash flow came in *Tables of Interest*, a book by Simon Stevan, a Dutch scientist and accountant, published in 1583. See Parker (1968).

5   Some companies also used other methods not discussed in this chapter. "Popular supplemental methods include sensitivity analysis, scenario analysis, inflation adjusted cash flows, economic value added, and incremental IRR." (Ryan and Ryan 2002, p. 362)

6   Ryan and Ryan's (2002) survey of 205 CFOs of Fortune 1000 firms in 2000 found that 83% considered their firm's weighted average cost of capital to be the most appropriate discount rate.

7   Shastri and Stout's (2008) survey of 720 IMA members working in industry in 2007 found that between 73% and 94% considered budgets to be either "somewhat useful" or "very useful" for each of the following: strategic planning, operational planning, operational control, communication, teamwork across subunits (the lowest score), motivation, and determining incentive awards.

8   You can see this works, because $TV = SP \times (AQ - SQ) + AQ \times (AP - SP)$, so $TV = SP \times AQ - SP \times SQ + AQ \times AP - AQ \times SP$. This simplifies to $AQ \times AP - SQ \times SP$ which is the total variance.

References

American Accounting Association. (1971). Report of the Committee on the Measurement Methods Content of the Accounting Curriculum [Supplement]. *The Accounting Review, 46*(4), 212–45.

Balakrishnan, R., & Sivaramakrishnan, K. (2002). A critical overview of the use of full-cost data for planning and pricing. *Journal of Management Accounting Research, 14*(1), 3–31.

Banker, R. D., Byzalov, D., & Plehn-Dujowich, J. M. (2013). Demand uncertainty and cost behavior. *The Accounting Review, 89*(3), 839–65.

Banker, R. D., Datar, S. M., & Kaplan, R. S. (1989). Productivity measurement and management accounting. *Journal of Accounting, Auditing and Finance, 4*(4), 528–54.

Edwards, E. O. & Bell, P. W. (1961). *The Theory and Measurement of Business Income.* Berkeley, CA: University of California Press.

Hall, M. (2010). Accounting information and managerial work. *Accounting, Organizations and Society, 35*(3), 301–15.

Harris, M., & Raviv, A. (1996). The capital budgeting process: Incentives and information. *The Journal of Finance, 51*(4), 1139–74.

IMA. (2014). *Conceptual Framework for Managerial Costing. Report of the IMA Managerial Costing Conceptual Framework Task Force.* Montvale, NJ: Institute of Management Accountants.

Kanodia, C., Bushman, R., & Dickhaut, J. (1989). Escalation errors and the sunk cost effect: An explanation based on reputation and information asymmetries. *Journal of Accounting Research, 27,* 59–77.

Luft, J., & Shields, M. D. (2009). Psychology Models of Management Accounting. *Foundations and Trends in Accounting, 4*(3–4), 199–345.

Padillo, J. M., & Diaby, M. (1999). A multiple-criteria decision methodology for the make-or-buy problem. *International Journal of Production Research, 37*(14), 3203–29.

Parker, R. H. (1968). Discounted cash flow in historical perspective. *Journal of Accounting Research* (Spring), 58–71.

Pike, R. (1996). A longitudinal survey on capital budgeting practices. *Journal of Business Finance & Accounting, 23*(1), 79–92.

Ryan, P. A., & Ryan, G. P. (2002). Capital budgeting practices of the Fortune 1000: How have things changed. *Journal of Business and Management, 8*(4), 355–64.

Shastri, K., & Stout, D. (2008). Budgeting: Perspectives from the real world. *Management Accounting Quarterly, 10*(1), 18–25.

Staw, B. M., & Hoang, H. (1995). Sunk costs in the NBA: Why draft order affects playing time and survival in professional basketball. *Administrative Science Quarterly, 40,* 474–494.

Part 3

Complications and Limitations

The next six chapters explain why accounting is an imperfect measurement system. Accountants must deal with a number of real-life complications. These include:

- The interaction between the act of measuring and the behavior of companies and employees (Chapter 6)
- The existence of several theoretically valid ways of valuing events (Chapter 7)
- The impact of uncertainty about the future on decisions about recognizing and valuing economic events (Chapter 8)
- The problem of allocating costs or benefits among products, or over time periods (Chapters 9 and 10)[1]
- The problem of controlling the processing of a large number of transactions to minimize errors (Chapter 11).

The following comment from the FASB helps set the stage for the next six chapters:

> Those unfamiliar with the nature of accounting are often surprised at the large number of choices that accountants are required to make. Yet, choices arise at every turn. Decisions must first be made about the nature and definition of assets and liabilities, revenues and expenses, and the criteria by which they are to be recognized. Then a choice must be made of the attribute of assets to be measured. . . If costs have to be allocated, either among time periods. . .or among service beneficiaries . . . methods of allocations must be chosen. Further, choices must be made concerning the level of aggregation or disaggregation of the information. . . . There are some who seem to harbor the hope that somewhere waiting to be discovered there is a comprehensive scoring system that can provide the universal criterion for making accounting choices. Unfortunately, neither the Board nor anyone else has such a system at the present time. Consequently, those who must choose among alternatives are forced to fall back on human judgment.[2]

One major problem that arises is that in financial accounting, the standard-setters had to set general rules for measurement. As we discussed in Chapter 1, there are different users and purposes for accounting. Any one rule is likely to be inappropriate for some users.

> The structure of accounting measurements disciplines individual measurements and makes them consistent and comprehensive. However, it also makes individual measurements less flexible and less adaptable to the changing needs of users. . . . Outside the structure of accounting measurements, R&D expense can be measured flexibly and adaptively depending upon the particular objective of the measurement. The measurement can vary greatly

depending upon whether it is used for budgeting, contract settlement, product costing, shareholder reporting, or tax computations. This is because fundamentally there is no such thing as the R&D expense independent of how the measure is to be used. The best measurement of R&D expense for one use may not be, and usually is not the best for another use. Nevertheless, the structure of accounting measurements forces the R&D expense to be uniquely determined at least within the structure. Since the structure is an integrating mechanism for thousands or even millions of measurements, it cannot withstand the complexity that might arise from indeterminate individual measurements.[3]

Accounting is not perfect, and the next six chapters will make that clear. However, as you read these chapters, it is important to keep a sense of perspective. As Tony Tinker wrote:

> Scorning conventional accounting's inability to produce measures that accurately depict a marginalist version of income and wealth is a celebrated, yet somewhat meaningless, pursuit for many accounting academics. (Criticizing something for lacking absolute perfection is a form of trivial idealism that has long since been abandoned in more mature sciences.)[4]

There is a purpose to having ideals, even if they cannot be met:

> To be sure, an ideal is not a goal we can expect to attain. But it serves to set a direction in which we can strive. Ideals are irrealities, but they are irrealities that condition the nature of real thought through their influence on human thought. . . . Ideals, though instruments of thought are not mere myths. For there is nothing false or fictional about ideals as such—only about the idea of their embodiment in concrete reality. Their pursuit is something which can be perfectly real and eminently productive.[5]

Notes

1   Part of the organization of this text was inspired by Yuji Ijiri, who noted three major issues in accounting measurement: "separability" problems (leading to arbitrary allocations); "multiplicity problems" (where more than one causal path leads to benefits or costs, creating ambiguity in valuation choices); and instability of causal networks (uncertainty). See Ijiri, Y. (1967). *The Foundations of Accounting Measurement: A Mathematical, Economic, and Behavioral Inquiry.* Englewood Cliffs, NJ: Prentice-Hall, Inc.
2   FASB. (1980). *Statement of Financial Accounting Concepts No. 2., Qualitative characteristics of accounting information.* Stamford, CT: FASB, para. 55.
3   Ijiri, Y. (1989). *Momentum Accounting and Triple-Entry Bookkeeping: Exploring the Dynamic Structure of Accounting Measurements.* Studies in Accounting Research # 31. Sarasota, FL: American Accounting Association, pp. 1–2.
4   Tinker, T. (1985). *Paper Prophets: A Social Critique of Accounting.* New York: Praeger Publishers, p. 179.
5   Rescher, N. (1993). *A System of Pragmatic Idealism. Vol. II: The Validity of Values.* Princeton: Princeton University Press.

6 Strategic Reaction to Measurement

Outline

Preliminary Thoughts

> The important difference between meteorological and financial predictions is that only exceptionally can meteorological predictions have an effect on the weather, but business or economic decision makers' predictions often affect their subjects. For example, the use of financial models to predict business failures look quite successful judged in the light of hindsight. . . But a prediction of failure can be self-fulfilling by restricting a company's access to credit.
>
> *FASB (1980, para. 55)*

The fact that measurement has real world effects means that people put pressure on accountants and standard-setters.

> Measures in accounting are not disinterested observations, but are always associated with the value notions of better or worse, desirable or undesirable. If we fail to recognize this evaluative nature of accounting measurements, it is easy to miss the pressures incident on the accountant from various interested parties.
>
> *Yuji Ijiri (1989)*

While the FASB has sought to be a neutral rule-maker, in fact we do not live in a world or economy where all parties have equal say. As the quote below indicates, the accounting system has typically been used in ways benefiting the more powerful.

The importance of giving due weight to the social context of accounting becomes even more apparent if we recognize that, to date, when accounting has affected the work-lives of employees, it has done so overwhelmingly on behalf of corporations and employers. Budgeting, motivating, coordinating and planning are methods for controlling the behavior of people within organizations.

Anthony Tinker, Barbara D. Merino and
Marilyn Dale Neimark (1982, p. 192)

The next quotations point out that there are often unintended consequences to measuring.

Financial controls can make hospitals more efficient. But they can also make them less humane.

Gareth Morgan (1988, p. 482)

In recent years, many serious criticisms have been directed at the control systems used by American corporations. Critics have observed that control systems tend to discourage new ideas, cause an excessive short-run orientation, stimulate data manipulation and other forms of gamesmanship, and cause management frustration and resistance.

Kenneth Merchant (1990, p. 297)

Finally, the last quote speaks to the dilemma faced by any professor or author who wishes to discuss topics such as budgetary slack, earnings management, or fraud. Anything we write can help good people detect and prevent these practices. However, our writings could also help those with improper motivations commit fraud. This is not a new dilemma—Rabbi Yohanan ben Zakkai, who died around the year 90 CE, spoke as follows:

Woe to me if I speak, woe to me if I don't speak. If I speak, perhaps deceivers will learn; if I don't speak, perhaps the deceivers will say: "The scholars are not experts in what we do!"

Rabbi Yohanan ben Zakkai (Katz and Schwartz 1998, p. 253)[1]

Learning Objectives

After studying this chapter you should understand:

1   How accounting measurement causes a chain of strategic reactions among managers and financial statement users
2   The process of setting accounting rules is affected by the reactions of companies, analysts, and markets to the impact of these rules, and that this is one reason for the complexity of accounting rules
3   The concepts of budgetary slack and expectations management
4   The nature of earnings management
5   The nature of off-balance sheet financing
6   The fraud triangle and risk factors for financial misrepresentation
7   The "principles versus rules" issue in standard setting.

Overview of Reactions to Measurement

According to game theory, a "one-person game" (also called a "game against nature") is a game where only one party acts strategically. A classic case is betting on whether it will rain tomorrow. Nature will act the same, regardless of what bets you make. Any game with two or more parties involves the interaction of the different parties' strategies. The accounting measurement system has many parties, and their actions affect each other. The "game" plays out over many time periods, so there is time for parties in the system to react to each other.

This chapter discusses how the reaction of people to measurement has impacted the accounting measurement system. It is extremely complicated. Before a measurement rule is put into effect, workers and companies try to influence it in their favor. Once a measurement starts to be used, workers and companies change their behavior. These changes may in turn cause other parties to react. Regulators may put in place new rules to stop what they see as abuse. Users of financial statements may change the degree of reliance they place on company reports. Company management may change their policies and controls once they see how employees respond to the new measurements. And then, of course, these changes may cause companies and employees to change their behavior once more.

I believe that when people know they are going to be evaluated by measurements, they react in one of the following key ways:

- They try to get the measurement system modified before it goes into effect. We speak of creating budgetary slack (or making "lowball" estimates of revenues) within companies, and of "expectations management" when companies try to influence the forecasts of outside analysts.
- They do what is desired of them. This may or may not have unintended consequences.
- They do what looks good on the measurement system, even if it differs from what is desired. In financial reporting, this is called "earnings management," and can be done both by adjusting accounting measures ("accruals management") and by making transactions that are primarily accounting-motivated ("real earnings management").
- They lie.
- They find ways to avoid being measured, such as by quitting a company, taking the company private to avoid SEC regulations, or convincing the managers or regulators to stop measuring something.

A non-accounting example may help make this clear. In 2001, the U.S. Congress enacted the "No Child Left Behind Act" (Title I of the Elementary and Secondary Education Act of 1965 (20 USC 6301 et seq.)). Its stated purpose was to "ensure that all children have a fair, equal, and significant opportunity to obtain a high-quality education." In particular, a major purpose of the law was to improve the ability of schoolchildren to read. Each public school would be judged on the scores of students on statewide reading tests, and there were significant penalties for schools whose students scored badly. In the years since this law was passed, we have seen all five of the behaviors listed above.

- There have been allegations that some states have changed their reading tests to be easier to pass, and various states have asked the U.S. Department of Education to waive some of the law's requirements.
- Many schools try hard to teach children to read better, which was the purpose of the law. However, in some cases there are unintended consequences, like spending less time on social studies, or on physical education.
- Many schools spend much more time teaching students how to take tests. Note that teaching children to pass reading tests is not the same thing as giving children a general love of reading, or the ability to do many types of reading.
- Some teachers and school systems lie. A 2013 article in the *Washington Post* said that there had been cheating scandals reported in 37 states and the District of Columbia. In Atlanta, the

school superintendent and 34 others were indicted. See Strauss (2013). In 2015, some of the teachers were convicted and sentenced to prison terms.

- Parents and teachers have tried to avoid being measured. Some teachers have left the public schools, and many parents have kept their children home on the test days.

Another example, that may be more familiar, is how students in a college class react to being graded in a course. Students have been known to show all five of the key behaviors:

- They lobby the professor in advance for easier exams.
- They study hard to learn the key aspects of the course.
- They try hard to prepare for what they think will be tested, which may not be all the key concepts of the course. For example, they may ask the professor for a clear list of what is and is not likely to be tested.
- Some students cheat.
- Students may try to avoid being marked by a professor known to be a hard grader by taking the course from other professors, or not taking the course at all.

The principles in this chapter extend far beyond accounting. Two well-known statements related to the problem are "Goodhart's Law" and "Campbell's Law." Campbell (1976) stated: "The more any quantitative social indicator (or even some qualitative indicator) is used for social decision-making, the more subject it will be to corruption pressures and the more apt it will be to distort and corrupt the social processes it is intended to monitor." (p. 49) Goodhart's Law was first expressed as "As soon as the government attempts to regulate any particular set of financial assets, these become unreliable as indicators of economic trends." (Goodhart 1975)[2] More informally, it is typically stated as "When a measure becomes a target, it ceases to be a good measure."

Step 0—Anticipation of Measurement

General

This section deals with three situations where people or companies, in anticipation of being measured in some way, try to influence the measurement rule in advance.

Lobbying Regulators

Companies devote considerable effort to keeping track of proposals that could affect how their performance is measured, and make their views known.

An obvious area is the definition of taxable income in the tax code. Companies make their views known on any proposal that affects which of their expenses are deductible and which of their revenues are taxable. At the time I write this chapter, an issue under discussion is what part of companies' worldwide income should be measured as pertaining to the United States.

Companies that are subject to rate regulation, such as electric utilities, are particularly sensitive to how their income is measured. They are typically allowed to set prices that will give them a "fair rate of return", and thus their prices depend directly on how their regulators define profits. They try to influence the regulatory accounting rules.

Before the FASB and IASB make new accounting pronouncements, they always ask for public comment, and usually hold public hearings. Often, the comments made by companies or governmental bodies cause the FASB and IASB to modify their proposals. Here are two examples of where that has happened.

Pension accounting has developed slowly over time, because of concerns of companies about how the recognition of liabilities for pension obligations would affect them. When companies first started offering pensions to employees on a large scale, many did not recognize the obligations to pay future benefits on their balance sheets. Instead, they simply recognized pension expense as they paid benefits to retirees. When the FASB began addressing this issue, many companies were concerned that if they suddenly had to show liabilities for future pensions, they would appear much less solvent. Also, fluctuations in the estimates of the pension liabilities would make their reported income appear more volatile. These concerns have affected the FASB's rules. As you will see in Chapter 8, the FASB adopted rules that keep certain fluctuations in the estimates of pension liabilities from affecting company income, and that reduce the impact of recognizing pensions on balance sheet ratios. Also, the accounting standard-setters moved very slowly on this process. The issue was first raised by one of the FASB's predecessors in 1955, and by another in 1966, but it was not until the FASB issued SFAS No. 87 in 1985 that companies were required to accrue pension expense systematically over the work lives of employees. However, the FASB did not require companies at that time to fully reflect the impact of pension obligations on their balance sheets, due to resistance by companies. The FASB explicitly noted that its statement was a compromise, and that full recognition of pension liabilities would be "too great a change from past practice" (FASB 1985, para. 107). It took 21 years, until 2006, for the FASB to require full balance sheet recognition of pension obligations in SFAS No. 158.

Accounting for employee stock options also was affected by corporate pressure. When a company gives an employee an option, the company says that the employee has the right to buy the stock at a fixed price, called the exercise price, for some fixed period of time. For example, a company may "grant" an option today, giving someone the right to buy stock starting two years from today, for a period of four years, at a price of $10. If the stock price rises to $100, these options can be extremely valuable. Many high-tech start-ups used stock options to attract employees, and there have been many stories of early employees becoming very wealthy.

Early accounting rules did not require companies to recognize any expense for stock options, as long as the options were not "in the money" at the date they were granted. This means that as long as the exercise price was set at the market value on the date of grant, there was no expense on the company's books. As more and more employee compensation began to be in the form of options, the FASB considered changing the standards. In the 1990s, the FASB proposed requiring companies to report the fair value of options granted as expenses. Companies protested, and lobbied Congress to block the rule. They argued that if such a rule was passed, companies would stop offering stock options, and that this would impair the ability of start-up companies to succeed. Ultimately, they claimed that America's competitiveness and its innovative culture would be damaged. The FASB backed down, and SFAS No. 123, as issued in October 1995, only required disclosure of the value of options granted, not recording an expense. In 2004, after the Enron scandal changed the political climate, the FASB revised SFAS No. 123 and required companies to record the fair value of options granted as an expense.

Budgetary Slack

When managers know that they will be judged on whether or not they meet budget targets, they are tempted to ensure that the budget targets are easily achievable. The difference between the targets they ask for, and what they actually think they can achieve, is called "*budgetary slack*." A review of the academic literature in 2000 (Hartmann 2000) found evidence that when top management relies more heavily on budget targets to judge performance, lower level managers tend to create more slack in their budgets.

There is also evidence that there is more slack and less honesty by lower level managers when they think that the budgeting process is a negotiating game. Since they expect that top management is also playing a game, and that top management's initial proposals are not totally honest, the lower level managers feel it is legitimate to build slack into their own initial positions. In situations when the lower level managers are actually setting the budget levels, they tend to set targets with less slack than when they expect top management to modify their proposals.[3]

Expectations Management

Company managers believe that a failure to report earnings that meet stock market expectations will hurt their company's stock price. One way to avoid this problem is to take steps to get analysts to reduce their predictions. Bartov and Cohen (2009) note: "Earnings expectations management" involves "walking down analyst earnings expectations so as to transform an otherwise negative earnings surprise into a positive one." (p. 506) Evidence suggests that companies are often successful in getting analysts to lower their expectations. See Cotter, Tuna and Wysocki (2006).

Step 1—Measurement (With or Without Preset Goals)

The FASB (1978) stated that its goal is simply neutral measurement, to help investors and creditors make decisions:

> The role of financial reporting requires it to provide evenhanded, neutral, or unbiased information. Thus . . . information that is directed toward a particular goal, such as encouraging the reallocation of resources in favor of a particular segment of the economy, are likely to fail to serve the broader objectives that financial reporting is intended to serve.
>
> (para. 33)

In some cases, the FASB has set new standards when something has become economically important, and existing measurement rules did not properly portray company financial performance. An example is the accounting for "post-retirement benefits" such as companies' promises to pay for the health insurance of retirees. This became economically significant in the U.S. over the later part of the 20th century, as more companies made these promises and as health care costs rapidly increased. Prior to the issuance of SFAS No. 106 in December 1990, companies did not have to recognize liabilities for these promises. SFAS No. 106 required companies to measure their likely obligations, and to begin recording the related liabilities.

In other cases, the FASB has acted to increase the consistency of accounting across different companies. For example, prior to the issuance of SFAS No. 2 in 1974 some companies treated their spending on research and development as an expense, while others treated such costs as the purchase of an asset. SFAS No. 2 required expensing these costs.

In other situations, the organizations setting measurement rules have explicit goals in mind. For example, management may decide to measure the amount of material being scrapped in order to focus attention on the efficiency of a process, and in order to identify ways of improving the process. A government may decide to measure the amount of property owned by its citizens in order to maximize its ability to collect taxes.

Step 2—Reactions to Measurement

General

If no one reacts to an accounting measurement at all, there was probably no point in making and reporting it. It is a general point of communication theory as developed by C. E. Shannon in the 1940s, that any communication would be meaningless if it was not meant to induce some reaction in the receiver (Bernhardt and Copeland 1970). These reactions are the topic of this section.

Real Behavior Changes—No Pre-Set Goal

The FASB has stated that its purpose in setting standards is to help investors and creditors make decisions, but not to help or hurt particular social policies. However, it would be wrong to say that the FASB does not expect its standards and accounting to influence behavior. In general, the FASB intends standards to have some of the following effects:

- To allow investors to more accurately compare companies.
- To allow investors and creditors to make more accurate investment and lending decisions about particular companies.
- To make the allocation of investment capital in the U.S. more efficient.

The widespread use of financial statements indicates that in general accounting standards have had these desired effects. Numerous academic studies indicate that stock markets do react to accounting information, implying the markets find the accounting reports helpful.[4] Studies also indicate that accounting reports are used by donors to nonprofit organizations in making donation decisions. See Parsons (2003). Apparently, donors give less money to organizations that report expense data that is seen as indicating inefficient use of donated funds.

While the FASB may not state a social goal, in some cases the likely consequences of its rules are obvious. As noted above, for many years companies that promised to pay medical insurance for employees after retirement did not accrue a liability in advance for these payments. They simply reported expenses at the time they paid the premiums. In 1990, the FASB issued SFAS No. 106, *Employers' Accounting for Postretirement Benefits Other Than Pensions*. This standard required companies to record an expense in the time periods in which the employees earned the rights to this post-retirement benefit, and to record the amount of the companies' obligations as liabilities on the balance sheets. The FASB's motivation for this statement was to inform users about the nature of the obligations. However, one could certainly predict that some companies would react by reducing the generosity of their promises to employees. Over time, fewer companies have been promising to cover post-retirement health benefits.[5,6]

The FASB (1980) also argues that the goal of neutrality in measurement is vital, regardless of the likely result of its rules.

> Many measurements relating to human beings—what they see when they step on a scale, what the speedometer registers when they drive a car, their performance in an athletic contest, or their academic performance, for example—have an impact on their behavior, for better or worse. No one argues that those measurements should be biased in order to influence behavior. Indeed, most people are repelled by the notion that some "big brother" . . . would tamper with scales or speedometers surreptitiously to induce people to lose weight or obey speed limits or would slant the scoring of athletic events or examinations to enhance or decrease someone's chances of winning or graduating. There is no more reason to abandon neutrality in accounting measurement.
>
> (para. 102)

The FASB knows that new standards will often require companies to change their record-keeping systems and to modify contracts that have accounting provisions. As a result, many FASB pronouncements give companies time to adjust, and do not become mandatory until one or more years after they are adopted.

Real Behavior Changes—Achieving Desired Goals

Intended Consequences

As noted above, often a measurement system is put in place in order to help meet some objective. Management often uses the combination of a budget and a system of reporting variances from budget targets to help communicate goals to managers, and to monitor performance. Budgets and variance reporting were discussed in Chapter 5. This can be successful in helping managers understand their tasks, as Yuji Ijiri (1967) notes:

> We often say that the goal of a business firm is to maximize profit. However, the concept of profit is far from being unambiguous. Therefore, even if a division manager knows that he should maximize profit, he does not know operationally what he should aim for. In this case, an accounting profit provides a means for him to simplify his environment by giving him this information. Another way that an accounting system determines the goals for a manager is by defining an area for him to pay attention to. For example, assume the accountants suddenly report scrap cost for the first time. The manager now creates a new goal that specifies his objective in regard to the control of scrap cost. . . . Furthermore, the accounting procedure, in addition to specifying goals or ends for a manager, may also help him define his means.
>
> (p. 158)

More recently, other researchers (Marginson and Ogden 2005) have noted that budgets can help provide structure and clarity to managers.

The FASB's standards are intended to help investors and managers make appropriate decisions. As discussed in Chapter 4, financial statement readers can use the information in the reports to make judgments about company profitability, leverage, solvency, and risk.

At other times, other standard-setters have had goals of helping particular industries. For example, Joni Young (1995) claims that during the 1980s, when rising interest rates and other economic changes caused many savings and loans banks to become unprofitable, the Federal Home Loan Bank changed the rules for deciding which banks were insolvent. She claims this was done to give the industry time to become profitable, and to avoid the costs to the government involved in shutting them down. Changes to the rules included more generous recognition of revenues on lending and deferring recognition of losses on mortgage sales.

Unintended Consequences of Managerial Accounting Measures

There is a long literature about unintended, dysfunctional consequences of relying on accounting performance measures. Some of the major issues are outlined below.

People can focus too much on the single item being measured. A 1956 study (Ridgway 1956) found that when people are judged on a single measure, they tend to place undue emphasis on this factor and ignore other important aspects of their jobs. If they are judged based on multiple measures, and this is not done carefully, the managers will focus on those measures that are easiest to meet, not those that are most important to the organization. An apocryphal (and probably untrue) story told years ago about a Soviet window factory that was judged solely on the number of windows produced. It responded by producing many very thin windows. Unfortunately, these often broke in shipping, so the central planners changed the goal. Now the goal was a low percentage of windows that broke during shipping. The factory responded by making thicker windows, that were resistant to breaking, but were, unfortunately, too thick to fit in the users' window frames.

Managers tend to adopt a short-term orientation, if they are measured too frequently (Gigler et al. 2014). There is little point making sacrifices today for future payoffs if you think you can only hold on to your job by meeting this month's targets.

If people are judged on their individual performance, that will reduce their incentive to act as "team players." Clearly, we see this happen in team sports, when a player is judged on a particular statistic. Demski et al. (2008) note that individual statistics can have a "corrosive effect" and that "Intuitively, the mere assembling of individual measures in our setting has the power to affect if not destroy synergy between the agents." (p. 171) A 1952 field study of factory supervisors (cited in Hartmann 2000) showed that one effect was forcing the supervisors to unduly narrow their attention to matters affecting their own department.

Accounting methods can sometimes lead to improper decision-making. Advocates of "lean" manufacturing techniques claim that conventional cost accounting techniques give managers an incentive to create excess inventories. When overhead is fixed, a higher volume of production means that less overhead cost is allocated to each item produced. This increases the apparent profit per unit. Also, higher volume produces favorable "fixed overhead volume variances," as discussed in Chapter 5. Advocates of "ABC" cost allocation systems claim that the use of conventional cost accounting procedures causes companies to overprice simple, high-volume products and underprice complex, lower volume products. See Chapter 10, where these claims are explained in more detail.

Frequent comparison to pre-set budgets can reduce the flexibility of an organization. Managers may become unwilling to take actions that risk causing them to miss monthly targets.

The pressure to meet targets can also produce undue stress in organizations. One result of this stress may be increased efforts to game the system, by building in managerial slack, or by improper reporting.

Unintended Consequences of Financial Measures

The FASB claims that its goal is simply to ensure that companies provide information useful to investors and creditors. However, the information will inevitably be used, and this will cause consequences. Here are some consequences that have been suggested as a result of particular accounting proposals or statements, by the FASB or other standard-setters:

- When the FASB required companies to report their expenditures on research and development as expenses, rather than assets, there were predictions that this would cause a reduction in American research, with adverse effects on the economy.
- When the FASB required companies to report liabilities for "defined benefit" pension obligations, and again for their obligations for post-employment retiree health insurance, there were predictions that this would induce companies to change their benefit plans, and reduce these benefits. Indeed, over time the frequency of these types of benefits has decreased. In 2012, a similar statement was issued by the Governmental Accounting Standards Board, for accounting by state and local governments, and again there is a prediction that this will cause governments to be less generous to their employees.
- When the FASB required companies to report the impact of certain changes in foreign exchange rates in income, companies responded by engaging in more trading in options and other instruments to "hedge" the risk of having to report an accounting loss.
- When the FASB required companies who had leased some of their equipment under certain types of arrangements to report these arrangements as if the companies had bought the equipment and taken out loans, the result was that companies showed higher assets, and higher liabilities. This changed certain key balance sheet ratios, and had an effect on whether

some companies were in compliance with their debt agreements. The result was to make certain types of leasing arrangements less attractive.

- When the FASB changed the rules on accounting for employee stock options, to require companies to show a greater expense when they granted the options, there were predictions that this would adversely affect both high-tech companies and their employees. The argument was that such companies had used stock options to get key talent, but that if the companies had to book expenses, they would stop granting the options. The indirect effect would be to inhibit one of the most innovative parts of the American economy.

- The way that electric utility commissions set rates for power companies is to allow the companies a "fair return" on the amount that they have invested in the assets used to produce power. This has the effect of encouraging companies to overinvest in equipment, and also to report (but not necessarily have) high expenses. See Tinker (1985).

- Donors to nonprofit organizations often judge the organizations by various accounting efficiency measures, such as the fraction of their expenditures that go to such "overhead" functions as central administration and fundraising. Organizations that try too hard to minimize overhead spending may lack enough infrastructure to perform their charitable functions effectively. See Pallotta (2008).

- The FASB required companies to report many financial assets and liabilities at fair value. During the 2008 financial crisis, the fair value of many investments fell drastically. Markets for certain types of financial instruments were not functioning well, even though some market participants thought that after a short panic, the markets would recover. A consequence was that some financial institutions seemed much less solvent than if they had been allowed to value assets at what they thought was a long-run true value, rather than the current day's depressed value. The role of fair value accounting on the 2008 crisis is discussed more fully in Chapter 7.

Behavior Changes to Achieve a Better Measurement, Rather Than Desired Goals

General

A common problem with using accounting measures to guide people's behavior is that the accounting measure is very often an imprecise measure of some real economic concept. This means that there is usually a difference between the true economic result of some action, and the way it is measured.[7] In this section, we discuss actions that managers take to exploit that difference. Here, the actions are neither illegal nor inherently dishonest. However, they are motivated more to achieve certain accounting measurements than the underlying economic goals. They are actions that fit the "letter of the law" but not the "spirit of the law." The general term for these actions is "*earnings management*," but this section also discusses actions to improve the appearance of balance sheet figures that do not affect reported earnings.

The two strategies that companies use to "manage earnings" are "*accruals management*" and "*real earnings management*." Accruals management involves purely accounting actions, such as changing to more favorable accounting policies, or changing accounting estimates in a way that achieves the desired accounting result. Real earnings management involves taking real actions, with real economic effects, primarily for accounting purposes. As an example, a company that wants to show a high level of cash on hand at year end might give its customers a slight discount for payments received before December 31.

Companies also use various techniques to make their balance sheets look better. A term for this is "*window dressing*." The idea here is that, just like people passing by a house only see its windows, readers only see balance sheets for one instant of time, so companies try to make the balance sheet at that instant look good. Companies also engage in "*off-balance sheet financing*" in order to look better on solvency and liquidity measures.

Research and casual experience indicate that companies can face significant costs for failing to meet market expectations.[8] A former head of the Securities and Exchange Commission, Arthur Levitt (1998), said in a speech:

> While the problem of earnings management is not new, it has swelled in a market that is unforgiving of companies that miss their estimates. I recently read of one major U.S. company that failed to meet its so-called "numbers" by one penny and lost more than six percent of its stock value in one day.[9]

Research has also identified other reasons that managers use "earnings management" techniques. These reasons include:

- Maximizing managerial compensation under employment contracts
- Avoiding violating debt covenants
- Avoiding political scrutiny
- Maintaining capital adequacy, and
- Managing timing of earnings impact related to new standards adoption.[10]

Note that different companies may want to "manage earnings" in different directions. In many cases, companies wish to show higher earnings, to achieve certain targets, or to affect the stock price. In other situations, managers have incentives to show lower earnings. They may wish to minimize taxes. They may wish to buy out certain shareholders, and hope that under-reporting earnings will help them to do so. They may wish to avoid criticism for being overly profitable. For example, a monopoly may wish to avoid seeming to have used its power to overcharge customers. Companies also sometimes wish to show a smooth pattern of earnings. They believe this makes them look less risky.

Outside the corporate world, there is also evidence that nonprofit organizations use "earnings management" techniques to try to appear more appealing to potential donors. In this situation, the focus is not on net income, but on various financial ratios used to judge the efficiency of the organization, such as the fundraising expenses as a percentage of donations.[11]

Earnings Management Using Accruals Management

Accruals management involves using the flexibility in the permitted methods of accounting measurement to achieve the desired results. When accounting rules are more flexible, there tends to be more earnings management.[12] There are a number of ways that accountants have used the accounting process for earnings management. Arthur Levitt (1998) described five methods he said were commonly used:

- "Cookie jar" reserves
- Abusive acquisition accounting
- Improper revenue recognition techniques
- "Big baths," and
- Improper uses of the idea of materiality.

A company can create "cookie jar" reserves when it creates excessive liabilities in good years. In those good years, the action to create the liabilities keeps income down. In worse years, the company can recognize that some of its liabilities are not needed. By the effect of the accounting equation, when the company reduces the liability to a more realistic level, something else has to change. No assets are affected, and no other liabilities are involved, so this has to increase income and therefore equity. This is not a new technique. It was described in a 1914 article in the *Journal of Accountancy* as creating "secret reserves." See Joplin (1914).

The basic accounting rule when one company acquires another is that it should record the assets it acquires, and the liabilities it becomes obligated for, at their fair values. If the acquirer undervalues the assets, then in later years, when it sells them, it will show gains. Similarly, if it overvalues the liabilities, then in later years, when it is able to pay them off for less than their recorded values, it will show more income than if the liabilities had been properly valued.

As we will discuss in other chapters, it is often unclear when revenue should be recognized. Companies that wish to report earnings quickly can use accounting techniques to recognize revenues more quickly than they have actually been earned.

"Big baths" occur when a company is already reporting a bad year. The idea is that, as long as you are getting wet, why not take a bath? A company that is taking a "big bath" records more losses than are appropriate during the year, in the belief that in future years, income will be helped. For example, a company might accelerate certain discretionary expenses into a bad year. The next year will have fewer of these expenses, and therefore will look better.

The last of the earnings management techniques listed by Levitt was abusing the idea of materiality. In essence, he claimed that some companies simply made up accounting adjustments that were small, by traditional measures, such as 2 cents per share for a company whose true earnings per share were $3.42, knowing that their auditors would not object to such small misstatements. However, these 2 cents could be the difference between missing analyst forecasts and meeting them.

A case that involved several of these techniques was that of the Sunbeam Corporation. It is described in Box 6.1.

Other people have noted other techniques for earnings management. These include *under-accruing estimated expenses* and *delaying the recognition of the loss of value of an asset*.[13] Often, expenses must be estimated. This is discussed in Chapter 8. In these circumstances, managers have the opportunity to pick estimates that are not in fact the most likely outcomes, but are plausible, and that help them achieve their accounting targets. Similarly, it is often unclear when economic changes mean that a company's assets have lost some of their value. In these cases, a company could have discretion over which period it will report the loss.

Earnings Management Using Real Earnings Management

"Real earnings management" occurs when companies take actions that help them achieve their accounting goals, but are not otherwise economically worthwhile. Examples of actions used for real earnings management include:

- Moving such discretionary expenses as advertising, training, research, or maintenance between periods, or cutting them temporarily
- Providing short-term price discounts or lenient credit terms to get customers to accelerate their purchases into the current period[14]
- Timing the sales of assets.[15]

Accounting rules call for recording expenditures on advertising and research as expenses in the period that the expenditures were incurred. However, there is often not much of an economic impact on a company if it delays spending on such items for a short period of time. For example, it really won't matter much if a company has its holiday party in late December or early January, but the timing of the party will affect the income in both years. Therefore, a company can "manage earnings" by moving a discretionary expenditure between fiscal years.

Box 6.1 Sunbeam—Deceptive Accounting: Restructuring, a Big Bath, and Revenue Recognition

The Sunbeam Corporation was doing poorly in 1996, so its Board hired Albert Dunlap as CEO. Dunlap had a reputation as a "turnaround specialist" who could help ailing companies by cutting costs and changing their strategies.

1996 was known by everyone to be a bad year, and Dunlap had only been hired partway through it, so he was willing to have the company take a "big bath." He hoped to have the company report much improved results in 1997, and wanted to try to sell the company at that point for a large gain. At the end of 1996, the company booked large "restructuring charges." According to the SEC, the company intentionally booked more expense than was appropriate, creating excessive "cookie jar" reserves of at least $35 million.

In 1997, the company reported profits of $189 million, much better than in prior years. Unfortunately, the improvement was not real. According to the SEC (2001), "at least $62 million of Sunbeam's reported income of $189 million came from accounting fraud." The company used the "cookie jar reserves" to inflate 1997 income by at least $35 million. The SEC claimed that Sunbeam engaged in various other improper accounting procedures in 1997. "Sunbeam's management engaged in guaranteed sales, improper 'bill and hold' sales, and other fraudulent practices." In a "bill and hold" arrangement, the company does not actually ship products to the customer at the time it sends a bill. Normally, accounting rules do not permit revenue to be recorded until goods are shipped, so these "bill and hold" arrangements were an abuse of revenue recognition rules.

The SEC also claimed that Sunbeam had engaged in other questionable techniques to inflate 1997 sales. The primary one was convincing customers to take delivery of much more product than they really wanted, usually by offering large discounts or pressuring the customers in some way. For example, customers who usually order a one-month supply are persuaded to order four months' supply. This is called "channel stuffing." It can give a temporary boost to sales, but what usually happens is that customers who have more inventory than they want in their warehouses order much less than normal in coming months until they bring their inventories down to normal. Sunbeams' sales in the first quarter of 1998 were low in large part because of the 1997 channel stuffing.

In the summer of 1998, after an article in *Barrons* questioning Sunbeam's accounting, the board of directors fired Dunlap and the company disclosed it had misstated its financial results.

The information in this exhibit is primarily from SEC 2001: Accounting and Auditing Enforcement Release No. 1393/May 15, 2001. Administrative Proceeding File No. 3-10481, In the Matter of Sunbeam Corporation.

Accounting rules typically say revenue should be recognized when the products are shipped to the customer, so if a company convinces more customers to buy in December, it will have more sales for the year. There is nothing wrong or illegal with offering customers incentives to buy during the year. However, the practice becomes earnings management when the company is offering economically unjustified terms to customers, just to shift the total amount sold between accounting periods.

Accounting rules often require companies to record certain assets on the books at their original, historical cost. This will be discussed in Chapter 7. In some cases, companies may own land or other assets for many years. Over time, their economic value has grown far above the value on the books. When the company sells the asset, it will report a gain. Economically, that gain has arisen over a long period of time, but for accounting purposes it is all reported on the day the asset is sold. This difference between the economic value of assets and the reported accounting value lets companies choose when they want to report the economic gains. In bad years, they can choose to sell some of these long-held assets.

Window Dressing

Companies often take actions to make their December 31 positions look better than their normal positions. For example, a company may normally have current assets of $15 million and current liabilities of $10 million. Its current ratio would be $15 \div 10 = 1.5$. If it wanted to have a higher current ratio, it could use some cash and pay some accounts payable. For example, if it paid $5 million of accounts payable, its current assets would now equal $10 million, and the current liabilities would be $5 million. The current ratio increases to 2.

Another example of window dressing occurs with mutual funds. These companies must report what securities they own as of the last day of the period. Mutual fund managers sometimes prefer to have balance sheets at the end of the period listing only very safe stocks. In this case, window dressing involves selling the more risky stocks just before year end, and replacing them with safer stocks. After the new period starts, the fund manager might sell the safe stocks, and replace them with riskier ones that are expected to have higher yields.

Off-Balance Sheet Financing

Companies need financing for all kinds of legitimate business purposes. However, they know that analysts and creditors use various solvency and liquidity ratios in judging them. Chapter 4 discussed such ratios as the debt to equity ratio and the capital structure leverage ratio. The more debt companies show on their balance sheet, the worse these ratios look. When companies are able to obtain funding without recording a liability on their balance sheets, this is called *"off-balance sheet financing."*

Here is an example. Assume a company buys equipment, for $10 million, and borrows $10 million to pay for the equipment. It expects the equipment to last 10 years. The loan needs to be paid back over a 10-year period, in monthly payments. Its assets increase by $10 million, and so does its debt. This transaction will cause its debt to equity ratio and its capital structure ratio to look worse. Also, since it now has more assets, it is harder to earn a high return on assets.

What would happen if, instead of buying the equipment, it rented the equipment for 10 years? Over the course of the 10 years, it would use the equipment. Since it doesn't own the equipment, then the equipment would not appear on its balance sheet. Since it does not have a loan outstanding, just a monthly rental obligation, it does not have to record a liability. Its total assets and its total debt are both lower than they would be if it borrowed and bought the equipment. However, the underlying economics of the lease deal are actually quite similar to a purchase, since the equipment is being leased for its entire useful life, and the total lease payments are likely to be very similar to what the payments on the loan would have been. As discussed below, the FASB has set rules to deal with this issue.

Companies have been very inventive in coming up with ways to achieve off-balance sheet financing. Some companies have sold receivables or inventory to financial institutions, and promised to buy them back later, at higher prices. More advanced classes in accounting discuss the use of affiliated companies controlled by the entity to achieve off-balance sheet financing.

Lying and Pretending to Meet Measures

Some actions go beyond earnings management, and involve lying in order to claim that accounting targets have been met. *Fraud* is defined as a deliberate omission or misstatement of material facts, with the intention that someone else will rely on the misstated facts. Fraud is not an accident; it is intentional. Producing materially fraudulent financial statements is illegal.

Why do people commit fraud? In 1953, Donald Cressey (1953) suggested that fraud is most likely to occur when three factors occur at once. First, a person believes they have a financial problem that they can't openly share. Second, they have the opportunity to secretly solve this problem by committing fraud. Third, they can find a way to rationalize to themselves that their actions are in some way justified. Auditing textbooks and auditing standards have taken Cressey's idea, and present it as the "*fraud triangle*." The idea is that fraud is most likely to occur in the presence of three factors:

• Pressures or incentives
• Opportunities to commit fraud
• Rationalizations

A CEO might feel *pressure* to commit fraud to keep up the company's stock price, or to avoid violating loan covenants. A CEO with generous stock options, or a bonus plan, might have a personal *incentive* to overstate earnings and boost the stock price. A CEO who wants earnings overstated can pressure the CFO and other executives.[16] A lower level manager may feel under pressure to meet budget targets in order to keep his or her job. The *opportunity* to commit fraud is often due to a lack of good outside oversight over the accounting process. We will talk more about controls over accounting in Chapter 11. It may also occur when the company's business operations involves hard to value transactions, which are difficult to audit.

People have various ways of rationalizing accounting fraud. A CEO who lies in order to hide the company's financial difficulty will often believe that, if the company just gets some more time, it can solve its problems. There have been numerous frauds that began when a company unexpectedly lost money. The company tried to hide the loss "temporarily," expecting to earn back the lost money. Instead, the company lost more and more money, until when it eventually could no longer hide the losses there was very little money left for creditors.

Some financial frauds result from lower level managers who are under extreme pressure from top management. A 1995 *Business Week* article suggested that this was the cause of a fraud at Bausch & Lomb. The article, discussing what managers said about the scandal, stated:

> Their tales provide a remarkably consistent picture: Driven by [CEO] Gill's fierce insistence on achieving double-digit annual profit growth, B&L's managers by the early 1990s increasingly resorted to what was expedient–often at the expense of what constituted sound business practice or ethical behavior. They gave customers extraordinarily long payment terms, knowingly fed gray markets, and threatened to cut off distributors unless they took on huge quantities of unwanted products. Some also shipped goods before customers ordered them and booked the shipments as sales, a possible violation of recognized accounting practices. For a period, the company also turned a blind eye to lucrative Latin American sales that may have indirectly aided money laundering.[17]

A manager who overstates his division's performance in order to get a bonus may feel that he is justified, because he is otherwise underpaid. Or he may believe that "everybody else does it" and it would be foolish not to do what others do. Or, perhaps, he is trying to protect the bonuses of other people in the division.

Box 6.2 presents a number of fraud risk factors, as enumerated by the AICPA in a statement of auditing standards. The factors are grouped by the three parts of the fraud triangle.

Box 6.2 Excerpts of Fraud Risk Factors Taken from AICPA Auditing Standard No. 122 Consideration of Fraud in a Financial Statement Audit

Incentives and Pressures

Financial stability or profitability is threatened by economic, industry, or entity operating conditions, such as ... the following:

- High degree of competition or market saturation
- High vulnerability to rapid changes ... in technology, product obsolescence, or interest rates
- Significant declines in customer demand
- Increasing business failures in either the industry or overall economy
- Operating losses making the threat of bankruptcy ... or hostile takeover imminent
- Rapid growth or unusual profitability

Excessive pressure exists for management to meet ... expectations of third parties

- Expectations of investment analysts ... significant creditors, or other external parties
- Need to obtain additional debt or equity financing
- Marginal ability to meet ... debt repayment or other debt covenant requirements
- Adverse effects of reporting poor financial results on significant pending transactions

The personal financial situation of management or those charged with governance

- Significant financial interests in the entity
- Significant ... compensation ... contingent upon achieving aggressive targets
- Personal guarantees of debts of the entity

Management or operating personnel are under excessive pressure to meet financial targets established by those charged with governance, including sales or profitability incentive goals.

Opportunities

Arising from the nature of the industry or the entity's operations

- Significant related party transactions not in the ordinary course of business
- The ability ... to dictate terms or conditions to suppliers or customers
- Assets, liabilities, revenues, or expenses based on significant estimates that involve subjective judgments or uncertainties that are difficult to corroborate
- Significant, unusual, or highly complex transactions

The monitoring of management is not effective

- Domination of management by a single person or small group.
- Oversight ... over the financial reporting process and internal control is not effective.

The organizational structure is complex or unstable.
  Internal control components are deficient as a result of the following:

- Inadequate monitoring of controls
- High turnover rates

- Employment of accounting, internal audit, or IT staff who are not effective
- Accounting and information systems that are not effective

Attitudes and Rationalizations

- Communication of inappropriate values or ethical standards
- Nonfinancial management's excessive participation in or preoccupation with the selection of accounting policies or the determination of significant estimates.
- Known history of violations of securities law or other law or regulation
- Excessive interest by management in maintaining or increasing the entity's stock price or earnings trend.
- The practice by management of committing to analysts, creditors, and other third parties to achieve aggressive or unrealistic forecasts.
- An interest by management in employing inappropriate means to minimize reported earnings for tax-motivated reasons.
- The owner-manager makes no distinction between personal and business transactions.
- Dispute between shareholders in a closely held entity.

Taken from Appendix A, paragraph A75, AICPA. (2015). *Clarified Statements of Auditing Standards, AU-C Section 240, Consideration of Fraud in a Financial Statement Audit.* New York: AICPA.

One problem with trying to pull off an accounting fraud is that the fundamental accounting equation always holds. Companies who wish to misstate earnings can never just misstate a single account, or the equation won't balance. If they wish to inflate income, they must also misstate something else. For example, a company overstating its income might also overstate accounts receivable, or inventory. In the Bausch and Lomb case, the creation of fictitious sales caused accounts receivables on the balance sheet to increase, since of course no payments were being received for the fictitious sales. A famous fraud from the 1930s, the McKesson Robbins fraud, involved overstating both receivables and inventory. In the WorldCom fraud, discovered in 2002, the company overstated its fixed assets by billions of dollars. In the Parmalat fraud, discovered in 2003, Parmalat overstated various assets, including cash supposedly on deposit with the Bank of America, by about $5 billion. Other companies have understated liabilities. These misstated balance sheet accounts are often difficult to explain.

Research (Ball and Watts 1972) also suggests that there is a problem with trying to pull off the kinds of fraud in which a company hides a loss in one year, and expects to have enough gains in the next year to cancel it out. Let's say a company had expected to have 2012 net income of $100 million. This year, sales were bad, and 2012 income was only $96 million. In some cases, the managers have expected the next year to be much better, for example $112 million. So they have lied, and reported 2012 income was $100 million (just as everyone expected). They hoped that when the real earnings in 2013 came in at $112 million, they could then hide their 2012 overstatement of $4 million by saying 2013 income was only $108 million. At that point the total of the two years' income that was reported would be the total of $208 million, and the company could report an honest balance sheet. Its need to lie would be over. The problem, according to research published in 1972, is that a company that has real earnings of $96 million in one year is far more likely to have the same disappointing earnings in 2013 than it is to have earnings of $112. In other words, the problems are more likely to get bigger once a fraud starts than to be covered up by future earnings.[18]

Avoiding Measurement

In some cases, managers who are unhappy about being measured within a company will quit. In other cases, they will lobby within the company to get the measurement system changed. For example, they may argue that the company's system of budgeting and holding managers to account for variances has dysfunctional effects. Some companies have moved away from using annual budgets to monitor performance, partly due to resistance from their employees. Others have adapted "continuous" budgeting techniques, which allow for frequent updating of budget targets. (See for example Frow, Marginson and Ogden 2010).

Companies may try to escape from what they regard as burdensome accounting rules. Some public companies "go private", and become exempt from the SEC's reporting requirements. Some private companies choose not to issue stock to the public, to avoid coming under SEC regulation. After the Sarbanes–Oxley Act was passed in 2002, with its tougher accounting requirements, people feared that fewer foreign companies would choose to register their stocks on U.S. exchanges.

Companies have also lobbied to get the FASB to change standards they do not like. An early example of this occurred in the 1970s. In December 1977, the FASB issued a pronouncement (SFAS No. 19) requiring oil and gas companies to use a form of accounting that would have required faster recognition of certain expenses of exploring for and developing new oil wells, and forbidding use of another method that had recognized these expenses more slowly. The SEC, reacting in part to lobbying by oil companies, announced that it would continue to allow the use of both accounting methods. The FASB backed down, and issued SFAS No. 25 in February 1979, allowing both methods.

More recently, during the financial crisis that started in 2008, both the FASB and the IASB came under strong political pressure to relax their rules on accounting for assets at "fair value." At this time, the markets for certain types of financial assets had collapsed. Some financial institutions were recording large losses on their holdings of these assets, since accounting rules required them to value them at what they could be sold for. The pressure from these companies led governmental authorities in both the U.S. and Europe to pressure the accounting standard-setters for relief. For example, the chair of the FASB faced hostile questioning by the House of Representatives Financial Services Subcommittee on Capital Markets (Morrison/ Foerster 2009). Both the FASB and IASB changed their rules to "clarify" that the requirement to use fair values only applied when there was a properly functioning "active market." When a company determined that the market was not properly functioning, it could use other methods to value its assets.[19]

Step 3—Reactions to the Reactions

General

The previous section discussed how people and organizations react to being measured. This section asks the next question—how do the various parties who rely on the measurements react, when companies and company personnel manage earnings, or lie, or behave in other dysfunctional ways?

Reactions by Management and Owners

Managers and owners use a large number of controls to try to prevent dysfunctional behavior, and to detect and correct it when it occurs. Chapter 11 discusses internal controls in detail. This section briefly describes some key steps that managers and owners take.

Clearly, top management can fire or otherwise penalize employees who are caught acting in a dysfunctional manner. Managers that are caught lying on their reports, or creating outrageous levels of budgetary slack, are likely to be quickly fired.

Top management often uses multiple measures of performance to try to prevent the dysfunctional behavior that arises when employees focus too much on a single measure. For example, the "balanced scorecard" contains not just financial measures, but also measures of customer satisfaction, and productivity, and efforts on training and innovation. While a manager who is under pressure to meet financial targets might be tempted to cut back on discretionary training cost, or on customer service, the manager would have to realize that cutting back in those areas adversely affects other parts of the balanced scorecard.

Top management uses incentive arrangements and contractual provisions to try to get employees to work in the desired manner. For example, contractual provisions tied to the overall profits of the company are meant to reward teamwork.

Top management can also take steps to encourage flexibility and innovation during the year. As noted above, Frow, Marginson, and Ogden (2010) found some companies use "continuous budgeting" techniques, whereby budget targets can be revised and updated to reflect changes in plan during the year. A study by Libby and Lindsay (2010) of 440 U.S. and Canadian business people found that a large number of their companies, even when they placed high emphasis on the budget, still made it possible to revise budget targets during the year. They concluded that:

> Our results indicate that only 12% of respondents in the Canadian high-budget-emphasis group and 17% of respondents in the US high-budget-emphasis group report that actual financial performance is rigidly compared against the pre-established budget target with no allowance for changes occurring in the competitive environment during the year. . . .
>
> In conclusion, the evidence does not support the . . . key assumption of the prevalence of the fixed performance contract in practice. In fact, it is remarkable how few firms use the budget in this way for performance evaluation. Instead, we find that subjectivity in performance evaluation or making allowances for non-controllable events is relatively widespread.
>
> (p. 64)

Reactions by Governments and Standard-Setters

Governments

There have been laws against fraud in business for many centuries, including some of the earliest law codes we know of.[20] In the United States, there are both Federal and state laws against fraud. Among the more important laws affecting accounting are the Securities Act of 1933, the Securities Exchange Act of 1934, and the Sarbanes–Oxley Act of 2002 (also known as the Public Company Accounting Reform and Investor Protection Act). The Securities Act of 1933 created the SEC and required companies who wished to sell new securities to the public to provide various information, including audited financial statements. The Securities Exchange Act of 1934 required public companies to make regular annual reports. Both these laws contain penalties for fraud. The Sarbanes–Oxley Act of 2002 increased the penalties for fraud, and also has other provisions meant to improve controls over company reporting. This act is discussed further in Chapter 11.

As has happened throughout the history of accounting, the U.S. laws were reactions to problems.[21] The 1933 and 1934 laws were passed in reaction to the practices of companies in the 1920s, which were considered part of the cause of the stock market crash of 1929, and the Great Depression. The Sarbanes–Oxley Act of 2002 was passed after a number of large U.S. companies were found to be reporting fraudulently. In particular, there were large and well-publicized frauds at Enron and WorldCom. See Boxes 6.3 and 6.4 for brief descriptions of these frauds.

Box 6.3 The Enron Fraud

Enron started as a gas pipeline company, in the 1980s. In the 1990s, after the energy markets in the U.S. were largely deregulated, Enron expanded its business. It began trading natural gas on commodity markets, and then expanded into other types of trading, including electric power. A large part of its business involved developing large energy facilities internationally. It also bought water utilities in various countries. The Enron Corporation was considered to be the seventh largest company in the U.S. by sales in 2001.

At the end of the third quarter of 2001, Enron reported a loss, and then later announced that it had overstated earnings for the previous four years. The company collapsed.

Enron used a variety of methods to overstate its earnings. Among other improper practices, Enron created "special purpose entities" which it controlled, but which were not considered part of Enron for reporting purposes. To avoid showing that it owned certain risky or unprofitable assets, Enron sold them to these special purpose entities. In some cases, Enron recorded gains on sales of assets to these entities.

At least 17 former Enron employees and five people from outside investment firms were found guilty of participation in the fraud, including Jeffrey Skilling, a former CEO, Andrew Fastow, the CFO, his wife Lea, and numerous other people. Kenneth Lay, the long-time CEO, died while his fraud conviction was on appeal, so under Texas law his conviction was voided.

The auditing firm, Arthur Andersen & Co., was charged with obstruction of justice. While its conviction was thrown out on appeal, Arthur Andersen & Co. went out of business in the aftermath of the scandal.

Box 6.4 The WorldCom Fraud

WorldCom was a telephone company that grew rapidly by acquisitions during the 1990s to become one of the U.S.'s largest telephone companies. Internet companies were booming in the 1990s, and companies that provided the necessary telephone service for them were also booming. By 2000, however, there was excess capacity in telephone capacity, and companies came under pressure to continue making profits. A second pressure on WorldCom was that it had been growing by acquisitions, and using acquisition accounting to improve its profits. By 2000, however, it had grown so large that it was difficult to find new companies to acquire that were large enough to affect its financial numbers. It tried to merge with Sprint, but the U.S. government barred this merger.

The company made accounting entries to inflate income. Instead of reflecting certain payments as expenses, it presented them as additions to fixed assets. According to the SEC complaint against its CEO, it overstated income by at least $9 billion over the period from 2000 to 2002.*

The fraud was discovered by the company's internal auditors.

After the fraud was disclosed, WorldCom declared bankruptcy. It was the largest bankruptcy in U.S. history at the time, larger than the recent Enron bankruptcy. The company later changed its name to MCI, and emerged from bankruptcy.

People convicted of fraud in connection with the WorldCom case include the CEO, the CFO, and four other accounting personnel.

*See www.sec.gov/litigation/complaints/comp19301.pdf (last accessed August 16, 2015).

When the SEC began operations in 1933, it favored accounting principles that it saw as more objective, and less subject to abuse by company managers. Some of the accounting principles favored by the SEC, in its efforts in the 1930s to reduce improper reporting, include:

- Revenue recognition when the transaction was realized. In the 1920s and earlier, it had been common for companies to recognize gains on assets they owned, due to increases in value. The SEC favored rules that delay recognizing these "holding gains" until the company actually sells the items
- Historical cost accounting. It favored the use of historical cost as a method of valuing assets and liabilities, because this method is easy to verify. See Brown (1975)
- Objectivity. The SEC favored accounting practices that rested upon objective, verifiable evidence
- Conservative bias. The SEC has tended to favor methods of accounting that are more *conservative*. For example, it has tended to favor methods of recognizing revenue that recognize revenue slowly, rather than quickly.

The SEC has also, from its inception, required companies to have audits of their financial statements by independent public accounting firms. The Sarbanes–Oxley Act gave the oversight of the relevant auditing rules to an agency called the Public Company Accounting Oversight Board. The belief is that independent auditors can reduce the likelihood of fraud.

The SEC has continued to try to reduce earnings management and fraud. In his speech about earnings management in 1998, Arthur Levitt not only listed what he saw as common earnings management techniques, but he also indicated what the SEC was intending to do about them. The SEC acted to change accounting and auditing rules related to acquisition accounting, revenue recognition, and materiality. The SEC staff began aggressively questioning companies suspected of managing earnings, and getting them to report more objectively.

Standard-Setters

Several accounting standards have clearly been designed to react to the ways that many companies were abusing the accounting rules. As noted above, the SEC favored the use of the realization principle for revenue recognition, and historical cost accounting, in the 1930s. The private sector standard-setters issued standards along these lines.

Also, for many years, FASB standards had a bias towards conservative accounting. This can be seen as a rational and reasonable way of countering management's incentive to be too optimistic. Various standards that are still in effect contain a conservative bias. For example, the standard on recognizing "contingent events" requires companies to book probable future losses, but does not allow them to book probable future gains until the gains actually occur. It should be noted that the FASB's conceptual framework for accounting, as discussed in Chapter 2, sees neutrality, not conservatism, as desirable in financial statements. Some scholars suggest that if the FASB wants published reports to be neutral, it needs to counteract management's aggressive tendencies with its own conservative bias.[22]

Here are some examples of standards that were set to reduce some kinds of perceived abuse:

- The FASB set several standards to regulate when revenues can be recognized in particular industries. These were seen at the time as ways to keep managers from being too aggressive and reporting revenues too soon. For example, there are special rules for franchising and for retail sales of homes.
- The FASB set several standards to limit the use of off-balance sheet financing. It has devoted a great deal of time to setting rules for accounting for leases, and has also addressed situations where companies try to obtain off-balance sheet financing by product financing arrangements or by selling receivables, with an agreement to buy them back.

The example of leasing is worth further discussion. In the section above on off-balance sheet financing, I described how a company might lease some equipment for its entire useful life, rather than buy it using borrowed money. Under the accounting rules in place in the 1960s, a company that bought equipment would have had to record the asset and the loan on its books, but a company who leased the equipment would not have shown the value of the equipment, or its lease obligation, on its balance sheet. In 1976, the FASB reacted to this abuse of accounting by issuing SFAS No. 13, which created the concept of a "capital lease." If a lease is considered a *"capital lease,"* it is accounted for basically as if the company had bought it for an amount equal to the present value of the lease payments. An asset is recorded on the books, and an obligation is also recorded. If a lease is not a capital lease, it is an *"operating lease."* The accounting for an operating lease is simple: each month, the company records a reduction of cash and a "lease expense" as it makes its payments. No asset appears on the balance sheet, and the obligation to make future payments is not shown as a liability.

The FASB then faced the problem of deciding when a lease was substantially the same thing, economically, as a purchase. Box 6.5 shows the four criteria it used from the point of view of the lessees (the people using the items).

The first two criteria make sense. If a lease transfers ownership, it is clearly like buying the asset. If the lease doesn't automatically transfer ownership, but buying the asset will be a terrific bargain at the end of the lease, then, again, the lease seems likely to result in a transfer of ownership. The third criterion focuses on the economic value of the asset. If the lease is so long that the lessee will enjoy most of the economic value of the asset, then this is an arrangement that effectively means the lessee is the only one who will ever get much benefit from the asset. The long lease gives the lessor the benefits an owner would have had. The cut-off for a lease being long is 75% of the expected life of the leased asset. The fourth criterion says that if the value of the lease payments is very high relative to the value of the assets, any rational person could have bought the asset for the same value. The cut-off is at 90% of the value. Therefore, the lease must be very similar to a purchase.

Box 6.5 Criteria for Classifying a Lease as a Capital Lease, per SFAS No. 13

For a lessee, a lease was a capital lease if any of the following four criteria were met:

a. The lease transfers ownership of the property to the lessee by the end of the lease term. . . .
b. The lease contains a bargain purchase option....
c. The lease term . . . is equal to 75 percent or more of the estimated economic life of the leased property. . . . [There is an exception for items leased late in their useful life.]
d. The present value at the beginning of the lease term of the minimum lease payments . . . equals or exceeds 90 percent of the . . . fair value of the leased property.

For a lessor, one of the above four criteria must be met, and also:

    a. Collectibility of the minimum lease payments has to be relatively predictable and
    b. There should be no major uncertainties about remaining costs the lessor must incur.

See www.fasb.org/jsp/FASB/Page/PreCodSectionPage&cid=1218220137031 (last accessed August 16, 2015).

For a lessor to say that they have sold the items, and recognize a gain on sale, they had to satisfy two additional criteria. This is consistent with the FASB having a conservative bias, and setting rules to prevent improper revenue recognition. Lessors had to show the lease payments were collectible, and that the lessors had minimal continuing costs related to the items they had leased, in order to recognize the lease as effectively a sale.

Reactions of Analysts and Stock Markets

Analysts are aware that the numbers provided by companies may be optimistic or fraudulent. The stock market tends to place lower valuations on companies whose earnings are seen as of "lower quality." It has also been suggested that analysts expect companies to use earnings management to meet their targets and therefore, when a company misses a target by a penny or two, the market assumes that things were in fact far worse. The analysts assume that the target was missed even after the managers did as much earnings management as they could.

A classic article in the economics literature by George Akerlof (1970) described the effects on markets where the buyer and seller have different information. In economics, this is referred to as "*asymmetric information*." It creates *information risk*. Buyers will be reluctant to buy when they believe the seller knows some secret about the product. The buyers wonder: "Why is he willing to sell at this price? Is there some problem I don't know about?" This doubt can either cause the buyers to offer a low price, or to stop buying altogether. In extreme cases, information asymmetry can cause markets to shut down entirely. In his 1998 speech on earnings management, Arthur Levitt raised this as a concern:

> The significance of transparent, timely, and reliable financial statements and its importance to investor protection has never been more apparent. The current financial situations in Asia and Russia are stark examples of this new reality. These markets are learning a painful lesson taught many times before: Investors panic as a result of unexpected or unquantifiable bad news. If a company fails to provide meaningful disclosure to investors about where it has been, where it is, and where it is going, a damaging pattern ensues. The bond between shareholders and the company is shaken; investors grow anxious; prices fluctuate for no discernible reasons; and the trust that is the bedrock of our capital markets is severely tested.
>
> Markets exist through the grace of investors.
>
> Today, American markets enjoy the confidence of the world. How many half-truths and how much accounting sleight of hand, will it take to tarnish that faith?[23]

The accounting scandals in 2001 and 2002, including the Enron and WorldCom frauds, shook public confidence in the stock market. This loss of confidence was one reason for major declines in the market. The passage of the Sarbanes–Oxley Act in July 2002 helped restore public confidence. However, some studies suggest that analysts remained skeptical of company reports for some time afterward. One study (Byun and Roland-Luttecke 2014) of companies that reported they had met or beaten their earnings target in the period after the scandals indicated their stock prices did not rise as much as theory would predict. The authors ascribe this to "temporary over-skepticism" by the market of the validity of company numbers.

There is also some evidence that the markets are able to recognize companies that report conservatively, and that the markets value this conservatism. The argument here is that where shareholders believe there is less risk of being misled by aggressive accounting, they are willing to pay more for the shares.[24]

Another reaction is that people have tried to develop tools to detect earnings management. There is a wide literature in accounting and auditing of models for identifying indicators of fraud or earnings management.[25] In a 2012 speech, the Chief Economist and Director of the SEC's Division of Risk, Strategy, and Financial Innovation announced that the SEC was developing an "audit quality model" to help it identify companies to look at more closely (Lewis 2012). There is some evidence that markets are at least partially able to spot fraud, because they seem to value the earnings of fraud firms less than normal earnings, in the periods before the fraud is revealed.[26]

Step 4—Reactions to the Reactions to the Reactions

Financial Accounting—Reactions to New Accounting Standards

This section takes the "game" of accounting one step further. Of course, operating managers and companies will respond to the actions of managers, governments, standard-setters, analysts and markets described in the last section. They may respond by doing what is desired, but they might also engage in more complicated earnings management, or more clever fraud.

In reaction to regulations and tax rules that favor particular types of transactions, companies change their operations to perform those particular actions. So, for example, if a regulation gives special benefits to a company with its "office" in a particular city, a company might establish an office there, even if almost no one ever uses that space. Waymire and Basu (2008) write that:

> The long-run effect of regulation and taxation on accounting can be to alter the causal relation between a transaction and its accounting treatment. As accounting becomes progressively more regulated, transactions become increasingly structured in anticipation of their subsequent accounting treatment. In addition, profitable transactions may be delayed or not undertaken if there is sufficient uncertainty about their current or future accounting treatment. The causality from transaction to accounting can thus reverse so that the relation now runs from accounting to transaction.
>
> (p. 101)

Here is one example of how a measurement rule can affect behavior. Assume a person owns a stock that has declined in value during the year, from $20,000 to $17,000. This is a real, economic decline in value. For tax purposes, this decline in value is not recognized until the person sells the stock. People often sell such stocks late in December, in order to report losses on their tax returns, and pay lower taxes. If the tax authorities allowed people to report losses without selling the shares, they probably would not sell them.

Leases provide another example. We have seen so far (Step 2) that managers reacted to the accounting rules of the 1960s by using leases as a form of off-balance sheet financing. This allowed them to obtain financing in ways that did not adversely affect common ratios used to judge solvency and leverage. In the 1970s, the FASB reacted to the widespread use of leases by issuing SFAS No. 13, and requiring companies to recognize certain types of leases as capital leases. This was discussed above, in Step 3. The FASB made very specific rules as to what a capital lease should be. These are shown above, in Box 6.5.

Companies reacted to SFAS No. 13 by changing the terms of their leases so they would either exactly meet the criteria to be treated as capital leases, or narrowly miss the requirements. One of the criteria states that if a lease extends for 75% or more of the expected useful life of the lease, it must be considered a capital lease. Similarly, SFAS No. 13 required that a lease be classified as capital if the present value of the minimum lease payments were 90% or more of the fair value of the leased equipment. Companies began changing their arrangements so that leases were for slightly shorter periods and the minimum lease payments were slightly lower, to avoid meeting the 90% criterion.

Sir David Tweedie, the first head of the IASB, used to joke that one of his goals in life was to fly on an airplane that actually appeared on the airline's balance sheet.[27] The point of the joke was that airlines try hard *not* to classify their aircraft leases as capital leases. The footnote on leases in the 2013 Form 10-K for Southwest Airlines says that "The Company had four aircraft classified as capital leases at December 31, 2013, compared to two aircraft classified as capital leases at December 31, 2012." The footnote then goes on to say that 160 other aircraft were accounted for as being under operating leases, with minimum lease payments totaling about $4.6 billion.

Financial Accounting—Reaction to Analyst and Market Skepticism

Trying to Demonstrate High-Quality Reporting

In Step 2, some managers were tempted to engage in earnings management or fraud in order to have their stock valued more highly. In Step 3, analysts and markets reacted to this "information risk" (the risk of relying on misstated information) by becoming more reluctant to buy stock.

In Step 4, one reaction by companies is to try to reassure the analysts and markets that they are in fact providing high-quality information. Good companies want to distinguish themselves from the bad companies. This is a reason that companies obtain audits, and that they will pay premium fees for audit firms with reputations for integrity and competence. Companies also will voluntarily disclose information and try to establish a reputation for transparency and complete disclosure.

Increased Pressure to Meet Analyst Forecasts

In Step 2, some managers used accrual or earnings management to meet analyst forecasts. In Step 3, analysts began assuming that managers used special efforts to meet their forecasts, and began assuming that earnings that came in even slightly below the forecasts were a signal of problems. The idea was that the true earnings must have been significantly below the forecast, because even with whatever tricks management used, they still couldn't reach the target. In Step 4, managers feel under even more pressure to meet the targets. This increases the likelihood of fraud or earnings management or of efforts to manage the analysts' expectations in advance.

Managerial Accounting—Reactions to Top Management Efforts to Control Employees

Trying to Demonstrate Honesty

In Step 1, top management set budget goals. In Step 2, some managers used actions to achieve the budget targets that hurt the company in the long run, and others lied about performance. In Step 3, top management used a variety of controls and incentives to try to punish dishonesty, and to give managers an incentive to operate in the company's best interests. In Step 4, those managers who want to be recognized and promoted and rewarded for their value will try to demonstrate their high quality. This is exactly parallel to the efforts of good companies to signal their quality to analysts. The higher quality managers will try to report clearly, will welcome internal audit inspection, and will try to establish reputations for honesty.

One researcher (Webb 2002) expressed the interactions this way:

> A budget is not an isolated, single-period event. Managers and their superiors may engage in repeated interactions about the budget and its contents. Budgets are reviewed and approved, performance is monitored and variances must be explained. This process can have consequences for future period performance evaluations, resource allocations and budget levels.

Because budgets have these implications that extend beyond the current period, managers' concern for their reputation is likely to influence budgeting decisions. Managers' budgeting decisions are also likely to be affected by the knowledge that results are reviewed against budget and they may be responsible for explaining variances.

(p. 363)

Trying to Obtain More Flexible Measurement Rules

One reaction by operating managers to new controls is to negotiate for more flexibility. Managers can legitimately argue that when rules are too restrictive, they will not be able to react properly to changes in customer demand, or unexpected production issues.

More Elaborate Efforts to Evade Controls

Unfortunately, some people will still feel a need to misrepresent their performance. Because they know that top management is monitoring certain statistics for signs of dysfunctional behavior, dishonest employees may try harder to hide their actions. For example, they may create fictitious documents, or involve outside parties in their actions. In the Bausch & Lomb case referred to earlier in this chapter, operating managers were trying to inflate their reported sales. To conceal the misrepresentation, they actually rented a special warehouse, and shipped goods to the warehouse, in order to have shipping documents to support their fraudulently recorded sales.

As another example, managers may act strategically on poorly designed compensation contracts.[28] For example, assume that a company gives a manager a bonus equal to 1% of her division's earnings, with a cap when the division's earnings reach $10 million. If the manager believes in November that her division could make $12 million for the current year, but that prospects for the following year are uncertain, she has an incentive to try to slow some sales down until January. After all, her bonus for the current year is the same whether her division makes $10.5 million or $12 million (or $200 million), and she is certain to achieve that in any case. However, next year's bonus is uncertain, and it could be very helpful to have the year start with a bang, due to the sales that she is going to defer into January.

Further Steps

This process can go on and on. When people react in some improper way to being measured, the standard-setters (or top management) respond with new rules and ways of auditing performance. In some cases these rules and audits work, but in other cases they lead to new dysfunctional behavior, and that can lead to another cycle of rules and responses. Dye, Glover, and Sunder (2015) list a total of 56 pronouncements that accounting bodies made on the topic of leases between 1949 and 2013, as the regulators tried to keep up with company efforts to game the system.

This cycle of reactions has caused people to suggest two very different approaches to the task of setting accounting standards. One approach is called "*rule-based*," and the other is called "*principles-based*." A rules-based approach provides a specific rule that accountants must achieve. There may be a specific numeric target. If this "bright line" is met, then a transaction falls into a particular category, and if the "bright line" is not crossed, then it is accounted for differently. On the other hand, a principles-based approach is less specific, and simply sets out the ideas behind the accounting treatment. The accountant is expected to use honest professional judgment to determine the accounting.

While there are many exceptions, and the differences in standards are becoming smaller, people tend to say that IASB historically followed a principles-based approach while the FASB

Box 6.6 Lease Classification Rules from International Accounting Standard 17

Classification of leases

A lease is classified as a finance lease if it transfers substantially all the risks and rewards incident to ownership. All other leases are classified as operating leases. Classification is made at the inception of the lease. Whether a lease is a finance lease or an operating lease depends on the substance of the transaction rather than the form. Situations that would normally lead to a lease being classified as a finance lease include the following:

1   The lease transfers ownership of the asset to the lessee by the end of the lease term.
2   The lessee has the option to purchase the asset at a price which is expected to be sufficiently lower than fair value at the date the option becomes exercisable that, at the inception of the lease, it is reasonably certain that the option will be exercised.
3   The lease term is for the major part of the economic life of the asset, even if title is not transferred.
4   At the inception of the lease, the present value of the minimum lease payments amounts to at least substantially all of the fair value of the leased asset.
5   The lease assets are of a specialized nature such that only the lessee can use them without major modifications being made.

Other situations that might also lead to classification as a finance lease are:

•   If the lessee is entitled to cancel the lease, the lessor's losses associated with the cancellation are borne by the lessee
•   Gains or losses from fluctuations in the fair value of the residual fall to the lessee (for example, by means of a rebate of lease payments)
•   The lessee has the ability to continue to lease for a secondary period at a rent that is substantially lower than market rent.

See www.ifrs.org/IFRSs/Pages/IFRS.aspx (last accessed August 16, 2015).

---

followed a rules-based approach. The rules for accounting for leases are a good example. As shown in Box 6.5 above, the FASB used "bright line" rules to determine if a lease was long enough, or if the lease payments were large enough, for the lease to be called a capital lease. In contrast, the IASB's criteria for classifying leases are shown in Box 6.6.

When you contrast the international standards to the U.S. ones, you see that they have mostly the same ideas. However, where the U.S. standards set specific targets, such as 75% and 90%, the international standard uses less precise terms, such as "the major part of the economic life" and "substantially all of the fair value" of the leased asset. The IASB leaves the interpretation of these terms to the professional judgment of the accountants and auditors.

The lease situation is hard because there are many possible lease terms, from one day to 200 years. In this case, it is clear how to classify extreme cases, but cases in the middle are harder. Dye, Glover, and Sunder (2015) note this logical issue was described by the ancient Greeks as the "paradox of the heap." If you start with a heap of sand, and take away the grains one by one, eventually you will no longer have enough sand to be described as a "heap," but it will be very hard to precisely define which grain of sand made the difference between "heap" and "not a heap." In this type of situation, it may be theoretically impossible for standard-setters to design rules that management cannot evade by redesigning the transactions.[29]

Is a principles-based approach better or worse than a rules-based approach? Each approach has supporters. Arguments for a principles-based approach include:

- It simplifies standard setting. Not every situation needs to be predicted as long as the main ideas are clear. IASB standards are shorter than FASB rules, and the IASB has not felt the need to issue as much specific guidance for particular industries as the FASB has.
- It discourages the kinds of actions that people take to just meet, or just fail, bright line standards. Under U.S. standards, a lease that is carefully structured to extend for 74% of an asset's useful life would be "operating" since it does not meet the 75% test, but it would probably be considered a capital lease under the international criterion of being for "the major part" of the asset's life.

The arguments for a rules-based approach include:

- It gives accountants a clear justification for their accounting. The U.S. is a society where there are many disputes, which often go to court. In court, it is relatively easy to point to a specific target, and explain that it simply requires a specific accounting action. It is harder to defend a professional judgment when the rules are not specific. To feel safe from arguments and challenges, many accountants want clear standards that give them "safe harbors." For the same reason, the tax law is often very specific, so it is easy for taxpayers and the IRS to decide if the rules have been followed
- There will be greater consistency in treatment of similar situations. To continue the example of leases, it may be that some accountants believe that a lease term of 51% is "the major part" of an asset's life, but that others would believe a lease must be for at least two-thirds of the life to meet this criterion. These different professional judgments will lead to inconsistent accounting.

As I write this chapter, the FASB and IASB are considering major changes to their standards on leases. In essence, their proposal (FASB 2013) would require companies to record an asset for the right to use an asset, and a related liability for lease payments, for all leases that are longer than 12 months. This seems to be their reaction to the way companies have abused the current rules on leases.

The same considerations affect managerial performance measurement. Top management could judge employees' performance strictly by pre-set numerical budget standards, or it could use a more flexible and subjective approach. The advantages of the numerical standards would be clarity and consistency, but people will be tempted to "game" the system. The subjective approach allows top management flexibility in judging performance, but may lead to complaints that judgments are unfair. Some employees may want the certainty of pre-set targets.

Something else that can happen is that the people who are being measured can try to re-educate the users to have more reasonable expectations. For example, companies can try to explain to the investment community that they should be judged on a long-term basis, not by monthly results. Sometimes, this can be successful. For example, Amazon.com argued in its early years that its goal was not short-term profitability, but, instead, to establish a major position in the marketplace. As another example, charities that have become tired of being judged by simplistic measures of how much they spend on overhead have tried to educate the public to focus, instead, on how the charities have helped the world. A Massachusetts highway sign making this point in 2014 is shown in Figure 6.1 below.[30]

Figure 6.1 A Massachusetts Highway Sign.

Concluding Comments

This chapter has presented the act of taking accounting measurements as part of a strategic process, involving reactions to measurements, and then further reactions. I want to complete the discussion by making several key points.

While the field of game theory provides useful insights, it is very dangerous to think of reporting as a game. When we play a game, we tend to suspend some of our normal ethical concerns. For example, in a game of poker, it is normal to pretend your cards are better, or worse, than they really are. There is some evidence that when managers think of reporting or the budgeting process as a game, they are less honest. (See Rankin, Schwartz, and Young 2008.) However, accounting reports affect real people, and there are real ethical requirements to report honestly. Arthur Levitt (1998) complained about this attitude of reporting being a game:

> Well, today, I'd like to talk to you about another widespread, but too little challenged, custom: earnings management. This process has evolved over the years into what can best be characterized as a game among market participants. A game that, if not addressed soon, will have adverse consequences for America's financial reporting system. A game that runs counter to the very principles behind our market's strength and success.

> Increasingly, I have become concerned that the motivation to meet Wall Street earnings expectations may be overriding common-sense business practices. Too many corporate managers, auditors, and analysts are participants in a game of nods and winks. In the zeal to satisfy consensus earnings estimates and project a smooth earnings path, wishful thinking may be winning the day over faithful representation.

He concluded his speech by saying:

> Numbers in the abstract are just that—numbers. But relying on the numbers in a financial report are livelihoods, interests, and, ultimately, stories: a single mother who works two jobs

so she can save enough to give her kids a good education; a father who labored at the same company for his entire adult life and now just wants to enjoy time with his grandchildren; a young couple who dreams of starting its own business. These are the stories of American investors.[31]

A second comment is that, while this chapter has spoken a lot about earnings management and fraud, it has also highlighted that there are strong economic and legal factors that induce honesty in both external and internal reporting. Managers and companies that establish reputations for honesty are rewarded, and a failure to be seen as credible presents companies and employees with real disadvantages.[32] Warren Buffett said "In the long run managements stressing accounting appearance over economic substance usually achieve little of either."[33]

Lastly, I want to return to the issue of how to teach about topics like earnings management and fraud. Ray Ball (2013) wrote:

> Yet the belief that an extraordinary proportion of accounting accruals are "managed" or "discretionary" is particularly troublesome, because it implies that most of what accountants do in practice—and of what we teach in accounting classes—consists of opportunities to manipulate.
>
> How do people who believe this literature teach their accounting classes to novice students? Do they start with: "Listen up, class. Most of what I am going to teach you this semester is how to cook the books. You will learn how to manipulate reported numbers to meet your objectives or those of managers generally. Some of what you will learn about reporting to users is not discretionary, but most is." If I thought that, I would quit.
>
> (p. 852)

I believe it is important for new students to understand that measurements create reactions, and some of those reactions are dishonest. However, I am *not* trying to help you "cook the books." Instead, I want to make you alert for the actions of others, and I also want you to understand that there are important economic and legal incentives for honest reporting.

I also want you to understand the pressures on the accounting system. That is why this is the first of the chapters on the limitations of accounting in Part 3 of the book. The standard-setters must consider, with every standard they set, how people will react.

Unresolved Issues and Areas for Further Research

1   How common is earnings management and fraud? By their nature, these are hidden behaviors, so it is hard to know how often they occur. There have been many studies of the topic, but many of these studies have serious flaws.[34] Graham, Harvey and Rajgopal's (2005) survey of 400 executives reported "A surprising 78% of our sample admits to sacrificing long-term value to smooth earnings." Dichev et al.'s (2013) study of 169 CFOs said that "in any given period, about 20% of firms manage earnings to misrepresent economic performance, and for such firms 10% of EPS is typically managed" (p. 30). The CFOs believe that 60% of earnings management increases income, and 40% is income-decreasing.

2   How common is it for managers to create budgetary slack to meet targets, or to use short-term, discretionary items to meet their targets? Again, it is hard to get evidence on this. There have been various studies that found evidence of these behaviors.[35]

The answers to these questions could in fact also affect behavior. If managers think "everyone else" manages earnings, they will be more likely to manage earnings themselves. On the other hand, if they believe the vast majority of earnings reports are objective and accurate, they will feel less pressure to "manage" their own company's earnings. This is the same pattern that we see in other behaviors, such as binge drinking or smoking on college campuses. Students who believe "everyone else does it" are more likely to binge drink or smoke than those who believe the behavior is uncommon.

3 What are the market consequences of earnings management? How does this behavior affect the overall markets, and the individual firms that practice it?[36]

4 What are the best techniques for detecting financial statement frauds?

5 What control systems and incentives make earnings management, or improper internal reporting, less likely?[37]

6 What budgeting processes, and subsequent performance evaluation methods, are likely to lead to the best results for organizations?[38]

Key Terms

Accruals management—This earnings management method uses the flexibility in accounting standards or estimates to affect earnings. For example, a company might underestimate its bad debts to improve income.

Asymmetric information—This exists when one side to a transaction has better information than the other. For example, company management knows more about the company than outside investors. Also, employees know more about their own performance than the supervisor.

Big bath—This earnings management technique, typically used by a company that is having a bad year, shifts losses from future years into the current period, and defers current revenues into future periods.

Budgetary slack—This is the difference between the targets set in a budget and what the manager actually expects to achieve. "Slack" makes it easy to achieve the budget level.

Capital lease—Capital leases are accounted for as if the company had actually bought the items. An asset is shown on the balance sheet for the present value of the leased assets, and a liability is shown for the obligation.

Cookie jar reserve—This earnings management technique involves recording excessive liabilities when profits are good. In some later year, the company corrects these excessive liabilities. The impact of reducing a liability is to increase income. These excessive reserves are waiting, like cookies in a jar, until management is hungry for them.

Conservative accounting practices—These accounting practices delay recognizing assets and income until they are very certain to be realized.

Expectations management—Companies try to convince analysts and investors what levels of earnings to expect the company to achieve.

Fraud triangle—Fraud is most likely when three factors exist: an incentive or pressure to commit fraud; an opportunity to deceive without being detected; and some rationale or explanation that will excuse the fraud in the perpetrator's mind.

Information risk—This is the risk of making a decision based on incorrect information. Information risk is increased by earnings management, budgetary slack, and fraud.

Off-balance sheet financing—This refers to a variety of ways that companies obtain financing without reporting their obligation to repay the financing on the balance sheet.

One-person game (also called a **game against nature**)—One person makes decisions about future events, but these decisions do not affect whether that event will actually occur. Example– deciding whether to bring an umbrella has no effect on whether it will actually rain.

Operating lease—These leases are accounted for as short-term rentals. A company records a lease expense each time it makes a lease payment. No asset is recorded for the value of the item leased. No liability is recorded for the future lease obligation. It is the opposite of a capital lease.

Principles-based accounting standards—These standards contain broad ideas of what they are meant to achieve, but do not set exact numerical criteria. Accountants must use professional judgment in applying these standards.

Real earnings management—This earnings management technique uses real transactions to achieve accounting targets. The transactions, or their timing, are made for accounting reasons more than economic reasons.

Rules-based accounting standards—These are very specific accounting standards, where very precise criteria must be met.

Window dressing—A company takes various steps at the balance sheet date to make the numbers look better than normal. Typically, there is little impact on earnings, but various ratios that use balance sheet data are improved.

Questions and Problems

Comprehension Questions

C1. (Strategic behavior) What is a one-person game? Why is budgeting not a one-person game?

C2. (Reaction to measurement) The chapter suggests that people can react to being measured in four different ways. Explain what each of the five ways involves.

C3. (Reaction to measurement) Explain what is meant by earnings management.

C4. (Earnings management) Explain the difference between accruals management and real earnings management.

C5. (Earnings management) Why might a manager try to "manage earnings" so that earnings appear:

    A. Higher than they really are

    B. Lower than they really are

    C. Smoother from year to year than they really are

    D. Extremely low this year, but higher next year.

C6. (Earnings management) Explain how earnings management differs from fraud.

C7. (Fraud) Can fraud be an accident? Why or why not?

C8. (Expectations management) Explain what expectations management is. How does it differ from earnings management?

C9. (Budgetary slack) What is budgetary slack? Why would a manager create budgetary slack?

C10. (Window dressing) What is meant by window dressing?

C11. (Fraud) Explain what the fraud triangle is.

C12. (Fraud) Give an example of an incentive or pressure that a company might have to report higher earnings.

C13. (Fraud) Give an example of an incentive or pressure that a company might have to report lower earnings.

C14. (Fraud) Give an example of an incentive a new CEO might have to take a "big bath" in the current year, and report very low profits or even losses.

C15. (Fraud) Give an example of something that increases the opportunity of a company to commit fraud.

C16. (Fraud) Give an example of something that a manager might use as a rationalization for overstating reported earnings fraudulently.

C17. (Forces encouraging honesty) What are some reasons that would cause a manager *not* to use earnings management or fraud when reporting its financial results to investors?

C18. (Forces encouraging honesty) What are some reasons that would cause a manager *not* to try to create large amounts of budgetary slack?

C19. (Types of accounting standards) Explain the difference between rules-based standards and principles-based standards.

C20. (Types of accounting standards) What are some *advantages* of a principles-based accounting standard system, compared to a rules-based system?

C21. (Types of accounting standards) What are some *disadvantages* of a principles-based accounting standard system, compared to a rules-based system?

Application Questions

A1. (Reactions to measurement) The chapter listed four ways that people react to a measurement that affects them: doing what the measurer wanted; doing something slightly different that is measured well; lying; and avoiding being measured. Note which type of behavior you think is being exhibited in each of 1 to 7 below. Also note if there are unintended consequences.

A business school wants to be better known for the intellectual quality of its faculty. It knows that schools are often judged on the quality and quantity of the faculty research professors. It begins measuring the number of articles that faculty publish in the top 10 peer-reviewed publications in their area. Professors are told that this is an important measurement for achieving tenure, and for being promoted. Some of the reactions are:

1 Professors make extra efforts in research during the summer, when they are not teaching, and publish more articles in top 10 journals

2 Professors reduce the time they spend preparing their classes, and spend more time on researching articles. They are able to publish more in top 10 journals

3 Professors who were known for publishing many short articles in less prestigious journals stop publishing in those journals, as they work on articles for top 10 journals. Instead of publishing eight articles in a five-year period, they are only able to publish one

4 Professors who have research ideas that will result in "top 10" articles help their friends by listing them as co-authors

5 The professors in a department agree to list some journals that are easier to publish in as "top 10" journals. The process of identifying "top 10" is subjective

6 Newly graduated doctoral students who are seeking their first job decide that it will be too hard to get tenure at this school, and take offers in other places

7 Professors who have tenure and were considering seeking promotion decide the standards are too high, and stop publishing altogether.

A2. (Reactions to measurement,) The chapter listed four ways that people react to a measurement that affects them: doing what the measurer wanted; doing something slightly different that is measured well; lying; and avoiding being measured. Note which type of behavior you think is being exhibited in each of 1 to 4 below. Also note if there are unintended consequences.

Some hospitals use "patient satisfaction surveys" to measure whether the patients treated by particular doctors or departments are happy with how the hospitals treated them. The goals of these measurements are to help identify both problems and good practices, and to make the doctors conscious of the need to consider how patients feel about their care. Some reactions are:

1 Some doctors began avoiding dealing with psychiatric patients, who are often more difficult to please

2 Some doctors began spending more time with patients, listening more carefully to their complaints

3   Some doctors began prescribing unnecessary tests, because patients are happier when they feel the doctor has "done something"

4   Some doctors made a point of asking patients who seemed happy with their care to fill out the surveys, but did not ask less happy patients to fill out the surveys.

A3. (Reactions to measurement) The chapter listed four ways that people react to a measurement that affects them: doing what the measurer wanted; doing something slightly different that is measured well; lying; and avoiding being measured. Note which type of behavior you think is being exhibited in each of 1 to 7 below. Also note if there are unintended consequences.

A university decided to collect survey information from students about the quality of the teaching by the professors. This information was to be used both to identify problems and for promotion and compensation decisions about professors. Surveys would be counted as long as there were at least 10 students responding. Professors distributed the surveys in class, and had a student collect the surveys and return them to the administration for processing.

1   Some professors started giving out cookies to students in the class before the surveys to put the students in a good mood.

2   Some professors tried to convince students who were doing poorly to drop the class before the time in the semester when the surveys were given out. Only students still in the class were counted.

3   Some professors spent more time preparing their classes, to ensure they were interesting and relevant.

4   Some professors spent extra time meeting students outside class, and giving extra help. This reduced the amount of time the professors were able to spend on research, and they published fewer articles.

5   Some professors made their courses easier, so more students would be happy with the course.

6   Some professors had the student who collected the surveys take out the four worst ratings and destroy them, before submitting the rest of the surveys to the administration.

7   A professor with a class of 11 students waited until a day when two students were absent to distribute the survey, knowing that the administration would ignore the results when there were only nine students.

A4. (Reactions to measurement) The chapter listed four ways that people react to a measurement that affects them: doing what the measurer wanted; doing something slightly different that is measured well; lying; and avoiding being measured. Note which type of behavior you think is being exhibited in each of 1 to 5 below. Also note if there are unintended consequences.

In December, 2014, the U.S. Department of Education asked for public comment on ways it was planning to measure two-year and four-year colleges in the United States.[39] The goal is to have a system of ratings of colleges as "high performing," "low performing," and "in the middle." Each college will be judged on: giving *access* to needy students; *affordability* after considering scholarships; and *outcomes*, "such as graduation and transfer rates, graduate earnings, and advanced degrees of college graduates." Assume that the Department of Education decides to measure "outcomes" for four-year colleges by the percentage of students who graduate in four years.

1   Schools increase the emphasis they place on advisement and tutoring, to help ensure students take appropriate courses.

2   Schools discourage students from taking internships while in school, since such students are likely to need an extra semester to graduate.

3   Schools take fewer students with low SAT scores. The schools are afraid these students will have a harder time finishing in four years.

4   Schools make it easier to graduate by making their classes and requirements easier.

5   Schools make it harder for their students to transfer to other colleges, since transfers to other colleges do not count as graduations.

6   Schools discontinue their engineering programs, which are normally five-year programs.

A5. (Reactions to measurement) The chapter listed four ways that people react to a measurement that affects them: doing what the measurer wanted; doing something slightly different that is measured well; lying; and avoiding being measured. Note which type of behavior you think is being exhibited in each of 1 to 5 below. Also note if there are unintended consequences.

In December, 2014, the U.S. Department of Education asked for public comment on ways it was planning to measure two-year and four-year colleges in the United States.[40] The goal is to have a system of ratings of colleges as "high performing," "low performing," and "in the middle." Each college will be judged on: giving *access* to needy students; *affordability* after considering scholarships; and *outcomes*, "such as graduation and transfer rates, graduate earnings, and advanced degrees of college graduates." Assume that one measure the Department of Education adopts to judge "outcomes" from four-year colleges is the percentage of graduates who earn more than some threshold dollar amount in the year after they graduate.

1   Schools encourage students to major in accounting, rather than sociology, because there are more job offers in accounting.

2   Schools discourage students from going on to graduate school, since the students will not earn much while in graduate school.

3   Schools improve the quality of their career counseling staff, and make greater efforts to match students with jobs.

4   Schools try to get rid of students early in their academic careers who the school feels will not be good job candidates. For example, the school makes it difficult for women who become pregnant to stay in school.

5   Schools admit fewer international students, since these students have difficulty getting U.S. employment and pay in their home countries is likely to be lower than U.S. salary rates.

A6. (Window dressing) The balance sheet of the Sunshine Corp. includes the following items (in dollars; the full balance sheet is not shown here):

Cash	50,000
Accounts receivable	30,000
Inventory	60,000
Total current assets	140,000
Noncurrent assets	260,000
Total assets	400,000
Current liabilities	100,000
Noncurrent liabilities	230,000
Equity	70,000
Total liabilities and equity	400,000

Assume the company had net income of $7,000 and sales of $90,000. The cost of goods sold was $60,000.

A.   Compute the current ratio. The formula for this is current assets divided by current liabilities.

B.   Assume the company uses $40,000 of cash to repay current liabilities just before year end. What would the current ratio be?

C.   Compute the number of days' sales on hand at the end of the year. The formula for this is 365 × (ending receivables ÷ sales.)

D.   Assume that, just before the end of the year, the company sells $10,000 of its accounts receivable to a financial institution, and receives cash of $9,500 in exchange. Compute the number of days' sales on hand at the end of the year after this transaction.

E.   Compute the number of days of inventory on hand at the end of the year. The formula is 365 × (ending inventory ÷ cost of goods sold.)

F.   Assume that, just before the end of the year, the company sells 25,000 of its inventory to another company in the business for the cost of $25,000, and secretly agrees to buy the inventory back after year end for $25,500. Compute the number of days of inventory on hand at the end of the year.

A7. (Off-balance sheet financing—leases) Shown below are summarized financial information for a retail company.

Current liabilities	$2,150	
Long-term debt	$500	
Other noncurrent liabilities	$1,000	
Shareholders' equity	$4,400	
Total	$8,050	Note—this also equals total assets.

All of this company's stores are leased. The company treated the leases as operating leases. If it had treated the leases as capital leases, the present value of the lease obligations would have been $3,000. Assume that of this $3,000, about $200 was a current liability and the rest is long term.

A.   Compute the ratio of liabilities to equity using the company's financial data, as shown in its balance sheet.

B.   Compute the ratio of long-term debt to equity using the company's data as shown on its balance sheet.

C.   Assume the company had treated the leases as capital leases. Compute the ratio of liabilities to equity.

D.   Assume the company treated the leases as capital leases, and considered the obligations to be debt. Compute the ratio of long-term debt to equity.

E.   Assume the company had net income for the year of $805. Compute the ratio of income to total assets, using the data as shown in the company's financial statements.

F.   What would be the ratio of net income to total assets if the company had capitalized the leases, and recognized additional assets of $3,000?

A8. (Earnings management incentives) Assume that the manager of a key division of the Dusk Corp. has a contract, that gives her bonuses based on the profits of her division.

It is now early December. In the current year, she believes her division is likely to earn $9 million without her taking any special actions to manage earnings. Her best forecast is that the earnings for the next year will also be about $9 million, so the two-year total is $18 million. She has the ability, by timing expenditures on things like research and training, to shift incomes somewhat. However, there are costs to doing this, so total two-year income will be lower than the $18 million total. She could shift the incomes to be $11 million in Year 1, and $6.5 million in Year 2, or $7 million in Year 1, and $10.5 million in Year 2.

Explain what behavior would be encouraged by the contract in each case:

A. Her bonus plan gives her 2% of the profits of the division each year.
B. Her bonus plan gives her 5% of any income over $9.5 million in either year. She receives no bonus for income below this level in either year.
C. Her bonus plan gives her a bonus of $60,000 as long as Year 1 earnings are over $6 million, and a bonus in Year 2 of 2% of profits.

A9. (Fraud triangle) For each of the items listed below, indicate if it is an example of: an incentive or pressure to commit financial fraud; opportunity; or rationalization. You may feel that some examples relate to more than one of the three parts of the triangle.

A. There has been a significant decline in customer demand this year.
B. The company believes most other companies in the industry manipulate earnings.
C. The CEO believes that if the company does not meet earnings this period, the company's lenders will shut it down. The CEO is optimistic that next year's earnings will be better, and any earnings problems are temporary.
D. The company's business and accounting are complicated, and the auditing firm does not understand some of the ways the company computes income. The auditing firm tends to accept the company's estimates without asking questions.
E. Each employee in the company is evaluated every 6 months. The company will fire the bottom 15% of employees, based on reported numbers.
F. The Board of Directors includes only people chosen by the CEO. The Board does little monitoring of the CEO's actions.

A10. (Accounting equation and fraud) The chapter mentioned that one problem that perpetrators of fraud have is that, when they inflate income, they must also misstate some other account so that the accounting equation will balance. In one real fraud, the company used all of the following methods to try to conceal a large overstatement of income. For each of the following, indicate how the fraud might be discovered:

A. The company claimed to have a large amount of inventory in Malaysia. In fact, the inventory did not exist.
B. The company claims to have made sales, on account, to certain customers. In fact, the accounts receivable are fictitious.
C. The company owed $20 million to two suppliers. It left these payables off its list of accounts payable.
D. The company claimed to have prepaid taxes of $12 million.

A11. (Ratio analysis and fraud) In Chapter 4, various ratios and other tools for analyzing financial statements were introduced. For each of the following examples, indicate if an unusual ratio might indicate the company misstating some asset or liability. Explain your answers.

A. Inventory turnover is much lower than normal.
B. Accounts receivable turnover is lower than normal.
C. The company seems to be paying its average accounts payable faster than normal, based on the reported amount of accounts payable at the end of the year.
D. The company's estimate of the amount of accounts receivable that it will not collect is much smaller this year than in prior years. (This means it is now expecting to collect a higher percentage of accounts receivable than normal.)

A12. (Fraud) According to charges made by the SEC, Enron Corporation engaged in a number of "prepay transactions" with Citigroup and J. P. Morgan Chase[41] between 1997 and 2001, totaling billions of dollars. In these cases, Enron sold certain commodities to a company owned by one of these banks, and received cash at the date of sale. Enron also agreed to buy back these commodities at a later time, for more money. The price Enron would pay in the future did *not* depend on any changes in the values of these commodities. The only risk the banks took was that Enron might not repay it, and in that case, the banks could sell the commodities at the market price.

A. How is a normal sale of commodities accounted for, in terms of the accounting equation? What are the effects on:

   a. Cash
   b. Inventories
   c. Sales
   d. Loans payable
   e. Cost of goods sold
   f. Operating cash flows
   g. Financing cash flows?

B. How is a borrowing normally accounted for? (Note that no entry is needed when a company "pledges" that its inventory will be collateral for a loan. The company still owns the inventory. However, it would disclose that the inventory is pledged.) What are the effects on:

   a. Cash
   b. Inventories
   c. Sales
   d. Liabilities
   e. Cost of goods sold
   f. Operating cash flows
   g. Financing cash flows?

C. The SEC claimed that these arrangements were disguised loans, and should not have been accounted for as true sales. In fact, the SEC cited one internal Chase email that said

   a. "WE ARE MAKING DISGUISED LOANS, USUALLY BURIED IN COMMODITIES OR EQUITIES DERIVATIVES (AND I'M SURE IN OTHER AREAS). WITH AFEW [sic] EXCEPTIONS, THEY ARE UNDERSTOOD TO BE DISGUISED LOANS AND APPROVED AS SUCH."
   b. Why should these transactions be accounted for as loans? Explain your answer.

D. What benefits, in terms of their financial statements, do you think that Enron was trying to achieve with these arrangements?

A13. (Fraud triangle.) This question applies the ideas of the "fraud triangle" to cheating by college students. For each of the following, indicate which part of the fraud triangle is involved: incentive or pressure; opportunity; rationalization. You may believe more than one part of the triangle is involved.

A. The professor does not allow students to use cell phones as calculators.
B. The entire grade for the course is based on a single test.
C. The professor reads the newspaper during exams.

D. Everyone knows the professor makes new exams each time, and there are three different versions of the exams.

E. A paper is a major part of the grade. The professor grades very strictly on English grammar. Some of the students are international students, and are not confident in their English.

F. Students believe that many other students are cheating.

G. Everyone knows the material in this course is unimportant. It is a required course, but there is no good reason anyone actually has to know this stuff.

A14. (Fraud triangle—turning it around to encourage good actions) The fraud triangle involves incentives or pressures; opportunity; and rationalizations. Assume a company believes that it would be good if many of its employees donate blood. It cannot order employees to give blood. How might the company use the three parts of the fraud triangle to increase participation:

A. How could it provide incentives?

B. How can it increase opportunity?

C. What rationales can it give employees to participate?

A15. (Fraud detection) A model for detecting fraud developed by Messod Beneish (1997) includes eight different factors. Listed below are some of these factors. Explain, for each one, why the factor is likely related to a company improperly reporting overly high earnings. Your answer might involve a pressure on the company to commit fraud, or it might consider whether the ratio is actually evidence that fraud has occurred:

A. A large increase in ending accounts receivable as a percentage of sales.

B. A firm that has a lower gross margin percentage this year than in prior years. The gross margin percentage equals the (sales–cost of goods sold) divided by sales.

C. Depreciation expense as a percentage of the related fixed assets is lower than in prior years.

D. The part of net income that is due to accounting accruals, rather than cash received, is growing compared to prior years.

E. An increase in the proportion of financing from debt, relative to equity.

A16. (Actions and reactions) In some cases, FASB standards seem to have been designed to prevent certain reactions by management to engage in "real earnings management" or "window dressing." Explain what actions the FASB may have been trying to prevent in these cases:

A. Classifying leases. The FASB says that a lease is a capital lease if, when the lease ends, the ownership transfers to the lessee. Why do you think the FASB then added a criterion that, even if the ownership is not transferred, the lease would be considered a capital lease if there was a "bargain purchase option" that made buying the asset very attractive to the lessee?

B. Earnings per share. This is a way of expressing how much of the company's income during the year relates to each share of stock. The rules for computing earnings per share say the earnings during the year are divided by the average number of shares that were outstanding during the year. Companies must compute this by considering the totals of shares outstanding on each day of the year. Why didn't the FASB let companies just use the number of shares outstanding on the first and the last days of the year for this computation?

Discussion Questions

D1. (Fraud detection tools) There has been academic research to develop a measure of the likelihood that a company's financial reporting is overly aggressive, and contains a high risk of fraud. Could there be any bad effects of creating such a fraud detection measure and making it widely available to the public?

D2. (Actions and reactions) When a company is found to have misstated its financial results, who do you think should be punished—the company, the officers, or both? Remember, while corporations are legally separate from their owners, payments by corporations are ultimately a cost to their shareholders.

D3. (Actions and reactions) Given that there are market pressures to behave honestly, is there any reason that we need to have government regulation of financial reporting by companies? Are market forces sufficient?

Notes

1   Talmud section Bava Batra 89b, as translated in Katz and Schwartz (1998). The Talmud was compiled between the first and seventh century of the Common Era. Yohannon ben Zakkai lived in the first century CE.

2   This quotation cited in Wikipedia: https://en.wikipedia.org/wiki/Goodhart%27s_law (last accessed August 19 2015).

3   See Rankin, Schwartz and Young (2008).

4   The seminal paper in this field is Ball and Brown (1968).

5   Arnold and Oakes (1998) discuss the relation between the FASB's decision to require measurement and recognition of OPEB costs and the rollback of benefits in many companies. They see a link, but not a strictly direct one. "Corporations were able to reduce resistance to employee benefit reductions by constructing RHB [retirement health benefits] and their accounting treatment as threats to corporate survival." (p. 146)

6   The Governmental Accounting Standards Board has moved even more slowly on requiring governments to accrue the full liabilities for these obligations. Its Standard No. 67, requiring such accrual of pension benefits, was issued in 2012, and became effective for fiscal years starting after June 15, 2014.

7   For further discussion of this point, see Hartmann (2000). Hartmann cites earlier work by Anthony Hopwood regarding certain inherent limitations of accounting measures of managerial performance. For example, not all management actions are measured, and companies rarely fully understand their economic cost functions.

8   See Bartov and Cohen (2009), American Accounting Association (2009) and Das, Kim and Patro (2011).

9   See www.cpajournal.com/1998/1298/Features/F141298.html (last accessed August 19, 2015).

10   For related research, see American Accounting Association (2009) and Walker (2013).

11   See for example Neely and Tinkelman (2014).

12   For a review of experimental studies supporting this finding, see Libby, Bloomfield and Nelson (2002).

13   See Bartov and Cohen (2009) and American Accounting Association (2009).

14   See Bartov and Cohen (2009) and Harrison and Fiet (1999).

15   Michael Chatfield (1977) noted that by making income recognition dependent on decisions to sell or not sell certain items, the adoption of the realization principle "permitted and encouraged the manipulation of periodic income figures" (p. 263)

16   See Feng et al. (2011). "CEOs of manipulation firms have higher equity incentives and more power than CEOs of matched firms. Taken together, our findings are consistent with the explanation that CFOs are involved in material accounting manipulations because they succumb to pressure from CEOs, rather than because they seek immediate personal financial benefit from their equity incentives." (p. 35)

17   Available at: www.businessweek.com/1995/43/b34471.htm (last accessed August 19, 2015).

18   To use technical language, earnings are more of a "random walk" than a "mean reverting process."

19   See FSP 157-E, issued March, 2009. More information available at www.fasb.org/news/nr031709.shtml (last accessed August 16, 2015).

20   Part of the ancient Code of Hammurabi, dating back to approximately 1750 BCE, is "If a herdsman, to whose care cattle or sheep have been entrusted, be guilty of fraud and make false returns of the natural increase, or sell them for money, then shall he be convicted and pay the owner ten times the loss." (Internet Sacred Text Archive 2011). The Biblical law codes also include various mentions of proper

measurement. For example, "Ye shall do no unrighteousness in judgment, in mete-yard, in weight, or in measure. Just balances, just weights, a just ephah, and a just hin, shall ye have." Leviticus 19:35-36. (The Jewish Publication Society of America 1955). See also Proverbs 11:1, Deuteronomy 25:13-16, Proverbs 20:10, or Micah 6:11.

21 Table 1.2 in Chapter 1 lists various developments in accounting that were reactions to financial crises or scandals.

22 Gao (2013a and 2013b).

23 Available at: www.cpajournal.com/1998/1298/Features/F141298.html (last accessed August 19, 2015).

24 See Francis, Hasan and Wu (2013).

25 See Beneish (1997). For a textbook discussion, see Wahlen, Baginski, and Bradshaw (2015). See also Dechow et al. (2011).

26 See Hui, Lennox, and Zhang (2014). "Our findings suggest that investors are able to accurately assess the probability of fraud and that such assessments affect the market's valuation of earnings even before it is publicly announced that fraud has occurred." (p. 627)

27 I heard him tell the joke at two different presentations.

28 See Pfeiffer and Velthuis (2009).

29 Dye, Glover and Sunder (2015) propose an "impossibility theorem" indicating that regulators can't stop managers from redesigning at least some transactions to circumvent rules when certain conditions exist. These include a situation where there are many transactions, some cases are close to some boundary, there are benefits to meeting the accounting target, and the cost of redesigning the transactions is a continuous variable.

30 Photo taken by Dan Pallotta. Used here with permission.

31 Available at: www.cpajournal.com/1998/1298/Features/F141298.html (last accessed August 19, 2015).

32 Work in game theory on repeated games may be relevant here. One strategy that has been found to be very effective in repeated situations is a "tit for tat" strategy, first developed by Anatol Rapoport in a tournament of computer programs to play a game. In the game, the choices were whether to act cooperatively or competitively. If both players acted cooperatively, they both got the highest rewards. However, if one player acted cooperatively, and the other acted competitively, then the cooperative player was hurt. If both players acted competitively, neither did well. The tit for tat strategy says that you should base your behavior this period on what happened last period. If the other player acted cooperatively last time, you should be cooperative this time, and if they hurt you by being competitive last time, you should hurt them this time. In experiments, this strategy usually results in both players acting cooperatively after a short period.

33 www.goodreads.com/quotes/tag/accounting (last accessed August 16, 2015).

34 Ball (2013) argues that many studies overstate the prevalence of earnings management. Zang (2006) suggests that managers use accruals management and real earnings management techniques as substitutes for each other. Bartov and Cohen (2009) suggest that earnings management became less frequent after various actions taken after the accounting scandals of 2001 and 2002.

35 For example, see Merchant (1990) and Harrison and Fiet (1999).

36 See Gunny (2010).

37 See Libby, Bloomfield, and Nelson (2002), Tessier and Otley (2012), Ittner and Larcker (1998) and Brown et al. (2014).

38 See Covaleski et al. (2006).

39 All quotations in this problem are from A New System of College Ratings—Invitation to Comment. U.S. Department of Education, issued December 19, 2014. www2.ed.gov/documents/college-affordability/framework-invitation-comment.pdf (last accessed August 16, 2015).

40 All quotations in this problem are from A New System of College Ratings—Invitation to Comment. U.S. Department of Education, issued December 19, 2014. www2.ed.gov/documents/college-affordability/framework-invitation-comment.pdf (last accessed August 16, 2015).

41 See http://www.sec.gov/news/press/2003-87.htm (last accessed August 16, 2015) and www.sec.gov/litigation/complaints/comp18252.htm (last accessed August 16, 2015).

References

Akerlof, G. A. (1970). The market for "lemons": Quality uncertainty and the market mechanism. *The Quarterly Journal of Economics, 84*(3), 488–500.

American Accounting Association. (2009). The impact of academic accounting research on professional practice: An analysis by the AAA Research Impact Task Force. *Accounting Horizons, 23*(4), 411–56.

Arnold, P. J., & Oakes, L. S. (1998). Accounting as discursive construction: The relationship between Statement of Financial Accounting Standards No. 106 and the dismantling of retiree health benefits. *Accounting, Organizations and Society, 25*(2), 129–53.

Ball, R. (2013). Accounting informs investors and earnings management is rife: Two questionable beliefs. *Accounting Horizons, 27*(4), 847–53.

Ball, R., & Brown, P. (1968). An empirical evaluation of accounting income numbers. *Journal of Accounting Research, 6*(2), 159–78.

Ball, R., & Watts, R. (1972). Some time series properties of accounting income. *The Journal of Finance, 27*(3), 663–81.

Bartov, E., & Cohen, D. A. (2009). The "Numbers Game" in the pre-and post-Sarbanes–Oxley eras. *Journal of Accounting, Auditing & Finance, 24*(4), 505–34.

Beneish, M. D. (1997). Detecting GAAP violation: Implications for assessing earnings management among firms with extreme financial performance. *Journal of Accounting and Public Policy, 16*(3), 271–309.

Bernhardt, I., & Copeland, R. M. (1970). Some Problems in Applying an Information Theory Approach to Accounting Aggregation. *Journal of Accounting Research* (Spring), 95–8.

Brown, C. D. (1975). The Emergence of Income Reporting. *International Journal of Accounting* (Spring), 85–107.

Brown, J. L., Fisher, J. G., Sooy, M., & Sprinkle, G. B. (2014). The effect of rankings on honesty in budget reporting. *Accounting, Organizations and Society, 39*(4), 237–46.

Byun, S. & Roland-Luttecke, K. (2014). Meeting-or-beating, earnings management, and investor sensitivity after the scandals. *Accounting Horizons, 28*(4), 847–67.

Campbell, D. T. (1976). *Assessing the Impact of Planned Social Change.* Hanover New Hampshire, USA: The Public Affairs Center, Dartmouth College.

Chatfield, M. (1977). *A History of Accounting Thought* (revised edition). New York: Robert E. Krieger Publishing Company.

Cotter, J., Tuna, I., & Wysocki, P. D. (2006). Expectations management and beatable targets: How do analysts react to explicit earnings guidance? *Contemporary Accounting Research, 23*(3), 593–624.

Covaleski, M., Evans III, J. H., Luft, J., & Shields, M. D. (2006). Budgeting research: three theoretical perspectives and criteria for selective integration. *Handbooks of Management Accounting Research, 2,* 587–624.

Cressey, D. R. (1953). *Other people's money; a study of the social psychology of embezzlement.* Glencoe, Ill: Free Press.

Das, S., Kim, K., & Patro, S. (2011). An analysis of managerial use and market consequences of earnings management and expectation management. *The Accounting Review, 86*(6), 1935–67.

Dechow, P. M., Ge, W., Larson, C. R., & Sloan, R. G. (2011). Predicting Material Accounting Misstatements. *Contemporary Accounting Research, 28*(1), 17–82.

Demski, J. S., Fellingham, J. C., Lin, H. H., & Schroeder, D. A. (2008). Interaction between productivity and measurement. *Journal of Management Accounting Research, 20*(1), 169–90.

Dichev, I., Graham, J., Harvey, C. R., & Rajgopal, S. (2013). Earnings quality: Evidence from the field. *Journal of Accounting and Economics, 56*(2–3), 1–33.

Dye, R. A., Glover, J. C., & Sunder, S. (2015). Financial engineering and the arms race between accounting standard setters and preparers. *Accounting Horizons, 29*(2), 265–96.

FASB. (1978). Statement of Financial Accounting Concepts No. 1, *Objectives of Financial Reporting by Business Enterprises.* Stamford, CT: FASB.

FASB. (1980). Statement of Financial Accounting Concepts No. 2, *Qualitative Characteristics of Accounting Information.* Stamford, CT: FASB.

FASB. (1985). Statement of Financial Accounting Standards No. 87, *Employers' Accounting for Pensions.* Norwalk, CT: FASB.

FASB. (2013). Proposed Accounting Standards Update (Revised) Leases (Topic 842)—*a revision of the proposed FASB Accounting Standards Update, Leases (Topic 840).* Norwalk, CT: FASB.

Feng, M., Ge, W., Luo, S., & Shevlin, T. (2011). Why do CFOs become involved in material accounting manipulations? *Journal of Accounting and Economics, 51*(1), 21–36.

Francis, B., Hasan, I., & Wu, Q. (2013). The benefits of conservative accounting to shareholders: Evidence from the financial crisis. *Accounting Horizons, 27*(2), 319–46.

Frow, N., Marginson, D., & Ogden, S. (2010). "Continuous" budgeting: Reconciling budget flexibility with budgetary control. *Accounting, Organizations and Society*, 35(4), 444–61.

Gao, P. (2013a). A measurement approach to conservatism and earnings management. *Journal of Accounting and Economics*, 55(2), 251–68.

Gao, P. (2013b). A two-step representation of accounting measurement. *Accounting Horizons*, 27(4), 861–6.

Gigler, F., Kanodia, C., Sapra, H., & Venugopalan, R. (2014). How frequent financial reporting can cause managerial short-termism: An analysis of the costs and benefits of increasing reporting frequency. *Journal of Accounting Research*, 52(2), 357–87.

Goodhart, C. A. E. (1975). Problems of monetary management: The UK experience. *Papers in Monetary Economics, Vol I*. Sydney: Reserve Bank of Australia.

Graham, J. R., Harvey, C. R., & Rajgopal, S. (2005). The economic implications of corporate financial reporting. *Journal of Accounting and Economics*, 40, 3–73.

Gunny, K. A. (2010). The relation between earnings management using real activities manipulation and future performance: Evidence from meeting earnings benchmarks. *Contemporary Accounting Research*, 27(3), 855–88.

Harrison, J. S., & Fiet, J. O. (1999). New CEOs pursue their own self-interests by sacrificing stakeholder value. *Journal of Business Ethics, 19,* 301–8.

Hartmann, F. G. (2000). The appropriateness of RAPM: Toward the further development of theory. *Accounting, Organizations and Society*, 25(4), 451–82.

Hui, K. W., Lennox, C., & Zhang, G. (2014). The market's valuation of fraudulently reported earnings. *Journal of Business Finance & Accounting*, 41(5–6), 627–51.

Ijiri, Y. (1967). *The Foundations of Accounting Measurement: A Mathematical, Economic, and Behavioral Inquiry*. Englewood Cliffs, NJ: Prentice-Hall, Inc.

Ijiri, Y. (1989). *Momentum Accounting and Triple-Entry Bookkeeping: Exploring the Dynamic Structure of Accounting Measurements*. Studies in Accounting Research # 31. Sarasota, FL: American Accounting Association.

Internet Sacred Text Archive. (2011). Code of Laws. Retrieved from www.sacred-texts.com/ane/ham/ham05.htm (last accessed August 16, 2015).

Ittner, C. D., & Larcker, D. F. (1998). Innovations in performance measurement: Trends and research implications. *Journal of management accounting research, 10,* 205–38.

Jewish Publication Society of America. (1955). *The Holy Scriptures According to the Masoretic Text: A New Translation*. Philadelphia: The Jewish Publication Society of America.

Joplin, J. P. (1914). The Ethics of Accountancy. *Journal of Accountancy*, 17(3), 187–96.

Katz, M. & Schwartz, G. (1998). *Swimming in the Sea of Talmud: Lessons for Everyday Living*. Philadelphia: The Jewish Publication Society.

Levitt, A. (1998). The numbers game. *The CPA Journal*, 68(12), 14–19.

Lewis, C. M. (2012, December 13, 2012). U.S. Securities and Exchange Commission. Retrieved from www.sec.gov/News/Speech/Detail/Speech/1365171491988#.VL-glSvF-So (last accessed August 16, 2015).

Libby, R., Bloomfield, R., & Nelson, M. W. (2002). Experimental research in financial accounting. *Accounting, Organizations and Society*, 27(8), 775–810.

Libby, T. & Lindsay, R. M. (2010). Beyond budgeting or budgeting reconsidered? A survey of North-American budgeting practice. *Management Accounting Research*, 21(1), 56–75.

Maremont, M. (October 23, 1995). Blind Ambition—Part I—How the pursuit of results got out of hand at Bausch and Lomb. *Business Week*, 78–92.

Marginson, D., & Ogden, S. (2005). Coping with ambiguity through the budget: The positive effects of budgetary targets on managers' budgeting behaviours. *Accounting, Organizations and Society*, 30(5), 435–56.

Merchant, K. A. (1990). The effects of financial controls on data manipulation and management myopia. *Accounting, Organizations and Society, 15*(4), 297–313.

Morgan, G. (1988). Accounting as reality construction: Towards a new epistemology for accounting practice. *Accounting, Organizations and Society, 13*(5), 477–85.

Morrison/Foerster (March 19, 2009). News bulletin: Mark-to-market update. Retrieved from www.mofo.com/~/media/Files/Resources/Publications/2009/03/MarktoMarket%20Update%20After%20Congressional%20Hearing%20__/Files/090319FASB/FileAttachment/090319FASB.pdf (last accessed August 16, 2015).

Neely, D. & Tinkelman, D. (2014). A Case Study in the Net Reporting of Special Event Revenues and Costs. *Journal of Governmental and Nonprofit Accounting, 3*(1), 1–19.

Pallotta, D. (2008). *Uncharitable: How restraints on nonprofits undermine their potential.* Hanover and London: UPNE.

Parsons, L. (2003). Is accounting information from nonprofit organizations useful to donors? Review of charitable giving and value-relevance. *Journal of Accounting Literature, 22*, 104–29.

Pfeiffer, T., & Velthuis, L. (2009). Incentive system design based on accrual accounting: a summary and analysis. *Journal of Management Accounting Research, 21*(1), 19–53.

Rankin, F. W., Schwartz, S. T., & Young, R. A. (2008). The effect of honesty and superior authority on budget proposals. *The Accounting Review, 83*(4), 1083–99.

Ridgway, V. F. (1956). Dysfunctional consequences of performance measurements. *Administrative Science Quarterly* (September), 240–7.

SEC. (2001). *Accounting and Auditing Enforcement Release No. 1393/May 15, 2001. Administrative Proceeding File No. 3-10481, In the Matter of Sunbeam Corporation.* Retrieved from: www.sec.gov/litigation/admin/33-7976.htm (last accessed August 16, 2015).

Strauss, V. (April 1, 2013). Atlanta test cheating: Tip of the iceberg? *Washington Post.* Retrieved from www.washingtonpost.com/blogs/answer-sheet/wp/2013/04/01/atlanta-test-cheating-tip-of-the-iceberg/ (last accessed August 16, 2015).

Tessier, S., & Otley, D. (2012). A conceptual development of Simons' Levers of Control framework. *Management Accounting Research, 23*(3), 171–85.

Tinker, T. (1985). *Paper Prophets: A Social Critique of Accounting.* NY: Praeger Publishers.

Tinker, A. M., Merino, B. D. & Neimark, M. D. (1982). The Normative Origins of Positive Theories: Ideology and Accounting Thought. *Accounting, Organizations, and Society, 7*(2), 167–200.

Wahlen, J. M., Baginski, S. P., & Bradshaw, M. T. (2015). *Financial Reporting, Financial Statement Analysis and Valuation: A Strategic Perspective* (8th ed). United States: Cengage Learning.

Walker, M. (2013). How far can we trust earnings numbers? What research tells us about earnings management. *Accounting and Business Research, 43*(4), 445–81.

Waymire, G. B., & Basu, S. (2008). *Accounting is an Evolved Economic Institution.* Hanover, MA: Now Publishers Inc.

Webb, R. A. 2002. The impact of reputation and variance investigations on the creation of budget slack. *Accounting, Organizations and Society, 27*(4), 361–78.

Young, J. J. (1995). Getting the accounting "right"; Accounting and the savings and loan crisis. *Accounting, Organizations and Society, 20*(1) 55–80.

Zang, A. Y. (2006). *Evidence on the tradeoff between real manipulation and accrual manipulation.* ProQuest.

7   Valuation Choices

Outline

- Preliminary Thoughts
- Learning Objectives
- Why Divergent Values Exist for Financial Accounting
- Values Used for Financial Reporting
- Values Used in Specific Accounts
- Implementing Fair Value Accounting
- Implementing Historical Cost Accounting
- Adjusting Historical Cost Accounting for Impairments
- Inflation and Financial Accounting
- Foreign Currency Translation Issues
- Values That Can Be Used For Managerial Accounting
- Impact of Valuation Methods on Behavior
- Unresolved Issues and Areas for Further Research

Preliminary Thoughts

What's aught, but as 'tis valued?
William Shakespeare (1602), Troilus and Cressida, Act II, Scene 2[1]

Here, then, is accounting wrestling with a dilemma: a purely cost balance sheet is unacceptable and a purely appraisal balance sheet is unacceptable. Result: a balance sheet which is often neither fish nor fowl, but containing not infrequently some items on an appraisal basis and some on a cost basis.

A.C. Littleton (1929, p. 148)

The balance-sheet of a large modern corporation does not and should not be expected to represent an attempt to show present values of the assets and liabilities of the corporation.
George O. May (1932), in a letter to the New York Stock Exchange, quoted in Flamholtz (1979, p. 131)

Once market structure departs from the textbook extreme of a perfect and complete set of markets, the very notion of a well-defined concept of value disappears. At that point, price guides are not available for all activities. . .. We hasten to add that if valuation is a true purpose, accounting is an abject failure on a worldwide basis. Economic and accounting values, where we have data, are virtually never well aligned.
John Christensen and Joel S. Demski (2003, p. 4)

Measurement concepts in financial reporting are sorely needed. A key role of accounting is to depict economic phenomena in numbers, i.e., to develop measurements to report in financial statements. It is shameful that neither is there a conceptual definition of accounting measurement nor are there concepts guiding standard setters' choice of measurement base. The Framework has a glaring hole until these concepts are developed.

Mary Barth (2013, p. 350)

[A] consequence of the basic role of equity accounting is that a measurement process which is completely arbitrary and useless for any decision can be very useful if all the parties agree to base the determination of their equities upon it. In operational accounting, the underlying economic phenomena related to the measure are what is important, while in equity accounting it is the consequence expected to result from the measure that is important. Therefore, apples can be added to oranges, pound for pound, if all interested parties agree to distribute the payoff. Theoretically meaningless allocations of costs and revenues can also be done and in some cases must be done in order to distribute the payoff.

American Accounting Association Committee on
Foundations of Accounting Measurement (1971, p. 34)

These six quotations point in various ways to the valuation issues that are the subject of this chapter. Shakespeare succinctly notes that to know what something is, we want to assign a value to it. The problem is that, for a long time, accountants have not settled on ways of assigning values. A.C. Littleton, writing one month before the 1929 stock market crash, wrote that accounting is unable to accept either cost or appraisal values for all balance sheet items. The next two quotations, from George May in 1931 and from John Christensen and Joel Demski in 2003, note that financial statements do not and cannot give the value of the corporation as an entity. Mary Barth, who was a member of the IASB from 2001 to 2009 and then academic advisor to the IASB until 2011, wrote in 2013 that the IASB's conceptual framework has a "glaring hole" because it does not settle on a single way of valuing financial statement items. In her article, she notes that currently financial statements contain different assets and liabilities measured with a variety of different valuation methods.

Does this mean that accounting is currently useless? The answer is no, for two reasons. First, even if financial statements do not show the value of the company, they provide information that readers can use to make their own valuations. This "information perspective" on accounting is probably the dominant academic view of the function of accounting.[2] A second is that, as long as accounting is done in a way that users understand, users can base contractual arrangements on the numbers. This point is made in the last quotation. An American Accounting Association committee noted that as long as two parties to a contract agree on a measurement system, they can use it to measure performance under their contract, regardless of how useful it is for other purposes.

Learning Objectives

After studying this chapter you should understand:

1 That a variety of different ways of measuring value are used in accounting
2 Which measures of value are used for key accounts
3 Reasons that certain methods of assigning values may be appropriate or inappropriate for particular financial or managerial reporting purposes
4 That inflation affects the usefulness of accounting measurements
5 That multinational companies face additional measurement issues due to changing foreign exchange rates
6 That different methods of measurement may encourage different reactions by managers.

Why Divergent Values Exist for Financial Accounting

In an ideal world, accountants would all use the same method of valuing every account. That would be simple, and we would all understand immediately what value applies to each item on the financial statements. In this ideal world, there would be *"perfect"* and *"complete"* markets for everything. A "perfect" market is totally efficient, with perfect information and zero transaction costs. A perfect market gives an accurate price at each instant in time. A company could always buy new assets at exactly the same price at which it sells items. It could also dispose of its liabilities by paying other people to take over these liabilities. Each company in the world would get the same benefit from using any asset. In such a world, the price you pay when you buy an asset would be exactly the same price you could receive when you sell the asset, and that price would equal the value you would receive by holding and using the asset. A world with "complete" markets has markets for every asset and liability.

For some assets, there are markets that are very close to perfect. For example, consider the market for U.S. Treasury bonds. Buyers and sellers of these bonds have the same information. There are low transaction costs in the market, and the bonds are traded constantly. The values of the bonds depend on the present value of the future bond payments, so the market price is very close to the amount of the discounted cash flows the bondholder would receive from the bonds by holding them until maturity.

For many other assets and liabilities, either markets do not exist or they are very imperfect. Some examples include: real estate; interests in research projects; machines that are used only for purposes of creating a single product; and liabilities for lawsuits against the company. Real estate, such as buildings, often takes a long time to sell, and it is hard to estimate in advance what a building can be sold for. A partly completed research project may be difficult to sell, because the potential buyers will not have complete information about its likelihood of success. Single-purpose machines are likely to be more useful to the company that owns them than they are to other companies. A company that wants to find someone to take over a liability for a lawsuit will likely find it difficult to do so, since any buyer would face the risk that the original company is hiding key information that affects the likelihood and amount of future payments.

When perfect and complete markets do not exist, then there may be very significant differences among the following measures of value:

1   The price at which someone could buy the asset now (an *"entry price"*).
2   The price at which the asset could be sold in orderly markets (an *"exit price"*).
3   The *"net realizable value"* that a company would receive by selling the asset in orderly markets, minus transaction costs.
4   The *"liquidation value,"* which is a sales value assuming the company must sell immediately.
5   The expected present value of future economic benefits to the company of holding the asset, which is sometimes referred to as its *"value in use."*

All of these values may need to be estimated, which adds a level of uncertainty to the process. It's not theoretically clear which measure to use. Issues of relevance, reliability, cost, and comprehensibility all arise. Also, the company may have made agreements that are based upon a particular measurement method. Therefore, different methods of valuing things are required by different accounting rules for different accounts, or for some accounts in different circumstances. It is unlikely that different users all have the same needs, so when there are not perfect and complete markets, it is impossible to find any one way of valuing assets, or computing income, that satisfies all users. See Beaver and Demski (1979).

All of these values may be different from what the asset originally cost the company. If it has held the asset for a long period of time then market values may have changed significantly.

Also, any value is expressed in units of currency, such as dollars. Accountants must consider how to adjust the values for inflation. When companies operate in more than one country, accountants must also consider how changing currency exchange rates affect accounting measurements.

Values Used for Financial Reporting

Overview

Both U.S. GAAP and IFRS use a variety of different values. In some cases GAAP and IFRS require companies to use a particular method of valuation. In other cases, companies are allowed to choose between two or more approved methods. The basic way GAAP and IFRS deal with the wide variety of values is as follows:

a. The value for each particular asset or liability is either specified by the rule-makers, or restricted to a few acceptable methods.
b. Companies must disclose which methods they use.
c. Companies must be consistent over time in using valuation methods. If they do change methods, they must disclose the effect of the changes.[3]

General Types of Values Used for External Accounting

Table 7.1 provides a summary of methods of valuation that are used in financial accounting. This section explains the nature of these methods, and some of their advantages and disadvantages. Other sections in this chapter indicate which methods must be used for particular accounts, and give additional details on how the fair value and historical cost methods are implemented.

Two methods in Table 7.1 focus on what a company must sacrifice to obtain an asset.[4] These methods are *historical cost* and *replacement cost*. Historical cost is what the company actually paid to acquire the asset in the past. It typically includes not just the price paid to the seller, but also ordinary and necessary costs to put the asset into place. For a purchase of Google common stock, historical cost would include brokerage fees. For the purchase of inventory, it would include shipping costs. Replacement cost is what it would cost the company to replace its assets now, including the costs to put the assets into place.

A primary advantage of historical cost is that it represents something that actually happened, and can be verified using records maintained by the company. If the company bought its assets in good-faith transactions, the price it paid represented the market value at the time the assets were bought. If the company sells its inventory quickly, the market price does not change much between the time the inventory is bought and when it is sold. The historical cost information is simple to use, since it does not require the company to make estimates or to obtain information about current market conditions. The information is objective. While there are many possible prices the company might have paid for its assets, Ijiri (1967) notes that the historical cost is unique—it is the cost that was actually paid. The objectivity of this measurement, and the ability to verify it, make historical cost especially useful for tax accounting.

There are several disadvantages to using historical cost information. When assets are held for a long period of time, or when the assets are items that are traded in volatile markets, the historical cost becomes less and less relevant to the current values of the items. For example, land that is owned by a company for 50 years is likely to have a historical cost that is far below its current market value.[5] As another example, an investment in the stock of a company could change in value significantly over a month. This means that historical cost information may not

Table 7.1 Summary of Types of Values

Type	Description
Sacrifice to obtain asset	
Historical cost	The amount actually spent in the past to obtain the asset.
Replacement cost	The estimated amount that has to be spent to replace the asset.
Market benefit from disposing of the asset	
Realized value	The amount actually received in a past transaction.
Fair value	For financial assets – the price that would be received on sale in an orderly transaction in the best market, without any deduction for transaction costs. For non-financial assets, it is the value of the asset in its highest and best use.
Net realizable value	The estimated amount that could be received in a future transaction, minus costs of making the transaction, in an orderly market sale.
Appraised value	An estimate by a qualified appraiser of the likely sale price.
Liquidation value	The amount that could be received in a future transaction, minus costs of making the transaction, assuming the item has to be sold immediately, in a "fire sale."
Benefit from using the asset	
Expected net present value of future cash flows (at the time of acquisition)	The expected value is a probability-weighted value. This method uses an estimate of the time value of money and the probability of receiving future cash flows to compute a value benefit expected to be obtained from using, not selling, the asset, as of the date the asset was acquired.
Expected net present value of future cash flows (at the balance sheet date)	This is the same as the prior method, using assumptions about probability and interest rates as of the latest balance sheet date.
Other valuation methods	
Nonrecognition	The asset is not recognized. In effect, it is assigned a value of zero.
Legally assigned values	The item is given a value specified by law.
Amortized (or depreciated) cost	The item is originally stated at historical cost. It is then reduced in value over time as the item is amortized or depreciated.
Lower of cost or market	The item is stated on either a cost basis or some market-related basis, whichever is lower.
Lower of cost or impaired cost	The item is stated at either the cost basis, or the cost basis adjusted for some expected impairment of the asset.

Note: If an asset was bought in a foreign currency, there are also choices as to whether to translate it at the current exchange rate or some past exchange rate. The above list also does not incorporate any inflation measurements into the values.

satisfy the FASB's criterion of relevance. A related problem is that when a company uses historical cost to account for assets that have very different economic values, managers may be able to exploit the difference between the economic and accounting values to manage income. This is discussed more fully below. A third problem is that historical cost information tends to overstate incomes in periods of inflation. A fourth problem is that a company's assets were bought at different points in time. This means that some assets are measured at 1980s costs while others are measured at 2014 costs. Adding costs from different years together to arrive at "total assets" is mathematically problematic.

Theoretically, replacement cost information would have some advantages over historical cost. The replacement cost method uses information as of the latest date, so it should be more relevant and less subject to distortion by inflation. Since all the assets are measured currently, it is mathematically valid to add them together to come to a total. The primary disadvantages of using replacement cost relate to the effort and the estimates needed to implement it. For some items, such as inventory that the company is constantly buying, it may already know the replacement cost. However, it would need to do considerable work to estimate the cost of replacing its factories, or its patents. Thus, while replacement cost has advantages in relevance over historical cost, it has disadvantages of: bookkeeping cost; subjectivity of estimates; and verifiability of the replacement cost data.

The next several valuation methods in Table 7.1 relate to the benefits a company can obtain from selling an asset. The *"realized value"* is what the company actually received in a past transaction. The *"fair value"* of a financial asset, as defined by the FASB in Codification Section 820, is the price when selling the asset in an orderly market, with willing market participants. Transaction costs are not considered. The *"fair value"* of a nonfinancial asset might either be a sales price or the value of the asset in its "highest and best use." *"Net realizable value"* is the value a company can obtain by selling an item, after deducting transaction costs. In some cases, when a company is going out of business, it is forced to sell at less than normal prices for its goods, and this lower than normal price is called *"liquidation value."*

The primary advantage of *"realized values"* is that they are based on real transactions which have already occurred. The company knows what actually happened. No estimation is needed, and the data is available in the company's bookkeeping system. The fact that realized values are objectively verifiable makes this method very useful for tax accounting. The limitation to using realized values is that they are not available to measure the values of assets that are still on hand, or liabilities that have not yet been paid off.

There are several advantages of measuring financial assets at fair value. First, it is relevant information, since these assets are likely to be sold at market prices. Second, it forces companies to report the gains or losses that were caused by the company's decision to hold on to these items. Under the historical cost method, such holding gains or losses would be ignored until the assets are sold. Third, since the financial assets are measured at fair value, there is less opportunity for a company to manage its earnings by selectively selling assets with holding gains. Fourth, all the financial assets are measured at current prices, so it is mathematically valid to add the values together into totals.

The major difficulty with using fair value to measure financial assets and liabilities arises because there are not perfect and complete markets for all financial assets and liabilities. This causes issues in measuring fair values reliably. The company must expend extra effort to obtain information about market prices each accounting period. The requirement to make various estimates affects comparability across companies that own similar assets, and can also create opportunities for earnings management. Also, fair value ignores transaction costs, which can sometimes be significant. A later section of this chapter discusses some of the issues in implementing this valuation method.

"Net realizable value" is similar in concept to "fair value" except that net realizable value is reduced for estimated transaction costs. Like fair value, net realizable value conveys relevant information about what an asset is currently worth. Like fair value, it requires the company to obtain information about potential selling prices each accounting period. Like fair value, it will require some estimates of possible selling prices.

An *appraised value* is an estimate of fair value, made by a qualified expert. Typically, appraisals are only needed where markets are not very liquid. For example, there are appraisers who specialize in valuing fine art, and appraisers who specialize in valuing commercial real estate. Therefore, appraisals contain a certain amount of subjectivity. Appraised values would need to be adjusted each accounting period. They are therefore a costly valuation method.

Liquidation value is an estimate of what the company could obtain for its assets if it were forced to sell them immediately, and what it would have to pay on its liabilities if it were forced to pay them immediately. Typically, accountants assume that a company will remain a "going concern" (see Chapter 2) and remain in business. Therefore the liquidation values are not considered relevant to evaluating ongoing businesses. Typically, accountants only use liquidation values when accounting for companies that are actually in the process of going out of business.

The next two methods in Table 7.1 relate to the "value in use" to a company of owning and operating an asset. Theoretically, the reason that a company buys a factory is to use it to produce products, which will eventually result in cash flowing in to the company. The value of owning and operating the factory can be measured by the discounted value of the expected (probability-weighted) future cash inflows from the asset, minus the cash outflows.[6] We looked at valuing capital investments using discounted cash flows in Chapter 5.

One of the two methods in Table 7.1 measures value by using the assumptions that existed at the date the asset was acquired, and does not change these assumptions over time. In essence, it is the *historical* estimate of the expected value in use as of the date the item was acquired. The second method updates the assumptions each period, as interest rates change and estimates of future payoffs change. It is basically an up-to-date estimate of the value of keeping the asset.

The primary advantage of the first method, which does not change assumptions, is simplicity. The company does not need to re-estimate future values each time it does accounting. The disadvantage is that, as conditions change, the historical estimates become inaccurate predictions of the actual value of keeping the asset, and can lead to poor decision-making.

Table 7.1 also contains five methods which are not well connected to either the value paid to acquire an asset, or what could be obtained by selling or using it. These five methods are: nonrecognition; legally set values; amortized cost; lower of cost or market; and lower of cost or impaired cost.

Nonrecognition means that no liability or asset is booked at all, even though economically there is an asset or liability. According to the FASB's conceptual framework, something should only be recognized if it meets the definition of an element of the financial statements (such as an asset or liability) and can be measured with reasonable accuracy. When the accounting standard-setters believe that there is great uncertainty in measuring an item, they may not allow recognition. For example, the FASB believes that, in general, research efforts are very uncertain of success, and their value cannot be measured with reasonable accuracy. Therefore SFAS No. 2 required most research spending to be recorded as an expense, not an asset. Traditionally, the FASB also leaned towards being conservative, which meant it tended to delay recognizing assets that were of uncertain value, but would recognize liabilities more quickly. As an example, if a company is engaged in a lawsuit, and might win a sizable award, usually accounting rules will not let the company recognize the expected value of this award until the court decision is actually final. However, if it expected to lose the lawsuit, it would be required to recognize a liability if the loss was "probable" and "reasonably estimable."

Nonrecognition has the advantage of limiting management's ability to overstate the value of a company by being overly optimistic about certain assets. Its disadvantage is that it causes financial statements to ignore some very important economic resources of companies. For example, by my reading of their public financial statements, the balance sheet of Coca Cola does not contain a value for its main brand name, and the financial statements of Google show it does not recognize the value of the software it developed.

In a few instances, there are legal requirements that certain items be stated at particular values. One example is that companies must record the par value of the common stock they issue in their financial statements. This was discussed in Chapter 4. In general, since legally set requirements are not closely connected to any particular economic decision models, they do not give decision-useful information. However, they may help users detect if the company is in compliance with some legal standard. For example, in some regulated industries, there are required minimum levels of equity that a company must keep on hand.

The *amortized cost* (or *depreciated cost*) method is used for a variety of items. The idea here is that the company owns an asset that provides service over a period of time, and slowly loses value over that period of time. Each accounting period, the company will recognize an "amortization" or "depreciation" expense for a small part of the asset's value, and will reduce the carrying value of the asset on the balance sheet. Amortized cost is used for such items as: factories; equipment; intangible assets with definite lives; natural resources being used up; or prepaid expenses being used up gradually. Methods of amortization for financial accounting are the topic of Chapter 9.

The advantage of amortized cost is that it is an organized and systematic way of allocating some part of the cost of having an asset to each time period that the asset is being used. The systematic nature of the amortization process reduces the chances for earnings management, and makes the process understandable to outside users. Also, it is a practical way to approximate the loss of value for certain types of assets over time, without the effort required to actually verify the fair value of each asset at the end of each accounting period. For example, a company knows that a truck used in a business will lose its value over time. Just keeping the value at the historical cost would not be helpful, since it would totally ignore this loss in value. A company that uses a depreciated cost method might assume it loses a tenth of its value every year for 10 years. While the actual net realizable value or the fair value may decline in different patterns, the differences in values might not be large enough to justify the extra effort needed to obtain price quotes on the truck each month.

The primary disadvantage is that the amortized cost value of the asset at any point in time may be different than what the asset could be sold for, and may also likely be different from the value of the asset in continued use. Therefore, the amortized cost value lacks decision-usefulness. An example of this arises with office buildings. A company that buys an office building will typically depreciate it over a period of 40 years. It is possible that over those 40 years, the value of the building may actually increase.[7]

The final two methods of valuation in Table 7.1 are blended methods. They both say a company should use the *lower* of cost or of some other method of valuation. The concept here is that a company should not overstate the value of its assets, but it also should not recognize gains on holding the assets until they are sold. The cost method will normally meet these criteria, unless that value of the asset has significantly decreased since it was purchased. Both of these methods require that a company recognize a lower asset value than the cost value in situations where it is unlikely that the asset will either be sold or used to obtain benefits equal to its cost. Note that these methods do not meet the FASB's desired criteria of neutrality. They require companies to *write down* assets when they lose value, but do not permit them to *write up* assets.

Values Used in Specific Accounts

This section describes what methods are either required or permitted for each major account. Box 7.1 provides a summary of how key accounts are measured.

Cash

Cash is assumed to be worth its face value. If the cash is in a foreign currency, it is translated at the exchange rate in effect on the balance sheet date.

Marketable Securities

In general, marketable securities are shown on the balance sheet at their fair value.

If a company owns debt securities, such as bonds, and intends to hold them until maturity, it can choose to record them on a cost basis.[8]

Box 7.1 Different Values for Different Accounts

Historical cost (less reductions for impairment or other problems)

Accounts receivable
Land
Some investments (without ready market)
Goodwill purchased from others
Other intangible assets with indefinite lives purchased from others
Accounts payable/deferred revenue

Historical cost, less amortization/depreciation and less impairment if necessary

Buildings and fixed assets other than land
Intangible assets with definite lives, purchased from others
Software development costs
Natural resources (oil wells, mines, etc.)
Bonds payable (premium or discount amortized)
Debt securities that the company intends to hold until maturity

Lower of cost or market (replacement cost)

Most inventories (U.S. GAAP)

Lower of cost or net realizable value

Most inventories (IFRS)

Present value or expected present value, original assumptions

Receivables or payables of longer than a year, with no stated interest
Capital lease assets and obligations, when created. Later these are amortized.

Expected present value, updated assumptions

Pension obligations and other post-employment obligations

Not recognized

Most research and development done internally
Gain contingencies
Most internally developed intangible assets

Fair value or net realizable value

IFRS, *not* GAAP, allows this for
    Property, plant and equipment
    Intangible assets

Investments in marketable securities
Investments in derivative instruments, such as options or forward or future contracts
Companies may choose to value their bonds payable at fair value

Financial Instruments

Options, forward contracts, and other financial instruments are carried at fair market value.

Accounts Receivable

Accounts receivable are carried on the books at their original value, with adjustments made, if needed, to reflect the likelihood that they will not be collected in full. At the time that the company makes a sale on credit, it records a receivable equal to the sales price. At the end of each accounting period, the company will decide how much of an adjustment for "bad debts" needs to be made to the value of the receivable. The balance sheet shows a value of the receivables minus an allowance for uncollectible accounts.

Inventories (Normal Products)

Inventories are normally valued at the lower of their cost or "market."[9] The purpose of carrying the inventory at cost is to keep companies from saying they have net income simply by buying inventory. Companies must wait until they actually sell the inventory before they can recognize revenue and therefore income. This makes measurements of revenue more reliable, and less subjective. The reason for requiring companies to use a lower "market" value is to force companies to recognize losses in those situations where their inventory is not easily marketable. Without this rule, companies' inventory balances would be higher than their economic value. Also, managers would be tempted to hold on to, rather than to sell, obsolete inventory items to avoid recognizing losses. With the lower of cost or market rule, companies cannot avoid recognizing the loss in economic value of obsolete items, whether or not they sell them.[10]

However, there is a complication in determining the cost of inventory. Let's assume an oil company got three shipments of oil during a month. The first shipment was 10,000 gallons at a cost of $2.50 per gallon, the second was 10,000 gallons at a cost $2.75 per gallon, and the third was 20,000 gallons at a cost of $3.00 per gallon. The three shipments went into three separate tanks. Now assume the company made one sale, of 10,000 gallons, for $2.80 per gallon. What was the cost associated with that sale, and what was the company's profit on it?

If it sold from the first shipment, which cost $2.50 per gallon, then it made $0.30 per gallon on the sale ($2.80 – $2.50), and made $3,000. If it sold from the second shipment, it made $0.05 per gallon ($2.80 – $2.75), and made $500. If it sold from the third shipment, it actually lost $0.20 per gallon ($2.80 – $3.00), or $2,000. So, the accounting profit depends on which oil it sold. From an economic point of view, this is kind of silly. The oil in all three tanks is identical. In reality, the cash flows are the same, no matter which oil we say was sold, and the sales value of the remaining 30,000 gallons of oil on hand is the same. So this situation is one where the manager can affect income simply by choosing which oil to sell, even though the choice of which oil to sell should be economically unimportant.

To prevent earnings management by arbitrarily saying which items were sold, GAAP and IFRS both require companies to use systematic ways of assigning costs to the items sold, regardless of which items were physically sold. Here are the major methods.

- *First in, first out* (FIFO). This method assumes that the company sells items in the order they were bought. The oldest items were sold first, and the items bought last are most likely to still be on hand at the end of the accounting period. This method is logical, and reflects the way most companies actually treat their physical inventory. In the example, the company would assume it sold 10,000 gallons that cost $2.50 each.
- *Weighted average cost.* This method computes an average cost of the items on hand. In the example, the three purchases were 10,000 gallons at $2.50, 10,000 gallons at $2.75, and 20,000 gallons at $3.00. It spent a total of $112,500 for 40,000 barrels, so the weighted average price per gallon was $2.8125.[11] This method is also logical, and reflects the fact that all the items are economically identical.

- *Last in, first out* (LIFO). This method assumes that the company sold the last items it bought first, and that the oldest items are the most likely to still be on hand at the end of the period. In this example, it would assume it sold 10,000 gallons that cost $3.00 each. The LIFO method is allowed under U.S. GAAP and for U.S. tax purposes, but is not allowed under IFRS. It normally is not the way that companies treat their physical inventory. However, one can come up with examples of situations where companies might treat physical inventories this way. In situations where inventory costs are rising, LIFO tends to result in higher cost of goods sold, and lower income than FIFO. Many companies choose to use it for tax purposes. Under U.S. law, companies that wish to use LIFO for tax purposes must generally also use it for financial reporting.[12]
- *Specific identification.* This method requires the company to specifically identify the individual item sold, and to track its cost. While this would seem to be the most intuitively sensible way to follow costs, in fact it has the problem of allowing earnings management. Also, where a company cannot individually track inventory items at low cost, it is impractical. For example, if the company in this example put all its oil into one tank, instead of keeping the three shipments in three different tanks, there would be no way to separately identify each gallon sold.

Box 7.2 presents an example of inventory accounting using these methods.

In practice, surveys of U.S. companies show few use specific identification. A survey of 500 companies (AICPA 2011) found that in 2010:

- 316 (63%) used FIFO for some or all of their inventories
- 166 (33%) used LIFO for some or all of their inventories
- 113 (23%) used average cost for some or all of their inventories.

Some other methods were reported less commonly.

Usually, firms using LIFO will tend to show lower inventory asset balances and higher cost of goods sold than companies using FIFO. Companies using weighted average cost will tend to show values that are in between the FIFO and LIFO levels. Box 7.2 has exactly those results. The inventory was lowest for LIFO at $80,000, and highest for FIFO, at $106,000. COGS is $460,000 using LIFO, and $434,000 using FIFO. While these differences can affect comparisons between companies, the differences in accounting methods are less important when companies keep their inventory levels low.

GAAP and IFRS use different ways of reflecting "market" value. IFRS requires companies to use the estimated net realizable value of inventory as the market value. GAAP has more complicated rules, but usually GAAP requires companies to use the estimated replacement cost of the items as the estimate of market value.[13]

Inventories—Standardized Products With Ready Markets

Certain commodities are highly standardized and widely traded. Examples include gold, crude oil, and wheat. Such commodities, where one unit is interchangeable with any other, are called *"fungible."* There are liquid markets for these items, so objective market prices are readily available. GAAP and IFRS allow these items to be carried at net realizable value.[14]

Land

Land is typically stated at historical cost for GAAP. Because land is assumed to last forever, it is not depreciated. However, if something has happened to impair its value, the historical cost

---

Box 7.2 Four Inventory Cost Methods

Assume the Edison Corp. starts the year with 13,000 units of steel wire on hand, at a cost of $10 per unit. During the year, it has the following purchases:

February 28	20,000 units, at $11 per unit
June 30	10,000 units, at $12 per unit
November 30	5,000 units, at $14 per unit.

The total cost of all the items available for sale during the year = $540,000.

Assume it sold a total of 40,000 units on December 10, leaving it with 8,000 units on hand. What was the cost of the 40,000 units sold, and what is the cost of the 8,000 units on hand?

FIFO

The cost of the 40,000 units sold would include:

$130,000 =	opening inventory of 13,000 at $10
220,000 =	February 28 purchases of 20,000 at $11
84,000 =	7,000 from the June 30 purchases at $12
$434,000	

The cost of the remaining 8,000 units = 3,000 units from June 30 at $12 + 5,000 at $14 = $106,000.

Note that we could also use the relationship ending inventory + COGS = cost of goods available for sale to find either the cost of goods sold or the cost of the ending inventory.

Weighted average

The total cost of goods available for sale = $540,000. The number of units available for sale = 13,000 + 20,000 + 10,000 + 5,000 = 48,000.

The average cost per unit = $540,000 ÷ 48,000 = $11.25 per unit.
The cost of the 40,000 units sold = $11.25 × 40,000 = $450,000.
The cost of the 8,000 units on hand = $11.25 × 8,000 = $90,000.
Alternatively, we could have found the cost of the 8,000 units on hand subtracting the cost of goods sold of $450,000 from the cost of goods available for sale of $540,000.

LIFO

The cost of the 8,000 units on hand = 8,000 at $10 = 80,000.

The cost of the items sold = 5,000 units from Nov 30 at $14 + 10,000 units from June at $12 + 20,000 units from February $11 + 5,000 units from opening inventory at $10 = $460,000. Alternatively, we could have found COGS as $540,000 of costs of goods available for sale − $80,000 of ending inventory.

---

value on the books may need to be written down to fair value as of the time of the impairment. For example, if laws changed in a way that prevented the company from using its land for the expected purposes, then it might need to record an impairment loss.

For IFRS, there are two options. Land can be adjusted each year to reflect net realizable value. If this is done, comprehensive income is also adjusted. IFRS also allows the same accounting method as U.S. GAAP.

Other Fixed Assets (Buildings, Equipment, etc.)

For GAAP, these assets are typically carried on the books at historical cost, minus depreciation that has been recorded over time. Depreciation methods are discussed in Chapter 9. If events have occurred to impair the value of the assets, then the carrying value of the assets should be written down to fair value at the date of impairment. After that date, depreciation will be based on the impaired value.

IFRS allows two options. Companies may carry these assets at depreciated cost, adjusted for impairments. Under IFRS, if there are later events which make the asset's value no longer impaired, then the company can increase the carrying value of the asset back to the original cost. As an alternative to using depreciated cost, IFRS Standard 16 permits companies to use a "revaluation model." If they use a revaluation model, and the fair value increases, the company will increase the asset account and will also increase accumulated comprehensive income. When fair values decrease, the company will decrease the asset account, and will reverse any related comprehensive income. If there is no related comprehensive income, the company will record an expense for the loss of value.

Rights to Use Assets Under Capital Leases

In Chapter 6, we discussed "capital leases." The situation with a capital lease is that the company does not own the leased property, it just rents it. However, the terms of the lease are such that economically, the company has similar use of the property as would an owner. Therefore, GAAP and IFRS require the company to record an asset for property under capital leases. The property is initially valued at the present value of the future minimum lease payments. That is presumably a good measure of the cost of the item. After it is acquired, depreciation is recorded that reduces the asset's carrying value.

Note that this is an example of using a present discounted value based on assumptions as of the date of the start of the lease. The present discounted value is not adjusted for later changes in interest rates.

Intangible Assets Created Internally

The types of assets that are included under this heading include the economic value that has grown from a company's brand names, the value of its workforce, the value of its customer list, and its research and techniques. None of these are recognized as assets. The basic issue here is the lack of an objective way to value them, and the temptation of management to be overly optimistic about them.

The only significant exception to this rule is the cost of internally developed software, after it has reached a stage of technological feasibility. The company would show a software asset at the cost of development, minus amortization over the expected life of the software.

Intangible Assets Purchased from Others

Intangible assets purchased from others that have a definite life are recorded at amortized cost, with the cost amortized over the expected useful lives of the assets. A patent would be an example of such an intangible asset. Intangible assets that have indefinite lives, and therefore might last for a very long time, are recorded at their cost, with no amortization.

If the value of an intangible asset is impaired, it should be reduced to fair value.

Investments in Other Companies

There are different methods used to value investments in other companies. These are discussed in more detail in more advanced accounting texts. Very briefly:

*   Small investments in stock of other companies, that do not give the entity significant influence over its actions, are recorded at fair market value. If the other company is not traded, and the fair value of its stock is not known, the stock is valued at the lower of cost or some impaired value.
*   Investments that give the entity significant influence over the investee (typically over 20% of the amount of the company's voting stock), are recorded using what is called the equity method. The investment is initially recorded at cost. Over time, the asset is increased by a share of the investee's earnings, and decreased by a share of the dividends paid by the investee.

Accounts Payable, Accrued Expenses and Short-Term Loans Payable

These items are typically stated at the amount the company has promised to pay for them.

Contingent Losses

A *contingent loss* situation exists when the company does not yet know the consequences of a past event. For example, the company is being sued for something that it did in the past, and does not yet know how much, if anything, it will have to pay in the lawsuit. The FASB rule is that if a loss is probable, and the company can reasonably estimate the loss, it should record the most likely amount it will have to pay. If the loss is possible, but is not considered "probable", then it is not recognized at all.

Contingent gains are not recognized.

Long-Term Estimated Liabilities for Pensions and Employee Post-Employment Benefits

These liabilities are measured at the expected future value of what will have to be paid out, using specified actuarial methods.

Long-Term Financial Liabilities, Such as Bonds

GAAP and IFRS offer companies a choice. They may either carry the bonds at the "amortized cost" basis, or they may adjust them to fair value each period.[15]

There are advantages and disadvantages of valuing bonds payable at fair value. The primary advantage is that the balance sheet will show the bonds at what the company would have to spend to pay the bonds off. That is relevant information.

The problem is that the effect of changes in a company's reputation on income is strange. For example, in 2008, during the fiscal crisis, people worried that General Motors would enter bankruptcy. The market price of its bonds fell. If it used the fair market method to record bonds payable, it would record a gain because it could now buy back its bonds cheaply. It seems odd that a company should show income due to people believing it would go bankrupt. In subsequent years, when General Motors survived, the values of its bonds increased. If it used the fair market method to record bonds payable, it would record a loss because of this recovery of public faith in its ability to survive. This is also an odd result.

Totals of Assets or Liabilities

What do you get when you add a fair value of $1 million to a 1960s historical cost of $1 million to a "lower of LIFO cost or market" figure of $1 million? While $1 + 1 + 1 = 3$, we have just added together three things in different units. Mathematically, that is not a sensible thing to do.

The result of using different methods of measurement for different types of assets and liabilities is that the various total and subtotal accounts end up poorly defined mathematically. This is a problem that has been pointed out by scholars at least since 1929.[16]

Not only is the total asset figure a blend of different valuation measures, but certain figures for particular asset types are also blends of valuation methods. An international company might value some of its inventory at LIFO cost and some at FIFO cost, before considering inventory that needs to be recorded at a lower market value. That means that the inventory total shown includes three different types of measurements.[17]

Another issue is that a collection of assets can have greater value than the sum of its parts, when there is synergy among the assets. So, even if we used fair value for every asset, Barth (2013) notes that the fair value for all the assets of the company, in aggregate, is probably not the same as the sum of the fair value of the assets if they were each offered for sale separately.

Implementing Fair Value Accounting

Trends in Accounting Standards

In the 1930s, the SEC and accounting standard-setters began moving towards a historical cost model. Stephen Zeff (2005a) noted that:

> From its founding, the SEC rejected any deviation from historical cost accounting in the body of financial statements. This position was a reaction to a widespread practice during the 1920s (prior to federal regulation) wherein listed companies would revalue their assets upward, often based on questionable evidence of market value. The abuse of this discretion, especially in the public utility field, was alleged to have misled investors when judging the values of their shares prior to the crash of 1929.
>
> (p. 20)

Historical cost offered a high degree of verifiability, and was seen as less subject to manipulation than was fair value accounting. At that time, the major assets that most companies were concerned with were inventories and fixed assets.[18] Over time, the relative importance of the manufacturing sector in the U.S. has declined while the financial sector has grown (Krippner 2005). This has made accounting for financial assets and liabilities more important.

Accounting standard-setters started to think about using some sort of fair values as early as the late 1940s.[19] Over recent years, the FASB and IASB moved towards fair value accounting for financial assets and liabilities. They first required marketable securities to be valued at fair value. Later, they required derivative securities (such as options and futures contracts) to be valued at fair value, and have given companies the option of recording other financial assets and liabilities at fair value. Mary Barth, a former member of the IASB, wrote in 2007:

> A review of the recent activities of the IASB reveals that the use of fair value in financial reporting is likely to increase. This is because as the board has debated particular

measurement questions, it has concluded that in some cases fair value meets the conceptual framework criteria better than other measurement bases considered. It is not because the board has a stated objective of changing accounting measurement to fair value for all assets and liabilities. Fair value is not a panacea and other measurement bases also have desirable characteristics. Thus, which basis the IASB will require in any particular situation is not a foregone conclusion.

(Barth 2007, p. 7)

Barth (2006) explains that fair value meets some key aspects of the IASB's conceptual framework. "Fair value accounting is the only comprehensive and internally consistent approach the IASB has identified" (p. 274). The Framework was discussed in Chapter 2. The following points are drawn from Barth (2006, 2007, and 2013):

- Relevance. Fair values represent current economic conditions. Historical costs represent past economic conditions. Research shows fair value has predictive value.
- Faithful representation of underlying economic reality. Market values are neutral.[20]
- Comparability. Presumably, all companies will refer to the same market. However, if companies use historical cost, they may have bought their assets at different times, so they may show different values for the same item. (Consider a share of Apple stock. A company that bought it the day it went public would show a very different historical cost than one who bought the stock yesterday. However, if the two companies used fair value, they would report the same values.)
- Consistency. Companies should use the same valuation method over time.
- Timeliness. The fair values change when economic conditions change.
- Facilitating stewardship because the financial statements reflect accurate values of the assets at management's disposal. Barth (2006) notes that "Such values are essential for determining performance ratios such as return on capital employed" (p. 275).
- If all assets and liabilities were measured at fair value, then the various totals and subtotals would be mathematically well defined. This is not true of amortized or adjusted historical cost, which includes not just cost data but various methods of amortization or methods of recognizing impairment.

However, the FASB and IASB recognize that reliability and the ability of managers to influence valuations are serious issues, so they are unlikely to require fair value measurements of all assets and liabilities in the foreseeable future.

Practicality Issues

There are not perfect and complete markets which allow valuing every possible asset. The FASB has noted various situations in which it is not practicable to obtain fair value measurements, and in those cases companies may use other methods of valuation.

There are a variety of issues that relate to finding fair values in particular situations. Various critics of fair value accounting have noted that the process can be difficult.[21]

Reliability of Inputs to Valuation

The FASB and IASB define fair value based on market conditions.[22] A financial asset's fair value is the amount that the company could sell it for, in an orderly sale, in the best normal market, to willing market participants. The fair value of a nonfinancial asset depends on the highest and best use of the asset. If the "highest and best use" is to sell the asset, then the fair value is what it can be sold for. If the highest and best use is to be used in the business, then the fair value depends on the future cash flows from keeping the asset. The fair value of a financial liability is what the company would have to pay a market participant to take that liability.

The main problem in implementing fair value accounting is not the theory, but the practice of coming up with numbers that meet these criteria. The FASB has said that companies should base valuation on market prices, not the intentions of the company doing the accounting.

Not all information about value is equally reliable. The FASB has directed companies to consider information in value in order of reliability. The FASB calls this the "*fair value hierarchy.*" There are three levels of reliability. Level 1 inputs are considered more reliable than Level 2, and Level 2 is more reliable than Level 3. Companies should use the most reliable of these three levels. The FASB defines these inputs as follows:

- *Level 1 Inputs.* "Quoted prices (unadjusted) in active markets for identical assets or liabilities that the reporting entity can access at the measurement date."
- *Level 2 Inputs.* "Inputs other than quoted prices included within Level 1 that are observable for the asset or liability, either directly or indirectly."
- *Level 3 Inputs.* "Unobservable inputs for the asset or liability."

Assume a company is trying to measure the values of debt securities it owns. If it owns U.S. 10-year Treasury bonds, it can probably find Level 1 inputs for them. Treasury bonds are traded daily, in active markets, and there are likely market prices for bonds identical to the ones the company owns. Let's say it also owns some City of Chicago 20-year bonds. It may be that those precise types of bonds did not trade on the exact last day of the year, so no Level 1 inputs are available. However, maybe those bonds did trade two days earlier. That might be a Level 2 input. Or, maybe very similar bonds were trading on the last day of the year. These might have been Chicago bonds with a different maturity date, for example. Those transaction prices would also be a Level 2 input. In other words, Level 2 inputs are observable, verifiable data, but they are not precisely for the identical assets or not on the precise date. Let's assume the company also had some installment notes from another company. These notes are not traded in any market, and no credit rating agency has rated them. To value these installment notes, the company would need to create its own estimates of credit-worthiness. Since the factors that go into that estimate are not verifiable from outside, they are Level 3 inputs.

The concerns about the reliability of fair value accounting are greatest for Level 3 inputs. For example, Enron Corporation in the late 1990s made some very specific and large energy contracts, involving millions of dollars. There was no marketplace in these contracts, so Enron valued them based on its own internal models. Such a situation creates an opportunity for earnings management or fraud. When Enron entered bankruptcy, it was found that many of its contracts were overvalued on its books.

In general, if a company acquires an asset in a market transaction, the assumption is that its fair value at the date acquired equals its cost. However, this might not be the case if the transaction is between related parties, or if one party to the transaction is forced to make the transaction.

Relation Between Fair Value Measurement of Assets and Income

The fundamental equation of accounting is that assets must equal liabilities plus equity. If accounting recognizes a change in the fair value of some asset or liability, it will have to recognize a change in equity. Usually, this means that income is affected, although the next section discusses some exceptions.

Assume that a company has a portfolio of marketable securities, which it records at fair value. During the year, it buys and sells some securities, and will have some "realized" gains or losses on what it sells. At the end of the year, the company will also look at all the financial marketable securities it still has, and will record a gain or loss for the change in value of these items. The income at the end of the year will have two components: one for the impact of the transactions during the year, and one for the changes in value of the securities still on hand.

As Barth (2006) notes: "The direct link between asset and liability measurement and income measurement means that expectations of the future that are incorporated into measures of assets and liabilities today are recognized in income today, not in the future when the cash flows actually occur" (p. 280).[23]

Volatility

Fair value fluctuates constantly, often for matters that management cannot control. Values depend on such factors as economic conditions, interest rates, and company credit ratings. Managers do not like being judged based on volatile measures that they cannot control. During the 2008 problems in the financial markets, many banks believed that the market prices for certain types of assets were unfairly low, due to panic selling. The banks were arguing that the market was not an orderly market, so market prices should not be trusted.

Managers are especially unhappy when they are forced to report swings in income on assets they have no intention of selling. For example, a company may have an investment in the stock of another company, and its strategy might be to hold that stock for many years. Over those years, the stock price will go up and down many times. Should a CEO's bonus be affected each time the stock price moves? As a second example, an insurance company may know that it must pay certain claims over a period of 20 or 30 years in the future. It buys bonds that will mature in time to pay the claims. It has no intention of selling the bonds before they mature. Should its CEO's bonus be affected because the market prices of these bonds go up and down? As another example, a company owns a subsidiary in Belgium. To put its balance sheet together, the company has to translate the books of the Belgian subsidiary from euros to dollars. Should the CEO's bonus be affected by swings in the value of the euro relative to the dollar?

The FASB has made five rules that reduce the impact of the volatility of market values on company income statements:

- If a company owns bonds that it intends to hold until they mature, it can account for them on an amortized cost basis, and ignore market fluctuations.
- If a company intends to hold marketable securities on a long-term basis, it must use fair value to record the assets, but the gains or losses from holding the assets are shown as part of "other comprehensive income" and not part of net income.
- There are special rules about the assets of companies' pension trust funds. These trust funds often hold very large amounts of assets, and the effect of the special rules is to allow companies an option to minimize the impact of market changes of the value of the pension assets on net income.[24]
- If a company owns foreign subsidiaries, changes in the market values of foreign currencies will affect the way that the values of these subsidiaries are translated into the U.S. dollars used in the financial statements. A later section of this chapter explains the issues. There are special rules that call for some of the effect of these changes in foreign currency markets to be shown as part of other comprehensive income, and not part of net income.
- Gains or losses from "*hedging*" are generally recognized in a way that reduces the volatility of income. "*Hedging*" is an activity a company uses to reduce its chance of loss. For example, a farmer may plant a crop of grain in April, and hope to harvest it August. The farmer expects to earn, at harvest time, $10 per bushel of the crop. If the market price falls before August to $7 a bushel, the farmer's profits will be hurt. The farmer can protect against

("hedge") this risk by making a forward contract with someone to sell grain in August at $10 per bushel. Now, if the price falls to $7, the farmer will earn less by selling his crop than the expected $10. However, the farmer now has the right to sell grain using the forward contract at $10 per bushel. The farmer can buy the grain at the August market price of $7, and sell it at $10. The gain on the futures contract cancels out the loss of profits on the physical grain the farmer has for sale. While the rules on accounting for hedges are complicated, the major idea is to make sure the gain or loss on the "hedge" is recognized at the same time as the gain or loss on the underlying transaction, so that they cancel each other out.

Implementing Historical Cost Accounting

What is Included in the Cost of an Asset?

The cost of an item includes everything that was sacrificed in order to get that item ready for use. In the case of inventory, the cost of inventory would include:

- The amount paid to the vendor as the purchase price
- Shipping charges to get the goods to the company's location
- Insurance or customs duties or other costs related to getting the items to the company's location
- For goods that the company makes itself, all normal costs associated with making the product. Chapter 10 deals with the complicated accounting issues involved in computing the costs of manufactured products.

In the case of a building that was purchased, the cost would include, among other items:

- The amount paid to the seller of the building
- The money spent for legal fees to buy the building
- Money spent to fix up the building and make it ready for its intended use.

In the case of a building that the company constructs itself, the cost would include, among other items:

- Architects' fees
- Construction costs for labor and materials
- Interest costs directly related to financing the construction.

Cost Can Include Future Obligations

In some cases, the cost to acquire an asset will include obligations the company assumes when it gets the asset. Here are two examples:

A company buys a building. It pays no cash on the day it buys the building. Instead, it signs a note, payable to the seller, promising to pay $10 million over the next 10 years, plus a reasonable rate of interest. Even though the company did not pay any cash today, the $10 million obligation is a cost.

An electric utility company builds a nuclear reactor to provide power. The utility company spent $100 million to build the reactor. It is expected to last 40 years. After 40 years, the utility company will have to spend another $50 million to take the reactor apart in a safe way. The present value of the obligation to spend $50 million in the future will be considered part of the cost of the nuclear reactor.

"Basket Purchases" and Goodwill

Often, a company will pay a single price, and will receive numerous items. The issue is how the single price should be split among the items that were acquired. The general rule is that the price should be allocated among the items based on the estimated fair value of the items acquired.

For example, assume a company spends $10 million, and acquires a building, the land under the building, and some equipment in the building, such as the heating equipment. For accounting purposes, the land, building and equipment need to be recorded separately. To decide how much of the $10 million total price to allocate to each asset, the company needs to estimate the fair value of the land, the building, and the equipment. Assume the company hires an appraiser, who estimates the land on its own is worth $2 million, the building is worth $8.5 million, and the equipment is worth $0.5 million. This adds up to $11 million, which means the appraiser thinks the company got a great deal by buying at $10 million. The company would apportion the $10 million purchase price as follows:

Land—$10 million × (2/11) =	$1,818,182
Building—$10 million × (8.5/11) =	$7,727,273
Equipment—$10 million × (0.5/11) =	$454,545
Total	$10,000,000

The rule when one company buys another company is different. In the case of buying another company, the acquirer must record all the *identifiable* assets and liabilities at their individual fair values. These would include cash, accounts receivable, and other assets that are normally carried on the books, as well as some items that are not normally recognized. Such additional identifiable items might include the value of customer lists, or brand names. Once all the identifiable assets and liabilities are added up, there will likely be some purchase price that has not yet been allocated. This excess purchase price is called *goodwill*.[25] It is considered to be a value that relates to the acquired business as a whole, not to any specific piece of it.

Several points should be made about the accounting treatment of goodwill. Clearly there is an economic basis to the idea that companies derive value from their reputations and the good feelings their customers, vendors, and employees have towards them, and to the synergy of their operations. This means the ongoing business can make higher economic returns than one would expect just by looking at the individual assets. However, accounting does not recognize goodwill as a company slowly develops it over time. It is only recognized when one company buys another. As an example, some years ago Disney bought the ABC network. ABC would not have shown goodwill on its balance sheet when it was an independent company, but Disney recognized goodwill after acquiring ABC. This means that many companies have an economic asset that is not on their accounting balance sheets. It also means that the balance sheets of different companies are hard to compare. Those that purchased part of their operations will show goodwill, while those that developed their own operations will not.

Another point is that goodwill is recorded as an intangible asset with an indefinite life. The goodwill could last forever. Companies do not amortize goodwill under conventional GAAP or under IFRS. Under conventional GAAP, companies must decide each year if the goodwill has been impaired in value. If it has, they must write it down. The theory here is that the goodwill of a major company like ABC may have an extremely long life, so amortization is inappropriate. On the other hand, as technology and the economy changes, sometimes a company will fall out of favor, and its goodwill will cease to have continuing value.

For smaller companies, the process of doing annual checks for impairment is burdensome. It requires hiring experts to obtain information about the value of businesses they acquired. Also, since tax rules allow the amortization of goodwill, the regular GAAP accounting creates differences between financial and tax accounting. The cost-benefit relation of this accounting may not be clear for small companies, since it is likely that any goodwill they obtain when buying other small companies will disappear quickly due to competition and economic changes. As a practical compromise, a different method for accounting for goodwill is allowed under both IFRS and AICPA frameworks for small and medium-sized organizations. The AICPA's (2013) framework for small and medium-sized organizations requires goodwill to be amortized over either the period used for tax purposes, or 15 years.[26] Under the IFRS for Small and Medium-Sized Entities (IASB 2009), goodwill must be amortized over its expected useful life. It the company can't estimate a life, it should use 10 years as the amortization period.

Transactions With Related Parties

Normally, we presume that a company makes the best deals it can when it buys and sells things. Therefore, we assume that the historical cost of an asset represents the result of a real negotiation between a seller and a buyer, and therefore was a true fair value at the time of the transaction.

When the buyer and the seller are "*related parties*", this assumption is no longer valid. A "related party" transaction may be influenced by something besides the economics of the deal in question. A parent company and its subsidiaries are related parties. The parent company may instruct the subsidiary to sell an asset to the parent at an artificial price, which does not reflect market value, for various reasons. The parent might want the subsidiary to look profitable, or to look unprofitable. Other examples of related parties include a company and its officers, a company and its owners, pension or other trusts controlled by a company, and common subsidiaries of the same parent company.

Here are two examples of related party transactions occurring at values that would not have occurred in "arms-length" transactions between independent parties.

Example 1. A corporation has two subsidiaries. One subsidiary processes cow hides into leather. The second subsidiary makes handbags out of leather. The handbag company buys leather from the first subsidiary. Assume the leather company is in a country with low income taxes, and the handbag company is in a place with high income taxes. There is a temptation for the parent company to order the handbag company to overpay for leather—this will reduce profits in the place with high taxes, and move the profits to a place with low taxes.

Example 2. The owner of a small company is also its president. Her time and skills are highly valuable. However, her company does not pay her a salary—she works "for nothing." Her company's business looks more profitable than it would if the company recognized the true value of her services. If she ever sold the company, the new owners would have to hire a CEO, and would find the company much less profitable.

The only special accounting rule for transactions with related parties is that the company should disclose the nature and amounts of material transactions it has with related parties.

Adjusting Historical Cost Accounting for Impairments

Companies that state assets at historical cost sometimes find that the assets have lost value, and that their historical cost seriously overstates the economic value of the assets. In this situation, we say the value of the assets has been impaired. Companies will either "write down" the assets for impairment, or will record some other type of "reserve" for the loss in value. Here are examples of events that cause companies to recognize their assets were impaired:

- Time Warner bought AOL in the late 1990s. AOL was the U.S.'s most popular internet service provider. AOL provided internet service for a fixed monthly fee, and most consumers dialed up each time they wanted to be connected. Time Warner recorded a large goodwill asset when it bought AOL. Later, the way that Americans connected to the internet changed, and the value of the AOL goodwill was considered impaired. Time Warner "wrote down" goodwill of about $98 billion in 2002.[27]

- A company has a large inventory of Model 3 of its product. It is about to start selling the new, improved Model 4. This will make it very hard to sell the Model 3 items. The company should create a reserve for obsolescence of its inventory.
- A company has $10 million in receivables from various customers. The company probably should create a reserve for uncollectible accounts, to reflect the reality that some accounts will not be paid in full.
- A telephone company has a factory designed to make one particular product. Demand for that product has fallen, and the company will stop producing it. The factory and equipment cannot be sold for the amount on the books for their amortized cost. The company should reduce the recorded value of the factory to its realizable value.

The purpose of adjusting values to reflect impairment is to make the financial statements more representationally faithful of underlying economic value when that value has fallen. While the FASB says that conservatism is not a goal of financial reporting, this practice does make financial statements more conservative. Note that under GAAP, historical cost values are reduced to reflect impairment of value, but they are *not* increased to reflect increases in value.

Inflation and Financial Accounting

The basic issue for accounting is that, when assets are stated at their historical cost, and all costs are measured in "nominal" dollars, inflation distorts the reported income and assets. Assume a company bought its inventory a year ago and bought its equipment three years ago. The income statement for the current year would reflect:

- Sales, measured in current year dollars
- Cost of inventory sold, measured in last year's dollars
- Depreciation on equipment, measured in the dollars of three years ago

When inflation is significant, the cost of inventory sold and the depreciation will be smaller than it would be in today's dollars. Income is therefore higher using nominal dollars than it would be if the costs were measured in inflation-adjusted dollars. This creates several bad effects:

- The company will pay more taxes than it should, based on the underlying economics.
- If the company pays out its accounting profits as dividends, it will soon go out of business. When the company needs to replace its inventory and equipment, it will have to buy them at the current dollar value. The cost of goods sold and the depreciation it reported were too small to reflect the replacement costs of these items.
- Investors will overestimate the true profitability of the business.

In addition, assets are shown on the balance sheet at unrealistically low values.

The problems related to inflation have been recognized for many years. The Indian writer Kautilya, writing around 300 B.C.E. discussed some of the accounting issues that arise with changing prices (Mattessich 1998). Articles in the U.S. in 1919, and in Germany during its inflationary period of 1928 and 1929 (Vangermeersch 1979), all discussed how inflation distorted income measurements.

IFRS has to be adaptable to conditions throughout the world. Since some countries have significant inflation, IFRS allows companies the option to make adjustments to reflect the effects of inflation. IAS Standard 16, Property, Plant, and Equipment, allows periodic revaluation of fixed assets when the fair value can be reliably measured. If this method is used, upward revaluations generally result in a direct adjustment of equity, not through the income statement.[28] IAS 29, Financial Reporting in Hyperinflationary Economies, calls for use of price-level adjusted statements in these economies. IAS 40, Investment Property, allows entities to use a fair value model to treat investment properties, rather than historical cost. Changes in fair value are included in income.

The U.S. has generally had relatively low rates of inflation. As a result, U.S. GAAP has basically ignored the changing purchasing power of the dollar. The tax rules also basically ignore inflation. There is some evidence that even with low inflation, ignoring inflation leads to distorted decisions. For example, Yaniv Konchitchki (2011) found that "stock prices do not fully reflect the implications of the inflation effects for future cash flows" (p. 1045). As another example, consider how even small rates of inflation lead to large effects over time. If a company still owned land it bought in 1964 that land would be on the balance sheet at a cost measured in 1964 dollars. According to Bureau of Labor Statistics tables, for every dollar needed to buy the land in 1964, you would need about $7.50 today.[29] That means the true value of the land is 7.5 times the amount shown on the balance sheet.

It is unclear whether the FASB will consider adjusting U.S. accounting to adjust for inflation. In 1979, the FASB issued SFAS No. 33, requiring large companies to report certain supplementary data on a constant dollar basis, but the FASB later repealed this requirement. Around the same time, the SEC temporarily required some large companies to provide data on the impact of inflation on their financial results, but then dropped this requirement (Zeff 2005b). In a 1984 concepts statement, the FASB indicated it would consider changes if inflation increased "to a level at which distortions became intolerable" (1984, para. 72). Adjusting for inflation would require extra accounting effort, and none of the methods to adjust for inflation are perfect. At the moment, the FASB is not under pressure to make this change in practice.[30]

Foreign Currency Translation Issues

Modern businesses are often multinational. They issue financial statements in one currency, but their worldwide operations include assets and liabilities that were bought in various currencies. The issue of how assets in various countries should be translated into a single currency is a complicated one, and beyond the scope of an introductory accounting course. The discussion here is to help you understand why many companies show an item related to foreign exchange translation as part of their "accumulated other comprehensive income."

Let's assume a French company owns a company located in the U.S. The French company produces financial statements that use euros. At the beginning of the year, the U.S. subsidiary had the following assets: $100 of cash, $100 of marketable securities, and land at a historical cost of $100. The total assets equaled $300. Assume there were no liabilities. Assume that only two things happen during the year: the U.S. subsidiary earns $5 of interest income; and the value of the euro changes from $1.25 to $1.50. The balance sheets of the U.S. subsidiary at the beginning and end of the year, in dollars, look like the following:

	Year 1	Year 2
Cash	$100	$105
Marketable securities	$100	$100
Land	$100	$100
Total assets	$300	$305
Equity	$300	$305

This is fine—everything balances. There was $5 of net income, which explains the increase in equity from $300 to $305. The problem comes when the French company tries to translate the U.S. statements. What exchange rate should it use for each asset?

It would seem sensible to translate the ending cash and marketable securities at the end of the year rate of $1.50. They should be stated at their fair value, and the change in exchange rates affected the fair value, in euros, of the dollar holdings. The $100 of cash at the start of the year was worth $100 ÷ 1.25 dollars per euro = 80€, but at the end of the year rate the $100 would only have been worth 66.67€. There was a loss in euros from holding onto dollars during the year. The same loss arises with holding onto the marketable securities. Since these items are recorded at fair value, it makes sense to record a loss.

Land is normally recorded at historical cost. In dollars, that was $100. In order for the French parent to report the land at its own historical cost, it would have to use the same exchange rate to translate the item as was originally in effect when the item was bought. In other words, it would have to use the historical exchange rate. Assume that was $1.25.

What would be the problem with translating the land at the new exchange rate of $1.50 per euro? In this case, we would say that the value of the land, in euros, had fallen from 80€ to 66.67€. This is probably economically false, because the land is probably now worth more than its $100 original cost in dollars. It does not make economic sense to multiply an out-of-date land value by an up-to-date translation rate, and claim to have an up-to-date value. The same problem arises with all assets that are carried at historical cost in the subsidiary's currency.

So let's assume that the company translates its $105 of cash and its $100 of marketable securities at the new exchange rate of $1.50 per euro, and its land at $1.25 per euro. The interest income will be translated at the average exchange rate during the year. The translated statements will not balance. Equity plus liabilities *in euros* won't equal assets *in euros*. Some balancing figure is needed to force the accounting equation to work in euros. Such a balancing figure is informally called a "plug." The more formal name is a "foreign currency translation adjustment."

There are accounting rules that prescribe which exchange rates are used for particular assets and liabilities. These accounting rules also specify when the balancing figures will be recognized as part of net income, and when they are instead recorded as part of other comprehensive income as a "foreign currency translation adjustment."

Values That Can Be Used For Managerial Accounting

Management has far more freedom in the choice of values it uses for internal decision-making than it does for external reporting. Management could, if it wished, keep track of the current sales value of its land and fixed assets. It could use inflation-adjusted accounting. In practice, rather than keep separate records for internal and external use, most companies use the same valuation practices for most of their assets for internal and external reporting.

Probably manufacturers' inventory is the most important area where companies use different valuation methods for internal and external use. For external reporting, companies have to use what is called "*full costing*" or "*absorption costing*" for their inventory. This means that the cost of each item of inventory contains, not just the materials and labor used to make it, but part of the overhead costs of the factory. However, for decision-making, the company may want to consider that fixed manufacturing costs are period costs, and not part of the inventory costs. This is called either "*direct costing*" or "*variable costing*."

In Chapter 5, the discussion of "relevant costs" indicated that companies should base their short-term decisions on only revenues and expenses that are directly affected by the decision. In most cases, fixed manufacturing costs will not vary based on short-term decisions. Therefore, companies may wish to use variable costing for short-term decision-making.

Impact of Valuation Methods on Behavior

Chapter 6 discussed how people react to being measured. Accounting regulators consider likely reactions when setting standards, and try to minimize dysfunctional effects and to reduce earnings management. This section shows how certain types of valuation impact actions.

Costing Methods and Production Levels

Let's assume that a company has fixed manufacturing costs of $10 million. If it uses variable costing, all of that $10 million is an expense during the year. If it uses absorption costing, then part of the $10 million in costs will be considered part of the inventory, and therefore an asset. This means income and retained earnings will be higher under absorption costing.

How much higher? That depends on the ending inventory. The higher the ending inventory level, the better the company will look under absorption costing. Therefore, absorption costing gives managers an incentive to overproduce. People who advocate "lean manufacturing" believe absorption costing is a very bad idea. It leads to excessive inventory, which can be expensive to store, and which is also at risk of becoming obsolete or damaged.

Goodwill, Acquisition Accounting and Earnings Management

When one company acquires another, GAAP and IFRS require the purchaser to record all the assets and liabilities acquired at their fair values. The fair values of assets will be based on estimates of what will happen in the future. For example, the fair value of accounts receivable depends on what portion is expected to be collected in the future. The fair value of contingent liabilities (such as lawsuits against the company) depends on the estimate of how much the company would pay out on those liabilities. If the purchase price is larger than the fair value of the net of all the assets and liabilities acquired, then any remaining amount is considered an asset called "goodwill." Goodwill is not amortized. It is checked periodically for impairment.

What happens in the years that follow the acquisition? Business will go on. The inventory will be sold. The receivables will be collected. The property will be depreciated. Any lawsuits or contingent liabilities will be paid off.

The accounting for the company will use the values as of the acquisition date to compute the impact of these actions on income. When the inventory is sold, the cost of goods sold will be based on the value assigned as of the date of the acquisition. When receivables are collected, if more are collected than expected at the date of acquisition, then the company will record a gain. The depreciation of equipment will be high if the equipment is assumed to have a high value at the date of acquisition, and lower if it is assigned a lower value.

The net effect of the accounting rules is this. A company that underestimates the fair value of assets as of the date of acquisition, and overestimates liabilities, will record higher goodwill than one that estimates accurately. In subsequent years, the company that underestimated the values of its assets, and overestimated the liabilities, will show higher income. Thus, companies that make acquisitions have an opportunity to engage in earnings management. In Chapter 6, one of the techniques of earnings management criticized by Arthur Levitt, head of the SEC, was "abusive acquisition accounting."

Historical Cost Accounting, Gains Trading and Impairment Accounting

Let's assume a company has two assets, each with a current value of $10 million. One of these was acquired at a cost of $8 million, and the other was acquired at a cost of $12 million. They are both shown on the balance sheet at their historical cost.

This difference between current value and historical cost gives management the ability to manage earnings by choosing which assets to sell. If management wants to show a gain of $2 million, it can sell the item that cost $8 million. It will have a realized gain of $10 million – $8 million, or $2 million. If the company instead wanted to show a loss of $2 million, it would sell the asset that cost $12 million. Note that in this case, economically both assets have the same value, of $10 million, so in theory it should not matter which one the company keeps and which it sells. Choosing to sell the items that have gains is called "*gains trading*."

In the 1990s, the FASB changed the accounting for marketable securities to require they be recorded at fair value in large part to limit "gains trading" (Laux and Leuz 2009). Ironically, Enron got the SEC to permit it to use fair value accounting for its energy contracts, by noting that fair value accounting would stop this kind of "gains trading." Fair value is also referred to as "marking" assets to their "market value," or "mark to market." Jeffrey Skilling, at that time Enron's chief operating officer, was quoted (Eichenwald 2005) as assuring the SEC that "Accrual accounting lets you pretty much create the outcome you want, by keeping the bad stuff and selling the good. Mark-to-market doesn't let you do this" (p. 59).

The FASB and IASB have made a variety of standards requiring companies to record impairments to assets. These standards attempt to reduce the temptation in historical cost accounting to "keep the bad stuff" and to avoid admitting that assets have lost value.

Impairment Rules and "Big Bath" Restructuring

Chapter 6 noted that sometimes managers have an incentive to show losses in a particular year, especially if they can explain the losses as something that will not recur in the future. Chapter 6 discussed the temptation of companies to take a "big bath" in certain situations, such as when a new CEO has just been appointed to replace one that was fired. Companies sometimes announced overly large "restructuring charges" in order to manage earnings.

Usually, a company would say that it had examined its businesses, and decided that a "restructuring," or major change, was needed. This would often involve deciding that certain fixed assets would no longer be as useful as previously thought, so impairment charges would be needed. Also, the company might need to reduce its workforce, creating a large contingent liability for severance pay. While many restructuring charges were actually economically appropriate, there was a widespread belief in the 1990s that other companies were overstating their problems in order to manage earnings. The companies would later indicate they had received greater value for their assets, and had paid less in severance, than they originally estimated. In a famous speech, the head of the SEC listed "big baths" as one of five common methods of managing earnings (Levitt 1998). The FASB later issued two statements (SFAS No. 144 in 2001 and SFAS No. 146 in 2002) that had the effect of making it harder for companies to record severance liabilities and asset impairments without strong evidence of the amounts that would actually be incurred.

Fair Value and Overvalued Assets

A major concern about the use of fair value is that managers could use the looseness of valuation measures to overstate assets and income. Indeed, Enron was an example of a company that did precisely that. It was allowed by the SEC to value the energy contracts it entered into at market value. These were not standardized contracts, and were often not tradable on external markets, so Enron set the accounting values of the contracts based on its own internal models. Part of the fraud at Enron was that the values of these contracts were overstated, resulting in overstated revenues and income (Eichenwald 2005).

In general, standard-setters and financial statement users have been very concerned about the chances of managers using estimates to manage earnings. In general, fair value was first allowed only for financial assets, where fairly objective market values were available. Two types of assets where there are clearly not complete and perfect markets are inventory and fixed assets. In these cases, the standard-setters have not allowed fair value accounting. In other situations, the standard-setters have required companies to disclose what types of data were used to arrive at fair value measurements.

Fair Value and Economic Behavior

There has been a great deal published about the relation between the shift towards fair value accounting and the 2008 financial crisis. Arnold (2009) wrote that "the solvency and survival of our major financial institutions now turns on how accountants value bank assets and the extent to which auditors require firms to consolidate off-balance sheet entities" (p. 803).

The basic argument that fair value accounting affected the fiscal crisis relates to the way that banks operate and the way they are regulated. To make money, when they receive financing through borrowing or through stockholder investments or receiving deposits from customers, they loan the money out or invest in other types of assets. They operate with high degrees of leverage, which increases their risk of failing. (Leverage was discussed in Chapter 4.) They are required to keep the level of "capital" above a certain percentage of their total assets. "Capital" is measured in a complex manner, but for the purposes of this section let's say it equals shareholders' equity. If the capital falls below the required percentage, banks are supposed to use their assets to pay off debt until the ratio of equity to total assets meets the required level. Remember, much of a bank's assets are loans it made to businesses and people. Assume the required ratio was 10%.

So, assume a bank has invested $100 million in a package of mortgage-backed securities. It needs to have related capital of 10%, or $10 million. Now, assume the fair value of these securities rises to $105 million, a 5% change in market value. Using fair market accounting, the bank would record income of $5 million. It would therefore now have capital equal to $10 + $5 = $15 million and the related asset is now $105 million. It has more capital than it needs—it only needs $10.5 million, but it has $15 million. It can make more loans, or it can buy more securities. So, when prices are rising, fair value accounting leads banks to expand their lending and to buy more securities. The greater demand for securities may increase their value further. In this case, the bank would lend $45 million to others, or buy more securities, raising its total assets to $150 million.

Now, assume the value of the assets falls from $105 million down to $92 million, a drop of $13 million. Using fair value accounting, the company would reduce the value of these mortgage loans to $92 million, and would also record a loss of $13 million. This $13 million loss changes its capital from $15 million to $2 million. At this point, the bank has capital of $2 million, and related assets on its books of $150 million minus $13 million, or $137 million. The required amount of capital is 10% of $137 million, or $13.7 million, and it only has $2 million.

What can the bank do? It can raise new equity capital, and some banks did sell shares to new shareholders. It can sell some of its assets and pay off debts, to reduce the $137 million of assets and also the amount of capital it needs to have. Many banks did this. The problem is that, when all banks try to sell at the same time, the prices of the mortgage-backed securities, and many other assets, will fall. This means the fair values of the banks' other assets will fall even more. This causes the banks to need to sell even more assets, increasing the problem. Another thing that banks could do was to try and get the rules changed. Indeed, in 2008, after the market for mortgage-backed securities collapsed, banks and other financial institutions argued that the new, lower market prices should not be accepted, because they were not "orderly" markets. The FASB and IASB allowed companies to deviate from using fair value where they could argue that the markets were not functioning properly.

The technical term is that the banks' behavior was "pro-cyclical." It enhanced the economic cycle, by having excessive buying while prices were rising, and excessive selling when prices were falling. The effect of one bank selling on the prices of assets, and thus on the actions of other banks, is "contagion." Thus, a major criticism is that fair value accounting reduced the stability of the banking system, and contributed to contagion and a collapse of credit markets when the value of mortgage-backed securities fell.[31] Empirical studies saw evidence of this effect in 2008 and 2009.[32]

A related criticism of fair value accounting is that it puts too much faith in market prices. It does not recognize that market prices might be irrational, and due to "speculative bubbles." In the period where the "bubble" is growing, this would lead to excessive bank lending and purchasing of the speculative assets. See McSweeney (2009). Some critics have said that the problem was especially severe in the case of the types of investments involved in the 2008 crisis because there were in fact not reliable markets for them. Many of the problem assets were valued using less reliable data than "Level 1" inputs.[33] As McSweeney (2009) wrote:

> Mark-to-market valuations of the now infamous "securitized" assets, such as collateralized debt obligations, were readily available and used. These assets were primarily traded through over-the-counter markets. . . . Yet, as we now know, those market valuations of largely opaque composite assets were often wildly overstated. In times of excessive exuberance current market values mirror and bolster valuations which ultimately must fall. Additionally, there is considerable management discretion in determining the timing and amount of asset valuation or revaluation, especially, for non-traded or infrequently traded assets....
>
> The claim that fair value accounting provides "faithful representation of reality" (Chartered Financial Analysts' Institute, 2008, and others), is wrong. Why? As valuations necessarily rely on expectations about hypothetical future events . . . that claim could only be true if markets (or accountants or other managers) had infallible powers of forecasting. But nothing and nobody has that power. It was inevitable that in bubble times the momentum of fair valuations of assets in general was towards over-valuation fuelled by the too-rosy and speculative expectations and added to that contagion.
>
> (p. 837)

Those who defend the GAAP accounting rules make two major points. The first is that part of the problem was not due to fair value accounting at all. Banks actually recorded many of their assets at cost, and did not do a good job of recognizing problems with their loans on a timely basis. Thomas Linsmeier, a member of the FASB, wrote (Linsmeier 2011) "the record of bank managers in recognizing losses has been exceedingly poor, as the generally 'healthy' balance sheets of New Frontier and so many other recently failed banks indicate" (p. 411). Indeed, Laux and Leuz (2009) note that the use of fair value would show indications of a drop in value faster than historical cost would, and could often be an early warning system. A second point is that bank regulators do not have to use rigid percentage capital ratios. They could have adjusted their regulatory requirements over the course of a business cycle. In other words, the accountants are simply the measurers, and it is the regulators' job to design appropriate decision models.

Unresolved Issues and Areas for Further Research

There are many unresolved issues related to the choice of valuation methods in accounting. GAAP and IFRS use a variety of different measures. Listed below are a few of the issues that arise that have not been discussed previously in this chapter:

1 To what extent can financial statement users "see through" different accounting methods, and compare companies that use different accounting measures? For example, the chapter indicated that in times of rising prices, companies that use LIFO will tend to have lower net income than companies that use FIFO to value their inventories. Does the stock market penalize companies for using LIFO, or does the stock market "see through" the differences in accounting?[34] As another example, can analysts use disclosures about advertising and research expenditures to correctly value companies, even though GAAP puts a zero value on internally developed intangible assets?[35]

2 In a number of cases, the current accounting rules will value an asset differently, depending on how a company intends to use it.[36] Here are two examples. The issue is whether it makes sense to use different ways of valuing assets, based on management's plans.

  a. If a company owns a bond, which it intends to hold until maturity, it can account for the bond at amortized cost, but if it intends to sell the bond, it must account for it at fair value.

  b. If a company owns a car, it would account for it at cost if it is a car dealer, but at amortized cost if it is intending to use the car in its business.

3 Can reliable ways be found for valuing internally developed intangible assets? For many modern companies, intangible assets such as software or brand names are a huge part of their overall value. The current accounting practice of not recognizing these assets at all leads to major distortions of their financial statements. However, so far the research indicates that reliable ways to measure the value of research and development and goodwill have not yet been found.[37] Or, is it possible that analysts are able to correct for this distortion by using other, disclosed, information?

4 Can ways be found to try to reflect the value of the synergy of having assets working together, rather than separately?[38]

Key Terms

Absorption costing—This inventory cost method includes an allocated portion of fixed manufacturing overhead, as well as direct labor and materials and variable overhead costs.

Amortized cost—This method of valuing fixed assets, intangible assets, and other items adjusts the historic cost of the item for amortization or depreciation that has occurred over time. For example, if a patent cost $3 million, and one third of its value has been amortized so far, its "amortized cost" would now be $2 million.

Appraised value—The value that an expert appraiser says an asset or liability is worth.

Basket purchase—This term refers to a situation where a company buys various assets for a single payment. For example, a company may buy a building together with its heating equipment. Typically, companies allocate the payment based on the fair value of the items received.

Complete markets—Markets that trade all the assets and liabilities a company has. The idea of complete markets simplifies economic theories but the real world does not have functioning markets for all assets and liabilities.

Contingent gains and contingent losses—These are gains and losses, related to some event that happened in the past, where the value depends on some future event. For example, the amount a company will pay on warranties for products sold depends on which products break in the future.

Depreciated cost—See amortized cost.

Direct costing—This cost method does not assign any of fixed overhead costs to items produced. Instead, fixed overhead costs are treated as period costs. The costs assigned to items produced include direct labor, direct materials, and variable overhead costs.

Entry price—The price to buy something. An example would be the cost of obtaining inventory.

Exit price—The price charged when a company sells something.

Expected net present value—This is the discounted value of the future cash payments from some asset, after considering the probability of receiving them. For a further discussion of present value, see Appendix B.

Fair value—The FASB and IASB define the fair value of a financial asset as the amount a company would charge as an exit price to sell the item, in an orderly market, to willing market participants. The fair value is not adjusted for transaction costs. The fair value of a nonfinancial asset may be the exit price to sell it, or it may be the "value in use" of the item.

Fair value hierarchy—The FASB and IASB have stated that companies should use information to compute fair value in order of how reliable it is. See **Level 1, 2, and 3 inputs**.

First in, first out (FIFO)—This method of computing the cost of inventory assumes a company sells its oldest items *first*. As a result, the ending inventory contains the most recently purchased items.

Full costing—See absorption costing.

Goodwill—From an economic standpoint, goodwill represents some extra value that a company has, beyond the value of its individual assets. It is a measure of the extra earnings power of the assets as they have been combined over their separate earning power. In accounting, goodwill equals the excess of the amount paid to buy a business over the net fair value of its separately identifiable assets and liabilities.

Historical cost—The cost that was incurred when an item was bought.

Last in, first out (LIFO)—This method of computing the cost of inventory assumes a company sells its newest items *first* and its oldest items *last*. As a result, the ending inventory contains items that were bought a long time ago and cost of goods sold contains the costs of more recently purchased items.

Level 1, 2, and 3 inputs—The FASB and IASB have defined three levels of reliability of information for valuation models. Level 1 is the most reliable of these levels, and Level 3 is the least reliable. Level 1 inputs, according to the FASB, include: "Quoted prices (unadjusted) in active markets for identical assets or liabilities that the reporting entity can access at the measurement date." An example would be stock exchange quotes for Apple stock, on today's date. Level 2 inputs are "Inputs other than quoted prices included within Level 1 that are observable for the asset or liability, either directly or indirectly." An example of a Level 2 input for the valuation of a shipment of oil might be a market price for a similar, but not identical, type of oil, delivered in a different location. Level 3 inputs are "Unobservable inputs for the asset or liability." Level 3 inputs contain factors that cannot be verified from outside market data.

Liquidation value—The value an asset would be sold for, or a liability would be settled for, if the company went out of business.

Lower of cost or market (GAAP and IFRS)—Both GAAP and IFRS require companies to record their inventory at the lower of the historical cost or some "market" measurement of the value of the inventory. "Market" is net realizable value for IFRS and is usually replacement cost for GAAP, although GAAP has some exceptions.

Net realizable value—The value that can be received from the sale of the item, after subtracting any transaction costs.

Nonrecognition—A practice of not recording the asset or liability at the time the financial statements are made. In effect, the asset or liability has a zero value.

Perfect markets—Markets where items are traded actively, with no transaction costs and where all parties to the markets have full information.

Realized value—The value that was received when the company disposed of the asset.

Related party—Related parties have some special relationship with the company that means the transactions may not be at "arms' length." One of the related parties can induce another into making a transaction at terms that would normally not be accepted. For example, the owners of a company have the ability to direct the company to sell products to them below cost.

Replacement cost—The cost to a company of replacing an asset it now has.

Specific identification—This inventory method identifies which particular inventory items were sold, and assigns the cost of those particular items to cost of goods sold.

Value in use—The expected value to the company of continuing to use, rather than sell, an asset.

Variable costing—See direct costing.

Weighted average cost—This inventory method assumes each item sold, and each item in ending inventory, has a cost equal to the weighted average of all items that were available for sale.

Questions and Problems

Comprehension Questions

C1. (Perfect and complete markets) What is meant by perfect and complete markets?

C2. (Perfect markets) Do you believe the market for used cars is a "perfect market"? Explain your answer.

C3. (Complete markets) Which of the following types of corporate assets do you think there are functioning "perfect" markets for? Explain your answer.

    A. U.S. Treasury bonds

    B. Inventories of standard grades of crude oil

    C. Inventories of men's suits

    D. Equipment used in the assembly line for cars the company makes

    E. The expertise of the company's workforce

C4. (Types of value) What is meant by "historical cost" valuation? Is it an entry price or an exit price?

C5. (Types of value) What is the FASB's definition of "fair value," for financial assets? Is it an entry price or an exit price?

C6. (Types of value) What is meant by "net realizable value"? How does it differ from the FASB's definition of "fair value" with regard to the treatment of transaction costs?

C7. (Types of value) How does the FASB say that the fair value of a nonfinancial asset should be determined?

C8. (Advantages/disadvantages of different types of value) Why do accountants usually not use liquidation value in financial accounting?

C9. (Advantages/disadvantages of different types of value) What are some good features of historical cost accounting?

C10. (Advantages/disadvantages of different types of value) What are some bad features of historical cost accounting?

C11. (Advantages/disadvantages of different types of value) What is "gains trading"? Why does it arise with historical cost accounting, but not with fair value accounting?

C12. (Advantages/disadvantages of different types of value) If there is rapid inflation, explain how this would cause the balance sheet assets to be understated for companies with large amounts of fixed assets that use historical cost accounting.

C13. (Advantages/disadvantages of different types of value) If there is rapid inflation, explain how this would cause income to be overstated for companies with large amounts of fixed assets that use historical cost accounting.

C14. (Advantages/disadvantages of different types of value) What are some good features of fair value accounting?

C15. (Advantages/disadvantages of different types of value) What are some potential problems with fair value accounting?

C16. (Advantages/disadvantages of different types of value—fixed asset) Compare the use of fair value accounting and historical cost accounting for an office building owned by a company, in terms of the following factors from the FASB's conceptual framework:

A.   Decision-usefulness (assuming the company intends to keep and operate the building)
B.   Decision-usefulness (assuming the company intends to sell the building in the near future)
C.   Neutrality of the value
D.   Verifiability of the value
E.   Representational faithfulness
F.   Comparability of values across various companies that own similar buildings.

C17. (Advantages/disadvantages of different types of value—Treasury bond) Compare the use of fair value accounting and historical cost accounting for a 20-year U.S. Treasury bond owned by a company, in terms of the following factors from the FASB's Conceptual Framework:

A.   Decision-usefulness (assuming the company intends to keep the bond until it matures)
B.   Decision-usefulness (assuming the company intends to sell the bond in the near future)
C.   Neutrality of the value
D.   Verifiability of the value
E.   Representational faithfulness
F.   Comparability of values across various companies that own similar bonds.

C18. (Values for particular accounts) Which valuation method is usually used for land used in the business?

C19. (Values for particular accounts) Which valuation methods are used for intangible assets that were:

•   Purchased from others, and have definite lives?
•   Purchased from others, and have indefinite lives?
•   Developed internally by the company?

C20. (Values for particular accounts) Which valuation method is usually used for recording fixed assets, such as buildings and equipment?

C20. (Values for particular accounts) Which valuation method is usually used for inventories?

C21. (Totals) Why does the chapter say that there are mathematical issues with the total assets on the financial statements?

C22. (Impairments) What is the reason that the FASB and IASB require companies to record impairments or losses in value in most asset accounts?

C23. (Consistency) Why is it important that companies use the same method of valuation consistently each year?

C24. (Measuring fair value) Explain what the FASB means by:

•   Level 1 inputs
•   Level 2 inputs
•   Level 3 inputs

C25. (Measuring fair value) Which estimate of fair value would you trust more—one based on Level 1 inputs, or one based on level 3 inputs? Explain your answer.

C26. (Volatility) What are some ways that the FASB and IASB have made "comprehensive income" more volatile as markets change than "net income"?

C27. (Costing methods) What is the difference between "absorption costing" and "direct costing"?

C28. (Costing methods) Why does "absorption costing" give managers more of an incentive than direct costing to produce excessive inventory?

Application Questions

A1. (Accounts and methods) For each of the following accounts, assuming there is no impairment, indicate whether they are normally accounted for under GAAP at fair value, historical cost, or amortized (depreciated) cost:

  A.   Accounts receivable
  B.   Inventories of a typical retailer
  C.   Inventories of fungible goods held by a commodities trader
  D.   Land used in a business
  E.   Cars used in a business
  F.   Cars held for sale by a car dealer
  G.   Investments in marketable securities
  H.   Financial instruments owned by a business
  I.   A patent bought from another company, with a remaining life of 6 years.

A2. (Accounts and methods) For each of the following items, assuming there is no impairment, indicate whether they would normally be accounted for using: nonrecognition; historical cost; amortized (depreciated) cost; or fair value.

  A.   A valuable brand name bought from another company. It has an indefinite life.
  B.   A brand name that is now valuable that was developed by the company over time. It has an indefinite life.
  C.   Goodwill acquired as part of buying another company.
  D.   Goodwill developed over the company's 30 years of operations.
  E.   A franchise to operate a McDonald's restaurant in a particular area. The franchise has an indefinite life, and was bought from the McDonald's Corporation.
  F.   The amount of money spent on a research and development project that is expected to lead to a useful new product. The new product is likely to have a market for many years.
  G.   A patent purchased from another company for a product that is likely to have a market for many years.

A3. (Accounts and methods—FASB Conceptual Framework) For each of the following accounts, explain whether you think that fair value would be more *relevant* than either historical cost or depreciated historical cost? Explain your answer.

  A.   Marketable securities the company is holding for sale in the near future.
  B.   Shares of stock in another company that the company is holding as a long-term investment. The intention is to hold this investment at least 10 more years.
  C.   Inventory of women's dresses held for sale.
  D.   Inventory of copper, of a type that is sold on commodities exchanges.
  E.   Machinery used in a factory. The factory is expected to be useful for many years to come.
  F.   Machinery used in a factory. The industry is very unstable, and it is possible the factory may need to be closed in the next two years.

    G. Advertising expenditures that have created favorable brand awareness in the public for the company's main product.

A4. (Accounts and methods—FASB Conceptual Framework) For the same items in the previous question, indicate which method (fair value or historical cost or depreciated historical cost) is more *verifiable*.

A5. (Accounts and methods—FASB Conceptual Framework) For the same items in question A3, indicate which method (fair value or historical cost or depreciated historical cost) is more *comparable across different companies*.

A6. (Fair value hierarchy) For each of the following pieces of information, indicate whether you think it is a Level 1, Level 2, or Level 3 input:

    A. The company owns stock in a company that is actively traded on NASDAQ. The information is the closing price on the stock on that date.

    B. The company trades in oil. It owns a large amount of oil that is similar to, but not exactly the same as, the kind of oil traded on commodities exchanges. Typically, the kind of oil on the exchange has sold for 10 cents per gallon more than the oil owned by the company. The company uses prices from the commodities exchange for similar oil, and reduces those prices by 10 cents to reflect the historical difference in prices.

    C. The company has made a contract to supply fuel to an important customer for a fixed price for two years. The company's internal models indicate the contract will have a profit of $200,000.

    D. The company has acquired another business, which sells clothing. GAAP requires it to value the inventory of the company it has acquired at fair value. The data the company uses is recent selling prices of the clothing from the stores it acquired.

    E. The company invests in a collection of home mortgages. Similar but not identical collections of mortgages are sold by certain dealers who specialize in putting together these packages of mortgages. To value the collection of mortgages it owns at December 31, the company used prices paid by dealers for similar collections of mortgages that day.

A7. (Historical cost—included costs) The Barker Corp. is a retailer. It made the following expenditures in February. Indicate which of them would become part of the cost of its inventory:

    A. The prices charged by suppliers for inventory shipped to Barker in February.
    B. The amounts Barker paid to advertise the goods for sale.
    C. The amounts Barker paid for shipping of inventory items to its stores in February.
    D. The amounts Barker paid for shipping of inventory items to its customers in February.
    E. The amounts Barker incurred to unpack inventory items received and get them ready for sale.

A8. (Historical cost—manufacturer—included costs) The Central Corp. is a manufacturer. It made the following expenditures in February. Assuming it uses the absorption costing method, which types of cost become part of the cost of its finished goods inventory?

    A. Direct labor cost, for people working on the products.
    B. Direct materials cost, for materials that become part of the product.
    C. Variable overhead cost, for other costs that vary directly with the amount produced.
    D. Fixed overhead costs.

A9. (Historical cost—manufacturer—included costs) Assume the same facts as the previous example, but now assume the company uses a variable costing method.

A10. (Historical cost—fixed assets) The Dexter Corp. buys a truck for use in its business. It incurs the following costs with respect to the truck in the first year. Which of these should be shown as part of the cost of the truck on the balance sheet? (Hint: only costs which are needed to get the truck ready for use are on the balance sheet.)

Amount paid to truck dealer	$100,000
Painting company name and colors on truck	$1,000
Sales tax on purchase of truck	$8,000
Gasoline for first year	$10,000
Liability Insurance coverage for first year	$6,000

A11. (Historical cost—building) The Early Corp. is building a new building for its operations. Which of the following costs should be shown as part of the cost of the building on the balance sheet?

Amount paid for construction workers' wages.
Amount paid for steel and building materials.
Amount paid as fines for violating safety regulations during the construction.
Amount paid for liability insurance during the construction period.
Amount paid for liability insurance after the construction was over.
Amount paid for interest on a construction loan, during the construction period.
Amount paid for interest on the construction loan, after the construction was over.

A12. (Historical cost—basket purchase) A company spent $6 million to buy a small farm. It hired an appraiser to advise it on the relative fair value of the farm assets. The appraiser indicated the following separate values:

Land	$4.5 million
Buildings	0.5 million
Equipment	0.5 million

Required: Allocate the purchase price to the three assets acquired.

A13. (Historical cost—basket purchase) The Knox Corp. bought four assets of the Tower Company for a combined price of $1 million. An appraiser stated that the items, if bought separately, would have had the following prices:

Asset A	$600,000
Asset B	$150,000
Asset C	$200,000
Asset D	$250,000

Required: Allocate the purchase price to the three assets acquired.

A14. (Purchase of business with goodwill) The Meade Corp. bought the Drum Corp. for a total price of $100 million. An appraiser stated that the separately identifiable assets of Drum Corp were, in millions of dollars:

Assets:	
Cash	2
Accounts receivable	8
Inventory	15
Property and equipment	30
Identifiable intangible assets	20
Liabilities:	30

Required: Compute the goodwill that would be recorded on the date of acquisition.

A15. (Acquisition of business, goodwill, earnings management) The Benning Corp. buys Dix Corp. for a total purchase price of $1 billion. Shown below are the values of the various assets and liabilities of Dix as of the date of the purchase, in millions of dollars, on the books of Dix as well as their estimated fair value.

	Book value	Fair value
Cash	125	125
Accounts receivable	270	265
Inventory	200	300
Other current assets	20	20
Land	50	150
Fixed assets, net of depreciation	100	80
Patents and other identified intangibles	1	300
Various liabilities	300	350

A.   Compute the goodwill that Benning will record after this purchase.

B.   Explain the likely reason why there would be large differences between the book value and the fair value of the following items as of the date of the acquisition:

   a.   Inventory
   b.   Land
   c.   Fixed assets, net of depreciation
   d.   Patents and other identified intangible assets

C.   When the inventory is sold in the next year, what will the company record as cost of goods sold, 200 or 300?

D.   When the patents are amortized in the future, will amortization be based on $1 or on $300?

E.   Is goodwill amortized under normal GAAP?

F.   In general, would future reported income be higher if the estimates of the values of the various assets acquired are *high*, leading to low goodwill, or *low*, leading to a high value assigned to goodwill? Explain your answer.

A16. (Inventory cost method—effects of different cost flow assumptions) Assume that the inventory record for the Gotham Steel Corp. show the following information:

January 1	Beginning inventory	10 units at cost of $100
January 23	Purchases	10 units at cost of $103
January 30	Sales	10 units, at a price of $110

A.   Compute the cost of goods available for sale

B.   Compute the cost of the ending inventory of 10 units under:

   a.   FIFO
   b.   LIFO
   c.   Weighted average cost

C.   Compute the cost of goods sold under

   a.   FIFO
   b.   LIFO
   c.   Weighted average cost

D.   Which method would show the highest and lowest cost of goods sold?

E.   Which method would the company probably prefer for tax purposes?

A17. (Inventory cost flow assumptions—modification of prior problem for lean inventory) Assume that the inventory records for the Gotham Steel Corp. show the following information:

January 1	Beginning inventory	10 units at cost of $100
January 29	Purchases	500 units at cost of $103
January 30	Sales	500 units at a price of $110

    A. Compute the cost of goods available for sale
    B. Compute the cost of the ending inventory of 10 units under:

        a. FIFO
        b. LIFO
        c. Weighted average cost

    C. Compute the cost of goods sold under

        a. FIFO
        b. LIFO
        c. Weighted average cost

    D. Which method would show the highest and lowest cost of goods sold?
    E. What is the percentage difference in cost of goods sold between the highest and lowest methods?

A18. (Inventory cost method) Assume that the Apex Tire Company's records showed the following information regarding one particular type of tires:

January 1	Beginning inventory	15 tires at cost of $70
February 15	Purchases	40 tires at cost of $72
March 15	Purchases	35 tires at cost of $75
Sales during January through March 31		80 tires at selling price of $100

You can assume all the sales were made on March 31. Compute the March 31 ending inventory, and the cost of goods sold for the quarter, if the company uses:

    A. The FIFO inventory method
    B. The LIFO inventory method
    C. The weighted average cost method.

A19. (Inventory cost method, perpetual inventory) Assume the same facts as the prior problem, with one change. In this case, the date the items were sold will matter to the way cost is computed.

    You should now assume that of the 80 items sold, 50 were sold on February 28, and the other 30 were sold on March 20. You should also assume that the inventory cost methods were computed at the dates of the sales. In other words, when the items were sold on February 28, the weighted average cost was the weighted average cost of the items available for sale at that date. LIFO and FIFO should both be computed using the earliest and latest items on hand at the February 28 and March 20 sales dates.

    Compute the March 31 ending inventory, and the cost of goods sold for the quarter, if the company uses:

    A. The FIFO inventory method
    B. The LIFO inventory method
    C. The weighted average cost method.

A20. (Lower of cost or market.) The Sheridan Corp. has the following products in inventory.

	Units	Cost per unit	Market per unit
Product A	1,000	$20	$22
Product B	1,000	$8	$7
Product C	3,000	$10	$11

A. For each product, find the lower of the cost or the market for that item.
B. Use your answers from part A to find the sum of the "lower of cost or market" values for the three items in inventory.
C. What is the total cost of the inventory?
D. What is the total market of the whole inventory?
E. Which is lower, total cost or total market?
F. Which is lower, your answer from part B, or your answer from part E?

A21. (Lower of cost or market.) The Grant Corp. has the following products in inventory.

	Units	Cost per unit	Market per unit
Product 1	100	$3	$4
Product 2	200	$4	$4.5
Product 3	300	$5	$3

A. For each product, find the lower of the cost or the market for that item.
B. Use your answers from part A to find the sum of the "lower of cost or market" values for the three items in inventory.
C. What is the total cost of the inventory?
D. What is the total market of the whole inventory?
E. Which is lower, total cost or total market?
F. Which is lower, your answer from part B, or your answer from part E?
G. GAAP and IFRS allow companies to compute "lower of cost or market" either on an item by item basis, or on total basis by department, or by a total basis for the whole inventory. In general, which method do you think will usually give the lowest inventory value? Why?

A22. (Upward revaluations of fixed assets—IFRS) IFRS, but not GAAP, allows companies to periodically revalue fixed assets to reflect changing fair values. Assume that the Meade Corp. has a building with a historical cost of $40 million. It bought the building 10 years ago. The Meade Corp. has been recording 1/40th of the historical cost as depreciation expense each year. (It assumed a 40-year life for the building.) At the current date, the Meade Corp. shows this building on its books at a net depreciated value of $40 million – $10 million of depreciation, or $30 million. It expects the building to last another 30 years, which agrees with its original estimate.

Assume that the Meade Corp. uses IFRS, and it now believes the building is worth $60 million.

A. What would be the effect of revaluing the building to a value of $60 million on the balance sheet assets?
B. Would be the effect of the revaluation from $30 to $60 million be shown in net income, or other comprehensive income, in the year of the change?
C. IFRS requires future depreciation to be based on the revalued amount. How much would depreciation expense be after the building was revalued?

A23. (Recognition of intangible assets) The Doubleday Corp. is very interested in professional sports. It engages in various transactions. For each of the following transactions, indicate if Doubleday will record an intangible asset at the time of the transaction. If it does, will the asset have to be amortized?

A. It pays Major League Baseball $200 million for the franchise to start a new baseball team in Sacramento, California.

B. It spends $20 million on television ads and other media costs to develop awareness of the team in the Sacramento area.

C. It spends $2 million designing logos and uniforms and other means of creating a "brand identity" for the new team.

D. It assembles a great group of coaches and managers. They all receive salaries every two weeks.

E. It assembles a great group of athletes to play baseball. It signs contracts with these players, under which the players are obligated to play for, on average, three years. The team has paid $20 million of bonuses to the players at the start of the contracts. It will also pay them salaries over the life of the contracts.

A24. (Recognition of intangible assets) Assume the Abner Company buys the New York Yankees baseball team for a very large amount of money. Indicate whether, under accounting rules, it should recognize any of the following as intangible assets after the purchase. If you believe the asset should be recognized, indicate if you think it has a definite or indefinite life:

A. The "franchise" that the New York Yankees have to play in the American League of Major League baseball. This franchise has no expiration date.

B. The value of having a coaching staff and management team in place. All of these people are paid on a twice per month basis.

C. Contracts with baseball players. On average, these contracts have three years left as of the date of acquisition.

D. The logos and designs that are trademarks of the New York Yankees.

E. The loyalty of many fans of the New York Yankees.

A25. (Gains trading) Assume that the Polk Corp. has investments in five assets which it bought on January 1, Year 1. Shown below are the amounts the assets cost, and their fair values on December 31, Year 1.

	Cost	Dec. 31 value
Asset 1	100	103
Asset 2	100	120
Asset 3	100	97
Asset 4	100	80
Asset 5	100	30
Totals	500	430

A. Economically, what was the company's gain or loss on holding this group of five assets for the year?

B. If it uses fair value to record the assets, will it recognize this gain or loss?

C. If it uses historical cost, and none of the assets are considered "impaired," will it recognize the gain or loss?

D. If it uses historical cost, and Asset 5 is considered "impaired," will it recognize a gain or loss? Explain.

E. Assume that the company has decided on December 31 that it wants to show as much income as possible. If it uses the historical cost method, and does not recognize any impairment, which assets should it sell in order to report the *largest* possible income?

F. Assume that the company has decided on December 31 that it wants to show as little income as possible during the year. It uses the historical cost method, without recognizing any impairment. For example, it might be trying to minimize its taxes. Which assets should it sell to minimize its reported income?

A26. (Fair value—marketable securities) Assume that the Pierce, Fenner Corp. owns stocks in other companies. Pierce, Fenner is holding these companies for short-term investment purchases, and hopes that the values of these stocks will rise. Here is some information on the market value of its stock holdings:

	Jan. 1, Year 1	Dec. 31, Year 1
Alpha Corp. stock	20,000	25,000
Beta Corp. stock	24,000	29,000
Gamma Corp. stock	10,000	1,000
Delta Corp. stock	17,000	20,000
Totals	71,000	75,000

A. Under GAAP and IFRS, companies are supposed to record their investments in marketable securities at fair value. The change in value of short-term holdings in marketable securities is shown as part of net income. What is the impact of the change in fair value during the year on Pierce, Fenner's:

a. Assets
b. Liabilities
c. Equity
d. Net income.

B. Pierce, Fenner would really like to avoid showing that it lost money on the stock of Gamma. Can it sell the stock on December 31 to avoid showing the loss? Explain your answer.

C. Pierce, Fenner would like to show as much income as possible. Can it maximize its income for the year by selling the Alpha, Beta and Delta stocks, and holding onto the Gamma stock? Explain your answer.

A27. (Historical cost and inflation) Assume the Longstreet and Jackson companies have identical factories and inventories as of the end of Year 5. If they sold their factories and inventories, they would receive precisely the same amounts. The only difference is that they bought the factories and inventories at different times. They both use historical cost accounting, and do not adjust their figures for changes in the purchasing power of the dollar. Both companies ignore inflation in their accounting. Inflation has been moderate, but was 5% in the latest year. You have the following data about the two companies:

	Longstreet	Jackson
Date of buying factory	Jan. 1, Year 0	Jan. 1, Year 5
Cost of factory	50 million	60 million
Current value of factory	63 million	63 million
Estimated useful life of factory	20 years	20 years
Average date of buying inventory	Jan. 1, Year 5	Dec. 25, Year 5
Cost of inventory	10 million	10.5 million

A. What would the depreciation expense be for each company in Year 6? (Assume the companies compute depreciation by dividing the cost by the estimated useful life.)
B. Assume that in the next year, each company sells its inventory. Which company will report the higher cost of goods sold?
C. Which company will look more profitable in Year 6? Explain.
D. Do you think the differences in Year 6 profits are useful in judging the relative performance of the managers of Jackson and Longstreet? Explain.

A28. (Full costing and absorption costing) Assume the James Corp. makes engine parts for cars. Some selected cost information is shown below:

Expected demand for the product	20,000 units
Fixed manufacturing costs	$20,000,000
Variable manufacturing costs	$35 per unit produced

A. Assume the company makes and sells the 20,000 units it expects to make and sell. No items are left in inventory.

    a. What are the total variable costs?
    b. What are the total fixed manufacturing costs?
    c. What were the fixed manufacturing costs per unit produced?
    d. What is the cost of goods sold? (Hint—all the items produced were sold.)
    e. What is the average cost per unit of the items sold?

B. Assume the company produces 40,000 units, but only sells 20,000. It has 20,000 units left in inventory.

    a. What are the total variable costs?
    b. What are the total fixed manufacturing costs?
    c. What were the fixed manufacturing costs per unit produced?
    d. Assuming the company uses the same cost per unit to value its ending inventory as it does to value the units it sold, what is the cost of the 20,000 units sold?
    e. What is the cost of the 20,000 units remaining in inventory?

C. Compare your answers to parts A and B above.

    a. Does the company show higher income when it produces 20,000 units or 40,000?
    b. Explain why the difference in reported income in parts A and B could lead to dysfunctional behavior for companies.

Discussion Questions

D1. (Valuation and Conceptual Framework) The FASB's Conceptual Framework describes certain desirable attributes of accounting data. See Chapter 2. These include: predictive value; representational faithfulness; neutrality; and comparability. They also note that information must be produced at reasonable cost. Using these concepts, discuss whether the FASB's decisions on values seem reasonable:

A. Marketable securities must be recorded at fair value
B. Inventory is recorded at lower of cost or market
C. Factory equipment is measured at depreciated cost
D. Internally developed intangible assets are not recognized
E. Land is recorded at historical cost

D2. (Fair value and historic cost) Look at the different types of measurements used for different assets and liabilities in Table 7.1.

    A.   Do you think there is a relation between the items that are accounted for using fair value and the existence of nearly perfect markets for those items?

    B.   Are there items accounted for at historical cost for which you believe there are nearly perfect markets?

D3. (IFRS and GAAP—lower of cost or market) Both GAAP and IFRS require companies to record inventory at the lower of cost or market. However, they define "market" differently. For GAAP, market is usually the replacement cost, but for IFRS, it is the net realizable value.

    A.   In general, which measure of "market" would you expect to be larger: replacement cost or realizable value? Explain.

    B.   Which measurement do you feel gives more relevant information to users? Explain.

    C.   Which method would normally be easier to verify? Explain.

    D.   Do you favor the GAAP or the IFRS approach? Why?

D4. (GAAP and tax rules) Under GAAP, companies must account for marketable securities at fair value. If the values change during the year, the companies report gains or losses. However, the U.S. income tax rules use historical cost to value investments, and companies do not report gains or losses until they sell the securities. Why would the tax authorities not want to use a fair value approach?

D5. (Inventories and conceptual framework) Under U.S. GAAP, the normal rule is that inventories are recorded at the lower of cost or market. However, there is an exception for certain fungible commodities, with a ready market, like gold or wheat or oil. Such items are recorded at fair value. Does this exception make sense, based on the ideas in the FASB's conceptual framework discussed in Chapter 2? (The conceptual framework listed various desirable characteristics of accounting information, including relevance, predictive value, representational faithfulness, freedom from error, neutrality, and comparability. It also considered the cost of measurement as a constraint.)

D6. (Accounting measurements and stock market valuations) As of the date that I am writing this chapter (January, 2015), the average market value of the stocks in the Standard & Poor's 500 Index is equal to 2.7 times the value of the equity as shown on those companies' balance sheets. Based on the discussion in this chapter of how accountants value assets, suggest two reasons why the market value of these companies is so much higher than the value of their equity on their balance sheets.

D7. (Impairment—IFRS and GAAP) Under both IFRS and GAAP, companies must recognize impairment losses in income if they believe their fixed assets have permanently lost value, and reduce the carrying value of the assets on the balance sheet. Under IFRS, if a company later decides that the asset has regained some value, it can record an adjustment to increase the carrying value of the asset, and to increase reported income. GAAP does not allow a company to recognize any increases in value after an impairment loss has been booked, until the asset is actually sold. Which accounting rule do you think is better? Explain your answer.

D8. (Impairment and conceptual framework) One of the criteria for desirable accounting information, according to the FASB's conceptual framework, is neutrality. However, while the FASB requires companies to recognize losses when it owns fixed assets whose value has decreased, it does not allow the companies to recognize increases in the value of these assets until they are sold. This is not a neutral treatment. What might be reasons that the FASB does not set neutral rules for recognizing both increases and decreases in values?

D9. (Volatility) In the chapter, there was a list of areas where the FASB has taken steps to keep net income from being affected by changes in fair value. These include special rules related to pensions, to long-term investments in securities, and changes in foreign exchange rates. Do you believe that it makes sense for managers to be judged on all the changes in values during the year, or do you agree with the FASB that certain changes should not be considered part of the net income computation? Explain your answer.

D10. (Inventory cost methods—rapid inflation) Assume the Royal Gas Corp. buys gasoline from a refinery, and sells it to local gas companies. It follows a policy of always selling its gasoline for 5 cents per gallon more than it paid, using a first in, first out (FIFO) assumption. Its records show the following with regard to its inventory:

January 1	Beginning inventory—100,000 gallons, at cost of $2.50 per gallon
January	Sales—90,000 gallons, at selling price of $2.55
	Purchases of 90,000 gallons, at average cost of $2.65
February	Sales of 90,000 gallons. 10,000 were sold at $2.55, and 80,000 at $2.70
	Purchases of 90,000 gallons, at average cost of $2.80
March	Sales of 90,000 gallons. 10,000 were sold at a price of $2.70, and 80,000 were sold at a price of $2.85
	Purchase of 90,000 gallons at a cost of $3.00 per gallon.

A. Using FIFO, compute the cost of goods sold, and the cost of the ending inventory of 100,000 gallons.
B. What was the total revenue?
C. What was the profit for the three months, on a FIFO basis? (Hint—it should equal 5 cents per gallon.)
D. If the company computed its cost of goods sold on a LIFO basis, with the assumption that all sales in a month occurred after the purchases in each month, compute the cost of goods sold, and the net profit or loss for the three months.
E. What did the company spend in cash on its total purchases for the period?
F. How much did cash increase or decrease during the period, assuming all revenues were in cash?
G. If you were running the business, do you think you would find the LIFO or the FIFO computations of profits more useful for decision-making? Explain your answer.

D11. (Impact of intangible asset accounting on comparability) Starbucks and Dunkin' Brands are competing companies, but they account for intangible assets differently. Starbucks is a company that has grown over time from its founding. It has made some acquisitions, and recorded some goodwill on the businesses it acquired, but the goodwill associated with the Starbucks name has not been recorded. Dunkin' Brands purchased the businesses of Dunkin' Donuts and of Baskin-Robbins (a chain of ice cream stores) in 2006. Some summarized information from the 2013 balance sheets of the two companies follows (in millions):

	Dunkin'	Starbucks
Goodwill	892	856
Other intangible assets	1,452	274
Total assets	3,235	10,753

A. Compare the intangible assets of the two companies as a fraction of total assets.
B. Explain why Dunkin' likely shows a much higher balance for intangible assets than does Starbucks. Is it because its brand names are economically more valuable than the Starbucks name?

C. How would the difference in the recognition of the intangible assets affect the comparison of the following ratios? (Which company is likely to look better?) For this question, ignore any amortization that might be taken on the intangible assets.

    a. Asset turnover
    b. Return on assets
    c. Debt to assets ratio

D12. (Research and development) In 1974, the FASB issued its statement saying that expenditures on research and development would be considered expenses, not assets. There were many people who were concerned that by not allowing companies to recognize these expenditures as assets, the FASB would discourage companies from doing research. The concern was that this accounting rule would have real, adverse effects on the U.S. economy. Should the FASB consider such arguments when setting accounting rules? Explain.

D13. (Bank leverage example and fair value) This is a simplified example. The actual regulations for banks are more complex.[39] Assume that regulators require banks to have equity equal to 5% or more of their total assets. Assume the Barney Bank has the following summarized balance sheet:

Cash on hand	1
Short-term Treasury debt and very safe assets	39
Investments in collaterized mortgages	<u>60</u>
Total assets	<u>100</u>
Customer bank deposits	40
Overnight borrowings—commercial paper	<u>54</u>
Total liabilities	94
Equity	<u>6</u>
Total liabilities plus equity	<u>100</u>

A. Does the bank meet the regulatory requirement with regard to the minimum amount of equity on hand?

B. Assume that the market value for securitized mortgages suddenly drops by 5%, and the value of the mortgages owned by the bank falls from 60 to 57.

    a. What would be the total assets?
    b. What would be the equity?
    c. Would the bank still meet the regulatory requirement for the minimum ratio of equity to total assets?

D. Some ways that a bank can increase its ratio of equity to assets are listed below. Comment on which you think may be seen as beneficial to the current shareholders, and which are likely not to be welcome to the bank?

    a. Selling off assets and using the money to pay off liabilities
    b. Selling new stock in the bank, at the price that the company can get at this time
    c. Revalue other assets to a higher value, thus increasing reported assets.

D14. (Accounting choices) The FASB and IASB allow companies to make some different choices on how they value assets and liabilities. For example, the chapter discussed different ways of figuring out the cost of inventory. Also, the IASB allows companies to use either the depreciated cost method of accounting for fixed assets or a fair value method. Some scholars have criticized the existence of choices of accounting methods. For example, R. J. Chambers (1965/1969) wrote that:

We all conform with road rules for the better regulation of traffic, and with the rules of language for the better understanding of one another. There is no reason why companies may not be made to conform with uniform rules for the derivation of comparable financial information for the better conduct of the securities markets.

(p. 223)

Do you think companies should be allowed to choose methods? Why, or why not?

Notes

1 Retrieved from http://internetshakespeare.uvic.ca/Library/Texts/Tro/ (last accessed August 18, 2015).
2 See Christensen and Demski (2003).
3 Due to changing FASB standards, changes in accounting principles are not uncommon. A survey of 500 companies' financial statements by the AICPA (2011) found that auditors noted a change in accounting principles 402 times in 2008, 290 times in 2009, and 112 times in 2010. Changes in FASB rules regarding income taxes and employee benefits explain the high number of changes in 2008 and 2009.
4 For simplicity, this section focuses on assets, but the same ideas apply to liabilities.
5 At two key historical periods when historical cost gained in popularity, prices were generally falling. This meant that businesses looked better under historical cost than under fair value accounting. One of these periods was the late 1800s. A price index quoted by Parker for the U.K. fell from 127 in 1873 to 91 in 1900. See Parker (1965). A second key period was the 1930s, when the SEC began operations. According to U.S. Bureau of Labor Statistics tables, the Consumer Price Index in the U.S. fell by about 19% from 1929 to 1940 before starting to rise again. See "Table 24. Historical Consumer Price Index for All Urban Consumers (CPI-U): U.S. city average, all items." Bureau of Labor Statistics, CPI Detailed Report Data for June 2015, Table 24, p. 70. Retrieved from www.bls.gov/cpi/cpid1506.pdf (last accessed August 18, 2015).
6 The term "expected value" is used here in its technical sense. If there are two possible outcomes, with different cash flows in each:

Expected value = (probability of the first outcome × its payoff)
+ (probability of the second outcome × its payoff).

7 Another disadvantage relates to adding the amortized costs of various assets together. This is similar to the problem of adding together the historical costs of assets bought at different times.
8 If the bonds were bought at a premium or discount to their eventual maturity value, this premium or discount is amortized over the life of the bond. The bond would then be said to be recorded at its "amortized cost."
9 According to Parker (1965), the practice became considered standard by the middle of the 19th century in Britain and the U.S. It was likely due to a long period of falling prices, and was in line with a conservative tendency in accounting at that time.
10 Frederick Gamble (1979) found an example of lower of cost or market for inventory being used as early as 1304.
11 Note that the weighted average is *not* found by simply averaging $2.50, $2.75, and $3.00. That would be an unweighted average of the costs per item. Instead, the weighted average computation looks at the total amount spent and the total number of units bought. The result is to put higher weight on the third purchase, of 20,000 gallons.
12 In 1938, when LIFO was first allowed for tax purposes in the U.S., prices were assumed to be cyclical, not steadily rising. Therefore, LIFO was not expected to give any permanent tax advantages. See Davis (1982).
13 The GAAP rules are more complicated, and sometimes require companies to use either net realizable value or net realizable value minus a normal profit margin. The exact rules are beyond the scope of an introductory course. Readers interested in the precise rules can check the FASB Codification Section 330-10-35 or an intermediate accounting text.
14 See FASB Codification, Section 330-10-35-15 and 16.
15 If bonds were initially sold at a price very different from their maturity value, there would have been a premium or discount recorded at the time of sale. This premium or discount would be amortized over the life of the bonds. The amortization affects interest expense.
16 See a reference in Chambers (1948/1969).

17 For other examples, see Barth (2013).

18 Companies were especially willing to switch to historical cost during the 1930s because there was deflation in the U.S. If they had stayed on a fair value method, they would have had to recognize losses on holding assets.

19 Ratcliffe and Munter (1980) looked at various historical pronouncements by accounting bodies. The American Accounting Association stated in 1936 and 1941 that historical cost was the only proper valuation, but by 1948 it was already accepting the idea of current value disclosures where they were materially different. By 1964 it was calling for current cost holding gains and losses to be reported in the primary financial statements. Accounting Research Study 1 of the AICPA called for current cost accounting, but this was too radical, and in 1962 the APB did not accept it. By 1979, in FAS 33, the FASB adopted supplemental reporting of current cost and constant dollar information. Ratcliffe and Munter also look at the works of various key authors. Hatfield in 1909 said current cost might be better than historical cost at times. Canning in 1929 looked to future cash flows. Hicks's 1946 concept of income implied not using historical costs.

20 Note that this assumes that markets themselves are neutral institutions. Tony Tinker (1985) argues that by accepting market prices, accountants implicitly commit to particular distributions of income and social resources.

21 See for example Benston (2008).

22 Unless otherwise noted, all references to FASB standards for fair value are to section 820 of the FASB Codification. See https://asc.fasb.org/ (last accessed August 18, 2015).

23 When assets are recorded at a discounted value, their recorded value will also change systematically over time as they are discounted for fewer future periods.

24 FASB Codification Section 715-30-35-20 allows companies to immediately recognize gains and losses as an option.

25 In the unusual case where the acquirer paid less than the total of the identifiable prices of the individual assets, goodwill can be negative. SFAS No. 141 requires companies to first allocate this negative goodwill to reduce the fair value assigned to various noncurrent assets acquired. If there is still any negative goodwill left, it is shown as an extraordinary gain in the income statement of the acquirer.

26 This is the same period as for tax purposes. See the Internal Revenue Code, Section 197.

27 *The Wall Street Journal*. Retrieved from www.wsj.com/articles/SB1043702683178461304 (last accessed August 18, 2015).

28 Under this method, the depreciation over the life of an asset would often be larger than its original cost. This may be one reason why the U.S. tax code does not allow upward revaluation of assets. Companies would have depreciation deductions over the life of the assets that are larger than the amounts they paid to buy the assets.

29 http://www.bls.gov/cpi/cpid1411.pdf (last accessed August 18, 2015).

30 Maurice Moonitz (1971) suggested that one reason accounting practice did not feel a need to build in inflation rules is that, between LIFO and accelerated depreciation, it had already taken steps to reduce the impact of inflation on reported profits. The Internal Revenue Code of 1954 allowed accelerated depreciation. I would also add that some modern trends in U.S. business reduce the impact of inflation. The manufacturing sector of the U.S. economy would be the sector most affected by the distortion in depreciation, and that sector has become relatively smaller over recent decades, while the service and financial sectors have grown. Also, companies have made greater efforts to reduce the amounts of the inventory they keep on hand. Faster turnover of inventory means that companies are likely recognizing cost of goods sold at very recent prices. Finally, to the extent that inflation results in overstating profits, it may be that managers do not mind this distortion, and therefore are not complaining to the FASB.

31 See De Jager (2014).

32 See for example Bhat, Frankel and Martin (2011).

33 See De Jager (2014). He cites a study by the SEC indicating that "this was especially true for investment banks where almost all derivatives and trading assets were at level 2 and not level 1" (p. 98).

34 See Libby, Bloomfield and Nelson (2002). Their summary of the related research led them to say:

"These studies focused on whether investors and others adjusted appropriately for the effects of accounting methods and disclosure alternatives. . . . Looking back on the earlier literature, it is readily apparent that the answer to this question is 'sometimes.' Some participants in nearly every study of this type demonstrate some degree of functional fixation; they do not fully adjust for differences in the effects of accounting alternatives on the bottom line. . . . As a consequence, firms that are in identical economic circumstances except for their choice of accounting alternatives are sometimes judged to be different."

(p. 783)

35 See Penman (2009).
36 See for example Leisenring et al. (2012). See also Barth (2013).
37 Wyatt's (2008) literature review concluded that "The evidence from a package of value-relevance and triangulation studies suggests research and development (R&D) is generally not reliably measured and may be less relevant in some contexts than others as well (e.g. established versus growth firms). Further purchased goodwill and some non-financial measures of brands and customer loyalty do not appear to be reliably measured" (p. 217).
38 See Barth (2013).
39 Interested readers should look at summaries of the "Basel III" international agreement, and rules of the U.S. Federal Reserve for U.S. banks. The rule in this problem is similar to one of the U.S. requirements in January 2015.

References

American Accounting Association. (1971). Report of the Committee on Foundations of Accounting Measurement [Supplement]. *The Accounting Review, 46*(4) 1–48.
AICPA. (2011). *Accounting Trends and Techniques*. New York: AICPA.
AICPA. (2013). *Financial Reporting Framework for Small- and Medium-Sized Entities*. New York: AICPA.
Arnold, P. J. (2009). Global financial crisis: the challenge to accounting research. *Accounting, Organizations and Society, 34*(6), 803–9.
Barth, M. E. (2006). Including estimates of the future in today's financial statements. *Accounting Horizons, 20*(3), 271–85.
Barth, M. E. (2007). Standard-setting measurement issues and the relevance of research [Supplement]. *Accounting and Business Research, 37*, 7–15.
Barth, M. E. (2013). Measurement in financial reporting: The need for concepts. *Accounting Horizons, 28*(2), 331–52.
Beaver, W. H. & Demski, J. S. (1979). The nature of income measurement. *The Accounting Review, 54*(1), 38–46.
Benston, G. J. (2008). The shortcomings of fair-value accounting described in SFAS 157. *Journal of Accounting and Public Policy, 27*(2), 101–14.
Bhat, G., Frankel, R., & Martin, X. (2011). Panacea, Pandora's box, or placebo: Feedback in bank mortgage-backed security holdings and fair value accounting. *Journal of Accounting and Economics, 52*(2), 153–73.
Chambers, R. J. (1948/1969). Accounting and Management. Reprinted in R. J. Chambers (1969), *Accounting Finance and Management*. Sydney, Australia: Hogbin, Poole (Printers) Pty. Ltd. (Original work published 1948).
Chambers, R. J. (1965/1969). Are the Stock Exchanges in Australia Meeting their Challenges. Reprinted in R. J. Chambers (1969), *Accounting Finance and Management*. Sydney, Australia: Hogbin, Poole (Printers) Pty. Ltd. (Original work published 1965).
Christensen, J. A. & Demski, J. S. (2003). *Accounting Theory: An Information Content Perspective*. Boston: McGraw Hill.
Davis, H. Z. (1982). History of LIFO. *The Accounting Historians Journal, 9*(1), 1–23.
De Jager, P. (2014). Fair value accounting, fragile bank balance sheets and crisis: A model. *Accounting, Organizations and Society, 39*(2), 97–116.
Eichenwald, K. (2005). *Conspiracy of Fools*. New York: Broadway Books.
FASB. (1984). Statement of Financial Accounting Concepts No. 5, *Recognition and Measurement in Financial Statements of Business Enterprises*. Stamford, CT: FASB.
Flamholtz, D. (1979). The structure of scientific revolutions and its implications for the development of accounting policy. Working Paper No. 27. In E. N. Coffman (Ed.), *The Academy of Accounting Historians Working Paper Series, Vol. 2 (Working Papers 21–40)*. Richmond, VA: Virginia Commonwealth University.
Gamble, F. E. (1979) [name of paper and paper number needed] In E. N. Coffman (Ed.), *The Academy of Accounting Historians Working Paper Series, Vol. 2 (Working Papers 21–40)*. Richmond, VA: Virginia Commonwealth University.
IASB. (2009). *IFRS for Small and Medium-sized Entities*. London: International Accounting Standards Board.
Ijiri, Y. (1967). *The Foundations of Accounting Measurement: A Mathematical, Economic, and Behavioral Inquiry*. Englewood Cliffs, NJ: Prentice-Hall, Inc.

Konchitchki, Y. (2011). Inflation and nominal financial reporting: Implications for performance and stock prices. *The Accounting Review, 86*(3), 1045–85.

Krippner, G. R. (2005). The financialization of the American economy. *Socio-Economic Review, 3*(2), 173–208.

Laux, C., & Leuz, C. (2009). The crisis of fair-value accounting: Making sense of the recent debate. *Accounting, Organizations and Society, 34*(6), 826–34.

Levitt, A. (1998). The numbers game. *The CPA Journal, 68*(12), 14–19.

Libby, R., Bloomfield, R., & Nelson, M. W. (2002). Experimental research in financial accounting. *Accounting, Organizations and Society, 27*(8), 775–810.

Leisenring, J., Linsmeier, T., Schipper, K., & Trott, E. (2012). Business-model (intent)-based accounting. *Accounting and Business Research, 42*(3), 329–44.

Linsmeier, T. J. (2011). Financial reporting and financial crises: The case for measuring financial instruments at fair value in the financial statements. *Accounting Horizons, 25*(2), 409–17.

Littleton, A. C. (1929). Value and price in accounting. *Accounting Review* (September), 147–54.

Mattessich, R. (1998). Review and extension of Bhattacharyya's modern accounting concepts in Kautilya's Arthśāsastra. *Accounting, Business, and Financial History, 8*(2) 191–209.

McSweeney, B. (2009). The roles of financial asset market failure denial and the economic crisis: Reflections on accounting and financial theories and practices. *Accounting, Organizations and Society, 34*(6), 835–48.

Moonitz, M. (1971). Inflation and the Lag in Accounting Practice: Critique. In R. R. Sterling & W. F. Bentz (Eds.), *Accounting in Perspective: Contributions to Accounting Thought by Other Disciplines.* Papers and Discussions from an Accounting Colloquium by the University of Kansas School of Business and the Arthur Young Foundation. Houston, Texas: Scholars Book Co.

Parker, R. H. (1965). Lower of cost and market in Britain and the United States: An historical survey. *Abacus, 1*(2), 156–72.

Penman, S. H. (2009). Accounting for intangible assets: There is also an income statement. *Abacus, 45*(3), 358–71.

Ratcliffe, T. A. & Munter, P. (1980). Asset valuation: An historical perspective. *The Accounting Historians Journal* (Spring), 73–8.

Tinker, T. (1985). *Paper Prophets: A Social Critique of Accounting.* NY: Praeger Publishers.

Vangermeersch, R. (1979). 36 classic articles from the 1905–1930 issues of the Journal of Accountancy. Working Paper No. 00. In E. N. Coffman (Ed.), *The Academy of Accounting Historians Working Paper Series Vol. 1 (Working Papers 1–20).* Richmond, VA: Virginia Commonwealth University.

Wyatt, A. (2008). What financial and non-financial information on intangibles is value-relevant? A review of the evidence. *Accounting and Business Research, 38*(3), 217–56.

Zeff, S. A. (2005a). The Evolution of U. S. GAAP: The Political Forces Behind Professional Standards— Part 1: 1930–1973. *The CPA Journal, LXXV* (1 January), 18–27.

Zeff, S. A. (2005b). The Evolution of U.S. GAAP: The Political Forces Behind Professional Standards— Part 2: 1973–2004. *The CPA Journal, LXXV* (2 February), 18–29.

8   Uncertainty

Outline

- Preliminary Thoughts
- Learning Objectives
- Pervasiveness of Uncertainty
- General Financial Accounting Responses to Uncertainty
- Estimation and Uncertainty in Specific Accounts
- Updating Accounts for New Information
- Discipline of the Accounting Process
- General Managerial Accounting Responses to Uncertainty
- Unresolved Issues and Areas for Further Research

Preliminary Thoughts

Assets are probable future economic benefits obtained or controlled by a particular entity as a result of past transactions or events. Liabilities are probable future sacrifices of economic benefits arising from present obligations of a particular entity to transfer assets or provide services to other entities in the future as a result of past transactions or events.

FASB (1985, p. Con6-1)

It is difficult to make predictions, especially about the future.

Various[1]

Under current accounting standards, almost all amounts recognized in financial statements today reflect some estimates of the future. This is not surprising because, by definition, assets and liabilities embody expected future inflows and outflows of economic benefits. . . . A review of recent activities at the International Accounting Standards Board (IASB) reveals that the use of estimates is likely to increase.

Mary Barth (2006, pp. 271–272)

In response to uncertainty, there has been a general tendency to emphasize purchase and sale transactions and to apply conservative procedures in accounting recognition.

FASB (1984, para. 50)

An undervaluation may be very conservative and praiseworthy from the standpoint of a creditor or of a management eager to add some cheap stock to its holdings, but the same undervaluation may seem outrageous and far from conservative to a stockholder desiring a just price for his stock.

Kenneth MacNeal (1939, pp. 51–52)

These five quotations set the framework for the topic of this chapter, which is how accounting deals with uncertainty about the future.

The first three quotations indicate that uncertainty is an important issue in financial accounting. The first quotation gives the FASB's definitions of assets and liabilities. Both definitions use the words "probable" and "future." This means that accounting is trying to predict what assets will be worth in the future, and how large a burden the company's liabilities will be when they are paid in the future. Because the ideas of probable future values and sacrifices are built into the definitions of assets and liabilities, the need to consider future events is pervasive in accounting. The second quotation reminds us that the future is uncertain and hard to predict. The third quotation tells us that the likely trend of standard setting will be to require more estimates of the future, not fewer. This trend is consistent with the trend noted in the last chapter, of the FASB and IASB moving toward measuring assets and liabilities at "fair value" and away from using historical cost measurements. "Fair values" are estimates of what an item can be sold for, or what its value will be in continued use.

The last two quotations relate to whether accounting should try to estimate the future in a neutral manner or in a more conservative one. Conservative accounting would tend to be slow to recognize gains, and would place higher standards on recognizing assets than liabilities. In 1984, the FASB's Concepts Statements noted that there had been a historical tendency to be conservative in accounting, and to wait until the time of sale to recognize revenues. However, the final quotation points out that conservative accounting is not neutral. A bank may be happy that a borrower states its assets and liabilities very conservatively, because that means that the company is more likely to have enough real economic resources available to repay its loans. However, someone who sold stock in the company for a low price, believing the company to be marginally profitable, is likely to be very upset when hearing that the company really was profitable, and that the stock changed hands at too low a price.

Learning Objectives

After studying this chapter you should:

1   Understand that uncertainty about the future affects many areas of financial and managerial accounting
2   Understand the arguments for and against conservative accounting practices
3   Understand how the accounting for various accounts is affected by uncertainty
4   Understand how changes in information about previous estimates are reflected in the financial statements
5   Understand that the accounting process will eventually force companies to fix previously incorrect estimates
6   Understand various ways that uncertainty affects managerial accounting practices.

Pervasiveness of Uncertainty

Investors and management want information about a company's assets, liabilities, revenues, and expenses on a timely basis. However, the company does not *know* exactly how its assets and liabilities should be valued until the assets are eventually sold and the liabilities are eventually paid off. Companies bought things, intending to use them to produce cash. The companies will not know for sure how much cash can be produced until some future date. Similarly, companies made commitments and accepted obligations that the companies will have to pay off in the future. The exact amounts they will need to pay may not be completely fixed until some future dates.

Except for cash, the value of almost every asset and liability depends on future events. Here are some examples. Table 8.1 has additional examples.

- Accounts receivable might not get collected.
- The values of marketable securities might change before they are sold.
- Inventory may become obsolete, or its value may change before it can be sold.
- Fixed assets may last longer, or for a shorter time, than was originally expected.
- Intangible assets, like patents for new products, may become immensely valuable, or they may totally lose value if the public does not like the new product.
- The company may have leased office space for a fixed amount of rent, for several years. The lease might have a penalty clause that says the company will have to pay extra amounts if it tries to move before the lease is over.
- The company may promise pensions after the employees retire. The value of this promise depends on how long the employees live, what they earn, and how long they work for the company.

Table 8.1 Accounts and Uncertainty

Account	*Uncertainty*
Accounts Receivable	Collectibility—Will customers pay?
Inventory	Salability—Can items be sold? What price will customers pay?
Land	Value—What will the land be worth, either by sale or through use?
Other fixed assets	Value—What will the assets be worth, either through sale or in use? Proper yearly depreciation – How long will the assets last, and what will they be worth when they are disposed of?
Investments	Value—What will the assets be worth upon sale?
Natural resources (oil wells, coal mines, etc.)	Existence—How much of the resource exists? For example, how much oil is actually underground in an oil field? Value—What will the assets be worth, either through sale or in use? Proper yearly depletion—How long will the assets last, and what will they be worth when they are disposed of?
Intangible assets	Value—What will the assets be worth, either through sale or in use? Proper yearly amortization—How long will the assets last, and what will they be worth when they are disposed of?
Contingent gains and losses	Probability of occurrence. Value if they do occur.
Employee vacation and sick pay	Probability and amount of obligation—How much of the amounts that employees have earned will actually be used in future periods?
Employee pensions and post-retirement benefits	Amount of obligation—How many employees will earn these benefits, and what will the company eventually have to pay for them?
Employee severance obligations	Probability and amount of obligation—Will the company actually fire employees? If so, what will be the amount of severance?
Asset retirement obligations	Amount of obligation—For example, coal mining companies have obligations to clean up the areas around their mines after they stop producing. The amount is hard to estimate.
Insurance obligations	Probability and amount of obligation—Insurance companies are uncertain as to the amounts and size of claims that they will have to honor for a time period until well after the end of the period.
Tax liability	Amount of obligation—If the company has taken some uncertain tax positions, what amount of taxes will eventually be due?
Warranty liabilities	Probability and amount of obligation—How many warranty claims will customers make, and what will it cost to honor the warranty?
Bonds and notes payable	Amount needed to satisfy obligation—Will the company pay the bonds off for a different amount than their stated face value?

Uncertainty affects the recognition and measurement of assets, liabilities, equity and income. Investors' demand for timely information means that accountants cannot wait for future events to occur, and must estimate values at the end of each reporting period. The estimates cannot be perfect, since the future is unknown.

The problem of estimating the values of particular assets and liabilities can be very tricky, because it can depend both on current market conditions and on company intentions. As an example, the SEC requires oil companies to disclose how much oil and gas "reserves" they have. The reserves are oil and gas that is believed to be underground and not yet pumped up. Some in the oil industry claim the SEC's methodology is overly pessimistic. Their reserve figures depend not just on the geology of how much is in the ground, but on whether it would be economically reasonable to pump them at a particular price. Also, the speed with which oil is pumped can affect the total amount that can be recovered from a particular oil well. So price assumptions, management plans, and geological studies all affect the reserve estimates.[2]

Two major questions arise:

- Should the estimates be neutral, or oriented towards some other objective?
- How should accountants deal with the inevitable fact that the future will be different from the estimates made now?

There are three main approaches that companies could take to estimating financial values. They could try to report neutral estimates, which have an equal probability of being too high and too low. They could try to be "conservative," and report estimates that are more likely than not to understate assets, overstate liabilities, or understate income. They could follow "aggressive" accounting, and report estimates that are more likely than not to overstate assets, understate liabilities, or overstate income. Clearly, the fact that estimates contain some subjective factors opens a door to earnings management or biased accounting by managers. Managers may also engage in "expectations management" by providing analysts with low forecasts of what the company expects its future earnings to be. (See Chapter 6.)

The uncertainty of future conditions also affects managerial accounting. Various managerial accounting techniques are designed to help companies cope with uncertain future conditions as the companies plan and run their businesses. Examples include the use of flexible budgets and complex methods of capital budgeting. Human reactions to uncertain future conditions also need to be considered. For example, managers may react to uncertainty by building extra "slack" into their budget proposals.

General Financial Accounting Responses to Uncertainty

Introduction

This section discusses several aspects of how financial accounting reacts to uncertainty. First, accrual accounting uses estimates of the values at which assets and liabilities will be realized in the future, assuming companies will continue in business. This is believed to result in more useful data than would be provided if accounting focused only on events that have already occurred and been settled in cash. Second, where estimates are highly uncertain, the normal accounting response is to "not recognize" the assets or liabilities. Third, accounting tends to assume that markets do a good job of estimating values. Fourth, accounting has struggled with whether it is appropriate to make estimates in a neutral manner, or whether estimates should be conservative. Finally, accounting uses additional disclosures to alert readers of important uncertainties.

Accrual Accounting Uses Estimated Values, Assuming Companies are Going Concerns

Under cash accounting systems, a company would only recognize revenues and expenses when cash moves. All cash-basis financial statements are based on past transactions. In contrast, accrual accounting requires companies to record events that have not yet been settled in cash, and thus that contain an expectation that cash will move in the future. As noted in Chapter 2, the "going concern assumption" in accounting means that we assume that the business will continue to operate normally in the future. For example, when a company sells to a customer on credit, the accounts receivable represents an expectation that the customer will send money in the future. When a company buys a factory, the going concern assumption means that the factory should be accounted for as if it will be used in the company's future operations, and not immediately sold in a bankruptcy proceeding. The reporting standards used in all countries use a mixture of reporting on past events and judgments about future values and events. See Biondi et al. (2012).

Academic research indicates that accrual accounting, even with estimates, provides decision-useful information. A committee of the American Accounting Association stated that: "There is no known way of improving financial reporting either by abandoning actual transactions (the past) or removing all subjective judgments about the future" (Biondi et al. 2012, p. 128). A review of studies that have looked at the relative effect of different financial statements on stock market prices of stocks (Nichols and Wahlen 2004) indicates they have generally found that the income statement, which includes estimates, has more impact than does the cash flow statement, which only contains information about past transactions. They also find that each of these statements provides some information to the markets that the other does not.

Nonrecognition Until Measurable With Sufficient Reliability

Chapter 2 discussed the general rules the FASB has set about when something should be recognized and recorded in a company's accounts. The FASB (1984) has stated that, in concept, an item should be recognized if, and only if, the following four criteria are met:

- The item meets the definition of an element of financial statements.
- It can be measured with sufficient reliability.
- The information is relevant; that is, capable of making a difference in user decisions.
- The information is reliable. It is representationally faithful, verifiable, and neutral.

These criteria help explain why some things are not usually recognized. As an example, assume a company is in discussions with a potential customer, about a deal that might be very profitable. Should it recognize profits now on this potential deal? The accounting answer would be: "No way." The deal has not yet been made, and it is not yet probable that it will be made. To be an asset there must be a "probable future benefit." The price is still to be decided, so the value of this potential contact cannot be measured with sufficient reliability. While the information may be relevant and interesting to potential investors, the profits from any potential deal are not verifiable, and may not be neutral due to natural optimism by managers. The accounting rules would require that nothing be recognized at this stage of the discussions.

Assumption That Market Measures are Appropriate

The accounting rules assume that markets do a fairly good job of pricing assets and liabilities. As we saw in the previous chapter, the FASB and IASB rely on market prices to set "fair value" of a variety of assets and liabilities. The "fair value hierarchy" in the previous chapter gave greatest weight to data that was from active markets for the particular assets being valued, and lesser weight to data that was less clearly linked to market prices.

This assumption that market prices are reliable also helps explain the difference in how internally created intangible assets are treated from how intangible assets are treated when a company purchases them from others. Let's assume Procter & Gamble spent money on advertising, and believes that it has established "brand awareness" with customers that will be very valuable in the future. Should it recognize a brand awareness asset? At the current time, the answer to this is "No." Companies may have a hard time demonstrating that the value of the brand awareness in the future is "probable," which would be necessary to meet the definition of an asset. Also, the techniques for measuring the value of brand awareness lack "sufficient reliability" and the underlying assumptions may not be verifiable. On the other hand, if it bought the rights to a brand from Colgate, it would record the brand as an intangible asset. The fact that two independent companies negotiated a price is considered to be a means for measuring the brand's value with sufficient reliability. The price paid is verifiable.

Conservatism

Historical Trends

In accounting, conservatism is a practice of dealing with uncertainty by choosing alternatives that show a less favorable balance sheet and income statement in the current period. Thus, a conservative balance sheet would tend to undervalue assets and to overvalue liabilities. A conservative income statement would understate revenues and overstate expenses. The result of conservatively slanted measurements is that, in the future, it is more likely that events will be better than the estimates, resulting in gains, than worse than the estimates, resulting in losses. Conservative estimating would fit with a generally risk-averse way of dealing with the world, which gives greater weight to losses than to gains. There is some evidence that risk-averseness has a biological basis.[3]

Accounting historians believe that conservatism in accounting was seen as very desirable in the 1800s and early in the 1900s, when the major users of financial statements were bankers and the owners of the business. The bankers used company balance sheets to decide whether the company had enough collateral to be worthy of getting a loan. Thus, the bankers wanted to make sure that a company claiming to have a certain amount of receivables, inventory, and fixed assets had *at least as much* as they were claiming. The bankers would be delighted to find out that the company really had more valuable assets than it claimed, because that meant the banker's loan was even safer. The bankers did *not* want to find out that the company's assets were understated, or that it had unreported liabilities, because that would mean the bank was less likely to get repaid. The owners were not misled by overly conservative balance sheets because they knew their own businesses well. See MacNeal (1939).

Several other factors led to conservative accounting over the first part of the 20th century. One was the adoption of income taxes. Conservative accounting resulted in lower reported taxable income, which in turn resulted in lower taxes. A 1919 article suggested that taxation enacted during World War I had a major impact on conservatism in accounting practice.[4] The regulators of railroads and electric utilities generally allowed these companies to set prices for their services that were enough to give the shareholders a reasonable rate of return. More conservative estimates of profits allowed the companies to justify higher prices.[5] A third factor was the reaction to the 1929 stock market crash, including the formation of the SEC. There was a belief that companies had overstated earnings in the 1920s, leading to excessive stock prices, and an eventual stock market collapse. Therefore, the SEC favored conservative accounting. There may also have been political reasons companies favored reporting more modest profits. For example, the early part of the 20th century saw government efforts to break up companies that were making monopoly profits, and also saw efforts by labor unions to force companies to pay out more money in wages and to keep less for shareholders.

From the 1930s until fairly recent times, conservatism was an important part of accounting standards. However, the FASB (1980) believes a shift in the users of financial statements has occurred, and statements should now follow a more neutral approach.

> Conservatism in financial reporting should no longer connote deliberate, consistent under-statement of net assets and profits. . . . The convention of conservatism, which was once commonly expressed in the admonition to "anticipate no profits but anticipate all losses," developed during a time when balance sheets were considered the primary (and often only) financial statement, and details of profits or other operating results were rarely provided outside business enterprises. To the bankers or other lenders who were the principal external users . . . understatement for its own sake became widely considered to be desirable, since the greater the understatement of assets the greater the margin of safety the assets provided as a security for loans or other debts. Once the practice of providing information about peri-odic income as well as balance sheets became common, however, it also became evident that understated assets frequently led to overstated income in later periods.
>
> (para. 93)

The last sentence in that quotation is important. Conservatism in one period of time will lead to overstating income in later periods of time. This chapter contains several examples that illustrate this point.

The FASB's conceptual framework says that *neutral* information is desirable. It does not, con-ceptually, favor either a conservative or an aggressive bias. In 1980, in its second Statement of Financial Accounting Concepts, the FASB stated "conservatism tends to conflict with significant qualitative characteristics, such as representational faithfulness, neutrality, and comparability" (1980, para. 92). In 2010, the FASB issued a restatement of Statement of Financial Accounting Concepts No. 2, and spoke even more firmly in favor of neutral measurement. See FASB (2010).

Example of the Problem of Excessive Conservatism

The Jackson Company sells cell phones on a retail basis. It buys cell phones from manufacturers (such as Apple and Samsung) for its stores. During 2015, it sold $10 million worth of phones and had related expenses of $8 million. Its management is thinking about how to state the remaining inventory of phones. These cost the company $500,000.

One manager says that since phone models change rapidly, it would be sensible to treat this inventory conservatively, and show its value at only $100,000. The impact of this decision would be to reduce income for 2015 by $400,000 (the cost of $500,000 less the expected value of $100,000), and to show a smaller inventory as of December 31, 2015. If the company actually sells these phones in 2016 for the $100,000 this manager expects, the 2016 financial statements will show a net profit of zero on these phones.

What if that manager is wrong, and after the company adjusts the inventory value to $100,000, the phones are actually sold for $600,000, as the company originally expected? Then the company's balance sheet at December 31, 2015 was understated, and the 2015 income statement has an unneeded expense of $400,000.

A banker who had loaned money based on the reported inventory value of $100,000 would not mind that the inventory was actually worth $600,000. However, a shareholder who sold her stock because of the company's low income in 2015 would be upset to find out that she sold her stock for too low a price.

Basically, any time an asset is understated *now* then future income can be expected to be *higher* than it would have been if the asset were stated correctly. The same is true for an over-stated liability—future income should be higher, when the company realizes that it had used an overly conservative figure. This means that financial statements that are conservative today will overstate future income. The future income will include both the income that really is earned in the future, and some income that was earned today, but not recognized yet. Most investors today use the income statement to help value the company. They do not want income shifted improperly between years. This is why the FASB favors neutrality in measurement.[6]

Disclosures

Companies make a variety of disclosures that help alert users to the existence of uncertainty in the financial statements. The FASB, in Section 275 of its Codification of Accounting Standards, requires companies to make disclosures about four types of risks and uncertainties. These are:

- *Risks inherent in the nature of the operations of the company*. The company has to alert the readers to the nature of its products or services, and its principal markets.
- *Use of estimates in the preparation of financial statements*. The company must alert users that GAAP financial statements include many estimates. Box 8.1 shows the related disclosure that Google made in its 2013 financial statements. Clearly, there are many accounts affected by estimates.
- *Certain significant estimates*. The FASB requires additional disclosure about any estimate when it is at least "reasonably possible" that the estimate will change in the near future, and the effect of the change in estimate would be material.
- Current vulnerability to what the FASB refers to as "*certain concentrations*" of the business. For example, if half of a company's business is dependent on one customer, the company is vulnerable to a decision by that customer to stop buying, or to that customer's bankruptcy. The FASB says companies should alert readers to concentrations such as: particular customers; particular products; particular suppliers; or particular regions. Box 8.1 contains Google's disclosure from 2013.

Section 450 of the FASB Codification also requires companies to disclose their best estimate of the loss, or the likely range of loss, for any contingencies that are "reasonably possible." Contingencies are discussed in more detail below.

In addition, auditors sometimes comment in their report on the presence of major uncertainties. A survey of 500 companies' reports in 2011 (AICPA 2011) showed 19 comments (3.8%) regarding significant uncertainties.

Estimation and Uncertainty in Specific Accounts

General

This section discusses the accounting rules related to uncertainty and estimation in particular accounts. You will see that the rules vary. This is partly due to whether the rules were set in a time when the FASB was more inclined to set conservative accounting rules than it is today. Another reason for the differences is that different levels of reliable market evidence exist for different accounts. Third, regulators are concerned about the possibility of earnings management. Finally, some ways of measuring assets require more estimation than others. For example, a historical cost measure of land does not require estimates, while an estimate of the "value in use" of the

---

Box 8.1 Excerpts of Footnote Disclosures from Google Inc.'s 2013 Form 10-K

Use of Estimates

The preparation of consolidated financial statements in conformity with U.S. Generally Accepted Accounting Principles (GAAP) requires us to make estimates and assumptions that affect the amounts reported and disclosed in the financial statements and the accompanying notes. Actual results could differ materially from these estimates. On an ongoing basis, we evaluate our estimates, including those related to the accounts receivable and sales allowances, fair values of financial instruments, intangible assets and goodwill, useful lives of intangible assets and property and equipment, fair values of stock-based awards, inventory valuations, income taxes, and contingent liabilities, among others. We base our estimates on historical experience and on various other assumptions that are believed to be reasonable, the results of which form the basis for making judgments about the carrying values of assets and liabilities.

Certain Risks and Concentrations

Our revenues are primarily derived from online advertising, the market for which is highly competitive and rapidly changing. In addition, our revenues are generated from a multitude of vertical market segments in countries around the world. Significant changes in this industry or changes in customer buying or advertiser spending behavior could adversely affect our operating results. In addition, for our Motorola Mobile segment, the vast majority of our Motorola products (other than some prototypes) are manufactured outside the U.S., primarily in China and Brazil.

Financial instruments that potentially subject us to concentrations of credit risk consist principally of cash equivalents, marketable securities, foreign exchange contracts, and accounts receivable. Cash equivalents and marketable securities consist primarily of time deposits, money market and other funds, including cash collateral received related to our securities lending program, highly liquid debt instruments of the U.S. government and its agencies, debt instruments issued by foreign governments and municipalities in the U.S., corporate securities, mortgage-backed securities, and asset-backed securities. Foreign exchange contracts are transacted with various financial institutions with high credit standing. Accounts receivable are typically unsecured and are derived from revenues earned from customers located around the world. In 2011, 2012, and 2013, we generated approximately 46%, 47%, and 45% of our revenues from customers based in the U.S., with the majority of customers outside of the U.S. located in Europe and Japan. Many of our Google Network Members are in the internet industry. We perform ongoing evaluations to determine customer credit and we limit the amount of credit we extend, but generally we do not require collateral from our customers. We maintain reserves for estimated credit losses and these losses have generally been within our expectations.

Form 10-K filings can be reviewed on the SEC website: www.sec.gov/edgar/searchedgar/companysearch.html (last accessed August 14, 2015).

---

land requires estimating future cash flows and selecting an appropriate discount rate. Therefore, the level of estimation needed is related to the way that the FASB required the asset to be valued.[7] See Chapter 7 for the different methods of valuation required by the FASB for particular accounts.

Accounts Receivable and Bad Debts

Any company that allows its customers to buy today and pay later is taking a risk that the customer will not pay. Clearly, the company generally expects customers to pay—giving credit to people you are sure will not pay you would be foolish. "*Bad debt expense*" is the loss caused by customers failing to pay. The accounting problem is that at the end of the accounting period, the company has a list of accounts receivable, adding up to some total, and the company is uncertain what will be collected in the future.

For companies that have fairly few and immaterial bad debts, it may make sense to just wait and see what gets paid. If it becomes clear that a customer will not pay an amount due, such as a $312 invoice, the company will "write off" this receivable. The accounting would be to recognize bad debt expense of $312, and to reduce the accounts receivable from this customer by $312. This is called the "*direct write-off*" method. It has the advantage of simplicity.

The FASB does not allow companies that have material amounts of bad debt experience to use the direct write-off method. Instead, they must use the "*allowance method*." The goal is to show the accounts receivable at an appropriate value at the end of the period, and also to match the bad debt expense to the same period as the related sales were made. The idea is that one of the costs that the company chose to accept, and which helped it make sales, was its decision to let customers pay on credit. Therefore, bad debt expense should be recognized in the same period as the sales, even if the company does not yet know which customers won't pay. Estimation is required.

Here is how the allowance method works:

a. The company already has an account in its ledger for accounts receivable. The company also probably also has another accounting record that lists every customer's account activity. This is called a *subsidiary ledger*, or a *subledger*. At any given time, the total of the amounts that the many customers owe (from the subledger) should equal the total asset "accounts receivable."

b. The company estimates that a certain dollar amount of accounts receivable will not be collected. There are many estimation methods that can be used here. The point is that the company *does not know which* customers will not pay. It therefore cannot adjust the accounts receivable subsidiary ledgers for particular customers.

c. To get the total receivables correct on the balance sheet, without adjusting particular customer accounts, the company sets up a new ledger account, called "*allowance for doubtful accounts*." The title is descriptive. This relates to accounts that may or may not prove uncollectible. The company does not know for certain. It does not list particular customers, but instead creates a general "provision" or "allowance" or estimate. The new ledger account is a balance sheet account, which modifies the accounts receivable asset account. It is shown as a reduction to the accounts receivable. Such accounts that modify other accounts are called "contra accounts."

d. Every period, the company makes an adjustment to its books to record the appropriate bad debt expense. This adjustment records an expense, and increases the allowance for doubtful accounts. Because the allowance for doubtful accounts is subtracted from accounts receivable on the balance sheet, the net effect of this adjustment is to reduce assets and reduce income. Companies use different methods of deciding the amount of the necessary adjustment. A common way is to try to predict the amount of the ending accounts receivable that will be uncollectible, and then to record whatever expense is needed to bring the allowance for doubtful accounts to that level.

e. When the company is certain that any particular bill will not be paid, it "writes off" that amount from its accounts receivable assets, and corrects the customer's account in the subsidiary ledger. It also reduces the allowance for doubtful accounts. Why? Because the account is no longer "doubtful"—it is certain to be uncollectible. This write-off entry has no effect on net income. It simultaneously reduces the total accounts receivable and the amount being subtracted from the accounts receivable. The net impact on total assets and income is zero.

f.   This means that bad debt expense is recognized through estimates at the ends of accounting periods, not when particular customers' bills go unpaid.

Box 8.2 shows bad debt accounting under the direct write-off and allowance methods.

This process recurs year after year. What we will see is that the expense recorded in any one year depends not only on the events of that year, but also on whether the preceding year's estimate was correct. A company that overestimates bad debt expense this year will show poorer income this year, but is likely to show higher income in the future when it reverses part of its allowance for

---

Box 8.2 Accounting for Bad Debts

Assume the Goctor Corp. has $3,000,000 of accounts receivable at the end of its first month of operations. During the month, it was not aware of any particular customers who are unable to pay. Based on its close knowledge of its customers, and based on industry experience, it believes that best estimate of the amount of uncollectible accounts is 2% of $3,000,000, or $60,000.

Also assume that in following months, it collects all but $55,000 of the $3,000,000 of accounts receivable, and decides the $55,000 is from two particular customers who will never pay.

Allowance method

In the first month, the company should record a bad debt expense, and set up an allowance for doubtful accounts, equal to $60,000. Ending assets would reflect a receivable of $3,000,000 minus an allowance for doubtful accounts of $60,000.

In later periods, it will record $55,000 of write-offs to specific accounts. It will reduce the accounts receivable by $55,000. It will also reduce the allowance for doubtful accounts by $55,000. The total assets of the company and its equity and its income are not changed at the time of any write-offs.

When the time comes to estimate bad debts in future years, the fact that the company over-estimated the first month bad debt expense by $5,000 will cause it to reduce bad debt expense in a later period by $5,000.

Direct write-off method

In the first month, since no particular accounts were written off, the company would not show any bad debt expense. Its balance sheet would include $3 million of accounts receivable, without any reduction for uncollectible accounts.

In later periods, as the $55,000 of specific bad debts become known, the company will reduce accounts receivable by $55,000 and will record $55,000 of bad debt expense.

Comparison of the two methods

If we look over the life of the company, both methods end up showing the same bad debt expense, of $55,000. They differ in timing. The allowance method anticipates the fact that some accounts will prove uncollectible, and records an expense earlier than the direct write-off method.

bad debts. A company that underestimates bad debts now will show higher income now, and can be expected to show worse income in the future, when these receivables are in fact not collected.

An example will help make this clear. Let's assume that the Pramble Company decides at the end of its first year in operations that $10 million of its accounts receivable are uncollectible. It recorded a $10 million bad debt expense, and set up an allowance for doubtful accounts of $10 million. Over the course of the next year, it "wrote off" specific accounts receivable that it learned were uncollectible. When Year 2 ends, the company will again look at its accounts receivable, and will record an entry to bring the allowance for doubtful accounts to its best estimate of the uncollectible amount. Assume that Year 2 sales and ending receivables are exactly the same as in Year 1. At the end of Year 2 it believes the right allowance for doubtful accounts will be $10 million again. What is the amount of the bad debt expense in Year 2?

The answer depends on whether the Year 1 allowance for doubtful accounts was correct. Let's look at three cases:

A. The Year 1 allowance of $10 million exactly predicted the Year 2 write-offs. If the company wrote off $10 million in specific customer accounts, at December 31, Year 2, the balance in the allowance for doubtful accounts would equal zero. (The opening balance was $10 million, and it was reduced in Year 2 by the write-offs of $10 million.) At the end of Year 2, Pramble would make an entry to increase the allowance for doubtful accounts from zero to the desired level of $10 million. $10 million minus zero = $10 million, so it would record a bad debt expense of $10 million.

B. The actual write-offs in Year 2 were only $8 million. All the other receivables as of December 31, Year 1, were collected. Before making any adjustment to record bad debt expense in Year 2, the allowance for doubtful accounts would have shrunk by the amount of the $8 million in write-offs, from an opening balance of $10 million down to $2 million. At the end of Year 2, the company wants the allowance for doubtful accounts to be $10 million. It therefore makes an entry of $8 million, and records $8 million of bad debt expense.

C. The actual write-offs in Year 2 were $11 million. Before making any adjustment to record bad debts at the end of Year 2, the allowance for doubtful accounts would have a balance equal to the $10 million opening balance, minus $11 million of write-offs. This is a balance of negative $1 million. At the end of Year 2, the company wants the allowance for doubtful accounts to be $10 million. It therefore makes an entry of $11 million to adjust it from negative $1 million to positive $10 million. Bad debt expense in the second period is $11 million.

In this example, part of the computation of the Year 2 bad debt expense related to the accuracy of the Year 1 estimate. In Case A, where the Year 1 estimate was exactly correct, the bad debt expense in Year 2 was $10 million. In Case B, the company's estimate in Year 1 was $2 million more conservative than it needed to be, so Year 1 income was understated by $2 million. The bad debt entry needed in Case B to get the reserve up to the required level in Year 2 was only $8 million, which is $2 million smaller than in the case where the Year 1 estimate was correct. Thus, Year 2 income was higher than it would have been with a correct estimate in Year 1. We get a similar picture of offsetting errors in Case C. Here, the company underestimated the bad debt expense by $1 million in Year 1, and the result was that the Year 2 bad debt expense became $11 million, instead of the $10 million in Case A.

Banks and Loan Loss Reserves

The same general ideas that govern accounts receivable apply to loans that banks make. For major banks, "loan loss reserves" can be huge numbers. They are somewhat subjective, so bank analysts must consider carefully whether the banks have made appropriate loan loss reserves.

Allowances for Sales Returns

Companies that allow customers to return goods after sale will also need to record an allowance for sales returns. This is similar to the allowance for doubtful accounts. It is another contra account, modifying accounts receivable. Again, the company needs to estimate the likely amount of the returns, and reduce income and net accounts receivables for the likely amount of the lost profits due to sales returns.

Inventory

When companies buy inventory, they hope to sell it at higher prices, but they are not certain they can do so. The normal rule in the U.S. for valuing inventory is to account for it at "the lower of cost or market." This was discussed in Chapter 7. This is clearly more of a conservative practice than a neutral one. For a profitable company, selling price is normally more than cost, so cost is a conservative measure. The idea of reducing the carrying value of inventory to reflect potential problems in selling it, but not increasing the value to reflect unexpected opportunities, is clearly not neutral.

The arguments for writing down inventory to market, when the market falls below cost, are:

- If the inventory value is not reduced, readers will be misled as to the true inventory value
- The loss in value relates to economic changes that have already occurred, so the company should recognize the loss now. If it fails to recognize the loss now, the loss in value will show up in later periods, when the inventory is actually sold and the company matches the high inventory carrying value with a low selling price.

Companies may need to "write down" their inventory to the market value for a variety of reasons. The inventory may be a commodity, like oil, whose price fluctuates. The inventory may also be of items that become obsolete. If the issue is obsolescence, companies may have a separate account for "inventory obsolescence reserves." This would be a "contra account", modifying the inventory balance.

Under U.S. rules, once a company "writes down" an inventory item to a "market" value, it cannot later increase the carrying value of the inventory item. Therefore, adjustments only go to decrease income, not to increase income. IFRS allows companies to reverse these write downs if the market value recovers.

IFRS is somewhat less conservative than U.S. GAAP. First of all, it uses the net realizable value of the inventory as the market value when doing the "lower of cost or market" test. This will normally be higher than the replacement cost, since the company usually buys at one price and sells at another, higher one. Second, under IFRS the company can write the inventory back up to its original cost value if conditions change.

If a company is too conservative, and records too large an adjustment for a "lower of cost or market adjustment" in one period, then its income in later periods will be helped when the estimation error is corrected. Box 8.3 is an example of such an overly conservative estimate being made.

Why have the FASB and IASB chosen to value inventory conservatively, rather than allowing companies to record their inventories at estimated fair value? The most likely explanation for requiring inventory to be accounted for at cost is concern over how managers would be able to distort reported earnings if inventory valuation was based on managers' estimates of fair values. Normally, there are not "perfect and complete" markets for a company's inventory, so fair value would depend in large part on estimates. They would also be recognizing income before completing an earnings process.

Box 8.3 Overly Conservative Accounting for Inventory—Cisco Systems in 2001*

During the 1990s, use of the Internet was expanding rapidly. Cisco Systems is a major supplier of computer equipment, and its sales grew rapidly during this period. However, around 2000 and 2001 growth in this industry slowed.

In April of 2001, Cisco announced it would write down its inventory by $2.2 billion. It later revised that figure to $2.8 billion for the fiscal year ended July 28, 2001. That meant that earnings in its 2001 fiscal year were reduced by $2.8 billion, on the assumption that certain inventory was worthless.

However, in the first quarter of the next fiscal year it reported selling some of this supposedly worthless inventory for $290 million. The impact of being too conservative in its 2001 books was to overstate the losses in the bad year of 2001 and overstate the degree of the recovery in the 2002 year by $290 million (ignoring taxes).

*Based on Levitt (2002).

Let's assume for example, that a clothing store was allowed to value its inventory at expected selling price. Assume it normally sold clothing for 50% more than it paid its suppliers. Every time it bought a pair of pants for $50, it would be recognizing an inventory worth $75, and an increase in equity of $25. That means that merely by buying inventory, it would be reporting profits, without actually selling them.

Similarly, the rule requiring companies to write inventory down to market values is needed to prevent managers from hiding the fact that some of their inventory is obsolete by simply refusing to sell it. If there were no requirement to write down inventory, the companies might hold on to bad inventory for years rather than recognize losses. This is similar to the issue of "gains trading" discussed in Chapter 7.

Note that there are different inventory rules for those types of inventory where there are nearly perfect markets. Items such as gold or fungible commodities that are traded on well-functioning markets are typically accounted for at fair value. See Chapter 7. This less conservative approach makes sense, since the existence of verifiable market prices limits the opportunity for earnings management through biased estimates.

For tax purposes, IRS rules make it difficult to recognize a loss in value of inventory until the inventory is actually sold. See Box 8.4.

Investments in Derivative Securities

Companies often buy a variety of "*derivative securities*" or "*derivatives*." These are securities or other instruments that have value based on potential price movements in something else. For example, an option to buy wheat in the future at a specified price "derives" its value from the movement in the "underlying" product, wheat. Some examples of derivatives are options, futures contracts, and forward contracts. Derivative contracts exist on many underlying items, including interest rates, commodity prices, stock prices, and foreign exchange. In some cases, the company has an obligation under its derivative contracts, while in other cases it may have an asset.

In general, derivative securities assets or liabilities are recorded at fair value. Because the value of derivatives can be very volatile, the SEC has required companies to make additional disclosures about them (Regulation S-K). One optional disclosure, under this rule, is sensitivity analysis of the potential losses resulting from hypothetical changes in interest rates, foreign currency exchange rates, commodity prices, or other market rates over a selected time period.

Box 8.4 Accounting and Society—Tax Rules, Inventory Obsolescence and Publishing

Before 1979, companies were able to take a tax deduction for obsolete or unsellable inventory based on an estimate, without actually selling the items off. In the 1979 case of Thor Power Tool v. Commissioner (*Thor Power Tool Co. v. Commissioner,* 439 U.S. 522 (1979)), the U.S. Supreme Court ruled that under the law, companies could not take a deduction simply because they thought they would be unable to sell an item. There needed to be strong evidence that the item's market value had decreased.

This decision had an impact on the publishing industry. At that time, the economics of publishing were such that it cost much less to publish many copies of a book at one time, than to publish the same number in several production runs. Therefore, publishers would routinely print many copies of a book at once, and hope they could sell them all over a period of years. If the initial sales of the book were slow, the publishers could take an obsolescence deduction to help them get some of their money back while they waited to see if the books would sell. Under the new rules, the publishers had to choose—either keep the books, and wait, and not take a deduction now *or* throw the books out to get the tax deduction.

Some people believe that the Thor Power Tool decision is one reason that, since the 1970s, publishers are less willing to take chances on books that would sell slowly, less willing to make large initial print runs of books, and faster to scrap their inventories of slow-selling books. See O'Donnell (1993).

Another option is to disclose a measure of risk called "value at risk" computed using certain financial models. Value at risk disclosures are meant to measure the maximum potential loss over some period of time, at a given probability of occurrence, due to changes in certain market rates.

Fixed Assets

Buildings, equipment, and other fixed assets are usually stated at their cost, minus depreciation. The issue of uncertainty is relevant here in two accounting decisions: computing depreciation, and determining if there is an impairment.

What should be the correct depreciation expense each period? The goal of depreciation is to systematically record expenses related to the cost of an asset (net of any money recovered when it is disposed of), over the useful life of the assets. Computing the right depreciation depends on estimating the useful life of the asset correctly and also on estimating any "salvage value" the company will receive when the item is disposed of. Both useful life and salvage value depend on future events, and must be estimated. In the case of a building, for example, the estimate of useful life may be quite long.

Here are some things the estimate of useful life depends on:

- How long will it take before the asset wears out through use?
- How long will it take before the asset becomes technologically obsolete, so that the company would want to replace it?
- How long will it be before the company changes in a way that makes it outgrow the capacity of this asset? For example, a small and growing company may outgrow its telephone system, and its building.

The estimate of what the salvage value will be depends in large part on how long the company means to own the asset, and also on how well the asset is cared for. For example, a company that uses a car in its business to make deliveries may expect to use the car for 12 years. In contrast, a major car rental company like Hertz may only want to have modern cars, and may plan on selling cars after two years. Clearly, the salvage value of a two-year-old car should be greater than the value of a 12-year-old car.

The estimates used in computing depreciation should be based on the best information available. If a company believes that events have happened that change the proper amount of depreciation (such as a change in estimated life of the asset) it should change the way it figures out depreciation for the current period and all future periods. Companies would not go back and revise previously issued income statements for this new information.

Has something happened that "impairs" the value of the fixed asset? Here, the company needs to decide if it is likely to continue to use these assets profitably in its business. For example, a cell phone manufacturer might decide that, due to competition from Apple, it can no longer use all its factories to make cell phones at a profit. If a company believes that such an impairment loss is probable, it needs to record a loss and adjust the carrying value of the fixed assets.

Research and Development Costs

Companies' expenditures on research projects are risky. At the time the company starts a project, success is highly uncertain. The FASB decided in SFAS No. 2, issued in 1974, that research and development was such an unpredictable activity that it would not allow companies to record their research and development expenditures as assets. The FASB standard is now found in Section 730-10-05-2 of the FASB Codification:

> At the time most research and development costs are incurred, the future benefits are at best uncertain. In other words, there is no indication that an economic resource has been created. Moreover, even if at some point in the progress of an individual research and development project the expectation of future benefits becomes sufficiently high to indicate that an economic resource has been created, the question remains whether that resource should be recognized as an asset for financial accounting purposes. Although future benefits from a particular research and development project may be foreseen, they generally cannot be measured with a reasonable degree of certainty. There is normally little, if any, direct relationship between the amount of current research and development expenditures and the amount of resultant future benefits to the entity. Research and development costs therefore fail to satisfy the suggested measurability test for accounting recognition as an asset.

There are some exceptions. One is costs incurred on computer software projects designed for sale or use by others after the software project has reached a stage of "technological feasibility."[8] Similarly, costs of software for internal use are shown as assets after the project has reached the "application development stage."[9] Another exception relates to research projects that have been purchased from other companies as part of a business combination.

Some companies do show sizable assets for internally developed software. The fiscal 2014 Form 10-K for Computer Associates shows it has included $407 million of internally developed software in its assets. However, some large companies do not show significant amounts of software development costs as assets. The accounting footnote from the Apple Computer Form 10-K for its fiscal 2014 year is quoted below.[10]

Software Development Costs

Research and development ("R&D") costs are expensed as incurred. Development costs of computer software to be sold, leased, or otherwise marketed are subject to capitalization beginning when a product's technological feasibility has been established and ending when a product is available for general release to customers. In most instances, the Company's products are released soon after technological feasibility has been established. Costs incurred subsequent to achievement of technological feasibility were not significant, and software development costs were expensed as incurred during 2014, 2013 and 2012.

Considering research and development an expense is clearly a very conservative approach—companies spend on research because they expect a return. Also, researchers have found that stock prices do include some recognition of the value of research and development spending, although it is unclear how accurately the stock market is able to value the economic benefits of research and development. See for example Lev and Sougiannis (1996). Box 8.5 discusses the controversy over the FASB's requirement to expense these costs.

Other Internally Developed Intangible Assets

The FASB does not allow companies to show assets for amounts spent to internally develop such assets as brand recognition, trademarks, and goodwill. Again, this is a very conservative approach. Some research indicates that it is possible to estimate brand values in a way that would be decision-useful and reasonably reliable. See Barth et al. (1998).

Box 8.5 Accounting and Society—The Case of Research

When the FASB decided in 1974 that research costs should be expensed, many people were worried that this would cause companies to do less research. If all U.S. companies cut back on research, the country's technological ability would be reduced, and the country would lose in competition with other countries.

Was this criticism correct? Research on the impact of the new rules on the amount of research done by U.S. firms was inconclusive. There is no strong evidence that firms reduced their research and development spending, or that market prices of companies that spent heavily on research and development were damaged.* Douglas Skinner (2008) compared the growth of spending on fixed assets, which are recorded as assets, to the growth of research and development spending, from 1980 to 2005. He found that:

> Over the period since 1980, aggregate capital expenditures have grown rather modestly, by a bit less than 50% overall. In contrast, spending on intangibles has grown considerably. Aggregate R&D spending increases steadily over this period, and is 250% higher in 2005 than it was in 1980. This is striking evidence both that R&D spending is now relatively more important in the economy and that its accounting treatment has not obviously adversely affected its growth.
>
> (p. 197)

*See Nix and Nix (1992). See also Skinner (2008).

Intangible Assets Acquired From Others

Companies record the costs of such intangibles as assets when they buy these assets from other companies. If the intangible assets have definite lives, they are amortized. If the assets are impaired, the carrying value must be reduced.

Why are these intangible assets recognized when internally developed intangible assets are not? The logic, apparently, is that since there was an arms-length purchase of these items, the probability of them having value is higher than for items developed by the company.

Under U.S. GAAP, the accounting remains conservative because of the requirement to record impairments, and because the accounting does not recognize any increase in value of the intangible assets.

In theory, IFRS is less conservative because IFRS allows the revaluation of intangible assets, if there is an active market for them. In practice, many intangible assets may not have markets that meet the IASB's standards. IAS 38 (Intangible Assets) requires that "the items traded in the market are homogeneous," meaning they are identical, but intangible assets like patents are often unique.

Natural Resource Assets

Some companies own valuable natural resource assets, such as oil wells, coal mines, copper mines, and forests. A major problem in accounting for an oil well is we don't really know how much oil is underground, and how much of that oil can be brought to the surface at reasonable cost. The same issue arises in any kind of mine where we won't know how much of the resource actually exists until after we finish the mining process. Therefore, when accounting for natural resources, the uncertainties include:

- The physical amount of the resource. No one knows how much oil is underground.
- The amount of the resource that can be economically produced. This depends in part on the technology used as well as the price that exists for the resource. For example, it may be reasonable to produce oil from a well when the market price is $100 a barrel but not when it is $50 per barrel.
- The prices at which the resource can be sold. Resource prices can change rapidly. During the last half of 2014, the market price for crude oil fell from over $100 per barrel to around $50.[11]

These uncertainties affect both the way that the oil well or gold mine asset should initially be measured, and the amount of "*depletion*" expense that should be recognized as the resource is used up. Typically, companies compute the amount of depletion expense per unit by dividing the carrying value of the resource by the number of units they expect to produce from the resource.

The accounting rules normally require companies to show their oil wells, coal mines, and other natural resource properties on their books at what they cost to find and develop, minus an accumulated "depletion" account. Cost of an oil well or a mine would include the cost of obtaining the land or the rights to mine on the land, and also costs of developing the well or mine. Companies vary in the extent to which they record exploratory costs as assets or expenses. Normally, the value of the natural resources in an oil well would be much larger than the cost to the company of finding the oil, buying the land, and drilling the oil well. This means that the accounting for these assets seems very conservative.

The values may not always be conservative. If one company buys mines from another, perhaps as part of buying the other company, then we would expect that the mines should change hands at a fair price, reflecting their actual value. Also, in some cases companies buy mineral rights in an auction or other open market process, which would also result in the resources being acquired at

---

Box 8.6 Examples of Accounting Policies for Natural Resources

From Exxon-Mobile's 2013 Form 10-K:

The Corporation uses the 'successful efforts' method to account for its exploration and production activities. Under this method, costs are accumulated on a field-by-field basis with certain exploratory expenditures and exploratory dry holes being expensed as incurred. Costs of productive wells and development dry holes are capitalized and amortized on the unit-of-production method.

Excerpts from Freeport McMoran Copper and Gold Inc.'s 2013 Form 10-K:

Property, Plant, Equipment and Mining Development Costs. Property, plant, equipment and mining development costs are carried at cost. Mineral exploration costs, as well as drilling and other costs incurred for the purpose of converting mineral resources to proven and probable reserves or identifying new mineral resources at development or production stage properties, are charged to expense as incurred. Development costs are capitalized beginning after proven and probable mineral reserves have been established. Development costs include costs incurred resulting from mine pre-production activities undertaken to gain access to proven and probable reserves, including shafts, adits, drifts, ramps, permanent excavations, infrastructure and removal of overburden. . . . Interest expense allocable to the cost of developing mining properties and to constructing new facilities is capitalized until assets are ready for their intended use. . . .

Depreciation for mining and milling life-of-mine assets, infrastructure and other common costs is determined using the unit-of-production (UOP) method based on total estimated recoverable proven and probable copper reserves (for primary copper mines) and proven and probable molybdenum reserves (for primary molybdenum mines). Development costs and acquisition costs for proven and probable mineral reserves that relate to a specific ore body are depreciated using the UOP method based on estimated recoverable proven and probable mineral reserves for the ore body benefited.

Included in property, plant, equipment and mining development costs is value beyond proven and probable mineral reserves (VBPP), primarily resulting from FCX's acquisition of FMC in 2007. The concept of VBPP has been interpreted differently by different mining companies. FCX's VBPP is attributable to (i) mineralized material, which includes measured and indicated amounts, that FCX believes could be brought into production with the establishment or modification of required permits and should market conditions and technical assessments warrant, (ii) inferred mineral resources and (iii) exploration potential.

Carrying amounts assigned to VBPP are not charged to expense until the VBPP becomes associated with additional proven and probable mineral reserves and the reserves are produced or the VBPP is determined to be impaired. Additions to proven and probable mineral reserves for properties with VBPP will carry with them the value assigned to VBPP at the date acquired, less any impairment amounts.

Form 10-K filings can be reviewed on the SEC website: www.sec.gov/edgar/searchedgar/companysearch.html (last accessed August 14, 2015).

a price reflecting their true economic value. Indeed, there is reason to believe that the winning bid in such auctions is often too high, meaning the cost is above the economic value.[12]

See Box 8.6 for footnotes from two companies about how they account for their natural resource costs. Freeport McMoran is a major mining company, and Exxon Mobil is a giant oil company. Both companies say they expense certain exploration costs, and both say they "capitalize" costs of developing productive wells or mines. When the companies say they "*capitalize*" certain costs, it means they recognize them as assets. Freeport McMoran also notes that the asset values for some of its properties include more than just these development costs, but also a "value beyond proven reserves" related to mines it acquired as part of the acquisition of another company.

There is a parallel between the accounting for natural resources and the accounting for intangible assets. When the assets are developed internally, they are likely to be shown on the books at a level below their fair value. If a mining company has two mines, with equal fair value, it would show different asset values for the mine it developed itself and a mine it bought as part of acquiring another mining company.

Contingencies

The FASB Codification (Section 450-10-20) defines a *contingency* as:

> An existing condition, situation, or set of circumstances involving uncertainty as to possible gain (gain contingency) or loss (loss contingency) to an entity that will ultimately be resolved when one or more future events occur or fail to occur.

As an example, let's assume that Able Company started selling a new product last year. Baker Company says that Able should not have done that, because Baker owns the patent for the product. Baker sues Able for $20 million. At the end of the year, the lawsuit has not yet been settled. The lawsuit is an "existing condition" and there is uncertainty as to how the lawsuit will end. It is a "loss contingency" for Able, and a "gain contingency" for Baker.

The definition of "contingencies" is not meant to include events that are totally in the future. For example, any company that owns beachfront property in Florida might, someday, have damage from a hurricane. That future event is not "an existing condition" within the FASB's definition of contingencies.

The FASB has made the following rules for contingencies:

1   Gain contingencies are not recorded as assets. However, there should be adequate disclosure of the nature of the contingency. The relevant standard says "Adequate disclosure shall be made of a contingency that might result in a gain, but care shall be exercised to avoid misleading implications as to the likelihood of realization."[13]

2   Loss contingencies should be recognized as liabilities when they are "*probable*" and the amount of the loss is "reasonably estimable."[14]

    a. The FASB's definition of "probable" is: "The future event or events are likely to occur."[15] This is fairly vague, but is usually interpreted as significantly more than a 50% probability. Under IFRS, in contrast, "probable" means a higher than 50% probability. Various studies have been done in the U.S. on how auditors and other accountants view these terms. Raghunandan, Grimlund, and Schpanski's 1991 study of 64 auditor firm partners from six firms found a mean probability of 70% as the threshold for "probable." The study also quoted three prior studies where the mean thresholds for "probable" were 59%, 68% and 68%.[16]

    b. If the reasonably estimable amount is a range, the company should accrue the most likely figure from within the range. If all figures in the range are equally likely, the company should record the lowest value in the range.

3   The FASB requires disclosure of loss contingencies if they are at least *"reasonably possible"* but does not require disclosure of contingencies which are *"remote."* "Remote" events are those where: "The chance of the future event or events occurring is slight." The FASB defines *"reasonably possible"* as those where: "The chance of the future event or events occurring is more than remote but less than likely."[17] It is not clear where, in practice, to draw the line between "remote" and "reasonably possible" events.[18] If possible, the disclosure should give the readers the magnitude of the likely loss.

The accounting for contingencies was first set out in SFAS No. 5, issued in 1975. In several ways, it does not reflect the FASB's and IASB's more recent thinking.

• The FASB, in its Statements of Accounting Concepts, favors neutral accounting over conservatism. However, the rules for recognizing contingent gains and losses are very different. Contingent gains are not recorded, but contingent losses are if they are probable and reasonably estimable. This difference in treatment is conservative, not neutral.
• The FASB has in recent years favored using a "fair value" approach that uses prices that would be paid to buy assets or to induce someone else to assume one of the company's liabilities. The amount of liability recognized under the loss contingency rules can be very different. Here is an example. Assume a company believes there is a 40% chance it could lose a particular lawsuit, and will lose $10 million if it loses. Under the contingency rules, since there is only a 40% chance of a loss, the loss is not probable, and no liability will be recorded. However, if the company wanted to find someone else to insure the possible loss, that other party would charge at least 40% of $10 million to cover the liability.
• The IASB uses a threshold of over 50% for something to be "probable." In some of its statements, the FASB also uses a "more likely than not" standard. However, it has never clearly specified what "probable" and "reasonably likely" mean in its contingency standards.

Unasserted Claims

Sometimes, a company will be aware that it has done something improper, and knows that it might be sued, but no one has sued it yet. For example, it might be aware that it has not lived up to one of its contracts, but the other company has not yet noticed the problem, or brought a lawsuit.

What are the accounting rules for this situation? The situation is tricky because in this case the accounting is likely to affect actions. People who might not otherwise know they could sue would learn of their rights from the company's financial statements.

The rules for accrual of a loss are the same as the general rules for contingent losses. The loss will only be accrued if it is probable and reasonably estimable. In judging if the loss is probable, the company can take into consideration the chance that the other company will never notice the problem, or will never make the claim. So, if a company believes there is very little chance the other party will recognize the issue, no accrual needs to be made.

The rules for disclosure are a little different than the normal rules for disclosing loss contingencies. The FASB normally does not require companies to disclose an unasserted claim if the party that could make the claim has not shown any awareness that the claim exists. Disclosure of such claims would only be required if it is "probable" that such a claim will be asserted, and there is a reasonable possibility that the outcome will be unfavorable.[19] The word "probable" has the same vague meaning here as it does in the contingency rules. The idea is that the disclosure rule is unlikely to hurt the company, because the other side is already likely to sue.

Uncertain Tax Positions

The corporate income tax laws are complex. It is not always clear at the time that a company files its tax return whether the tax authorities will agree with how the company has computed its taxes. The FASB has created special rules to deal with accounting for what are called "uncertain tax positions." The rule is: "An entity shall initially recognize the financial statement effects of a tax position when it is more likely than not, based on the technical merits, that the position will be sustained upon examination."[20]

This differs from the normal rules on recognizing unasserted claims in three ways. First, the FASB is using a "more likely than not" standard, which means more than 50% probability. This is more specific than the vague "probable" term used in the contingency rules. Second, companies cannot assume that the tax authorities are unlikely to notice the issue. This is different from the rules for unasserted claims, which only require accrual of liabilities if it is probable that the claims will be asserted. Third, the FASB is allowing companies to recognize favorable results of these uncertain tax benefits, but the normal contingency rules do not allow accrual of gain contingencies.

Does it make sense that the rules for uncertain tax positions are different from the normal rules for unasserted claims? From a public policy standpoint, it makes sense not to consider the probability that the government will notice the issue. The U.S. tax system is based on companies computing taxes themselves, and audits by the IRS are relatively infrequent for most companies. If the FASB only required recognizing potential tax problems if there was a high probability of a tax audit occurring and the auditor seeing the problem, then few companies would record liabilities for these uncertain positions.

There is no clear reason why the FASB in this rule uses a "more likely than not" standard rather than the "probable" standard used in the general contingency rules.

In 2006, when the FASB first required companies to disclose their uncertain tax positions, there was considerable concern that the FASB was handing the IRS a "road map" to use in selecting companies for audits. The concern was that the IRS would select those companies for audits based on which ones said they had uncertain tax positions, and would then request copies of the working papers that indicated what was questionable about the company's position. There have been few academic studies so far on the effect of the FASB rules, but they suggest that companies have tended to become somewhat less aggressive in their tax positions.[21]

Warranty Reserves

When you buy something, you often are given a "warranty", which is a promise that the product will in fact work for some period of time. If the product does not work, the seller will have to fix it for the buyer.

The existence of these warranties is important to the buyers. Imagine going shopping for a car, costing $40,000 and being told that the manufacturer was unwilling to guarantee it would work for more than a day. You would not buy that car.

Logically, the cost of providing the warranty is just as much of a cost of making and selling cars as is the cost of the steel in the car. Both costs are necessary to the process of making and selling cars. This means that accountants want to estimate and record warranties in the periods when sales occur for two reasons:

- The cost of providing the warranty should be matched to the revenues that the warranty promise helped make possible.

- The warranty promise meets the definition of a contingent liability. It creates a probable future sacrifice of economic value. The "existing condition" is that cars have been sold, some of which were defective. The eventual cost of fixing them is not known for sure.

Normally, the decision to record a liability for warranties follows the same ideas as those used for contingencies.[22] Because companies sell many products, based on their past history they are able to tell that it is probable that some products will break, and they can reasonably estimate the likely costs of honoring the warranties.

The accounting for warranties proceeds as follows.

- At the time the products are sold, the company will record a warranty expense, and will set up a liability.
- Later, when the items break, the company will spend cash, and will reduce the amount of the warranty liability. As long as the original estimate of the liability was correct, the company will not have to record any more warranty expense.
- If it turns out that the original liability recorded was *higher* than the actual costs, then the company will "reverse" part of the original entry. That will cause expenses in the future to be lower.
- If it turns out that the original liability recorded was *less* than the actual costs, then the company will have to record additional warranty expenses in future periods.

Box 8.7 shows an example of accounting for warranties.

Part of the footnote for warranties for General Motors, from its 2013 Form 10-K, is shown in Table 8.2. It shows the activity that affected the warranty balance each year. This included both estimated new warranty liabilities and payments on existing liabilities, adjustments to previous estimates, and some other factors like the impact of exchange rates.

Obviously, estimating the future warranty claims can be difficult. For some companies, that are making new and innovative products, they may not have any past experience to use as a guide. If companies overestimate the expense in the year of sale, they will understate their net assets that year, and that year's income. Future years' income will look better. If companies underestimate the warranty costs, their future earnings will show extra expenses. In Table 8.2, the figures indicate that General Motors had a pattern of under-accruing its warranty expense, since the "adjustments to pre-existing warranties" were positive figures in each of the three years shown.

Financial Guarantees

Companies will sometimes guarantee the debt or performance of some other company. For example, Company A may guarantee some lender that Company B will pay its debts. If Company B actually pays its debts, then Company A does not have any further duties. If, on the other hand, Company B is unable to pay its debts, then Company A must pay the debt. Clearly, at the time the guarantee is issued, there is uncertainty over whether Company A will ever have to make a payment.

The rules for accounting for guarantees are that a company who makes the guaranty should recognize a liability that is the larger of the "fair value" of the guaranty or the amount that would be recognized as a loss contingency.[23] The logic of this becomes clear with an example.

Assume that Shaky Corp. wants to borrow $3 million from National Bank. National Bank is nervous about making the loan, because Shaky Corp. has been in financial difficulty, and has a 5% chance of failing. Shaky goes to the Helpful Guarantee Corp., and asks Helpful to guarantee the loan. Helpful decides that a 5% chance of failure on $3 million means the expected value of failure is $150,000. Helpful is in the business of making these guarantees. It wants to make a

---

Box 8.7 Example of Warranty Costs

The Lu and Meng Corp. made sales of $50,000,000 in 2014 of products with warranties that expire in 2016. These warranties are not separately sold, but are a necessary part of making its sales. Based on its past experience, it expects to have warranty costs equal to 1% of the amount sold, or $500,000. It believes these costs meet the FASB's standards of being probable and reasonably estimable.

Assume that it actually paid claims of $100,000 in 2014; $250,000 in 2015; and $125,000 in 2016.

During 2014, it would record two different entries. First, it would recognize its warranty liability by recording a warranty expense equal to $500,000, and setting up a liability account of $500,000. Second, it would record the use of cash to pay warranty claims. It would reduce cash by $100,000 and reduce the warranty liability by $100,000. Note that the actual payment of claims does not add to the expense. At the end of 2014, the warranty liability = $500,000 − $100,000 = $400,000.

During 2015, it would record the payment of $250,000 in claims. It would show a reduction in cash, and a reduction in warranty liability. Again, the payment of claims did not involve recognizing any more expense—it is merely paying down a liability. At the end of 2015, the warranty liability would equal its starting balance of $400,000 minus the $250,000 of claims paid, or $150,000.

During 2016, it would record the payment of an additional $125,000 in claims. Again, cash would be decreased, and the warranty liability is decreased. The payment of claims does not involve recognizing any more expense. After the claims are all paid, the remaining warranty liability = the starting balance of $150,000 minus the 2016 claims paid of $125,000, which is a balance of $25,000.

At the end of 2016, the warranties all expire. No customers can claim any more money. This means that the company no longer needs a warranty liability of $25,000. It had overestimated the amount of claims that would be required. The way to fix the books is to reduce the liability to zero, and to record a $25,000 negative amount to warranty expense. It may seem odd to record a negative expense, but it is the normal way to deal with this situation. That way, over the three-year life of the warranties, the company has recorded a total of $475,000 of expense, equal to the original $500,000 estimate, minus the $25,000 correction at the end of 2016. The total expense equals the cash actually paid.

What would have happened if the original estimate was too low, instead of too high? For example, what if the 2016 payments were $160,000, instead of $125,000? In this case, the company would first record the warranty payments normally, by reducing cash and reducing the warranty liability. The warranty liability at the start of 2016 was $150,000, so the first $150,000 of payments would be charged to that account, bringing the liability to zero. The remaining payments in 2016 would be recorded as additional warranty expense.

---

profit on its overall business, so it prices its services more than the expected value of the losses. Helpful charges Shaky $180,000 for a guarantee, and National Bank makes the loan.

In this case, what must Helpful record when it makes the guarantee? First, it has received $180,000 of cash from Shaky. Second, it has to consider how to record the guarantee. The rules say that Helpful must record the larger of the fair value of the guarantee obligation or what would be required by the contingency rules. The fair value would be what Helpful would have to pay a competitor to take over this guarantee. Assuming there is a competitive market for guarantees that would probably be about the same $180,000 that Helpful charged. At the time this guarantee

Table 8.2 Excerpts from General Motors Form 10-K in 2013 Regarding Warranties
All figures in millions.

	2013	2012	2011
Beginning balance	$7,204	$6,600	$6,789
Warranties issued and assumed in period	3,181	3,394	3,062
Payments	(3,063)	(3,393)	(3,740)
Adjustments to pre-existing warranties	123	539	565
Effect of foreign currency and other	(231)	64	(76)
Ending balance	$7,214	$7,204	$6,600

Form 10-K filings can be reviewed at: www.sec.gov/edgar/searchedgar/companysearch.html
(last accessed August 14, 2015).

was issued, under the contingency rules, it would not record any liability. The chance of Shaky defaulting on its loan is only 5%, so it is not "probable" that Helpful would have to pay under this guarantee. However, at some later time, if the chance of Shaky going bankrupt increases to the point where it is "probable," the guarantee would have to be valued at the amount that Helpful expects to pay to National Bank.

Pension Plans

Many U.S. companies and state and local governments have promised their employees pensions under what are called "defined benefit pension plans." The companies have promised to pay the employees a pension for the rest of the employees' lives, with a value that depends on how much the employees earn when they retire.

If we follow the same logic used with loss contingencies, the company would need to record a pension liability if it is probable that it will have to pay pensions, and if the amounts are reasonably estimable. The FASB believes that in general these conditions are met, and therefore companies are required to record liabilities, over the period that employees work, for the pensions that will eventually be paid to those employees. Companies are required to record a liability based on actuarial estimates of the amounts that will need to be paid. Because the liabilities will be paid in the far future, they are shown at present value.

Pensions present two different but related issues for managers and analysts.

The first is that it is hard to estimate the amount of the liability. It will depend on events that will take place over perhaps 70 or 80 years. Future inflation and future trends in people's lifespan will have an impact. The values are estimated by specialists—pension actuaries—using certain approved methods. The values depend on assumptions, and those assumptions are based on professional judgment.

The second problem is that the amounts of pension liabilities, and the assets that companies have put in trust to satisfy these liabilities, can be huge. For very large companies, the obligations and related assets can be in the tens of billions of dollars. For example, the Ford Motor Form 10-K for 2013 showed total obligations under defined benefit pension plans of about $74 billion and assets in trust to pay for these benefits of about $65 billion.

The large size of the pension assets and liabilities means that they could have a big, and usually unfavorable, effect on such balance sheet ratios as return on assets or the ratio of assets to equity. The combination of the size of pensions and the difficulty in estimating them also means that income can be affected in major ways by relatively small changes in assumptions. For example, look at what happens when you change an estimate of a $74 billion liability by 1%. A 1% change doesn't seem like much, but you will need to adjust income by $740 million.

Since Ford's reported net income for the year was about $7.2 billion, $740 million is a little bit more than 10% of income.

Companies did not want their income to be moved up and down each quarter by minor changes in actuaries' assumptions. They also did not want the various balance sheet ratios to be affected by large amounts of pension assets and liabilities. This has led to complicated accounting for pension plans, which is beyond the scope of an introductory text. The key points are:

- Companies must value the pension plan liabilities at the present value of what is actuarially expected to be paid.
- Companies value the assets that they have put in trust to pay these benefits based on their fair value.
- The balance sheet does *not* show both the pension plan liability and the value of the pension assets. Instead, the balance sheet shows only the difference between the two. If the assets are larger, the net difference is shown as an asset. If the obligation is larger, the difference is shown as a liability. For Ford, in 2013, the plan obligations of $74 billion were about $9 billion larger than the plan assets of $65 billion, so the liabilities section of its balance sheet showed a net liability related to these plans of $9 billion. This "netting" of the asset and the liability reduces the impact of pension plans on the various balance sheet ratios.
- The income statement does *not* have to include all changes in the values of these estimated pension assets and liabilities. Companies have the option to show all these changes in income,[24] but they may also use an option to "smooth" the expense each period to exclude most of the variability that could occur from changing estimates. In particular, the full impact of changes in actuarial estimates, and the full impact of changes in the market value of plan assets, does not have to be included in the net income of the current year. According to a January 20, 2015, *Wall Street Journal* article, only about 30 companies choose to reflect the full impact of changes in values in their current income. As an example of the large size of these changes, the *Wall Street Journal* reported that AT&T would record an extra pension expense of $7.9 billion dollars due to changes in assumptions about interest rates and about how long people would live.[25]
- The expense each period includes:
  - Service cost—an actuarial estimate of what employees earned this period
  - Interest cost—interest accrues on the outstanding pension liability, just like on any other liability
  - Small factors to slowly recognize any changes in estimates related to the pension plan investment performance or the value of the plan liability to the employees.
- To make the balance sheet balance, the company must record some of the matters that affect the pension plan in "other comprehensive income." Other comprehensive income is used to record the difference between adjustments that were made to pension liabilities due to, for example, a change in the actuary's estimates, and the smaller amount of that change in estimate that affected net income during the year.

Other Post-Employment Benefits

Often, companies or governments have also promised employees certain other benefits after the employees retire. The most important one is health insurance.

The issues are similar to those for pensions. The only real difference is that future health care costs are even harder to estimate than future pension costs. In order to predict them, you would not only need to predict what employees will earn the benefits, you also have to predict how healthy the retirees will be, what medical costs will be, and whether some of those costs will be

---

Box 8.8 Accounting and Society—Accounting Rules and the Elderly

Some people believe that the requirements by the FASB and the Government Accounting Standards Board to measure and report liabilities for pensions and for other post-employment benefits is causing companies and governments to eliminate pensions and promises of health benefits to retirees. This is an example of a case where an accounting rule can have real effects on company actions, and people's lives. The FASB would argue that it is simply acting as a neutral measurer—it is up to companies to make their decisions, once they know the facts.

SFAS No. 36, issued in 1980, required disclosure of the accumulated benefit obligation and the related assets. SFAS No. 87, issued in 1985, required the recording of pension expenses based at least in part on the actuarial obligation. Did these statements cause a reduction of the number of defined benefit pension plans?

The data definitely show a shift away from defined benefit pension plans after 1980. A 2009 study indicates the percent of private sector employees covered by defined benefit ["DB"] plans fell from 38% in 1980 to 20% in 2008.* In contrast, the proportion of private sector employees covered by defined contribution plans such as 401(k) plans rose from 8% to 31%. The authors claimed that, if this shift continued, "there would be more losers than winners, and average family incomes would decline" (Butrica et al. 2009, p. 19).

However, this study does *not* cite changed accounting rules as a cause of the shift. Instead, it cites tax rules allowing employees to take tax breaks for contributing to defined contribution plans, an increased number of workers in service industries relative to manufacturing jobs, and worker demand for more portable plans with transparent investment features.

* Butrica et al. (2009). Bureau of Labor Statistics tables for March 2014 indicate the percentage of private sector workers with defined benefit plans fell to 16%. See Table 2: Retirement benefits: Access, participation, and take-up rates, private industry workers, National Compensation Survey, at www.bls.gov/ncs/ebs/benefits/2014/ownership/private/table02a.pdf (last accessed August 18, 2015).

---

offset by government programs. The normal rule is that for a liability to be accrued it must be "reasonably estimable" and in this case that was clearly debatable. However, the FASB decided that financial statements would be more meaningful with some accrual for this obligation than no accrual at all.

The requirement to account for other post-employment benefits was controversial. The FASB started requiring accrual of these costs in SFAS No. 106, issued in 1990. Companies resisted recording this liability for three reasons: it was large, it was very difficult to estimate, and usually the companies had not been putting assets in trust to service the liabilities. This meant that there were not any assets to net against the liabilities. However, SFAS No. 106 required companies to record the liability.[26]

As with pensions, the full impact of certain changes in assumptions or other events related to other post-retirement benefits is not shown in net income. There is some "smoothing" of net income. The remaining impact of these changes is shown in "other comprehensive income." Box 8.8 discusses the social impact of the pension and post-employment accounting rules.

Revenue Recognition—General

In some businesses, there is very little uncertainty in determining when to recognize revenue. For example, a restaurant that sells food for cash knows at the end of each day what its sales are. Its earnings process is quick, and completed by the end of each day. It also collects money from customers in cash or in highly collectible credit card receipts, so there is little uncertainty about the value of what it has collected.

Other businesses may have long processes involved in creating and delivering goods to customers, with long periods for collection, and perhaps also periods in which the customers can return goods. For example, consider a company that has made a contract with the U.S. Air Force to make and deliver 500 of a new type of fighter planes in three years. There are numerous uncertainties. The company may be unable to make the planes at the expected cost. It may make planes that do not meet the Air Force's specifications, and which the Air Force refuses to accept. The Air Force may have its budget cut, so that the number of planes that are eventually delivered may have to change. Because of these uncertainties, it is unclear when the company should recognize revenue. Should it record some when it got the contract? Should it recognize some revenue as it manufactures the planes, or when it delivers them, or as it receives payments, or only after all the planes are delivered and the Air Force has said it is satisfied?

The FASB for many years based its revenue recognition rules on three tests. There had to be a substantially complete earnings process; the revenue was either realized in cash or was "realizable"; and the amount of the revenue had to be reasonably estimable. Revenue was considered "realized" or "realizable" if the company received a valid account receivable or some other asset.

The effect of these rules was that revenue was *not* normally recognized in various situations where its eventual amount was highly uncertain. These situations included situations where the customer had not yet taken delivery. The idea is that customers might change their minds, making collection uncertain. Also, the earnings process was not complete until delivery.

There were also a number of special situations with special rules. These included:

- *Right of return.* In situations where the company has delivered products, but the customer has the right to return the products, normally a company would record revenue and record an allowance for sales returns. However, if it can't estimate the amount of sales returns with reasonable accuracy, it may have to wait to recognize revenues until it can estimate the returns.
- *Long-term contracts.* In most long-term contract situations, companies should recognize revenue as they do the work, based on the percentage of completion of the job and the estimated total project profits. However, where the company cannot reliably estimate either its stage of completion or the eventual project revenues and costs, it must wait to recognize profits until the project is complete.
- *Sales on an installment basis.* In most cases, a company should record revenues at the time goods are sold, even if the customer will pay over a period of time. However, it was often very hard to predict what fraction of retail installment sales would eventually be collected. If a company could not reliably estimate its bad debts at the time of sale, it was allowed to recognize a portion of the revenues and income as each installment payment was received.

The FASB has recently announced new revenue recognition standards that will go into effect for fiscal years starting after December 16, 2018. Under this new guidance, the focus of revenue recognition will be on a company fulfilling its "performance obligations." The new standard deals with uncertainty mainly through its rules on recording the price of the revenue transactions. The standard basically says that the recorded revenue should only include amounts that are probable of not later being reversed when uncertainties are resolved.[27]

Updating Accounts for New Information

What happens when new information becomes available, and estimates change? Since the purpose of financial reporting is to give users timely, decision-useful information, it seems logical that financial statements should contain the most up-to-date estimates.

The relevant accounting rules are as follows:

1   New information should be used to change estimates that affect the current period, and all related future periods. This makes sense—those periods should be reported with the best available information.
2   New information about estimates should *not* be used to restate prior years' financial statements. This is not quite so clear. One could argue that the readers are entitled to the most accurate picture possible of the past years as well. However, the FASB and its predecessor organization, the Accounting Principles Board, decided that it was more important not to confuse readers by constantly restating past financial statements. They noted that there are many estimates in every financial statement, and every year some of them must be incorrect. Therefore, if we started on restating past years' figures for incorrect estimates, we would never stop.[28]
3   The effects of changes in estimates will affect the current year and possibly future years as well.
4   There should be appropriate disclosure in the footnotes when changes in estimate have a material effect on the financial statements.

Here are two examples.

In April, 2010, there was an explosion and fire at the Deepwater Horizon, an oil rig in the Gulf of Mexico owned by the BP group. Eleven people died, and oil flowed out of the well for 87 days before the oil well was capped. BP faced claims by many people affected by the oil spill, and by the relatives of the people who died. In its 2010 financial statements, BP estimated that this incident would result in a loss of approximately $41 billion, before taxes.[29] Since 2010, various claims have been made and tested in the courts. In its 2013 Form 10-K, BP has a six-page footnote related to this matter. It said that the pre-tax cost related to this disaster has increased to $42.7 billion, without counting "liabilities of uncertain timing and amount." The difference between the original estimate of $41 billion and the 2013 estimate of $42.7 billion was accounted for as expenses in the years when the estimate was increased. Any future changes in estimate will be shown as expenses in the periods when the estimates are changed.

Assume that a company bought an office building in New York City in 2005, and paid $130 million for the building, not counting any price paid for the land under the building. The company originally estimated the building would have a useful life of 40 years, and would then be sold for $10 million. Based on these original estimates, the company computed depreciation expense each year. The depreciation was computed as (the cost – the salvage value) divided by the estimated useful life. This would equal $(130 – 10) ÷ 40 = \$3$ million per year. By the end of 10 years, the company had recorded $30 million of depreciation on the building. Its net book value after 10 years would equal the $130 million cost minus the $30 million of depreciation. $130 million – $30 million = $100 million.

At this point, the company decides that the building will last 60 years, not 40. When it is sold, it will likely sell for $20 million, not $10 million. The company does *not* change the past accounting. Instead, the company uses the new assumptions to depreciate the building from year 11 onwards. The building has a book value of $100 million at the time the estimate was changed. It has a remaining life of 60 years – the 10 years that have passed, or 50 years. It will have a sale value at the end of $20 million. The depreciation each year will be computed as $(100 – 20) ÷ 50$ years $= \$1.6$ million per year.

Discipline of the Accounting Process

The accounting process will eventually force companies to recognize the impact of incorrect estimates in income. This occurs because information eventually comes about the true values of the recorded assets and liabilities. For many assets, the true value becomes known when they are disposed of or sold. Inventory is an example. For some liabilities, the true value becomes known when they are paid off. For other assets and liabilities there may be good ways to check the recorded values against some kind of outside evidence. When the ending balance sheet is corrected, the accounting process will automatically force the reported *cumulative* income to be correct, even though income in any particular year may be wrong.

To understand this, let's consider a particular account, inventory, for three years. For inventory, and all the other balance sheet accounts, the following equation always holds:

Ending balance = Beginning balance + additions − subtractions

For inventory, the additions are purchases, and the subtractions are cost of goods sold and adjustments like the obsolescence charge.

Assume the Onyo Corp. is a new company, with no beginning inventory. At the end of its first year it has inventory with a cost equal to $100 million. Onyo Corp. estimates that $20 million of the inventory is obsolete, and can't be sold. Therefore Onyo records an allowance for obsolete inventory on its balance sheet of $20 million, and records an expense in Year 1 of $20 million for obsolescence. Its balance sheet will show a net balance for inventory of $100 million − $20 million = $80 million.

Let's look at what happens in Year 2 if Onyo is only able to sell $70 million of the year 1 inventory (at cost), and has to throw away the rest. At the end of Year 2, Onyo has none of this inventory left. It started with a balance of $80 million for these items, and ends with a balance of zero. It *must* record $80 million of expense related to these items to comply with the equation linking the beginning and ending balances. It would have to show a cost of goods sold in Year 2 of $80 million.

Is its cumulative accounting correct? Well, at the end of Year 2 it shows zero remaining inventory for these items, which is correct. There should be $100 million of costs showing as expense over the two years, since $100 million of inventory cost is now gone, and in fact the two years show a total of $100 million in expenses. Year 1 has $20 million of obsolescence expense, and Year 2 has cost of goods sold of $80 million.

The accounting for the two individual years is not correct. Year 1 should have shown $30 million of obsolescence expense, instead of the incorrect estimate of $20 million. If the Year 1 estimate had been made correctly, and the Year 1 ending inventory balance was $70 million, then the Year 2 expense would be $70 million.

The same logic holds for any other asset or liability account. When an estimate causes the balance in one year to be wrong, then income will also be wrong in that year. When new information comes in, and the ending balance in some future year is corrected, there will be an adjustment to income that offsets the original error. This means that as long as the balance sheet items are periodically verified, the impact of incorrect errors cannot be hidden forever.

General Managerial Accounting Responses to Uncertainty

Management accountants use a variety of tools to help companies cope with the impact of uncertainty on planning and operations. A few of the key tools are listed in this section. Some are discussed in more detail in other sections.

Capital budgeting decisions often involve large investments and uncertainty about future returns. Chapter 5 discussed some of the tools that companies use to evaluate potential investments. Often, companies react to a more uncertain environment by being more selective on investments, choosing only the least risky projects, or those with the quickest payback period. Organizations in more uncertain environments also tend to use more sophisticated budgeting techniques.[30]

Chapter 5 also discussed budgets. One way companies deal with uncertainty is by using flexible budgets. Flexible budgets adjust the budgeted levels of expenses and expected profits as sales volumes change.

Another way companies deal with uncertainty in the budgeting process is by budgeting some "miscellaneous" or "contingent" expenses. For example, a company rarely knows in advance what repairs will be needed during the next year, but is prudent to budget that something will break, or that there will be bad weather at some point. Individual managers may also try to build "slack" into their budgets, to make it less likely that they will fail to meet the targets.

When considering decisions, companies also perform a variety of "what-if analyses" to examine the impact on future financial statements of a variety of outcomes.

Companies use a variety of procedures to try to manage risks related to fluctuations of key markets. For example, a company may have borrowed at variable interest rates, and may face risks if interest rates rise. Companies may also be hurt if the prices of key commodities change, or if foreign exchange rates move significantly. Management accountants try to track companies' exposure to various types of risk. One tool used is to compute the "value at risk." This is meant to statistically predict the largest loss likely during some specified time period, which has a likelihood of some specified probability. For example, a company may try to keep its one-day, 95% probability value at risk to $3 million.

Manufacturers also face uncertainties in predicting demand. If they are not able to produce all the goods that are demanded, they will lose sales. Companies use different ways of dealing with this uncertainty. Some produce extra inventory during slow periods, in order to have inventory on hand when customer demands peak. Others have a larger production capacity than is needed in normal periods, in order to meet peak demands. Still others make arrangements with other firms that let the company outsource orders in peak periods.

Unresolved Issues and Areas for Further Research

This chapter has discussed a number of different ways that uncertainty and the need to estimate affect accounting. Questions that would benefit from additional research include the following:

1   How useful are the estimates in financial statements to users? Fair value measures tend to be more volatile than historical cost measures. Lev, Li and Sougiannis (2010) noted that while accounting estimates can provide useful forward-looking information to investors, they could also be misleading because of difficulties in estimating and because of managerial misuse of estimates. They point out that: "Given the ever-increasing prevalence of estimates in accounting data, particularly due to the move to fair value accounting, whether these opposing forces result in an improvement in the quality of financial information is among the most fundamental issues in accounting" (p. 779).

2   Are there benefits to conservative accounting? The FASB has stated that, conceptually, it prefers accounting to be neutral. However, many accounting practices remain conservative. There have been different types of research on this question. One strain of research finds that conservatism causes companies' income to be less persistent over time. Less persistent income is typically not valued as highly in the stock market.[31] Another strain of research looks at comparative stock performance of more and less conservative accounting. One study (Francis, Hasan and Wu 2013) reported that during the financial crisis starting in 2008 there was "a significantly positive and economically meaningful relation between conservatism and firm stock performance" (p. 319).

3   How well do users understand the various disclosures that are made of risks and uncertainties? For example, how do users interpret the disclosures of contingent liabilities that are "probable?"

4   Are there better ways to measure the riskiness of certain company positions, such as their investments in derivative securities? For example, the "value at risk" statistic is often used by companies, but some critics have argued that it understates risk, and that this was a factor in

companies making unduly risky investments before the 2007–2008 problems in the financial markets. See Nocera (2009).

Key Terms

Allowance for doubtful accounts—This account modifies the balance of accounts receivable for an estimate of uncollectible accounts. It is increased by bad debt expense and decreased when specific accounts are written off.

Allowance for sales returns—This account modifies the balance of accounts receivable for an estimate of accounts receivable that will not be collected because customers will return items.

Allowance method of computing bad debts—This accounting method requires the company to estimate the amount needed as a general allowance for bad debts and for bad debt expense in the same period as related sales. An alternative method is the direct write-off method.

Bad debt expense—This expense reflects the fact that some accounts receivable will not be collected.

Budgetary slack—Budgetary slack is the difference between the budget target that managers must meet and what the managers really expect to achieve. For example, if a manager convinced the company to adopt a budget that provided $100,000 for telephone expense, which the manager expected to be $80,000, there would be $20,000 of slack.

Change in estimate—This occurs when a company changes its estimate of the value it placed on some asset or liability after it was reported in the financial statements. The effect of changing estimates must be recorded in the period of the change, or over future periods, depending on the nature of the change in estimate.

Concentrations of risk—FASB requires companies to disclose certain risks that are due to the business being focused ("concentrated") in certain areas. For example, a high degree of reliance on a single customer would be a concentration of risk.

Contingent gains and losses—These are matters where some past event has occurred, but the amount that the company will pay or receive depends on some future event. For example, a claim for a tax refund may be contingent upon a court decision.

Depletion—Depletion is an expense recognized as natural resource assets are used up.

Direct write-off method of accounting for bad debts—This accounting method recognizes bad debt expense when the company identifies specific customers who are highly unlikely to pay. This method is not usually allowed under GAAP.

Reserve—This term is sometimes used to describe a liability established for such items as warranty claims or lawsuits.

Salvage value—This is the value that the company expects to obtain at the end of the economic life of a fixed asset.

Value at Risk—This is a statistical measure of the likely maximum loss in some period of time that has an x% probability of occurring. The validity of this measure of risk depends upon various statistical assumptions.

Questions and Problems

Comprehension Questions

C1. (Definitions of assets and liabilities) Explain how the FASB's definitions of assets and liabilities involve a need to estimate future events.

C2. (Neutrality, aggressiveness, and conservatism) Explain the difference between "aggressive," "neutral" and "conservative" accounting.

C3. (Who benefits from conservative accounting?) Which of the following financial statement users would likely be happy with a "conservative" way of measuring net income? Explain.

   A. Managers who are paid bonuses based on earnings
   B. Current shareholders wishing to sell their stock
   C. Potential shareholders seeking to buy stock
   D. Tax authorities
   E. Lenders to the company who make loan decisions based on reported results
   F. Managers who are trying to take a company private, and buy out public shareholders

C4. (General responses to uncertainty—going concern) Explain how the "going concern assumption" relates to the fact that accounting usually does not require companies to use liquidation values to account for assets.

C5. (General response to uncertainty—nonrecognition) In general, what criteria must be met before something is recognized as an asset?

C6. (General response to uncertainty—market prices) Why does the FASB require various assets to be recorded at the "fair value," which is based on market data, but does not require any assets to be recorded at "appraised value"?

C7. (Conservatism) Do the FASB's Concepts Statements favor conservative or neutral accounting? Why?

C8. (Conservatism) Assume a company has a choice between a neutral or a conservative method of recording an asset this year. Explain which method is likely to give rise to higher income:

   A. This year
   B. In following years

C9. (Disclosures) What are some examples of disclosures companies must make about risks and uncertainties?

C10. (Disclosures) Why would financial statement users be concerned if a company disclosed that half of its sales were to a single customer?

C11. (Accounts receivable) What uncertainties affect the measurement of accounts receivable?

C12. (Bad debts) What is the allowance method of accounting for bad debts?

C13. (Bad debts) Explain the difference between the allowance method of accounting for bad debts and the direct write-off method.

C14. (Bad debts) What type of account is the allowance for doubtful accounts? Where is the allowance for doubtful accounts shown on the balance sheet?

C15. (Inventory) What uncertainties affect the measurement of inventory?

C16. (Inventory) What is the "lower of cost or market" rule? Why is this a conservative practice?

C17. (Inventory) What is one reason a company might need to "write down" its inventory from cost to market?

C18. (Inventory) Assume a company has an inventory of items that it bought for $40 each. They can now be sold for only $15 each. Can the company hide the fact that it has a loss on these items by simply not selling them, and continuing to value its inventory at cost? Explain.

C19. (Derivatives) What are derivative securities? What is the general rule for valuing them in accounting?

C20. (Derivatives) What uncertainties affect the valuation of derivatives like options and futures contracts?

C21. (Fixed assets) What uncertainties affect the measurement of fixed assets like factories and equipment?

C22. (Fixed assets) What are some factors affecting the estimated useful life and salvage value of fixed assets?

C23. (Research and development) What is the FASB's general rule regarding accounting for research and development costs? Why do you think it decided on this treatment?

C24. (Research and development) Is the treatment of research and development costs in accounting aggressive, neutral, or conservative? Explain.

C25. (Intangible assets) Is the treatment of intangible assets under GAAP aggressive, neutral, or conservative? Explain.

C26. (IFRS and GAAP) IFRS allows some assets to be revalued upwards. Examples include intangible assets and fixed assets. GAAP does not allow these upward revaluations. Which system is more conservative? Explain.

C27. (Natural resources) What uncertainties affect the measurement of natural resources like oil wells and copper mines?

C28. (Natural resources) What are the normal accounting rules for recording and measuring natural resource assets?

C29. (Contingencies) Explain what is meant by "loss contingencies" and "gain contingencies"?

C30. (Contingencies) Explain the FASB rules for recording:

  A. Liabilities for loss contingencies
  B. Gain contingencies

C31. (Contingencies) Explain whether the FASB requires accrual or disclosure or both for loss contingencies that are:

  A. Remote
  B. Reasonably possible
  C. Probable

C32. (Unasserted claims) What are the criteria for recording a liability for an unasserted claim?

C33. (Uncertain tax positions) Can a company record a benefit for taking an extreme position on its tax returns that has no legal support, because the company believes there is only a 1 in 20 chance of being caught by the IRS? Explain.

C34. (Guarantees) Assume the Reb Company guarantees the debt of the Sac Company. Reb believes there is only a 1% chance of having to pay any money on this guarantee. Does Reb need to record a liability? Explain.

C35. (Pension plans and other post-retirement benefits) What are some significant uncertainties related to companies' promises to pay their employees pensions and other benefits after retirement?

C36. (Pension plans) Why are pension plans a significant issue for managers and analysts?

C37. (Pension plans and other post-retirement benefits) Why did the FASB require that the effects of certain events be shown as part of other comprehensive income, not in net income?

C38. (Revenue recognition) What are the general criteria for recognizing revenue?

C39. (Change of estimates) Under GAAP, if a company learns that its estimate for inventory obsolescence last year was too high, should it revise the previous year's financial statements? Explain.

C40. (Impact of change in estimate) Assume a company estimated that its bad debt expense for 2014 should be $100 million, and established an allowance for bad debts of $100 million. What will be the effect of this estimate on the 2015 income if it turns out that the "correct" amount of bad debt expense for 2014 should have been:

  A. $85 million
  B. $105 million
  C. $100 million

Application Questions

A1. (Bad debt accounting) In 2014, the Holmes Corp. had total accounts receivable of $73 million. At the end of that year, it believes that it will collect all but 2% of this balance. However, it is not yet aware of any customers in particular who are not going to pay.

In 2015, the Holmes Corp. learns that six accounts that existed in 2014, with a total value of $1.3 million, will not be paid. It "writes off" these accounts in 2015. All the rest of the 2014 receivables are collected in 2015.

A.   Under the direct write-off method, what bad debt expense would be recorded in:

    a.   2014
    b.   2015
    c.   The two years combined?

B.   Under the allowance method, what bad debt expense would be recorded in:

    a.   2014
    b.   2015, as it learns of the six bad customers?
    c.   2015, as it learns that the rest of the receivables are collectible?
    d.   The two years combined?

C.   Which method is more conservative?

A2. (Bad debt accounting) The Schnur Company uses the allowance method of accounting for bad debts. In 2014, the Schnur Company had sales of $90 million on credit. Based on its historical experience, it expects that it will collect all but 1% of these amounts. Over the course of the year, it makes entries to record $900,000 of bad debt expense and to increase the allowance for doubtful accounts.

During 2014, it becomes aware of $330,000 of amounts from specific customers that are not collectible.

A.   What will be the balance in the allowance for doubtful accounts at the end of 2014?
B.   Assume that in 2015, it writes off another $400,000 of specific accounts, and collects all of the remaining receivables related to 2014 sales.

    a.   Was the 2014 bad debt expense too high or too low?
    b.   What will be the effect of the 2014 misestimate on 2015 income?

C.   Assume that in 2015, it writes off another $900,000 of specific accounts, and collects all of the remaining receivables related to 2014 sales.

    a.   Was the 2014 bad debt expense too high or too low?
    b.   What will be the effect of the 2014 misestimate on 2015 income?

A3. (Inventory obsolescence) The Cohen Corp. has inventory at a cost of $450 million worth of Model 7 of its popular tablet at the end of fiscal year 2014. It is planning to announce the sale of Model 8 in a month. Once Model 8 is announced, it will not be able to sell Model 7 profitably. It expects that it will only be able to sell the $450 million of inventory for $300 million.

A.   What reserve for inventory obsolescence, if any, should be booked in 2014?
B.   Assume that it records a reserve of $150 million, and sells the inventory for the expected price of $300 million. What will be the expense affecting income in

    a.   2014?

    b.   2015?

    c.   Combined between the two years?

C.   Assume that in 2014, Cohen records a "conservative" reserve for inventory obsolescence of $200 million. In 2015, it sells the inventory for $300 million. What will be the expense affecting income in

    a.   2014?

    b.   2015?

    c.   Combined between the two years?

D.   Assume that in 2014, Cohen records an "aggressive" reserve for inventory obsolescence of $50 million. In 2015, it sells the inventory for $300 million. What will be the expense affecting income in

    a.   2014?

    b.   2015?

    c.   Combined between the two years?

A4. (Contingencies) For each of the situations listed, indicate whether FASB rules would require the company to: accrue a liability; disclose a contingency, but not accrue a liability; both accrue a contingent liability and disclose it; neither accrue nor disclose it. Explain.

A.   The company owns a factory in California. Since California sometimes has earthquakes, how should the company account for the possibility of future earthquake damage?

B.   The company is being sued for labor law violations in previous years. The company believes it is probable it will have to pay, and believes the best estimate of the loss is $8 million.

C.   The company is being sued by a customer who says the company sent defective products. The company believes the products were actually OK, but anything can happen in a lawsuit. The company's lawyers say it is reasonably possible the company could have to pay $1 million.

D.   The company is being sued under the securities laws for misleading financial statements. The company's lawyers say the chance of losing the case is remote.

E.   One of the company's factories exploded on December 30. 15 people were killed. No one has actually sued yet, but the company's lawyers say that lawsuits are highly likely to come, and the company will probably have to pay damages of from $50 to $80 million. All numbers within that range are equally likely.

F.   Same as point E above, but the attorneys say it is just too early to make any reliable estimate of the likely amount the company will have to pay.

A5. (Contingencies) The Schwalb Corp. is involved in several lawsuits. For each case below, indicate if it is required to: accrue an asset; accrue a liability; make no accrual, but make a disclosure; make neither a disclosure nor an accrual. Explain.

A.   It is suing the Wu Corp. for $15 million. Schwalb's attorneys say a victory in court is probable, and that it will likely get $12 million on this lawsuit.

B.   It is suing the Thomas Corp. for $10 million. Schwalb's attorneys say that a victory in court is reasonably possible, and that if it wins it will most likely get between $3 and $9 million.

C. The Chen Corp. is suing Schwalb for $50 million. Schwalb's attorneys say the chance of losing this suit is so small as to be remote.

D. The Nehru Corp. is suing Schwalb for $32 million. Schwalb's attorneys say it is reasonably possible that Schwalb will lose, but the amount of the loss cannot be reasonably estimated.

E. Six employees are suing Schwalb for violating labor laws. Schwalb's lawyers believe that Schwalb will probably lose $12 million.

A6. (Contingencies) The Kuttner Corp. is sued in 2014 for violating patent laws. In 2014, the Kuttner Corp. decides that a loss is probable, and records an expense of $23 million. What is the effect on income in 2016 if the case is settled in that year for:

A. $23 million
B. $20 million
C. $30 million?

A7. (Warranty accounting) The Kaufman Car Company sells cars with a warranty that they will work properly. Based on its historic experience, it expects the cost of honoring this warranty to be about 1% of sales. In 2014, it makes $500 million of sales. Assume all the warranties for these cars expire at the end of 2016. The actual costs to fix the cars was $1,700,000 in 2014, $2,000,000 in 2015, and $1,200,000 in 2016. What expense would the company record:

A. In 2014, as it sells the cars?
B. In 2014, as it pays the $1,700,000 in claims?
C. In 2015, as it pays the $2,000,000 in claims?
D. In 2016, as it pays the $1,200,000 in claims?
E. At the end of 2016, when the warranties expire?
F. In total, over the 2014–2016 period?

A8. (Warranty accounting) The Snyder Company sells equipment with a warranty that it will work properly. Based on its historic experience, it expects the cost of honoring this warranty to be about 2% of sales. In 2014, it makes $300 million of sales. Assume all the warranties expire at the end of 2015. The actual costs to fix the equipment were $2,800,000 in 2014 and $3,300,000 in 2015.

A. What is the effect of the decision to record warranty expense in 2014 on Snyder's assets, liabilities, and equity for 2014? Is income affected?
B. What is the effect of paying the 2014 claims on Snyder's assets, liabilities, and equity in 2014? Is income affected by paying the claims?
C. What is the effect of paying the 2015 claims on Snyder's assets, liabilities, and equity in 2015? Is income affected by paying the claims?
D. What is the effect of the warranties expiring in 2015 on Snyder's assets, liabilities, and equity in 2015? Is 2015 income affected? (Hint—when the warranties expire, the warranty reserve needs to be adjusted down to zero)
E. Over the course of two years, what did Snyder show as warranty expenses?
F. Over the course of two years, how much cash did Snyder pay for warranty costs?

A9. (Research and development) The Rosen Company spends $30 million on a research project. How much of this spending can be recognized as an asset if:

A. The chance of having a successful product is 40%, with profits of $600 million if the project is successful?

B.   The chance of a successful project is 90%, with profits of $40 million if the project is successful?

C.   The chance of making a successful project is 10%, but the profits if it is successful will be $1 billion?

A10. (Software costs—one project) FASB rules allow a company to record amounts spent developing software to be recorded as an asset after the project has reached the stage of "technical feasibility." Any software assets have to be amortized over the expected life of the software product. Both Alpha Corp. and Beta Corp. spent $120 million on a project in 2014, and developed products with a useful life of three years. Alpha says that technological feasibility was reached very late, and expenses the $120 million. Beta says technological feasibility was established early, and records all $120 million as an asset. Assume both companies start selling their product on January 1, 2015.

A.   What expense will Alpha record:

   a.   In 2014
   b.   In 2015
   c.   In 2016
   d.   In 2017
   e.   In total, from 2014 through 2017?

B.   What expense will Beta record:

   a.   In 2014
   b.   In 2015
   c.   In 2016
   d.   In 2017
   e.   In total, from 2014 through 2017?

C.   Which method is more conservative?

A11. (Software costs—multiple projects) This is a variation of the preceding problem. In that problem, both companies had a single project. This problem assumes the companies have a new project every year. This is more like the position of real software development companies.

Assume that Alpha and Beta both began operations in 2010. Each year from 2010 through 2014, they spent $120 million on software projects. Alpha always expenses the costs in the year they are spent. Beta always amortizes the costs over three years, beginning in the year after it made the expenditures. After 2014, both companies stop spending on new software.

A.   Fill out the following chart:

Year	Spending	Alpha expense	Beta expense
2010	$120 million		
2011	$120 million		
2012	$120 million		
2013	$120 million		
2014	$120 million		
2015	0		
2016	0		
2017	0		

B. Which company would have higher income in:

    a. 2010
    b. 2015
    c. 2017?

C. In 2014, which company would likely have a higher return on equity? (From Chapter 4, return on equity = net income ÷ average shareholders' equity. This means that return on equity depends on the equity as well as the income.)

A12. (Pensions) Under FASB rules, explain whether the full effect of each of the following factors that affect the pension plan is shown in net income, or whether part of the effect is in "other comprehensive income."

A. Employees worked during the year, and the company's actuaries say that the "service cost" related to their work increased the present value of the pension liability by $30 million.

B. Because more of the employees have become very stressed, they have started smoking heavily. The company's actuaries have changed their estimates, and believe that the employees will die sooner, and therefore have decreased their estimate of the pension liability by $40 million.

C. The pension liability was stated last year at its present value. Over the course of the year, the obligation has come one year nearer to having to be paid. The "interest costs" of discounting the liability less is $5 million.

D. The pension plan has investments in the stock market. This year the stock market rose much more than the normal 5% earnings expected by the actuaries.

A13. (Pensions) Navistar International makes a variety of vehicles, including farm equipment. It has various defined benefit pension plans. Table 8.3 shows its statement of comprehensive income for the three years ended in October 2012 to 2014. The schedule is from the company's Form 10-K. Because the income was negative each year, it is titled a statement of comprehensive loss.

The items in this statement related to pensions largely relate to changes in estimates made by the actuaries.

A. What was the effect of the pension plans on comprehensive income in 2013?

B. What was the net loss in 2013 on the income statement?

C. What would the net loss have been on the income statement if all effects of pension plans were shown in net income?

Table 8.3 Navistar International Consolidated Statements of Comprehensive Loss (USD $)

In millions, unless otherwise specified	12 months ended October 31		
	2014	2013	2012
Net loss	$ (619)	$ (898)	$ (3,010)
Other comprehensive income (loss):			
Foreign currency translation adjustment	(52)	(51)	(125)
Unrealized gain on marketable securities	1	0	0
Defined benefit plans (net of tax of $(2), $(233), and $14)	(388)	552	(256)
Total other comprehensive income (loss)	(439)	501	(381)
Total comprehensive loss	$ (1,058)	$ (397)	$ (3,391)

D. Would the net loss on the income statement have been significantly different in each year if the full effect of pension plans had to be shown in net income? Explain.

A14. (Tax—uncertain positions) Tori Corp. has taken several different positions on its tax returns. Under FASB rules, indicate if it can show a benefit for these positions in its financial statements:

A. The law is unclear as to whether certain entertainment expenses are deductible. Some other companies are currently suing, and courts will decide on the issue soon. Tori deducted them. An IRS agent has noticed the deduction, and is questioning it. Tori's accountants believe that there is a 40% chance that when the courts decide, the deduction will be allowable.

B. Same as "A," but Tori has not yet been audited by the IRS, and believes there is only a 10% chance that it will be audited.

C. Same as "A," but Tori's accountants believe there is a 75% chance the courts will allow the deduction.

D. The law says that only half of the cost of business meals is deductible. Tori has deducted 100% of the cost. Tori believes that the odds of the IRS auditing companies of its size are only 1 in 20.

Discussion Questions

D1. (Conservatism) Early in the 20th century, the main providers of capital to U.S. corporations were banks and other lenders. Later, the sale of stock grew in importance. How do you think that shift may have influenced the desirability of conservative methods of accounting?

D2. (Conservatism) In the U.S., the idea of conservatism in accounting was taken for granted by many people. However, conservative accounting has not always been accepted. After the end of the civil war in China in 1949, the new rulers established a communist economic system and needed a new accounting system. The idea of using conservatism was apparently rejected, with the new rulers seeing conservative accounting as a way that business owners hid profits from workers and from tax authorities. Is there any fairness in this view?

D3. (Nonrecognition) The FASB sometimes deals with uncertainty by not recognizing certain items in the financial statements. This uncertainty may explain the rule that companies cannot record their expenditures on internally developed intangibles as assets. However, in other cases the RASB requires companies to record highly uncertain amounts as liabilities. For example, the estimates of what companies will have to pay for post-retirement medical benefits are very uncertain. Is there a good reason for the different treatments of these two items?

D4. (Impact of accounting policies vary with the company's growth) Both Microsoft and Google report in their Form 10-Ks that they basically expense all software costs when incurred. Why do you think they may choose to do this, rather than to try to record some of their software costs as assets?

(Hint—Look at application question A11. In this question, two different companies use different policies for accounting for software costs. One immediately expenses its costs, but the other amortizes them over three years. If you work through the question, you will see that the company that immediately expenses its costs has higher costs in its early years, while it is growing; the same costs in a period of stability; and lower costs in the later, declining years. Also, because it had lower income in the early years, the company that immediately recognized its software costs as expense shows higher return on equity in later years.)

D5. (Contingencies) Let's assume that a company is being sued. The company's auditor asks the lawyer who is defending the company what the odds are of losing the case, and what the company is likely to have to pay. The lawyer says: "I am not going to answer that question. If I tell you the likely settlement is $10 million, you will put that in the financial statements, and then the people who are suing are going to know we think they will win, so they won't drop the suit. What is worse, we will have zero chance of settling the lawsuit for a low amount. The other side will take $10 million as a starting point for their negotiations. Your footnote will cost the company, which is my client, money."

    A.   Do you think the lawyer has a point?
    B.   What is the purpose of disclosing contingencies?
    C.   Do you see any way to resolve the different needs of the outside investors for information with the concerns of the company's attorney?

D6. (Contingencies and uncertain tax positions) Normally, a company will not record a liability for an unasserted claim unless it is probable that the claim will be asserted, and that the company will end up paying. The FASB's rules on uncertain tax positions are different, because the accountant must assume that the IRS will notice the position and will challenge it. Do you think this difference in rules makes sense?

D7. (Contingencies—IFRS and GAAP) The IASB has defined "probable" to mean more than a 50% chance. The FASB has not given any exact definition of the term "probable." As was noted in the chapter, various researchers have done studies of what auditors and other accountants think is "probable." In these studies, the threshold between "reasonably possible" and "probable" is typically over 60%. Do you think that the FASB should adopt the IASB's definition of what is "probable"? Why, or why not?

D8. (Natural resources) For the Exxon Corporation:

    A.   Look up the market value of Exxon stock as of the end of the last year.
    B.   Find Exxon's Form 10-K, and compute the "book value" of the outstanding shares. To do this, divide the shareholder's equity by the number of shares outstanding.
    C.   Which is larger, the market or the book value?
    D.   What factors in the accounting for natural resources might help explain this difference?

D9. (Intangible assets) For Google Corp.:

    A.   Look up the market value of its common stock as of the end of the last year.
    B.   Find its 10-K, and compute the "book value" of the outstanding shares. To do this, divide the shareholder's equity by the number of shares outstanding.
    C.   Which is larger, the market or the book value?
    D.   What factors in the accounting for intangible assets might help explain this difference?

Notes

1 This has been attributed to a variety of people, including Confucius, Mark Twain, and Will Rogers.
2 See Ball, Cummins, and Bahree (2005).
3 "Neuroeconomic research suggests a strong pattern of brain behavior consistent with the principle of conservatism; specifically, the brain processes gains and losses differentially." (Dickhaut et al. 2010, p. 243).
4 Robert Montgomery, in *Journal of Accountancy*, as cited by Vangermeersch (1979).
5 See Tinker (1985).
6 Some scholars have argued that in order for financial statements to show neutral measurements, one must consider both the actions of managers and the accounting rules. If managers tend to be biased

upwards in their estimates of income, then these scholars say that the accounting rules need to have an opposite bias to counteract the management bias. Thus, they argue that conservative accounting rules are needed to arrive at neutral reports. This argument is clearly stated in Gao (2013). For another study indicating managers tend to be overconfident in their estimates, see Ahmed and Duellman (2013).

7 See Barth (2006).

8 See Section 985-20-25 of the FASB Codification.

9 See Section F350-40-25-2 of the FASB Codification.

10 Footnotes for Microsoft Corp., Adobe Systems and Google Inc. were similar in indicating no material amounts were shown as assets.

11 Per statistics on http://online.wsj.com/mdc/public/page/mdc_commodities.html?mod=mdc_topnav_2_3012 (last accessed August 18, 2015).

12 See Thaler (1988). "The winner's curse is a concept that was first discussed in the literature by three Atlantic Richfield engineers, Capen, Clapp, and Campbell (1971). The idea is simple. Suppose many oil companies are interested in purchasing the drilling rights to a particular parcel of land. Let's assume that the rights are worth the same amount to all bidders, that is, the auction is what is called a common value auction. Further, suppose that each bidding firm obtains an estimate of the value of the rights from its experts. Assume that the estimates are unbiased, so the mean of the estimates is equal to the common value of the tract. What is likely to happen in the auction? Given the difficulty of estimating the amount of oil in a given location, the estimates of the experts will vary substantially, some far too high and some too low. Even if companies bid somewhat less than the estimate their expert provided, the firms whose experts provided high estimates will tend to bid more than the firms whose experts guessed lower. Indeed, it may occur that the firm that wins the auction will be the one whose experts provided the highest estimates. If this happens, the winner of the auction is likely to be a loser. The winner can be said to be "cursed" in one of two ways: (1) the winning bid exceeds the value of the tract, so the firm loses money; or (2) the value of the tract is less than the expert's estimate so the winning firm is disappointed." (p. 192).

13 FASB Codification, 450-30-50.

14 FASB Codification, 450-20-05-05.

15 FASB Codification, 450-20-20.

16 See also Harrison and Tomassini (1989).

17 FASB Codification, 450-20-20.

18 One experimental study found that the probability threshold that auditors used depended on the magnitude of the item that was being considered. As the magnitude of the item increased, the mean threshold for their subjects fell from 40% to 13%. See Raghunandan, Grimlund and Schpanski (1991). Harrison and Tomassini (1989) found a mean threshold of 16% for items to be "reasonably possible."

19 FASB Codification, 450-20-50-6.

20 FASB Codification, 740-10-25-6. The amount of benefit recognized is the largest amount that meets the "more likely than not standard."

21 See Blouin, and Robinson (2011).

22 See FASB Codification, Section 460-10-25-6. There are, however, different rules for warranties that are sold separately from the products. Under the newly issued revenue recognition rules, contained in FASB Codification, Section 606-10-55-34, separately sold warranties would be seen as a separate "performance obligation" requiring the company to stand ready to fix the items for some period of time. Instead of recognizing a "warranty liability," the company would record "unearned revenue" or "deferred revenue" at the time of selling this warranty. It would recognize revenue over the warranty period. It would also recognize expenses as it had to fix broken items.

23 FASB Codification, Section 460-10-25-4.

24 FASB Codification, Section 715-30-35-20.

25 Beckerman and Monga (2015). The article says that about 30 companies choose to report the full impact of pension changes in current income. As another example, a January 22, 2015 earnings release by Verizon, which also reports the full impact of pension assumption changes in earnings, reported that without such factors, its fourth quarter earnings per share for 2013 and 2014 would have increased from 66 cents to 71 cents, but that, because there were positive changes in pension estimates in 2013 and negative ones in 2014, the GAAP figures dropped from earnings of $1.76 in 2013 to a loss of 56 cents per share in the fourth quarter of 2014. See www.verizon.com/about/news/verizon-reports-high-quality-customer-additions-4q-caps-year-position-drive-continued/ (last accessed August 18, 2015).

26 The FASB allowed companies to record the liability over a period of years, giving them some time to place offsetting assets in trust before they had to start showing the liability for these post-employment benefits. See SFAS No. 106.

27 FASB Codification 606-10-05-04(c).

28 See Accounting Principles Board Opinion No. 20. "Restating financial statements of prior periods may dilute public confidence in financial statements and may confuse those who use them." Available at http://clio.lib.olemiss.edu/cdm/ref/collection/aicpa/id/367 (last accessed August 18, 2015).

29 From BP Group Form 10-K for 2010. 10-K Forms can be sourced at: www.sec.gov/edgar/searchedgar/companysearch.html (last accessed August 14, 2015).

30 See Verbeeten (2006).

31 See Chen et al. (2013). See also Basu (1997).

References

Ahmed, A. S., & Duellman, S. (2013). Managerial overconfidence and accounting conservatism. *Journal of Accounting Research*, *51*(1), 1–30.

AICPA. (2011). *Accounting Trends and Techniques*. New York: AICPA.

Ball, J., Cummins, C., & Bahree, B. (2005, February 24). Big oil differs with SEC on methods to calculate the industry's reserves. *Wall Street Journal*, C1, C3.

Barth, M. E. (2006). Including estimates of the future in today's financial statements. *Accounting Horizons*, *20*(3), 271–85.

Barth, M. E., Clement, M. B., Foster, G., & Kasznik, R. (1998). Brand values and capital market valuation. *Review of Accounting Studies*, *3*(1–2), 41–68.

Basu, S. (1997). The conservatism principle and the asymmetric timeliness of earnings. *Journal of Accounting and Economics*, *24*, 3–37.

Beckerman, J. & Monga, V. (2015, January 20). AT&T to take $7.9 billion pension hit. *Wall Street Journal*. Retrieved from http://www.wsj.com/articles/at-t-estimates-some-fourth-quarter-charges-1421449286 (last accessed August 18, 2015).

Biondi, Y., Glover, J., Jamal, K., Ohlson, J. A., Penman, S. H., Sunder, S., & Tsujiyama, E. (2012). Some conceptual tensions in financial reporting: American Accounting Association's Financial Accounting Standards Committee (FASC). *Accounting Horizons*, *26*(1), 125–33.

Blouin, J., & Robinson, L. (2011). Academic research on FIN 48: What have we learned? Prepared for the *Financial Accounting Foundation's Post-Implementation Review of Financial Accounting Standards Board Interpretation* (48), 1–41.

Butrica, B. A., Iams, H. M., Smith, K. E., & Toder, E. J. (2009). The disappearing defined benefit pension and its potential impact on the retirement incomes of baby boomers. *Social Security Bulletin*, *69*(3), 1–27.

Chen, L. H., Folsom, D. M., Paek, W., & Sami, H. (2013). Accounting conservatism, earnings persistence, and pricing multiples on earnings. *Accounting Horizons*, *28*(2), 233–60.

Dickhaut, J., Basu, S., McCabe, K., & Waymire, G. (2010). Neuroaccounting: Consilience between the biologically evolved brain and culturally evolved accounting principles. *Accounting Horizons*, *24*(2), 221–55.

FASB. (1980). Statement of Financial Accounting Concepts No. 2, *Qualitative Characteristics of Accounting Information*. Stamford, CT: FASB.

FASB. (1984). Statement of Financial Accounting Concepts No. 5, *Recognition and Measurement in Financial Statements of Business Enterprises*. Stamford, CT: FASB.

FASB. (1985). Statement of Financial Accounting Concepts No. 6, *Elements of Financial Statements*. Stamford, CT: FASB.

FASB. (2010). Statement of Financial Accounting Concepts No. 8, Conceptual Framework for Financial Reporting—Chapter 1, *The Objective of General Purpose Financial Reporting*, and Chapter 3, *Qualitative Characteristics of Useful Financial Information* (a replacement of FASB Concepts Statements No. 1 and No. 2) (pp. 1–14, 16–22). Norwalk, CT: FASB.

Francis, B., Hasan, I., & Wu, Q. (2013). The benefits of conservative accounting to shareholders: Evidence from the financial crisis. *Accounting Horizons*, *27*(2), 319–46.

Gao, P. (2013). A measurement approach to conservatism and earnings management. *Journal of Accounting and Economics*, *55*(2), 251–68.

Harrison, K. E., & Tomassini, L. A. (1989). Judging the probability of a contingent loss: An empirical study. *Contemporary Accounting Research*, *5*(2), 642–8.

Lev, B., & Sougiannis, T. (1996). The capitalization, amortization, and value-relevance of R&D. *Journal of Accounting and Economics*, *21*(1), 107–38.

Lev, B., Li, S., & Sougiannis, T. (2010). The usefulness of accounting estimates for predicting cash flows and earnings. *Review of Accounting Studies*, *15*(4), 779–807.

Levitt, A. (2002). *Take on the Street: What Wall St. and Corporate America Don't Want You to Know/What You Can Do to Fight Back*. Random House LLC.

MacNeal, K. (1939). *Truth in Accounting*. Houston, Texas: Scholars Book Co.

Nichols, D. C., & Wahlen, J. M. (2004). How do earnings numbers relate to stock returns? A review of classic accounting research with updated evidence. *Accounting Horizons*, *18*(4), 263–86.

Nix, P. E., & Nix, D. E. (1992). A Historical Review of the Accounting Treatment of Research and Development Costs. *The Accounting Historians Journal*, 51–78.

Nocera, J. (2009, January 4). Risk Mismanagement. *The New York Times Magazine*. Retrieved from www.nytimes.com/2009/01/04/magazine/04risk-t.html?pagewanted=all (last accessed August 18, 2015).

O'Donnell, Jr., K. (1993). How Thor Power Tool Hammered Publishing. Retrieved from www.sfwa.org/2005/01/how-thor-power-hammered-publishing/ (last accessed August 18, 2015). First published in the *Bulletin of Science Fiction and Fantasy Writers of America*, *27*(1).

Raghunandan, K., Grimlund, R. A., & Schpanski, A. (1991). Auditor evaluation of loss contingencies. *Contemporary Accounting Research*, *7*(2), 549–69.

Skinner, D. J. (2008). Accounting for intangibles—a critical review of policy recommendations. *Accounting and Business Research*, *38*(3), 191–204.

Thaler, R. H. (1988). Anomalies: The winner's curse. *The Journal of Economic Perspectives*, *2*(1), 191–202.

Tinker, T. (1985). *Paper Prophets: A Social Critique of Accounting*. NY: Praeger Publishers.

Vangermeersch, R. (1979). 36 classic articles from the 1905–1930 issues of the Journal of Accountancy. Working Paper No. 12. In E. N. Coffman (Ed.), *The Academy of Accounting Historians Working Paper Series Vol. 1 (Working Papers 1–20)*. Richmond, VA: Virginia Commonwealth University.

Verbeeten, F. H. (2006). Do organizations adopt sophisticated capital budgeting practices to deal with uncertainty in the investment decision? A research note. *Management Accounting Research*, *17*(1), 106–20.

9   Allocations in Financial Reporting

Outline

- Preliminary Thoughts
- Learning Objectives
- The Allocation Problem in Accounting
- Allocations Affecting Revenues
- Allocations Affecting Expenses
- Allocations of Tax Expenses and Benefits
- Allocations Among Related Entities
- Impact of Improper Allocations
- Unresolved Issues and Areas for Further Research

Preliminary Thoughts

And from the beginning there was a contradiction between the continuity assumption and the periodicity assumption. . . . The one tells us to look at operations as a continuous flow; the other says we must break this flow into comparable time segments. The root of the period problem is that in assigning revenues and expenses to time intervals, the accountant is doing something that is absolutely necessary but is at the same time quite arbitrary and artificial.

Michael Chatfield (1977, p. 98)

Nine tenths of the problems of the accountant are due to this demand to express results in terms of years. The accountant is wrestling with it. That it has not been solved is apparent to anyone who opens a text on the subject or enters into the intricacies of the income tax.

A. C. Littleton (1933, p. 11)

Most of the figures generated by accounting systems are the results of allocations. Accountants always allocate the cost of nonmonetary inputs to one or more years, and to one or more organizational activities. . . . There appears to be an implicit assumption in almost all of this literature that allocation of some sort will always be appropriate. However, in most circumstances where the accountant might wish to allocate a cost or revenue a number of conflicting allocation methods might be available to him, each of which is no more and no less defensible than any other.

American Accounting Association Committee on Foundations of Accounting Measurement (1971, p. 8)

Present research indicates that most accounting allocations of costs and revenues are arbitrary.

American Accounting Association Committee on Foundations of Accounting Measurement (1971, p. 23)

It is this inconsistent and arbitrary nature of accounting practices which pushes bright students toward other disciplines where logic plays a more basic role.

American Accounting Association Committee on Foundations of
Accounting Measurement (1971, p. 45)

These five quotations help frame the topic of this chapter. Michael Chatfield points out that one of the key assumptions of accounting is that businesses are continuing concerns. We have seen the "going concern" assumption before, in Chapters 2 and 8. However, accountants are also required to report results of operations in particular periods. In order to report on the income of a period, they must try to separate ("*allocate*") the effects of certain events on particular months or years. You will see in this chapter that accountants may also have to allocate money between various products or items, as well as between time periods. The next three quotations all indicate that no good solution to this "allocation problem" has been found. The final quotation suggests that people who insist on perfect answers to problems like this may not want to become accountants!

Learning Objectives

After studying the material in this chapter, you should understand:

1   The need for allocation to different time periods in accounting
2   Typical ways accountants allocate revenues between time periods and among products
3   Methods of allocating the costs of long-term operating assets to expenses through depreciation, depletion, and amortization
4   Methods for allocating prepaid assets and deferred costs to income over time
5   How income taxes are allocated to particular time periods and to different types of income
6   How expenses are allocated among related entities
7   That improper allocations can lead to incorrect decisions and can be related to earnings management.

The Allocation Problem in Accounting

The "Allocation Problem"

"*Allocation*" is a process of taking one total number, and dividing that total into parts which we then associate with particular time periods, or with particular products, or with other particular things we are interested in. Here are some examples:

•   A company buys a machine that will be used to produce its products for several years. How should the cost of the machine be divided and assigned to particular time periods? Or should the cost of the machine be allocated to items sold, not to time periods?
•   A company like Starbucks rents a store location. Should it allocate a little piece of the cost of rent to each cup of coffee sold?
•   A company works on providing a service or product for a client over a period of several months. It gets one payment for this project. How much of the payment should be considered revenue in each month?
•   A food processing company buys large amounts of cotton seeds. It crushes the seeds, and gets both cotton seed oil and cotton seed meal. It sells these two products separately. How much of the cost of the cotton seeds should be allocated to the cotton seed oil, and how much to the cotton seed meal? There are many examples of production processes

where a single "joint" input is used to produce more than one product. Chapter 10 discusses this issue.

Historically, the problem was not important when most businesses had short lives, but became important once businesses began investing in expensive assets that would last for many years. For example, when the British East India Company was formed in 1600, it invested in ships and also in buildings and forts in India. It faced the problem of trying to decide how much its profits were each year. The company needed to decide how much of the costs of its buildings and forts were expenses in the year they were built, and how much cost should be allocated to the other years when they were used. According to Frederick Gamble, as quoted in Coffman (1979) the first book recommending allocating income and expense into the accounting periods to which they pertained was written by Lodovico Flori, in 1636.

Unfortunately, there is no theoretically best way to allocate costs among time periods or between items. Therefore, accounting uses arbitrary rules to deal with these situations. The American Accounting Association committee that looked at this problem in 1971 defined "arbitrary" measurement to exist when: another numeral could have been assigned; the choice of numerals affects the economic decision; and no conclusive argument is used to defend the numeral actually chosen. It said that "Unfortunately, many of the accounting's . . . measurements are arbitrary. For example, any assignment of joint costs to two or more resulting products is arbitrary" (American Accounting Association 1971, p. 23).

Methods of Dealing With the Allocation Problem

The accounting standard-setters have responded to the problem by defining certain methods of allocation that are allowed in certain areas. For example, they specify certain acceptable methods of depreciation and ways of treating costs of inventory. Companies can choose among the acceptable alternatives. FASB typically requires companies to disclose what policies they use and to use allocation methods consistently from year to year.[1]

How should individual accountants who work for companies choose an allocation method? The AAA committee (1971) gave the following practical advice:

- If only one allocation method is in current use, do what everybody else does. (For example, a company that purchases insurance for three years will usually recognize the same expense each month each for 36 months. This is what everyone does.)
- If a limited choice exists, and one helps the organization (e.g. for tax purposes) use the one that helps the company.
- If a limited choice exists, with equal results to the company, use the one with lowest clerical cost.[2]
- The hard cases are when varying methods exist, and different parties are affected differently. "No general solutions exist, nor do any appear to be immediately forthcoming. The best that the accountant can do is to accept the results of negotiation or the choice of the dominant party among the contending interests, i.e. trim his sails to the prevailing winds. This is not a satisfactory answer" (American Accounting Association 1971, p. 37).

The AAA committee (1971) also strongly recommended that companies be *consistent* in whatever practices they adopted. They noted that inconsistent accounting methods "make people distrust accounting and create more disputes on the distribution of payoffs" (American Accounting Association 1971, p. 45).

The hope is that if users understand what companies are doing, the users can make appropriate decisions. The danger is that users will not fully understand the nature of the allocations, and will be misled into bad decisions.

Allocations Affecting Revenues

Introductory Comments

For some modern companies the process of earning revenues has numerous steps, which can take months or years to complete. Steps might include: designing a product; finding a buyer; making the product; delivering the product; collecting cash; and providing services such as technical support or repairs to the customer after delivery. The accounting issue is when in this process to recognize revenue: at the beginning; during the process; or at the end? For other companies, a single deal with a customer may involve numerous products or services that the company must deliver at different times. How should the customer payment be divided among the various products and services?

Here are some examples:

1   A cattle rancher owns animals which take about two years to grow and become ready for sale. Their economic value gets bigger as they grow. Should the rancher wait to recognize revenues until the animals are sold, or should the rancher recognize some revenue each month as the cattle grow bigger?

2   A computer services company sells its client a new software package, which it delivers immediately, and also promises its client free upgrades for three years as well as technical support help for three years. There is one price for this whole package of services. How much of this price should be allocated to the day the company sold the package, and how much must wait to be recognized until the company delivers the upgrade services and the computer technical support services?

3   L.L. Bean sells shoes and clothing and other products over the internet. It allows people to return clothes and shoes that do not fit. Should it recognize revenue on its sales: when people order the shoes and give their credit card payments; when L.L. Bean delivers the shoes; or when it is sure people will not return the shoes?

4   A construction company agrees to build a bridge over the Hudson River for the State of New York for $5 billion. The project is expected to take three years. How much revenue should be recognized when the contract is signed, how much should be recognized as the work is done, and how much should be recognized when the job is finished?

Revenue recognition policies can have a major effect on companies' reported results. Remember that stock analysts are often interested in growth in revenues. They also look at such measures as asset turnover and profit margin, which are affected by how revenues are measured.

General Rules Related to Revenue Recognition

Because analysts care about reported revenues, managers have incentives to do "earnings management" on revenues. Studies of accounting frauds indicate that about half involve revenue recognition issues. Therefore, the SEC, FASB and IASB have made numerous rules related to when revenues are recognized. Chapters 2 and 8 have discussed the revenue recognition rules. To review, the basic GAAP criteria for recognizing revenues are that revenue should not be recognized until:

* An earnings process is substantially complete, and
* The revenue is "realized or realizable."

In practice, an earnings process is normally considered not substantially complete until a service has been delivered to the customers. Where numerous products are sold at once, part of the revenue is recognized when each service or product is delivered.

The second part of the FASB's revenue recognition rule means the company must be able to reasonably estimate how much it will collect from customers. The company may have to wait on recognizing revenue, even if it has delivered the products, under certain circumstances:

- Payment is unpredictable. In some cases, companies give generous credit terms, and can't predict how much customers will actually pay. In these circumstances, the company must delay recognizing revenue until cash is received.
- The likelihood of the customer returning the product is unpredictable but expected to be high.

The SEC staff (SEC 1999) interprets the GAAP rules to mean that revenue should only be recognized when all four of the following conditions are satisfied:

- There is persuasive evidence that there is actually an agreement between the buyer and seller. The SEC was worried about situations where a company made a product with a particular customer in mind, but that customer had not yet actually ordered the product.
- Delivery has occurred or services have been rendered. The SEC was concerned that some companies were recognizing revenues before they had actually finished the earnings process by delivering the goods.
- The seller's price is fixed or determinable. The SEC was worried that companies were reporting revenues based on estimates of what the sales price would be, before the sales price was actually agreed upon.
- Collectibility is reasonably assured.

Basic Situation—One Product, One Payment

This is the simplest situation. A company sells a single product to a customer, in return for a single payment. As long as collectibility is reasonably estimable, the company recognizes revenue when the product is delivered to the customer. For example, a book publisher would recognize revenue on a book sold to Barnes & Noble when it ships the books to Barnes & Noble. It normally does not matter if the customer has paid in advance, or agrees to pay later. In each case, revenue is recognized when the product is delivered.[3]

Chapter 8, in discussing uncertainty, indicated that sometimes there is major uncertainty about whether customers will pay and whether they will return goods they don't want. Normally, this does not stop a company from recognizing revenue at the time of sale. Instead, companies set up "allowances for doubtful accounts" and "allowances for sales returns" to avoid overstating their income and receivables.

Situation 2—One Product, Delivered at Start, Payments in Installments Over Time

General

In this situation, the company is giving the customer one product, and will be paid in installments over time. For example, a company may sell furniture to customers on an "installment plan" that allows customers to pay in equal monthly payments over three years. The issue here is how much of the revenue should be recognized at the time the furniture is delivered, which is the date the customer makes the first payment.

If the company can reliably estimate the collectibility of its receivables, it should record the revenues as of the date it delivers the furniture. It should also record an expense for the cost of the furniture.

The complication comes when the company cannot reliably estimate collections. In those situations, two other accounting methods have been used in the past, the "*installment method*" and the "*cost recovery method.*" The "*cost recovery method*" is also called the "*deposit method.*" Box 9.1 provides an example of how a sale would be treated under these three methods. In Box 9.1, a machine that cost $9 million is sold at a price of $12 million during Year 1. The $12 million will be paid in four installments, received during Years 1, 2, 3, and 4. We are ignoring payments for

---

Box 9.1 Example of Revenue Recognition—Three Methods

Situation

The Gao Corp. sold a large piece of equipment to the Scodes Corp. for $12 million during Year 1. The equipment had cost Gao $9 million. Scodes promises to pay in four installments, of $3 million each, from Year 1 through Year 4. (Also assume that Scodes pays additional interest payments in return for being given four years to pay.) What gross revenue and gross profit will be recorded each year?

Time of sale recognition

The revenue in Year 1 = $12 million
Cost of sales in Year 1 = $9 million
Gross profit in Year 1 = $3 million
There is no revenue, cost of sales, or gross profit related to this sale in Years 2, 3, or 4.

Installment method

Expected gross profit on the sale = $12 million revenues − $9 million cost of sales = $3 million.
  Gross profit needs to be allocated to each payment.
  Each yearly payment is $3 million, which is 25% of the $12 million total expected revenues.
  Therefore, 25% of the revenue, cost, and gross profit are recorded each year. As a result:

	Revenue	Cost of sales	Gross profit
Year 1	3,000,000	2,250,000	750,000
Year 2	3,000,000	2,250,000	750,000
Year 3	3,000,000	2,250,000	750,000
Year 4	3,000,000	2,250,000	750,000
Totals	$12,000,000	$9,000,000	$3,000,000

Cost recovery method

Under this method, equal amounts of revenue and cost of sales are recognized until after the total cash payments equal the cost of the items. In this example, at the end of Year 3 the total collections = $9 million, which is exactly equal to the cost of the equipment. This means no gross profits are recognized until Year 4. In Year 4, the $3 million installment payment is revenue, and there are no more costs to record.

	Revenue	Cost of sales	Gross profit
Year 1	3,000,000	3,000,000	0
Year 2	3,000,000	3,000,000	0
Year 3	3,000,000	3,000,000	0
Year 4	3,000,000	0	3,000,000
Totals	$12,000,000	$9,000,000	$3,000,000

interest—any interest earned would be separately accounted for. Under normal accounting, the revenue and cost of sales would both be recognized at the time of sale, resulting in Year 1 gross profits of $3 million. Under the installment and cost recovery methods, some of the gross profit is recognized later.

Installment Method

In this method, a portion of the revenue and the cost of the sale are recognized as each installment is received. The process is as follows:

- The company decides what the total revenues, cost of sales, and gross profits are that it expects on the installment sales made in the year. In the example in Box 9.1, total revenues are expected to be $12 million, total costs of sales are expected to be $9 million, and therefore total gross profits are expected to be $3 million.
- Each year, the company compares the total cash received to the expected amount of cash received. In Year 1, the total cash received was $3 million, which is 25% of the expected total cash received. Because this is a simple example, in every year the installments are the same 25% of the total.
- Each year, the company multiplies the total expected revenue and the total expected cost of sales by the percentage computed in the previous step to come up with the amount of revenues and cost of sales to recognize for the year. In this case, 25% of the expected total revenues of $12 million = $3 million, and 25% of the expected total cost of sales of $9 million = $2,250,000. The result is that a gross profit of $3,000,000 − $2,250,000 = $750,000 is recognized in each year.

If the company were to realize that the customer was not going to make any more payments, it would have to write off any remaining receivables.

Cost Recovery Method

This method is also called the deposit method. Under this method, the company recognizes equal amounts of cost of sales and revenues as installments are received, until the cumulative total of money collected equals the cost of the item sold. After that point, the company recognizes the installments as revenue, and stops recording cost of sales.

In the example in Box 9.1, the cost of the item sold was $9 million. The installments received equal $9 million at the end of Year 3. That means that for Years 1, 2, and 3 the company receives $3 million each year in cash, and recognizes $3 million in revenue and $3 million in sales each year. As a result, gross profits for each of Years 1, 2, and 3 are zero. In Year 4, when the $3 million installment is received, it is recognized as revenue, and there are no more costs to match it against. Gross profit in Year 4 is $3 million.

Comparison of the Methods

Over the life of the company, all three methods showed the same total revenues, total cost of sales, and total gross profit. The difference among the methods is timing. They allocate the revenues and cost of sales to different time periods.

With a single sale, the least conservative method is to recognize the revenues at the time of sale. That method, in this example, recognized all the $3 million of the gross profit expected on the sale in Year 1. The most conservative method is the cost recovery method, which waited until Year 4 before recognizing any gross profit. The installment method, which recognizes some gross profit as each installment is received, is less conservative than the cost recovery method but more conservative than the method of recognition at the time of sale.

It is important to realize that, for companies that have been in business for some time, you should *not* assume that the company with the most conservative method will always show the lowest income. Box 9.2 illustrates this point. In this situation, the company makes similar sales to those in Box 9.1 each year for five years, and then stops. Box 9.2 shows the revenues, cost of sales, and gross profits by year under each method.

The "conservative" methods show low gross profit in the early years, as the company grows, but higher income in the years of decline. In Years 4 and 5, when the company is at a steady level of sales, all three methods show the same gross profit of $3 million. In fact, if we considered ratios like return on equity, the conservative methods would look better in Years 4 and 5. Return on equity compares income for the period to the shareholders' equity, and the conservative methods recognized less income in Years 1, 2, and 3, meaning the shareholders' equity was lower.

Situation 3—One Product, Delivered at End, Work Done Over Time Under a Long-Term Contract

Assume that a company works for a long time on a project, such as building a bridge. Construction is expected to take four years. How much of the revenue should be shown as earned each year, while the work is being done, as opposed to when the bridge is finished? It seems unfair to say a company earned nothing for four years, while it worked on the bridge, and all the revenue was earned on the last day. On the other hand, it would be bad to report making profits for the first three years, if the project was actually unprofitable.

So here are the rules:

1   Under both U.S. GAAP and IFRS, if the company believes the project will lose money, it must recognize the loss as soon as it knows about the loss. The loss is *not* allocated over the life of the project—it is recorded immediately as soon as the company knows about it. If the estimated amount of the loss changes, the change in estimate is booked as soon as the company knows about it.

2   Under both U.S. GAAP and IFRS, if the company believes the project will make money, and the company can reasonably estimate both the costs of the project and the percentage of the project that is complete each period, then the company must use the "percentage of completion method." Box 9.3 has an example. Basically, this means that the contract profit is allocated to the time periods when the work is actually being done. If the estimated profit changes, the past entries are not changed. Instead, the new estimate is used to figure out the cumulative amount of profit that should have been recognized, and there is a "catch-up" in the period when the estimate changes.

3   If the company believes the project will make money, but the company cannot reliably estimate the costs or the percentage of the project that has been done, then the company cannot use the percentage of completion method.

    a. GAAP requires companies to use the "completed contract" method. Under this method, the profits are not recognized until the project is complete. This method is not generally allowed for taxes, because it would result in later tax payments.

    b. IFRS requires companies to use the cost recovery method.

In the example in Box 9.3, a company is doing a three-year project, for which it will bill $400 million. When it starts the project, it expects to make a gross profit of $40 million, after incurring costs of $360 million. Over three years, it finishes the project. During the project, it

Box 9.2 Example of Revenue Recognition—Continuing Business

Situation—Assume the same situation as in Box 9.1 is repeated every year for five years. Each year, from Year 1 through Year 5, Gao sells Scodes a $12 million machine that cost $9 million. For each machine, Scodes pays over four years. After Year 5, sales stop. Shown below is the pattern of sales, cost of sales, and gross profit under the three methods.

Time of sale recognition

Each year from Year 1 to Year 5 there is a sale, treated as in Box 9.1.

	Revenue	Cost of sales	Gross profit
Year 1	12,000,000	9,000,000	3,000,000
Year 2	12,000,000	9,000,000	3,000,000
Year 3	12,000,000	9,000,000	3,000,000
Year 4	12,000,000	9,000,000	3,000,000
Year 5	12,000,000	9,000,000	3,000,000
Year 6	0	0	0
Year 7	0	0	0
Year 8	0	0	0
Totals	$60,000,000	$45,000,000	$15,000,000

Installment method

Each year, from Year 1 to Year 5, there is a single new sale. In Year 2, the total revenues and costs include both the effects of the Year 1 sale and also the Year 2 sale. Each year thereafter until Year 8 includes the effect of more than one year's sale.

	Revenue	Cost of sales	Gross profit	Years' sales included
Year 1	3,000,000	2,250,000	750,000	Year 1
Year 2	6,000,000	4,500,000	1,500,000	Years 1 and 2
Year 3	9,000,000	6,750,000	2,250,000	Years 1, 2, 3
Year 4	12,000,000	9,000,000	3,000,000	Years 1, 2, 3, 4
Year 5	12,000,000	9,000,000	3,000,000	Years 2, 3, 4, 5
Year 6	9,000,000	6,750,000	2,250,000	Years 3, 4, 5
Year 7	6,000,000	4,500,000	1,500,000	Years 4 and 5
Year 8	3,000,000	2,250,000	750,000	Year 5
Totals	$60,000,000	$45,000,000	$15,000,000	

Cost recovery method

Each year after Year 1 includes revenues and costs from more than one year.

	Revenue	Cost of sales	Gross profit	Years' sales included
Year 1	3,000,000	3,000,000	0	Year 1
Year 2	6,000,000	6,000,000	0	Years 1 and 2
Year 3	9,000,000	9,000,000	0	Years 1,2,3
Year 4	12,000,000	9,000,000	3,000,000	Years 1,2,3,4
Year 5	12,000,000	9,000,000	3,000,000	Years 2,3,4,5
Year 6	9,000,000	6,000,000	3,000,000	Years 3,4,5
Year 7	6,000,000	3,000,000	3,000,000	Years 4 and 5
Year 8	3,000,000	0	3,000,000	Year 5
Totals	$60,000,000	$45,000,000	$15,000,000	

Box 9.3 Long-Term Contract Gross Profit Recognition Under Two Methods

Situation

The Fillmore Corp. has a contract to build an airfield for the U.S. Air Force over three years. The total contract price is $400 million. At the beginning of the contract, Fillmore estimates that the work will cost a total of $360 million, and that Fillmore will earn a gross profit of $40 million on the job. Fillmore gets various progress payments over the three years.

In the first year, Fillmore does 25% of the work and spends $90 million. At the end of the year, it continues to believe the total cost will be the same.

In the second year, Fillmore does enough more work that the project becomes 80% complete. Because of some cost increases, Fillmore now believes the job will cost a total of $380 million.

In the third year, Fillmore finishes the job. The total costs are $382 million.

Completed contract

Under the completed contract method, no gross profit is recognized until Year 3, when the job is complete. At that time, Fillmore will recognize a gross profit of $400 million – $382 million = $18 million.

Percentage of completion

Under this method, gross profit is recognized so that the cumulative gross profit recognized equals the (percentage of completion) times (the expected final gross profit).

In Year 1, the job is 25% complete. The expected gross profit = $40 million. Therefore, in Year 1, the company recognizes 25% of $40 million as gross profit, which equals $10 million.

At the end of Year 2, the job is 80% complete. The expected gross profit = $400 million – $380 million = $20 million. This means that the cumulative gross profit, for Years 1 and 2 together, should equal 80% of $20 million, or $16 million. The Year 2 gross profit equals the cumulative gross profit of $16 million minus the gross profit already recognized in Year 1 of $10 million. $16 million – $10 million = $6 million of Year 2 gross profit.

At the end of Year 3, the job is done. The total gross profit earned on the job is clearly = $400 million – $382 million. This = $18 million. That means that the cumulative gross profit must be brought to $18 million in the books. In the first two years, a total of $16 million has already been recorded. The Year 3 gross profit is $18 million – $16 million = $2 million.

---

changed its estimate of the eventual final cost. After the second year, it thought the project would cost $380 million. When the project was over, it ended up costing $382 million.

When we compare how the project would be accounted for under the two methods, we see that the total gross profit over the three years is the same, but the timing of recognizing it is different. Under the completed contract method, all the gross profit was recognized at the very end. This seems unfair to the company in the early years. Clearly, it was doing something productive, but was not recognizing benefits for this. Under the percentage of completion method, some gross profit was recognized each year. However, because the company changed its estimates of the costs of the project over the three years, the pattern of recognizing income is not exactly the same as the percentage of the work done that year. The gross profit recognized and the percentages of work done were as follows:

	Gross profit	**% of work done in that year**
Year 1	$10 million	25%
Year 2	$6 million	55%
Year 3	$2 million	20%

In this case, due to the early optimistic cost estimates, the company recognized more gross profit in Year 1 than it would have if it had estimated accurately, and there was less gross profit left to be recognized in the two later years.

The example in Box 9.3 did not show results with the cost recovery method. Under that method, the amount of gross profit recognized would depend on the payment schedule. No gross profit would be recognized until the total payments exceeded the estimated total costs.

Box 9.4 is an example of the accounting policy for long-term contracts. It is from the 2013 financial statements of KBR, Inc., a major construction company. It uses the percentage of completion method.

Clearly, for a single contract, the completed contract method is more conservative. However, for an ongoing business, this does not mean that in any particular year it would have higher income using the percentage of completion method. Box 9.5 shows how gross profit would be recognized using the two methods for a company that has identical projects for five years and then has no more projects. Over the early years, profits are higher if it uses the percentage of completion method. At a certain point, when new contracts are starting as fast as old contracts are finishing, both methods give the same income. Once the new contracts start declining, the completed contract method shows higher income.

Situation 4—Services and Payments Over Time

In this situation, the company provides services over time. The company also receives multiple payments. It would be possible for the company and its customer to come up with different payment plans which all have the same economic net present value but differ in their timing. For example, consider a landlord and tenant who are negotiating a five-year lease agreement.

Box 9.4 Excerpt of Accounting Policy Disclosure—from KBR, Inc. 2013 Financial Statements*

Contracts. Revenue from contracts to provide construction, engineering, design or similar services is reported on the percentage-of-completion method of accounting. Depending on the type of job, progress is generally measured based upon man-hours expended to total man-hours estimated at completion, costs incurred to total estimated costs at completion or physical progress. All known or anticipated losses on contracts are provided for in the period they become evident. Claims and change orders that are in the process of negotiation with customers for additional work or changes in the scope of work are included in contract value when collection is deemed probable and the value can be reliably estimated.

*KBR Inc. Form 10-K for the fiscal year ended December 31, 2013, p. 54. Information available at www.sec.gov/Archives/edgar/data/1357615/000135761514000005/kbr1231201310k.htm (last accessed August 18, 2015).

Box 9.5 Long-Term Contract Gross Profit Recognition—Multiple Projects

Situation—The RBK Corp. starts operations in Year 1. It makes a three-year contract with a customer, for a price of $10 million and with expected costs of $7 million. Assume that it does the work under the contract as scheduled, and completes one-third of the work each year. Now, assume it enters into new contracts, just like the first one, in Years 2, 3, 4, and 5. It then stops making new contracts after Year 5. Each contract is completed on schedule, at the expected costs. What gross profit would the company recognize each year?

Completed contract—For each contract, the gross profit is $3 million. The gross profit on each contract would only be recognized when it is done, in its third year. The overall picture is:

Year	Gross profit	Gross profit recognized on contracts from which years?
1	0	
2	0	
3	3,000,000	Year 1
4	3,000,000	Year 2
5	3,000,000	Year 3
6	3,000,000	Year 4
7	3,000,000	Year 5
Totals	$15,000,000	

Percentage of completion—Each contract is completed over a three-year period. Due to the simple numbers in this example, the RBK Corp. earns $1 million each year it works on each contract. (Each contract has a total gross profit of $3 million, and that is earned one-third each year.)

Year	Gross profit	Gross profit recognized on contracts from which years?
1	1,000,000	Year 1
2	2,000,000	Years 1 and 2
3	3,000,000	Years 1, 2 and 3
4	3,000,000	Years 2, 3 and 4
5	3,000,000	Years 3, 4, and 5
6	2,000,000	Years 4 and 5
7	1,000,000	Year 5
Totals	$15,000,000	

They might agree on equal monthly installments for the 60 months. Alternatively, they might agree on two months' "free" rent at the start, and higher payments for the remaining 58 months. As a second example, a health club might offer two different yearly plans. Under one plan, the customer makes a large payment up front, and small payments each time she uses the health club. The other plan requires a smaller payment up front and higher payments each time the customer uses the club.

The basic idea of the accounting rules in these situations is that the revenue recognition should be based on the services provided, not when cash moves. If the landlord is providing the same services all 60 months, then the rental revenue each month should be the same. Whether the customer pays 60 equal monthly payments or 58 somewhat larger ones has no effect—the same monthly revenue should be recognized each month. If the health club gives its customer the right to 12 months of service, the fees should be recognized as revenue equally over the 12 months. If health club membership fees are "for life," then the health club would recognize them over the average expected membership period. For example, the 2013 financial statements of Life Time Fitness state:

> We . . . receive a one-time enrollment fee (including an administrative fee) at the time a member joins. The enrollment fees are nonrefundable after 14 days. Enrollment fees and related direct expenses, primarily sales commissions, are deferred and recognized on a straight-line basis over an estimated average membership life of 33 months, which is based on historical membership experience.[4]

Situation 5—One Payment, Multiple Products or Services Delivered Over Time

Let's consider a company that makes agreements with customers under which the company gets one contract price but delivers a variety of products. This issue arises in a number of industries. A good example is the computer industry. The International Business Machine Corporation ("IBM") 2012 financial statements gave this example:

> A client may purchase a server that includes operating system software. In addition, the arrangement may include post-contract support for the software and a contract for post-warranty maintenance service for the hardware. These types of arrangements can also include financing provided by the company. These arrangements consist of multiple deliverables, with the hardware and software delivered in one reporting period and the software support and hardware maintenance services delivered across multiple reporting periods.[5]

The accounting issue is how to allocate the revenue fairly across the different products delivered, and to allocate the revenue into appropriate time periods. If there were no rules, there would be a temptation for managers to allocate the revenue in a way that helped them manage earnings. For example, a company trying to look good in the current year might say that most of the revenue should be allocated to items delivered early in the contract, with little being deferred until the later years.

The FASB has made special rules for accounting for arrangements with "*multiple deliverables*."[6] A "deliverable" is a product or service given to the client. For IBM, in the example they provided, there were five separate "deliverables": a server; operating software; post-contract software support; maintenance for the server; and financing. There are basically four steps:

1 The company should separately recognize revenue for any particular delivered item if it is something that would have value to the customer on a standalone basis, and if delivery is under the control of the seller. Items are considered to have standalone value either if there are companies selling the items separately, or if the customer could resell it separately.

2 At the start of the arrangement, the company should normally allocate the total consideration to the various "deliverables" based on their relative selling price. The selling price should be based on objective evidence of the seller's own practices, where possible. This is called "*vendor-specific objective evidence.*" If the seller does not have its own prices for separate items, it can use evidence of what other companies sell the items for. If it does not have either of these types of evidence, it can use its best estimates.

3 Revenue for each deliverable is recognized based on when the company meets the revenue recognition rules for that deliverable. In the IBM example, the company should recognize revenue for the server when it delivers it to the client. The software support, hardware maintenance, and financing services are earned over a period of time.

4   The company should disclose key information about the types of products and services that it accounts for under this method, and the general timing of revenue recognition for significant types of deliverables.

Box 9.6 is an example of revenue recognition following this guidance.

Allocations Affecting Expenses

Product Versus Period Costs

"*Product costs*" relate directly to particular products or services that the company sells. A retailer that buys clothes from a manufacturer and sells them to consumers would consider the amounts paid to the manufacturer for the clothes as product costs. The manufacturer of the clothes would consider labor and fabric, among many other things needed to make the clothes, as product costs.

Box 9.6 Example of Revenue Recognition With Multiple Deliverables

Assume that Whiz-Bang Computer Systems signs a contract with New York City under which Whiz-Bang will provide the following products and services that together will allow New York City to better process its employees' payroll:

- Computer servers (separate value $50,000,000, to be delivered Day 1, Year 1)
- Initial Training to New York employees to operate the system (separate value, $1,000,000, to be delivered Month 1, Year 1)
- Software license, to use software for five years (separate value $45,000,000, to be delivered Day 1, Year 1, but used over five years)
- Software support and updates for five years ($4,000,000 value, delivered over five years.)

The total contract price is $95 million. This is a bargain for New York, since the total of the four separate "deliverables" = $100 million ($50,000,000 + $1,000,000 + $45,000,000 + $4,000,000).

The $95 million contract price would be allocated as follows:

- $47,500,000 to hardware ((50/100) × $95 million), recognized at time of sale
- $950,000 to initial training ((1/100) × $95 million) recognized at the time the training was done
- $42,750,000 to the software license ((45/100) × $95 million), recognized over the five years of the license.
- $3,800,000 ((4/100) × $95 million) to the software support and updates, recognized over the five years of the contract.

By year, Whiz-Bang would record the following revenues:

Year 1	$57,760,000 = $47,500,000 + $950,000 + (1/5)($42,750,000) + (1/5)($3,800,000)	
Year 2	$9,310,000 = (1/5)($42,750,000) + (1/5)($3,800,000)	
Year 3	$9,310,000	Same as Year 2
Year 4	$9,310,000	Same
Year 5	$9,310,000	Same
Total	$95,000,000	

Product costs are considered to be part of the inventory asset until the items are sold, and then are considered part of the cost of sales.

"*Period costs*" are costs that are incurred during a period of time, that are not directly related to making or buying inventory. These are allocated to expenses in several different ways:

- Some are directly related to the process of selling, and are considered to be expense in the same time period as the related sale was made. For example, salespeople's commissions are recognized in the time period of the sale.
- Some relate to a time period, and are recognized in the time period for which they were incurred. For example, if a company rents an office in January, the company would recognize the rent applicable to January in January. Under GAAP, the expense is a January expense, regardless of whether the rent was paid during January, before the month started, or after it ended.
- The costs related to buying long-term assets are allocated to expense systematically. This is discussed more fully in a later section.

Allocating Prepaid Assets to Expenses

Companies often pay for services such as insurance and rent in advance. At the time they make the payment, they record a reduction in cash, and an increase in "prepaid assets." Over time, they need to allocate a part of what they paid to expenses. Usually, this is simple. For example, if a company pays $12,000 for a one-year automobile liability insurance policy, it should allocate 1/12 of the cost to insurance expense every month. The effect of this accounting on the fundamental accounting equation is shown below.

Day 1, when insurance is purchased:

Total assets do not change because $12,000 of cash bought $12,000 prepaid insurance.
Liabilities and equity are not affected.

Each month afterwards, for 12 months:

Total assets decrease by $1,000 (which = 1/12 of the amount paid for insurance).
An expense of $1,000 is recorded, which reduces equity by $1,000.
Liabilities are not affected.

Long-Term Operating Assets

General Principles

The accounting for land, buildings, natural resources like oil wells, and intangible assets all follows the same logic.

When these items are acquired for cash, the company adjusts its books to record the asset acquired, and to decrease cash for their cost.[7] There is no expense at the time of purchase.

Costs of simply repairing and maintaining these assets are considered to be expenses in the period in which they are incurred. For example, a car rental company has expenses for oil and car repairs. It can sometimes be difficult to distinguish between an action that should be considered a repair and one that should be "capitalized" as an addition to the asset. The general rule is that unless the action either makes the asset more productive than it originally was, or extends its life from the original expectation, it is a repair or maintenance expense. Under this standard, painting a building is a maintenance expense, but adding on a new wing to a building should be considered making the building asset bigger.

The following is United States Steel Corporation's 2013 footnote explaining its accounting policies for maintenance and repair expenses:

U. S. Steel incurs maintenance costs on all of its major equipment. Costs that extend the life of the asset, materially add to its value, or adapt the asset to a new or different use are separately capitalized in property, plant and equipment and are depreciated over the estimated useful life. All other repair and maintenance costs are expensed as incurred.[8]

Some assets are considered to have indefinite lives, and for these assets the company does not record any amortization or depreciation of the cost. Such assets would include: land; goodwill; trademarks and other intangible assets with indefinite lives; and works of art. If the values become impaired, the company would record an impairment loss.

Most assets do have definite lives. For these assets, the company needs to allocate *the net cost of owning* them over the periods they are used. The net cost of owning the asset equals the original cost of the asset minus whatever "*salvage value*" or "*residual value*" the company will receive when it sells the item, or plus any special costs needed to dispose of the item. Here are three examples:

- A car rental company buys cars for use in its car rental business. It normally uses them for a period of two years. Because it maintains the cars well, it is able to sell them off after two years at an average price equal to 60% of the cars' original cost. Its net cost of owning the cars would therefore be only 40% of the original purchase price of the cars (100% cost − 60% salvage value). It would need to allocate this net cost over the two years the cars are used.
- A drug company buys a patent for a new blood pressure medicine for $3 million. The patent will legally expire after six years. When it expires, it will have zero value. The drug company needs to allocate all $3 million to expense over six years, since the salvage value of an expired patent is zero.
- A coal mining company buys the right to mine coal on a piece of land for $20 million. It expects to use the mine for eight years. After it is done using the mine, it will not own the land. The law requires the coal company to clean up the mine site, so it will not pollute the nearby streams. The company estimates the clean-up costs will be $2 million. The company needs to allocate $22 million to expense over the time it uses the mine, equal to the $20 million original cost plus the $2 million needed to clean up the site at the end of its useful life.

Even though the basic principles of dealing with different long-term assets are similar, there are differences in terminology. "*Depreciation*" is the term for allocating the net cost of owning fixed assets like buildings and equipment to expense. "*Amortization*" is the equivalent term for intangible assets, and "*depletion*" is the equivalent term for natural resources like oil wells.

Every period, accountants record an expense to allocate these costs. At that same time, they increase a "contra asset account." A "contra asset account" modifies the balance in an asset account. We have already seen the allowance for bad debts and an allowance for inventory obsolescence as contra accounts. The three "contra asset accounts" used to track the total amount of allocated costs related to long-term operating assets are:

- "Accumulated depreciation," which modifies fixed assets
- "Accumulated amortization," which modifies intangible assets
- "Accumulated depletion," which modifies natural resources

Accountants need to keep track, for each of the individual operating assets, of both the cost and the accumulated amounts of costs which were allocated to expense in the past.

Depreciation, Amortization, and Depletion Methods

As Box 9.7 indicates, the idea of depreciation has not always been accepted as appropriate. For some time, people questioned whether it was appropriate to depreciate buildings or certain other assets, like railroad track beds. However, since the early part of the 20th century, it has been

---

Box 9.7 The Idea of Depreciation Through History

One of the earliest records of depreciation expense was for a Scottish canal in 1764. There is no history of American companies recording depreciation until around the 1830s. When railroads developed, they had large amounts of fixed assets. Some began recording depreciation, but the practice was not consistent.

Until the late 1800s in the U.K and the early 1900s in the U.S., most companies did not record depreciation. Some companies thought it was wrong to both record depreciation on an asset and the costs of repairing it. For some of the major assets at the time (buildings, railroad tracks, and canals) the argument was that if they were well maintained they would not lose value over time. Several U.S. Supreme Court decisions took this position. The most widespread method of accounting for fixed assets of railroads from the mid-1800s until the early 20th century was the retirement method. Under this method, expenses due to using up the assets were recognized at the time the assets were retired.

In both countries, the adoption of depreciation seems to have been related to regulations or tax factors. In the U.S., the prices railroads could charge customers were often regulated. Railroads were not allowed to charge prices that gave them more than reasonable rates of profits. By recording depreciation expense, railroads reported lower profits and could charge higher prices. The adoption of corporate income tax laws in the U.K. in 1878 and in the U.S. in 1909 gave companies another incentive to report higher expenses. The U.K. law originally only allowed depreciation for equipment, not for buildings. The U.S. Supreme Court decided in a 1909 decision that depreciation was a valid expense, reversing several prior decisions that were skeptical of the idea of depreciation.

It was not clear whether depreciation should be based on replacement cost or historical cost. If the purpose of recording depreciation is to measure the value lost in a period, then replacement cost would be better. In the U.S. the depreciation is based on historical cost. Scholars believe that this decision is largely based on tax reasons. It is easier to administer a historical cost system, and the government collects more tax revenue if the depreciation is limited to the original cost of the item. Under IFRS, companies are allowed to revalue assets and to compute depreciation on the revalued figure.

Various different methods of depreciation were used in the early 20th century. The straight-line method of depreciation became the most common method after the 1929 stock market crash. The Revenue Act of 1943 allowed accelerated depreciation to help increase construction of wartime facilities. With post-World War II inflation, companies felt the straight-line method did not give adequate expenses. The Revenue Act of 1954 gave companies some relief from the impact of inflation by allowing higher depreciation in early years.

Depreciation also was not immediately used for all types of organizations. The FASB did not require not-for-profit organizations to record depreciation until SFAS No. 93, issued in 1987. State and local governments follow special rules, which basically do not recognize depreciation as a cost that needs to be covered through annual budgets.

The discussion in this box is largely based on the following articles: Woodward (1956); Watts and Zimmerman (1979); and Bookholdt (1978).

normal practice in the U.S. to depreciate fixed assets and to assume that all fixed assets except land will lose value.

The FASB Codification 360-10-35 explains the purpose of depreciation as follows:

> The cost of a productive facility is one of the costs of the services it renders during its useful economic life. Generally accepted accounting principles (GAAP) require that this cost be spread over the expected useful life of the facility in such a way as to allocate it as equitably as possible to the periods during which services are obtained from the use of the facility. This procedure is known as depreciation accounting, a system of accounting which aims to distribute the cost or other basic value of tangible capital assets, less salvage (if any), over the estimated useful life of the unit . . . in a systematic and rational manner. It is a process of allocation, not of valuation.

Note that by saying that depreciation is *not* a process of valuation, the FASB is indicating that at any time the "*book value*" of an asset, after considering depreciation, is not meant to equal its fair value. The purpose of depreciation is to rationally allocate the cost of owning an asset to time periods. Ideally, it should be allocated "equitably" to periods when services are obtained from the assets.

In general, accountants would normally try to pick a method of depreciating fixed assets that tracks either the items the asset produces or the time periods over which it loses its value. What causes an asset to lose value over time? Accountants typically cite three different reasons: usage; obsolescence; and capacity limitations.

- *Usage*. This is sometimes also referred to as "wear and tear." Some assets physically wear out, and as they age they become less and less valuable. A car engine will eventually wear out if the car is driven. In the case of natural resources, usage decreases the amount of resources remaining. The amount of oil left in an oil well decreases over time as people pump out the oil.
- *Obsolescence*. Some assets lose value because companies would prefer newer, more up-to-date items. For example, most companies decide to replace their computer systems because newer systems have better features, not because the old systems wore out.
- *Capacity*. A company may outgrow certain assets. For example, a new company might acquire a telephone system that can handle up to 50 employees. When it grows, that system will no longer be adequate for its needs.

The way that assets lose value depends both on the type of asset and the way the assets are used. For example, a car is subject to both wear and tear and to obsolescence. For a company like Hertz Rent-A-Car, which tries to have up-to-date models for rent, obsolescence is the key factor that leads it to replace cars. The "Rent-A-Wreck" car rental company would presumably not worry about the appearance of its cars and would be more concerned with using them until they wear out.

The FASB has given companies fairly broad discretion to choose methods of depreciation that fit its concepts. For financial accounting purposes, most companies use either the "*straight-line*" method of depreciation, the "*units of production*" method, or an "*accelerated*" method of depreciation.[9] A study of 500 companies by the AICPA (2011) found that, in 2010, 492 used the straight-line method for some or all of their fixed assets, 15 used the units of production method, 25 used accelerated methods, and a few used other methods.

For tax purposes, most U.S. companies use the "Modified Accelerated Cost Recovery System" ("MACRS") that is permitted by the tax law. The MACRS system was designed to encourage companies to invest in equipment, by allowing large tax deductions in the early years of the assets' life. Because it is not trying to allocate the costs fairly as the assets are used, the MACRS usually assumes very short useful lives for assets. Therefore, the FASB usually does not allow MACRS to be used for financial accounting.[10]

How do these methods work? Box 9.8 provides an example. Assume the Strand Company bought a truck on January 1, Year 1 for a cost of $90,000. The company expects the truck to last eight years, during which time the company will also drive the truck 500,000 miles. When the truck is eventually sold, the company expects to receive $10,000.

Box 9.8 Depreciation Using Different Methods

Situation—A truck is bought on January 1, Year 1.
Cost = $90,000
Expected life, in years = 8 years
Expected life, in miles driven = 500,000
Expected salvage value = $10,000
Miles driven: 75,000 in Year 1, and 60,000 in Year 2

Straight-line method

The depreciation each period is the same.

Expense = (cost – salvage) ÷ (estimated useful life)
Expense = ($90,000 – $10,000) ÷ 8 = $10,000 each year.
Total over 8 years = $80,000

Units of production method

There are two equivalent formulas for computing the depreciation. We will use

Expense = [(cost – salvage value) ÷ (expected life in units)] × units produced this period

The quantity in brackets is the depreciation cost per mile driven = ($90,000 – $10,000) ÷ 500,000 miles = $0.16 per mile.
Year 1 depreciation = $0.16 × 75,000 = $12,000
Year 2 depreciation = $0.16 × 60,000 = $9,600

Double declining balance method

Depreciation in any period = 2 × [Cost – prior accumulated depreciation] ÷ estimated life
Year 1 = $22,500 = 2 × (90,000 – 0) ÷ 8
Year 2 = $16,875 = 2 × (90,000 – 22,500) ÷ 8
Year 3 = $12,656 = 2 × (90,000 – 22,500 – 16,875) ÷ 8
Year 4 = $9,492 = 2 × (90,000 – 22,500 – 16,875 – 12,656) ÷ 8
Year 5 = $7,119 = 2 × (90,000 – 22,500 – 16,875 – 12,656 – 9,492) ÷ 8
Year 6 = $5,339 = 2 × (90,000 – 22,500 – 16,875 – 12,656 – 9,492 – 7,119) ÷ 8
Year 7 = $4,005 = 2 × (90,000 – 22,500 – 16,875 – 12,656 – 9,492 – 7,119 – 5,339) ÷ 8
Year 8 = $2,014 = The remaining depreciation to reach a total of $80,000
Totals $80,000

The straight-line method is the most common method used for companies in their financial reporting. An equal expense is computed each time period. If you graph the expense against time, you would see a straight horizontal line. The formula for expense is:

Depreciation expense each period = (cost – expected salvage value) ÷ useful life.

The logic of the straight-line method is that the usefulness of the asset is reduced in about equal amounts each month the item is in use. This might make economic sense in many situations. Perhaps the asset becomes technologically obsolete at a steady rate. Perhaps the asset is being used at a steady pace, and is physically wearing out about the same amount each month. Perhaps the reasons that most companies use straight-line depreciation in financial reporting is that it is simple, and that it seems like a straightforward and honest way of dealing with the situation.

In the example in Box 9.8, the straight-line method results in expense of $10,000 each year.

A second common method is the unit of production method. The logic here is that depreciation will be recorded each time an asset is issued. This would make economic sense if the asset loses value based primarily on wear and tear, and the wear and tear was different in different time periods. For example, an oil company may not use the machinery around an oil well at all in a year when it chooses not to take oil out of that well, but may use the machinery extensively in other years. The formula to compute depreciation expense here can be stated in two mathematically equivalent ways:

Expense = (cost – salvage value) × [(units produced this period) ÷ expected life in units)]

Or

Expense = [(cost – salvage value) ÷ (expected life in units)] × units produced this period.

The first formula multiplies the net cost of using the asset by the fraction of its use that occurred this year. In the example in Box 9.8, the truck was used 75,000 miles in Year 1, and its expected total life in miles is 500,000. That means 15% of its useful life was consumed in Year 1. 15% of the net cost of ownership of $80,000 = $12,000.

In the second formula, the quantity in brackets gives us the depreciation per mile that we should record over the life of the truck. The net cost of $80,000, divided by the 500,000 mile useful life, implies the depreciation per mile should be $0.16. Since the truck was driven 75,000 miles in Year 1, the depreciation expense for year 1 = $0.16 × $75,000 = $12,000. The two methods give us the same result.

The depreciation expense will vary between years, depending on how much the truck is driven. In the example in Box 9.8, the truck is driven 60,000 miles the second year, so the Year 2 depreciation expense is $9,600.

The third general method of depreciation is accelerated depreciation. Here, the idea is that it is appropriate to take more depreciation in the early part of the asset's life. One argument for doing this is that assets may be most productive in their early lives, so it makes sense to match more expense against revenues at that time. Another argument is that some assets lose value most quickly in the early part of their lives. For example, they may lose value quickly in Years 1 and 2 when they change from being fashionable new cars to being older cars, but would not decline much in value between Years 7 and 8. Another argument for accelerated depreciation is that it is one means of keeping the overall cost reported for an asset, including both depreciation and maintenance costs, steady over time. The idea is that maintenance costs rise as assets get older. To keep the overall costs of ownership constant, depreciation expenses should fall.

There are several different accelerated depreciation methods. The one shown in Box 9.8 is called the "double declining balance" method.[11] The formula for computing the expense in any year is:

Expense = 2 × [cost – accumulated depreciation from prior years] ÷ (estimated useful life)

The name of this method makes sense when you consider the formula. The quantity in the brackets is the "declining balance." Each year, as accumulated depreciation increases, the quantity in the brackets will get smaller. You can see that in Box 9.8. The "double" in the name of the method refers to the "2" in the formula. Multiplying by two doubles the expense from what it would be otherwise. Notice that salvage value is not part of the formula.

The first year, there is no accumulated depreciation from prior years, so the quantity in the brackets is simply the cost of the asset. In Box 9.8, the first year depreciation under this method = $2 \times [90,000 - 0] \div 8 = \$22,500$. This is much larger than the straight-line depreciation of $10,000. With the double declining balance method, the depreciation expense gets smaller every year. In the second year, it has fallen to $16,875. By the fourth year, it is $9,491, which is smaller than the straight-line value. Over the life of the asset, the total depreciation must equal the net cost of owning the asset, which equals cost – salvage value. In the example in Box 9.8, the net cost = $90,000 – $10,000 = $80,000. In the final year, the depreciation expense was not computed using the regular formula, but instead was computed as the number that brought the total accumulated depreciation to $80,000.

Most companies amortize intangible assets using the straight-line method, and assume there is zero salvage value. The FASB Codification Section 350-30-35-6 states that:

> The method of amortization shall reflect the pattern in which the economic benefits of the intangible asset are consumed or otherwise used up. If that pattern cannot be reliably determined, a straight-line amortization method shall be used.

Most companies compute depletion of natural resources using the unit of production method. This follows the FASB's guidance (Section 932-360-35-3) for oil and gas that "The costs of an entity's wells and related equipment and facilities and the costs of the related proved properties shall be amortized as the related oil and gas reserves are produced." This method makes more sense than basing depreciation on time periods, since companies may choose to let oil wells stay unused for long periods.

Partial Years

For simplicity, all examples in this book of depreciation or amortization use full years. In Box 9.8, for example, the asset was bought on the first day of the year. In real life, companies will often acquire assets at various dates during the year, and they would pro-rate the annual figures as appropriate to record depreciation for the fraction of the year they actually use the assets. Companies that buy large numbers of similar assets sometimes use simplifying assumptions to reduce the record-keeping burden, such as assuming that all assets were bought halfway through the year.

Changes in Estimates

Depreciation, amortization, and depletion are all computed using estimates of such factors as the service life of an asset, the amount of oil in an oil well, or the salvage value of a building. What happens when a company learns new information and revises these assumptions?

This situation was discussed in Chapter 8. The company will *not* change past financial statements. Instead, it will treat the book value on the day it changes its assumptions as the "cost" of the asset. It will use its new assumptions about the asset's salvage value and remaining life to compute depreciation over the remaining years of the asset's life. See the example in the "Updating Accounts for New Information" section of Chapter 8.

Gains and Losses on Disposals of Operating Assets

Let's consider how to account for the disposal of an operating asset, like a building or a patent or an oil well. Let's assume that the truck from Box 9.8 was sold at the end of Year 2 for $62,000. The company needs to record the following:

- It has $62,000 more cash.
- It no longer has a truck, so the cost of the truck of $90,000 should be removed from the books.
- Since it no longer has the truck, the accumulated depreciation related to the truck should be removed from the books. The amount of the depreciation accumulated depends on what method was used. Under the three methods in the example:
  - Straight-line depreciation resulted in $20,000 of accumulated depreciation through the end of Year 2
  - Units of production resulted in $21,600 of accumulated depreciation
  - Double declining balance resulted in $39,375 of accumulated depreciation
  - A gain or loss needs to be recorded for the difference between the cash received and the (cost – accumulated depreciation) disposed of.

The "cost – accumulated depreciation" is the "*book value*" of the asset. The book value and the amount of gain or loss on disposal both depend on how much depreciation was taken before. Let's look at the gain or loss for the three different depreciation methods. In each case, the gain or loss = cash received – (cost – accumulated depreciation).

Straight-line
Gain or loss = $62,000 – ($90,000 – $20,000) = a loss of $8,000

Units of production
Gain or loss = $62,000 – ($90,000 – $21,600) = loss of $6,400

Double declining balance
Gain or loss = $62,000 – ($90,000 – $39,375) = $11,375 gain.

It is worth noting what is happening here. At the start of Year 1, the company spent $90,000 for this truck, and two years later it sold it for $62,000. Owning this truck for two years cost this company a net amount of $28,000 in cash. That is the real cost of owning the truck, and under all three depreciation methods, the books eventually have to reflect $28,000 as the cumulative cost. Under the straight-line and units of production depreciation methods, the company had depreciated less than $28,000 through the end of Year 2. Therefore, at the end of Year 2, under these methods the company had to recognize losses to bring the total expenses up to $28,000. Under the double declining balance method, it had already recorded expenses of $39,375. That was too high. Therefore, at the time of disposal, an $11,375 gain was recorded to bring the cumulative net expense back down to $28,000. The gain or loss on sale acts like a correction of the previous incorrect estimates included in the depreciation computation.

The accounting for throwing away an asset, rather than selling it, is the same as what we have just seen, except that the cash received is zero.

Conservatism and Choice of Depreciation Methods

Accelerated depreciation methods show depreciation expense more quickly for any particular asset than the straight-line method. Therefore, they are more conservative than straight-line. How they compare with the units of production method would depend on the timing of production.

However, this does not mean that a company using accelerated depreciation will always show lower income than a company using straight-line. How their income compares will depend on whether they are in a growth period, a steady state, or in decline. Box 9.9 is an example. In the period when the amount of fixed assets is growing, accelerated depreciation gives higher depreciation expense. Once the level of fixed assets stabilizes, and new assets are added at the same rate that old ones become fully depreciated, the expense is the same. In the period when assets are being added more slowly than they are becoming fully depreciated, accelerated depreciation gives a lower expense. This means that whether a method produces higher or lower income depends on the growth phase of the company. This same point was made in Boxes 9.2 and 9.5 about different revenue recognition methods.

Allocations of Tax Expenses and Benefits

General

This section is a simplified presentation of a complex topic, normally treated in detail in intermediate accounting courses. The purpose of this discussion is to help you understand the general principles dealing with the accounting for taxes, and to help you understand both the tax expense shown in company income statements and the "deferred tax" assets and liabilities that appear on balance sheets.

In the U.S., most businesses are not subject to income tax. For example, a business organized as a partnership does not pay income tax. Instead, the income is assumed to "pass through" to the

---

Box 9.9 Depreciation for a Company With Multiple Asset Additions

Situation—The Stratford Corp. buys a machine in Year 1, on Day 1, with a cost of $30,000, a three-year life, and no salvage value. In each of Years 2, 3, 4, and 5 it buys an identical machine. It does not buy any additional machines in Years 6 or 7.

The accounting for the first machine

Using straight-line depreciation, the depreciation expense each year would = $10,000.
Using double declining balance, the expense would be as follows:
Year $1 = 2 \times (30,000 - 0) \div 3 = \$20,000$
Year $2 = 2 \times (30,000 - 20,000) \div 3 = \$6,667$
Year 3 = $3,333 (to add to $30,000)

The accounting for the Stratford Corp.

Expense by year, two methods

Year	Straight-line	Double Declining Balance	Machines being depreciated
1	$10,000	$ 20,000	Year 1 purchase
2	20,000	26,667	Years 1 and 2
3	30,000	30,000	Years 1, 2, 3
4	30,000	30,000	Years 2, 3, 4
5	30,000	30,000	Years 3, 4, 5
6	20,000	10,000	Years 4, 5
7	10,000	3,333	Year 5
Total	$150,000	$150,000	

partners, and each partner is taxed each year on his or her share of the partnership's income. The tax law is similar for businesses organized as "limited liability corporations" and "Subchapter S partnerships." The businesses are not taxed, but the income "passes through" to their owners. Also, when a business is owned directly by a single owner (a "sole proprietorship") and not through a corporation, the tax on the business is combined with the owner's personal taxes. This section of the text is not discussing these various "pass through" entities. Instead, it is discussing the income taxes on U.S. corporations that are not able to claim "Subchapter S" status. These are sometimes referred to as "C" corporations, referring to a section of the tax law. They tend to be the larger companies, and include almost all publicly traded companies. According to the IRS, approximately 2,263,000 corporate tax returns for "C" corporations were filed in the U.S. in 2013.[12] In the U.S., the corporate income tax rate is normally 35%.[13]

If the tax authorities measured income the same way the FASB does, then when companies earn $100 in revenues, their taxes would rise by $35, and when they incur $100 in expenses, their taxes would fall by $35. In other words, earning revenues has a tax consequence, and so does incurring expenses. Under both GAAP and IFRS, accounting rules exist to account for these tax consequences.

The primary complication with the accounting is that revenues and expenses are often recognized in different time periods for tax and book purposes. The time that taxes are actually paid depends on the tax rules. However, GAAP and IFRS want to recognize the related tax liabilities or assets based on when the related revenues were earned and the related expenses were incurred.

Examples

This topic can be very abstract. To understand what is meant by differences in the timing of recognizing revenues and expenses, it helps to look at two examples.

Example 1—Investing in Stock

Assume that the Sibyll Corp. invested $10,000 in the stock of Apple, Inc. in February 2002 when it was selling at $1.55 per share. As of January 2015, the stock is worth $113.56 per share. This means that over about 13 years, the value of Sibyll's investment has increased from $15,500 to $1,135,600. For accounting purposes, Sibyll records its investment at fair value. Each year, from 2002 until January 2015, Sibyll recorded some gains or losses to reflect the changing market value of the stock. This means that over the 13 years, Sibyll's books showed over $1.3 million in gains. If it sells the stock in 2015, the gain it will show in 2015 is *not* the entire increase in value of the investment, but instead the change in value between December 31, 2014 and the date of sale.

What about the tax accounting? Under tax law, Sibyll has no gain and no loss until it sells the stock. If it sells the stock in 2015, it will have to pay a tax of 35% on the total increase in value since 2002.

So, in this example, all the tax payment would come in the thirteenth year, even though the value of the Apple stock has grown each year over the period. GAAP and IFRS want to recognize the increasing tax liability each year that is a consequence of the value of the stock increasing. Under GAAP and IFRS, each year from 2002 through 2014, as the stock grew in value, Sibyll would record tax expense and would record a "deferred tax liability."

Example 2—Net Operating Losses

It is fairly common for companies to lose money in a year. For accounting purposes, they would simply show a loss. The tax treatment is more complicated.

The idea behind the tax laws is that it is fair to tax a business on its income over a period of years on a net basis, but that the government won't actually subsidize businesses that always lose money. Imagine a company that earns $2 million in Year 1, loses $2 million in Year 2, makes $3 million in Year 3, and loses another $2 million in Year 4. By the end of Year 4, its net earnings (minus its losses) equal only $1 million. It would be unfair for the government to tax it at 35% for the Year 1 and 3 profits, and not allow it to offset those taxes by considering the Year 2 and Year 4 losses.

If the company has previously reported positive income on its tax returns, it can use losses to offset some of its previously reported taxable income, and get a refund of taxes paid in one of the two prior years. This is called "carrying back" the loss. In this example, the company would pay taxes in Year 1, because it made $2 million that year. In Year 2, it would "carry back" its Year 2 loss of $2 million. When you apply the Year 2 loss to the Year 1 profit, the net result is zero income. The company would claim a refund at the end of Year 2 for its Year 1 taxes. In Year 3, because it has profits, it would pay taxes based on the $3 million it earned. In Year 4, the company lost $2 million, and it would "carry back" that loss to partly offset the Year 3 income. At the end of Year 4, it would claim a partial refund of its Year 3 tax payments. As a result of these "carry-backs", after four years the company would only owe taxes on the net earnings of $1 million.

What about companies that have not previously made money? They have no prior income to carryback the losses against. The tax law does not give them any right to an immediate refund. Instead, the law allows them to "carry forward" their losses for up to 20 years and use these losses in future years to reduce the income that they would otherwise report to the IRS in those future years.

So, in the case of a new company that has lost money and can't carry the losses back against past income, the IRS will not send it a refund. However, for accounting purposes, it seems unfair to record its pre-tax losses without considering that it may be able to use those losses to reduce its future taxes. For accounting purposes, the ability to use the carryforwards in future years would be considered a "deferred tax asset," and the net loss would be reduced by the amount of the expected future tax benefit.

Like other assets, the company might have to record a charge if it is not likely to be realized. For example, a company that is constantly losing money would record a deferred tax asset, but would also establish a "valuation allowance" to reduce its carrying value.

General Rules for Allocating Tax Expenses Between Periods

This topic can get complicated, but in this text we will ignore some of the complications. As a general matter, there are two parts of the tax expense that companies recognize each year.

- *Current income taxes.* The current taxes are based directly on what the company reports to the IRS on its tax returns. If the company will owe taxes, this is an expense. If it is expecting a refund, this is a "tax benefit."
- *Deferred income taxes.* The deferred part of the tax expense results from differences in when the tax laws and GAAP recognize various revenues or expenses.
  - When the tax laws recognize net income earlier than GAAP, the result is that the company will pay taxes before GAAP would have required it to. In essence, it is "prepaying" its taxes, and needs to record a deferred tax asset.
  - When tax laws recognize net income later than GAAP, this means that even though under GAAP there was income in early years, the actual tax payments will be made in later years. The company must record a "deferred tax liability" in these situations.

Table 9.1 provides examples of some common causes of deferred tax liabilities and assets. One of the items mentioned is depreciation. Earlier in this chapter, we saw that most companies use

Table 9.1 Examples of Common Deferred Tax Assets and Liabilities

When tax law recognizes revenues earlier than GAAP:	
Customer deposits are recognized as taxable income when received, but considered deferred revenue for GAAP until services are provided.	Deferred tax asset
When tax law recognizes expenses later than GAAP:	
GAAP requires accruing contingency loss when probable, but the loss is not deductible for tax purposes until paid.	Deferred tax asset
Various GAAP expenses are not deductible for tax until realized (sick pay, bonuses, bad debts, etc).	Deferred tax asset
GAAP requires recording deferred compensation expenses when people work, but they are not deductible for tax purposes until employees are paid.	Deferred tax asset
Net operating losses are recorded for GAAP, but companies with no carrybacks cannot use the losses to reduce taxes until future years.	Deferred tax asset
When tax law recognizes revenues later than GAAP:	
Sale is treated using the installment method for tax, but recognized at time of sale for GAAP.	Deferred tax liability
Increase in value of marketable securities is treated as income for GAAP as it occurs, but not taxed until securities are sold.	Deferred tax liability
When tax recognizes expenses earlier than GAAP:	
Depreciation is recorded using the MACRS system for tax but the straight-line method for books.	Deferred tax liability

straight-line depreciation for their GAAP reporting but use an accelerated depreciation method on their tax returns. This means that, in the early years of the assets' lives, most U.S. companies are claiming higher depreciation deductions than the amount of straight-line depreciation expense they report for financial reporting. However, for book purposes it makes sense to not only record the same depreciation expense each year, but the same tax benefit from depreciation each year. This results in the companies needing to record a deferred tax liability, to reflect the fact that in the later years of these assets' lives there will be very small depreciation deductions for tax purposes.

Companies must disclose in the footnotes the amount of tax expense and also the factors that gave rise to deferred tax assets and liabilities.

Impact of Uncertainty on Deferred Tax Assets

Basically, one can consider deferred tax assets to be future tax deductions. If the company has profits in the future, then these deductions will be valuable. However, if the company does not have enough future taxable income, then the deductions will not be valuable. The FASB requires that companies set up a valuation allowance if it is "more likely than not" that part of the deferred tax asset will not be usable.

Amazon.com is a good example of how uncertainty affects the accounting for deferred tax assets. Amazon.com was incorporated in 1994 and went public in 1997. In its early years, its stated goal was to increase its market share and to grow, not to make profits. In fact, it reported losses in its early years. Its 2003 financial statements showed various deferred tax assets, totaling $1,500,175,000. This included $897,665,000 worth of net operating loss carryforwards. Because Amazon had a history of losses, it was not "more likely than not" that it would become profitable, and be able to use these deferred tax assets. Accordingly, Amazon.com recorded a valuation allowance of $1,495,908,000, which almost totally offset the deferred tax assets.

As with any estimate, a company may later change its mind as new facts emerge. At that time, the company will change its valuation allowance, and there will be an effect on net income.

In 2004, Amazon.com started to make money, and it changed its mind about its ability to use the deferred tax assets to offset future taxes. Its 2004 income statement included a benefit of $233 million from reducing its valuation allowance. In 2004 and some later years, Amazon.com was able to use its early losses to reduce its tax payments.

Allocations Among Related Entities

The final type of allocation discussed in this chapter occurs between accounting entities that are related to each other. For example, there may be different companies with common ownership, or different departments within a company. If there are costs that are incurred to provide services for two or more of these entities, what is the best way of allocating them? As an example, a multinational company may have a single worldwide tax department. Should the salaries in that department be charged to each part of the company, and if they are charged, how should they be allocated? A similar issue occurs when different parts of a large organization buy and sell to each other. The prices charged are called "*transfer prices.*" The transfer prices charged affect which parts of the company enjoy profits.

It should be noted that this is mostly an issue for managerial and tax reporting rather than financial reporting. Usually, financial reports are done on the entire group of related entities as a whole, and therefore only the total costs affect the overall financial statements. However, diversified companies also report data in their footnotes for particular segments of their business. The method of allocating central expenses to these segments can affect investors' perception of the operating segments' profitability. Researchers have noted two types of abuses of allocations among segments. In some cases, overly low amounts of expenses were allocated to segments to help hide poor performance. In other cases, where management did not want competitors to realize how profitable segments were, researchers saw evidence of excessive amounts of expenses being allocated to those segments. See Lail, Thomas and Winterbotham (2014).

The issues with regard to managerial accounting are discussed in the next chapter.

Impact of Improper Allocations

At the start of this chapter, I quoted Michael Chatfield as saying that in making allocations, the accountant is doing something that was necessary, but something that is also arbitrary and artificial. This chapter has discussed a variety of uses of the allocation process. Accountants find it necessary to allocate revenues, expenses, and taxes into periods, and to allocate revenues and expenses among organizations. Unfortunately, the process of allocation can also cause problems. This section lists some of the issues that can occur.

1   Managers can use the allocation process to report overly conservative or overly aggressive income. Since the allocation process depends on a number of estimates and judgments, management can use biased estimates to manage earnings.

2   The fact that companies are allowed to use different accounting methods can lead to a lack of comparability between companies.

3   The use of inappropriate accounting methods could lead to poor measures of profitability. For example, a company performing a long-term contract using the completed contract method might report zero income for several years, while it was in fact performing valuable work.

4   The use of improper allocations or transfer prices among parts of a large company can aid tax avoidance, and may also distort the profitability of particular segments of the company.

5   Some users question whether the practice of depreciating particular fixed assets and amortizing certain intangible assets makes economic sense. For example, it is common to depreciate commercial buildings over lives of 30 to 40 years, but in fact many commercial buildings

gain in value over time. Doubt about the usefulness of the depreciation and amortization processes is one reason some analysts use a measure called "EBITDA." "EBITDA" stands for "earnings before interest, taxes, depreciation and amortization."

Unresolved Issues and Areas for Further Research

There are many issues related to accounting allocations that would benefit from further research. Several are outlined below:

1   Which allocation methods are the closest to an accurate measurement of economic income?
2   Are financial statement users confused by the different allocation measures used by different companies, or are they able to effectively compare the results of companies that use different methods?
3   How do different methods of allocating costs within a group of related organizations affect the performance of the group?
4   How much tax is being avoided by transfer pricing and expense allocations among related companies?
5   Are there ways for tax authorities to easily identify abusive allocations of income for tax purposes among related entities?

Key Terms

Accelerated depreciation—Accelerated depreciation methods compute high amounts of depreciation early in the life of an asset and lower levels in later years. The double declining balance method is an example.

Accumulated depreciation—This contra account modifies the related fixed asset accounts. At any time, it shows the cumulative amount of depreciation recognized to date for these assets.

Allocation—This is a process of assigning parts of a single balance to various objects or accounts or time periods.

Amortization—Amortization is the term used for allocating the cost of intangible assets to time periods.

Book value of a fixed asset—This equals cost minus accumulated depreciation. This is the value at which a fixed asset is "carried" on the balance sheet.

Completed contract method—This method of accounting for long-term contracts waits to recognize gains until the work is substantially complete. If losses exist, they are recognized immediately.

Cost recovery method—This revenue recognition method recognizes equal amounts of expenses and revenues until the installment payments received equal the total expected costs of the deal. Revenue and gross profit are recognized when payments beyond the initial cost are received.

Current income taxes—The income tax payable or receivable on the tax return for the year is the "current" income tax.

Deferred income tax assets and liabilities—Deferred income tax assets and liabilities result from differences in the timing of recognizing revenues and expenses under GAAP and tax rules. When net income is recognized *earlier* under tax rules than under GAAP, the result is a deferred tax asset. When net income is recognized *later* under tax rules than under GAAP, the result is a deferred tax liability.

Deferred income tax expense (or benefit)—This is the part of the income tax expense (or benefit) that is *not* included on that year's tax return. Deferred income tax expense is caused by differences in the timing of recognition of revenues and expenses under GAAP and tax rules.

Deposit method—This is another name for the cost recovery method. See the entry above.

Depletion—Depletion is the process of allocating the net cost of owning natural resources to inventory and to expense.

Depreciation—Depreciation is the process of allocating the net cost of owning fixed assets such as buildings to expense over their useful lives.

Double declining balance method—This accelerated method of depreciation bases the depreciation expense on the beginning carrying value of the fixed asset. The "rate" of depreciation is double the straight-line rate. Double declining balance would multiply the beginning carrying value by the rate to compute the annual depreciation expense.

Installment method—The installment method recognizes revenue and costs on sales as installment payments are received from the customer.

Multiple deliverables—The company must perform several services, or deliver several services, as part of a single contract.

Percentage of completion method—Under this method of recognizing revenues and costs on long-term contracts, the company recognizes revenues and costs each year based on the estimated total profits from the contract, the current stage of completion of the project, and the revenues and costs already recognized.

Period costs—These costs are not directly related to making the product by a manufacturer or buying it for a merchandising company. They are expensed during periods of time, and are not treated as part of the inventory asset.

Product costs—These are costs of manufacturing a product or the cost of purchasing it from a vendor. These costs are considered part of inventory until the items are sold.

Residual value—This is the same as "salvage value."

Salvage value—The estimated amount of money expected to be received when the company disposes of an asset.

Straight-line method—The method of depreciation that records an equal expense each year, based on the asset's cost, expected salvage value, and expected useful life.

Transfer price—The price at which one member of a group of related companies or divisions sells an item, or provides a service, to other members of the group.

Units of production method—This method of depreciation or depletion allocates costs equally to each item produced, based on cost of the asset; production figures for the year and estimates of the total amount of likely production in the life of the asset; and salvage value.

Vendor-specific objective evidence—This is a type of evidence used in allocating revenues when there are multiple deliverables. It is objective evidence of how the seller of the services or products would price them if sold separately.

Questions and Problems

Comprehension Questions

C1. (Allocation) Why do accountants try to allocate costs of buildings, equipment and other operating assets to several time periods, instead of considering them expenses when they are purchased?

C2. (Allocation—revenues) What are the different methods of allocating revenues for a contract when the customer pays with installments?

C3. (Revenue recognition) What are the FASB's general criteria for when revenues should be recognized?

C4. (Revenue recognition) One of the criteria for revenue recognition is that the revenue is "realized or realizable." Does this mean that a company should never record revenue until it has received cash from the customer? Explain.

C5. (Revenue recognition—single payment, services over time) An insurance company sells home insurance to customers. The typical insurance contract calls for the insurance company to receive payment first. Once payment is received, the insurance company provides insurance for 12 months. Should the insurance company recognize the full amount of the cash received as revenue at the time the cash is received, or allocate the revenue over the 12 months of the policy? Explain your answer.

C6. (Installment and cost recovery methods) What are the installment and cost recovery methods of recognizing revenues? When is it appropriate to use one of these methods, rather than recognizing revenue when goods are shipped to customers?

C7. (Installment, cost recovery, and immediate recognition) Which of these three methods of recognizing revenue and costs on installment sales arrangements is the most conservative? Which is the least conservative? Explain your answer.

C8. (Long-term contracts) When is income or loss earned on a long-term contract recognized under the following methods?

A. Completed contract, when the contract is expected to be profitable
B. Completed contract, when the contract is expected to lose money
C. Percentage of completion, when the contract is expected to be profitable
D. Percentage of completion, when the contract is expected to lose money

C9. (Long-term contracts) Which of the following methods of accounting for long-term contracts is most conservative, and which is least conservative, assuming the contract will be profitable?

A. Percentage of completion
B. Completed contract (an alternative under U.S. GAAP)
C. Cost recovery (an alternative under IFRS)

C10. (Long-term contracts) When are the following methods appropriate for accounting for long-term contracts?

A. Percentage of completion
B. Completed contract
C. Cost recovery

C11. (Similar services over time) Assume that a landlord offers to rent office space to an accounting firm for three years, for a total amount of rental of $360,000. The lease will start on November 1, Year 1. The landlord tells the accounting firm it can either pay a monthly rental of $10,000 each month for 36 months, or it can pay no rent for the first two months, and pay rent of $10,589 for the remaining 34 months. If the accounting firm chooses the second option, and pays no rent in November and December Year 1, would it be able to say for GAAP purposes that it had no rent expense in Year 1? Explain your answer.

C12. (Multiple deliverables) What is the general rule for accounting for a contract under which a company delivers several products to a customer?

C13. (Period and product costs) What is meant by the terms "period costs" and "product costs"?

C14. (Repairs and maintenance versus costs of fixed assets) What is the general rule that distinguishes between costs of maintaining a fixed asset and costs that are considered to add to the carrying value of the fixed asset?

C15. (Depreciation—causes) What are three major reasons that fixed assets may lose value to a company over time?

C16. (Straight-line depreciation) What is meant by straight-line depreciation? What is the formula for computing the expense each period?

C17. (Units of production depreciation) What is meant by units of production depreciation? What is a formula for computing the expense as production occurs?

C18. (Double declining balance depreciation) What is meant by double declining balance depreciation? What is the formula for computing the expense each period?

C19. (Double declining balance depreciation) This question deals with salvage value.

A. Does the formula for double declining balance contain a factor for salvage value?

B. How does an accountant using the double declining balance method of depreciation ensure that the asset is not depreciated so much that the book value becomes less than the salvage value?

C20. (Terminology) What differences, if any, are there between the following terms? When is each one used?

A. Amortization
B. Depletion
C. Depreciation

C21. (Book value) What is meant by the "book value" of a fixed asset?

C22. (Disposals of fixed assets) How is the gain or loss computed when a company sells a fixed asset, such as a machine?

C23. (Disposals of fixed assets) Would the gain or loss on the sale of a fixed asset, partway through its expected life, be different if the company used straight-line depreciation than it would be if the company used accelerated depreciation? Explain your answer.

C24. (Changes in estimates for depreciation) When a company changes its estimates of the remaining useful life of a machine, what effect does this have on the accounting for:

- Periods in the past, for which the company has already published financial statements?
- The current and future periods?

C25. (Intangible amortization) What method do companies typically use to amortize intangible assets that have fixed useful lives?

C26. (Depletion) What method do companies typically use to compute depletion of natural resources like coal mines?

C27. (Deferred taxes) What is meant by a deferred tax asset? Give an example.

C28. (Deferred taxes) What is meant by a deferred tax liability? Give an example.

C29. (Deferred taxes) Assume that the Reardon Corp. is being sued by the Jarvis Corp. At the end of Year 1, Reardon believes it to be probable that it will eventually have to pay Jarvis $10 million. That means that this lawsuit meets the GAAP rules for a loss contingency, and an expense must be recorded in Year 1. However, the tax rules do not allow Reardon to take a tax deduction until it actually makes a payment. Reardon expects that the lawsuit will end in Year 3. Reardon also believes that when it makes the payment to Jarvis in Year 3, Reardon will be able to take a tax deduction for the $10 million. The tax rate is 35%, so Reardon's tax will be reduced by $3,500,000 when it takes this deduction.

A. For GAAP purposes, does it make sense to record the $3,500,000 tax benefit in Year 1 or in Year 3? Explain your answer.

B. On the balance sheet, should Reardon record a deferred tax asset or a deferred tax liability in Year 1?

C30. (Deferred taxes—net operating losses) What is meant by the following terms:

    A. Net operating loss carryback
    B. Net operating loss carryforward.

C31. (Deferred taxes—valuation allowance) What is meant by a "valuation allowance" on deferred tax assets? What standard of probability is used to decide if a valuation allowance is needed?

Application Questions

A1. (Revenue recognition methods) Match the appropriate revenue recognition technique to the situation:

Immediate recognition when goods are delivered
Installment or cost recovery method
Percentage of completion method
Completed contract method

    A. A company is building a road on a long-term contract. It is able to estimate the eventual cost of the project, and the total amount of work required, and how much work has been completed so far.
    B. A company sells goods on credit, and is able to estimate reliably the sales returns and bad debts.
    C. A company sells goods on credit, on an installment basis, and the amount of bad debts is unpredictable.
    D. A company is building a new fighter plane for the Air Force. Because the technology is so advanced, the company is unable to reliably predict the total cost of the job.

A2. (Revenue recognition) For each of the following situations, would GAAP require that revenue be recognized: at the start of the period; at the time of delivery of goods or services; evenly during a period of time; or at the end of the period? Explain your answers.

    A. A manufacturer sells electronics products like televisions to retail stores. It gives the retail stores 60 days to pay for the electronics. The company is able to predict collections with reasonable accuracy.
    B. A book publisher sells books to retail bookstores, and allows the bookstores to return any unsold books within 60 days for full credit. A presidential candidate has just written a book, and the publisher is printing and shipping a million copies. No one knows how popular the book will be. Should revenue be recognized at the date of shipment or should it be recognized only after the 60-day period is past?
    C. A company provides computer support services. It collects payment in advance, and provides support as needed over a 12-month period.

A3. (Revenue recognition—installment sales) The Garcia Corp. is a real estate developer. In Year 1, it sold a house to Michael Sukul for $200,000, in return for five yearly installments of $40,000 each, plus interest. The first installment was paid at the time of sale. The house cost Garcia $115,000 to build. Compute the revenue and cost of sales that Garcia would recognize each year from Year 1 to Year 5 if it used:

    A. Immediate recognition at time of sale
    B. The installment method
    C. The cost recovery method

A4. (Revenue recognition—installment sales) The Lozito Corp. sold a $6,000 set of bedroom furniture to a customer. The customer agreed to pay the balance in four payments of $1,500, plus interest. The first payment was at the time of delivery. The cost of the bedroom furniture to Lozito was $4,000. Compute the revenue and cost of sales that Lozito should record as it receives each payment, if it used:

A. Immediate recognition at time of sale
B. The installment method
C. The cost recovery method

A5. (Revenue recognition—one payment up front) Macumber Corp. publishes a monthly magazine. On January 20, Year 1, it receives a check from a customer for a three-year subscription to the magazine, for $144. Macumber begins sending the magazines out in February, Year 1, and continues to send one per month through January, Year 4.

A. In January, Year 1, how much of the $144 payment should be considered revenue, and how much should be considered deferred revenue?
B. In February, Year 1, how much should be recognized as revenue?
C. After 11 months, at the end of December, Year 1, how much revenue would Macumber have recognized, in total, for this subscription?
D. After 11 months, at the end of December, Year 1, what is the deferred revenue balance from this subscription?
E. What is the deferred revenue balance at December 31, Year 2?
F. What is the deferred revenue balance at December 31, Year 3?

A6. (Multiple deliverables) Assume that on the first day of Year 1, Chuck Laboratory Systems, Inc. signs a contract with the state of California under which Chuck Laboratory Systems will provide the state with:

- Computer equipment, to be delivered in Year 1, that cost Chuck $200,000
- Computer software, written by Chuck Systems, to be delivered in Year 1
- A promise to provide maintenance and software support for three years

The total contract price is $1,000,000. Chuck Systems estimates that, if it sold these services separately, it would have charged $250,000 for the computer equipment, $800,000 for the software, and $150,000 for the maintenance and support services.

A. Compute the amounts of revenue that Chuck Systems should allocate to:

a. The computer equipment
b. The software
c. The maintenance and support services

B. Compute the total amounts of revenue that Chuck Systems should recognize in:

a. Year 1
b. Year 2
c. Year 3

A7. (Long-term contracts—estimated costs don't change) Anker Corp. is building an office building under a long-term contract. The total construction contract price is $40 million. Anker estimates that its costs will total $32 million. The contract is expected to take three years to complete.

A. In the first year, costs are $8 million. Anker estimates that the job is about 25% done. What gross profit will it recognize under:

    a. The percentage of completion method?
    b. The completed contract method?

B. In the second year, costs are $16 million. Anker estimates that the job is now 75% done. Anker continues to believe the total cost of the job will be $32 million. What gross profit will it recognize under:

    a. The percentage of completion method?
    b. The completed contract method?

C. In the third year, costs are $8 million, and the contract is completed. What gross profit will Anker recognize under:

    a. The percentage of completion method?
    b. The completed contract method?

D. What are total gross profits under the two methods?

A8. (Long-term contracts—estimated costs change during contract) Donnelly Corp is building a highway for the State of Maine. The total contract price = $100 million. The project is expected to take three years. Donnelly expects to incur $80 million of costs, and therefore it expects the gross profit on the project to be $20 million.

A. In the first year, costs are $16 million, and Donnelly believes it is 20% complete. Donnelly continues to believe that total costs will equal $80 million. What gross profit will Donnelly recognize in Year 1 under:

    a. The percentage of completion method?
    b. The completed contract method?

B. In the second year, construction was slower than expected, due to bad weather and to some unexpected construction problems. Donnelly spent $29 million in Year 2, bringing the total costs to date to $45 million (including the $16 million from Year 1). Donnelly now believes the project is 50% done, and that the total project costs will equal $90 million. What gross profit will Donnelly recognize in Year 2 under:

    a. The percentage of completion method?
    b. The completed contract method?

C. In the third year, there are some extra unexpected costs. Donnelly spends $47 million in Year 3, and finishes the project. The total costs over three years equal $92 million. What gross profit will Donnelly recognize in Year 1 under:

    a. The percentage of completion method?
    b. The completed contract method?

A9. (Allocation of operating lease payments) Daiva Corp. signs an agreement to rent office space to Jarvis Ltd. The lease is for 10 years. Under the terms of the lease, the "base rent" is:

$2,000 per month in years 1, 2, and 3
$3,000 per month in years 4 through 7
$4,000 per month in the last three years

A. What is the average monthly rent for the 10-year period?
B. Under GAAP, what should the company record as monthly rent expense in Year 1?

C. How should the receipt of each $2,000 payment of rent in Year 1 be reflected in the fundamental accounting equation? What assets, liabilities, or revenues are affected?

D. How should the receipt of each $4,000 payment in Year 10 be reflected in the fundamental accounting equation? What assets, liabilities, or revenues are affected?

A10. (Product and period costs) Classify each of the following as either period costs or product costs of a refrigerator manufacturer. Note that overhead costs related to manufacturing are considered product costs:

A. Rent on the headquarters building
B. Accounting department salaries
C. Materials used to make the refrigerator motors
D. Labor used to assemble the refrigerators
E. Research on new product designs
F. Advertising
G. The cost of heating the manufacturing facility

A11. (Repairs and maintenance versus capitalized costs) For each of the following indicate whether the cost should be considered an expense in the period incurred, or whether it should be accounted for as adding value to a fixed asset. Explain your answer.

A. A company that provides limousine service spends money to change a regular car into a "stretch" limo with room for three more passengers.
B. A company that provides taxi service spends money to replace the battery of a taxi.
C. A company that owns an office building adds an additional wing to the building.
D. A company that owns an office building replaces an old roof that was leaking with a new roof.

A12. (Prepaid expenses) The Kwang Corp. paid $72,000 on July 1, Year 1, for a four-year property insurance policy.

A. At the time it makes the $72,000 payment, how does this payment affect the accounting equation? What assets, liabilities, or expenses are affected?
B. Each month, as Kwang records some insurance expense, how is the accounting equation affected? What assets, liabilities, or expenses are affected?
C. What amount of this payment should it allocate to expense in:

    a. The last six months of Year 1?
    b. Year 2?
    c. Year 3?
    d. The first six months of Year 4?

A13. (Straight-line and declining balance depreciation methods) On January 1, Year 1, the Obremski Corp. paid $14,000 for a machine that it expects to have a four-year life, and to have salvage value of $2,000. Compute the appropriate depreciation expense each year from Year 1 through Year 4.

A13. (Straight-line and declining balance depreciation methods) On January 1, Year 1, the Wierciak Corp. paid $23,000 for a machine that it expects to have a five-year life, and to have salvage value of $3,000. Compute the appropriate depreciation expense each year from Year 1 through Year 5.

A14. (Units of production method) In Year 1, the Taslitsky Corp. paid $25,000 for a machine. It expects to use this machine to produce 300,000 units of its product. It expects the salvage value to be $5,000. Compute the depreciation expense for years in which it produced:

A.   40,000 units
B.   75,000 units
C.   0 units
D.   90,000 units

A15. (Depletion) A company expects to use a coal mine for several years, and the company plans to take 20,000 tons of coal out of the mine. The cost related to the mine is $6,000,000.

A.   What depletion expense should be recognized per ton of coal that is mined?
B.   What would be the depletion expense in a year when the company mined 5,000 tons of coal?

A16. (Gains or losses on sales of fixed assets) The Narkaj Corp. bought a machine in year 1, for a cost of $10,000. It expected the salvage value to be $1,000, and it expected to use the machine for nine years. It actually sold the machine after two years for a price of $7,500.

A.   If it used straight-line depreciation, what would be the book value of the machine after two years?
B.   If it used straight-line depreciation, what would be the gain or loss on the sale of the machine?
C.   If it used double declining balance depreciation, what is the depreciation expense for:

   a.   Year 1?
   b.   Year 2?

D.   If it used double declining balance depreciation, what would be the book value at the end of the second year?
E.   If it used double declining balance depreciation, what would be the gain or loss on the sale of the machine?

A17. (Deferred taxes) In Year 1, the Natole Corp. sells a building that it has owned for many years for a gain of $50 million. The buyer agrees to pay Natole half the purchase price in Year 1 and the other half (plus interest) in Year 2. For GAAP, the entire gain is recognized in Year 1. For tax purposes, Natole is using the installment method, and will report half the gain in Year 1 and half in Year 2.
   The tax rate is 35%.

A.   How much tax will Natole pay because of this transaction in:

   a.   Year 1?
   b.   Year 2?

B.   For GAAP accounting purposes, how much should the tax expense be in:

   a.   Year 1?
   b.   Year 2?

C.   For GAAP purposes, will Natole show a deferred tax asset or a deferred tax liability at the end of Year 1? Explain.

A18. (Deferred taxes) In Year 1, Zhang Corp. records a $300,000 expense on its books for vacation pay that has been earned by its employees, for vacations they have not yet taken. The tax law will not allow Zhang to take a deduction for vacation pay until the employees take their vacations. Assume that employees do take the vacations in Year 2. The tax rate is 35%.

A. How much of a tax savings will Zhang have because of this employee vacation pay in:

    a. Year 1?

    b. Year 2?

B. For GAAP accounting purposes, what tax benefit related to the vacation pay will Zhang record in

    a. Year 1?

    b. Year 2?

C. For GAAP purposes, will Zhang show a deferred tax asset or a deferred tax liability at the end of Year 1?

Discussion Questions

D1. (Comparing depreciation methods) You are comparing the financial statements of two manufacturers. The two companies have exactly the same machines, bought at the same times. The machines typically last eight years. Straight Company uses straight-line depreciation, and Fast Company uses accelerated depreciation. Which company would you expect to show higher depreciation expense in each of these situations? Explain your answers.

A. Both companies are in their first year of operations.

B. Both companies are 20 years old, and are expanding every year.

C. Both companies are 20 years old, and stopped expanding after their 10th year. They have been replacing machines as old ones wear out, but not adding new ones.

D. Both companies are 20 years old, and they are shrinking. They are not replacing their machines as fast as they wear out.

D2. (Depreciation concepts) Rockefeller Center is a building complex in midtown Manhattan that was originally built by the Rockefeller family in the 1930s. According to Wikipedia, construction costs were reportedly about $250 million, and the land was later purchased for $400 million. In 2000, the land and buildings were sold for about $1.85 billion.[14] This means that the original owners of Rockefeller Center made a great deal of money over the approximately 60 years they owned it. However, if they were like most property owners, they recorded depreciation each year on the $250 million cost of the buildings.

A. Do you think recording depreciation expense on buildings is appropriate for financial statement purposes? Explain.

B. Do you think that, as an analyst, you would consider depreciation of office buildings to be relevant and useful information? Explain.

C. Would it make sense for the new owners to compute depreciation assuming zero salvage value? If not, what salvage value would you consider appropriate?

D3. (Revenue recognition in cattle ranching) The introduction to this chapter mentioned several issues in allocation, including cattle growing. Assume that Heather Cattle Ranch buys young calves at an age of six months, and then feeds them until they are three years old. It then sells the cattle.

    A. Economically, when does the increase in value of the cattle occur? As they grow, or at the time of sale?

    B. Should it recognize revenue for accounting purposes as the cattle grow (and become more valuable) or only when it sells them? Explain.

    C. For tax purposes, revenue is recognized at the time of sale. Can you explain why you think the tax law uses this rule?

D4. (Depreciation for tax purposes) The text explained that, for tax purposes, companies take depreciation much more quickly than they recognize it for GAAP. Why do you think the tax law allows this fast depreciation? Do you think it is good public policy?

D5. (Inconsistencies in accounting—long-term contracts) Your friend complains to you that she is unable to figure out what the FASB wants. In its Concepts Statements, it says it wants neutral, not conservative accounting. But then it doesn't treat gains and losses on long-term contracts equally. If you have a long-term contract, and you expect it to lose money, you recognize all the loss at once, but if you expect it to make money, you recognize the gains slowly, as you do the work. Is she right? Is the FASB inconsistent? Can you think of a good reason for not treating profitable and unprofitable contracts the same?

Notes

1 The idea of allowing different accounting methods, but insisting on consistency and disclosure, has been attributed to George O. May, and was implicit in the NYSE and AICPA correspondence in 1934, according to Carey (1979).

2 For example, if a company could either consider small tools to be an expense when they are bought, or consider them to be fixed assets, it is easier to simply expense them. If they were treated as assets, the company would have to make monthly depreciation entries, and would have to compute a gain or loss when they are disposed of.

3 Chapter 12 introduces a complication. In some cases, the ownership of the books legally changes from seller to buyer at the time the products are shipped, and at other times it changes when the products are delivered. For this chapter, we assume the date of shipment is the key date.

4 Life Time Fitness Inc. Form 10-K for the fiscal year ended December 31, 2013, p. 48. Available at www. sec.gov/Archives/edgar/data/1076195/000107619514000004/ltm201310k.htm (last accessed August 18, 2015).

5 IBM financial statements for the fiscal year ended December 31, 2012. Available at www.sec.gov/Archives/edgar/data/51143/000104746913001698/R9.htm (last accessed August 18, 2015).

6 FASB Codification 605-25-25-5 and 605-25-30.

7 If they are bought in a more complicated fashion, for example using loans or trade-ins of other assets, the entry becomes more complicated, but the basic point is that the asset is established for its cost.

8 United States Steel Corporation, Form 10-K for the fiscal year ended December 31, 2013, p. F-12.

9 Some methods which are now rarely used include recording depreciation in proportion to the revenue expected from an asset and the "retirement method," in which depreciation is only recorded when the asset was retired from use. The FASB also forbids use of "annuity" methods, in which depreciation gets systematically larger over time.

10 FASB Codification Section 360-10-39-9.

11 One alternative method of accelerated depreciation is to replace the "2" in the computation formula with some other number greater than 1, such as 1.5. When 1.5 is used, that is called 150% declining balance depreciation. Another method, discussed in intermediate accounting texts, is "sum of the years' digits" depreciation.

12 IRS. 2013. IRS Data Book, Table 1. See http://www.irs.gov/uac/SOI-Tax-Stats-Collections-and-Re-funds,-by-Type-of-Tax-IRS-Data-Book-Table-1 (last accessed August 18, 2015). According to this table, there were 4,580,000 Subchapter S returns and 3,626,000 partnership returns, so there are more of both of these types of pass-through entities than of corporations subject to income tax. According to other IRS data I have seen, corporations subject to tax tend to be larger and have a disproportionately large share of overall U.S. business revenues and income.

13 Lower rates apply to income below certain thresholds.

14 http://en.wikipedia.org/wiki/Rockefeller_Center (last accessed on January 27, 2015).

References

American Accounting Association. (1971). Report of the Committee on Foundations of Accounting Measurement [Supplement]. *Accounting Review*, *46*(4) 1–48.

AICPA. (2011). *Accounting Trends and Techniques*. New York: AICPA.

Bookholdt, J. L. (1978). Influence of nineteenth and early twentieth century railroad accounting on development of modern accounting theory. *The Accounting Historians Journal* (Spring), 9–28.

Carey, J. L. (1979). The CPA's professional heritage, part II. Working Paper No. 5. In E. N. Coffman (Ed.), *The Academy of Accounting Historians Working Paper Series, Vol. 1 (Working Papers 1–20)*. Richmond, VA: Virginia Commonwealth University.

Chatfield, M. (1977). *A History of Accounting Thought* (revised edition). New York: Robert E. Krieger Publishing Company.

Coffman, E. N. (Ed.) (1979). *The Academy of Accounting Historians Working Paper Series, Vol. 2 (Working Papers 21–40)*. Richmond, VA: Virginia Commonwealth University.

Lail, B. E., Thomas, W. B., & Winterbotham, G. J. (2014). Classification shifting using the "corporate/other" segment. *Accounting Horizons*, *28*(3) 455–77.

Littleton, A. C. (1933). *Accounting Evolution to 1900*. New York: American Institute Publishing Company.

SEC. (1999). Staff Accounting Bulletin No. 101. *Revenue Recognition in Financial Statements*.

Watts, R. L. & Zimmerman, J. L. (1979). The demand for and supply of accounting theories: The market for excuses. *The Accounting Review*, *54* (2), 273–305.

Woodward, P. D. (1956), Depreciation—The development of an accounting concept. *Accounting Review* (January), 71–6.

10   Cost Allocations in Managerial Accounting

Outline

- Preliminary Thoughts
- Learning Objectives
- Overview
- Basic Manufacturing Cost Concepts
- Allocating Costs of Joint Products
- Allocating Overhead and Fixed Costs to Products
- Allocating Costs Among Divisions
- Unresolved Issues and Areas for Further Research

Preliminary Thoughts

> The objective of managerial costing is to provide a monetary reflection of the utilization of business resources and related cause and effect insights into past, present, or future enterprise economic activities. Managerial costing aids managers in their analysis and decision making and supports optimizing the achievement of an enterprise's strategic objectives.
>
> *IMA (2014a, p. 5)*

> The problem: there is no perfect cost accounting but there are many interesting ideas.
>
> *Thomas Schildbach (1997, p. 261)*

> If assets are converted into other enterprises within an enterprise, as when raw materials are converted into finished products, or buildings or equipment are constructed by an enterprise for its own use, the multiplicity of costing conventions that can be used, all within the boundaries of generally accepted accounting principles, make it impossible to attach a unique cost to the finished asset.
>
> *FASB (1980, para. 65)*

> There is substantial confusion about what is the best or most appropriate approach for organizations to measure and report costs for managerial decisions. One would think that now in the 21st Century this situation would be resolved, but debates continue, even among management accountants, about which approach to use.
>
> *IMA (2014a, p. 3)*

> Organizations seeking to maintain or improve their competitiveness need cost information that is accurate and relevant. In the past, companies planned and controlled their operations using accounting information that was assumed to accurately reflect the costs of their products and services. . . . In fact, this was often not the case. The costing systems of many

companies, with their broad averaging allocation of indirect costs, masked by an illusion of precision, were actually providing misleading information to decision makers. This resulted in suboptimal decision making by these companies' managers.

IMA (2014a, p. 1)

This chapter deals with the problems of allocations in managerial accounting. As we saw in Chapter 9, accountants are often forced to allocate costs or revenues for financial reporting, even though there is no clear economic theory that can guide us. The same situation applies in the problems of allocating costs to products, and in allocating certain costs among the divisions of a company.

These five quotations set the themes for this chapter. The IMA outlines some of the important functions that managerial cost information should assist with. Cost information should help managers understand the cause and effect relationships that determine profitability, and is needed for planning, decision-making, and control. Unfortunately, as Thomas Schildbach says in the next quotation, there is no perfect cost accounting. The next two quotations, from the FASB and from the IMA, confirm this. The FASB says there is no one unique way to assign costs to manufactured products, and the IMA says that even in the 21st century, there are debates among management accountants about the best methods. From the point of view of the student, this makes the topic complicated. You need to become familiar with some of the approaches that have been suggested. As Schildbach says, "there are many interesting ideas." So, for each of the major topics in this chapter, you will see that several different approaches are used in practice. Courses in cost accounting and in management provide greater depth to the discussion than is done here.

The last quotation points out why the topic is important. Accountants produce measurements of costs, and these measurements get used. When there are different methods of measuring, they will lead to different decisions. People have suggested that bad methods of allocating costs have led to such bad decisions as:

1   Setting the wrong prices on products and services. Companies may overprice simple products, and lose sales to competitors. Or, companies may underestimate their costs of producing products, and end up losing money by selling unprofitable products

2   Producing too much inventory. Some costing systems may give managers too much incentive to keep production levels high, and that can result in excessive inventory levels. Inventory costs money to store, and is at risk of becoming obsolete. Proponents of "lean manufacturing" processes want systems that result in incentives to minimize inventory

3   Failing to recognize waste and to recognize opportunities to improve production processes. Methods of cost accounting differ in whether they give managers insights into inefficiencies. They also differ in how they look at the activities that contribute to product cost, or into the factors that need to be addressed to improve the speed of production

4   Failing to have different divisions of a company act in a way to maximize overall profits. When different divisions of a company buy and sell from each other, situations can arise in which the best action from a company-wide perspective is not the action that is best from the point of view of one of the divisions.

Learning Objectives

After studying the material in this chapter, you should:

1   Understand the reasons that costs are allocated to products in managerial accounting.
2   Understand the basic terminology involved in assigning costs to products.

3   Understand the issues involved in assigning joint costs to joint products, and several methods now used to allocate these costs.

4   Understand the issues involved in allocating overhead costs to products, and several methods now used to allocate these costs, including: traditional absorption costing; activity-based costing; and resource consumption accounting. Throughput accounting is also introduced, in an appendix.

5   Understand the issues involved in transfer pricing and cost allocation among divisions of decentralized organizations, as well as methods now used to set transfer prices.

Overview

Cost accounting developed later than financial accounting. By some accounts, it first began to be used extensively by manufacturers during the Industrial Revolution to help companies determine rational ways to price their products.[1] Over the course of the 20th century, several variations of cost accounting were developed to help companies make better pricing decisions and also to help control costs. In addition, the principles and techniques of cost accounting were used beyond the manufacturing environment, to help service and merchandising companies. Now, hospitals or airlines use the ideas of cost accounting to identify their most and least profitable products and services, and to identify ways of reducing costs.

Cost accounting was developed to help solve particular problems. Because these problems were different in different industries, and in different parts of the world, a variety of different practices arose. For example, the textile manufacturing done in Britain and the United States during the Industrial Revolution tended to use large amounts of direct labor but relatively simple machinery to make the products. Control of labor costs was important, and the cost of the machinery was not large. In Germany, much early manufacturing involved the chemical industry, which had very expensive machinery and used less labor. Therefore, accounting needed to track the utilization of the expensive factory equipment. In Japan, after World War II, land was expensive, making inventory expensive to store. Also, the major Japanese companies rarely fired workers, so labor costs did not vary much. In Japan, there were strong pressures to minimize inventory levels (Hutchinson and Liao 2009).

Over the course of the 20th century, manufacturing processes changed in several ways.

- Product variety. From 1913 to 1925, Ford Motor Company's famous "Model T" car came in only one color—black.[2] Car companies now make cars with a wide variety of colors and other optional features. This means that cars differ in their costs. It also means that factory resources are being used to produce a variety of different outputs. This creates the issue of "joint costs" which need to be allocated.

- Speed. Production processes have also become faster, meaning there is less inventory that is partly completed.

- Relative importance of inputs. Over time, production processes have tended to be more highly mechanized. From an accounting point of view, that means that direct labor is a less important input, and that the "overhead" costs of machine use, inspection, factory maintenance, and supervision have become relatively more important. These overhead costs are not directly traceable to particular products, and need to be allocated.

- Outsourcing. Companies have become more willing to rely on outside companies to provide them with components, instead of manufacturing items themselves.

- Organization. Many companies have tried to give more autonomy to employees and supervisors at lower levels of the organization, for example on the "shop floor." This change in authority means that information flows have to be designed to serve both the "shop floor" decisions and the upper level managers who monitor the entire organization.

This chapter starts by explaining some basic cost accounting concepts. These concepts are then used to explain some of the problematic issues that arise in three different tasks. One task is deciding how to "split up" costs that were used to produce more than a single product. For example, an oil refinery buys crude oil, and splits it into many different petroleum products (gasoline, jet fuel, kerosene, and so on.) The issue is how much of the cost of the crude oil and of the refinery equipment should be allocated to gasoline as opposed to the other outputs. The second task is allocating overhead to products produced. People have developed several different techniques for doing this. A "traditional" method was used early in the 20th century, and several other methods have been developed to try to overcome some weaknesses in that method. The third issue is how costs are assigned among the divisions of a decentralized company.

Basic Manufacturing Cost Concepts

Categories of Costs

Let's consider a factory that makes men's cotton shirts and women's cotton blouses. There are many different inputs involved in running the factory, and making the garments.

Some of these inputs are directly used every time the company makes a garment. For example, some worker must spend time sewing the sleeves onto the garment. Each garment contains cloth and buttons.

Some other inputs to the process are not directly related to any particular garment. These are "*indirect*" costs. For example, the factory needs to be heated, and there needs to be electric light so the workers can see. The factory building will wear out over time. The company pays for insurance and property taxes on the factory building. These inputs that do not have direct connections to particular items produced are often referred to as "*overhead*" or "*factory overhead.*"

Typically, cost accounting deals with three major categories of costs, which relate to different types of inputs.

"*Direct labor*" is the cost of the workers' time spent making the products. We will assume that the direct labor cost includes wages, payroll taxes, and also such other employee benefits as health insurance. For this example, it would include the time spent by employees cutting the cloth and sewing the cloth into shirts and blouses.

"*Direct materials*" is the cost of the materials that are included in the final product. For the shirt and blouse factory, direct materials would include the cotton cloth used in the shirt, as well as buttons and thread used to sew the shirts together.

"*Overhead*" is the category for the many different indirect costs involved in running the factory and producing clothing. "*Variable overhead costs*" vary directly with the level of production. For example, the company might believe that certain costs of operating machinery vary with the number of garments produced. "*Fixed overhead costs*" do not vary, in the short term, with levels of production. For example, the property taxes on the building typically are the same whether the company produces a lot or just a little.

Cost Hierarchies

It is often useful to think about costs that occur at different levels of the organization. One way of thinking about costs has a "hierarchy" of four levels.

Unit level costs arise each time a unit is produced. An example might be the cotton that goes into a shirt.

Batch level costs include all the unit costs, and also include costs that are incurred when a batch of items is produced. For example, a beer brewing company might have costs to clean out big vats between every batch of a thousand gallons of beer.

Product level costs include all the batch costs, and also include other costs that are incurred when the company decides to produce a particular product. These costs might include product development costs and special equipment.

Facility level costs include all the product costs incurred at the facility, but also include the other costs needed to keep the factory facility operational.

When managers make decisions, it is important that they consider costs at the correct level of the hierarchy. For example, if they are considering closing a factory, all facility level costs are relevant. On the other hand, if they are trying to decide whether to accept a special order for additional batches of an existing product, then the batch level costs would likely be relevant, while many of the product and facility level costs would not.

Note that the amount of allocation effort needed to properly assign costs is lowest for the facility level costs, and greatest for the unit level costs. For example, the salary of a factory security guard is clearly a facility level cost. That is an easy accounting task. Allocating part of that salary to each item produced by the factory is clearly a much more complicated task.

Cost Drivers

A "*cost driver*" is something that is believed to cause costs to increase. Formally, the IMA (2014b) has defined a cost driver as "A measure of activity that is a causal factor in the incurrence of cost to an entity. Examples include direct labor hours, machine hours, beds occupied, computer time used, flight hours, miles driven, and contracts" (p. 313).

In a clothing factory, the number of garments produced is a logical cost driver for raw materials cost, and also for direct labor cost. The number of different types of raw materials needed may be a cost driver for the company's purchasing function. It takes more time for the purchasing department to order a variety of types of raw materials than a small number of them.

Stages of Production

It takes time to manufacture the clothing. First, the company buys cloth, thread, and buttons. Then, it cuts the cloth. Then, it sews the parts of the cloth together. We typically speak of a manufacturer as having three types of inventory, depending on the stage of production of the products.

Raw materials are items that the company has not yet started to work on. This company might have large rolls of cotton cloth and many buttons in its raw materials inventory.

Work in process consists of items that the company has started to work on but has not yet finished. This company might have some cloth that has been cut to the right sizes to make sleeves for shirts and blouses, but has not yet been sewed onto finished shirts. For simple operations like making shirts, quantities of work in process may be small. For complex items with many components, or for items which involve slow chemical aging processes, work in process will be larger.

Finished goods are items that have finished the manufacturing process, and are ready for sale.

Job and Process Cost Systems

A "*job cost system*" is typically used in a business that produces a variety of different products, in distinct batches or "jobs." For example, a printing company might produce 3,000 different novels in a year. It prints many copies of one novel, and then changes its production line to produce copies of the next novel. The different novels have different numbers of pages, use different sizes and qualities of paper, and have different covers. The book company might want to track the costs of producing each type of novel as a separate "job." A law firm or accounting firm would separately track costs it performs for each project for each client.

A "*process cost system*" is typically used in businesses that produce a large amount of identical items on a continuous basis. For example, a company that transforms crude oil into gasoline and fuel oil and other products would typically use a process cost system. Here, there is no need to track individual "jobs" because each gallon of gasoline looks like every other gallon. Instead, all the production for a month is considered part of a continuous process.

Flow of Costs During the Period

For accounting purposes, whether a company uses a job cost system or a process cost system, the company will track the costs of items as they move through the stages of production. Accountants speak of costs moving through the manufacturing process in the same way that physical items being produced move through the system. For the clothing factory example, the costs related to the raw materials inventory consist of what the company paid to buy the cloth, threads, and buttons, and the freight cost to get them into the company's factory. Conceptually, the cost of getting the work in process items into their partly completed stage would include the cost of direct materials in these garments, plus some labor and some overhead costs. The finished goods inventory would include all the items that were used to compute the cost of work in process items, plus additional costs needed to complete them.

A critical point is that the normal *costs* of making the inventory are not *expenses* until the inventory is sold or scrapped. Inventory is an asset. This means that some of the costs that were used to make products each period have to be allocated to the ending inventory, and some costs relate to cost of goods sold (an expense). If more costs are allocated to inventory, expenses are lower, and income is higher. If fewer costs are allocated to inventory, then expenses are higher, and income is lower.

An equation that relates beginning to ending inventory is the following:

Beginning inventory + raw materials purchased + direct labor + manufacturing overhead – cost of goods sold (including shrinkage) = ending inventory

In this equation, the beginning and ending inventories each include three parts: raw materials, work in process, and finished goods inventories. A company can physically count the items on hand at the beginning and end of the period that are in each stage of production. It must use accounting records to assign costs to these items. The costs assigned to beginning and ending inventories include raw materials, direct labor, and overhead. Once the company computes a cost for its ending inventory, it computes the cost of goods sold. You can see from this equation that higher costs assigned to ending inventory result in a lower computed value for cost of goods sold.

Inventory shrinkage is a term used to measure a variety of types of loss of inventory. It can include theft, but also includes spoilage and other unexplained factors that reduce the inventory. Usually, for external reporting, shrinkage is combined with cost of goods sold.

Allocating Costs of Joint Products

In many cases, a company will use a single input to produce more than one product. A classic example is the production of meat. Upton Sinclair's 1906 novel *The Jungle* involved workers in a meat packing factory in Chicago. The company would buy hogs, kill them, and then cut them up. Part of the hog was sold as ham, part as bacon, part as leather, part as sausage meat, and other parts had other uses. As Sinclair wrote, "They use everything about the hog except the squeal." The accounting question is how much of the cost of buying and cutting up the hog should be allocated to each of the many products.

Other examples might include:

- Oil refineries take crude oil, heat it, and separate out a variety of petroleum products, such as kerosene, jet fuel, heating oil, benzene, gasoline and so forth.

- Dairies take cow's milk and separate it into such products as cream, whey, whole milk, cheese, and butter.
- Cotton seeds are crushed to produce cottonseed oil and cottonseed meal.

In technical language, we refer to the many products that come from this process as "*joint products*" because they are produced jointly from the same process for some period of time.

The "*split-off point*" is the point at which the two products incur different costs. For example, in the case of the hog, after the company splits the hog into different pieces, it will incur different costs in turning some of the meat into sausages than it will in turning the skin into leather. In the case of a dairy, after cream is separated from milk, the cream must undergo further processing to become butter or cheese.

"*Joint costs*" are the costs incurred up until the split-off point.

From an economic point of view, there is no point in trying to allocate the joint cost of buying the hog to the various products. Pricing should be based on what customers will pay. Any decisions about production should be based on looking at the total costs of producing all the products that come from a hog, and comparing these costs with the total revenues. In other words, the economic decisions should be made at the level of the hog, not the level of each of the products. The same logic applies to any other joint product. A committee of the American Accounting Association (1971) wrote, with regard to two (imaginary) joint products, one liquid and one solid:

> None of the internal economic decisions which might be made with regard to these two products, such as whether to make or buy, determination of selling price, capital budgeting decisions for related equipment, or cost control decisions, will be enhanced by allocation of the joint costs to the individual products. In this sense, such allocations are pointless for economic decision purposes. Indeed, there is a danger that if such allocations are made, some economic decision makers may take them seriously, be confused, and make inappropriate decisions. Because of this, allocations of joint costs are to be discouraged for internal economic decision purposes.
>
> (p. 35)

However, there are various accounting purposes which make it is necessary to try to allocate costs to the unit or product level. In particular, it is necessary to use unit level costs to value the ending inventory for financial reporting purposes. Also, the company may sometimes need to show that the prices it charges for particular items are reasonable with regard to their costs.

Three different approaches are used to allocate the joint costs among significant joint products, and other methods are used to deal with assigning costs to minor "*by-products*." Let us assume we are trying to allocate the costs of an $80 barrel of crude oil among three petroleum products: two units of gasoline; two units of heating oil; and one unit of jet fuel. Assume that the gasoline can be sold for $20 per unit ($40 in total), the jet fuel can be sold for $16, and the heating oil can be sold for $22 per unit ($44 in total). The total selling price of all the joint products = $100. As long as the $100 in selling prices exceeds the combination of the $80 purchase price for crude oil and the costs of the refining process, the refiner can make money.

Method 1—Allocation by unit volumes. In this method, we allocate the joint costs based on the volume of the products produced. In this example, one barrel of crude oil results in five units of output: two of gasoline; two of heating oil, and one of jet fuel. Using this method, 2/5 of the cost of the crude oil would be allocated to gasoline, 2/5 to heating oil, and 1/5 to jet fuel. The allocations of cost would be:

Gasoline	$32
Heating oil	$32
Jet fuel	$16

An advantage of this method is simplicity. A disadvantage is that it is likely to make certain products look unprofitable. Some petroleum products have low sales value, and if they are assigned a cost based just on volume, it will look like the company is losing money on them. In this example, the cost and the selling price of the jet fuel are each $16, so it appears the company makes no profit on jet fuel. It appears that the profit on gasoline = $40 − 32 = $8, and the profit on heating oil = $44 − 32 = $12.

Method 2—Allocation by relative sales value at split-off. In this method, the costs are allocated based on market prices of the various products. Here the amount of cost allocated to each product, and the profit on sales, are as follows:

	Costs	**Profits**	
Gasoline	$80 × (40/100) = $32.00	$40 − $32 =	$ 8.00
Heating oil	$80 × (44/100) = $35.20	$44 − $35.20 =	$ 8.80
Jet fuel	$80 × (16/100) = $12.80	$16 − $12.80 =	$ 3.20
	Total cost $80.00	Total profit	$20.00

This method has several benefits, and is recommended by various authorities.[3] One benefit is its simplicity. It also includes in the analysis information about how valuable each of the joint products is. None of the products are seen as unprofitable, as long as the overall process of making all the products is profitable.

Method 3—Using relative net realizable value at point of split-off. This method is very similar to using the relative sales price. The difference is that "*net realizable value*" equals the selling price minus the costs involved in completing and selling the items. If the selling costs are minor, the two methods will give the same results. If selling costs differ among the products, then less joint cost will be allocated to the products with higher selling costs after the split-off point.

This method is slightly more complicated to compute than the previous method, since companies need to estimate selling costs and the costs to bring the items to a salable state.

This method will result in equal gross margin percentages for each of the joint products.

A theoretical objection is that this method uses information and costs after the split-off point to allocate costs at the time of the split-off.

By-products are items that are not produced as the main purpose of the manufacturing process, but may have some minor sales value. For example, in the process of cutting wood into chairs and tables, a furniture company will probably have some scrap wood and sawdust. It may be able to sell these by-products for minor amounts of cash. Companies use two different ways of allocating costs to these by-products.

One method is not to record any revenue from the sales of the by-products. Instead, when the items are sold, cash is increased and the company records the amount of cash received as a reduction in the costs of making the other joint products. In this example, the money received from selling wood scraps would be considered a reduction in the joint costs involved in making furniture.

A second method is to allocate just enough costs to the by-product as to bring the net profit on the by-product to zero. This has a very similar effect to the first method, since in both cases there are fewer costs being allocated to the furniture produced.

Allocating Overhead and Fixed Costs to Products

Overview

Companies need to allocate costs to products for financial accounting, for tax purposes, and for managerial accounting reasons.

The IMA (2011) has summarized the research on how companies allocate as follows:

> Survey evidence and research shows that firms design systems to allocate fixed costs (sometimes termed capacity costs) for several reasons. First, allocation is required for valuing inventories and for computing income as per the generally accepted accounting principles (i.e., the *inventory valuation* role). Second, managers use cost allocations when making decisions related to product planning and resource planning (i.e., the *product costing* role). Third, firms employ cost allocations to induce desired behavior and to dissuade or "tax" undesired behavior (the *behavior modification* role).
>
> (p. 3)

The "inventory valuation" role is needed for both financial accounting and for tax reporting. The financial statements and tax returns need to have measurements of ending inventory and of the cost of goods sold. For this purpose, the accountants need to determine which parts of the materials, labor, and overhead costs of the period should be considered to apply to the items that have been sold during the period, and which parts are related to the ending inventory. It is not conceptually difficult to trace the materials and labor costs to the individual units produced. The conceptual difficulty comes in allocating overhead costs such as heating the factory building, usage of factory machines, depreciation on the factory building, the purchasing function of the factory, and factory supervision. In modern manufacturing operations, these overhead and indirect costs are a large part of the total cost.

It would be much easier if we could decide to treat all overhead costs as period costs. In that case, we would not have to allocate them to products, and would not have to assign any of them to the ending inventory. Some accountants have advocated using such methods for management accounting. These accountants would only include such "direct costs" as raw materials and direct labor (and possible overhead costs that vary with production) in computing the product costs. We will discuss these methods later. However, the FASB, the IASB, and the U.S. tax authorities all insist that inventory be computed in a way that includes some rational and systematic allocation of overhead. They believe that including overhead in product cost is necessary to avoid materially understating ending inventory and overstating cost of goods sold. See Boyd and Cox (2002).

The "product costing" role is essential to management. Managers need cost information for decision-making, for control, and for evaluation. Managers need cost information to determine which products are profitable to make at current market prices. Cost information is also helpful in deciding how to improve production processes and production scheduling. The ability to compare actual costs to expected costs is very useful in the control and evaluation functions. Some of the decisions managers make require information from different cost hierarchies. For example, assume a company that takes milk and uses it to jointly produce whey (the part of the milk after the cream is removed) and cheese needs to make decisions about how much to produce. Since it produces these two products jointly, it makes sense to consider both the revenues and the costs on a combined basis.

The major problem that can arise in cost accounting is when the costs that are measured lead managers to make bad decisions. Here are two examples:

- If a company makes numerous products, including both high-volume, simple products and lower volume, complicated products, some systems will overestimate the costs of the high-volume products and underestimate the costs of the complicated products. As a result, the company may set incorrect prices. It will overprice the simple products, and will lose sales to its competition because its prices are too high. It will price the complicated products too low. This will help the company sell these items, but unfortunately it may actually lose money on them.

- The method of allocating costs may encourage managers to keep production levels high. When you have fixed costs, the fixed cost allocated to each unit is lower at high levels of production. This can lead to overproduction, and excessive levels of inventory. Inventory can be expensive to store, and the company is also at risk of having its inventory become obsolete or damaged.

The "behavior modification" role for cost accounting uses cost accounting reports to give managers incentives to plan operations to meet specific management goals. These might include: using labor efficiently; using expensive machines at near their capacity; keeping inventory levels low; reducing bottlenecks in production; or using support services more efficiently.

The different methods of cost accounting discussed in this chapter each have advantages and disadvantages. No perfect method, that provides all the desired information without leading to any bad decisions, has yet been created.

Traditional Full Absorption Costing

The Basic Process

Under both U.S. GAAP and IFRS, inventory costs must include the related direct costs of materials and labor plus allocated overhead costs. This requirement is called "*full absorption costing*" or "*absorption costing*" because the costs of the products produced must contain ("absorb") all of the production costs. The FASB has forbidden companies to use an alternate method, called "*direct costing*," which only assigns the direct labor and materials costs to the units produced. U.S. tax rules also require absorption costing.

This is how the process works.

1   The company keeps track of the raw materials cost for each item produced, and assigns those costs to particular items or batches of items produced.
2   The company keeps track of labor time spent directly on producing items, and assigns these direct labor costs to particular items or batches of items produced.
3   The company keeps track of its other production-related spending, and accumulates these costs in what are called "cost centers" or "overhead pools." For example, during a year it will use cost centers or overhead pools to keep track of the costs for a plant maintenance staff, a production scheduling department, a materials receiving staff, insurance on the building, property taxes, and numerous other activities and functions.
4   The company assigns or "applies" the overhead costs in each cost center to items produced based on the activity of one or more "cost drivers." This is the critical and complicated step. It is discussed below.
5   At the end of the period, the costs that are assigned to those items still on hand are shown on the company's books as an asset, inventory. The costs that are assigned to items that have been sold or that have been scrapped are expenses, typically called cost of goods sold.
6   At the end of the period, 100% of the costs incurred for raw materials, direct labor, and overhead must have been assigned either to the ending inventory or the cost of goods sold. If any costs have not yet been assigned, the accountants must make entries in the books to assign them to inventory or cost of goods sold.

Some studies suggest that up to around 40% of companies use this method, although it is hard to get good data on the frequency of use.[4]

Over-Applied and Under-Applied Overhead

A practical problem that companies face in using absorption costing is that overhead costs are incurred unevenly throughout the year. For example, real estate taxes might be paid quarterly, and property insurance might be paid once per year. Heating costs are seasonal, and some repairs occur randomly during the year. As a result, companies usually do not try to apply overhead costs as they occur. This would make the amount of overhead cost applied per unit fluctuate wildly throughout the year, and the resulting measurements would not be helpful to decision-makers. Instead, companies try to estimate a "predetermined overhead rate." They compute this rate per unit of activity of some cost driver as follows:

Predetermined overhead rate = (budgeted annual overhead) ÷ (budgeted level of activity)

Note that companies typically use a budgeted level of activity here, which is always lower than either the practical capacity or the theoretical capacity.[5] This is a difference between the traditional full absorption method and the activity-based costing and resource consumption methods discussed later.

Companies using traditional absorption costing also use cost drivers whose activity level has a logical relation to the overhead cost. Some typical cost drivers include:

1   Number of units produced
2   Direct labor hours. This is a sensible cost driver for overhead costs that directly relate to the number of employees working, and the time they spend working. For example, if people are using up certain supplies while they work on the production, then the use of these supplies is related to the hours worked
3   Direct labor dollars. This would be a sensible cost driver if the overhead costs are affected both by the number of hours worked, and also the pay level or skill level of the workers. This might make sense as a cost driver for certain bonus or vacation pay expenses
4   Machine hours. Here, activity is measured by the number of hours key machines are being used. This might be logically related to such costs as energy usage or machinery maintenance.

So, for example, assume a company expects to produce 1,000,000 widgets during the year, and expects its overhead costs to total $9,000,000. If it uses the number of items produced as a cost driver, its predetermined overhead application rate would be $9 per widget (= $9,000,000 ÷ 1,000,000 widgets).

Assume that it actually produces 995,000 widgets, and its overhead costs were $9,001,000. Of the widgets produced, 100,000 are still on hand at the end of the year, and the rest were sold. What would its accounts look like?

It would actually have spent $9,001,000 on overhead costs. During the year, it would have used its predetermined overhead rate to apply the inventory. It would have "applied" $9 of overhead costs to each of the items produced. The total amount of inventory "applied" would equal $9 × 995,000 = $8,955,000. Of this total, $900,000 ($9 × 100,000) has been applied to items in inventory, and the $8,055,000 remainder has been considered part of cost of goods sold.

Because the company applied overhead costs using an estimated rate, and the actual spending and activity were slightly different from the budget, it will end the year with $46,000 (= $9,001,000 – $8,955,000) in "under-applied" overhead costs. If it is considered material, companies will usually divide the under-applied overhead costs between ending inventory and cost of goods sold, based on the relative numbers of units sold and still on hand. In this example, 100,000 of the 995,000 items produced are still on hand, so 10.05% (100,000 ÷ 995,000) of the under-applied overhead would be treated as an addition to ending inventory, and the rest would be considered an addition to cost of goods sold.

In the above example, there were under-applied overhead costs because production activity was slightly below the targeted level. It is just as likely that a company could have over-applied overhead costs, if the production level was above the targeted level. It could also have over-applied overhead if the actual costs were below the budgeted costs. If there are over-applied costs, a year-end entry would be needed to reduce cost of goods sold and ending inventory.

Often, companies believe that there would be no material error in allocating the entire amount of over-applied or under-applied overhead to cost of goods sold, instead of allocating part of the amount to inventory. If companies budget accurately, the amount of over- or under-applied overhead will be small. Also, when companies keep low levels of inventory, and "turn over" their inventory quickly, the large majority of the over-applied or under-applied inventory should be allocated to cost of goods sold, with only a small amount left for inventory. In the example above, 90% of the under-applied overhead of $46,000 = $41,400, and the 10% to be allocated to inventory = $4,400. Depending on whether the company assigns all the under-applied overhead to cost of goods sold, or 90% of the under-applied overhead, the cost of goods sold would vary from $8,096,400 ($8,055,000 + $41,400) to $8,101,000 ($8,055,000 + $46,000). The difference between these two figures is very small as long as ending inventory is small.

Product Mix Decisions Using Traditional Full Absorption Costing

Assume the Oneida TV Company makes four models of television: a 22 inch model; a 32 inch model; a 40 inch model; and a 47 inch model. Table 10.1 shows key data for this company. The numbers of units to be produced and the total dollar figures are rounded to the thousands. The per unit figures are not rounded. The four different models of television vary in the amount of labor they use, the average wages of the workers, and the amount of machine processing time.

In this example, the company is budgeting to make a profit. The budgeted total revenues are $371 million, and the budgeted total costs are $357.6 million, leaving a budgeted profit of $13.4 million. Exhibit 10.1 shows budgeted profits per product, using overhead costs per direct labor hour to allocate the $100 million of overhead. Based on this analysis, three of the products are profitable, but the cost per unit for the smallest televisions is higher than the sales price.

What we will see is that different methods of allocating overhead can lead to different total costs per unit, and that in turn can lead managers to make differing decisions.

Table 10.1 Oneida TV Company—Budgeted Data Numbers other than per unit figures are in thousands

	22 inch	32 inch	40 inch	47 inch	Totals
Units	100	300	400	200	1,000
Expected sales price per unit	$180	$310	$400	$500	NA
Budgeted revenues	$18,000	$93,000	$160,000	$100,000	$371,000
Direct labor hours per unit	1	1.25	1.25	1.5	NA
Direct labor $ per hour	35	36	40	42	NA
Machine hours per unit	0.1	0.2	0.25	0.3	NA
Raw materials per unit	80	160	230	300	NA
Total labor costs	$3,500	$13,500	$20,000	$12,600	$49,600
Total raw materials costs	$8,000	$48,000	$92,000	$60,000	$208,000
Total budgeted direct costs	$11,500	$61,500	$112,000	$72,600	$257,600
Total overhead costs*	$7,843	$29,412	$39,216	$23,529	$100,000
Total costs	$19,343	$90,912	$151,216	$96,129	$357,600
Expected profits	$(1,343)	$2,088	$8,784	$3,871	$13,400

* Overhead is allocated based on number of direct labor hours at $78.43 per direct labor hour.

In the example, the company used direct labor hours as the cost driver. Here are four different predetermined overhead rates the company might choose to use:

Per unit made	$100	(= $100 million total overhead ÷ 1 million units budgeted)
Per labor hour	$78.43	(= $100 million ÷ total labor hours (not shown))
Per labor dollar	$2.02	(= $100 million ÷ $49.6 million)
Per machine hour	$434.78	(= $100 million ÷ total machine hours (not shown))

Because the four products use labor and machine hours in different proportions, and because the wages of the workers differ, these four different overhead allocation bases would produce different unit costs. Let's look at what overhead would be applied to the 22 inch televisions under these four bases:

Basis	Allocated overhead per unit	
Per unit	$100	(= $100 per unit)
Per labor hour	$ 78.43	(=1 hour per unit × $78.43 per hour)
Per labor dollar	$ 70.70	(= 1 hour per unit × $35 per hour × $2.02)
Per machine hour	$ 43.48	(= 0.1 machine hours × $434.78)

Table 10.2 shows how the per unit total costs, and the resulting profits per unit, for the four products would vary based on the method of allocating overhead costs. In this example, the differences are sometimes substantial. The 22 inch televisions have a profit per unit of $21.52 when overhead is allocated based on machine hours, but a loss of $25 per unit when overhead is allocated based on the number of units produced.

Issues With Traditional Full Absorption Costing

People have raised the following issues with traditional full absorption costing:

- The allocation of overhead may not follow actual cause and effect relationships. Differing allocation bases can give very different costs.

Table 10.2 Oneida Television Company Example, Continued Differing Costs and Profitability Depending on Overhead Allocation Bases (All figures are in USD $)

	22 inch	32 inch	40 inch	47 inch
Allocated overhead per unit, differing allocation bases				
Units	100.00	100.00	100.00	100.00
Direct labor hours	78.43	98.04	98.04	117.65
Direct labor $	70.70	90.90	101.00	127.26
Machine hours	43.48	86.96	108.70	130.43
Total unit costs, differing allocation bases				
Units	215.00	305.00	380.00	463.00
Direct labor hours	193.43	303.04	378.04	480.65
Direct labor $	185.56	295.73	380.81	490.02
Machine hours	158.48	291.96	388.70	493.43
Budgeted price per unit	180	310	400	500
Profit (loss) per unit, differing allocation bases				
Units	(25.00)	5.00	20.00	37.00
Direct labor hours	(13.43)	6.94	21.96	19.35
Direct labor $	(5.56)	14.27	19.19	9.98
Machine hours	21.52	18.04	11.30	6.57

- Allocating fixed costs may lead managers to make bad short-term decisions, since fixed costs are usually not relevant to short-term decisions.
- The method creates incentives for managers to overproduce.
- The method can also fail to highlight the presence of unused or excess capacity.
- It ignores capacity bottlenecks and treats all cost areas equally.

The example we just used is useful for illustrating some of these criticisms of traditional absorption costing.

The example showed that the cost per unit can be heavily influenced by the choice of cost driver used to allocate costs. Exhibit 10.2 shows a range of differing values. There is an old saying that a man with a clock knows what time it is, but a man with two clocks is never sure. In this case, the differing figures are confusing.

In this case, we allocated all the $100 million of overhead using a single cost driver. However, it is not logical to assume that all overhead costs are "driven" by the same factors. There are various ways to try to deal with this issue. As we will see, both activity-based costing and resource consumption accounting (RCA) use numerous different cost pools and cost drivers. It is common for companies that use traditional full cost methods to keep costs in separate overhead "cost pools," and to use different cost drivers to allocate these pools. The goal is to get an allocation that better represents causal relationships. For example, supervisory personnel salaries might be logically allocated based on direct labor hours, and machine depreciation and maintenance might be allocated based on machine hours.

A second criticism of full absorption costing is that it can provide poor information for making short-term decisions. As an example, managers should not make decisions on dropping products based on full cost data. In the Oneida example, the company makes four products, and currently earns net profits of $13.4 million. What would happen if the company decided to drop the "unprofitable" 22 inch televisions? What we will see is that profits actually go down, not up. This happens as long as the company tries to eliminate a product which has revenues greater than its variable costs. This is totally consistent with the "relevant cost" analyses we did in Chapter 5, because the "full costs" did not separate out fixed costs from variable costs.

Let's assume that the company stops buying the materials used in the 22 inch television, and also fires the employees who make it, but that the overhead is fixed, and remains at $100 million for the factory. The company loses the $18 million of revenues from the 22 inch televisions. It reduces labor costs by $3.5 million and materials costs by $8 million. The net result is that profits fall by $6.5 million as a result of eliminating the "unprofitable" product.

If management makes the mistake of using full costs for deciding which products to retain, the company can go into what is called a "death spiral" of reducing models until it becomes unable to cover its fixed overhead. We have just seen what would happen if the 22 inch model is eliminated. What would happen next? With the 22 inch product gone, the company will now apply the remaining overhead to fewer units—just the other three remaining models. The total units produced falls from 1,000,000 to 900,000. With three models, the overhead application rates change as follows:

Basis	Old rate	New rate
Units	$100	$111.11
Labor hours	$78.43	$ 85.11
Labor dollars	$2.02	$ 2.17
Machine hours	$434.78	$454.55

In this example, the Oneida Company has been allocating overhead based on direct labor hours. The unit cost of the 32 inch television would then be computed at $311.38, which is higher than the budgeted selling price of $310. Management might then make the erroneous decision to eliminate the "unprofitable" 32 inch product. Because the overhead is fixed, this will be a terrible decision. The remaining two products will have revenues of $260 million, direct costs of labor and materials of $184.6 million and the company will still have the overhead of $100 million. The company as a whole will have a $24.6 million loss.

Another criticism of full absorption accounting is that it can lead managers to overproduce. In the Oneida example, based on the budgeted volume, the 22 inch television appeared unprofitable. However, what would have happened if management decided to make more televisions? In that case, the $100 million of overhead would have been spread over more units, and the cost per unit would be lower. With a higher production goal, the 22 inch televisions could look profitable. In general, under absorption costing, fixed cost per unit and total cost per unit always fall with higher production levels.

Note that, if the full amount produced is not sold, the remaining items are part of ending inventory. Inventory is an asset. As a result, part of the $100 million of overhead would become part of an asset, and would not be allocated to expenses. This makes the company appear more profitable. There is some evidence that managers sometimes manage earnings by deliberately overproducing.[6] Of course, there are costs of having excessive inventory, and these have not yet been considered. The items may prove unsalable, and the company may incur sizable storage costs and interest costs to finance its investment in inventories.

Finally, one criticism of the traditional method is it does not highlight unused capacity. In the Oneida example, the company budgeted to produce a total of one million units. The overhead allocation factors were all based on this budget. Overhead costs were spread over the budgeted one million units. What if, in fact, the factory could make three million units, and the budget is for only a third of the actual capacity? The company is incurring costs to maintain a much bigger facility than it plans on using. Nothing in the traditional method highlights the fact that managers are leaving most of the factory unused. As we will see, RCA and activity-based costing both try to separately measure the cost of unused capacity.

In the Oneida example, there was no information about the details of the production processes for these four models, and no consideration of constraints on production. We assume Oneida could produce as much as it wanted of each product, and did not consider that producing one product might interfere with production of the others. In particular, we did not consider whether the different models could be produced at equal speed through the process that is the binding constraint. However, where there are capacity constraints, a proper decision on which products to produce needs to consider these factors.

Activity-Based Costing ("ABC")

The ideas that we discussed about traditional full absorption costing are helpful in understanding *activity-based costing*. In the 1970s and 1980s, company experience and academic research showed that manufacturing overhead was becoming relatively more important in modern companies, and that overhead costs were caused by a variety of different factors other than simply the volume of production. For example, Gosselin (2006) finds that overhead costs were related to such activities as "logistics (moving materials), balancing (meeting purchasing, materials planning, and human resource requirements), quality (engineering and quality control), and change (engineering change orders)" (p. 643). According to the IMA (2014b), another factor affecting the problem of allocating costs was the increasing trend by companies to produce large varieties of products, instead of mass producing identical items.

According to Gosselin (2006), these changes in the manufacturing environment led to dissatisfaction with traditional methods of allocating overhead, often by labor hours. There was a desire to allocate these different types of overhead costs in ways that reflected how they were related to particular products. Companies began allocating costs based on a variety of different underlying overhead activities, and this became known as "*activity-based costing.*" Articles in the *Harvard Business Review* by Robin Cooper and Robert S. Kaplan in the late 1980s publicized the ABC method. ABC has attracted some very strong supporters, but has also been criticized for its difficulty of implementation and for certain limitations. According to Gosselin (2006), "Activity-based costing (ABC) is considered by many academics and practitioners as one of the most important innovations in management accounting of the twentieth century along with variance analysis, return on investment, and the balanced scorecard" (p. 641). On the other hand, Thomson and Gurowka (2005) say it has also been referred to as "yesterday's hope" and "pure snake oil" (p. 28).[7] The gap between the claims of its proponents, and the fact that ABC has only been adopted by a minority of companies, is sometimes called the "ABC paradox."[8]

So how does it work? There are some variations in practice, but basically activity-based costing is a multiple-step process.

Step 1—Identify significant overhead activities. For example, a company might identify materials purchasing as an activity. Other activities might include inspecting items, moving materials into storage, unloading raw materials, ordering materials, paying employees, and so on.

Step 2—Assign costs to "activity cost pools." For example, salaries of the people who order supplies and certain other related costs would be assigned to the materials purchasing activity.

Step 3—Decide on appropriate cost drivers relating each activity to product lines or to some other level of the cost hierarchy.

Step 4—Compute predetermined overhead allocation rates based on practical capacity. This may be larger than the budgeted capacity.

Step 5—Allocate overhead costs to product lines or other cost objects during the year.

Step 6—Account for any unapplied or over-applied overhead.

Table 10.3 presents an application of both traditional costing and ABC for a company that makes two products. One is its "regular" model, and the other is a "deluxe" model. The company makes 90,000 units of the regular model, and 10,000 units of the deluxe model. The deluxe model requires somewhat more material costs and a little more labor. It also requires more than a proportionate share of certain supporting activities. In this example, there are five supporting activities: moving materials; generating purchasing orders; inspecting finished items; setting up machinery to make new batches; and supervising direct labor. The basis for allocating the overhead costs in the traditional method in this example is the number of units produced. For ABC, each of the five supporting activities is allocated using a different activity driver. The only costs allocated based on the number of units produced are the costs of inspecting them.

The first steps in an ABC analysis involve identifying the activities and the activity cost drivers. That is done in the first part of Table 10.3. An activity driver is identified for each of the five activities. The materials moving activity is driven by the number of moves. The purchasing activity is driven by the number of different purchase transactions. The quality control activity is driven by the number of items needing to be inspected. The engineering change costs are driven by the number of machine "set-ups." The supervisory costs are driven by the number of hours worked by direct labor workers.

The next step is to use the budgeted capacity levels of each activity to compute the rates to charge each product for each activity. This is also done in the top part of Table 10.3. The results are shown in the last column. For example, the company computes that moving costs should be charged at $110 per move. (This equals the budgeted $77,000 in moving costs divided by the 700 moves that can be done.)

The middle section of Table 10.3 computes product costs using ABC. The raw materials and direct labor costs are measured directly from the company's records. The five different overhead activities are allocated individually. The deluxe items use more than their proportionate share of moving costs, purchase orders, set-ups, and labor hours, so they have higher per unit allocations of overhead for each of these activities than the regular items. The total product costs computed

Table 10.3 Activity-Based Costing Example

Overhead activities and cost drivers				
	Budgeted cost	Activity-based cost driver	Capacity activity level	Cost per activity
Moving materials	$77,000	# of moves	700	$110
Purchasing	$90,000	# purchase orders	1,000	$90
Quality control/inspecting	$100,000	# items produced	100,000	$1.00
Changes—setups	$120,000	# set-ups/changes	300	$400
Supervision and other	$400,000	# labor hours	160,000	$2.50
Total overhead:	$787,000			

Product costs—allocated by ABC		
	Regular model	Deluxe model
Raw materials per item	$20.00	$25.00
Direct labor per item	$23.00	$30.00
Moving (540 moves for regular, 160 for deluxe)*	$0.66	$1.76
Purchasing (700 orders for regular, 300 for deluxe)	$0.70	$2.70
Quality control (90,000 regular units, 10,000 deluxe)	$1.00	$1.00
Changes (250 setups regular, 50 deluxe)	$1.11	$2.00
Supervision & other (130,000 hours regular, 30,000 deluxe)	$3.61	$7.50
Total cost per unit	$50.08	$69.96

Product costs—allocated by units made		
	Regular model	Deluxe model
Units produced	90,000	10,000
Raw materials per item	$20.00	$25.00
Direct labor per item	$23.00	$30.00
Per unit overhead, if based on average overhead per unit	$7.87	$7.87
Total cost per unit	$50.87	$62.87

* For the ABC analysis, the costs per unit were computed by multiplying the number of activities times the cost per activity, then dividing by the number of units. For example, the moving cost per unit for regular items = (540 moves) × ($110 per move) ÷ (90,000 units) = $0.66.

are $50.08 for regular items and $69.96 for the deluxe items. There is approximately $8 per item more of overhead allocated to the deluxe than to the regular items.

The last section of Table 10.3 shows product costs if the company allocated all the overhead using a single cost driver, the number of units produced. The overhead allocated to all the items is the same, and as a result the costs of the two types of items are closer together. The cost of the regular items is $50.87 and the cost of the deluxe item is $62.87. While the difference for the regular item is relatively small ($50.87 versus $50.08), the cost for the deluxe item of $69.96 per ABC is 10% higher than the cost using the traditional, volume-based method.

There are several points to make about this example.

The types of results found in real life tend to be similar to what was seen in this example. Traditional volume-based cost methods tend to *overestimate* the costs of relatively simple products produced in large volume, like the "regular" model. They tend to *underestimate* the costs of more complicated items produced in small volumes. The relative size of errors in costing tends to be greater for the small-volume, complicated items.

A key point is that ABC focuses attention on the use each product makes of various activities. This helps management understand its cost structure, and the different types of demands different products make on the supporting facilities. This can help management better align its pricing and product production decisions to the underlying costs. There are some studies that suggest the major part of the benefits of an ABC system are derived from just the process of identifying the activities, and understanding their relationship to different products.[9] So, in this example, the fact that management will regularly see reports with costs of moving materials and purchasing will likely induce it to think of ways to make these activities more efficient.

Because the costs assigned to each product depend on the number of times the product uses that activity, each product manager has a motivation to use the activity less. This may be beneficial to the company. However, there is also a possible adverse effect. For example, assume purchasing department costs are allocated based on the number of different purchase orders processed. A manager might try to reduce the purchasing department overhead allocated to her product by ordering fewer but larger batches of raw materials. This could lead to a build-up of inventory waiting to be processed.

The activities may also cut across department lines. This means that accounting at the activity level may differ from the accounts that are aligned with the way managers are supervised.

Another point is that the ABC process is complicated. The company must separately identify and track the costs of numerous activities. It must also compute rates for applying the activity costs to particular products. Since the underlying logic is that there are different cost drivers for different activities, the results should be more accurate when the company identifies a large number of different activities, each with costs driven by a single cost driver. In this example, there were only five overhead activities. In real life, many more can be defined.

A third point is that the ABC process needs to be updated whenever the company changes its processes. For example, if the company changes its ways of ordering materials, the total number of process orders will change, and therefore the rates for applying costs from the purchasing department to products will change. Similarly, if the company reduces staffing in the purchasing function, even if the number of orders in the year stays the same, the cost per purchase order will change.

A variant of ABC, called time-driven activity-based costing, has been developed that is easier to implement and to update. It is beyond the scope of this text.[10]

A fourth point is that ABC mixes together fixed and variable costs. The cost of the purchasing function includes occupancy costs that are probably fixed, and labor costs that are probably partly variable and partly fixed in the short term. In ABC each cost is allocated as if it varies proportionately to the activity driver, and that may not be strictly correct.

Finally, it should be noted that ABC is a full absorption cost method, but the method of allocating costs is different from the traditional method. Under the traditional method, budgeting higher production led to lower allocated overhead charges per unit. ABC bases the overhead allocation not on budgeted production, but on the practical capacity. This means there is less of an incentive to budget excessively high levels of production, since the budget does not affect the cost per unit. However, managers still have an incentive to produce at high levels, since they do not want to end the year with unapplied overhead due to producing at volumes less than the capacity.

While the ABC approach started as a method of analyzing product costs, it can be easily expanded to help with other issues. For example, a company can include selling costs in the analysis, to get a better idea of the profitability of particular products. It can also use the same approach to identify costs related to serving particular customers, or the costs of receiving items from different vendors. Several examples of uses of ABC are included in the application questions at the end of this chapter.

Resource Consumption Accounting ("RCA")

How Does it Differ From Other Methods?

Resource consumption accounting ("RCA") is a third method of allocating costs to products. It is discussed here in general terms, without numerical examples. It is newer than ABC, and it is not clear how widely adopted it is. It was introduced in articles by Anton van der Merwe[11] and is described in the website of the RCA Institute.[12] It is a combination of ideas from ABC and from German cost accounting. The German cost accounting system is known as "Grenzplan-kostenrechnung" and is generally referred to in English as GPK. Its origins go back to shortly after World War II.[13] The description in this section is largely based on Balakrishnan, Labro and Sivaramakrishnan (2012a).

Like ABC, this process involves looking closely at various overhead costs, and allocating them separately. Conceptually, it differs from ABC in several ways, which are noted below.

The beginning step in the process is to form cost pools by grouping together resources. For example, particular machines or groups of workers might be considered resource pools. Thus, while ABC creates cost pools for particular activities, RCA creates cost pools for particular resources. The RCA cost pools tend to be small, and one manager will often be responsible for more than one cost pool.

For each cost pool, costs are characterized as either fixed or proportionate, with regard to some cost driver. Separate rates are used to charge out the fixed and proportional parts of the resource pool's costs. Again, this is a difference from ABC. In ABC, the accountant did not need to separately track what parts of the cost of, for example, the purchasing activity was fixed, and which was incurred proportionately as the number of purchase orders rose. Proponents of RCA see this closer attention to cost behavior as a major advantage.

The fixed portion of each resource pool is allocated based on a theoretical capacity level of activity. This is larger than either the budgeted capacity used by traditional costing methods or the "practical capacity" used in ABC. The reason this is done is because managerial choices affect how much of the theoretical capacity is in fact being used. If managers choose not to run the facility near capacity, then there will be significant under-applied overhead under this method, which will be treated as additional operating expenses. The low utilization of facilities will be noted in management reviews of performance.

The proportionate costs in each resource cost pool are allocated using output-based drivers that have logical causal relations to the use of the resources. Each type of resource cost is allocated using a single cost driver. Usually, the driver is based on physical quantities for that pool, such as units of machine time or hours of labor, and not on either outputs measured in dollars, like direct labor dollars, or on units of the final products produced. The idea is that there is a stronger causal relation with these quantitative measures than with dollar measures.

Part of the costs in a resource cost pool may have been allocated to it from other cost pools. For example, some of the costs of having a group of machines ready for use may have been allocated from a pool consisting of costs of having a staff of mechanics in the factory. The records keep track of which of these allocated costs are fixed, and which will vary proportionately as the resource is used.

RCA measures depreciation using the replacement costs of the equipment and assets, not their historical costs.

What Are the Benefits of RCA?

A major benefit is that, by separating out fixed and proportional costs, RCA provides managers with more relevant information for making decisions.

Under RCA, performance reports compare the activity of each resource pool with "flexible budgets." The idea of a "flexible budget" is that the budgeted amount of each proportional cost is adjusted to reflect the actual activity. For example, if the company was producing 10% less than expected, the budget for a proportional item like materials is adjusted to be 10% lower. Also, the rate of allocating fixed costs is based on the theoretical capacity, so overhead charges per unit are steady over time. Changes in volume do not create variances in per unit allocations of fixed costs. The combination of using a flexible budget approach to variable costs and basing fixed overhead charges on theoretical capacity means that the measured variances of unit costs from budgets are due to factors other than volume. This means managers can concentrate on such other causes of variances as changes in production efficiency or changes in input prices.

Also, RCA highlights the cost of leaving some capacity idle (Hutchinson and Liao 2009). This occurs because the amount of fixed costs is allocated based on theoretical capacity. Whenever actual production is below capacity, there will be under-applied costs. These costs are typically charged to expense in the period, not added to inventory. There can be both good and bad effects of this attention to unused capacity. It can make managers use their capacity more efficiently. However, managers may be motivated to overproduce, which creates costs for the firm.

Survey results indicate that German managers tend to be relatively happy with their cost accounting systems.[14]

What Are Some Drawbacks of RCA?

RCA requires companies to create large numbers of cost pools, identify numerous cost drivers, and separately track fixed and proportional costs. This method involves a great deal of effort, and is feasible only with good computerized cost management systems.

Given the effort required to set up the system, it is most useful for highly routine factory operations that do not change much over time.[15]

Of course, some costs do not behave as either exactly fixed or exactly proportional. This creates inaccuracies in the cost measurements.

Like traditional absorption costing and ABC, RCA does not consider the impact of capacity constraints when comparing product costs.

Throughput Accounting

See the appendix to this chapter for a discussion of throughput accounting. This is a method that focuses on short-term decisions, and is meant to help companies keep their production processes lean and avoid overproducing inventory.

Recap—How Do These Cost Systems Compare?

In each area, the methods are discussed in the order of best to worst.[16]

Simplicity and Clerical Effort

Any method that does not require allocation of costs to products is easier than a full absorption method. Throughput accounting does not require tracing any costs except tracing totally variable costs to products. It is therefore the simplest of the methods.

Traditional absorption costing requires allocating overhead costs to products. However, it typically requires less effort than either ABC or RCA. Traditional absorption costing uses only a few cost centers, and only a few cost drivers.

ABC requires the company to consider a variety of drivers for various activities. A number of companies that adopted ABC later dropped it due to the efforts involved. RCA typically requires tracking more cost centers than traditional systems, and also requires keeping track separately of fixed and variable costs. Updating the ABC system as systems change and efficiencies are developed is a difficult task. Various studies document firms having difficulty implementing ABC, and often deciding to drop the method due to implementation difficulties.[17]

RCA tends to have even more cost centers and data requirements than ABC systems, and Balakrishnan, Labro and Sivaramakrishnan (2012b) call updating a resource consumption system for changes in efficiencies "a daunting task" (p. 27). A further complication with RCA is that some companies that use it base depreciation on replacement cost, instead of historical cost. Estimating replacement cost is an additional task.

There may be ways to reduce the effort required to use ABC and RCA. As noted earlier, time-driven ABC is a new method designed to be easier to use. Also, it may be possible to use fewer activity cost centers and fewer resource cost centers than are typically used, without losing a great deal of accuracy. An IMA study on designing effective cost systems (IMA 2011) indicates that usually a reasonably small number of cost centers will result in reasonable information for decisions. Also, the same IMA study says that in situations where a relatively few resources account for most of the overhead costs, a simple system with cost drivers for those key resources may perform as well as a more extensive ABC system.

Logic of the Link Between Product Costs and Manufacturing Activities

There are three ways in which RCA is arguably the best system in logically relating manufacturing activities and resources to product costs. First, it tends to use more cost pools, each of which can have different drivers. Second, it keeps fixed and variable costs distinct. Third, it bases depreciation costs on the replacement costs of assets, not their historical cost.

ABC has more defensible allocations to product cost than traditional absorption costing. It separately considers a wide variety of activities involved with products, and uses separate cost drivers for each.

Traditional absorption costing has tended to make the simplifying assumption that there are only a few cost pools and cost drivers. It has also tended to combine both fixed and variable costs in cost pools. As a result, the causal link between incurring overhead costs and product costs is often weak.

Information for Short-Term Product Decisions

In Chapter 5, we saw that a number of short-term decisions should be based only on "relevant costs," which were the costs that would vary based on the decision. Typically, fixed costs are not relevant to short-term decisions, such as deciding on whether to accept a special order. Opportunity costs are relevant.

The throughput accounting method includes only "totally variable costs," and therefore is the closest method to the ideal of only including relevant costs. The analysis also includes considering opportunity costs. It is the only method to explicitly consider the impact of production constraints on the product mix.

RCA separates out variable and fixed cost components, which would be helpful to a manager trying to use only relevant costs. A difference between RCA and throughput accounting is that RCA assumes that direct labor and some overhead costs are variable costs. In fact, many factories would be reluctant to cut employees' pay or workloads when there are temporary changes in production. Instead, the factories might reassign the workers. Also, RCA does not consider opportunity costs. Instead, it tends to assume there is some level of unused capacity.

Both traditional absorption costing and ABC include some allocated fixed costs in the costs of production, which means that the resulting figures include some irrelevant costs. This is a problem for these methods. Neither method explicitly considers opportunity costs.

Long Term Decision-Making on Product Mix

Surveys taken in the 1980s and 1990s indicated that the majority of firms surveyed used full cost data to set list prices and to make long-run decisions on which products to produce.[18] Note that here the focus is in the long run, and in the long run there are no fixed costs. Firms face a very difficult problem in deciding on their optimal capacity and product mix, especially since future demand and prices are uncertain. Under certain assumptions about the production process, full absorption cost might be theoretically justifiable. It can provide information useful in finding approximate solutions to this problem. The 2002 literature review by Balakrishnan and Sivara-makrishnan suggests that the theoretical usefulness of full cost data depends critically on the level of uncertainty of demand, and the ability to flexibly adjust capacity and "tactical" prices for short-term fluctuations in demand. Firms that use full cost information for capacity planning and long-term decisions, but react to short-term conditions using marginal cost pricing do better than firms who use full cost for all pricing decisions. This finding is completely consistent with our discussion of relevant costs in Chapter 5.

Traditional absorption costing, ABC, and RCA all consider fixed costs as part of product costs. In contrast, throughput accounting does not consider fixed costs to be part of product costs. This may lead to incorrect long-term decisions when throughput accounting is used.

Consideration of Production Bottlenecks and Constraints

The only method that considers the impact of particular processes on the overall productive capacity of the factory is the throughput method. The focus of analysis in this method is on how changes in production or product mix affect the production through the most con-strained part of the operation. Its focus is on increasing throughput, while the other methods tend to focus on reducing cost or increasing capacity utilization. The other methods do not separately analyze conditions at the constrained process from conditions at the other processes.

Incentives to Overproduce Versus Incentives to Fully Utilize Capacity

A major claimed benefit of throughput analysis is that it is compatible with keeping production levels "lean." Managers do not have incentives to overproduce, because all overhead and labor costs are considered period expenses. None of these expenses can be "hidden" by being assigned to ending inventory.

All three full absorption methods assign some overhead costs and labor costs to ending inventory. This means that managers can "manage earnings" and show lower cost of goods sold by overproducing. There is some evidence that in fact full absorption cost systems do create incentives for overproduction. One study of the U.S. auto industry (Brüggen, Krishnan and Sedatole 2011) found evidence of a relation between cost measurement systems and apparent excess production.

One impact of this different focus arises when managers look at reports and variances from budgets. Under a throughput analysis, it is important that the constrained operation be operat-ing at peak capacity, since that affects the rest of the plant. It is not desirable for the processes immediately before it to be operating at peak capacity. These areas need to have some excess capacity ("sprint capacity") in order to ensure that there is always a stockpile of partly completed parts ready for the constrained operation. A traditional analysis might result in one of two dys-functional effects. It might criticize the prior operations for having low capacity utilization rates. Managers responding to that criticism would tend to overproduce, leading to build-ups of work in process inventory waiting to be processed by the constrained operation. Alternatively, managers might react by reducing capacity. While operations are normal, this would be acceptable, but if anything caused delays in ordering materials, or in processing items in early stages of produc-tion, the company would not be able to use "sprint capacity" to ensure that the production at the constraint process stayed steady.

One IMA publication (IMA 2006) explains how certain measurements can motivate managers to create excess production:

> Traditional measurements associated with mass production include both financial and nonfinancial measurements, such as labor efficiency, machine utilization, earned hours, overhead absorption, purchase price variance (PPV), and similar measurements. Use of these measurements may motivate nonlean behaviors. Does this mean that these traditional measurements are bad metrics? No. They are perfectly good metrics if you want to be a traditional mass producer. They are inappropriate if you wish to be a lean manufacturer. There is nothing wrong with these tools, but they are the wrong tools for a lean enterprise.
>
> What behaviors are motivated by such measurements as earned hours, labor efficiency, and machine utilization? The metrics are designed to motivate people to maximize the amount of standard hours earned in any one day or week. They motivate people to make large quantities. They also motivate people to manufacture large batches of products so as to minimize the effect of change-over time. The production people will make large batches, manufacture out of sequence, and "cherry pick" production jobs that yield high earned hours. There may also be a tendency to make quantity at the expense of quality, which leads in turn to the need for increased inspection. In short, these measurements motivate people to do the opposite of lean manufacturing. They will motivate people to build inventory in order to maximize their efficiency and make large batches instead of single-piece flow. These measurements will undermine a company's move to lean processes.
>
> (pp. 13–14)

Probably the method that creates the greatest incentive to overproduce is RCA, which highlights the extent to which production each period falls below the theoretical capacity. Managers using this system are likely to try to avoid showing production shortfalls.

Does this mean that RCA is not appropriate? It depends on the manufacturing environment. Remember, RCA was developed for the German manufacturing environment, where companies had to make large, long-term investments in facilities. At the time these were brought on line, they would typically have excess capacity. It makes sense in this situation to think in a long-term manner, and to try to use these large facilities efficiently. In contrast, throughput accounting has a short-term focus, and assumes that capacity is constrained.[19]

Whereas RCA is the worst of the methods when we are concerned about providing an incentive to overproduce, it is the best of the methods if the company is concerned about not fully utilizing its expensive fixed assets. Under RCA, overheads are allocated based on theoretical capacity. This normally will result in a company reporting considerable under-applied overhead, because actual production is beneath theoretical capacity. ABC applies overhead based on practical capacity, and would typically have less under-applied overhead. Traditional methods apply overhead based on budgeted production, and would tend to have low amounts of under-applied overhead.[20]

Helps Identify Controllable Costs

Both ABC and RCA analyze the company's activities at a very detailed level. Their focus on what drives the usage of different overhead activities and resources can help management identify inefficiencies and waste. In particular, the manager of a cost system would realize that his or her area was being charged each time it used a particular overhead service or resource. This would motivate the manager to use the overhead departments more efficiently.

Managers who use activity-based management techniques try to find ways to make the necessary activities more efficient, and to reduce the amount of time on activities that do not add value to the process. Such "non-value added" activities might include time spent on: scheduling production; moving goods from one production process to another; waiting until the next stage of production is ready; inspecting goods for defects; storing goods; handling customer complaints, or dealing with warranty claims.[21]

Throughput accounting and traditional absorption costing are probably less useful in highlighting how overhead costs are incurred, or what activities increase use of them. This is not to say that managers using these methods cannot look for ways to improve efficiencies, but these accounting systems do not tend to focus management attention on details of overhead costs.

What do we Know About Errors in Cost Systems in Real Life?

Given that there are advantages and disadvantages of various systems, what do we know about what kinds of real world losses have been caused by these imperfect systems?

It may be that in practice businesses are able to live relatively comfortably with imperfect systems. A simulation study by Balachandran, Balakrishnan and Sivaramakrishnan (1997) looked at the relative performance of four methods in solving a product mix problem, compared to a mathematically computed perfect solution. On average, the full cost, resource-based decisions, and a variety of throughput methods all produced profits between 79% and 90% of the mathematical benchmark. An IMA (2011) study that cited these results saw them as comforting and as an indication that "product costs do not entail an unacceptable loss relative to the optimal economic decision. . . . The insight is that, while the calculated product cost is only an approximation of the underlying opportunity cost, it serves us well" (p. 5).

Another study cited by the IMA (2011) suggests that relatively more products are undercosted rather than overcosted, "with large amounts of overcosting for a few "big-ticket" (in dollar terms) products, and small amounts of undercosting for a larger number of cheaper products. The practical implication is that firms that rely on a few high-value product lines for the bulk of their profit should be particularly careful to refine their cost systems, as there is a strong possibility that the accounting system overestimates the real cost of these products" (p. 7). There is less concern about the many products that are slightly under-costed.

While the impact of different methods may not be large, businesses should try to maximize their profits. A variety of studies comparing firms using ABC to firms using traditional methods find advantages for ABC. One simulation study in an industry with relatively high overhead costs found that "ABC captures manufacturing characteristics and resource usage more accurately than traditional costing and through-put accounting and results in higher profit, lower inventory, and better customer service for both the short and long term."[22] A study by Kennedy and Affleck-Graves (2001) reported that:

> [F]or a sample of U.K. firms, we show that firms adopting activity-based costing techniques outperform matched non-ABC firms by approximately 27 percent over the three years beginning on January 1 of the year in which the ABC techniques are first implemented. . . . Further analysis suggests that ABC adds to firm value through better cost controls and asset utilization, coupled with greater use of financial leverage.
>
> (p. 19)

However, it is not clear how ABC compares to the other, more modern, systems. One study (Schildbach 1997) comparing ABC measures of full cost to those produced by German cost systems (which are similar to RCA) found differences tended to be rather small.

Some other studies support throughput accounting as superior when there is constrained production capacity.[23] In particular, Balachandran, Balakrishnan and Sivaramakrishnan (1997) compared decision-making using four methods, and found advantages to throughput accounting.

However, the relative success of the methods depended on the situation. The throughput method did relatively better when there were constraints in production and products shared production processes, and the resource-based method did better when the products shared resources. Similarly, Souren, Ahn and Schmitz (2005) indicate that several aspects of the decision situation will affect whether throughput accounting gives superior product mix decisions. For example, if there is more than one binding constraint, or if direct costs other than totally variable costs are tightly related to throughput, throughput accounting will not yield an optimal solution.

What should you, as a future manager, take away from this long section on cost accounting? There are a few major points. First, you should understand there are several ways of measuring costs. You should be cautious about making decisions, and should not believe any one cost figure is "the truth." Second, the right cost system for a company depends on its environment and the types of behavior management wants to encourage. The best system for encouraging lean inventory levels is probably not the best method for ensuring that expensive equipment is kept fully utilized. Third, as a manager you need to understand the incentives and signals that other managers are receiving. If you understand that one accounting method might encourage overproduction, for example, you can take steps to prevent overproduction.

Allocating Costs Among Divisions

Introduction

Most modern companies are both complex and decentralized. It is common for one division to sell to another, or for a central administrative function to be performed on behalf of various divisions. What "*transfer price*" should one division charge another? Should the headquarters allocate costs to divisions, and, if it does, what methods should the company headquarters use for allocating these costs?

This is rarely a problem for financial accounting. Typically, the financial statements that companies produce for outside investors and lenders are "*consolidated*" financial statements. Consolidated financial statements bring together the accounts of all the subsidiaries and divisions controlled by the "parent" company into a single set of financial statements. In these statements, the intercompany and interdivisional dealings offset each other. For example, if the headquarters allocates a cost to its Australia division, there is less expense on the separate books of the headquarters, but more on the books of the Australia division. The total expense of the whole group is unaffected. It is standard practice under GAAP and IFRS for the effects of intercompany dealings to be "eliminated" from consolidated financial statements.

However, the allocation of costs among divisions and subsidiaries can have important effects for legal purposes, for tax purposes, and for management of the individual divisions.

Legally, there may be creditors of a particular subsidiary who are not creditors of other parts of the company. If, for example, the Australia subsidiary declares bankruptcy, its creditors do not have the right to make claims against other parts of the consolidated group. Therefore, the creditors of the Australian subsidiary would be helped if that subsidiary made money dealing with other parts of the consolidated group, and would be hurt if it lost money. The method of pricing intercompany transactions and allocating costs would affect these creditors.

As a general matter, the allocations should be systematic and logical. When allocations are done badly, they can lead to incorrect judgments about profitability. People have also claimed that improper allocations have been used to help companies avoid paying third parties amounts that are due them. Box 10.1 contains excerpts from *The Atlantic* magazine describing how Hollywood movie studios allocate corporate costs when computing the net profits from particular movies. Artists and actors whose contracts entitle them to a percentage of the "net profits" from a movie have long claimed that the allocations of corporate expenses to individual movies were excessive.

Box 10.1 Excerpts From Article on "Hollywood Accounting"

How Hollywood Accounting Can Make a $450 Million Movie 'Unprofitable'

by Derek Thompson, September 14, 2011

Here is an amazing glimpse into the dark side of the force that is Hollywood economics. The actor who played Darth Vader still has not received residuals from the 1983 film "Return of the Jedi" because the movie, which ranks 15th in U.S. box office history, still has no technical profits to distribute.

How can a movie that grossed $475 million on a $32 million budget not turn a profit? It comes down to Tinseltown accounting. As Planet Money explained in an interview with Edward Jay Epstein in 2010, studios typically set up a separate "corporation" for each movie they produce. Like any company, it calculates profits by subtracting expenses from revenues. Erase any possible profit, the studio charges this "movie corporation" a big fee that overshadows the film's revenue. For accounting purposes, the movie is a money "loser" and there are no profits to distribute.

Confused? Imagine you're running a lemonade stand with your buddy Steve. Your mom says you have to share half your profits with your sister. But you don't wanna! So you pretend your buddy Steve is actually a corporation – call him Steve, Inc. – charging you rent for the stand, the spoon, etc. "Dang, mom, I don't have any profits, I had to pay it all to Steve, Inc.!" you say when you come home. But the money isn't gone. It's as good as yours – in your best friend's pocket. So: "Return of the Jedi" is a $475 million lemonade stand.

Hollywood can't really work like this, you're thinking. But it does. Last year, the website Techdirt revealed a balance sheet from "Harry Potter and the Order of the Phoenix", which, under Hollywood accounting, ended up with a $167 million "loss" even though it's one of the top grossing films of the last decade. Warner Bros. charged about $350 million in distribution, advertising, and interest fees to this external corporation. . . .

This brings us back to Darth. "Return of the Jedi" made almost half a billion dollars. But Return of the Jedi, Inc., still has no profit to pay its famous villain because the movie corp has paid so much of its revenue back to the studio in distribution fees. Here's actor David Prowse, via Techdirt:

"I get these occasional letters from Lucasfilm saying that we regret to inform you that as Return of the Jedi has never gone into profit, we've got nothing to send you. Now here we're talking about one of the biggest releases of all time," said Prowse. "I don't want to look like I'm bitching about it," he said, "but on the other hand, if there's a pot of gold somewhere that I ought to be having a share of, I would like to see it."

Most corporations try to make a profit by limiting costs. Movies corporations manage to record a loss by maximizing costs. Only in Hollywood, indeed.

www.theatlantic.com/business/archive/2011/09/how-hollywood-accounting-can-make-a-450-million-movie-unprofitable/245134/ (last accessed August 18, 2015).

For tax purposes, often each separate subsidiary is responsible for its own tax return. For a worldwide company, such as Apple, the total tax it pays can be significantly affected by which countries the income is earned in. If the money is considered to be earned by subsidiaries located in jurisdictions with low tax rates, Apple will pay less tax on a worldwide basis than if the money was earned by subsidiaries in high-tax countries. The pricing of intercompany transactions and the allocation of expenses can affect the locations in which income is considered earned. Tax authorities have been very concerned with this issue. For example, the European Union has investigated the way that companies shift income into Luxembourg and Ireland, which have low tax rates, from other EU countries.[24]

Typically, the managers of parts of decentralized companies are judged on the performance of the subsidiaries or divisions that they control. If they can charge other parts of the company high prices, their own division will look more profitable. If they are asked to pay other divisions high prices for inputs, they may not wish to buy from these divisions. A problem is that the decisions that local managers make, based on their own local interests, may not be optimal from the point of view of the overall company.

Let's consider an example. Assume Oneida Corp. has two subsidiaries.

One subsidiary, Leather Corp., takes cow hides and makes them into leather. It has variable cost per unit of $60 and fixed costs per unit of $30. It normally sells its products for $100 per unit. It has excess capacity. The other subsidiary, Handbags, makes women's handbags out of leather. Handbags needs leather. It can buy the leather from Leather Corp. or it can buy from outside suppliers at $96 per unit.

Is it best for the overall company if Handbags buys externally, or internally? For the company as a whole, it is clearly better for Handbags to order from its sister company. The variable cost of new leather is $60. The cost for buying from outside suppliers would be $96.

However, unless management takes some special action, Handbags would choose to order from outside. It knows that the outside price is $96, and that Leather Corp. normally charges $100. Handbags' costs will look lower if it orders from outside.

Market Prices as Transfer Prices

One possible solution is to tell divisions to use external market prices as transfer prices. In this case, Leather should charge Handbags $96 per unit.

This method has several advantages. It is relatively simple to administer. Also, managers of the different companies tend to see this as a fair method. The market price is set by outside forces, and is not the result of anyone within the company favoring one division over another. The market prices can be verified, making them more trustworthy than any computations done inside the company.

Unfortunately, this method has disadvantages.

In some cases, there will not be reliable external market prices. This can arise, for example, when a company produces a patented drug that external companies do not make. Or it is possible that the lowest outside prices are from suppliers with poor records for quality or reliability.

A second problem is that the external prices typically reflect the full costs of competing companies. As we have seen in prior chapters, and also in this chapter, for many short-term decisions the important consideration is the variable cost. In the example, if Leather sets a price of $96, Handbags will see the price as the same as it would pay outside suppliers, and might choose to buy from outside. For the company as a whole, this is unfortunate, since the variable cost of producing a unit is only $60 for Leather.

Variable Costs as Transfer Prices

What would happen if the price that Leather charged Handbags was Leather's variable cost of $60? Clearly, Handbags would choose to buy from its sister company for $60 rather than paying $96 to outsiders. This is the right decision from the point of view of the consolidated company. An advantage of this method is that it leads to the correct decisions on intercompany buying from a consolidated standpoint.

There are drawbacks to this approach. One is that Leather is charging such a low price that it does not receive any contribution towards covering its fixed costs. While this is not a problem in the short term, with excess capacity, it would become a problem for Leather if it has capacity limitations, and also if this situation becomes the pattern for long-term pricing. If it has capacity limitations, each item it produces and sells for $60 to Handbags means it can sell fewer at $100 to outsiders. The managers of Leather will be unhappy at losing possible profits.

Also, it is a more complicated method because it requires companies to carefully compute variable costs. As we have seen in the previous section, different cost allocation methods can come up with different cost computations. This makes the figures harder to verify.

Variable Costs Plus Opportunity Costs as Transfer Prices

If Leather does not have any capacity problems, selling to Handbags will not cause it to lose any other sales. In that situation, opportunity costs would be zero. Again, Leather would sell at $60 per unit, and Handbags will happily buy at that price.

On the other hand, if making the products for Handbags causes Leather to turn away highly profitable orders, it would increase its charges to Handbags to recover the opportunity costs. This method therefore has advantages over simply using variable costs. It makes it more likely that the company will make the right decisions when capacity is limited, and also protects the managers of the selling division from opportunity costs.

A difficulty is that the company must not only estimate variable costs, but also the opportunity costs. Again, this method does not compensate Leather at all for its fixed costs. If this becomes the major long-term method of pricing Leather's output, Leather will report losses.

Absorption Cost as the Transfer Prices

In this method, Leather would charge Handbags the full cost of its products, including both fixed and variable costs. In this particular case, the price would be $90. Handbags would find this better than the external price of $96, and would choose to buy from Leather. In this case, that is the right decision from the consolidated group's perspective.

A disadvantage is that this method will sometimes lead to improper decisions from the group standpoint, because fixed costs are theoretically irrelevant. If the facts of this case changed, and outside suppliers could sell inputs to Handbags at $80, instead of $96, then Handbags would be facing a choice of $80 from outsiders and $90 from Leathers. It would buy from outside. From a consolidated standpoint, that is the wrong decision, since the variable costs are only $70.

As a long-term pricing policy, this method means that Leather would not lose money. That is an advantage, from the point of view of Leather's management, over the methods that use variable cost. Of course, Leather is still not making any money, and its management presumably would like at least some positive amount of profits on these deals.

Absorption Cost Plus Markup as a Transfer Price

This method is very similar to the prior one. In this case, Leather would charge its full cost of $90 plus some normal "markup" price. That has the advantage of ensuring that the Leather division makes some money. As long as this price is under the $96 outside price, the Handbags group will also see buying from Leather as advantageous.

This method has a similar drawback to the previous method—it still considers fixed costs as part of the transfer price, which can lead to incorrect decisions. The company may end up buying from outside even when the outside price is higher than the Leather division's variable costs of production.

Negotiated Values

A company could simply let its subsidiaries and divisions negotiate their own prices. In this example, the management of Leather might use the same logic we used in Chapter 5 in considering special order decisions. Leather might decide that, for a special offer, it could offer a lower price than its normal $100 price, and lower than the external price of $96, but higher than its variable cost of $60. The management of Handbags would negotiate on a price with the management of Leather, and would likely come up with something between $96 and $60.

An advantage of this system is that it respects divisional autonomy. The managers of both divisions are likely to see the resulting prices as fair.

There are some clear disadvantages. This method can waste management time on negotiating prices. In some cases, these negotiations can create dissension within the company. It may also result in prices that do not lead to the correct decisions, from a central perspective, as to buying externally.

Unresolved Issues and Areas for Further Research

Clearly, there are many opportunities to better understand what companies are doing, and to improve practice in the way that companies allocate costs. Here are some examples:

1   Research is needed to better understand how methods of allocating joint costs affect companies' decisions in producing and pricing joint products.
2   Research is needed to better understand what cost allocation methods companies are currently using, and why the companies chose those methods.
3   Research is needed to better understand the causal links between particular activities and uses of resources and the costs of production.
4   Research is needed on when various different cost methods produce more accurate short-term and long-term decisions.
5   Research is needed on when various cost methods produce such dysfunctional activities as building excessive inventories and earnings management.
6   Further progress is needed in combining the best features of different costing methods into a single system, and in reducing the costs of implementing these systems.
7   Research is needed into the transfer pricing used by companies.
8   Research is needed into how the transfer prices used by multinational companies affect their tax liabilities.

Key Terms

Absorption costing—A method of assigning overhead costs to products which ensures that all overhead costs are assigned to (or "absorbed by") some units produced. This is also called "full absorption" costing.

Activity-based costing ("ABC")—A method of assigning costs to products that begins by identifying various activities in the facility, and then identifying the factors that drive the costs of each of those activities to particular products.

Applied overhead—This represents the part of the overhead costs incurred for the period that have been allocated to ("applied to") items produced.

Batch level costs—These are costs that are incurred each time a company produces a particular batch of a product. An example might be the set-up costs to prepare machinery to produce a particular batch, or costs to transport a batch of completed products to the storage area.

Behavior modification role—One purpose of cost accounting is to provide incentives that cause people to change their behavior. For example, a system that highlights unused capacity may induce managers to try to find ways to use the capacity, or to sell off unneeded capacity.

By-products—These are items that are produced incidentally as part of a production process, and are not the intended major purposes of the production process. A commonplace example might be the use of leftover turkey after Thanksgiving to make sandwiches the next day.

Cost driver—Something that is considered to be causally related to the incurrence of an overhead or resource cost. Commonly used cost drivers include the volume of items produced, the amount of labor or machine hours spent in producing items, or the levels of certain types of overhead activities.

Cost hierarchy—This term refers to the fact that costs are incurred at various levels of production. A common hierarchy refers to unit level costs, batch level costs, product level costs, and facility level costs.

Direct costing—This is a costing method in which only the direct costs of production are assigned to units produced. Typically, the direct costs are direct labor and direct materials. This method is not acceptable for GAAP.

Direct labor—This is the labor work done that is closely linked to the production of the products. For example, direct labor in the making of wooden chairs would include the labor of workers who cut and shape wood, but would not include the labor of people who clean the factory or perform supervisory functions.

Direct materials—These are materials that become part of the items produced. In a factory making wooden chairs, direct materials might include wood, glue to hold the wood together, and paint.

Facility level costs—In a cost hierarchy, these are costs needed to keep a factory facility operational. They might include factory supervisory salaries, building depreciation, building heating costs and other costs related to the entire facility.

Finished goods inventory—This is the part of the inventory consisting of items that have finished production and are ready for sale.

Fixed overhead—This is the portion of the overhead costs which is fixed in the short term, and does not vary with levels of production.

Full absorption costing—See **absorption costing**.

Indirect costs—These are costs that are related to production, but are not directly incorporated in the final product. Indirect costs would not include direct labor and would not include direct materials, but would include overhead costs in the factory.

Inventory shrinkage—This term is used for the difference between the inventory that is expected to be present and the actual inventory on hand. Common reasons for shrinkage include spoilage, theft, and errors in inventory accounting.

Inventory valuation role—One of the uses of cost accounting is to provide values for ending inventory for financial accounting purposes.

Job cost system—A method of tracking costs that accumulates costs for each "job order" or "project." This would typically be used by a manufacturer or service company that does projects or special batches of items for particular customers. An alternative method is a *process cost system*.

Joint costs—These are costs that are applicable to more than one product produced in a process.

Joint products—These are two or more products that are produced from a single process. For example, oil refineries separate crude oil into a number of petroleum products, such as kerosene and heating oil.

Net realizable value—This is the amount of money that a company ends up with ("realizes") after selling an item, and paying any expenses related to the selling process. It equals the selling price minus the related selling expenses.

Overhead—Factory costs that are not directly related to producing individual items. In this text, I have treated factory costs other than direct materials and direct labor as overhead.

Predetermined overhead rate—This is the rate at which overhead is "applied" ("allocated") to each item produced. It is "predetermined" because the rate is set at the beginning of the period, based on some estimated figures for overhead costs and for production levels.

Process cost system—This is a method of tracking costs when a company makes a large number of identical items. It is an alternative to the *job cost system*.

Product costing role—One purpose of cost accounting is to help companies decide the true cost of producing products.

Product level costs—These costs occur at the level of a cost hierarchy related to deciding to produce a product. The costs of product design might be an example.

Raw materials inventory—This is the part of the company's inventory that consists of materials that the company has not yet begun to process into products.

Split-off point—This is the stage in a production process where the company begins to perform different procedures on joint products. For example, a dairy company may take milk and separate it into skim milk and cream. That is a split-off point. Some of the cream may be further processed into butter.

Unit level costs—In a cost hierarchy, these costs are incurred each time a unit is produced. Direct materials are an example of a unit level cost.

Variable overhead—These are overhead costs that vary with the level of production.

Work in process inventory—This is the part of the inventory that relates to items that have begun, but not yet finished, the production process. Under absorption costing, the cost of work in process would include some costs for direct materials, direct labor, and overhead.

Questions and Problems

Comprehension Questions

C1. (Impact of inaccurate cost allocations) How can inaccurate allocations of costs to products lead to bad pricing decisions?

C2. (Impact of cost allocation methods) How do some cost allocation methods give managers an incentive to produce too much?

C3. (Changes in production) How have some of the changes in the production environment over the last century made it more difficult to assign costs to products?

C4. (Basic terms) Explain what is meant by the terms:

   A. Overhead
   B. Direct labor
   C. Direct materials

C5. (Cost hierarchy) Explain what is meant by each of the following terms related to the "cost hierarchy":

   A. Unit level costs
   B. Batch level costs
   C. Product level costs
   D. Facility level costs

C6. (Cost drivers) Explain what is meant by a cost driver.

C7. (Cost drivers) Assume that one of the overhead costs in a factory is machinery maintenance. Which of the following might make reasonable cost drivers for allocating this cost? Explain your answer:

    A. Number of units produced.
    B. Direct labor hours
    C. Direct labor dollars
    D. Machine hours worked

C8. (Stages of production) What types of costs (materials, overhead, and direct labor) would you expect to be included as part of the cost of inventory at each of the following stages of production? Explain your answer.

    A. Raw materials inventory
    B. Work in process inventory
    C. Finished goods inventory

C9. (Cost systems) Explain what types of production are appropriate for job cost systems, and when process cost systems are appropriate.

C10. (Flow of costs) At the time that a company incurs costs in making products, are these costs considered expenses? At what point in the production and sales process are the costs of production considered an expense?

C11. (Flow of costs) Give an equation relating beginning inventory, various manufacturing costs, ending inventory, and cost of goods sold and shrinkage.

C12. (Joint products and joint costs) Explain what is meant by the terms

    A. "Joint products"
    B. "Joint costs"
    C. "Split-off point"

C13. (Joint products and joint costs) Explain why economists consider the allocation of joint costs among joint products to be irrelevant to economic decision-making.

C14. (Joint products and joint costs) What are the three different approaches that are sometimes used to allocate joint costs among joint products?

C15. (By-products) What methods are used to allocate joint costs to by-products?

C16. (Allocating costs to products—reasons) Explain what is meant by the following three reasons firms allocate fixed costs to products:

    A. Inventory valuation role
    B. Product costing role
    C. Behavior modification role

C17. (Product costing) What is the difference between "absorption costing" and "direct costing"?

C18. (Applying overhead) How does a company compute a "predetermined overhead rate?

C19. (Applying overhead) What is meant by "under-applied overhead"? Why would a company have under-applied overhead at the end of the year?

C20. (Absorption costing) What are some issues or problems that have been raised with regard to traditional full absorption costing methods?

C21. (ABC) What is different about ABC, when compared to traditional full absorption costing? What benefits do people claim for ABC?

C22. (ABC) What are some problems or limitations with ABC?

C23. (RCA) What makes resource consumption accounting different from other methods? What advantages do people claim for RCA?

C24. (RCA) What are some drawbacks or limitations of RCA?

C25. (GAAP and cost methods) Respond to the following questions:

    A. Does GAAP require full absorption costing?

    B. Does the throughput method use full absorption costing for decision-making purposes? Explain.

    C. Can throughput accounting be modified to comply with GAAP? Explain.

C26. (Throughput accounting) What are some advantages people claim for throughput accounting?

C27. (Comparisons of methods) Which method or methods of cost accounting seem to have relative advantages with regard to:

    A. Simplicity

    B. Logically relating cost drivers to activities

    C. Making short-term product decisions

    D. Making sure long-term pricing and planning decisions consider all costs

    E. Highlighting decisions that leave part of the facility's capacity unused

    F. Reducing the risk of overproduction of inventory?

C28. (Transfer pricing) Explain why transfer prices between subsidiaries are, or are not, a problem from the perspective of:

    A. Financial accounting for the consolidated group of companies

    B. Creditors of particular subsidiaries

    C. Tax authorities

C29. (Transfer pricing) Explain some advantages, or disadvantages, of using each of the following transfer pricing rules:

    A. Market prices

    B. Variable costs

    C. Full absorption costs

    D. Negotiated prices

Application Questions

A1. (Types of costs) The Erie Shoe Factory has various costs during the year. Indicate for each whether it is a direct labor cost, a direct materials cost, a variable overhead cost, or a fixed overhead cost.

    A. Leather that is used to make the shoes.

    B. Salary of the factory supervisor.

    C. Salaries of the people who make the shoes.

    D. Cost of heating the factory.

    E. Cost of energy for the machines that are used to make the shoes. The machines are used only as shoes are made.

    F. Depreciation on the factory building (computed using straight-line method).

    G. Depreciation on factory machines (computed using unit of production method).

A2. (Cost hierarchy) The Niagara Paint Company makes different paint products, which it sells in one gallon containers. For each of the following, identify whether it is best described as a unit level cost, a batch level cost, a product level cost, or a facility level cost.

    A. Cost of washing equipment and setting up between different colors of paint. It typically makes 5,000 gallons of paint at a time. After each 5,000 gallons, the equipment must be washed and serviced.

    B. Cost of the container for each gallon of paint.

    C. Cost of the chemicals in each gallon of paint.

    D. Cost of identifying and testing the chemical formula for a particular color of paint it decides to add to its product line.

    E. Cost of heating the factory, which makes many different paint products.

A3. (Cost drivers) The Iroquois Trucking Company is freight business. It is trying to understand what causes certain of its costs to vary between months. For each of the following, suggest whether the most logical cost driver is: the number of miles it must drive its trucks; the total salaries of its truck drivers; or the number of truck drivers it has:

    A. Fuel costs for the trucks.

    B. Highway tolls it pays.

    C. Medical insurance costs for the drivers. (It must pay $400 per month for each driver that works during the month.)

    D. Payroll taxes. (Payroll taxes for this company are typically 8% of salaries.)

    E. Supervision of the drivers.

A4. (Cost systems) Which of the following companies would probably use a job order cost system, and which would probably use a process cost system?

    A. A law firm that needs to keep track of the time and other costs of each lawsuit that it works on.

    B. A beer company that brews 5 million gallons of beer each year. It sells only two kinds of beer.

    C. A car repair shop that bills each customer for the materials and labor used to repair the car.

    D. A steel company that makes many tons of very standard products each year.

    E. A printing company that makes many different kinds of printed materials for clients during a year, and charges each client prices based on the costs of their orders.

A5. (Stages of production) The Noel Denim Jeans Corp. makes blue jeans. Identify for each of the following whether the item would be part of the raw materials inventory, the work in process inventory, or the finished goods inventory.

    A. Rolls of denim fabric which Noel has bought from other companies, which have not yet been cut or otherwise worked on.

    B. Completely sewn blue jeans, packaged and ready for shipment.

    C. Cloth that has been cut, but has not yet been sewn into blue jeans.

    D. Blue jeans that have been sewn together, but do not yet have zippers or buttons.

A6. (Stages of production) For the four items in question A5, identify whether the company should have allocated overhead and labor costs to these items. (Remember that overhead is allocated to items once work has begun, but not to raw materials.)

A7. (Relation of beginning and ending inventory) For each situation below, identify the missing number that is needed to make the relationship between beginning and ending inventory work.

Beginning inventory + Raw material purchased + Direct labor + Overhead
– Cost of Goods sold & shrinkage = Ending inventory

A.	10,000	5,000	3,000	6,000	–19,000	?
B.	12,000	100,000	40,000	28,000	?	10,000
C.	20,000	30,000	?	16,000	–98,000	18,000
D.	?	80,000	40,000	20,000	100,000	50,000

A8. (Joint products—unit volume and relative sales value methods) A cheese-making factory buys milk, and turns the milk into two major products: cheese and butter. Here are some facts regarding its production during the year:

Pounds of cheese produced	1,000,000
Pounds of butter produced	2,000,000
Selling price per pound of butter	$2
Selling price per pound of cheese	$3
Joint costs of making the butter and the cheese	$7,500,000

A. Compute the factory's total amount of revenue for the year.
B. Compute the factory's total costs for the year.
C. Compute the total profits for the year.
D. If the joint costs are allocated based on the number of pounds of products produced:

    a. How much of the joint costs would be allocated to butter?
    b. What would be the profit or loss associated with making butter?
    c. How much of the joint costs would be allocated to cheese?
    d. What would be the profit or loss associated with making cheese?

E. If the joint costs are allocated based on the relative sales value of the butter and cheese:

    a. How much of the joint costs would be allocated to butter?
    b. What would be the profit or loss associated with making butter?
    c. How much of the joint costs would be allocated to cheese?
    d. What would be the profit or loss associated with making cheese?

A9. (Joint products—unit volume and relative sales value methods) An agricultural products company buys soybeans, and separates out the soybean oil from the solid parts of the soybeans. The solid part is called soybean meal. Here are some facts regarding its production during the year:

Kilograms of soybean meal produced	4,000,000
Kilograms of soybean oil produced	6,000,000
Selling price per kilogram of soybean oil	$5
Selling price per kilogram of soybean meal	$2
Joint costs of making the two products	$30,000,000

A. Compute the factory's total amount of revenue for the year.
B. Compute the factory's total costs for the year.
C. Compute the total profits for the year.
D. If the joint costs are allocated based on the number of kilograms of products produced:

    a.   How much of the joint costs would be allocated to soybean oil?

    b.   What would be the profit or loss associated with making soybean oil?

    c.   How much of the joint costs would be allocated to soybean meal?

    d.   What would be the profit or loss associated with making soybean meal?

E.   If the joint costs are allocated based on the relative sales value of the two products:

    a.   How much of the joint costs would be allocated to soybean oil?

    b.   What would be the profit or loss associated with making soybean oil?

    c.   How much of the joint costs would be allocated to soybean meal?

    d.   What would be the profit or loss associated with making soybean meal?

A10. (Predetermined overhead rates) Knox Corp. is budgeted to spend $80,000 on manufacturing overhead in 2016. What would be the predetermined overhead rate if it based the computation on:

A.   Budgeted direct labor hours of 60,000?

B.   Budgeted machine hours of 160,000?

C.   Budgeted direct materials costs of $480,000?

A11. (Predetermined overhead rates) Ontario Corp., has budgeted to spend $130,000 on manufacturing overhead in 2016. Compute the predetermined overhead rates per hour or per dollar of materials cost that it would use if the computation is based on:

A.   Budgeted direct labor hours of 65,000.

B.   Budgeted machine hours of 195,000.

C.   Budgeted direct materials costs of $520,000.

A12. (Applying manufacturing overhead) Huron Corp. has three manufacturing divisions, as shown in the exhibit below. Each division has its own cost accounting system, and forecasts the data for 2016 shown in Table 10.4.

A.   Compute the predetermined overhead rate for each division.

B.   If Division A actually incurred $80,000 in overhead costs, and used 61,000 machine hours, compute the amount of under or over-applied overhead costs.

C.   If Division B incurred $135,000 in overhead costs, and used 279,000 units of materials, compute the over- or under-applied overhead.

D.   If Division C incurred $100,000 in overhead, and used 60,000 labor hours, compute the under- or over-applied overhead.

A13. (Applying manufacturing overhead) Black Corp. has three manufacturing divisions, as shown in the exhibit below. Each division has its own cost accounting system, and forecasts the data for 2016 shown in Table 10.5.

Table 10.4 Huron Corp. Forecast Cost Data for 2016

	Division A	Division B	Division C
Materials to be used (units)	240,000	280,000	60,000
Direct labor hours	90,000	120,000	50,000
Machine hours	60,000	37,500	22,500
Total budgeted overhead	$75,000	$140,000	$90,000
Method of allocating overhead	Machine hours	Material used	Direct labor hours

Table 10.5 Black Corp. Forecast Cost Data for 2016

	Division 1	Division 2	Division 3
Materials to be used (units)	200,000	250,000	50,000
Direct labor hours	10,000	15,000	15,000
Machine hours	50,000	40,000	20,000
Total budgeted overhead	$100,000	$150,000	$120,000
Method of allocating overhead	Machine hours	Material used	Direct labor hours

A. Compute the predetermined overhead rate for each division
B. If Division 1 actually incurred $120,000 in overhead costs, and used 61,000 machine hours, compute the amount of under- or over-applied overhead costs.
C. If Division 2 incurred $145,000 in overhead costs, and used 255,000 units of materials, compute the over- or under-applied overhead.
D. If Division 3 incurred $110,000 in overhead, and used 14,000 labor hours, compute the under- or over-applied overhead.

A14. (Cost allocation—traditional full absorption costing) The Green Corp. makes two products, a Big Product and a Small Product. Facts about the production process and cost are given below.

Total factory overhead costs	$10,000,000
Raw material costs per unit of Big	$4
Raw material costs per unit of Small	$1
Direct labor costs per unit—either Big or Small	$3
Direct labor hours per unit, either Big or Small	0.1
Number of units produced in month	
Big	3,000,000
Small	2,000,000

The company uses direct labor hours as the cost driver to allocate overhead.

A. Compute the total labor hours in the month to produce:

a. Big
b. Small
c. The company's total production

B. Compute the amount of overhead cost that Green will allocate per unit produced to:

a. Big
b. Small

C. Compute the per unit cost that Green will assign to:

a. Big
b. Small

A15. (Cost allocation—traditional full absorption costing) The Red Corp. makes two products, a Fancy Product and a Simple Product. Facts about the production process and cost are given below.

Total factory overhead costs	$60,000,000
Raw material costs per unit of Fancy	$3.00

Raw material costs per unit of Simple	$2.50
Direct labor costs per unit—Fancy	$6
Direct labor hours per unit—Fancy	0.2
Direct labor dollars per unit—Simple	$3
Direct labor hours per unit—Simple	0.1
Number of units produced in month	
Fancy	10,000,000
Simple	20,000,000

The company uses direct labor hours as the cost driver to allocate overhead.

A. Compute the total labor hours in the month to produce:

    a.   Fancy
    b.   Simple
    c.   The company's total production

B. Compute the amount of overhead cost that Red will allocate per unit produced to:

    a.   Fancy
    b.   Simple

C. Compute the per unit cost that Red will assign to:

    a.   Fancy
    b.   Simple

A16. (ABC) The Blue Company makes two products, regular and premium. Data for the company and its products is in Table 10.6. Using the data provided:

A. Compute the rates to charge for each activity:

    a.   Moving (per move)
    b.   Purchasing (per purchase order)
    c.   Inspecting (per unit)
    d.   Supervision (per labor hour)

B. Compute the total overhead that will be allocated to Premium units, including the costs of moving, purchasing, inspecting, and supervision.
C. Compute the per unit overhead cost that will be allocated to Premium units.
D. Compute the total cost per unit for Premium units, including labor, overhead, and raw materials.
E. Compute the total overhead that will be allocated to Regular units, including the costs of moving, purchasing, inspecting, and supervision.
F. Compute the per unit overhead cost that will be allocated to Regular units.
G. Compute the total cost per unit for Regular units, including labor, overhead, and raw materials.

A17. (Comparison of traditional full absorption costing to ABC) Use the same facts as in question A16. Now assume the company does not use ABC, but allocates total overhead based on either labor hours or on units produced.

A. If the company allocates total overhead based on direct labor hours, what will be the overhead per unit allocated to:

    a.   Regular units?
    b.   Premium units?

Table 10.6 Blue Company Data

Overhead activities and cost drivers

	Budgeted cost	Activity-based cost driver	Capacity activity level
Moving materials	$90,000	# of moves	180
Purchasing	$150,000	# purchase orders	1,000
Quality control/inspecting	$100,000	# items produced	140,000
Supervision and other	$400,000	# labor hours	150,000
Total overhead:	$750,000		

Other data

	Regular	Premium
Raw materials per item	$22.00	$26.00
Direct labor per item	$20.00	$25.00
Units produced	100,000	40,000
Labor hours per item	1	1.25
Number of moves	120	60
Number of purchase orders	500	500

B. If the company allocates total overhead based on the number of units produced, what will be the overhead cost per unit allocated to:

    a.   Regular units?

    b.   Premium units?

A18. (ABC and analyzing customers) The Buffalo National Bank is trying to analyze the profitability of its business of providing checking account services to customers. It is dividing its customers into three groups, based on the average size of their checking accounts: high, medium, or low. The overhead activities associated with checking accounts, and the annual costs, are as follows:

	Amounts	Cost driver
Opening and closing bank accounts	$300,000	# accounts opened/closed
Issuing monthly statements	400,000	# checking accounts
Processing regular transactions	2,500,000	# regular transactions
Providing ATM services	1,100,000	# ATM transactions
Other	500,000	# checking accounts
Total	$4,800,000	

Some additional data is as follows:

	Low	Medium	High	Total
Number of accounts opened/closed	14,000	5,000	1,000	20,000
Number of checking accounts	65,000	10,000	5,000	80,000
Number of transactions processed	21,500,000	2,500,000	1,000,000	25,000,000
ATM transactions provided	3,700,000	500,000	200,000	4,400,000

A. Compute the cost of each of the five activities per unit of the cost driver:

    a.   Opening and closing accounts

    b.   Issuing statements

    c.   Processing regular transactions

    d.   Providing ATM services

    e.   Other

B. Using the activity cost rates from the previous part, and the number of times each activity occurs, compute the *total overhead cost* that would be assigned to:

    a.   Low accounts
    b.   Medium accounts
    c.   High Accounts

C. Assume that Buffalo Bank wants to charge a fee high enough to cover its costs. Using your answer from the previous part, and the number of checking accounts in each type, compute the fee per checking account that Buffalo Bank would need to charge to equal the overhead cost *per checking account* for:

    a.   Low accounts
    b.   Medium accounts
    c.   High accounts

D. The preceding parts of this problem used an ABC analysis to compute overhead costs per account. In this part, assume the Buffalo Bank decides to charge all its 80,000 checking accounts the same fee. Compute the fee that would be needed per checking account to allow Buffalo Bank to cover its overhead costs.

E. Compare your answer in Part D with your answers in Part C. For which types of accounts would Buffalo Bank be charging too high, or too low, a fee if it charged equal amounts to all types of customers?

A19. (ABC and supplier costs) Assume that a car manufacturing company has two different suppliers, Red and Green, for a fuel pump that it uses in its cars. Problems with the suppliers can cause two types of problems: warranty claims for defective products, and delay costs due to late shipments of parts from the suppliers. Some data related to the company is provided below:

Total repair costs during the year due to defective fuel pumps	$1,400,000
Total delay costs due to late shipments of fuel pumps	$600,000

Information related to the parts from the two suppliers:

	Red Company	Green Company
Price per item charged for fuel pumps	$100	$102
Units purchased	250,000	750,000
Defective units	10,000	4,000
Late shipments	20	10

A. Compute the activity cost rate for:

    a.   Repair costs per defective unit
    b.   Delay costs per delay

B. Compute the total amount of repair costs that should be allocated to:

    a.   Items bought from Red Company
    b.   Items bought from Green Company

C. Compute the total amount of delay costs that should be allocated to:

    a.   Items bought from Red Company
    b.   Items bought from Green Company

    D. Compute the amount *per unit* that should be allocated to items bought from Green company for:

        a. Repair costs
        b. Delay costs

    E. Compute the amount *per unit* that should be allocated to items bought from Red company for:

        a. Repair costs
        b. Delay costs

    F. Which is the low cost supplier? Explain your answer.

A20. (Transfer pricing) Assume that Parent Corp. has two subsidiaries, Brother Corp. and Sister Corp. Brother Corp turns wheat into flour. Sister Corp. uses flour to make bread. Sister Corp. can buy flour from other suppliers for $0.50 per pound. Brother normally sells its flour for $0.55 per pound. Brother has variable costs per pound of $0.44 and fixed costs per pound of $0.06. Its price of $0.55 per pound gives it a profit of $0.05 per pound.

    Assume Brother does not have any capacity constraints.

    A. If Brother sets a price to Sister of $0.55 per pound, Sister will buy its flour from outside suppliers. What will the variable cost per pound be for the group of companies as a whole for each pound of flour Sister makes into bread?

    B. If Brother sets a price to Sister of $0.50 per pound, and Sister buys at that price:

        a. What profit will Brother make on a full cost basis?
        b. What is the difference between Brother's selling price and its variable costs per pound?
        c. Would Brother want to make this deal? What is its benefit in making the sale?
        d. Would Sister want to make this deal? What is its benefit in buying from Brother, rather than buying from outside?
        e. What will be the variable cost per pound for the group of companies as a whole for each pound of flour Sister makes into bread?

    C. If Brother sets a price to Sister of $0.44 per pound, and Sister buys at that price:

        a. What profit will Brother make on a full cost basis?
        b. What is the difference between Brother's selling price and its variable costs per pound?
        c. Would Brother want to make this deal? What is its benefit in making the sale?
        d. Would Sister want to make this deal? What is its benefit in buying from Brother, rather than buying from outside?
        e. What will be the variable cost per pound for the group of companies as a whole for each pound of flour Sister makes into bread?

Discussion Questions

D1. (Allocating costs to divisions) Stride University has three campuses, in New York, Boston, and Philadelphia. The university overall is running a deficit of $10 million. The accounting system indicates that the New York location is making profits of $3 million, Boston is making profits of $1 million, and Philadelphia is losing $14 million. The faculty in New York have voted to ask the President to close the Philadelphia operation to cure the university's overall fiscal problems. Using ideas from this chapter, explain what additional information you would want to have before making this decision.

D2. (Lean accounting) The proponents of lean accounting, and of "just-in-time" inventory management techniques, argue for keeping inventory at the lowest possible levels. What are reasons that, instead, a company might want to keep significant levels of inventory on hand?

D3. (Cost allocation among contracts) Assume that a university receives a grant from the U.S. Defense Department to cover the costs of a research project. Which of the following indirect costs do you think it would be fair for the university to allocate to this grant? Explain your answers.

A.   Part of the university's heating costs.
B.   Part of the university's fund-raising costs.
C.   Part of the university's bookkeeping and audit costs.
D.   Part of the university's personnel department costs.

D4. (Allocating costs to divisions) Assume that a company operates subsidiaries in two countries with different tax rates. The company has the opportunity to set transfer prices between the two subsidiaries in a way that saves the company taxes. These transfer prices are different from what the company would set if there were no tax advantages. Comment on whether you believe the company's actions are ethical.

Notes

1   See Chatfield (1977). See also Littleton (1933). An early user of cost accounting was Josiah Wedgwood, founder and owner of the famous English pottery business. See Soll (2014).

2   See http://www.thehenryford.org/exhibits/showroom/1908/model.t.html (last accessed August 18, 2015).

3   See for example Horngren, Datar and Rajan (2015). A contrary view is from Yuji Ijiri (1967), who sees no reason to use a selling price as a measure of the sacrifices needed to create the product.

4   See the discussion of research in Balakrishnan, Labro and Sivaramakrishnan (2012a).

5   FASB's SFAS No. 151, issued in 2004, required fixed overhead costs to be allocated based on "normal capacity," which is adjusted for normal maintenance. "Normal capacity is the production expected to be achieved over a number of periods or seasons under normal circumstances, taking into account the loss of capacity resulting from planned maintenance" (para. 2). Costs that are due to excess capacity are expensed, not inventoried. International standards, in particular IAS No. 2, also require overhead costs to be allocated based on normal capacity.

6   Gupta, Pevzner and Seethamraju (2010) find that inventories of firms with high fixed manufacturing overhead tend to move in ways consistent with earnings management. They also find that analysts do not seem to identify this earnings management and the stock market does not identify it.

7   See also Gosselin (2006) for a discussion of studies on reasons companies have implemented or chosen not to implement ABC.

8   See Gosselin, M. (2006). Balakrishnan, Labro, and Sivaramakrishnan (2012a) cite research indicating that ABC is used by a sizable minority of companies.

9   Using this information in decision-making, even if not incorporating it into the cost accounting system, is called "activity-based management" ("ABM").

10   Time-driven activity-based costing was introduced by Robert S. Kaplan and Steven R. Anderson in 2004. See Kaplan and Anderson (2004). According to Balakrishnan, Labro, and Sivaramakrishnan (2012a), time-driven ABC should normally give the same product costs as the regular ABC method.

11   See Balakrishnan, Labro and Sivaramakrishnan (2012a).

12   www.rcainstitute.org/ (last accessed August 18, 2015).

13   See Sharman (2003).

14   See Friedl et al. (2009).

15   See Sharman (2003).

16   This section is based on several published articles that compare the merits of the different cost systems. See: Grondskis and Sapkauskiene (2011); Balakrishnan, Labro and Sivaramakrishnan (2012a and 2012b); Gupta, Pevzner and Seethamraju (2010); and IMA (2011).

17   See for example Wegmann (2008).

18   See Balakrishnan and Sivaramakrishnan (2002).

19 Various authors have pointed out that it could be useful to blend some of the features of the different methods. See, for example, Chapman and Kern, A. (2012).
20 Balakrishnan, Labro, and Sivaramakrishnan (2012a). See also Tse and Gong (2009).
21 See Heitger, Mowen and Hansen (2008). The idea for including inspection and warranty claims in this list is that if goods were made right the first time, there would be no need for inspection, and there would be no customer complaints or warranty claims.
22 Lea (2007), p. 1188. For another study of the better ability of ABC to set appropriate prices, see Cardinaels, Roodhooft and Warlop, L. (2004).
23 See Boyd and Cox (2002).
24 See for example the October 7, 2014 BBC story "Amazon faces European Union tax avoidance investigation" www.bbc.com/news/business-29519631 (last accessed August 18, 2015). It mentions investigations into Apple, Starbucks, and Fiat.

References

American Accounting Association. (1971). Report of the Committee on Foundations of Accounting Measurement [Supplement]. *Accounting Review, 46*(4) 1–48.

Balachandran, B. V., Balakrishnan, R., & Sivaramakrishnan, K. (1997). On the efficiency of cost-based decision rules for capacity planning. *Accounting Review, 72*, 599–619.

Balakrishnan, R., Labro, E., & Sivaramakrishnan, K. (2012a). Product costs as decision aids: An analysis of alternative approaches (part 1). *Accounting Horizons, 26*(1), 1–20.

Balakrishnan, R., Labro, E., & Sivaramakrishnan, K. (2012b). Product costs as decision aids: An analysis of alternative approaches (part 2). *Accounting Horizons, 26*(1), 21–41.

Balakrishnan, R., & Sivaramakrishnan, K. (2002). A critical overview of the use of full-cost data for planning and pricing. *Journal of Management Accounting Research, 14*(1), 3–31.

Boyd, L. H., & Cox III, J. F. (2002). Optimal decision making using cost accounting information. *International Journal of Production Research, 40*(8), 1879–98.

Brüggen, A., Krishnan, R., & Sedatole, K. L. (2011). Drivers and consequences of short-term production decisions: Evidence from the auto industry. *Contemporary Accounting Research, 28*(1), 83–123.

Cardinaels, E., Roodhooft, F., & Warlop, L. (2004). The value of activity-based costing in competitive pricing decisions. *Journal of Management Accounting Research, 16*(1), 133–48.

Chapman, C. S., & Kern, A. (2012). Reflections on the research and practice of costing. *Irish Accounting Review, 19*, 23–9.

Chatfield, M. (1977). *A History of Accounting Thought* (revised edition). New York: Robert E. Krieger Publishing Company.

FASB. (1980). Statement of Financial Accounting Concepts No. 2, *Qualitative Characteristics of Accounting Information*. Stamford, CT: FASB.

Friedl, G., Hammer, C., Pedell, B., & Kupper, H. U. (2009). How do German companies run their cost accounting systems? *Management Accounting Quarterly, 10*(2), 38.

Gosselin, M. (2006). A review of activity-based costing: technique, implementation, and consequences. *Handbook of Management Accounting Research, 2*, 641–71.

Grondskis, G., & Sapkauskiene, A. (2011). Cost accounting information use for product mix design. *Economics & Management, 16*, 48–53.

Gupta, M., Pevzner, M., & Seethamraju, C. (2010). The implications of absorption cost accounting and production decisions for future firm performance and valuation. *Contemporary Accounting Research, 27*(3), 889–922.

Heitger, D. L., Mowen, M. M., & Hansen, D. R. (2008). *Fundamental Cornerstones of Managerial Accounting*. Thomson South-Western.

Horngren, C. T., Datar, S. M., & Rajan, M. V. (2015). *Cost Accounting—A Managerial Emphasis* (15th ed). Boston: Pearson.

Hutchinson, R., & Liao, K. (2009). Zen Accounting: How Japanese Management Accounting Practice Supports Lean Management. *Management Accounting Quarterly, 11*(1), 27–35.

Ijiri, Y. (1967). *The Foundations of Accounting Measurement: A Mathematical, Economic, and Behavioral Inquiry*. Englewood Cliffs, NJ: Prentice-Hall, Inc.

IMA. (2006). *Statements on Management Accounting—Accounting for the Lean Enterprise: Major Changes to the Accounting Paradigm*. Montvale, NJ: Institute of Management Accountants.

IMA. (2011). *Designing an Effective Cost System*. Montvale, NJ: Institute of Management Accountants.

IMA. (2014a). *Conceptual Framework for Managerial Costing*. Report of the IMA Managerial Costing Conceptual Framework Task Force. Montvale, NJ: Institute of Management Accountants.

IMA (2014b). Statements on Management Accounting. *Implementing Activity Based Costing*. Montvale, NJ: Institute of Management Accountants.

Kaplan, R. S., & Anderson, S. R. (2004). Time-driven activity-based costing. *Harvard Business Review*, *82*(11), 131–8.

Kennedy, T., & Affleck-Graves, J. (2001). The impact of activity-based costing techniques on firm performance. *Journal of Management Accounting Research*, *13*(1), 19–45.

Lea, B.-R. (2007). Management accounting in ERP integrated MRP and TOC environments. *Industrial Management & Data Systems*, *107*(8), 1188–211.

Littleton, A. C. (1933). *Accounting Evolution to 1900*. New York: American Institute Publishing Company.

Schildbach, T. (1997). Cost accounting in Germany. *Management Accounting Research*, *8*(3), 261–76.

Sharman, P. A. (2003). Bring on German cost accounting. *Strategic Finance*, *85*(6), 30–8.

Soll, J. (2014). *The Reckoning: Financial Accountability and the Rise and Fall of Nations*. New York: Basic Books.

Souren, R., Ahn, H., & Schmitz, C. (2005). Optimal product mix decisions based on the theory of constraints? Exposing rarely emphasized premises of throughput accounting. *International Journal of Production Research*, *43*(2), 361–74.

Thomson, J., & Gurowka, J. (2005). Sorting out the clutter—ABC, ABM, TOC. *Strategic Finance*, *87*(2), 27–33.

Tse, M., & Gong, M. (2009). Recognition of idle resources in time-driven activity-based costing and RCA models. *Journal of Applied Management Accounting Research*, *7*(2), 41–54.

Wegmann, G. (2008). The activity-based costing method: Development and applications. *The IUP Journal of Accounting Research and Audit Practices*, *8*(1), 7–22.

Appendix to Chapter 10 on the Theory of Constraints and Throughput Accounting

This appendix discusses a different way of thinking about factory processes and costs than the methods in the body of the chapter. The methods discussed in this appendix are especially useful to companies trying to use "lean" production techniques, and trying to avoid building excessive inventory.

The *theory of constraints* was developed and popularized by Eliyahu Goldratt beginning in 1984.[1] The theory of constraints focuses on understanding the limiting constraints in production processes, and taking these constraints into account when making all decisions.

In this appendix, we will first discuss some basic terminology, then discuss how the theory of constraints applies to production processes, and then discuss "throughput accounting."

Basic Terminology—Capacity, Production Constraints and the Idea of Throughput

The IMA (2014) has defined "capacity" as "the physical facilities, personnel, and processes available to meet the product or service needs of customers. Capacity generally refers to the maximum output or production ability of a machine, person, process, factory, product, or service" (p. 31). We will be using the term in this sense of the maximum output that can be made.

Often, a production process involves numerous steps. For example, the process of making steel wire may involve buying iron and other raw materials, melting them together in a giant furnace to form liquid steel, and shaping the steel into wires. The company may have a different maximum amount that it can process through each of these steps in a day. A manufacturer's ability to produce steel wire is limited by the *slowest* of these operations.

As an example, assume that a steel company is able to unload 300 tons per day of raw materials into the facility, that it is able to melt 120 tons, and it is able to shape 200 tons of liquid steel per day into wires. How much wire can it produce in a day? It will only be able to produce 120 tons of wires, because that is the most its furnaces are able to produce. The furnace operation is the "binding constraint" or "bottleneck" that limits the production.

To maximize production, the company's management should make sure that it keeps the furnaces working constantly at a rate of 120 tons per day. It is not necessary for the unloading operation to unload 300 tons of raw materials each day, since that is far more than can be melted. In fact, it would be bad if the company unloaded 300 tons of raw material each day, since that would result in large piles of materials waiting to be melted. That would clutter the facility, and cost money to store. It is only necessary to unload enough materials each day to allow the furnaces to process 120 tons, and to keep a reasonable size extra *"buffer"* inventory on hand in case there is some delay in receiving deliveries in a day. It is also unnecessary for the company to keep the staff and machines needed to make 200 tons of wire out of molten steel each day, since the furnaces cannot melt that much steel. Keeping the unneeded extra wire-making capacity is unduly expensive.

Managing Using the Theory of Constraints

Companies that try to manage operations using the theory of constraints tend to focus on three variables.[2]

The first is *throughput*. "Throughput" is the selling price of the amount processed through the binding constraint, minus the "*totally variable cost*" of producing this output. Usually, totally variable cost only includes raw materials cost. The companies that use this method tend to treat direct labor as fixed in the short term. The idea is that most companies will not in fact send workers home on slow days, but instead will find something else for them to do.[3]

Companies should try to maximize the throughput. If they must choose between different products to make, they should choose based on the dollars of *throughput per hour through the binding constraint*. For example, assume that Product A has a price of $5, and raw materials costs of $2. Ignoring overhead and labor, the profit margin per item is $3. Now assume that Product B has a price of $10, and raw materials costs of $3. Ignoring overhead and direct labor, the profit margin per item is $7. At first, it looks like the company should focus on Product B, because it has a higher profit margin per item. However, the theory of constraints would argue that a complete analysis must consider the speed of processing through the constraint.

Assume that 60 items of Product A can be produced per hour, but only 20 items of Product B. The throughput per hour for Product A = 60 units × ($5 − $2), or $180. The throughput per hour of Product B = 20 × ($10 − $3) = $140. The company will make less money if it produces Product B, even though it has a higher profit item per item made, because it can't produce as many items.

The second variable is *operating expenses*. For this method of accounting, operating expenses include all the period expenses of the facility, as well as selling expenses, direct labor, and overhead costs. This leads to the following equation:

Operating profits = throughput − operating expenses.

This means that both increasing throughput and decreasing operating expenses can increase profits. While the profit equation indicates that reducing operating expenses will increase profits, companies must be careful when reducing spending on overhead, labor, and selling efforts to avoid inadvertently reducing throughput. Selling efforts, direct labor, and overhead functions are not directly tied to the number of units produced, but spending on these functions may be necessary to keep the facility productive at its capacity level. For example, if all the supervisors are fired, then operating expenses will decline, but probably the steel company would become less efficient, and would no longer be able to melt 120 tons of steel per day.

The third variable is the company's *investment in inventory and facilities*.[4] All other things being equal, it is best to have less company money tied up in inventory and factories. It costs money to store inventory, and there is always the chance that inventory will be stolen or become obsolete. There is also an opportunity cost in having money tied up in excessive equipment and facilities. There is a point to maintaining some extra "buffer" inventory on hand in the stages of the production process before the constraint, to ensure the constraining process continues to operate when there are interruptions in production at earlier stages. It is also useful to keep some extra capacity ("*sprint capacity*") in the stages of the process before the constraint, to allow production to catch up if there were interruptions. However, it is wasteful to maintain excess capacity or excess inventory after the constraining stage of production.

Throughput Accounting

Background

This section describes a method of accounting that is compatible with the theory of constraints. The description follows Bragg (2012). Throughput accounting is a relatively new approach, and shares some characteristics with what is known as "lean accounting." Both systems are concerned with constraints, and both systems seek to help management avoid production of excessive inventory. However, a full discussion of "lean accounting" is beyond the scope of this text.[5]

Throughput is defined as the revenue from production minus the totally variable costs. In the examples that follow, only raw materials are treated as totally variable. In particular, direct labor is *not* regarded as a totally variable cost, because in practice most factories try to keep their employees steadily employed. If there are temporary lulls in production of one product, most facilities find other work for their employees to do, rather than fire them.

Operating expenses include overhead costs and any other costs that are not directly variable. Operating profit is equal to throughput minus the operating expenses.

The focus of this method is on understanding how decisions affect overall profit. For decision-making purposes, the operating expenses are *not* allocated to individual units of product. This is very different than other methods we saw. Those methods allocated labor and overhead to products. They were "full absorption" methods, and throughput accounting is not.

Example of Analysis Using Throughput Accounting

The following example for the Seneca TV Company shows how a throughput analysis can work. The company makes four different models of television. The company can run one eight-hour shift each day. This amounts to approximately 10,000 minutes per month.

The Seneca Company production process has one constraining operation, which limits the total number of units it can produce. All four types of TV must pass through this one constraining operation. The four types of TV are handled by the operation at different speeds. The smallest TVs take only four minutes, but the largest take 12 minutes.

Given that the company can't produce all the items it can sell, and that each model has different costs and prices, how should Seneca decide what to make? A throughput analysis of the problem starts by computing the throughput for each model per minute that it uses the constraining operation. In this example, the smaller TVs have higher throughput per minute of use of the constraint, and the larger TVs have lower throughput per minute. The company should produce all it can of the models with the highest throughput per minute. Table 10A.1 follows this logic, and the company decides to make all it can sell of the three smaller models, but only makes 216 of the largest models. The result is a total throughput of $66,660, and a profit after operating expenses of $7,660.

Note that this analysis focuses on throughput per minute, not throughput per product. In this example, the throughput per unit of product produced is larger for the bigger TVs, not the

Table 10A.1 Seneca TV Company—Throughput Profit Analysis—Optimal Product Mix

Product	Throughput $/minute of constraint	Required constraint usage in minutes	Units of scheduled production and demand	Constraint utilization in minutes	Throughput per product
22 inch TV	$8.00	4	600/600*	2,400	$19,200
32 inch TV	$7.50	6	500/500	3,000	$22,500
40 inch TV	$6.00	10	200/200	2,000	$12,000
47 inch TV	$5.00	12	216/400	2,592	$12,960
		Total planned constraint time		9,992	
		Maximum constraint time		10,000	
			Throughput total		$66,660
			Operating expense total		$59,000
			Profit		$7,660

*The first figure is the number produced, and the second is the number demanded.

Table 10A.2 Seneca TV Company—Throughput Profit Analysis Non-Optimal Product Mix

Product	Throughput $/minute of constraint	Required constraint usage in minutes	Units of scheduled production and demand	Constraint utilization in minutes	Throughput per product
22 inch TV	$8.00	4	50/600*	200	$1,600
32 inch TV	$7.50	6	500/500	3,000	$22,500
40 inch TV	$6.00	10	200/200	2,000	$12,000
47 inch TV	$5.00	12	400/400	4,800	$24,000
		Total planned constraint time		10,000	
		Maximum constraint time		10,000	
			Throughput total		$60,100
			Operating expense total		$59,000
			Profit		$1,100

*The first figure is the number produced, and the second is the number demanded.

smaller ones. Throughput per unit varies from $32 for the smallest TVs to $45 for the 32 inch models to $60 for the two largest units. If the managers decided to produce all they could of the items with the highest per unit throughput, they would have made a suboptimal decision. Profits would fall, because the extra profits from making more 47 inch TVs would be more than offset by the lower production of 22 inch TVs. Table 10A.2 shows the analysis.

Usefulness for Decision-Making

The usefulness of throughput accounting is in helping management make short-term decisions in an environment where there is some constraint on production. If we think back to the discussion of "relevant costs" in Chapter 5, it was important in decision-making to ignore sunk or fixed costs. Throughput analysis assumes that most factory level costs are fixed. In Chapter 5, we also indicated that opportunity costs needed to be considered when comparing alternative actions. Throughput analysis incorporates the need to consider the impact of decisions about one product on the profitability of other products. In the example above, the decision to produce more 47 inch TVs would cause the company to incur the opportunity cost of producing fewer small TVs.

Throughput analysis can be used for a number of other decision problems. Here are some examples:

- Whether to accept a special order from a customer at a discounted price. The items produced in this special order would have a lower price than normal, but the same raw materials cost, so the throughput per unit and the throughput per minute would be lower than the normal production. The order should be accepted only if the overall throughput for the company would be higher if it is accepted than if it is not accepted.
- Adding or dropping a product. The company would need to recompute the throughput analysis, taking into account the changes in the product mix. Adding or dropping a product might affect operating expenses. It will also affect the production of other items through the constraint process, because the company should strive to produce the items with the highest throughput per minute at the constraint.
- Whether to add capacity at the constraint. For example, a company may consider whether to hire people to work during the "break time" of the regular employees. This would allow the production line to keep functioning during breaks. In a throughput analysis, the result would be to increase the total amount of the capacity of the process. In our example, it would increase the available minutes per month from 10,000 to some higher

number. This would increase total throughput per month. The wages for the new employees would add to operating expenses. The company should hire the extra employees only if the increase in throughput is more than the increase in operating expenses.

- Whether to increase capacity in the factory *after* the constraining process. (This is referred to as "downstream" capacity.) A company may consider investing in increasing the capacity of processes that come after the constraining process. Usually, a throughput analysis will argue against such investments. Because this investment will not affect the speed of production through the constraining process, it will leave throughput unchanged. If there are extra operating expenses associated with this downstream capacity, profits will be lower. Even if there are no extra operating expenses, the profit per dollar of investment will be lower.

- Whether to increase capacity in the factory *before* the constraining process. (This is referred to as "upstream" capacity.) A throughput analysis may find such investments worthwhile if they help ensure that there is always enough material ready for use at the constraining process. In the example in Table 10A.2, we assumed that there could be production at the bottleneck for 10,000 minutes per month. Any interruptions in the process before the bottleneck that reduce the company's ability to use that process to, for example, 9,000 minutes per month on average, affect its profits. Investments in upstream capacity must be evaluated based on their effect on the likely average throughput, their impact on operating expenses, and the amount of investment required. If they improve the expected profit per dollar of investment, they are worthwhile.

There are limitations to the usefulness of this method. Throughput accounting is not interested in product costs for valuing ending inventory. It does not allocate overhead or most labor costs to products for purposes of decision-making. Instead, most of the costs allocated to products under the other methods are considered period costs under throughput accounting. Because it considers almost all costs except raw materials to be fixed, it does not explore the links of these costs to product costs in the short term.

Throughput Analysis and GAAP

In the analyses we have done so far, we did not allocate any labor or overhead costs to individual items of products produced. We considered these to be operating costs of the periods. Only the raw materials costs were included in the cost of inventory. This approach is forbidden under GAAP, which requires the allocation of labor and overhead costs to products produced. As a result, managers who wish to use throughput accounting for internal decision-making must do additional accounting to comply with GAAP.

One way to handle the problem is to use extra accounts. A company might divide its work in process inventory between two accounts: "materials in work in process"; and "allocated costs in work in process." Similarly, it could divide its finished goods inventory into two accounts, one for the raw materials component and one including allocated costs. For reporting under GAAP, it would report inventory using all the materials and overhead costs. For internal analysis, it would only consider the materials components of inventory to be assets, and would consider all changes in the allocated costs of inventory to be part of operating expenses.[6]

How should overhead be allocated to these special inventory accounts? It is unlikely to matter much, especially if companies keep inventories low. Since managers are not using this information to make decisions, but merely to comply with accounting rules, it would seem reasonable to use the simplest allocation method, involving the least bookkeeping effort and expense. Studies indicate that in Japan, where companies have traditionally tried to be "lean," the most common method is traditional full absorption costing.[7]

Problems Related to Throughput or the Theory of Constraints

Comprehension Questions

C1. (Theory of constraints) In the theory of constraints:

    A. What is meant by a constraint? Why does the constraining process limit the company's overall production?

    B. Why would a company want to keep some extra inventory on hand at the stage of production before the constraint?

    C. Why would a company want to have some extra "sprint capacity" in stages of production before the constraint?

    D. Is there a purpose to keeping extra processing capacity at processing stages after the constraint?

C2. (Theory of constraints) What is meant by "throughput"? What costs are considered in the computation of throughput?

C3. (Throughput accounting) In this method:

    A. Define throughput

    B. Indicate whether direct labor is used in the computation of throughput or of operating expenses

C4. (Throughput accounting) Using throughput accounting, would a manager tend to choose which products to produce based on their throughput per unit produced, or based on their throughput per minute at the constraint? Explain your answer.

C5. (Throughput accounting) What are some advantages people claim for throughput accounting?

C6. (Throughput accounting) What are some drawbacks or limitations of throughput accounting?

Application Questions

A1. (Throughput accounting cost concepts—throughput) A company can produce 400 units per hour through its process. It can sell each unit for $10. It had totally variable costs of $3 per unit, and other costs per unit of $5. Compute the throughput per hour.

A2. (Throughput accounting concepts—operating expenses and operating profits) The Oneida Corp. runs its production line 16 hours per day, and an average of 22 days per month. This gives it 352 hours of production each month. Additional facts are as follows:

Number of units produced per hour	2,000
Selling price per unit	$5
Total variable costs per unit	$2
Operating costs per month	$1,800,000

    Compute:

    A. Throughput per month

    B. Operating profit or loss per month

A3. (Throughput and special order) Mohawk Corp. makes four products. The Table 10A.3 below shows the key data for these four products.

    Currently, Mohawk is making 300 units of Product C. The throughput per unit is $4.50 × 8 minutes per unit = $36. A customer wants to make a special offer for an additional 300 units,

Table 10A.3 Mohawk Company—Throughput Profit Analysis

Product	Throughput $/minute of constraint	Required constraint usage in minutes	Units of scheduled production and demand	Constraint utilization in minutes	Throughput per product
Product A	$6.00	3	700/700*	2,100	$12,600
Product B	$5.00	5	600/600	3,000	$15,000
Product C	$4.50	8	300/300	2,400	$10,800
Product D	$4.00	2	1250/5,500	2,500	$10,000
		Total planned constraint time		10,000	
		Maximum constraint time		10,000	
			Throughput total		$48,400
			Operating expense total		$42,000
			Profit		$6,400

*The first figure is the number produced, and the second is the number demanded.

at a reduced price. If Mohawk accepts the order, it will receive total throughput per unit on the items in the special order of $28 per unit.

A. Compute the throughput per minute on the additional 300 units.
B. Compute the constraint utilization for the 300 additional units.
C. Compute the incremental throughput from these 300 additional units.
D. Compute the reduction in throughput from Product D that will be required to make room for these extra 300 units of Product C.
E. Compute the net change in profits from accepting the special order.

A4. (Throughput analysis) Assume the same facts for the Mohawk Company as the previous question. The throughput per unit for product A is $18. Currently, it takes three minutes at the constraint procedure to make one unit of A, so the throughput per minute is $6. The Mohawk Company is considering a change in its operating procedures. If it makes this change, it will be able to process Product A through the constraint in two minutes per unit, instead of three minutes per unit. However, the operating expenses will rise by $2,000 per period. What will be the net change in profits if it makes the change? (To solve this, you need to compute the changed amount of throughput of Product D as well as the change in the operating expenses.)

Notes

1   See Goldratt (1990) and Goldratt and Cox (1984). Wikipedia indicates that Wolfgang Mewes had written earlier about some of the key concepts, including the importance of identifying bottlenecks in production. See http://en.wikipedia.org/wiki/Theory_of_constraints, accessed February 14, 2015.
2   For a more complete explanation of the ideas in this section, see Bragg (2012).
3   Some writers have interpreted "totally variable cost" to include only direct raw materials. This was not the original intent. See Balderstone and Keef (1999).
4   Companies using this approach would measure their investment in inventory using only the raw materials costs. The labor and overhead costs are considered period operating costs.
5   Interested readers should refer to IMA (2006). See also Hutchinson and Liao (2009) as well as Kennedy and Widener (2008) for a discussion of the links between lean accounting concepts and the accounting and production practices of Toyota.
6   See Bragg (2012).
7   Hutchinson and Liao (2009).

References

Balderstone, S., & Keef, S. P. (1999). Exploding an urban myth. *Management Accounting: Magazine for Chartered Management Accountants, 77*(9), 26–7.

Bragg, S. M. (2012). *Throughput Accounting: A Guide to Constraint Management*. Hoboken, NJ: John Wiley & Sons.

Goldratt, E. M. (1990). *Theory of Constraints*. Croton-on-Hudson, NY: North River.

Goldratt, E. M., & Cox, J. (1984). *The Goal: Excellence in Manufacturing*. North River Press.

Hutchinson, R., & Liao, K. (2009). Zen Accounting: How Japanese Management Accounting Practice Supports Lean Management. *Management Accounting Quarterly, 11*(1), 27–35.

IMA. (2006). *Statements on Management Accounting—Accounting for the Lean Enterprise: Major Changes to the Accounting Paradigm*. Montvale, NJ: Institute of Management Accountants.

IMA (2014). *Statements on Management Accounting. Implementing Activity Based Costing*. Montvale, NJ: Institute of Management Accountants.

Kennedy, F. A., & Widener, S. K. (2008). A control framework: insights from evidence on lean accounting. *Management Accounting Research, 19*(4), 301–23.

11 Controlling Measurement and Reporting to Minimize Errors

Outline

- Preliminary Thoughts
- Overview
- Learning Objectives
- Causes of Incorrect Reports
- Places Misstatements Arise
- General Types of Accounting Controls
- Special Accounting Controls

    ○ Double-Entry Accounting as a Control
    ○ Accounting Information Systems
    ○ Reconciliations
    ○ Management by Exception and Variance Investigations
    ○ Auditing

- Limitations of Control Systems
- Accounting Controls in a Broader Context

    ○ Historical Perspective
    ○ The COSO Framework for Internal Controls

- Unresolved Issues and Areas for Further Research

Preliminary Thoughts

Monday was actually the busiest day of the season for UPS—more than 34 million packages delivered. Last Monday was the busiest for FedEx—about 23 million packages delivered.
Michael Chesney (2014)[1]

There is a tendency in many physical and social systems towards increasing disorganization, or inefficiency, if they are, or become, isolated from sources of energy which counteract the tendency. The tendency is expressed in the second law of thermodynamics, and it has been applied by analogy in many other fields. It is styled the principle of increasing entropy.
Raymond J. Chambers (1969, p. 235)

Glendower: "I can call spirits from the vasty deep."
Hotspur: "Why, so can I, or so can any man;
But will they come when you do call for them?"
William Shakespeare, Henry IV, Part 1, Act III, Scene 1

Accounting has been around a long time and shows no sign of declining in importance. This suggests it has a comparative advantage relative to the vast array of alternate information sources. . . . Its strength is that it is designed to be difficult to manipulate. It is designed to be and generally is audited.

John S. Christensen and Joel S. Demski (2003, p. 436)

This chapter deals with the problems of ensuring that the many accounting measurements that companies make each year are made, compiled, and reported accurately.

The first quotation shows the enormous numbers of transactions that modern companies engage in. On a single day in December, 2014, UPS delivered 34 million packages. It needed to accurately and promptly bill these deliveries.

The second quotation notes that any system will, if left unattended, tend to become disorganized. To keep systems organized, constant efforts are required. The accounting system is no different.

The quotation from Shakespeare points to the difference between simply giving a command, and actually getting results. Anyone can *say* they can call demons to come to them, but actually getting them to come is different. This chapter deals with some techniques that are used to ensure business processes actually work the way management wants them to.

The final quotation suggests that one important feature of accounting systems, as sources of information, is they are designed to be reliable and hard to manipulate.

Overview

In Chapter 2, one of the desirable attributes of information, according to the FASB (2010), was "representational faithfulness." "Representational faithfulness" requires that information be as "free from error" as possible. Like any process that involves many people, and is conducted under time and cost pressures, the accounting process is subject to error. This chapter discusses steps companies take to reduce the number of errors, and to minimize the effect of errors or intentional distortions on their financial reports. Errors and intentional distortions reduce the usefulness of reports.

An analogy to radio or telephone communications may be useful. When you listen to the radio, you hear both the organized radio waves carrying voices or music which the radio station is trying to transmit, which are called the "signal," and some random radio waves, called "noise." When there is a lot of noise, the signal is hard to understand. The noise could arise accidentally, or from someone's efforts to interfere with the signal. Communication scientists try to maximize the amount of signal, and minimize the noise, to ensure that listeners can hear programs clearly.

Accidental errors and intentionally dishonest reporting both create "noise" in accounting signals. Readers are less willing to use reports if they believe the data in the reports is either biased or unreliable. To make accounting reports useful, accountants need to find ways to maximize their accuracy. Businesses like UPS and FedEx use systematic accounting processes, as well as a variety of procedures, called internal controls, to ensure that their businesses function in accordance with management's wishes and that the reporting systems produce highly reliable information. These accounting systems and internal controls make it possible for investors to rely on company financial statements.

This chapter outlines the basics of accounting systems and internal controls. It also introduces some common control techniques, including reconciliations, documentation procedures, segregation of duties, and periodic audits. These techniques help prevent and detect errors. It discusses limits to the effectiveness of internal controls, as well as factors which affect the reliability of the control system. This chapter focuses on how the reliability of accounting reports is maximized. A final section relates accounting controls to the broader context of how company managers control their operations.

Learning Objectives

After studying this chapter, you should understand:

1 The difference between inadvertent errors and fraud
2 The basic goals of internal control systems
3 The nature of preventive and detection controls
4 General types of control procedures, such as separation of duties and documentation
5 The basics of the double-entry bookkeeping system, and how it enhances control
6 The basics of how accounting information systems accumulate information
7 How accountants use reconciliation processes, such as bank reconciliations, to enhance accuracy of recorded amounts
8 The roles of internal and external auditors
9 Inherent limitations of internal control systems
10 How accounting controls fit into a broader context of managerial control systems.

Causes of Incorrect Reports

Accounting reports can be inaccurate and misleading for a variety of reasons. For purposes of this chapter, we will consider three basic causes.

1 The basic accounting theory and rules can be faulty and fail to describe economic reality. Even if an accountant carefully follows these rules, the resulting reports will not be useful to the readers. Various defects in accounting theory have been discussed in previous chapters. They include, for example, the fact that GAAP accounting does not record most internally created intangible assets on balance sheets. This type of problem is not the focus of this chapter.
2 Accountants can make inadvertent errors in recording transactions or applying accounting rules. Numbers can be copied or added incorrectly. Computations of depreciation or taxes can include errors. Because errors are inadvertent, they could either make the company look better or worse.
3 A company may intentionally misstate its results. Intentional misstatements differ from errors in various ways. While errors have a random effect on reported results, intentional misstatements do not—they are meant to achieve a particular accounting result. Also, fraud often involves misstatements in a variety of accounts, all adding together to achieve a desired result. Errors are random, and errors in various areas of the company tend to cancel each other out. Finally, fraud perpetrators typically try to conceal intentional misstatements, often with fake documentation. In contrast, those people committing errors do not realize they have made the errors, and accordingly make no efforts to conceal them.

This chapter uses "misstatements" as a general term, including both errors and intentional misstatements. The term *irregularity* is also used for intentional misstatements.

Places Misstatements Arise

Accounting is a process involving recognizing that events have occurred, classifying them, recording them, summarizing them, and reporting. Inaccuracies can arise at each step of the process.

The Recognition Phase

A variety of misstatements can occur at the recognition phase.

A company can fail to recognize that an event has occurred. For example, it can fail to recognize that the value of an asset has decreased, and fail to write down the asset to its fair value. It could fail to make such routine adjustments of its books as:

- recording the using up of prepaid insurance
- recording depreciation or amortization
- recording accrued interest receivable or payable.

A company might make the mistake of recording the same event more than once. It could record the same sale twice.

A company might recognize an event in the wrong time period. For example, it might improperly recognize a January sale as having occurred in December.

Classification Issues

When a company spends money, it is often either buying an asset or incurring an expense. Errors in classifying the expenditure can directly affect income. If a company says its expenditure was for the purchase of an asset, when it really was an expense, it will overstate equity and net income.

Companies also tend to use a large number of categories to classify expenses. Errors can arise in categorizing expenditures between these categories. For example, salary costs might be direct factory labor, factory overhead, selling expenses, or administrative expenses.

Recording

For information to be accurately included in the accounting process, it must be recorded properly. Even if the first person to see the transaction makes the correct recognition and classification decisions, the transaction still must be entered into the accounting system. Errors that can occur include:

- failing to record a transaction. Box 11.1 provides an egregious example
- recording a transaction twice
- recording a transaction with the wrong date
- recording the incorrect amount of the transaction
- recording the transaction in the wrong accounts
- recording the transaction backwards. In this error, the right accounts are affected, but the accounts that should have been increased were decreased.

Summarization

Accounting information is initially recorded in what is called a *journal*. A journal is basically a list of transactions or events, and includes the key aspects of these events: the date; the accounts involved; the amounts each account is increased or decreased; and an indication of the nature of the event. This initial recording of the event is called a *journal entry*. A variety of problems can occur in summarizing information after it is first recorded in journals.

Information from journals is typically copied ("*posted*") into *ledgers*, which summarize the activity in each account. While a sales journal, for example, might contain the sales transactions that occurred during a month in order of their occurrence, a "*general ledger*" would contain separate accounts for every classification of asset, liability, equity, revenue, dividend, and expense that the company has, sorted by account. Errors that can occur in this copying ("posting") process include:

Box 11.1 Failing to Record Transactions—The Case of the Cash Sent to Iraq

The following excerpts from an article in *The Guardian* in 2007 relate to an extreme example of cash being spent without adequate records.

How the US sent $12bn in cash to Iraq. And watched it vanish.

Special flights brought in tonnes of banknotes which disappeared into the war zone

The US flew nearly $12bn in shrink-wrapped $100 bills into Iraq, then distributed the cash with no proper control over who was receiving it and how it was being spent.

The staggering scale of the biggest transfer of cash in the history of the Federal Reserve has been graphically laid bare by a US congressional committee.

In the year after the invasion of Iraq in 2003 nearly 281 million notes, weighing 363 tonnes, were sent from New York to Baghdad for disbursement to Iraqi ministries and US contractors. Using C-130 planes, the deliveries took place once or twice a month with the biggest of $2,401,600,000 on June 22, 2004. . . . Henry Waxman, a fierce critic of the war, said the way the cash had been handled was mind-boggling. "The numbers are so large that it doesn't seem possible that they're true. Who in their right mind would send 363 tonnes of cash into a war zone?"

The money. . . came from Iraqi oil sales, surplus funds from the UN oil-for-food programme and seized Iraqi assets.

"One CPA [Coalition Provisional Authority] official described an environment awash in $100 bills," the memorandum says. . . .

". . . Cash payments were made from the back of a pickup truck, and cash was stored in unguarded sacks in Iraqi ministry offices. One official was given $6.75m in cash, and was ordered to spend it in one week before the interim Iraqi government took control of Iraqi funds.". . .

The memorandum concludes: "Many of the funds appear to have been lost to corruption and waste . . . thousands of 'ghost employees' were receiving pay cheques from Iraqi ministries under the CPA's control. Some of the funds could have enriched both criminals and insurgents fighting the United States."

According to Stuart Bowen, the special inspector general for Iraq reconstruction, the $8.8bn funds to Iraqi ministries were disbursed "without assurance the monies were properly used or accounted for". . . .

However, evidence before the committee suggests that senior American officials were unconcerned about the situation because the billions were not US taxpayers' money. . . . Retired Admiral David Oliver, is even more direct. The memorandum quotes an interview with the BBC World Service. Asked what had happened to the $8.8bn he replied: "I have no idea. I can't tell you whether or not the money went to the right things or didn't—nor do I actually think it's important."

Q: "But the fact is billions of dollars have disappeared without trace."

Oliver: "Of their money. Billions of dollars of their money, yeah I understand. I'm saying what difference does it make?"

www.theguardian.com/world/2007/feb/08/usa.iraq1 (last accessed August 18, 2015).

- Copying the incorrect figures
- Copying figures into the wrong accounts
- Copying figures into the right accounts, but with their sign reversed

- Failure to copy data from journals to ledgers
- Double-copying figures from journal to ledgers

The information in the ledgers needs to be added up, and then the figures need to be used to create financial reports. Errors can arise in adding the data, or copying it into the financial reports.

For large companies, which have a parent company and numerous subsidiaries, errors can also arise in the process of adding together the results and accounts from the various subsidiaries into a single consolidated report.

Reporting

Even if a company has carefully kept its books, misstatements can arise in the process of preparing financial reports. Such errors include:

- Copying information improperly
- Adding information in reports improperly
- Failing to include necessary footnotes or disclosures
- Placing accounts in the wrong section of reports. For example, including certain operating cash flows in the investing cash flow section of the statement of cash flows would be an error.

This is also the stage at which "*management override*" is most likely to occur. Management override is the term used when management instructs employees to ignore the normal accounting processes. Top management may instruct employees to make improper entries in accounting records to achieve the desired results. Box 11.2 is an example.

Box 11.2 WorldCom Fraud—An Example of Management Override

During the 1990s WorldCom grew rapidly by acquiring other companies, and became the second largest provider of long distance telephone service in the United States. In the 1990s, internet and telecom companies were booming. At the turn of the century, the revenues and stock prices of telecom and internet companies, including WorldCom's, came under pressure.

Beginning in 1998, the CEO and CFO of WorldCom overrode the normal controls by directing accounting staff to make improper accounting entries. As described in a 2003 *Wall Street Journal* article, three mid-level accounting people initially resisted making the false accounting entries, and then caved in under pressure. The article cites an internal report at WorldCom after the scandal broke that indicated that "dozens of employees knew about the fraud at WorldCom but were afraid to speak out."

The entries improperly reduced expenses, overstated assets, and overstated income by billions of dollars, over several years. After the fraud was uncovered, WorldCom filed for bankruptcy.

In addition to the CEO and CFO, four other accounting personnel were found guilty of aiding the fraud.

Pulliam, S. (2003, June 23). A staffer ordered to commit fraud balked, then caved. *Wall Street Journal*, p. 1.

General Types of Accounting Controls

Internal Controls in General

"Internal controls" are the set of policies and procedures companies use to ensure that the company is functioning in accordance with the wishes of management. Typically, accountants list four goals or objectives of internal control systems:

1 *To encourage adherence with company policies*—This means that employees should know what management wants them to do, and that management should be confident that employees are actually doing what they are supposed to be doing. For example, a movie theater's managers may want to sell tickets for a particular price, with discounts for students and senior citizens. The managers need a method of telling the employees what the prices are, and some way of ensuring that employees charge the right prices. The theater might use a memo to the employees to inform them of the pricing policy. One way to reduce the risk that employees might forget to offer student discounts is by advertising the prices, and posting signs, so that students ask for the discounts.

2 *To ensure operations are conducted efficiently and effectively*—"Efficiency" means that the job gets done. "Effectiveness" means that the job gets done at a low cost. UPS could not have delivered 34 million packages in a single day without effective and efficient delivery and billing procedures.

3 *To safeguard company assets*—Companies need procedures to keep assets from being lost, damaged, or stolen. Factory equipment needs to be serviced regularly. Inventory needs to be guarded to prevent theft, and protected from damage from fire, high or low temperatures, rodents and insects. Cash needs to be kept safe from loss or theft. Key computer files need to be protected from viruses, and backed up regularly.

4 *To ensure accurate and reliable financial reporting*—Errors in financial reporting can cause major problems. Companies may make improper decisions, such as failing to bill customers who ordered goods, or paying bonuses to people who don't deserve them, or stopping production of products which they (incorrectly) believe to be unprofitable. Errors in financial reporting may cause the company embarrassment and legal penalties if the companies file incorrect tax returns or financial reports.

General Types of Accounting Controls

Controls that are meant to prevent errors and intentional misstatements are *"preventive controls."* Other controls are meant to discover any errors or intentional misstatements that have occurred. These are *"detection controls."* In general, it is cheaper to prevent errors from happening than to let them happen, and then find them afterwards. Once accounting errors occur, bad things can happen—people can be paid the wrong amount, customers can be undercharged or overcharged. Finding errors takes time, and the errors may embarrass the company and cause difficulties for its customers, employees, or suppliers.

Five categories of control activities are frequently cited in accounting texts: segregation of duties; authorization procedures; physical controls; documentation and record-keeping; and independent review. I have added three others: employee policies related to hiring, training, and supervision; process design features to avoid errors; and loss limitation procedures.

Segregation of duties (also called *separation of duties*) means that different people should be responsible for the steps of authorizing transactions, recording them, and actually handling the assets related to a transaction. It is good practice to split these duties between different people, both so that errors can be caught and to discourage dishonest activity. Often, businesses will use machines or computers to double-check work. For example, cash registers keep a record of the money received, which serves as a double-check on the cashier. Turnstiles keep count of the number of people passing through them.

Authorization procedures should be established so that transactions and policies are authorized by the appropriate level of management. Management should decide for example, what types of goods are for sale, and at what prices and credit terms. It should have policies on who can take money out of company bank accounts, and who is authorized to handle and move inventory.

A company should establish *physical control over assets and records*. This may seem obvious. Money should be kept locked up, or in bank accounts. Warehouses and company offices should have adequate locks and security guards. Computer databases should be properly protected against loss and hackers.

Appropriate *documentation and record-keeping* should be performed. See Box 11.3 for a historical example. Companies must have records that indicate clearly what actions they took. Companies use documents on sales, purchases, employment, and so forth both as the basis of their bookkeeping entries and also as legal evidence of how they and their customers, vendors, and employees have performed. Companies also use documents to communicate information.

Another very important type of control is to have *regular independent reviews and checks on performance and on accounting records*. Work by lower level employees should be reviewed by supervisors. Top management should review accounting reports to see if they make business sense, or if they contain implausible numbers. A management technique called "*management by exception*" states that managers should focus their attention on unusual or unexpected numbers. Some unusual numbers are, of course, simply errors in accounting, so reports which highlight the unusual are very useful for identifying errors. Managers use various reports to ensure that the accounting system is functioning properly. For example, companies frequently compare actual performance to budgets and to past results, and investigate variances. Companies frequently prepare "*exception reports*," which list transactions that are unusual in some way.

People other than those who maintained the accounting records should check to see if the records match outside sources of information. The process of comparing two sets of figures and explaining any differences is called "*reconciliation*." There are many ways companies can check their records. The company's accounting records of its bank activity can be reconciled with bank statements. The company's accounts receivable records can be checked by asking customers if they agree with the company's records. The recorded accounts payable can be compared to

---

Box 11.3 George Washington's Advice to his Grandson Regarding the Importance of Documentation

"Another thing I would recommend to you—not that I want to know how you spend your money—and that is, to keep an account book, and enter therein every farthing of your receipts and expenditures, the doing of which will initiate you into a habit from which considerable advantage would result. Where no account of this sort is kept there can be no investigation, no correction of errors, no discovery, from recurrence thereto, where too much or too little has been appropriated to particular uses."

George Washington kept personal account books from 1749 until his death in 1799. Cloyd (1979) says "He recorded all his expenditures listing each item as the expenses were made with receipts provided." (p. 89)

From a letter from George Washington to his adopted grandson, George Washington Parke Custis, January 11, 1797, cited in Cloyd (1979).

statements sent by vendors. The inventory records can be checked by comparing the company records to physical counts of the inventory.

The use of auditors to perform these checks is discussed in a later section.

Another important category of controls are the procedures for *hiring, training and supervising employees*. Maybe the most obvious and important internal control procedure of all is to hire competent employees. There must be enough employees to handle the work. They must be educated and trained, so that they understand management's policies. Employees must have a clear set of duties, so that everyone understands who is responsible for performing each task. Supervisors must be available to answer questions and help handle complicated or unexpected situations. Where appropriate, employees should have copies of policy manuals to help them process transactions accurately.

Another general category of controls is *process design features to prevent errors*. One way to illustrate this is by a non-accounting example. It would be a problem if a car owner put diesel fuel into a car designed to run on regular gasoline. Car manufacturers and gas stations have designed the fuel tanks and the gas pumps to prevent car and truck owners from making this mistake—the diesel fuel hoses do not fit into the fuel tanks of cars that use gasoline. Here are two accounting examples:

- Computerized accounting systems will not allow an accountant to make an entry to the books unless the entry leaves the basic accounting equation in balance.
- Most computerized order entry systems prevent errors in spelling the names of states, by using drop-down menus.

Another step businesses take to protect themselves from theft is to limit the amount of assets at risk at any time—they use *loss limitation procedures*. For example, well-run companies deposit the money they receive into the bank promptly, so there is never a large amount of cash on hand. Companies also put limits on the amount of cash which is kept in bank accounts used by branch managers or other mid-level employees, and limit the ability of certain people to sign large checks. These controls help ensure that, if these people stole, the amount of money stolen will be limited.

Companies may also obtain insurance against employee theft and dishonesty.

Table 11.1 summarizes a variety of common procedures that companies can take to either prevent or detect errors and irregularities. Some of the procedures listed are explained later in this chapter. The use of computer technology to initially record transactions and to summarize data has enormously enhanced the ability of companies to process large amounts of data quickly and accurately.

Note that while some procedures are effective against both types of problems, some additional procedures are useful for detecting intentional misstatements. For example, requiring key employees to take vacations is a way to ensure that other people get a chance to see the key records in their absence.

Because cash is easily stolen, companies typically use a variety of procedures to reduce the likelihood that employees or others will steal cash. Box 11.4 lists some of the most common procedures. A basic step is to try to avoid using actual currency to do business, but, instead, to use checks to pay bills and to get customers to pay by check or wire.

Perhaps the most important thing managers can do to prevent irregularities is to create the proper business environment. A well-run company pays attention to controls and treats its customers, employees, and suppliers fairly. Management is known to pay close attention to details, so people know there is a significant risk of being caught if they steal or distort records. When people are treated fairly, they have less of a motive to steal from the company. They will be less afraid of reporting honestly if they know that management will treat them fairly than if they expect management to fire anyone who reports bad news.

Table 11.1 Common Procedures for Preventing and Detecting Errors and Irregularities

Preventing errors	Preventing irregularities
• Hire qualified people • Have training programs and policy manuals • Have adequate supervision available • Use computerized processing • Authorization and approval procedures • Assign clear responsibility for tasks • Test of new computer programs • Use standard data input formats • Make "chart of accounts" available to staff	• Clear management policies against fraud • Background checks on new employees • Security guards, locks, etc. • Approval and authorization procedures • Separation of duties • Close management attention to business and control system
Detecting errors	**Detecting irregularities**
• Supervisory review of work done • Have a second person (or machine) check the work • Review trial balance for equality of debits and credits (see below) • Compare general ledger balances to subsidiary ledgers (see below) • Review the trial balance for unreasonable amounts and balances • Compare financial results to predicted or budgeted amounts • Periodic counts of assets and reconciliations to accounting records • Compare accounting records to source documents	• All the procedures for detecting errors are also useful for detecting irregularities • Periodic rotation of duties • Mandatory vacations • Special-purpose investigations by auditors • Special logs and exception reports on computer transactions • Encourage employees to report irregularities

Special Accounting Controls

Double-Entry Accounting as a Control

Debits and Credits Explained

Double-entry bookkeeping is a system of accounting, based on the fundamental accounting equation, that is used worldwide to record and summarize accounting events. It was developed in Italy at some point in the 1300s, and was first described in print by Luca Pacioli, in 1494 in a mathematical text titled *Summa de Arithmetica, Geometria, Proportioni et Proportionalita*.[2] The key to the system is that every entry to the accounting records must affect two or more accounts, and must leave the equation "assets = liabilities + equity" balanced. This method is described in detail in Appendix A. This section presents the basics of the system.

"*Accounts*" are created to accumulate information for each of the categories of things that the company wants to keep track of. For example, a company will have accounts for money in banks, accounts receivable, revenues, and expenses.

The record containing the details of all the accounts that together comprise the accounting equation for the company is called the "*general ledger*." Traditionally it was a book, but in modern times it is usually a computer file.

You can think of the record for any particular account in the general ledger as being written on one sheet of paper, with two columns. One column lists the opening balance, and all the events and transactions that have increased the account during the year. For a bank account, this column might include deposits the company has made and interest it has earned on this account.

Box 11.4 Various Common Controls Regarding Cash

General:

- Minimize the amount of currency on hand by making regular bank deposits.
- Utilize the banking system as much as possible for making payments and receiving customer payments.
- Keeping cash on hand in a safe.

Disbursements by check:

- Have a list of authorized signers.
- For large transactions, require two signers.
- Keep unused checks locked up.
- Avoid hand writing checks. Use a computerized check system so the check is properly recorded when it is generated. This ensures the accounting records show the actual amounts and payees of the checks.
- Require that supporting documentation be given to check signers along with checks.
- Periodically compare the checks that clear the bank with the disbursement records, and investigate any discrepancies.

Customer receipts:

- Encourage customer payments by check or wire.
- In retail environments, where currency is received, use cash registers which record the transactions as they are made, and generate customer receipts. Compare the cash in the register at the end of each shift with the amount predicted by the cash register's records.
- When checks are received by mail, the mail should be opened by employees other than those who keep accounting records.
- The checks should be immediately stamped "for deposit only" to the company's bank account. The mailroom should make a list of checks received, and should send the list to the accounts receivable department and the actual checks should go to the treasury department, which should deposit them in the bank on a daily basis.

Reconciliation procedures:

- Bank statements should be reconciled by employees with no other cash-related duties.
- Any petty cash funds should be periodically checked to ensure no cash is missing.
- Customer complaints regarding errors in their accounts should be investigated by employees who do not keep the accounts receivable records.
- Vendor complaints regarding their accounts should be investigated by employees other than those keeping disbursement accounts.
- Significant variations from budget should be investigated.

The other column lists all the items that have decreased the account during the year. For a bank account, these might include payments the company has made from the account, and fees charged to the company by the bank. The net balance in the account can be found by taking the beginning balance, adding all the increases, and subtracting all the decreases.

The term for an item on the left side of an account is a "*debit*." It may be helpful to repeat to yourself, at this point, "debits are on the left."

An item on the right side of an account is a "*credit*." We can also use these terms as verbs—we speak of debiting and crediting accounts.[3] A basic rule of double-entry bookkeeping is that the total debits in the company's general ledger must equal the total credits. It turns out that this is mathematically equivalent to requiring that assets = liabilities plus equity. Proofs are given in Appendix A.

The tricky part of the system, for people first learning accounting, is that some accounts increase with entries on the left side of the account (debits) while others increase with entries on the right (credits). Here are the basic rules:

1   Debits and credits offset each other. When an account includes a debit of $100 and a credit of $8, the balance will be a $92 dollar debit. In each of the following sections, I only list what increases an account. Remember, if a debit increases an account, a credit will decrease it.
2   The total debits must always equal the total credits.
3   Asset accounts increase with debits.
4   Liabilities, which are in many ways the opposite of assets, increase with credits.
5   Equity accounts increase with credits.

   a. Since revenues represent increases in equity, revenues increase with credits.
   b. Since expenses and dividends decrease equity, they increase with debits.

One of my colleagues teaches students to remember the word "dead" as a memory aid, to remember that Debits increase Expenses, Assets, and Dividends. If you can remember that, you can figure out everything else.

It is important to realize that "debit and credit" do *not* correspond to "good and bad." Both assets and expenses are increased by debits. Both revenues and liabilities are increased by credits. Debits and credits are simply tools for ensuring events are recorded in a way that keeps the accounting equation in balance.

Appendix A contains a more thorough explanation of the system, and more examples.

Journal entries

In the double-entry bookkeeping system, transactions are initially recorded ("entered") in records called *journals*. The actual notation made in the journal is called a "journal entry." Classically, a journal entry shows: the date of the transaction; the name of the account or accounts being debited, the amounts being debited; the names of the accounts being credited; the amounts being credited; and some explanation of the entry. It is common to abbreviate the word "debit" with "dr." and "credit" with "cr." It is also common to record the debit accounts first, and more to the left, than the credit amounts.

For example, to record a collection of an accounts receivable from the John Smith Company on July 1, 2015, a company might record the following entry:

    Dr. Cash   10,000
        Cr. Accounts receivable   10,000
    Collection of amount due from John Smith Company

Since cash is an asset account, and it increased, the company has debited the cash account. Accounts receivable has been decreased by this payment from the John Smith Company. To record a decrease in an asset account, the company has credited the account.

A second example would be to record an accrual of payroll expense that employees have earned, but which the company has not yet paid. The appropriate journal entry might be as follows:

    Dr. Salary expense $13,482
        Cr. Accrued salaries payable $13,482
    To accrue three days' pay for employees as of December 31, 2015.

In this entry, the accountant needed to increase salary expense. Debits increase expense accounts. At the same time, a larger liability needed to be recorded. Credits increase liability accounts.

This is a topic that typically requires significant time to master. If you are confused, see Appendix A. It has much more detail on double-entry bookkeeping. In this text, I am not expecting that the readers will become accountants and will actually be making journal entries. However, it is important to understand how the system enhances control. In Chapter 12, I use journal entries to illustrate the accounting for transactions. The entries are a compact and clear way of showing how a transaction is recorded.

Summarizing and Reporting Information

Companies have many transactions each day. Classically, the process of recording and summarizing information goes through the following steps:

1   Each transaction is recorded when it occurs, either manually or by a computerized system, in a way that identifies the transaction and the related debit and credit amounts. Classically, this was done in a "journal" but may now be done in a more integrated computer system.
2   Information on each transaction is copied ("posted") to the appropriate account in the general ledger. The ledger is sorted by account, not by date.
3   The information for all the accounts in the ledger is totaled to find their balances.
4   The company prepares what is called an "unadjusted trial balance", which is a listing of all the ledger accounts, and their balances. The total debits should equal the total credits. If the debits do not equal the credits in the trial balance, then the accountants will search for an error in recording or processing information.
5   After reviewing the unadjusted trial balance, the company makes adjustments to the ledger using journal entries. Each entry contains debits and credits. The company makes these adjusting journal entries for two reasons. The first is to correct any errors or problems that are noted when reviewing the trial balance. For example, the company may realize that a legal expense was improperly classified as an advertising expense. Second, companies routinely make adjustments to bring the records into line with accrual accounting. We discussed these kinds of adjustments in Chapter 2. Examples of adjustments include those to record:

    a. The using up of prepaid assets
    b. Interest or other revenues earned, but not yet received in cash
    c. Depreciation and amortization
    d. Expenses (such as interest or taxes) that have been incurred which have not yet been paid in cash
    e. Earning some revenue that previously had been treated as unearned

6   The company prepares a new, "adjusted," trial balance.
7   The company uses the adjusted trial balance as a basis for preparing financial statements.

Control Features of Double-Entry Bookkeeping

Double-entry bookkeeping has several very important control features.

First, it forces accountants to understand the nature of transactions before recording them. It is not enough to know that cash has increased. That will only allow the accountant to debit cash, but the accountant must also find an account to credit. To do so, the accountant must understand where the cash came from. Modern computerized accounting systems will not permit entries to be made unless the debits equal the credits.

Second, the system forces the accountant, when preparing an overall report of all the activity, to include all the accounts. If any accounts are left out, the total debits will not equal the total credits. Historically, this feature of ensuring that a listing of accounts was complete was one of the major reasons that double-entry bookkeeping was adopted. Winjum's (1972) review of English accounting records for the early 1500s to 1750 indicates the major advantage drawn from double entry was that it helped businessmen see all their records in a systematic way. Apparently, many bankruptcies in the 1500s occurred because owners lacked knowledge of what assets and liabilities their businesses had.

Third, the requirement that total debits must equal total credits is a powerful error-detection device. It allows accountants to detect such errors as: copying a number improperly; adding figures in the ledger improperly; and improperly copying what should be a debit as if it were a credit.

Finally, the system produces reports that serve as a basis for managerial review. We have already discussed the basic financial statements, including the balance sheet and income statement. For large companies, these tend to be highly summarized. A key output of the double-entry system for control purposes is the "*trial balance*", which lists the ending debit or credit balance of every account in the general ledger. Clearly, total debits must equal total credits. In addition, a trial balance provides management with the opportunity to examine every account for reasonableness. Such a review can often identify errors. For example, if an expense account, which should have a debit balance, has a credit balance, then something is wrong. If an account which should have activity does not show activity, then, again, something is wrong.

Accounting Information Systems

When double-entry accounting was first used, in the 1300s, accounting was performed by people writing in ink in large books. Times have changed dramatically, primarily in the last 75 years with computerization. This section briefly describes some features of accounting information systems that improve the efficiency and accuracy of financial accounting.

All accounting systems feature the ability of users to find out where the final totals come from. Someone must be able to find the numbers that were combined to produce the total, and to find out where each of these numbers came from. There should be some documents or explanations for everything that is entered into the accounting system. A term that is used to describe this ability to verify the outcome of the accounting system is "*audit trail*." In computerized systems, audit trails include logs or other records that indicate whether key programs or databases have been altered, and by whom.

To ensure that employees knew what accounts should be used to record transactions, companies use accounting policy manuals and "*charts of accounts*." The "chart of accounts" is a listing of the various accounts that should be used. For example, a company might want to separately keep track of its sales by product, and would therefore have a separate account in its chart of accounts for each product. In modern times, a company may expand this chart of accounts into a dictionary of terms to be used to enter transactions into a database.

Accounting systems often assign the accounting for different types of transactions to different people or departments. For example, one group of bookkeepers might deal with sales transactions, while a different one dealt with payroll transactions. This makes training of employees easier, and is a convenient way of dividing the workload. Each group might record transactions in a separate, specialized journal. For example, an organization might have separate journals, kept by different groups of employees, for: cash disbursements; payroll; sales; raw material purchases; and cash receipts.

With modern systems, often transactions are initially recorded by a computer. This could be done by a scanner, using a barcode, at a cash register. It could be done by an on-line system that takes your order for a plane ticket. This computerization of the initial input has improved the speed and accuracy of accounting. There are simply far fewer input errors.

Modern accounting systems have totally eliminated the need for humans to add and copy numbers once they have been entered in accounting systems. Computers, once programmed, quickly and accurately copy information from the point where they were initially recorded into ledger accounts, and then summarize the information and copy it into the form of financial statements. Computerization has vastly reduced the errors in summarizing accounting data. This has transformed the work life of management accountants. As Kuleza (1997) wrote "number crunching and data collection alone are a thing of the past. Now our profession has entered the realm of financial management, business strategy, information technology, and information management" (p. 57).

Increasingly, accounting systems are being integrated into wider systems, such as "enterprise-wide resource planning systems," that produce a variety of managerial outputs as well as accounting reports. While such systems are often hard to install, there is mixed evidence of various benefits to enterprise-wide planning systems.[4]

Reconciliations

Double-entry bookkeeping systems and accounting information systems help ensure that accounting information is internally consistent. Numbers that are supposed to "add up" actually "add up." Relations that are supposed to work, such as the accounting equation, actually work. However, this internal consistency does not tell us if the reports from the accounting system agree with reality external to the company. I can make up a random 100 transactions, feed them into a computerized accounting system, and get balanced, internally consistent reports. However, since the events were fictitious, so are the reports. The process of *reconciliation* compares accounting reports to other sources of information, and explains any differences. It is important in ensuring that accounting reports agree with reality.

Companies routinely check a number of accounts on their books against other sources of information. Examples include:

* Reconciling recorded bank account balances to bank records
* Reconciling recorded amounts of investments held by banks and brokers to the bank and broker statements
* Asking customers to confirm the recorded amounts of accounts receivables
* Asking employees to confirm recorded amounts paid to them
* Checking recorded amounts of accounts payable with statements sent by vendors
* Checking recorded amounts of inventory against actual counts of the inventory
* Checking recorded amounts of equipment against physical counts of the fixed assets.

This section focuses on bank account reconciliations. Bank reconciliations are an extremely useful tool for detecting a wide variety of errors and irregularities. Obviously, cash receipts and cash disbursements are a large part of any company's business. Companies deposit their receipts in bank accounts, and pay almost all their bills by check. Traditionally, banks sent monthly statements to their customers, listing all the deposits, checks, and other activities affecting the bank account. Now, banks make activity visible on-line in real time. This means that a company's bank provides the company with information that serves as an independent check on the company's own cash disbursement and receipt journals.

The bank reconciliation process involves comparing the bank's records with the company's records. Most transactions which occur each month are recorded the same by both the company's accounting system and the bank. However, some transactions may have been recorded differently. Understanding what transactions have been recorded differently, and why, is the heart of the bank reconciliation process.

Transactions can be recorded differently by the bank and the company for four reasons:

Reason 1. The transactions appear properly on the company's accounting records, but due to normal time lags in processing, the bank has not recorded them yet. Therefore, these items appear in the company's books, but do not appear on the bank statements. The two most common examples of this situation are *outstanding checks* and *deposits in transit*.

Outstanding checks are checks which the company has written and mailed, but which have not yet been presented for payment to the company's bank. The company knows it wrote them, and expects them to be paid, but the bank is not yet aware of them.

Deposits in transit are deposits which the company has sent to the bank near the end of the month, and which were not recorded by the bank by the close of business on that day. These deposits may be in the mail, or they may have been left in a night deposit box.

The transactions in this category do not represent any sort of errors or problems. They are properly recorded on the company's books. The bank will record them properly as soon as the outstanding checks are presented for payment, and as soon as it receives the deposits in transit. Normally, the company's accountant does not have to take any action with regard to these items.[5]

Reason 2. The transactions represent actions taken by the bank, which appear properly on the bank statement, but which have not yet been recorded by the company. The company first learns about these items when it receives the bank statement. Therefore, the company must record the items in order to bring its records into agreement with the bank's. Examples of these items include: bank fees; returned customer checks;[6] and interest earned on deposits.

Reason 3. Items have been recorded properly by the company, but the bank has made errors. It is now fairly rare for banks to make errors in processing transactions, but it does happen occasionally. The company should ask the bank to fix the problem. Since the company's records are correct, no adjustments are needed in the company's books.

Reason 4. Items have been recorded properly by the bank, but the company has made errors in recording or summarizing them. There are many types of possible errors. Someone may forget to record a check that was mailed out. Someone may record a check for the wrong amount. Someone may forget to record a deposit. Someone may record a deposit for the wrong amount of money, or as being deposited on the wrong date. All the deposits and checks may be correctly recorded, but the accountant may have added them together incorrectly. All of these types of errors were far more likely with manual systems than they are with modern computerized check-writing systems.

Since the bank treated these items correctly, and since bank statements summarize data accurately, the books and the bank statement will disagree until the errors in the company's books are found and fixed. This means the bank reconciliation is a powerful tool for detecting certain types of errors. Any error affecting the *balance* of the cash account will affect the bank reconciliation.

Irregularities involving unrecorded disbursements are easy to detect in performing bank reconciliations. For example, assume a dishonest company payroll manager writes an additional check to herself every pay period for $2,000, and never records it. The accountant who performs the bank reconciliation will see that the bank has paid certain checks, for $2,000 each, which are not recorded as disbursements on the company's books. The accountant would then look at the canceled checks, see that they were paid to the payroll manager, and begin an investigation. Similarly, if a dishonest employee stole incoming cash receipts on the way to the bank, the bank statements would show lower deposits than the company's records, and the company would investigate.

Other irregularities in cash disbursements may require the accountant performing the bank reconciliations to perform some additional tests. For example, assume that a dishonest accounts payable manager writes a $2,000 check to himself every month, but records it in the company's books as a monthly payment to an insurance company. The company's books would record a $2,000 check, and the bank would honor a $2,000 check. The cash balance in the books would agree with the bank records. There would not be a difference between the "book" and "bank" balances to alert anyone doing the bank reconciliation that the cash disbursement had been improper. The accountant doing the reconciliation could detect this kind of irregularity by comparing the payees listed in the cash disbursement journal with the payees on the canceled checks returned by the bank.[7] Another test which is sometimes performed is to see if the check has actually been endorsed by someone other than the payee listed on the front.

It should be noted that a thorough bank reconciliation process can not only detect irregularities, it can help prevent them. Irregularities generally occur when employees have both a motive to steal and an opportunity. If employees know that bank statements are being carefully and competently examined, they are less likely to try to steal.

Boxes 11.5 and 11.6 show two different common formats used to prepare bank reconciliations. The first, which is often shown on the backs of bank statements, is in a single column. It starts with the bank statement balance and adds or subtracts various items to arrive at the company's ledger balance. The second is in two columns. In one column, the accountant starts with the company's ledger balance, and adds or subtracts items as necessary to come to what the "true" available balance should be. For example, it would subtract bank fees it had not previously recorded, and would add in interest it had earned on its deposits. In the second column, the accountant starts with the balance on the bank statement, and adds or subtracts items the bank will record once it knows about them. For example, the accountant adds deposits in transit, and subtracts outstanding checks. The result is a "true" balance that will be available at the bank, once the bank learns about certain items. The totals for the two columns should agree. This is

---

Box 11.5 Typical Bank-Supplied Bank Reconciliation Form

Balance per bank statement

Plus: Deposits in transit
Plus: Any fees charged or other deductions listed on the bank statement not yet recorded
   by the company.

Subtotal

Less: Outstanding checks
Less: Interest earned on the account not yet recorded by the company
Less: Any items increasing the bank balance not yet recorded by the company

Total

The total should agree with the company's records. If not, the company should check for errors.

Box 11.6 Recommended Bank Reconciliation Format

Bank records	**Company accounting records**
Month-end balance per bank statement	Month-end balance per company ledger
Plus: deposits in transit	Plus: interest earned not previously recorded
Plus: other items not yet recorded by bank	Plus: any other additions to cash in the bank statement, not yet recorded
Less: outstanding checks	Less: bank fees charged not yet recorded
	Less: returned customer checks not yet recorded.
Plus or minus: any bank errors	Plus or minus: any errors in the company records
= Adjusted total per bank	= Adjusted total per books

---

the format typically recommended by accounting textbooks, because it clearly shows, in the company column, all the items that the company will need to correct in order to get its books to reflect economic reality.

While we have been discussing bank reconciliations, accountants use the same formats to reconcile other accounts. For example, the same format could be used to reconcile a vendor's monthly statement with the company's accounts payable records.

Outside verification is not as effective for some types of errors as for others. Customers and employees are far more likely to inform you of errors which cost them money than of errors in their favor. Also, complicated errors may be harder for outsiders to catch. For example, employees are more likely to notice an error in the number of hours they worked than in the amount of federal income tax withheld from their pay.

Management by Exception and Variance Investigations

Managers use accounting reports to understand the performance for the period. The review of the reports by managers often reveals problems in accounting, and the feedback from managers will allow the company to fix these errors.

A widely known management technique is *"management by exception."* The concept here is that managers have limited time, and that they probably don't need to spend time on things that are operating routinely, and going according to plan. They should devote their time to "exceptions," such as events that cause the company to be doing much better or worse than was expected. Managers following this method compare current recorded results with the results from prior periods, and with budgets, and investigate any reported results that deviate from expectations. While the primary purpose of this technique is to focus management attention on real operational problems, it also helps identify accounting errors.

On a detailed operational level, companies often compute the "variances" between expected and actual manufacturing performance. Chapter 5 discussed variance analysis. We saw that companies can compute the variance between actual performance and budgeted performance, and can break this down into the impact of changes in prices and changes in efficiency. Once managers compute variances, they will investigate and try to understand the real operational causes of the variances. If the variances are due to errors in accounting for the current period, this investigation will bring these errors to light.

Auditing

Auditing is a process of checking to see if there is sufficient evidence to judge that particular statements are correct. In this section, we are focused on how auditing is used to check whether the company's records and reports of its financial activities are correct.

In general, there are two different types of auditors. Some companies in regulated industries, such as banks and insurance companies, are also audited by government auditors.

Large companies typically have *internal auditors*. These are company employees, who periodically check that key procedures in the company are performed properly, and that accounting records are being accurately kept. They typically report to someone high up in the company organization, and ideally are independent of the departments or processes they are auditing. Sometimes, they report to the audit committee of the Board of Directors. While they are an important part of the company's accounting control system, internal auditors perform additional tasks that go beyond the accounting control process. For example, they often assess the efficiency and effectiveness of various company programs and processes.

"*External auditors*" are independent certified public accountants who work in "*public accounting firms.*" Companies hire external auditors to audit their financial statements. Public companies in the U.S. are required by law to include audit reports with their annual securities filings on Form 10-K. Many other companies, government entities, and nonprofit organizations also choose to hire external auditors to examine their financial statements.

The basic economic function of the external audit is to increase the credibility of the company's financial statements to outside users. The users face an "information risk" that the financial statements were either prepared incompetently or dishonestly. The fact that the financial statements have been checked by people who have a reputation for both expertise in accounting and independent and objective judgment reduces this risk, and makes users more willing to trust financial statements. The profession of public accounting was first established in the United Kingdom, in the 1800s, and came to the U.S. in 1896 when New York created the Certified Public Accountant designation.[8]

Because it would take too long and would be too expensive, external auditors do not check every item that a company records and do not look for errors that are not material. Instead, they work on a sample basis, and focus their efforts on areas where they believe the risk of errors or fraud is greatest. They then form an opinion as to whether they believe the financial statements are fairly stated, in accordance with generally accepted accounting principles. They seek "reasonable assurance," not total certainty, that the financial statements are free of material errors. An example of such an audit opinion, for Starbucks, is shown in Box 11.7.

You should note what the auditors say and do not say. The first paragraph indicates that the company is responsible for the financial statements, and the auditors are responsible for doing an audit and expressing an opinion. The auditors are not issuing a guarantee that the financial statements are correct, merely an opinion. The second paragraph says what the auditors did to form an opinion. They followed standards set for audits, and gathered evidence which they believe is enough to give them "reasonable assurance" about the financial statements. The third paragraph states that, in their opinion, the financial statements are fairly presented in accordance with generally accepted accounting principles in the United States, "in all material respects."

Starbucks got a good audit report. The technical term for an audit report where the auditors say they did enough work, and believe that the financial statements are fairly presented is an "*unqualified*" audit report. Informally, people will refer to a "clean" report. Not all reports are unqualified. If auditors believe the financial statements have material inaccuracies, they may give what are called "*qualified*" or "*adverse*" reports, depending on the seriousness of the issue. If the auditors are unable to do enough work to obtain evidence about the financial statements, they may give "*qualified*" reports, or may "*disclaim*" an opinion and say they are unable to form any judgment.

Box 11.7 Sample Auditors' Report—Public Company

REPORT OF INDEPENDENT REGISTERED PUBLIC ACCOUNTING FIRM

To the Board of Directors and Shareholders of Starbucks Corporation
Seattle, Washington

We have audited the accompanying consolidated balance sheets of Starbucks Corporation and subsidiaries (the "Company") as of September 28, 2014 and September 29, 2013, and the related consolidated statements of earnings, comprehensive income, equity, and cash flows for each of the three years in the period ended September 28, 2014. These financial statements are the responsibility of the Company's management. Our responsibility is to express an opinion on these financial statements based on our audits.

We conducted our audits in accordance with the standards of the Public Company Accounting Oversight Board (United States). Those standards require that we plan and perform the audit to obtain reasonable assurance about whether the financial statements are free of material misstatement. An audit includes examining, on a test basis, evidence supporting the amounts and disclosures in the financial statements. An audit also includes assessing the accounting principles used and significant estimates made by management, as well as evaluating the overall financial statement presentation. We believe that our audits provide a reasonable basis for our opinion.

In our opinion, such consolidated financial statements present fairly, in all material respects, the financial position of Starbucks Corporation and subsidiaries as of September 28, 2014 and September 29, 2013, and the results of their operations and their cash flows for each of the three years in the period ended September 28, 2014, in conformity with accounting principles generally accepted in the United States of America.

We have also audited, in accordance with the standards of the Public Company Accounting Oversight Board (United States), the Company's internal control over financial reporting as of September 28, 2014, based on criteria established in *Internal Control — Integrated Framework (1992)* issued by the Committee of Sponsoring Organizations of the Treadway Commission and our report dated November 14, 2014 expressed an unqualified opinion on the Company's internal control over financial reporting.

/s/ Deloitte & Touche LLP
Seattle, Washington
November 14, 2014

Because Starbucks is a large public company, subject to standards of the Public Company Accounting Standards Board ("PCAOB"), the auditors' report shown in Box 11.7 is different from that of a private company in two ways. First, the audit report for a private company would refer to "generally accepted auditing standards," which are set by the American Institute of Certified Public Accountants, rather than to standards set by the PCAOB. Second, only public companies have to have auditors report on their internal controls. The last paragraph of the report in Box 11.7 refers to the internal controls report for Starbucks, which is shown in Box 11.8.

If you examine Box 11.8, you will see that the auditors state, in the fourth paragraph, that the auditors believe that Starbucks maintained effective controls over financial reporting, "in all material respects," as of the end of its fiscal year. This is a favorable, or "unqualified," report. A significant number of public companies each year do not receive such reports, but instead the

Box 11.8 Auditor's Report on Internal Controls—Public Company

REPORT OF INDEPENDENT REGISTERED PUBLIC ACCOUNTING FIRM

To the Board of Directors and Shareholders of Starbucks Corporation

We have audited the internal control over financial reporting of Starbucks Corporation and subsidiaries (the "Company") as of September 28, 2014, based on criteria established in *Internal Control — Integrated Framework (1992)* issued by the Committee of Sponsoring Organizations of the Treadway Commission. The Company's management is responsible for maintaining effective internal control over financial reporting and for its assessment of the effectiveness of internal control over financial reporting, included in the accompanying Report of Management on Internal Control over Financial Reporting. Our responsibility is to express an opinion on the Company's internal control over financial reporting based on our audit.

We conducted our audit in accordance with the standards of the Public Company Accounting Oversight Board (United States). Those standards require that we plan and perform the audit to obtain reasonable assurance about whether effective internal control over financial reporting was maintained in all material respects. Our audit included obtaining an understanding of internal control over financial reporting, assessing the risk that a material weakness exists, testing and evaluating the design and operating effectiveness of internal control based on the assessed risk, and performing such other procedures as we considered necessary in the circumstances. We believe that our audit provides a reasonable basis for our opinion.

A company's internal control over financial reporting is a process designed by, or under the supervision of, the company's principal executive and principal financial officers, or persons performing similar functions, and effected by the company's board of directors, management, and other personnel to provide reasonable assurance regarding the reliability of financial reporting and the preparation of financial statements for external purposes in accordance with generally accepted accounting principles. A company's internal control over financial reporting includes those policies and procedures that (1) pertain to the maintenance of records that, in reasonable detail, accurately and fairly reflect the transactions and dispositions of the assets of the company; (2) provide reasonable assurance that transactions are recorded as necessary to permit preparation of financial statements in accordance with generally accepted accounting principles, and that receipts and expenditures of the company are being made only in accordance with authorizations of management and directors of the company; and (3) provide reasonable assurance regarding prevention or timely detection of unauthorized acquisition, use, or disposition of the company's assets that could have a material effect on the financial statements.

Because of the inherent limitations of internal control over financial reporting, including the possibility of collusion or improper management override of controls, material misstatements due to error or fraud may not be prevented or detected on a timely basis. Also, projections of any evaluation of the effectiveness of the internal control over financial reporting to future periods are subject to the risk that the controls may become inadequate because of changes in conditions, or that the degree of compliance with the policies or procedures may deteriorate.

In our opinion, the Company maintained, in all material respects, effective internal control over financial reporting as of September 28, 2014, based on the criteria established in *Internal Control — Integrated Framework (1992)* issued by the Committee of Sponsoring Organizations of the Treadway Commission.

We have also audited, in accordance with the standards of the Public Company Accounting Oversight Board (United States), the consolidated financial statements as of and for the fiscal year ended September 28, 2014, of the Company and our report dated November 14, 2014 expressed an unqualified opinion on those financial statements.

/s/ Deloitte & Touche LLP
Seattle, Washington
November 14, 2014

auditors issue "adverse" reports listing one or more material weaknesses in the controls over financial reporting.

While this was a favorable report, you may also notice that the auditors say various things that limit the strength of their report. They do not say there are no weaknesses in controls, just that the weaknesses are not "material." They do not test all controls, but only those related to financial reporting. Their report is limited to the controls as of the end of the fiscal year, and they do not indicate whether controls were worse earlier, or have become worse later. They did not check everything, but instead followed appropriate professional guidance to obtain reasonable assurance about the functioning of controls. They also note that there are inherent limitations to any system of internal controls.

Limitations of Control Systems

In spite of the efforts that have been made to control the accounting process, companies do sometimes produce incorrect or fraudulent accounting reports. Why don't accounting controls always work? There are a number of reasons that the controls can fail.

The first issue is *cost*. Any business needs to balance the costs of installing controls against the benefits that they will provide. Companies may decide that the benefits of implementing certain kinds of controls are too small to justify the costs, and so may decide to live with imperfect controls. For example, stores which have historically had few losses due to shoplifting may decide not to hire security guards, and may accept a certain level of shoplifting losses as part of the cost of doing business. Because some of the inventory has been stolen, the reported balances of inventory on hand will be wrong.

A second problem arises with *unusual or non-routine events*. Most control systems are designed for routine transactions. For example, companies routinely make sales, pay bills, collect customer payments, and pay their employees. They have policies to make sure these transactions happen smoothly and are recorded properly. However, there may be no special systems in place for transactions or events which happen infrequently, and these transactions are therefore more likely to be recorded improperly.

Errors may also arise with items requiring *difficult or subjective computations*. It is harder to record transactions or events that require subjective estimates of amounts, or complex computations, than transactions where there is clear and simple evidence of the amounts. For example, it is fairly easy to record a monthly payment of an electric bill. In contrast, consider the computation of income tax expense. Determining the tax expense requires a complex computation, involving numerous other pieces of accounting information as well as knowledge of all the applicable state, federal and foreign tax rules. An internal control system may require that the people computing the taxes be trained, and that supervisors check their work. However, no system can eliminate the chance that people may simply misunderstand a complicated rule. Not surprisingly, recorded tax expense is far more likely to be incorrect than the recorded utility expense.

Some accounting entries require *subjective estimates*. In some cases, in order to apply the revenue recognition and matching principles, we have to make estimates about the future. In other cases, we may have no precise methods of measuring the transactions, and may have to use estimates. (We considered the issue of uncertainty in Chapter 8.) By their very nature, balances based on subjective estimates are more likely to be wrong than balances based on objective evidence. Controls are less able to function properly when objective evidence is unavailable.

A major inherent limitation in internal accounting controls is the *ability of top management to override the control system*. There have been many cases where managers wanted to report high profits, even though their companies were not doing well, in order to affect the price of the company stock. In these situations, top management deliberately misstates the company's financial results.

In other cases, *control systems may be subverted or avoided by lower level employees*. A control like the separation of duties can be subverted if the employees who have the different duties collude together. Employees may subvert accounting controls either to hide stealing, or to report better results than have actually been achieved. If management gives rewards (such as big bonuses and promotions) based on meeting quarterly sales or profit goals, and fires people who fail to meet tough sales or profit targets, it puts enormous pressures on people to report certain numbers. Most people will report honestly, but others will be tempted to report dishonestly. We discussed this issue in Chapter 6.

Irregularities are harder to detect than errors. Errors occur by accident, and no one is trying to hide the fact that they occurred. Irregularities happen because people are trying to steal from the company, or manipulate the reporting system. People who commit irregularities often try to hide what they did, often by destroying documents, or creating phony documents or accounting records. Some irregularities involve more than one person, acting in collusion. As a result, many irregularities are never caught. While many irregularities are caught by the organization's control system, others come to light by accident, or when the perpetrator confesses.

Accounting Controls in a Broader Context

The focus of this chapter has been on how controls are used in business now to maximize the accuracy of accounting reports. This section briefly provides some broader context.

Historical Perspective

History and Internal Controls

There is evidence of internal control techniques and auditing being adopted early in history, perhaps as early as 3000 BCE. Temples in ancient Egypt and Babylonia required that counts of incoming donations of grain and other offerings be counted separately by two different scribes. Some of the earliest written records are clay tablets used to document the terms of transactions (Newman 1979).

As industry became more complex, and operated over greater distances, more control techniques were developed. For example, Johnson and Kaplan (1987) noted that railroads in the 19th century developed a number of internal control techniques that are still used today. One was the use of prenumbered documents, such as tickets. Because the tickets were numbered, the accountants could check to see if all tickets issued had been recorded. Railroads also placed limits on the amounts of funds provided to the bank accounts at each branch, to give local managers the funds they needed to operate while limiting the amount of money that any one manager could steal.[9] Indeed, some scholars believe that internal controls were necessary for the development of large, vertically integrated corporations around the start of the 20th century.

Johnson and Kaplan (1987) write that controls were needed to allow managers to understand these complex organizations, and to ensure that employees paid attention to the owners' goals.

While the development of internal controls has mostly occurred naturally, as companies see a need for them, there have also been significant government influences. In 1977, in reaction to some scandals, the United States enacted the Foreign Corrupt Practices Act. This act, among its other provisions, required companies to establish effective systems of internal control. At the time, there were not any general standards of what this meant. The act was largely ignored by companies, in part because they had no duty to report on whether they had complied. The Sarbanes–Oxley Act of 2002 reaffirmed the need for large public companies to have effective systems of internal control over financial reporting, and added two reporting requirements.[10] Each quarter, the CFO and the CEO of the company must certify that they believe the internal controls are operating properly, or must describe the weaknesses. Once a year, the company's auditors must also report on the internal controls. We have seen an example of such a report in Box 11.8.

The internal control reporting requirements of the Sarbanes–Oxley Act were very controversial, because companies found that they needed to spend large amounts of money to comply, especially in the first year. This is a major reason that Congress has not required smaller public companies to comply with these rules.[11]

There has been a great deal of academic research on the costs and benefits of the Sarbanes–Oxley Act. Coates, John, and Srinivasan (2014) reviewed 120 studies and report the following main findings regarding costs and benefits:

Costs

- Initially, the direct costs of complying with the rules were substantial.
- The costs have fallen over time, partly in response to changes in implementation rules set by the PCAOB.
- The research on whether there were significant indirect costs of the act, such as reduced risk-taking in the U.S., is inconclusive.
- There is also only weak evidence for such possible disadvantages as a reduced number of companies going public or reduced numbers of foreign companies registering in the United States.

Benefits

- Financial reporting quality has improved since the Sarbanes–Oxley Act, but it is hard to be sure that the act was the cause of the improvement.
- Financial statement users appear to have used reports of internal control weaknesses, and the stock markets have reacted negatively to companies that report them. The markets also react positively when companies report having fixed control weaknesses.
- Survey evidence suggests that the act has improved investor confidence in financial statements.

Coates, John, and Srinivasan (2014) report survey evidence that many informed observers, such as corporate officers and investors, believe the law has had net benefits and has not been a significant problem.

History and Auditing

Auditing also has a long history. Newman (1979) notes that in the Middle Ages, in England, lords who owned manors often used auditors to check on whether the stewards running the manors were acting honestly.

Auditing has often developed as a reaction to economic problems and company bankruptcies. In the United States, a major reason for the development of the auditing profession came from bankruptcies in the railroad industry in the 1870s. Much of the money invested came from the United Kingdom. After many railroads were found to be insolvent, the British investors began demanding audited financial statements, and several large British accounting firms established branches in the United States. These branches later grew into firms that still dominate the auditing profession in the United States.[12]

Box 11.9 Accounting Scandals of the Early 2000s

Beginning in 2001, a string of major corporate frauds shook public confidence.

Enron

Enron grew rapidly during the 1990s, and was seen as an innovative and growing company in the field of trading energy, especially natural gas. Its reported revenues placed it in the top ten of the Fortune 500 companies. In 2012, it was discovered that Enron had used several techniques to overstate its assets and income and understate its liabilities. It rapidly went into bankruptcy. Several people were found guilty of criminal offenses.

WorldCom

WorldCom, a major telecommunications company, overstated its income and assets by billions of dollars between 1998 and 2002. After the fraud was discovered in 2002, WorldCom entered bankruptcy. It emerged from bankruptcy later, and changed its name to MCI. Several people, including the top executives, were guilty of criminal offenses.

HealthSouth

HealthSouth is a major health care organization, with headquarters in Birmingham, Alabama. In 2003, it was discovered to have been overstating its income for a long period of time. At least 15 accounting and tax executives pleaded guilty to fraud, including five chief financial officers. Amazingly, a jury found the CEO not guilty. The company survived the fraud scandal.

Adelphia

Adelphia was a large regional cable TV provider. Even though it was a public company, it was largely controlled by a single family. In 2002, the public learned that several large loans had been taken out for the company, primarily for the benefit of the family, not the company. After the fraud was revealed, the company went bankrupt. Several people were found guilty of criminal offenses.

Parmalat

Parmalat is an Italian dairy company founded in 1961 that grew into a multinational corporation. It was largely run by its founder. The company misstated its financial results both to appear more profitable than it was and to hide the fact that corporate money was being siphoned off for the use of the founder. The fraud was uncovered in 2003. The founder was sentenced to prison, and charges against eight other defendants were settled out of court.

The requirements for audits of public companies also came as reactions to economic problems. The first requirement that the financial statements of public companies be audited was enacted into law in the 1930s, in reaction to the many bankruptcies that followed the stock market crash of 1929. The requirement for an auditor's report on the effectiveness of the internal control systems of large public companies was enacted as part of the Sarbanes–Oxley Act of 2002, in reaction to the accounting scandals at Enron, WorldCom, and other companies in 2001 and 2002. See Box 11.9.

The COSO Framework for Internal Controls

In Box 11.8, the auditors refer to "criteria established in *Internal Control — Integrated Framework (1992)* issued by the Committee of Sponsoring Organizations of the Treadway Commission." These criteria are usually referred to as the "COSO" criteria or COSO Framework for Internal Controls. The Committee of Sponsoring Organizations includes five private organizations: the American Institute of Certified Public Accountants; the American Accounting Association; Financial Executives International; the IMA; and the Institute of Internal Auditors.[13] The vast majority of U.S. companies use the COSO Framework to judge the effectiveness of their internal control systems.

This framework sees three major categories of objectives of internal controls in organizations: ensuring effective and efficient *operations*; ensuring accurate *reporting*; and ensuring *compliance* with laws and company policy. Note that this framework of internal controls goes well beyond accounting control—accurate reporting is only one of three objectives, and accounting reports would be part of a broader set of reports that the company makes. For example, a company might produce reports on its activities to improve its impact on the environment or the local economy.

To achieve these objectives, companies should use internal control systems with five key components. These are interrelated, and affect each other. The five components[14] are:

1 *The overall control environment.* This component relates to factors that have a pervasive effect throughout the company. The attitude of top management towards controls and towards ethical behavior is a key factor. The degree to which a Board of Directors and an audit committee oversee management is important. Bonus and compensation policies should be compatible with controls, and not set in a way that would encourage improper behavior or reporting. General computer systems and related controls should be in place to support operations and to ensure effective reporting.

   An example of a company with a poor overall control environment was Enron. Its top managers were focused on reporting earnings that would support a high stock price, and its internal policies put great pressure on employees to report high earnings.

2 *Risk assessment procedures.* The company should have procedures to understand the risks it faces in both its operations and its reporting processes. Operating risks are often related to the risk that reports will be incorrect. For example, a company that makes loans to people with poor credit should recognize that it has a business risk of not being repaid, and that it also has the risk of overestimating the collectible accounts receivable in its financial statements. The COSO Framework does not tell companies not to take risks, just that they need to understand the risks they are taking. The point is that the company should manage itself in such a way that it only takes the risks that management wants to take.

3 *Control activities.* These are various procedures that a company takes to ensure that activities are properly conducted and reports are properly prepared. A previous section of this chapter listed a variety of common procedures. These include separation of duties, authorization procedures, having adequate documents, having proper physical safeguards over key assets and documents, and regular independent review of documents.

4   *Information and communication systems.* In order to properly control a company, management must establish methods of communicating to employees what it wants done. This can be through policy manuals, or notices, or through goals and budgets. Management also needs to have information systems that tell it what is happening in the business. Clearly, the accounting information system is usually a vital part of the internal information system.

5   *Monitoring.* This component of the COSO Framework refers to the methods management uses to ensure that it knows whether the other four components are working. How does management know that the computer controls it established are working, or that the people who are supposed to assess risks are actually doing their jobs? A variety of monitoring procedures can be employed. One is the use of internal auditors to check that controls are in place. Additional procedures are regular supervisory reviews of how employees are performing their duties. In addition, when a company investigates variances from budget and from expected performance, it will often find that these are caused by breakdowns in various controls.

Note that while the COSO Framework is addressed to a broad area of controls, which go well beyond accounting controls, in order to comply a company will need good accounting controls. For example, good controls on the overall accounting information systems would be part of having an adequate control environment. Appropriate communication of budget targets to employees, and reports of financial results, are essential parts of the communication and information component. Accounting control activities, such as proper documentation of transactions, are part of the "control activities" component. Procedures such as having independent reconciliations of key accounts, and investigating variances, are important monitoring activities.

One final comment is worth making. You may not intend to be an accountant, and may think that you don't need to understand the COSO Framework. This is incorrect. Under the Sarbanes–Oxley Act, Congress required both CEOs and CFOs of large public companies to personally certify that their companies had adequate controls over financial reporting. As a result, many CEOs have asked the various managers reporting to them, not just the accounting departments, to certify that controls in their area are adequate.

Other Broad Concepts of Control

There is a large literature about how companies control their activities, and how accounting and accounting controls fit into this broader context. This section is meant merely to point out some of the major themes of this research.

Much has been written on how companies manage risk. Some risks come from the nature of the business, such as the risk a movie studio takes that the public will not like its movies. Other risks arise from employees not following company policies, or failing to comply with laws. Having proper internal controls is therefore part of a comprehensive risk management strategy.

The literature on management control systems indicates that there is often a tension between management maintaining control of operations and allowing operating managers adequate flexibility. Management needs to use procedures that are "tight" enough to ensure that employees adhere to its policies, but the policies must be "loose" enough to allow employees to innovate and to respond to unexpected events.[15] A management that is too focused on deviations from budgets or from standard production targets may not be allowing its employees enough flexibility to react to changing conditions.

There is an extensive literature on how "reliance on accounting performance measures" (abbreviated "RAPM") affects company performance and employee behavior.[16] Such measures include variance analyses and comparisons to budget. This literature suggests that companies differ in their reliance on these measures for various reasons, such as top management style and also the degree to which the company functions in a rapidly changing industry.

One influential way of looking at controls was developed by Simons, who defined four "*levers of control*" used by management.[17] The first "lever" is the ability of management to shape the "*belief systems*" of the company. Management needs to communicate the important company values, and the purpose and direction it wants the members of the organization to follow. Setting budget goals would be an accounting control that relates to the belief systems. "*Boundary systems*" establish rules as to what activities are acceptable, and which are off-limits. Related accounting controls might include budget limits on expenditures, or requirements that only certain people are authorized to sign checks. "*Diagnostic control systems*" help management monitor and control the implementation of its plans. Clearly, accounting reports of performance relative to budget, or variance reports on production, fit into this category. In addition, activities like reconciling accounts would help diagnose errors in the accounting system. The fourth "lever of control" is the use of "*interactive control systems*" to learn about, and respond to, opportunities and threats that arise as conditions change. Again, such accounting activities as comparing performance to budget and to expectations would be part of interactive control systems.

The point of this short section is that accounting controls are part of a broader effort by management to control the operations of the company.

Unresolved Issues and Areas for Further Research

There are a large number of areas where researchers are actively trying to better understand how the accounting process can be better controlled. Here are some examples:

1. How can information systems be improved, to make them faster, cheaper, and better able to keep management informed of events?
2. How do internal control systems affect employee motivation? What is the right balance between "tight" and "loose" controls in particular situations?
3. Have government efforts to affect internal controls, such as the requirements of the Sarbanes–Oxley Act, been effective?
4. How can information systems be better secured from hackers and other unauthorized users?
5. How often do serious misstatements of financial information occur? What are the major causes, and how can these misstatements be detected and prevented?
6. What are the major costs of internal controls, and how can these costs be reduced without reducing their effectiveness?
7. What makes auditing effective, or ineffective? How can the auditing process be improved?

Key Terms

Account—A record that contains the effects of events affecting a particular element of financial statements. For an example, a company may establish an account for all matters affecting land, or a loan payable to a bank, or its electricity expense.

Adjusted trial balance—A listing of the balances of all the accounts in the general ledger, prepared after the accounts have been adjusted for normal accrual entries.

Adverse report—A report by the company's auditors that states that the auditors do *not* believe the financial statements are presented fairly and in accordance with generally accepted accounting principles.

Audit trail—The records and source documents that give evidence for how a company arrived at figures in its financial statements.

Auditor's report—A statement by independent certified public accountants giving their opinion of whether the company's financial statements were fairly presented.

Chart of accounts—A listing of the names of the various accounts in the company's general ledger, prepared to help accounting staff know how to account for particular transactions.

COSO Framework—A widely used way of judging companies' internal control systems. It is based on work done by various organizations, which together are the Committee of Sponsoring Organizations of the Treadway Commission.

Credit—In the double-entry bookkeeping system, credits are entries on the right side of an account. They are the opposite of debits. Credits increase liabilities, revenue, and owners' equity accounts.

Debit—In the double-entry bookkeeping system, debits are entries on the left side of an account. They are the opposite of credits. Debits increase asset, expense, and dividend accounts.

Deposit in transit—These are bank deposits that a company has recorded on its books on a particular date, but which were not processed and recorded by the bank until a later date.

Detective control—Types of internal controls which are designed to detect an error or irregularity after it has occurred.

Disclaimer—An audit report in which the auditing firm says it is unable to give an opinion on the financial statement, usually because the firm was unable to do enough testing.

Double-entry bookkeeping—A system of bookkeeping that is based on recording transactions using a debit and credit system. Each transaction or event is recorded in a way that keeps the basic accounting equation in balance, and keeps the total debits equal to the total credits.

Effectiveness—The degree to which the company actually accomplishes the tasks it set out to do.

Efficiency—The degree to which a company accomplishes tasks at low cost, and minimizes wasted money or wasted effort.

Error—An unintentional misstatement of accounting measurements.

General ledger—The accounting record which includes all the accounts used by the company. The general ledger contains accounts for all assets, liabilities, revenues, expenses, dividends, and equity accounts.

Intentional misstatement—A misstatement caused by the deliberate action of some person. It is not an error, which is unintentional.

Internal controls—Sets of policies and procedures that help a company ensure that the company's objectives will be achieved.

Irregularity—See intentional misstatement. An irregularity could also include stealing of company assets.

Journal—An accounting record used to record transactions as they occur.

Journal entry—A record in a journal of a particular transaction. A typical journal entry will show the date of the event, the accounts debited and credited, the amounts debited and credited, and an explanation of the transaction.

Management by exception—A style of management that focuses on unexpected events or results.

Management override—Actions by top management to make lower level employees ignore the usual internal controls, and to either enter into improper transactions or to account for transactions improperly.

Misstatement—An accounting result or balance that is incorrect.

Outstanding check—A check written and mailed by a company, which has not yet been processed by the company's bank. The amount of the check has not yet been deducted by the bank from the company's bank account.

Preventive control—An internal control designed to prevent errors or irregularities from occurring.

Qualified report—A type of auditor's report that says that, in the auditor's opinion, the company's financial statements are fairly presented, except that the auditor has some reservation ("qualification") regarding a particular matter. For example, the auditor may disagree with how the company estimated one particular asset account, or the auditor might not have been able to gather enough evidence to test one account.

Segregation (or separation) of duties—An internal control practice that involves making sure that certain responsibilities are divided among different people. No one person should have the ability to authorize events, keep custody of related assets, and control the accounting for these events.

Trial balance—A listing of all the accounts in the general ledger, showing their names, balances, and whether they are debits or credits.

Unadjusted trial balance—A trial balance prepared before the company has done its routine entries to ensure the accounts are on the accrual basis, and before management has reviewed the accounts for apparent errors.

Unqualified report—An auditor's report that indicates the auditors did enough work to form an opinion, and that they believe the financial statements are fairly presented, in accordance with generally accepted accounting principles.

Questions and Problems

Comprehension Questions

C1. (Causes of incorrect reports) What are three reasons accounting reports can be inaccurate and misleading?

C2. (Causes of incorrect reports) Why is it usually easier to detect unintentional errors than fraudulent misstatements of accounting reports?

C3. (Summarization of accounting information) What is the difference between a journal and a general ledger? Describe how each is used.

C4. (Internal controls) What are the four main objectives of an internal control system?

C5. (Internal controls) What is the difference between preventive controls and detective controls?

C6. (Internal controls) Explain what is meant by "segregation of duties."

C7. (Internal controls) Explain what is meant by "authorization controls."

C8. (Internal controls) What is meant by the term "reconciliation"? Give an example of a type of reconciliation commonly done in accounting.

C9. (Internal controls) The chapter says that one of the best things that managers can do to help prevent irregularities is to create the proper business environment. Explain how this idea relates to the idea of the fraud triangle discussed in Chapter 6.

C10. (Double-entry bookkeeping) What types of accounts are increased with debits?

C11. (Double-entry bookkeeping) What types of accounts are increased with credits?

C12. (Double-entry bookkeeping) What is a journal entry? What information is usually needed to make a journal entry?

C13. (Double-entry bookkeeping) What is the difference between an "unadjusted trial balance" and an "adjusted trial balance"?

C14. (Double-entry bookkeeping) What are some features of double-entry bookkeeping that help in detecting errors in accounts?

C15. (Accounting information systems) What is meant by the term "audit trail"?

C16. (Bank reconciliations) Explain why "deposits in transit" and "outstanding checks" cause the company's cash records to differ from the bank's records of activity in a bank account.

C17. (Investigating variances) What is management by exception?

C18. (Auditing) Explain what "internal auditors" and "external auditors" are. Why is it normal for published auditors' reports to come from external auditors?

C19. (Auditing) Explain how "information risk" is related to the economic purpose of having audits by public accounting firms.

C20. (Auditing) Explain what is meant by the following types of auditors' reports on financial statements:

    A. Unqualified
    B. Qualified
    C. Adverse
    D. Disclaimer

C21. (Auditing) Auditors do not claim to have examined all of a company's transactions, and to have found them all to be totally accurately reported. Explain what auditors actually do claim to have done.

C22. (Limitations of control systems) Explain some limits to control systems.

C23. (Sarbanes–Oxley) Explain what the Sarbanes–Oxley Act required companies to do with regard to reporting on their internal control systems.

C24. (COSO Framework) What are the three objectives of internal controls, according to the COSO Framework?

C25. (COSO Framework) Explain what the COSO Framework means by:

    A. The control environment
    B. Risk assessment procedures
    C. Control techniques
    D. Information and communication processes
    E. Monitoring.

C26. (Simon's levers of control) Describe Simon's (2013) four "levers of control."

Application Questions

A1. (Times misstatements arise) For each of the following situations, indicate at which phase of the accounting process the misstatement arose (recognition, classification, summarization, or reporting):

    A. Even though the general ledger and the trial balance had the correct balance for cash, top management ordered the accounting department to inflate the reported cash and the reported net income in the financial statements by $30 million.
    B. Due to a computer error, every time the company sold a bottle of milk, the cost of goods sold was recorded as zero instead of the correct cost.
    C. Due to a computer error, when the company spent money on travel expense, it was recorded as telephone expense.
    D. The company keeps manual books. Even though each transaction was appropriately listed in the ledger, the accountant added the total travel expenses incorrectly and used the incorrect figure in the trial balance.

A2. (Intentional misstatements versus errors) For each of the following misstatements, indicate whether it is best described as an error or as an intentional misstatement.

    A. A customer was buying 15 items. The cashier counted them wrong, and recorded a sale of 14 items.
    B. A cashier told her friend that if the friend bought six items, the cashier would only charge for one.

C. The company has a complex tax return. The company's accountant inadvertently forgot to include one type of revenue, and this resulted in the company paying lower taxes.

D. The company's accountant knew that the law does not allow a company to deduct the full value of certain business entertainment costs from the tax return, so the accountant classified them as "printing expenses" and deducted them, thus reducing the tax payable.

A3. (Preventive and detective controls) For each of the following, indicate if it is best described as a preventive control or a detective control. Explain your answers.

A. The company does background checks on potential new employees.
B. The company counts the inventory on hand once per month, and compares the records with the inventory on hand, to identify missing inventory.
C. The company looks at all the canceled checks that have been returned by the bank, and compares who actually cashed the check with the person the check was supposed to be paid to.
D. The company only allows high-level, trusted employees to sign company checks.

A4. (Preventive and detective controls) For each of the following, indicate if it is best described as a preventive control or a detective control. Explain your answers.

A. The company segregates certain duties in handling cash. The people who receive checks, and put them into the bank, are *not* the ones who keep the records for accounts receivable.
B. The company periodically looks at all accounts receivable that have been written off, to make sure that they were only written off for good reasons. (A company might be worried that an employee had stolen incoming checks, and then had claimed the customers had not paid, and were "bad debts," to hide the thefts.)
C. The company reconciles all bank accounts each month, and looks for unexplained checks that were written.
D. The company uses firewalls and access controls to protect its computer systems from hackers.

A5. (Types of accounting controls) The text discusses five major types of accounting controls: authorization controls; segregation of duties; having adequate documentation; physical controls; and independent reviews and reconciliations. Indicate which of these controls best describes each of the following company policies:

A. Each time a sale is made to a customer, a sales receipt is printed. A copy of the sales receipt is kept by the company.
B. The people who are authorized to sign checks for the company are different from the people who keep the cash disbursement records, and from the people who reconcile the bank accounts.
C. Company checks are kept in a locked cabinet until they are used to make payments.
D. No sales personnel can accept an order of more than $10,000 without the permission of the Vice President for Sales.
E. Twice each year, the internal audit department reviews all write-offs of customer accounts to ensure they were written off for valid reasons.
F. Once per year, the company counts the inventory on hand, and compares the count to the amounts recorded on the company's records.

A6. (Types of accounting controls) The text discusses five major types of accounting controls: authorization controls; segregation of duties; having adequate documentation; physical controls; and independent reviews and reconciliations. Indicate which of these controls best describes each of the following company policies:

A. Before any journal entry is recorded, it must be approved by the company Controller.
B. Company policy requires that whenever an accounting staff person prepares a journal entry, the staff person must also put into a folder the evidence and source documents that support the journal entry.
C. Access to the company's information systems is limited to people who have valid passwords.
D. The internal audit department periodically checks the records to ensure that all employees who received overtime pay had actually been present during the hours they claimed to have worked.
E. Employees fill out time sheets each week, indicating what tasks they performed, and how long each task took.

A7. (Debits and credits) Indicate whether the following accounts increase with debits, or with credits:

A. Bank loans payable
B. Printing expense
C. Dividends to shareholders
D. Land
E. Prepaid expenses
F. Wages payable to employees
G. Sales revenues
H. Interest revenues
I. Common stock (an equity account)

A8. (Debits and credits) Indicate whether the following accounts increase with debits, or with credits:

A. Cash
B. Taxes payable
C. Telephone expense
D. Account payable
E. Retained earnings
F. Service fees revenues
G. Gain on sale of building
H. Accounts receivable

A9. (Journal entries) Make journal entries to record the following events, each of which occurred on September 1, 2015. Each journal entry should include the date, the names and amounts for each of the accounts debited and credited, and a brief description.

A. The company provided $10,000 of services to a customer, and received cash.
B. The company provided $5,000 of services to another customer, on credit terms.
C. A customer paid the company $3,000, reducing the company's accounts receivable.
D. The company borrows $23,000 from a bank, and promises to repay the loan in one year.
E. The company receives a telephone bill for $2,578. It does not pay the bill right away, but records an expense and an accrued expense payable.

A10. (Journal entries) Make journal entries to record the following events, each of which occurred on October 1, 2015. Each journal entry should include the date, the names and amounts for each of the accounts debited and credited, and a brief description.

A. The company paid $56,000 in cash dividends to shareholders.

B. The company sold computers to customers for $78,000 in cash. The computers had cost the company $60,000. (Note—This entry will affect cash, sales, cost of goods sold, and inventory.)

C. The company's employees earned $36,000 in salaries, which the company paid in cash.

D. The company paid an accounts payable of $4,891.

E. The company computed its taxes for the year, and realized the expense was $57,000. The company has not yet paid the taxes.

A11. (Bank reconciliation)

A. Prepare a bank reconciliation for the Lutz Corporation as of December 31, using the following facts:

- The bank statement showed a balance of $112,000.
- The company's ledger showed a balance of $110,000.
- $15,000 of checks written by the company had not yet been received by the bank. (They are outstanding checks.)
- The company had deposited $12,000 on December 31, which was not processed by the bank until January 2.
- The bank had charged the company $1,000 in fees and interest which the company had not yet booked.

B. What corrections, if any, should Lutz record in its books?

A12. (Bank reconciliation)

A. Prepare a bank reconciliation for the May Corporation as of December 31, using the following facts:

- The bank statement showed a balance of $29,000.
- The company's ledger showed a balance of $20,000.
- $13,000 of checks written by the company had not yet been received by the bank. (They are outstanding checks.)
- The company had deposited $3,000 on December 31, which was not processed by the bank until January 2.
- The bank statement showed a check of $1,000 had been processed by the bank but had not been recorded in the company's records.

B. What corrections, if any, should May record in its books?

A13. (Auditors' reports). The text described four major types of auditors' reports: unqualified; adverse; disclaimers; and qualified reports. For each of the following excerpts from an auditor's report, indicate which type of report it is.

A. "In our opinion, the accompanying financial statements are fairly stated, in accordance with generally accepted accounting principles. . ."

B. "In our opinion, except for the error in accounts receivable described below, the accompanying financial statements are fairly stated, in accordance with generally accepted accounting principles. . ."

C. "Because we were not appointed as auditors until after the end of the fiscal year, we were not able to obtain enough evidence to form an opinion about the financial statements, and accordingly, we do not express an opinion on the fairness of the financial statements. . . ."

D. "In our opinion, the accompanying financial statements are not presented fairly, in accordance with generally accepted accounting principles."

A14. (Limits of controls) The text indicated the following reasons that controls may not prevent all misstatements:

- Management override
- Cost considerations
- Subjective estimates
- Difficult computations
- Unusual or non-routine events that normal controls do not cover
- Subversion by lower level employees
- Irregularities may be well hidden

For each of the examples below, indicate which of these limitations apply:

A. A company measured the time worked by factory employees by having them place a time card in a special clock when they came and left. Employees cheated the company by having friends "clock out" for them an hour or two after they actually left. As a result, the reported time worked, and wage expense, was higher than it should have been.

B. A publishing company printed a large number of copies of a politician's autobiography. It did not record any reserve for non-salable inventory. In fact, the book was unpopular, and the inventory was overstated.

C. The top management was upset that the company's third quarter earnings were going to be below what analysts expected. Top management ordered the accounting staff to record a lower tax expense than the company actually expected to pay.

D. A department store has decided that it is better off tolerating a certain level of shoplifting than trying to hire enough guards to stop this problem. As a result of thefts by customers, the inventory actually on the shelves is always somewhat lower than the company's records indicate.

A15. (Limits of controls) The text indicated the following reasons that controls may not prevent all misstatements:

- Management override
- Cost considerations
- Subjective estimates
- Difficult computations
- Unusual or non-routine events that normal controls do not cover
- Subversion by lower level employees
- Irregularities may be well hidden

For each of the examples below, indicate which of these reasons apply:

A. Banks usually have a number of controls to ensure they only loan money to reliable people. Several years ago, it was reported that the Kabul Bank of Afghanistan had made large loans to friends and relatives of bank officers, at the direction of top management, and these loans were not going to be repaid. As a result, the bank had been overstating the value of its assets.

B.   A company set difficult targets for the profitability of each store. Local store managers reacted by overcounting the inventory in their stores, and undercounting the cost of goods sold.

C.   The company operates in 35 countries. It made an error in computing its worldwide taxes because the tax staff did not fully understand the relation between Chinese and U.S. tax laws.

D.   A purchasing manager arranged with a friend to overbill the company on certain office supplies by 5%. The purchasing manager prepared phony documents that made it look like the company was getting a good price, when in fact it was not.

A16. (COSO Framework) The text lists five components of the COSO Framework: an overall control environment; risk assessment procedures; specific control activities; information and communication systems; and monitoring. For each of the following, indicate which part of the COSO Framework it relates to:

A.   The company uses appropriate passwords to limit access to key databases.

B.   The company has a Board of Directors that is actively involved in the oversight of management.

C.   The company has a code of ethics for employees.

D.   The internal audit department regularly checks to see if the company's policies on using computer passwords are being followed.

E.   The company has decided that it should not grant credit to certain types of customers, because the chance of uncollectible accounts is too great.

F.   Top management receives regular monthly reports of expenses and revenues for each department.

A17. (COSO Framework) The text lists five components of the COSO Framework: an overall control environment; risk assessment procedures; specific control activities; information and communication systems; and monitoring. For each of the following, indicate which part of the COSO Framework it relates to:

A.   The company requires segregation of duties between people who write checks and people who reconcile the company bank accounts.

B.   The company's internal auditors check each year to make sure that all bank reconciliations are being made on a timely basis.

C.   The company has hiring and promotion policies that encourage ethical behavior.

D.   The company has appropriate locks and security procedures to protect inventory from theft.

E.   The company has decided that it is not cost-effective to keep track of office supplies as they are used, since the chance that errors could be material is very low.

F.   Top management lets lower management know about changes in policies by writing and sending formal memos.

A18. (Simon's levers of control) Simon's (2013) four "levers of control" are: beliefs; boundaries; diagnostic controls; and interactive controls. For each of the following, identify the applicable "lever of control."

A.   A salesman is not allowed to offer a customer more than $1,000 in credit without receiving authorization from a credit manager.

    B.   The company tells employees they are all part of a team, and that they will all share in the company's success. The company makes all employees eligible for a profit-sharing plan to demonstrate its commitment to this team philosophy.

    C.   The company regularly counts the inventory on hand to see if any is missing or stolen.

    D.   The company regularly performs usage variance analysis on materials used in production, and involves workers and managers in discussions of why variances have occurred and what can be done to improve performance.

A19. (Simon's levers of control) Simon's (2013) four "levers of control" are: beliefs; boundaries; diagnostic controls; and interactive controls. For each of the following, identify the applicable "lever of control."

    A.   A computer system will not allow an accountant to make a journal entry where the debits do not equal the credits.

    B.   A public accounting firm tells all of its new hires that it is vital for the firm to act at the highest possible ethical level, and that the firm's reputation for integrity is critical.

    C.   A company performs bank reconciliations to identify any errors in recording cash disbursements or receipts.

    D.   The company's top managers and lower level managers regularly discuss the company's performance, compared to budget, and consider whether the budget should be changed to reflect changed circumstances.

A20. (Internal controls that prevent or detect issues) The chapter discussed a number of different types of internal accounting controls, such as: authorization procedures; segregation of duties; physical controls; proper documentation; regular independent review; designing processes to prevent errors; and personnel policies. For each of the following situations, suggest some kind of control that might have either detected or prevented the problem. Explain your answer.

    A.   Last month, the company agreed to sell 20,000 units of product to a customer for $7 each. The customer now says that it only agreed to buy 2,000 units, and the price was $5 each.

    B.   The company's computer system was hacked, and its accounts receivable records were erased.

    C.   A salesperson sold $5 million of products to her brother, on credit, and then left the country after the goods were shipped. The goods were never paid for.

    D.   A dishonest bookkeeper at a small company wrote checks made out to himself, and recorded them as various types of expenses.

    E.   The company's ledger is out of balance. The journal entries made this month contained more debits than credits.

A21. (Internal controls that prevent or detect issues) The chapter discussed a number of different types of internal accounting controls, such as: authorization procedures; segregation of duties; physical controls; proper documentation; regular independent review; designing processes to prevent errors; and personnel policies. For each of the following situations, suggest some kind of control that might have either detected or prevented the problem. Explain your answer. Often, there is more than one possible control.

    A.   Warehouse employees have been stealing valuable inventory items, such as televisions.

    B.   A company sells electronics. Every day, one salesperson makes some sales for cash, pockets the money, and does not record the sales. The customers have done nothing wrong. For these sales, the company loses the value of the electronics that the customers walk out with.

C. A bookkeeper wrote out 46 checks to vendors in one day. Accidentally, the bookkeeper forgot to record one $8,000 check in the company's disbursement journal.

D. Workers in a company are entitled to be paid extra when they work overtime. Employees routinely claim to work two hours per day more than they actually do.

E. A dishonest bookkeeper has been stealing checks that customers send in to pay for items they have bought. The bookkeeper does not deposit these checks in the company bank accounts, but the bookkeeper makes accounting entries to say that the cash was received, and to reduce the amounts the customers owe. The bookkeeper also reconciles the bank account, and hides the fact that the bank does not show these deposits.

Discussion Questions

D1. (Ethics) What would you do if the company CFO ordered you to make an incorrect entry, and said that if anything went wrong, he would be the one who went to jail? Would you make the entry? Quit? Take some other action? Explain your answer.

D2. (Internal controls) We have all had experiences of buying on-line. Thinking of the last few times you ordered something, what types of internal control procedures do you think the seller built into the process?

D3. (Auditing) In the U.S., auditors do not guarantee that financial statements are correct. Instead, they say they have done enough work to provide reasonable assurance, and then give an opinion that they believe the financial statements are presented fairly. This means that, when the financial statements are incorrect, the auditors are not held legally responsible unless they are found to have been negligent or to have been part of a fraud. Do you believe that the auditors should in fact be held responsible for all material misstatements, whether or not the auditors acted negligently? Explain your answer.

D4. (Auditing) In the U.S., auditors are hired by the companies they audit. This seems to create an incentive for auditors to try to please their clients, and might reduce their aggressiveness in challenging management representations. Would it be better if audits of public companies were performed by government-paid auditors, who would presumably be more independent?

D5. (Sarbanes–Oxley) Under the Sarbanes–Oxley Act, large public companies were required to comply with Section 404, which required auditors to comment on their internal controls. As noted in the chapter, this was expensive. In 2012, Congress changed the law so that companies with market capitalizations of under $700 million do not need to report on internal controls for the first five years after they go public. What do you see as good and bad points of this change in the law?

Research Questions

R1. (Auditing) Go to the latest version of *Accounting Today*'s special edition listing the 100 largest public accounting firms.

A. For the top six firms, what percentage of their revenues came from accounting and assurance, from tax, and from other services?

B. What are the six largest firms, in terms of revenues from auditing and assurance?

C. What is the largest firm? What are its total number of partners and professional employees?

R2. (Auditing) Under the Sarbanes–Oxley Act, the PCAOB not only is required to regulate U.S. public accounting firms that audit public companies, but is also supposed to regulate foreign accounting firms that audit foreign companies registered in the U.S. Go to the PCAOB's website (pcaobus.org)[18] and click on the tab labelled "International." Answer the following questions:

A. Approximately how many foreign audit firms are currently registered with the PCAOB?
B. What is the nature of the reciprocal arrangement that the PCAOB has reached with regulators in China?

Notes

1 Retrieved from www.wboc.com/story/27697765/ups-fedex-look-to-not-repeat-2013-christmas-delivery-problems (last accessed August 18, 2015).
2 Bendetto Cotrugli wrote an earlier Italian treatise on double-entry bookkeeping in 1458, but this was not published until the 1500s. See MacNeal (1939).
3 The derivation of these terms, and of the abbreviations for them, is unclear. The Latin debitum means "debt," and the creditum means "thing entrusted to one." See Baladouni (1984).
4 See Dechow and Mouritsen (2005).
5 However, if checks are not cashed for a long period of time, the accountant may wish to follow up with the payees to see if they have been lost. If deposits remain in transit for more than a few days, the accountant should investigate what has happened to the cash.
6 Sometimes checks which a company receives from customers are not honored by the customer's bank. The most common reason is that the customer does not have enough money in its account to cover the check. The bank statement will show a separate debit item for each returned check. The bank generally returns the check to the company which deposited it. The company needs to take two actions. It should adjust the cash account and accounts receivable to indicate that the customer's payment was invalid. The company then should contact the customer and make arrangements to receive a valid payment.
7 The accountant might also reconcile recorded insurance payments to the amount due on the actual insurance policy, and notice that the recorded payments were more than the true cost of the insurance.
8 See Newman (1979).
9 The technical term is that these were "imprest" bank accounts. See Johnson and Kaplan 1987.
10 Smaller public companies are not required to comply with these requirements.
11 The Dodd—Frank Act of 2010 removed the internal control reporting for companies with market capitalization of less than $75 million. In 2012, Congress allowed companies to defer reporting on internal controls for up to five years after going public, except for those with market capitalizations over $700 million or revenues and non-convertible debt over $1 billion. See Coates, John & Srinivasan (2014).
12 The so-called "Big Four" auditing firms (PWC, Ernst, Deloitte, and KPMG) all have British roots, although their current form reflects various mergers over their history.
13 See the COSO website, www.coso.org. Accessed on April 9, 2015. All description of the COSO Framework in this section is based on McNally (2013).
14 The COSO's 2013 framework expanded upon this to list 17 different principles that relate to these five components. A full explanation is beyond the scope of this text.
15 See, for example, Frow, Marginson and Ogden (2005) and Henri (2006).
16 See for example Hartmann (2000).
17 Simons, R. (2013). Simons also discussed this topic in several prior works. As of the date I wrote this chapter, April of 2015, GoogleScholar already showed over 2,400 citations of this 2013 work. See Tessier and Otley (2012) for an attempt to extend Simon's analysis.
18 Last accessed August 18, 2015.

References

Baladouni, V. (1984). Etymological observations on some accounting terms. *The Accounting Historians Journal*, *11*(2), Fall. 101–9.
Chambers, R. J. (1969). *Accounting Finance and Management*. Sydney, Australia: Hogbin, Poole (Printers) Pty. Ltd.

Chesney, M. (2014, December 23). UPS & FedEx look to Not Repeat 2013 Christmas Delivery Problems. *WBOC16*. Retrieved from http://www.wboc.com/story/27697765/ups-fedex-look-to-not-repeat-2013-christmas-delivery-problems (last accessed August 18, 2015).

Christensen, J. A., & Demski, J. S. (2003). *Accounting Theory: An Information Content Perspective*. Boston: McGraw Hill.

Cloyd, H. M. (1979). George Washington as an Accountant. *The Accounting Historians Journal* (Spring), 87–91.

Coates, I. V., John, C., & Srinivasan, S. (2014). SOX after ten years: A multidisciplinary review. *Accounting Horizons, 28*(3), 627–71.

Dechow, N., & Mouritsen, J. (2005). Enterprise resource planning systems, management control and the quest for integration. *Accounting, Organizations and Society, 30*(7), 691–733.

FASB. (2010). Statement of Financial Accounting Concepts No. 8, Conceptual Framework for Financial Reporting–Chapter 1, *The Objective of General Purpose Financial Reporting,* and Chapter 3, *Qualitative Characteristics of Useful Financial Information* (a replacement of FASB Concepts Statements No. 1 and No. 2) (pp. 1–14, 16–22). Norwalk, CT: FASB.

Frow, N., Marginson, D., & Ogden, S. (2005). Encouraging strategic behaviour while maintaining management control: Multi-functional project teams, budgets, and the negotiation of shared accountabilities in contemporary enterprises. *Management Accounting Research, 16*(3), 269–92.

Hartmann, F. G. (2000). The appropriateness of RAPM: Ttoward the further development of theory. *Accounting, Organizations and Society, 25*(4), 451–82.

Henri, J. F. (2006). Organizational culture and performance measurement systems. *Accounting, Organizations and Society, 31*(1), 77–103.

Johnson, H. T., & Kaplan, R. S. (1987). *Relevance Lost: The Rise and Fall of Management Accounting*. Boston, MA: Harvard Business School Press.

Kuleza, C. S. (1997). "It's not your father's management accounting!" *Management Accounting* (May), 56–9.

MacNeal, K. (1939). *Truth in Accounting*. Houston, Texas: Scholars Book Co.

McNally, S. (2013). The 2013 COSO Framework & SOX Compliance: One approach to an effective transition. *Strategic Finance* (June), 1–8.

Newman, M. S. (1979). Historical development of early accounting concepts and their relation to certain economic concepts. Working Paper No. 11. In E. N. Coffman (Ed.), *The Academy of Accounting Historians Working Paper Series, Vol. 1 (Working Papers 1–20)*. Richmond, VA: Virginia Commonwealth University.

Pulliam, S. (2003, June 23). A staffer ordered to commit fraud balked, then caved. *Wall Street Journal*, p. 1.

Simons, R. (2013). *Levers of Control: How Managers Use Innovative Control Systems to Drive Strategic Renewal*. Boston, MA: Harvard Business School Press.

Tessier, S., & Otley, D. (2012). A conceptual development of Simons' Levers of Control framework. *Management Accounting Research, 23*(3), 171–85.

Winjum, J. O. (1972). *The Role of Accounting in the Economic Development of England: 1500–1750*. Champaign, IL: Center for Education and Research in Accounting, University of Illinois.

Part 4

Introduction to a Case Study

Part 4 focuses on the business and accounting issues of a fictional company. It is mostly meant to help you integrate the material from the first 11 chapters. However, it also introduces some new topics, including different forms of organizations that businesses use; employees and independent contractors; and methods companies use to obtain financing.

12 Rebeli Press, Inc.—The First Year

Outline

- Preliminary Thoughts
- Learning Objectives
- The Plan
- Legal Considerations

    o   Form of Organization
    o   Employees or Contractors
    o   Taking Money out of the Business

- Getting Ready to Operate
- Operating and Selling
- Analyzing the Results
- Budgeting for Year 2
- Thinking About Expansion
- Relating the Case to Earlier Chapters

Preliminary Thoughts

> "Hey, Eli, let's start a publishing business."
> "Rebecca, you're crazy. That's a tough business. We'll go broke."
> "Trust me. I've got a plan."

And that is how we start the story of Rebeli Press, a company started by a brother and sister and specializing in magazines and books related to cats and dogs.

This chapter will trace the first year of the company, including its foundation, its initial financing, employment and contractor arrangements, and its basic operating and sales activities. The activities will be described using both text and journal entries. The chapter concludes with analysis of the first year's operations and its plans for the next year.

Unlike the previous chapters, which are theoretical, this chapter is devoted to dealing with practical details related to typical activities involved in a business.

Learning Objectives

After studying this chapter, students will:

1   Be familiar with the advantages and disadvantages of forming businesses as proprietorships, partnerships, and corporations

2   Understand the concepts of C corporations, limited liability corporations, and Subchapter S corporations

3   Understand the basic legal rules for determining whether workers are employees or independent contractors

4   Understand the basic payroll taxes and benefit costs applicable in the U.S.

5   Gain practice with the use of debits and credits to record transactions

6   Become more familiar with the process of analyzing financial statements

7   See how many of the concepts in the earlier chapters apply to a particular business

The Plan

"OK, Rebecca, what's the plan? You do know that publishing is risky and competitive? I'd heard somewhere that nine out of 10 new businesses fail."

"There is risk, but it's not nearly as high as 90%. The figures from the Small Business Administration are that over half of new businesses survive more than five years, and about one third make it for 10 years or more."[1]

"That may be true for businesses in general, but isn't publishing really tough? I read this article called 'The 10 awful truths about book publishing' by Steven Piersanti.[2] His figures are a few years old, but he says the average book has a less than 1% chance of being stocked in a bookstore. One source says that in 2013 there were over 304,000 different titles published in the U.S.[3] So how are we going to succeed?"

"First of all, we're going to focus on pet owners. We can get the rights to publish in book form the stories of Lorimer and Oscar, the two cutest cats ever, as well as Fred the golden retriever. Those will separate us. Second, we'll also publish a magazine, the *Rebeli Pet Monthly*. There will be nothing like it."

"OK, Rebecca, I guess there is a chance of success. There are an awful lot of pet owners in the U.S."

"Yes. About a third of the population has a cat or a dog, and those people really care. The American Veterinary Medical Association[4] says about 63% of pet owners think of their pets as family members. And we don't need that many people. I've done some break-even analysis, and if we price the books at $18 and the subscriptions at $80 a year, we would only need book sales of around 15,000 copies and two or three thousand magazine subscribers to cover our marketing and production and other costs, and to make a small profit. If the sales go higher, we can make a lot of money."

"OK, I'll agree to do this. But are there ways we can limit our risk if things don't go right?"

"Yes, Eli, there are. We'll be careful about the form of business we choose, so that we don't become personally liable for the debts of the business. We'll also try to operate the business with very little operating or financial leverage until we're confident it can succeed. We'll set things up so we have a low break-even point at first. That way we won't lose much if sales are low. We won't buy or operate our own printing plant—we'll contract the work out. And we will rent equipment and offices rather than buying them. To the extent possible, we'll use contractors instead of employees to ensure we have variable, not fixed, costs. You look confused. Don't worry, I've taken an accounting course, and can explain these ideas to you. . ."

Legal Considerations

Form of Organization

Rebecca and Eli made an appointment to see a legal advisor, Gene, for advice on how to form their new business. Gene explained in an email that the basic choices for small businesses are

Box 12.1 Basic Types of Business Organization in the U.S.—Proprietorships

Description
This is a business with a single owner. The business is not legally distinct from the owner.

Advantages:
It is simple to set up a proprietorship.

No separate tax filings are required. The business's taxable income and deductions are reported on the owner's personal tax return.

There is no "double taxation" of business and individual income.

Disadvantages:
The proprietorship form is not appropriate if there is more than one owner. If the owner wants to bring in additional owners, the business form needs to change into a partnership or corporation.

The business entity does not have a life separate from the owner of the business.

The owner can be sued for any debts of the business. The owner has "unlimited liability" for the business's debts.

Box 12.2 Basic Types of Business Organization in the U.S.—Partnerships

Description
A partnership is formed by the agreement of two or more parties.

The partnership technically would end each time new partners are added, or old partners leave.

In a "general partnership," each partner has the right to:

- Make contracts and agreements for the business
- Participate in making partnership decisions
- Share in the profits and losses of the business, at a rate determined by the agreement.

Advantages:
Partnerships are a flexible form of organization, which can be set up to allow for different ways of sharing profits and losses.

Partnerships can be formed without some of the formalities needed to create corporations.

Partnerships are not subject to income tax at the partnership level. The partnership's income and deductions are instead reported as being earned by the various partners, who must report these items on their personal income tax returns. This means there is no "double taxation" of partnership income.

Disadvantages:
General partners have unlimited personal liability for the debts of the partnership. (Some partnerships are "limited partnerships," with some partners whose liabilities and management rights are limited.)

The life of a partnership is tied to the lives of its partners. Technically, a partnership may end when the partners change due to admitting new partners or old ones dying or leaving.

There are usually limits on how a partnership interest can be sold or transferred. Existing partners usually would have to approve the admission of new partners.

sole proprietorships, partnerships, and corporations. He sent them the information about each type of business, and asked them to study the material before their meeting.

Some extracts from their conversation are shown below:

GENE: "So, as I understand it, you two want to set up a business, with yourselves as equal owners. Right now it is small, but you hope that it can grow. If it grows, you may want to bring in new owners. Is that right?"

ELI: "Yes. I am worried that if it fails, I could be held responsible for the business's debts."

GENE: "Then you and Rebecca should incorporate your business. A primary advantage of the corporate form of business is that it is a legally separate entity. It is responsible for its own debts. That's different than either a proprietorship or a general partnership. In those forms of business, the creditors can try to collect their debts from the owners—partners have unlimited liability for the partnership's debts.

"I'm not going to talk about proprietorships to you, since those are one-person businesses, and there are two of you. But the material I sent (Boxes 12.1, 12.2, and 12.3) indicates that most of the considerations relevant to partnerships and proprietorships are the same."

ELI: "Besides limited liability, are there other reasons we should form the business as a corporation?"

GENE: "Yes. One is that a corporation theoretically has an indefinite life—its life is not tied to who the owners are. That's different than a partnership. Technically, a partnership has to be re-formed each time a partner leaves it, or a new partner enters it. Another important one for you two is that it's easy to transfer ownership of shares in a corporation. You hope to grow the business, and eventually maybe even go public. It's easy for any shareholder to sell his or her stock to anyone else. That's very different from a partnership. All the partners would have to agree on someone new becoming a partner. Also, if you brought someone in as a partner, they might have the right to make business decisions. Unless a partnership agreement is specific, usually any partner can take actions that are binding on the whole partnership. You may not want that."

REBECCA: "So why does anyone create partnerships? It must be tough to have unlimited liability."

GENE: "There are some good things about partnerships. They are easy to set up, and the partners can agree to split the work, and the profits and losses, in all sorts of different ways. Also, for federal and state income tax purposes, they are '*pass-through entities*.' That means that partnerships don't actually pay tax on their income. Instead, they report to the government how much of the partnership income is allocable to each partner, and the partner shows that income on his or her individual tax return. To put it another way, for tax purposes income just 'passes through' the partnership to the partners, without the partnership paying a separate tax. In contrast, for a corporation, there may be 'double taxation'—a corporate income tax paid each year when the corporation earns money, and a tax the shareholders have to pay when they receive dividends.

"Technically, to form a corporation you have to file with the state, and get approval of a corporate charter, but this is fairly cheap and automatic. There are services on-line that will help, or I will do it for you for a fee."

ELI: "How big are these taxes on corporate income and dividends?"

GENE: "The normal corporate income tax rate is 35%. Usually, individuals pay tax at either 15% or 20% capital gains rates when they receive dividends, depending on their income."

REBECCA: "That's pretty high! Now I'm wondering why anybody creates a corporation instead of a partnership."

GENE: "Congress has created two special rules, which help most small businesses enjoy the major legal advantages of the corporation form while avoiding double taxation. These are the Subchapter S rules and the limited liability corporation rules. Limited liability corporations

---

Box 12.3 Basic Types of Business Organization in the U.S.—Corporations

Description

A corporation is a legal entity, chartered by a state, and owned by one or more persons. A corporation is legally separate "person" from its owners. The corporation can make contracts, and be sued, separately from its owners.

Typically, shareholders have the following legal rights:

- To receive information about the company.
- To receive an equal amount of dividends per share with other shareholders, if and when dividends are paid.
- To have one vote per share in any matters voted on by shareholders.
- To receive an equal amount per share with other shareholders, when the company ends and any assets that remain, after paying off creditors, are distributed.

Advantages:

The owners of stock in a corporation are not liable for the debts of the business. The most that the owners can normally lose is the amount they have already invested in the company. This is referred to as "limited liability."

The corporation has an indefinite life, which is not affected by the death of owners, or by transfers of ownership. This gives corporations greater stability than partnerships.

The management and decisions of a corporation are made by its Board of Directors and officers, not by individual shareholders. This means that shareholders, unlike partners, are not at risk by a single shareholder's bad business judgments.

It is easy for shareholders to transfer their shares. They do not need the approval of other shareholders.

It is typically easier to raise large amounts of capital using the corporate form than the general partnership form.

It is possible, using different classes of stock, to give different voting rights or shares in profits to different groups of shareholders.

Disadvantages:

The formation and closing of a corporation requires more formality than the formation and closing of a partnership, including registration with a state.

There is "double taxation" of income of regular, or "C," corporations. There is a corporate income tax, usually 35%, on corporate income. When corporations pay dividends to shareholders, the dividends are taxable to the shareholders in their individual tax returns. Usually, these dividends are taxed at capital gains rates, which are lower than ordinary income tax rates. The U.S. capital gains rates in 2015 were 20% for individuals in a 39.6% tax bracket, and 15% for most individuals.

---

are usually referred to as LLCs for short. Both these types of corporations are pass-through entities, like partnerships, for tax federal income tax purposes. Some but not all states also treat them as pass-through entities. The companies that actually have to pay the federal corporate income tax are referred to as 'C corporations.' The names 'S' and 'C' refer to sections of the tax law.

"Oh. There's one other good thing about pass-through entities. If your business loses money in the early years, which some businesses do, you can use the losses in a pass-through entity on your personal tax returns to reduce your taxes. That's not possible with a C corporation.

"I sent you some material comparing 'S corporations' and LLCs. That's Table 12.1. Did you get a chance to look it over?"

REBECCA: "Yes. They look pretty similar to us. Both are pass-through entities. Right now we only have two owners, so it's not a problem that the S corporation is limited to 100 shareholders, and that only individuals can be shareholders. If we wanted to have corporations as shareholders, I guess that maybe we would favor an LLC. I see that S corporations only allow one kind of stock, and LLCs can have different types with different rights, but that's not an issue right now. So we don't have a strong preference. Do you have a recommendation?"

GENE: "Like you say, it seems like a close call for your situation. I understand that these days, more new businesses are choosing LLCs than S corporations, but in your case I think maybe an S corporation makes sense. In New York, it's a little more costly to form an LLC, since you have to announce it in newspaper ads. If you decide to pay yourselves salaries, there may be a minor savings on employment-related taxes in the Subchapter S form. It is perfectly normal for owners of S corporations to also be employees of the corporations, but technically owners of LLCs are not employees, and are considered self-employed. This can result in them having to pay self-employment taxes on money they earn working for their companies, and the bill ends up a bit higher than what the taxes work out to be for the owner-employees

Table 12.1 Choosing Between Subchapter S and LLC

	Subchapter S corporation	*LLC*
Ease of creating	Easy	Slightly harder, depends on state. In New York, LLCs must publish certain information in two newspapers.
Limited liability?	Yes	Yes
Avoids federal double taxation?	Yes	Yes
Avoids state federal double taxation	Depends on state. New York State and City tax S corporation income.	Depends on state. Usually avoids double taxation.
Legally separate from owners?	Yes	Yes
Can owner deduct losses on personal return?	Yes, but more limited than LLC	Yes
Indefinite life	Yes	Depends on state—in some states death of an owner could require dissolution of the LLC
Limits on total number of owners?	100	No limit
Restrictions on who owners can be?	No owners can be non-U.S. Owners basically must be individuals, not corporations or trusts.	No restrictions
Sharing of profits	All shares must have equal rights	Different types of shares with different rights are allowed
Transferability of ownership	Easy—no permission of other owners needed	Harder—permission of other owners needed
Self-employment taxes	May have advantage. The owners may be paid as employees, and rates may be lower.	May have disadvantage. Owners can't be employees, and are subject to self-employment tax.

This table incorporates ideas from www.bizfilings.com/learn/llc-vs-s-corp.aspx (last accessed August 18, 2015) and www.newyorksmallbusinesslaw.com/new_york_small_business_l/2012/04/choosing-between-an-s-corporation-and-an-llc.html (last accessed August 18, 2015).

Box 12.4 IRS Statistics on Types of Business Organizations in the U.S. in 2012

The total number of business tax returns = 32,783,232
 The most important types of business returns were:

Proprietorships	23,553,850 (72%)
Corporations	5,840,821 (18%)
Partnerships other than LLCs	1,177,208 (3%)
LLCs	2,211,353 (7%)

Among the corporations, there were 4,205,452 S corporation returns and 1,617,739 C corporation returns. Thus, S corporations were about 72% of corporation returns (ignoring LLCs), and 13% of all business returns, and C corporations were 28% of corporation returns and 5% of all business returns.

   C corporations have a disproportionate amount of the business receipts. Their receipts of over $22 trillion were almost 70% of the total business receipts of $32 trillion.

All data are from the IRS SOI Tax Stats—Business Tax Statistics, retrieved from www.irs.gov/uac/SOI-Tax-Stats-Integrated-Business-Data (last accessed August 18, 2015)

---

of S corporations. And, if you do later decide to bring in new owners, it's usually easier in the S corporation form."

ELI: "Why does any business use the 'C' form of corporation, and pay corporate income taxes?"

GENE: "The way the law works, the LLC and Subchapter S forms are generally not appropriate for big companies that have many shareholders. The law specifically won't allow the S status for companies with over 100 shareholders. While there is no specific numerical limit on shareholders in LLCs, there are other features that make it hard for them to have a large number of owners. For example, in some states, if an owner dies, the company is supposed to be dissolved. That is clearly not workable for a public company with thousands of shareholders! So, the bottom line is that the really big companies in the U.S. do pay corporate income taxes, and most other businesses are one kind of pass-through entity or another. If you look at the last thing I sent you on business taxes, Box 12.4, you'll see that C corporations only account for about 5% of the business tax returns the IRS receives, but these 5% of returns include about 70% of the total revenues."

REBECCA: "So, when we make it big, can we switch from being an S to being a C corporation?"

GENE: "Yes. No problem, except then your company will have to start paying corporate taxes on the income earned after you convert to being a C corporation. You'll need some tax advice at that time."

Employees or Contractors

GENE: "Have you guys thought about whether you plan to have employees, or use independent contractors?"

REBECCA: "We want to keep our fixed commitments to a minimum. I'd prefer not to have people on fixed salaries, since we'd have to pay them whether business was good or bad. So we'd prefer to hire people just as we need them. So, we'll treat everybody as independent contractors, and just pay them for the tasks they do, or the hours they work."

GENE: "I understand the idea, but the law is more complicated than that. Legally, it is not always clear whether someone is considered an independent contractor or an employee."

ELI: "Who cares? Why does it matter?"

GENE: "There are big differences in taxes and other legal considerations whether someone is legally an employee or a contractor. This is something that trips up a lot of businesses, which is why you should look at Table 12.2.

"If someone is an independent contractor, you don't have to pay them any employee benefits, and you don't have to pay the taxes that are required of employers. The main ones are social security and Medicare, which together amount to about 7.65% of income up to a limit, and state and federal unemployment taxes. Together, people often refer to the social security and Medicare taxes as FICA taxes.

"If they are an employee, you do have to pay these taxes.

"Also, if they are employees, you are responsible for deducting the income taxes and social security and Medicare taxes that the employees owe to the state and federal governments from their paychecks each period, and sending these taxes on to the governments. This is not a separate expense to you, but if you fail to do the withholding, there are large penalties.

Table 12.2 Treatment of Employees Versus Independent Contractors

	Employees	*Contractors*
Degree of control	Both objectives and methods	Only objectives—contractors choose their own methods
Self-employment taxes	N/a	Paid by the contractor. The 12.4% social security tax up to a limit ($118,500 in 2015), and the Medicare tax of 2.9% (which increases by 0.9% for earnings over $200,000).
Social security tax—paid by employee	6.2% social security (FICA) on wages up to a limit ($118,500 in 2015). 1.45% Medicare tax, increasing to 2.35% for wages over $200,000.	N/A
Social security tax—paid by employer	Same as for employee, except that the Medicare tax is limited to 1.45%.	N/A
Unemployment compensation—federal	6.0% of first $7,000 of wages per employee per year. However, employers can credit their state unemployment compensation payments against the federal tax. A minimum would be 0.6% federal tax.	N/A
Unemployment compensation—state	Varies. For New York State, in 2015, the rates ranged from 2.1% to 9.9%, depending on experience, on earnings up to around $10,500 in 2015.*	N/A
Employee benefits	The normal rules are that when benefits exist, they should be made available fairly. Benefits might include medical benefits, life insurance, pensions, and stock options. If a company is large enough, the Affordable Care Act requires it to either provide health insurance or to pay a special tax to the IRS.	N/A

* www.labor.ny.gov/ui/bpta/contribution-rates.shtm (last accessed August 18, 2015) and www.labor.ny.gov/ui/employerinfo/quarterly-reporting.shtm (last accessed August 18, 2015).

Box 12.5 IRS Guidance on Employee Versus Independent Contractor

"People such as doctors, dentists, veterinarians, lawyers, accountants, contractors, subcontractors, public stenographers, or auctioneers who are in an independent trade, business, or profession in which they offer their services to the general public are generally independent contractors. However, whether these people are independent contractors or employees depends on the facts in each case. The general rule is that an individual is an independent contractor if the payer has the right to control or direct only the result of the work and not what will be done and how it will be done. The earnings of a person who is working as an independent contractor are subject to Self-Employment Tax.

"If you are an independent contractor, you are self-employed. . . .

"You are not an independent contractor if you perform services that can be controlled by an employer (what will be done and how it will be done). This applies even if you are given freedom of action. What matters is that the employer has the legal right to control the details of how the services are performed.

"If an employer–employee relationship exists (regardless of what the relationship is called), you are not an independent contractor and your earnings are generally not subject to Self-Employment Tax.

"However, your earnings as an employee may be subject to FICA (Social Security tax and Medicare) and income tax withholding."*

Excerpts from "Independent Contractor (Self-Employed) or Employee?"**

Common Law Rules

Facts that provide evidence of the degree of control and independence fall into three categories:

1   Behavioral: Does the company control or have the right to control what the worker does and how the worker does his or her job?
2   Financial: Are the business aspects of the worker's job controlled by the payer? (These include things like how worker is paid, whether expenses are reimbursed, who provides tools/supplies, etc.)
3   Type of Relationship: Are there written contracts or employee type benefits (i.e. pension plan, insurance, vacation pay, etc.)? Will the relationship continue and is the work performed a key aspect of the business?

Businesses must weigh all these factors when determining whether a worker is an employee or independent contractor. Some factors may indicate that the worker is an employee, while other factors indicate that the worker is an independent contractor. There is no "magic" or set number of factors that "makes" the worker an employee or an independent contractor, and no one factor stands alone in making this determination. Also, factors which are relevant in one situation may not be relevant in another.

The keys are to look at the entire relationship, consider the degree or extent of the right to direct and control, and finally, to document each of the factors used in coming up with the determination.

*Source: www.irs.gov/Businesses/Small-Businesses-&-Self-Employed/Independent-Contractor-Defined (last accessed August 18, 2015).
**Source: www.irs.gov/Businesses/Small-Businesses-&-Self-Employed/Independent-Contractor-Self-Employed-or-Employee (last accessed August 18, 2015).

"What happens with a lot of businesses is that they try to save money by saying the people who work for them are independent contractors. If the people are later found to be employees, there can be big penalties—including the taxes that should have been paid and interest and penalties. And sometimes the people who were treated as contractors sue for the medical premiums or other benefits they felt they should have gotten."

REBECCA: "OK, so what's the legal rule?"

GENE: "You won't like my answer. It's not clear. The idea is that if someone is an employee, the boss has a lot of control, and can tell them how to do their job—when to come in, what tools to use, who to work with, and so on. With a contractor, as long as the thing they promised to do gets done, they set their own rules and ways of doing the job. I've given you some material from the IRS that lets you know what they look for. See Box 12.5. My advice—be careful! It is more expensive to treat people as employees, but it's safer for you."

ELI: "Is treating somebody as a contractor the same as what people mean when they say someone is paid 'off the books'"?

GENE: "No. The idea of someone being paid 'off the books' is that you are hiding the transaction from tax authorities. I strongly discourage my clients from doing this. It is illegal, and you are taking a significant risk. Also, your hope is to grow this business. That means you will be getting more attention later, from possible investors, and they will want to know that you are running the business cleanly and not taking legal risks.

"Whether you pay someone as a contractor or as an employee, the payments should be 'on the books.' You are required to report the payments to the IRS every year and send a copy of this information to the workers, so they can do their own tax returns. For employees, you will use a W-2 Form, and for contractors who you pay more than $600, you will use a Form 1099-MISC.

Taking Money Out of the Business

ELI: "We had one other question for you, Gene. How do Rebecca and I get money from our business, assuming it makes money?"

GENE: "I'm glad you're thinking positively, and assuming there will be money. . . . There are several ways owners of small businesses get money. You both plan to work for the business, so it is appropriate for you to be paid salaries. There could also be bonuses if the work is good or the business is doing well. The business should make employment agreements with you, and withhold taxes on your pay, just like any other employees. Of course, if you have legitimate business-related expenses, the business should cover those. Finally, the Board of Directors of your company can declare dividends as long as the dividends do not reduce the retained earnings below zero."

REBECCA: "Is there any reason we should favor one method of taking out money over another?"

GENE: "A lot depends on the situation. Money that comes out of the business to you as dividends will not be subject to social security and other payroll taxes. In fact, it won't be taxed at all. The income was already taxed when the company earned it, so there is no tax on Sub S or LLC or partnership distributions to partners. So, some owners of Sub S corporations used to like to pay themselves almost zero salaries, and take the earnings out as dividends. However, the law now says that if salaries to owners are not what the IRS considers 'reasonable,' then it will impose penalties and will charge payroll taxes on the dividends. So, be careful to pay yourselves some reasonable salaries.

"Also, I know you guys will want to make sure you split money fairly, to reflect not just the money you invested, but also the value of your time. Any dividends have to be paid in the same proportion as the share ownership. Right now, you plan to be equal owners, so the dividends have to be the same for both of you. But it could be that one of you ends up working much more on the business than the other. In that case, it would be fair for the person who works more to get more money. Dividends can't be set that way, but salaries certainly could be set any way you feel fairly reflects the value of the work done.

"If your company was a C corporation, there might be a temptation to take the money out as salaries and bonuses. That would help the owner-shareholders avoid double taxation. Their salary is a deduction at the corporate level, reducing the corporate income tax. So, a lot of small companies manage to keep corporate income taxes down by paying bonuses to reduce corporate income. Again, there is a risk. If the IRS believes the bonuses are disguised dividends, it can impose penalties.

"Finally, at some point you might sell your stock to somebody. Any profits would be taxed at capital gains tax rates, which are lower than regular individual tax rates.

"Good luck, and come back when you want more advice."

Getting Ready to Operate

This part of the company's story is told through journal entries that summarize activity. It may be helpful to review the discussion of debits and credits in Chapter 11 or Appendix A.

Initial Incorporation, Investment and Financing

Rebecca filed papers with New York State setting up the corporation. She paid the various filing fees herself, from her own bank account, since the company did not yet legally exist. She also filed a variety of other papers, for example registering the company for purposes of state sales tax. Once the state approved the corporate charter, she and Eli held an initial shareholders' meeting to authorize the issuance of shares to herself and Eli. They elected themselves the two members of the Board of Directors. They held an initial board meeting. She became CEO, and he became CFO. The Board also authorized the opening of a bank account. They felt a little bit silly going through these formalities, but their lawyer had told them it was important to observe the appropriate legal formalities, since legally the corporation was separate from the two of them.

Rebecca and Eli each found a way to come up with $25,000, and each bought 500 shares of $1 par value common stock on January 2, 2016. The certificate of incorporation of Rebeli Press, Inc. authorized the issuance of up to 1 million shares of common stock, which is far more than they need at the current time. The result of their purchase of stock is Journal Entry 1 ("JE 1"). The effect is to increase both assets and equity. Income is not affected.

The cash was deposited in a corporate bank account, with Rebecca and Eli as the authorized signers.

JE 1

Jan. 2, 2016	Dr. Cash	50,000	
	Cr. Common stock, $1 par		1,000
	Cr. Additional paid-in capital		49,000

To record sale of 1000 shares of $1 par for $50 each.

Rebecca now asked the company to reimburse her for the various filing fees involved in setting up the business. The company wrote a check from its bank account. The following entry reflects the reduction in cash and the recording of start-up expenses.

JE 2

Jan. 2	Dr. Start-up expenses	1,000	
	Cr. Cash		1,000

To reimburse Rebecca for start-up expenses and filing fees.

[Note—the original cash disbursement journal would include the check number and payee, as well as the ledger accounts being debited and credited.]

Rebeli Press's strategy, at least to start, is to avoid owning fixed assets, such as printing equipment or buildings or factories. It will pay other companies to actually print its books and magazines, and will rent office space and equipment.

Rebeli Press knows it will need more financing. However, it needs to be able to tell other lenders or investors a convincing story, and to show it has something worthwhile to market. The company next uses some of its cash to buy the rights to publish various books, including what it hopes will be its great hits, *The Amazing Adventures of Oscar and Lorimer* and *Beyond Frisbee: Golden Retrievers in Sports*. It makes arrangements with authors that give it the sole rights to publish certain works for 10 years. The authors will be entitled to royalty payments for each book sold. JE 3 shows that these transactions decrease cash and increase the intangible asset "publishing rights". Liabilities, equity, and income are not affected.

JE 3
Jan. 5   Dr. Publishing rights   30,000
*   Cr. Cash   30,000*
To record the rights to publish various books for 10 years

Note that over the course of 10 years, the publication rights will run out, so the company needs to record regular amortization expenses. The total $30,000 cost would be amortized on a straight-line basis over 10 years, which amounts to a rate of $250 per month. Rebeli Press must make monthly journal entries to record this expense. JE 4 is a summary of the effect of 12 such entries for the first year.

JE 4
12 months   Dr. Publishing rights amortization expense   3,000
*   Cr. Accumulated amortization, publishing rights   3,000*
Summary of 12 monthly amortization entries of publishing rights

Rebecca and Eli tell their family and friends about their business, and show them copies of the books they plan to issue. They succeed in borrowing a total of $100,000 from their family and friends. The business signed notes promising to repay the loans at December 31, 2018. Interest of 5% per year has to be paid monthly, including a full calendar month's interest in the first month.

One uncle asked if he could buy $50,000 in stock, instead of making loans. Rebecca and Eli decided they'd prefer to borrow the money. They did not want to share voting power and profits with another shareholder at this point, especially one who would own 50% of the total shares. They preferred borrowing. Lenders do not get to vote on corporate matters, and do not share in profits.

Note that if the business does poorly, the law requires that lenders be paid back before shareholders. Losses will be charged to equity before they affect the creditors. Therefore, while the family members are taking a risk, they are taking a somewhat smaller risk than Rebecca and Eli. The lenders are entitled to interest, whether or not the company is profitable, and if the business goes bankrupt, the lenders have preference over the shareholders in dividing up any remaining money. JE 5 shows how the transaction affects cash and liabilities. Equity and income are not affected. Over time an interest expense should be accrued, but there is no expense at the moment the loan is taken out.

JE 5
Jan 15, 2016   Dr. Cash   100,000
*   Cr. Loans payable in 2018   100,000*
To record borrowing money for a 3-year term at 5%

Over the course of the year, Rebeli Press will record monthly and pay monthly interest expense on this loan. For simplicity, we will assume that a full month's interest was due for January. The interest would be 5% of $100,000 for a full year, or $5,000. Monthly interest would be $416.66. JE 6 is a summary of the 12 months' interest entries.

JE 6

12 months	*Dr. Interest expense*	*5,000*	
	Cr. Cash		*5,000*

A summary effect of the 12 monthly interest payments of $416.66 each on the $100,000 loan

Operating and Selling

Office Staff and Officers

Rebeli Press hires a part-time employee, Sam, to do office work, including some bookkeeping, at a salary of $3,000 per month. Because the employee is part-time, Rebeli Press is not paying for any employee benefits. However, it still must pay for the employer's part of social security taxes, Medicare taxes, and federal and state unemployment insurance taxes. It also has to withhold some money from Sam's paychecks for the social security, Medicare, and state and federal income taxes that Sam is liable for. The amount to be withheld depends upon a number of factors.

Rebeli Press also agrees to pay Eli and Rebecca salaries of $10,000 each per year, and some medical insurance premiums. It chooses to use a separate ledger account to keep track of their pay as officers, and another to keep track of their benefits. These salaries are obviously low, but the company is unsure if it will make money, and both Rebecca and Eli are able to continue to do other, outside work to cover their living expenses.

On each payroll date, Rebeli Press has to do a lot of computations to get all this right. Then, they have to make sure that the company pays the correct net pay for the three people, and pays the various government entities the right amounts of employer taxes and withheld taxes from employees. Not surprisingly, many companies hire payroll services to do the computations and to send in the right payments to the tax authorities. Others have set up computerized systems to handle the detail computations. Rebecca and Eli decide that they don't want to be bothered with the details of payroll, so they make a contract with a payroll service. On each pay period, Rebeli Press sends the payroll service enough money to cover the employees' net pay, the various withheld taxes, and the employer taxes. It would make journal entries each pay period to record salaries and to record payroll taxes for Sam and for the officers.[5] JEs 7 and 8 summarize the entries for the whole year related to Sam and the officers' pay. The effect of these entries is to reduce assets, to reduce income, and to reduce owners' equity.

JE 7

Various dates	*Dr. General salary expense*	*36,000*	
	Dr. Payroll tax expense	*4,000*	
	Cr. Cash		*40,000*

Summary of entries over 12 months to record Sam's salary at $3,000 per month, plus various payroll taxes.

JE 8

Various dates	*Dr. Officers' salary expense*	*20,000*	
	Dr. Officers' benefits	*12,000*	
	Dr. Payroll tax expense	*2,000*	
	Cr. Cash		*34,000*

A summary of the pay and medical insurance benefits paid for officers during 2016.

Other Office and General Costs

Rebeli Press rents space in a shared office facility for $2,000 per month. The landlord also required a security deposit of $4,000 in advance, which Rebeli Press considers a noncurrent asset. It makes monthly payments during the year, which are summarized by JE 9. The entries reduce cash and income and equity.

JE 9

Various dates	*Dr. Office rent expense*	*24,000*	
	Dr. Security deposit	*4,000*	
	Cr. Cash		*28,000*

To record payment of rent 12 times per year at $2,000 each as well as a $4,000 security deposit

The company also buys an insurance policy, with a two-year term. The policy will protect the company against losses due to damage to its property, and also against liability claims if it hurts or damages someone. The insurance policy includes coverage to protect the company against claims that materials it publishes may be libelous. This is potentially important for a publisher.

The purchase of the insurance is treated as the purchase of a prepaid asset, and therefore JE 10 does not affect income. Insurance expense is recorded as the insurance is used up. Over the course of the year, the company makes monthly entries to reduce the prepaid insurance asset, and to record insurance expense. These monthly entries are summarized in JE 11.

JE 10

January 18	*Dr. Prepaid insurance*	*4,000*	
	Cr. Cash		*4,000*

To record purchase of a two-year insurance policy, effective January 1, 2016 and expiring Dec. 31, 2017.

JE 11

Various dates	*Dr. Insurance expense*	*2,000*	
	Cr. Prepaid insurance		*2,000*

The summary effect of 12 entries made monthly throughout the year that collectively reflect the using up of 1 year's prepaid insurance. Each month's entry would be for $166.66.

In keeping with the idea of keeping fixed costs low, Rebeli Press decides to lease the office equipment it needs for the first year, on a short-term basis of $500 per month. The leases do not qualify as capital leases. The monthly lease payments are summarized in JE 12.

JE 12

Various dates	*Dr. Equipment lease expense*	*6,000*	
	Cr. Cash		*6,000*

A summary of 12 monthly payments of $500 each under operating leases.

During the course of the year, Rebeli Press has a variety of other operating costs. JE 13 summarizes them. Rebecca and Eli decide it is not necessary to keep separate accounts for each of these items, so they use a single account called "other operating costs." For financial statement purposes, they will show these together with the start-up costs.

JE 13

Various dates	*Dr. Other Operating Expenses*	*9,000*	
	Cr. Cash		*9,000*

A summary entry for various minor costs incurred during the year.

Doing Business—Advertising, Printing and Selling

Rebeli's business plan involves two types of products. It will sell books to bookstores, and it will sell monthly magazines. In order to find customers, it has to incur marketing expenses. It is a small company, so it can't take out expensive TV or magazine ads, but it has promotional expenses in appearing at book fairs and sending out copies for reviewers in order to get noticed. It also spends some on social media to help get noticed. For accounting purposes, even if the marketing may have a positive impact for a long period of time, it has to be recorded as an expense at the time the marketing is done. JE 14 shows the effect of these costs on cash and income.

JE 14
Various dates   Dr. *Marketing expenses*   *8,000*
                          Cr. *Cash*   *8,000*

While Rebeli Press owns the rights to various books, it also has to spend some money in order to get the books ready for printing. The books need to be edited, and formatted properly. Some design costs need to be incurred. Rebeli hires outside independent contractors to do this editing, formatting and design work. It makes separate contracts with each of these contractors, and pays them by the assignment they complete. The contractors it works with do this kind of work for other publishers as well. Because these are independent contractors, there are no payroll taxes due for their work.

These types of costs are called prepublication costs. Accounting rules consider these costs of getting books ready for production to be assets, which can be amortized over the expected period in which the books will generate sales. Rebeli expects that its books will probably have the vast majority of their sales in the first two years, so it chooses to amortize these costs over two years, with a full year's amortization taken in the first year. JE 15 shows the effect of spending for these costs, at the time that Rebeli pays for them. JE 16 shows the impact of amortizing the costs over an estimated two-year life. Note that JE 15 does not affect income, but JE 16 does.

JE 15
At payment dates   Dr. *Prepublication costs—books*   *5,000*
                              Cr. *Cash*   *5,000*
To record payments for costs related to getting books ready to print, such as editing and design

JE 16
Monthly entries   Dr. *Book prepublication cost amortization*   *2,500*
                            Cr. *Accum. amortization—prepublication costs—books*   *2,500*
To amortize the costs over a two-year period.

In keeping with its strategy of minimizing its risks, Rebeli Press has chosen not to print books in advance, and hold them in inventory. Instead, it will send orders to other companies that will print and ship the books for it each time it receives an order. The advantages of this decision to do "printing on demand" are that Rebeli Press has to spend less cash up front on books, and it has less risk of being stuck with an inventory of books that don't sell. The principal disadvantage is that it incurs a higher cost per book printed. If it made larger orders, its suppliers would charge it a lower cost per copy.

Rebeli Press sells its books in traditional printed versions, to various bookstores. It allows the bookstores up to 60 days to pay, and it also allows the bookstores to return unsold books.[6]

In its first year, Rebeli Press sells 15,000 copies of *The Amazing Adventures of Oscar and Lorimer* and *Beyond Frisbee: Golden Retrievers in Sports* to bookstores for $18 each. JE 17 shows the summary effect of these sales, and JE 18 shows the related costs it incurs. For each book, the costs were approximately $5 for printing, $3 for shipping, and $2 for author royalties.

JE 17

Various dates	Dr. Accounts receivable	270,000	
	Cr. Book sales		270,000

To record various sales on account.

JE 18

Various dates	Dr. Cost of goods sold—printing	75,000	
	Dr. Cost of goods sold—shipping	45,000	
	Dr. Royalties expense	30,000	
	Cr. Accounts payable		120,000
	Cr. Royalties payable		30,000

Things are looking great! The sales of $270,000 are higher than the related costs of $150,000. However, there is an issue. The printers want to be paid immediately, but the bookstores are not required to pay their bills for 60 days. Rebeli could run short of cash. It therefore applies for a working capital line of credit from its bank. The bank is willing to give the business a $50,000 line of credit, with 8% interest payable monthly, based on the sales and costs it has. The bank also requires the company to give it a security interest in the accounts receivable as collateral.[7] Assuming that the interest cost in the first year was $4,000, JE 19 and JE 20 show the effects of the borrowing and the interest expense in the first year. The initial borrowing does not affect income. Interest expense is recorded over time, while the loan is outstanding.

JE 19

Date of borrowing	Dr. Cash	50,000	
	Cr. Bank line of credit		50,000

To record borrowing $50,000 under line of credit.

JE 20

Monthly	Dr. Interest expense	4,000	
	Cr. Cash		4,000

Summary for various interest payments on line of credit.

Over the course of the year, Rebeli Press received various payments totaling $212,000 from bookstores, and it paid its suppliers and the authors the amounts due to them. JE 21 and JE 22 show these cash transactions in summary form. Note that these do not affect income. Also, note that not all of the $240,000 in accounts receivable has been paid—$28,000 is still uncollected at the end of the year. Similarly, Rebeli Press has not paid all of its accounts payable and royalties payable. $15,000 of the original $120,000 in accounts payable is still a liability at year end, and so is $6,000 of the original royalties payable of $30,000.

JE 21

Various dates	Dr. Cash	212,000	
	Cr. Accounts receivable		212,000

Receipts of payments related to the $240,000 of book sales on account.

JE 22

Various dates	Dr. Accounts payable	105,000	
	Dr. Royalties payable	24,000	
	Cr. Cash		129,000

Payments of various amounts related to the $120,000 of accounts payable and $30,000 of royalties payable related to book sales.

At the end of the year, Eli looked over the accounts for the various customers who had not paid their bills in full. The remaining accounts receivable were $28,000 in total. Of this, Eli thought that it was probable that there would be $3,000 of sales returns from bookstores that had ordered too many copies, and another $1,000 of bad debts related to a bookseller that was facing bankruptcy. JE 23 records the related allowance for doubtful accounts and reserve for sales returns. Note that "sales returns" is an adjustment to a revenue account, not an expense. It is a contra revenue account. Typically, companies report their sales on their income statements "net" of sales returns. Both "allowance for sales returns" and "allowance for doubtful accounts" are contra asset accounts, which modify the amount of reported accounts receivable. When these allowances are material, companies are required to disclose the amounts.

JE 23

December 31	Dr. Bad debt expense	1,000	
	Dr. Sales returns	3,000	
	Cr. Allowance for sales returns		3,000
	Cr. Allowance for doubtful accounts		1,000

To record estimated allowances for returns and bad debts

Rebeli Press also started a magazine business, aimed at cat owners who dislike dogs. On July 1, it launched the *Puppy-Hater Monthly*, with an annual subscription price of $80. JE 24 summarizes the various marketing and prepublication costs that were incurred in preparing the magazines. Certain prepublication costs are considered to apply to the entire first 12 months of journals, and are amortized over 12 months, starting July 1. JE 25 shows the amortization of these costs. The marketing costs are considered expenses when incurred.

JE 24

June	Dr. Prepublication costs—magazine	11,000	
	Dr. Marketing expenses	20,000	
	Cr. Cash		31,000

To record various magazine-related costs

JE 25

July–Dec	Dr. Amortization prepublication costs—magazines	5,500	
	Cr. Prepublication costs—magazines		5,500

Summary of entries amortizing magazine prepublication costs over first six months of a one-year period starting July 1.

By July 1, Rebeli Press had received $240,000 in payment for 3,000 one-year subscriptions, at $80 each. At the time the subscriptions were received, Rebeli Press recorded unearned revenue— income was not affected at this date. See JE 26. Each month, as it shipped out magazines, it recorded revenue and reduced the unearned revenue account. See JE 27 for a summary entry.

JE 26

July 1	Dr. Cash	240,000	
	Cr. Unearned revenue		240,000

To reflect receipt of payment for 3,000 subscriptions at $80 each.

JE 27

July–Dec.	Dr. Unearned revenues	120,000	
	Cr. Magazine sales		120,000

To recognize subscription revenue earned July through December

To print and ship the magazines during the year, Rebeli Press incurred printing costs of $30,000 and shipping costs of $15,000, which it paid during the year. Rebeli Press decided that for this magazine, it would hire writers and artists as independent contractors on a contract basis, who were not entitled to royalties. JE 28 is a summary entry.

JE 28

July–Dec.	Dr. Cost of goods sold—printing	30,000	
	Dr. Cost of selling—shipping	15,000	
	Dr. Contract writing and editing costs	20,000	
	Cr. Cash		65,000

To record costs of writing, printing, and shipping magazines.

Analyzing the Results

A Year-End Decision

It is the end of December, and Rebecca and Eli are looking over the books.

Eli uses the bookkeeping software to print out an income statement (Table 12.3). It shows that their business had accounting profits of $7,000 for the first year.

They decide to declare a dividend of the entire income of $7,000, and write checks of $3,500 to each other. Eli records JE 29, below.[8] They wish each other a happy new year and they go off to celebrate New Year's Eve and the survival of their business for the first year.

JE 29

December 31	Dr. Dividends	7,000	
	Cr. Cash		7,000

To record dividends of $3,500 each to the two owners.

Table 12.3 Income Statement for the Year Ended December 31, 2016

Net sales:	
Books (net of returns)	$267,000
Magazines	120,000
Total revenues	387,000
Direct publication and selling expenses:	
Printing	105,000
Shipping	60,000
Royalties	30,000
Marketing	28,000
Contractor editing and writing expenses	20,000
Amortization of prepublication costs and publishing rights	11,000
Total direct publication expenses	254,000
Gross margin from publications	133,000
Other operating expenses	
Administrative staff payroll and related payroll taxes	40,000
Officer salaries and benefits	34,000
Rent	24,000
Equipment lease	6,000
Insurance	2,000
Bad debt expense	1,000
Other operating and start-up costs	10,000
Total operating expenses	117,000
Net operating income	16,000
Interest expense	9,000
Net income	$7,000

Reading the Basic Financial Statements

Early in January, they prepare several other reports. Table 12.4 is a statement of changes in owner's equity. Table 12.5 is a year-end balance sheet. Table 12.6 is a cash flow statement, prepared using the direct method of reporting operating cash flows. Table 12.7 reconciles operating cash flows with net income.

The income statement shows a total of $387,000 in net revenues on the accrual basis. The $267,000 from book sales equals $270,000 of sales on account, minus estimated sales returns of $3,000. The $120,000 of magazine sales equals the part of the $240,000 of subscriptions received which the company earned by sending out magazines during 2016.

Rebeli Press had $254,000 of direct publication and selling expenses, on the accrual basis. The printing and shipping expenses are the largest, and they are recognized as the company prints and ships books. Royalties are also recognized as the books are shipped. So these three types of costs are directly variable with sales. The other three types of publication and selling expenses (marketing, contractor editing and writing, and amortization of intangible assets) are less closely linked to the volume of books sold.

The gross margin from publications was $133,000, or 34.4% of net revenues. From this $133,000 of gross margin, Rebeli Press deducted $117,000 of operating expenses, to arrive at net operating income of $16,000. Rebeli Press incurred a total of $9,000 in interest expense on its two loans, leaving net income of $7,000. The net income was 1.8% of net revenues.

Table 12.4 Statement of Owners' Equity, for the Year Ending December 31, 2016

	Common stock at par	Additional paid-in capital	Retained earnings	Total equity
Beginning of year	$0	$0	$0	$0
Initial sale of stock	1,000	49,000		50,000
Net income			7,000	7,000
Dividends paid			(7,000)	(7,000)
End of year	$1,000	$49,000	$0	$450,000

Table 12.5 Balance Sheet for the Year Ended December 31, 2016

Current assets		**Current liabilities**	
Cash	$246,000	Accounts payable	15,000
Accounts receivable, net	54,000	Royalties payable	6,000
Prepaid insurance	2,000	Unearned revenues	120,000
Prepublication costs, net	8,000	Bank demand loan payable	50,000
Total current assets	310,000	**Total current liabilities**	191,000
Other assets		**Other liabilities**	
Publishing rights, net	27,000	Term loan payable in 2018	100,000
Security deposits	4,000	Total liabilities	291,000
		Stockholders' equity	
		Common stock at $1 par	1,000
		Additional paid-in capital	49,000
		Retained earnings	0
		Total stockholders' equity	50,000
Total assets	$341,000	**Total liabilities and equity**	$341,000

Table 12.6 Statement of Cash Flows for the Year Ended December 31, 2016

Operating cash flows:	
Cash received for magazine subscriptions	$240,000
Cash received for books sold	212,000
Payments made for printing and shipping	(214,000)
Royalties paid	(24,000)
Salaries, payroll taxes, and benefits paid	(74,000)
Rent and office security deposit payments	(28,000)
Equipment lease payments	(6,000)
Payments for insurance	(4,000)
Interest payments	(9,000)
Payments for other operating costs	(10,000)
Net operating cash flows	83,000
Investing cash flows:	
Purchase of book rights	(30,000)
Financing cash flows:	
Sale of stock	50,000
Borrowing under term loan	100,000
Borrowing under line of credit	50,000
Cash dividends paid	(7,000)
Net financing cash flows	193,000
Net increase in cash	246,000
Cash, beginning of year	0
Cash, end of year	$246,000

Table 12.7 Reconciliation of Net Income to Operating Cash Flows For the Year Ended December 31, 2016

Net income	$7,000
Non-cash items in net income:	
Amortization of publication rights	3,000
Changes in various assets and liabilities:	
Minus: increase in accounts receivable	(54,000)
Minus: Increase in prepaid insurance	(2,000)
Minus: Increase in prepublication costs	(8,000)
Minus: Increase in security deposit	(4,000)
Plus: Increase in accounts payable	15,000
Plus: Increase in unearned income	120,000
Plus: Increase in royalties payable	6,000
Net operating cash flows	$83,000

No income tax is shown here. As a Subchapter S Corporation, Rebeli Press owes no federal corporate income tax. As a New York company, Rebeli would owe state corporate income tax. For purposes of this example, due to the low income and the relatively low rate of state income tax, we assume the tax rounds to zero.

Table 12.4 is a statement of owners' equity for the year. It is fairly simple. The business started with zero balances in equity. Rebecca and Eli invested a total of $50,000 in the business. It earned $7,000 in net income, and they withdrew $7,000 in dividends, so the ending shareholders' equity is $50,000.

The return on common shareholders' equity = 7000 ÷ (50,000 average equity) = 14%.

Table 12.5 is a balance sheet at the end of the first year. The largest single asset is the $246,000 in cash. The accounts receivable are $55,000 minus a $1,000 allowance for doubtful accounts, leaving a net balance of $54,000. There is $2,000 of prepaid insurance, comprised of the original $4,000 policy minus the $2,000 of coverage used up during 2016. The prepublication costs, net of amortization, are presumed to only apply to items sold in 2016 and 2017. Therefore, at the end of 2016, they are shown as a current asset, since their value will be used up within a year. In contrast, the publishing rights had an original 10-year life, and they are shown as noncurrent assets.

The company has several kinds of liabilities. Its largest liability is the unearned revenues related to magazine subscriptions. It received $240,000 in one-year subscriptions in July 2016, so at December 31, 2016, it has an obligation to produce and mail six more months of magazines. The accounts payable and royalties payable represent amounts due, and not yet paid, to printers and authors related to books sold in 2016.

The other liabilities are the two loans. Because the bank can demand repayment of its loan at any time, it is a current liability. The other loans are not due until 2018, so they are noncurrent liabilities.

There are $310,000 of current assets, which is more than the $191,000 of current liabilities. As a result, Rebeli Press has "working capital" of $119,000, and a "current ratio" (current assets divided by current liabilities) of 1.62.

The ending equity is $50,000.
Total assets are $341,000.
The ratio of liabilities to equity is 291,000 to 50,000, or 5.82.

If we assume that the company started the year with assets equal to $150,000 (the $50,000 of contributions by the owners plus the $100,000 initial loan), then average total assets for the year equal (150,000 + 341,000) ÷ 2, or $245,500.

The asset turnover equals total revenues ÷ average total assets, or $387,000 ÷ 245,500, which equals 1.58.
The return on assets (ROA) for the year = (net income + interest expense) ÷ average total assets
$$= (7,000 + 9,000) \div 245,500 = 6.52\%$$

Notice that the ROA of 6.52% is much less than the return on common equity of 14% computed above. This occurs even though, for the purposes of computing ROA, we added back the interest expense to the net income, but for the computation of return on equity we simply used net income. The higher return on common equity is due to the presence of capital structure leverage. Capital structure leverage = average total assets ÷ average common equity. In this case, it equals 245,500 ÷ 50,000, or 4.91.

Table 12.6 is a cash flow statement, prepared using the direct method. Over the course of the year, cash increased from zero to $246,000. Rebeli Press generated $83,000 in cash flow from operations. It invested $30,000 in long-term intangible assets, the rights to publish books. It got most of its cash through financing activities. It borrowed $150,000, and it issued shares for $50,000. It paid $7,000 in dividends, which reduce the net cash flows from financing activities. Under U.S. rules, the interest payments on the debt reduce operating cash flows.[9]

The operating section of the cash flow statement shows the major types of cash movements.

Cash inflows related to cash actually received for the sales of books and magazines. Note that these figures are different from accrual-basis sales figures. For the magazines, when customers pay for a subscription, the cash they pay counts immediately as an operating cash inflow, but the company does not recognize revenues until it ships magazines. As a result, you can see that the cash flow statement shows $240,000 of cash inflows from magazines, while the income statement shows accrual-basis revenues of $120,000.

Similarly, the operating cash outflows shown reflect actual cash movements, and are not on the accrual basis. For example, the payments for insurance of $4,000 in the cash flow statement represent the full payment for the two-year insurance premium, while the accrual-basis insurance expense in the income statement of $2,000 represents the part of the insurance premium that applied to 2016.

Table 12.7 is a reconciliation of net income to operating cash flows. If companies report cash flows using the direct method, this is a required statement. It shows the major reasons why the operating cash flows of $83,000 are so much higher than the net income of $7,000. The biggest two differences relate to the magazine subscriptions and the sales of books on account. Rebeli received $240,000 of subscription payments, all of which are counted as part of operating cash flows, but only $120,000 of which were treated as earned for purposes of computing net income. The difference, of $120,000, is an increase in unearned income. When books were sold on account, Rebeli Press reflected the sales as part of net income, even if some of the money was not yet collected by year end. In contrast, the cash flow statement would only include cash actually received. Therefore, the increase in accounts receivable is a reconciling item—it is caused by sales made for which cash has not been received by year end.

Further Analysis

Rebecca and Eli thought about the financial statements, and made several observations.

1   The returns from the business to them were larger than the $7,000 in dividends. In addition, they had received the value of $34,000 in salaries and medical insurance. This total of $41,000 was still not a lot for two people to live on. On the other hand, it is a high percentage return on a $50,000 investment. However, that might be an overly optimistic way to look at their business, since the $50,000 was simply the cash they invested, and gave no value to the time they invested.
2   Their business is more leveraged than they had expected. The ratio of liabilities to equity is 5.82. If this continues, they may have difficulty borrowing.
3   When they first set up the company, an uncle had wanted to buy $50,000 in stock, rather than loan them $50,000. Rebecca and Eli insisted on borrowing, and now have mixed feelings about their decision to borrow from him. This decision increased the financial leverage of their company. If the uncle had made a $50,000 stock purchase, rather than a loan, then equity would be $100,000 and liabilities would be $241,000, so the ratio of liabilities to equity would be much lower, 2.41 rather than 5.82. Income would have been $2,500 higher, or $9,500, since there would have been less interest expense. On the other side, the uncle would have bought 50% of the stock, so Rebecca and Eli would no longer have had control. Also, in 2016 the increase in leverage helped them. Their share of the net income for the year, if the uncle bought stock, would have been their half of total income (with the lower interest expense) of $9,500, or $4,750. That is less than the $7,000 of income they had from the company when they were the only shareholders.
4   They are surprised that the total asset turnover is only 1.58. They had expected it to be higher, since they were trying to avoid owning fixed assets and inventory. They realized that the two largest assets were cash and accounts receivable, and that a key to improved asset turnover would be managing these two assets.
5   They can probably repay the working capital loan from the bank, as long as their magazine business is good. The magazine subscriptions provide them cash in advance of their needs. Repaying the loan would both help the total asset turnover and make the company look less leveraged. They will also save on interest expenses. However, they will keep the agreement with the bank giving them a line of credit, so they can borrow when they need money.
6   They also realized that they missed the opportunity to invest their cash and earn interest income.

Budgeting for Year 2

Rebecca and Eli decide to try to set a budget for the new year, before things get busy. They know that things are likely to change over the course of the year, because their business is so new, but they make the following assumptions:

1 Their book business will grow by 100%. They assume they will find new books for this year that will have the same level of sales that the previous books had, and that the books they introduced in 2016 will have sales in the current year equal to the first year's level. They will again incur marketing costs of $8,000 and will again spend $30,000 to buy rights to new books. They will continue to amortize publishing rights over 10 years. The bad debts and sales returns will be the same percentages of book sales as they were in 2016.
2 The magazine business will have the same number of subscribers, and the same pricing. However, since it will exist for a full year, rather than the six months in 2016, the revenues and variable expenses on an accrual basis will be double the figures for 2016.
3 Printing, shipping and royalty costs per book and magazine will be the same.
4 They will pay $4,000 less in interest, since they will not use the line of credit from the bank, and will actually earn $1,000 in interest.
5 They assume that various costs will not increase even though their volume of book sales rises. Such costs include: rent, officer salaries and benefits, Sam's salary and payroll taxes, insurance, equipment leases, and other operating expenses. Also, they will not have the $1,000 in start-up expenses again in 2017.

They use these assumptions, and produce the budget draft shown in Table 12.8.

The results are startling. These assumptions produce a budgeted income of $160,000, as compared to $7,000 in 2016. Their assumptions that sales would double led to more than a 22-fold increase in income. This business will actually pay them a nice amount, between the $160,000 in profits and their $34,000 in salaries and benefits.

How could profits increase so much more than sales? The answer is from the ideas of cost–volume–profit analysis we saw in Chapter 5, as well as the ideas of operating and financial leverage. In 2016, the gross margin from the publications of $133,000 was not that much more than the operating expenses of $117,000. In other words, the company was just above the break-even point. In 2017, the assumed levels of sales bring the company far above its break-even point, and, if the operating costs do not increase with sales, then profits increase rapidly. The company was also operating with a relatively small amount of its financing from the owners' equity. It had large financial leverage through the unearned revenues and the term loan. When operating profits increase, and a company has high financial leverage, then net income will increase much faster in percentage terms than operating income.

Thinking About Expansion

Looking at the draft budget, Rebecca and Eli realize that if they can increase the scale of their business even more, they could make even more money. But increasing the scale of the business might mean investing more money in new book titles, incurring large marketing costs, and perhaps even investing in their own printing production facilities. This will take cash—lots of cash. They go back to see Gene, for more advice.

GENE: "I'm glad to hear things have been going so well! I emailed you a summary of the ways that businesses come up with cash for expansion. It's Table 12.9. Did you get a chance to look at it?"

Table 12.8 2016 Budget—First Draft All figures in thousands

	Books	Magazines	General	Total	Comments
Sales	<u>534</u>	<u>240</u>		<u>774</u>	Double book sales and sales returns. Magazine revenue for full year
Printing	150	60		210	These vary directly with sales.
Shipping	90	30		120	
Royalties	60	N/A		60	
Contractor editing and writing		40		40	
Prepublication costs	10	11		21	
Bad debts	2			2	
Publishing rights amortization	6			6	Reflects the additional titles published
Marketing	<u>16</u>	<u>20</u>		<u>36</u>	Book marketing doubles, since there are twice as many titles. Magazine is steady.
Total costs directly related to publishing and selling	<u>334</u>	<u>161</u>	=	<u>495</u>	
Contribution from publishing	<u>200</u>	<u>79</u>	=	<u>279</u>	
Other costs and expenses					
Administrative payroll-related			40	40	These are all assumed to not increase with volume.
Officers' compensation			34	34	
Rent			24	24	
Equipment lease			6	6	
Insurance			2	2	
Other operating costs			9	9	
Total operating expenses	=	=	<u>115</u>	<u>115</u>	
Net operating income	<u>200</u>	<u>79</u>	(115)	164	
Interest expense	–	–	(5)	(5)	Assumes only one loan.
Interest income	=	=	<u>1</u>	<u>1</u>	Assumes minor earnings.
Net income	<u>200</u>	<u>79</u>	<u>(119)</u>	<u>160</u>	

REBECCA: "Yes, we looked at. But it's very summarized and seems general. Please help us understand what would be best for our business."

GENE: "OK. When businesses are trying to come up with money for expansions, there are four main ways they do it. The first is to use money that is generated by their own operations. If the operations are generating enough money, this is usually the preferred method. In 2016, you could have chosen to leave the profits of $7,000 in the business, instead of declaring a dividend. In 2017, if your business is profitable, you can leave some in the business. Also, you have managed to set up your magazine business in a way that gets you cash from customers before you have to pay all the related printing and shipping costs. That was helpful. So, by earning positive profits and by getting customers to prepay for magazines, your business is generating operating cash. The great thing about this is you are getting cash without paying anybody interest, and without sharing control of your company with anybody.

ELI: "That's all true, but the cash won't be enough for the expansion we're considering."

GENE: "That's often the case. A second source of cash that companies can use is to sell off some investments. Again, the benefit is that there are no interest costs, and you are not sharing control of your company."

Table 12.9 Ways of Getting Cash for Expansion

Operating the business	Save income from operations—generate retained earnings. Business model that receives cash from customers before payments to vendors are due.
Investing activities	Generate investment income. Sell existing investments.
Borrowing	Bank lines of credit—often at variable rates. Commercial paper—these are tradable, very short-term notes payable. Repurchase agreements—typically, a company sells a security and promises to repurchase it, in a short term, for more money. Promissory notes—These may be payable in a single payment or in installments. Bonds—These are tradable notes, which specify a payment date and a regular fixed dollar interest payment. There are several important varieties of bonds: <ul><li>"Secured" or "mortgage" bonds are those where a company has set aside particular assets as collateral for the bonds.</li><li>"Convertible" bonds allow the owner of the bond to convert the bond into a set number of shares of common stock.</li><li>"Callable" bonds can be bought back by the company that issued them at a set price.</li></ul>
Leasing	Leases can be seen as equivalent to secured installment promissory notes, with the leased property as the collateral.
Equity financing	Common stock. Preferred stock—There are several important varieties of preferred stock: <ul><li>"Voting" versus "nonvoting" – The voting rights of preferred stock can vary from none to being equivalent to common shareholders to having more voting power than common shareholders.</li><li>"Convertible" preferred shares give the shareholders the option of converting the preferred stock into a set number of common shares.</li><li>"Cumulative" versus "noncumulative" – The difference occurs if a company decides not to pay dividends in a year. In later years, "cumulative" preferred shares are entitled to catch up on the missed dividends, but noncumulative shares are not.</li></ul> Stock options—These give their holders the right to buy a set number of shares at a particular price, for a particular period of time.

REBECCA: "Gene, our company doesn't have investments. We have nothing to sell."

GENE: "Then the two main alternatives are debt and equity financing.

"Debt financing means borrowing, one way or another. When you borrow, you will have to pay interest, and you will have to repay the loans when they come due. If you do not make the payments, your business will be in default, and the lenders can push your company into bankruptcy. That is one major risk with debt financing.

"A second issue that arises is that the lenders will try to put conditions on their loans. These are called 'loan covenants.' They may want you to personally guarantee the loans, or they may say you can't pay dividends unless your profits are over a certain level. So, when you borrow, you may have to accept conditions you don't like.

"A good thing about debt financing is that the interest on loans is tax deductible.

"Something that may be good or bad is that when you borrow, your business has more financial leverage."

ELI: "Explain financial leverage again, please."

GENE: "Sure. The basic idea is that the interest cost is fixed, and does not depend on sales. If times are good, and your business is earning more on its assets than the interest rate on the loan (after the tax deductions), then it helps you to borrow and buy more assets. If your business is not doing so well, and your assets are not earning a return greater than the after-tax interest rates, then financial leverage can hurt you."

REBECCA: "You sent us material that shows several different ways to borrow. What are the advantages and disadvantages?"

GENE: "In your current situation, of being a new and small business, you will probably only be able to deal with banks or similar financial institutions. The choices you will have will basically be between short-term borrowings under lines of credit and longer term loans. The advantage of the lines of credit is that they are flexible. You only borrow as you need money, and you can repay it when you have cash on hand. The advantage of the longer term loans is that you can be sure of a particular interest rate for a longer period of time, and also you don't have to worry about a bank suddenly asking for its money back.

"You may also be able to get some equipment using leases. A lease can act just like borrowing under an installment loan. You will need to make monthly payments, and if you default the leasing company will take back its equipment."

ELI: "What are these other items—commercial paper, and bonds?"

GENE: "These are probably not something that a small business will be able to use. Bigger companies use these two methods of raising money. Companies use bonds when they want to borrow money, but not all from the same person. Instead of making one big debt agreement, they sell a lot of bonds. Each bond, on its face, specifies a certain amount of money that the company will pay, at some future date. The company will also pay interest of a fixed dollar amount periodically, usually twice per year. Anyone who buys these bonds can sell them to other people. They are tradable. This makes them attractive. Someone who buys a 20-year U.S. Treasury bond does not necessarily want to wait 20 years to be repaid, so they are happy that they can sell their bonds to brokers or other people any time they want. Commercial paper is similar, but usually has a very short-term maturity, from one day to maybe a couple of weeks."

ELI: "Why can't we use these methods?"

GENE: "Well, to have publicly traded bonds, you'd have to register with the SEC, which is time-consuming and expensive. And people usually only want to buy commercial paper from big, well-known companies with good credit ratings."

ELI: "Just out of curiosity, why did you list various types of bonds?"

GENE: "The point is that people who want to borrow by selling bonds want the best deal they can get, and the people who are willing to lend, by buying the bonds, also want the best deal they can get. The features of the bonds represent a compromise. Borrowers want to pay low interest, and lenders want high interest. Borrowers want to be able to call the bonds back if interest rates move in their favor, while lenders are happier if the bonds cannot be called back. Lenders would like collateral, and borrowers usually don't want to give collateral."

REBECCA: "What are our choices on equity financing?"

GENE: "The simplest thing to do is to issue more common stock. If you two have more money, invest more of your own money. That will make the company's leverage ratios look better, and you will keep control.

"If you sell common stock to anyone else, there are pluses and minuses. The plus is that the company will be less leveraged, and less risky. Shareholders are not guaranteed any particular dividends, so shareholders who are disappointed in the company's earnings will not result in the company going bankrupt. That's different from lenders who don't get their interest payments. The minus is that these shareholders have the same rights per share as you do. They get to vote for the Board of Directors, and if you sell a lot of stock, you will no longer have majority ownership."

ELI: "What about preferred stock? You listed several kinds of preferred stock."

GENE: "Preferred stock is stock that has some special right that common stock does not have. The most typical kind of preferred stock has preferential rights to dividends, and to any money left when the company goes out of business. The Board of Directors never has to declare a dividend, but if it does declare dividends, typically each share of preferred is entitled to some set payment, such as 4% of a par value of $100, before dividends get paid to common shares. Also, if the company goes out of business, preferred gets paid first.

"Note that preferred shareholders have an intermediate level of rights between common shareholders and bondholders. Preferred shareholders are entitled to dividends before common shareholders, but, unlike bondholders, they can't put your company into bankruptcy if there are no dividends.

"Dividends are not tax-deductible.

"In some companies, preferred stock may have no voting rights. In other companies, it can have special, extra voting rights. This is one way that founders of companies try to keep control even as they sell stock to other people.

"I listed various types of preferred stock. Just like the situation with bonds, the preferred shareholders want the best deal they can get, and may ask for a variety of extra features. The common shareholders would not want to give these features. The actual terms of the preferred stock depends on bargaining."

REBECCA: "So, if our company has both preferred and common stock, we might be able to bring in more shareholders while keeping voting control?"

GENE: "Yes, that's correct. But there is a complication. You set up your company as Subchapter S. The rules are there can only be one class of stock for Sub S companies, so your company would become a C corporation, subject to federal income taxes."

ELI: "You've given us a lot to consider. I see you also listed stock options in your table. Explain this."

GENE: "A stock option gives somebody the right to buy a specified number of shares of stock, at a specific price, for some set period of time. Start-up companies have used options as a way of attracting talented employees. Your company will not pay cash. Instead, if the company succeeds, and the stock becomes worth a lot, the employees will "exercise" their options and buy stock cheaply. If you do give employees these options, you will want to see an accountant to help you compute how to record the related compensation expense."

REBECCA: "Thanks. I see there a lot of ways companies raise money. We'll figure out what works best for us."

Relating the Case to Earlier Chapters

This is a simple company, but the accounting is affected by several of the issues that were discussed in Chapters 6 through 11. It also uses the financial and managerial accounting tools discussed in Chapters 4 and 5.

Chapter 4 introduced a variety of financial analysis measures, including leverage measures. Rebecca and Eli use these measures at the end of 2016.

Chapter 5 introduced the basics of cost–volume–profit analysis and budgeting. The budget for 2017 builds on these ideas, and shows how profits can increase quickly after a break-even point.

Chapter 6 indicated that, whenever people are measured, there are temptations and pressures for people to act in a way that makes the measurements look favorable. In this situation, Rebecca and Eli are both the managers and the owners. There are still several situations where the way they categorize events can be affected by how they think that others will react to the reports.

- It was not always clear whether they should treat people who do particular work as employees or as independent contractors. To save on payroll taxes, there is a temptation to classify people as independent contractors.

- At the end of the year, when they realized the company had profits of $7,000, they chose to pay themselves a dividend. They could, instead, have declared bonuses. The money they receive is the same, but the accounting is different. If they had declared bonuses, there would have been zero remaining profits. An outsider looking at the income statement would, perhaps, view the company less favorably. Also, bonuses would have been subject to payroll taxes, but dividends are not subject to these taxes.
- Several estimates affected net income. If Rebeli Press was trying to get bank loans, or new investors, it might be tempted to skew these estimates towards higher income. If it were trying to save on taxes, it would be tempted to skew the estimates towards lower income. Estimates affect the recording of sales returns, bad debt expense, and amortization of prepublication costs and publishing rights.

Chapter 7 dealt with values. In this case, some issues in valuation deal with the intangible assets. Rebeli Press recorded the publication rights at what it paid for them, minus accumulated amortization. If the books turn out to be major hits, these assets will have economic values higher than the company's balance sheet indicates. Also, GAAP does not allow companies to show values for internally developed intangible assets. Its 2016 marketing efforts and its successful magazine launch may have created favorable goodwill and brand awareness, but these do not appear on the balance sheet. Also, Rebecca and Eli are now smarter business people than they were when the year began, but their increased skill level is not an asset for accounting purposes.

Another issue relates to Rebecca and Eli's compensation. This year, the business basically paid them what it could afford to pay them. The value of their services might have been very different. The company did not attempt to see what it would have had to pay on the market to get similar quality management services. Therefore, we don't know if the company's income statement is showing too high, or too low, a figure for officer's pay on an economic basis.

When valuation experts look at private companies, they often try to "normalize" officers' compensation and benefits. Their goal is to measure the company's earnings power as if the company was paying non-shareholders a fair compensation value to perform the same work (Fishman et al. 2015). This can be difficult, and has sometimes been disputed in court cases. One court, in trying to find a formula to separate dividends from compensation, wrote that "A formula should reasonably compensate for the work done, the performance achieved, and the experience and dedication of the employee, while at the same time allowing investors a satisfactory return on equity. . ."[10]

Chapter 8 deals with uncertainty. From a business point of view, Rebecca and Eli have been dealing with uncertainty from the start. It affected their choice of the form of their business, and their decisions to avoid fixed assets and inventory, and to rely on print-on-demand publishing methods. It led them to buy liability insurance. Uncertainty also affected the parties they dealt with. Their relatives chose to take somewhat less risk by making loans rather than the greater risk of buying stock. The bookstores who purchased books had the right to return the books if they can't be sold. Their landlord required a security deposit, in case they defaulted on their lease. Their bank charged an interest rate reflective of its risk, and obtained a security interest in the accounts receivable which would help the bank if Rebeli Press defaulted on its loan.

The particular accounts of Rebeli Press that are affected by uncertainty include:

- The allowance for sales returns. Sales returns have to be estimated.
- The allowance for doubtful accounts. Bad debt expense must be estimated.
- Prepublication costs. The appropriate amortization period must be estimated.
- Publication rights. The appropriate amortization period is the lesser of the expected period in which the books will sell, or the period set forth in the contract with the authors of 10 years.
- Contingent liabilities. In this case, Rebeli Press does not believe there are any contingent liabilities that meet the criteria of being "probable" and "reasonably estimable." However,

there is the chance that the tax authorities will decide that certain people who have been treated as independent contractors are really employees. Also, it is possible that something they published will have exposed the company to lawsuits. For example, something might have been libelous, or might have infringed someone else's copyrights.

Chapter 9 dealt with allocations in financial accounting. Here the prepaid insurance, the magazine subscriptions, the prepublication costs and the publishing rights needed to be allocated across time periods.

Chapter 10 dealt with allocations of cost in managerial accounting. Because Rebeli Press was not doing its own printing, at first glance the material in Chapter 10 was not relevant to it this year. However, while Rebeli Press does not have manufacturing overhead, there is a case to be made that the books and magazines could not have been produced without efforts by Rebecca and Eli, and their efforts would likely not have been productive if there was no office and no office equipment. So, if we wanted to judge the true cost of producing magazines, and the true cost of producing books, we would need to allocate some of the operating costs to each product. One way to make such allocations would be based on the owners' time spent, but that would require Rebecca and Eli to spend time on tracking their activities. Better accounting would take more effort. . . The cost-benefit relation is not clear in this case.

Chapter 11 dealt with internal controls, including double-entry bookkeeping. This chapter has used journal entries throughout, to help familiarize you with this basic accounting tool. Internal controls tend to be less important in very small businesses, where the owner directly supervises matters, than in larger companies. However, even in this simple example, there is a need for controls. The officers need controls to be comfortable that Sam the bookkeeper is doing his job competently and honestly. They also need to be sure that other business matters are being handled in accordance with the company policy. Here are some examples of applicable controls:

- Rebeli Press has told the bank that Rebecca and Eli are the only authorized check signers. This provides some protection if Sam were to write unauthorized checks.
- Rebecca keeps the unused checks in a locked cabinet, which Sam does not have a key to.
- Rebecca and Eli open the mail, and handle all correspondence with the bookstores who are customers. This would make it difficult for Sam to steal incoming customer checks and conceal these thefts.
- While Sam keeps the company's books, Eli reconciles the cash receipts and disbursements records to the bank statements every month. This will help uncover errors or irregularities in the company records.
- The company uses an outside payroll service to compute pay each pay period, and to make the applicable withholding payments to the government. The outside company is expert, and therefore the chance of inadvertent errors is reduced.
- Eli reviews the reports from the payroll service periodically, to ensure that only authorized payments are being made.
- Sam has a listing of activity that should happen on a regular basis, such as payments of interest and rent. This will help avoid inadvertently failing to pay important bills.
- Eli and Rebecca review monthly income statements and bank activity for unusual or unexpected items.
- While Sam can handle routine customer orders, Rebecca must approve credit terms for all new bookstore customers.
- The company prints and sends monthly accounts receivable statements to its bookstore customers.

Together, these controls help reduce the risk of errors or irregularities.

Hopefully, the point you will take away from this case is that accounting is helpful and necessary for owners to measure and understand the results of a business. However, measurement is complicated, and the accounting model is imperfect. Even for a simple business, interpreting financial reports requires an understanding of the measurement issues.

Key Terms

Bonds—A form of borrowing in which the borrower sells (or "issues") certain contractual promises in return for cash. The key promises are to pay a certain "face amount" when the bonds "mature," and to pay periodic set amounts as interest. Bonds are usually sold in standardized amounts, such as $1,000, and are tradable.

C corporation—A corporation that is subject to Federal corporate income tax.

General partner—A partner in a partnership whose rights to manage the company, and to share in profits and losses, are not limited. Unless a partnership agreement specifically defines categories of limited partners, with limited liability and limited shares of profits and losses, all partners are considered general partners.

Independent contractor—some person or business that does work for a company, but is not subject to as much detail control as the company would have over its own employees.

Limited liability—This term applies to the shareholders of corporations. In general, if a corporation has insufficient assets to pay its debts, the shareholders have no obligation to contribute any extra money to make up the shortfall. The most the shareholders can lose is the amount they have already invested in the company.

LLC—A limited liability corporation is one organized under applicable state law that enjoys the major advantages of a corporation, but is treated as a pass-through entity for tax purposes. The owners of LLCs enjoy limited liability for the debts of the business.

Limited partner/limited partnership—Some partnerships are organized in a way that separates partners into two classes: general partners and limited partners. General partners have rights to manage the business, and have unlimited liability for partnership obligations. Limited partners typically have little or no ability to manage the business. Their share of income is often different from that of general partners. They also have limited liability for the obligations of the partnership.

Pass-through entity—This term applies to various forms of business organizations. Federal taxes are *not* charged to the businesses. Instead, their income or losses is considered to "pass through" them, and is considered to have been received by their owners.

Preferred stock—Stock that differs in some rights from common stock. For example, it may have different rights to vote or to dividends, or to distribution of corporate assets when the company goes out of business.

Proprietorship—A business owned by a single person.

Subchapter S corporation—a corporation that has elected to be taxed in accordance with Subchapter S of the federal income tax code. Subchapter S corporations are pass-through entities for federal income tax purposes.

Unlimited liability—This term means that, if a business lacks the funds to pay its debts, the owners of a business are liable for these debts.

Questions and Problems

Comprehension Questions

C1. (Forms of business—partnership) Briefly list some advantages and disadvantages of doing business as a partnership.

C2. (Forms of business—corporation) Briefly list some of the advantages of doing business as a corporation.

C3. (Shareholders' rights) What are some of the rights of shareholders in a corporation?

C4. (Double taxation) What is meant by the term "double taxation" of corporate income?

C5. (Pass-through entities) What is meant by the term "pass-through entity"?

C6. (Pass-through entities) Which of the following are "pass-through entities" for federal income tax purposes?

A. Proprietorships
B. Partnerships
C. C corporations
D. Limited liability corporations
E. Subchapter S corporations

C7. (Forms of business organization) Based on IRS data, rank the following types of business organization tax returns from least to most common in the U.S.:

A. Proprietorships
B. S corporations
C. LLCs
D. C corporations
E. Partnership returns, other than LLCs filing as partnerships

C8. (Forms of business organization) Why do most small businesses choose not to be C corporations?

C9. (Employees and contractors) Explain briefly what you understand the factors are that would cause someone to be classified as an employee of a business, and not as an independent contractor.

C10. (Employees and contractors) Explain briefly what costs a business has with regard to an employee that it does not have with regard to independent contractors.

C11. (Owner compensation) Explain the effect on net income, and on employment taxes, of an S corporation paying:

A. A dividend to shareholders
B. Salaries to shareholders who work for the company

C12. (Factors to reduce risk) Explain how the following steps, taken by Rebeli Press, are related to its efforts to reduce risks:

A. Doing business as a corporation, not a partnership.
B. Trying to use independent contractors as needed, rather than hiring employees on yearly salaries.
C. Renting office space, rather than buying an office.
D. Using a "print-to-order" business model, rather than printing in large quantities and keeping inventory.

C13. (Intangible assets) Explain why Rebeli Press was able to record the prepublication costs and the publishing rights as assets. (You may need to refer back to Chapter 2 for the asset definition.)

C14. (Payroll taxes) What are the Medicare and social security taxes? Are they charged to both the employee and the employer, or just the employee?

C15. (Intangible assets) Explain why Rebeli recorded the following costs the way it did:

    A. Costs of doing marketing were considered expenses, even though they may have future value.

    B. Prepublication costs, such as editing, were recorded as assets, and amortized.

    C. The purchase of publication rights were recorded as assets, and amortized.

    D. The company has not recognized any increase in value of the publication rights, even though the books are successful.

    E. The company has not recognized any value for the name Rebeli Press, even though it is becoming known.

C16. (Sales returns) Explain how estimated sales returns are reflected in the income statement, and in the balance sheet.

C17. (Ways of generating cash) Explain how a company can generate cash by:

    A. Operations

    B. Investing activities

    C. Borrowing

    D. Issuing shares

C18. (Ways of generating cash) Why is leasing listed in Table 12.9 as a means of generating cash?

C19. (Bonds) Would the borrower or the lender prefer that a bond be:

    A. Convertible to common stock at the option of the bondholder?

    B. Callable by the company whenever it wants, at a set price?

    C. Secured by particular assets as collateral?

C20. (Bonds and preferred stock) Are the following payments tax deductible by a corporation?

    A. Payments of interest on bonds.

    B. Payments of dividends on common stock.

    C. Payments of dividends on preferred stock.

Application Questions

A1. (Forms of business organization) For each of the following, indicate if it is true of a general partnership, a corporation, or both.

    A. Owners have unlimited liability for the business's debts.

    B. Owners have limited liability.

    C. Owners have the right to make contracts on behalf of the business.

    D. The business cannot be created until a state approves a charter for the business.

    E. May be subject to dual taxation.

A2. (Forms of business organization—types of corporations) Three different types of corporations are LLCs, S corporations, and C corporations. They have some features in common, and some differences. For each of the following comments, indicate which types of corporations it applies to. Note that some questions will refer to more than one type of corporation, so your answer might involve one, two, or all three of these types.

    A. Shareholders have limited liability for corporate obligations.

    B. The number of shareholders is restricted to 100.

    C. There can only be one class of stock.

    D. There are no federal income taxes paid by the business. Instead, corporate income and losses "pass through" to the owners.

E.   Federal income taxes are paid by the business, and in addition shareholders must pay taxes on any dividends they receive.

A3.   (Double taxation) Assume that the Zhang Corporation is subject to federal corporate income tax. If the Zhang Corporation earns $1000 in 2016:

A.   Compute the federal corporate income tax at a 35% rate.
B.   Assume that the company pays out all the after-tax income as dividends to its shareholders, and that the shareholders must pay 15% capital gains taxes on the dividends they receive. Compute the taxes that will be due on these dividends.
C.   Compute the amount of dividends that the shareholders will keep, after paying their individual income taxes.
D.   Now assume the Zhang Corporation is a pass-through entity, and the income of $1,000 is reported on the tax return of its shareholders. It pays out all the $1,000 as dividends, which are taxed at ordinary income tax rates. Assume the shareholders pay tax at the top individual tax rate, of 39.6%. How much of the $1,000 in income will the shareholders keep, after taxes?
E.   What is the difference, in terms of the amount of earnings kept by the shareholders, between your answers in C and D above?

A4.   (Employees and contractors) Assume that Rebeli Press needs secretarial help. It can hire its own secretary, or it can pay a temporary help agency to supply a secretary. If it hires its own secretary, it will pay an annual salary of $35,000. Assuming a normal work year is about 2,000 hours, this is a pay of about $17.50 per hour. It will pay $6,000 towards health insurance. It will also pay the following taxes:

Social security tax of 6.2%
Medicare tax of 1.45%
State and federal unemployment taxes of 6% of the first $7,000 in wages.

A.   Compute the payroll taxes that will be applicable for a full year.
B.   Compute the total cost of hiring the secretary as an employee, including payroll taxes, salary, and medical benefits.
C.   Compute the approximate cost per hour, using a 2,000 hour year.
D.   Assume that the company could obtain a temporary secretary, through a temporary agency, at a cost of $21 per hour. Should the company hire its own employee, or obtain help through the temporary agency? Explain your answer.

A5.   (Employees and contractors) For this question, refer to the tables indicating factors the IRS says are relevant to deciding whether someone is an employee, or a contractor. For each factor, indicate whether you feel the factor indicates the person is an employee, indicates the person is a contractor, of if you feel the factor is not relevant to this decision.

A.   The workers must come in at the hours set by the person who pays them.
B.   The workers keep no set hours, but just need to get their work done.
C.   The workers use their own tools and methods.
D.   The workers must use tools and methods prescribed by the person who pays them.
E.   The worker gets vacation pay and sick leave.
F.   The worker is working for several different companies in the same month, and advertises her services publicly.

A6. (Payments to owners) Two ways that owners can get money from their business are by declaring dividends on their shares, and by paying salaries and bonuses. For each of the following, indicate whether it is true or false.

A. Dividend payments to owners must be made in proportion to the amount of shares held by each owner.
B. Dividend payments to owners are subject to FICA and other employer payroll taxes.
C. Bonuses paid to shareholders must be made strictly in accordance with the amount of shares each owner owns.
D. Dividends paid by the company reduce net income.
E. Bonuses paid by the company reduce net income.

A7. (Debits and credits) For each of the following journal entries, briefly describe what event you believe it describes.

A. Dr. Cash
      Cr. Accounts receivable
B. Dr. Equipment
      Cr. Cash
C. Dr. Salary expense
      Cr. Cash
D. Dr. Royalties expense
      Cr. Royalties payable
E. Dr. Insurance expense
      Cr. Prepaid insurance.

A8. (Debits and credits) For each of the following transactions or events, write a journal entry in proper form. Be careful to debit and credit the proper accounts.

A. The company makes a sale of books on account of $2,000. (Ignore the related costs.)
B. The company receives a shipment of $3,000 worth of books from a printer, which the company stores as inventory. The company has bought these books on account, and will pay for them in 25 days.
C. The company pays a $5,000 dividend in cash to its shareholders.
D. The company has electricity expense of $230, which it pays in cash.
E. The company borrows $20,000 in cash from a bank.

A9. (Debits and credits) Indicate whether you would use a debit, or a credit, to do each of the following:

A. Record an increase in a cash account.
B. Record an increase in a revenue account.
C. Record a decrease in a liability account.
D. Record an increase in an expense account.
E. Record a decrease in an asset account.

A10. (Financial statement analysis) Using the financial statements given for Rebeli Press, in Tables 12.3 to 12.7, compute the following ratios. (See Chapter 4 for the definitions of these ratios.)

A. Profit margin for ROA.
B. Profit margin for return on common equity.
C. Time interest earned.

D. Accounts receivable turnover. For this purpose, only compare the accounts receivable to the book sales.

A11. (Financial statement analysis—leverage) Using the financial statements given in the text for Rebeli Press, compute the following ratios. See Chapter 4 for their definitions.

A. The operating leverage effect. Here, you should assume that the only variable operating expenses are shipping, printing, and royalties.
B. The financial leverage effect.
C. The total leverage effect.
D. Compare the company's operating and financing leverage effects. Which are larger?

A12. (Cost–volume–profit analysis) When you compare the entries that recorded the sales of 15,000 of books, and the related costs, you will see that on average Rebeli Press received a price of $18 per book. There were three variable costs. On average, printing cost $5 per book, royalties were $2, and shipping was $3.

In order to publish and sell the books, Rebeli Press incurred additional costs, which do not vary by book sold; publication rights of $30,000, prepublication costs of $8,000, and marketing of $5,000. These costs total $43,000.

Using these facts, answer the following. You may wish to refer to Chapter 5's discussion of cost–volume–profit analysis.

A. What was the contribution margin per book, in dollars?
B. What number of books did Rebeli Press need to sell in order to "break even" and cover the other costs of $43,000?
C. If Rebeli Press reduced its price to $16 per book, what number of books would it need to "break even," with the same $43,000 in other costs?

A13. (Cost–volume–profit analysis) Rebeli Press chose to sell its books through traditional bookstores, at a price of $18 per book. Rebeli press also considered the alternative of selling its books on-line through a major on-line bookselling site, at $16 per book. If it chose to do this, the on-line site would do the printing and shipping, and would keep $12 from every sale. It would give Rebeli $4, from which Rebeli would have to pay royalties of $2 to the author.

A. For on-line sales, what would be the contribution margin per book, in dollars?
B. What number of on-line books did Rebeli Press need to sell in order to "break even" and cover the other costs of $43,000?
C. Compare the number of books it would have to sell using this on-line site to the number it would have to sell to bookstores when its contribution margin per book is $8.

A14. (Cost–volume–profit analysis) In the chapter, Rebeli Press sold paper copies of its books to bookstores at a price of $18 each, and had a contribution margin per copy of $8. Assume that, instead, it could sell e-books through one of the major on-line bookselling companies. It would not have to incur printing or shipping costs per copy, which were a total of $8 per books. The deal would be as follows. Each e-book would sell for $9. Of this amount, the on-line seller would keep $4, and the author would receive $2, leaving Rebeli Press with $3 per copy.

A. What number of books would Rebeli Press need to sell in order to "break even" and cover its publication rights, prepublication, and marketing costs, which total $43,000?
B. How does this compare with the number of print copies it needs to sell to bookstores, at a contribution per book of $8, to break even?

    C.   Given the greater number of copies it would need to sell, does it make sense for Rebeli Press to sell e-books? Why, or why not?

A15. (Different financial leverage) In the case, Rebeli Press obtained $50,000 of financing by selling stock to Rebecca and Eli, and also borrowed $100,000 at 5% interest from their friends and family. Assume that instead of lending money, these family and friends had bought stock. In this case, the company would have had less liabilities and less interest expense. Instead of owning all the common stock, Rebecca and Eli would, together, own one third of the stock. Using the Rebeli financial statements, compute what the following figures would be, assuming that the family and friends bought stock instead of loaning money. You should also assume that all the income was distributed as dividends at the end of the year.

    A.   Total operating income
    B.   Total interest expense
    C.   Net income
    D.   Dividends that pertain to Rebecca and Eli, together
    E.   Shareholders' equity at the end of the year
    F.   Return on common equity
    G.   Return on assets
    H.   Ratio of liabilities to equity

A16. (Different budgeting) In the chapter, Rebecca and Eli assumed their sales would double. Redo their budget, using the same assumptions they made about all accounts except the following. Assume that sales and the variable costs of printing, shipping, royalties grow only 50%. Compute:

    A.   Total direct publication expenses
    B.   Gross margin from publications
    C.   Total operating expenses
    D.   Net income

Discussion Questions

D1. (Business form) You may sometimes read about brokers or investment companies that offer their customers the chance to invest in limited partnerships. For example, you will sometimes see interests offered for sale in limited partnerships that invest in new movie projects, or in oil and gas exploration. Why do you think that people would want to invest in these projects as limited partners, rather than as shareholders in corporations?

D2. (Business form—classes of stock) Some corporations have one single class of stock. Others have more than one class, with different rights. For example, a company might have $100 par value preferred stock, which is entitled to a 4% annual dividend on its par value before any dividends can be paid on common shares. Preferred stock might also vary in voting rights. In some cases preferred stock has extra voting rights, and is used to help one group keep control. In some recent public offerings, such as Facebook's, the original shareholders kept extra voting rights to help control the company. One reason Alibaba chose to make its initial public offering in the U.S. is that U.S. stock exchanges allow such arrangements, while Chinese exchanges do not. Questions:

    A.   Would you as an investor be more, or less, willing to invest in common stock if you knew that the founders kept extra voting rights?
    B.   Do you think stock exchanges should allow arrangements where a small number of preferred shareholders keep control of a company? Why, or why not?

D3. (Employees and contractors) The chapter discussed the distinction between employees and independent contractors from the point of view of Rebeli Press, not from the point of view of the workers. From the worker's point of view, what do you see as advantages and disadvantages of being an employee, instead of an independent contractor?

D4. (Holding inventory) In this case, Rebeli Press decided not to keep books in inventory, but, instead, to order books printed as it needed them. It made this decision even though its cost per copy would have been lower if it ordered books in larger quantities.

    A. What characteristics of the publishing industry made it decide to use this higher cost method of printing books?

    B. What factors might exist that would lead a company to decide that it is more sensible to produce in advance, and to keep an inventory of items on hand?

D5. (Owners taking money out) In this case, Eli and Rebecca received three types of benefits from Rebeli Press: salaries; medical insurance; and dividends. They could have chosen to make a different mix of these payments. For example, they could have paid a year-end bonus, instead of giving themselves dividends. They could also have decided that the company would not pay for medical insurance. Instead, they would have received higher dividends, from which they could have paid their own insurance.

    Tax rules treat dividends, salaries, and benefit payments differently. Dividends are not deductible by a corporation, but salaries and benefit payments are. Businesses can fully deduct employee medical insurance costs from their taxes, but usually individual taxpayers cannot. Salary and bonus payments are subject to employer payroll taxes, and the individual has to pay social security taxes and Medicare taxes on them. These taxes do not apply to dividend payments.

    A. If you were an owner, would you try to take money out in a way that minimized taxes?

    B. Do you see a decision characterizing a year-end payment in a way that minimizes taxes as being unethical?

D6. (Taxes and financing) Under the tax laws, interest expense is deductible, but dividend payments are not. Some people have argued that this is provides businesses an incentive to borrow rather than to sell shares, and has caused the U.S. economy to be too reliant on borrowing. Do you see this as a problem? Why, or why not?

Notes

1 Small Business Administration, Office of Advocacy (2014).

2 Piersanti, Steven (2015). The 10 awful truths about book publishing. Retrieved from: http://outthinkgroup.com/the-10-awful-truths-about-book-publishing (last accessed June 2, 2015).

3 Bowker. (2014). Traditional print book production dipped slightly in 2013. Retrieved from: www.bowker.com/news/2014/Traditional-Print-Book-Production-Dipped-Slightly-in-2013.html (last accessed August 18, 2015).

4 American Veterinary Medical Association. (2012). *U.S. Pet Ownership & Demographics Sourcebook (2012)*. Retrieved from: www.avma.org/KB/Resources/Statistics/Pages/Market-research-statistics-US-Pet-Ownership-Demographics-Sourcebook.aspx (last accessed June 2, 2015).

5 The figures for payroll taxes here are a rounded illustrative approximation, and are not meant to be exact figures. Also, typically a company does not pay all the withheld taxes and benefits on the same date as it pays the employees their net pay. It is common for a company to make an entry of the following form on the date it pays its employees:

Dr. Salary expense (for the gross pay)
Dr. Payroll tax expense (for employer taxes)
Dr. Benefits expense (for employer costs of various benefits)
    Cr. Cash (for the net pay to employees)
    Cr. Withheld taxes payable (for the employees taxes, withheld from their pay)

Cr. Employer payroll taxes payable
Cr. Benefits payable

Since a company will often keep a separate ledger account for each type of benefit it offers, and each type of tax, this can be a long journal entry.

Later, when it makes payments of the withheld taxes, the employer payroll taxes, and the various benefits, it will debit the respective liability accounts and credit cash.

6 A legal and accounting issue that arises with sales is whether the transfer of legal ownership of the items legally takes place when the seller ships the items, or when the buyer receives them. If the ownership changes at the place of shipment, then the buyer is responsible for shipping costs and for any losses that occur before delivery. If the ownership changes at the delivery, then the seller is responsible for shipping costs and for any losses or damage to the items until they reach the buyer's location. The seller should also consider items that it shipped part of its inventory until they are delivered. "FOB" is an abbreviation that is often used in contracts to indicate where the place of ownership changes. For example, if Rebeli Press, in New York, shipped books to a Chicago bookstore, with terms "FOB Chicago," that would indicate that ownership did not transfer until the books reach the buyer's business in Chicago.

7 Banks may also ask for personal guarantees from the owner-shareholders, so that if the company fails they can also try to collect from the personal assets of the owners. Even though, legally, shareholders are not responsible for the debts of a corporation, in practice such guarantees mean that the shareholders do end up with substantial personal risk.

8 For public companies, the process of declaring and paying dividends is more complicated. There are many shareholders, and the company needs time to know who the owners are at any particular date, and to make out and send the checks. Typically, the board of a public company meets on a particular date and "declares" that it will send dividends of a certain amount per share to the "owners of record" on some specified date (the "record date") between the "declaration date" and the "payment date." Between the date of declaration and the date of payment, the companies will show the unpaid dividends as a liability. Equity is reduced on the declaration date.

9 IFRS would permit companies to show interest expense as either a financing cash flow or an operating cash flow.

10 *L&B Pipe & Supply Company v. Commissioner*, TC memo 1994-187 (1994).

References

American Veterinary Medical Association. (2012). *U.S. Pet Ownership & Demographics Sourcebook (2012)*. Retrieved from www.avma.org/KB/Resources/Statistics/Pages/Market-research-statistics-US-Pet-Ownership-Demographics-Sourcebook.aspx. (last accessed June 2, 2015).

Bowker. (2014). Traditional print book production dipped slightly in 2013. Retrieved from: http://www.bowker.com/news/2014/Traditional-Print-Book-Production-Dipped-Slightly-in-2013.html (last accessed August 18, 2015).

Fishman, J. E., Pratt, S. P., Griffith, J. C., & Hitchner, J. R. (2015). *PPC's Guide to Business Valuations, Vol. 1* (25th edition). Carrolton, TX: Thomson Reuters Checkpoint.

IRS. (2015). Independent contractor (self-employed) or employee? Retrieved from: http://www.irs.gov/Businesses/Small-Businesses-&-Self-Employed/Independent-Contractor-Self-Employed-or-Employee (last accessed August 18, 2015).

Piersanti, Steven. (2015). The 10 awful truths about book publishing. Retrieved from: http://outthinkgroup.com/the-10-awful-truths-about-book-publishing (last accessed June 2, 2015).

Small Business Administration, Office of Advocacy. 2014. Frequently asked questions. https://www.sba.gov/sites/default/files/FAQ_March_2014_0.pdf (last accessed June 2, 2015).

Appendices

Appendix A   Record-Keeping Systems

Outline

Preliminary Thoughts

What advantage does he derive from the system of bookkeeping by double-entry! It is among the finest inventions of the human mind."

Johann Von Goethe (1824, ch. X, p. 28)

Double-entry bookkeeping came from the same spirit which produced the systems of Galileo and Newton, and the subject matter of modern physics and chemistry. By the same means it organizes perceptions into a system, and one can characterize it as the first cosmos constructed on the basis of mechanistic thought. Double-entry bookkeeping captures for us the cosmos of an economic, more precisely, a capitalistic world by the same means that later the great natural scientists used to construct the solar system and the corpuscles of the blood. . . Double-entry bookkeeping is based on the methodological principle that all perceptions will be manipulated only as quantities, the basic principle of quantification which has delivered up to us all the wonders of nature, and which appeared here for the first time in human history in all its clarity. Without too much difficulty, we can recognize in double-entry bookkeeping the ideas of gravitation, of the circulation of the blood, of the conservation of energy and others which the physical sciences have discovered . . . we cannot regard double-entry bookkeeping without wonder and astonishment, as being one of the most artistic representations of the fantastic spiritual richness of European man.

Werner Sombart (1919)

The two quotations are obviously extremely high praise, and at first it would seem surprising that Goethe, a great poet and scientist, and Sombart, an economist and sociologist, would write such enthusiastic endorsements of a bookkeeping system. After all, isn't bookkeeping dull?

The basic answer is that bookkeeping is necessary to understanding a business, and the double-entry system is an elegant and logical way of performing this task. The double-entry system is extremely flexible, and can handle any sort of business. It forces the accountant to think clearly about what is happening in any transaction in order to record it. It also has error-checking features that help to ensure that accounts are accurate and complete.

This appendix expands upon the discussion in Chapters 2 and 11, and explains in detail the double-entry system of bookkeeping that is the predominant method of record-keeping in the world. While there were other methods of bookkeeping that have been used in the past, the double-entry method has several advantages.

Learning Objectives

1   Understanding how accountants use debits and credits to categorize increases and decreases in accounts.
2   Being able to record transactions using journal entries.
3   Understanding how information in journal entries is summarized in ledgers.
4   Being able to create entries to adjust accounts for events other than transactions.
5   Understanding the functions of a trial balance.
6   Understanding the accounting cycle.
7   Understanding how to prepare balance sheets, income statements, and statements of changes in owners' equity from a trial balance.
8   Understanding the historical importance of the double-entry system.
9   Understanding modern changes in record-keeping and possible future changes.

Double-Entry Bookkeeping—Debits and Credits

General Points

The double-entry bookkeeping system relies on the concept of the fundamental equation of accounting. This was introduced in Chapter 2. The equation is:

assets = liabilities + equity.

This equation provides a way of focusing on the financial aspects of a business. The left side of the equation shows the company's assets, and the right side indicates where the financing came from. Another way of looking at the equation is that it shows both the company's assets, and the claims of creditors and owners on the assets.

In Chapter 2, we saw how various events or transactions would affect this equation. The key point to remember is that any time the accountant records an event in a company's books, the equation must stay in balance. So, for example, if a company borrows $1 million from a bank, the accountant should recognize that the assets are now larger, because the company has more cash, but the liabilities are also larger, because there is an obligation to repay the loan.

The need to keep the equation in balance means that the accountant never records a change in just one account. Most frequently, there must be changes in two accounts, which is why this is called "double-entry" bookkeeping. The process forces the accountant to think about *why* an account is changing. It is not enough to know that cash has increased by $1 million. The accountant can't just increase cash by $1 million, and leave the rest of the equation unchanged, because then it won't balance. The accountant has to know why cash changed. Was it because accounts receivable were collected? Was it because of sales? Was it because of a loan? The accountants cannot record anything unless they know both sides of the entry, and can keep the equation in balance.

Conceptually, the accountants could simply use a giant spreadsheet with the accounting equation written out horizontally in the columns at the top. The accountants could then record each transaction by adding a row to the spreadsheet showing how it affects the equation. The problem is that this would be incredibly clumsy. Large companies may have thousands of different asset, liability, expense, and other accounts, and thousands of daily transactions. So, a system is needed that can:

- Deal with a large number of accounts
- Deal with a large number of events that need to be recorded
- Allow the bookkeeping work to be split among various workers or locations
- Facilitate error-checking
- Focus on the key items of interest to the owners—their equity and their income

The double-entry system was developed hundreds of years ago, and satisfies these requirements.

Debits and Credits

T Accounts

Chapter 2 explained that accountants classify economic activity into certain key elements. These include: assets; liabilities; equity; revenues and gains; losses and expenses; investments by owners; and distributions to owners. Companies may need to classify their activity using many different specific categories of these elements. For example, a company may keep cash in 12 different banks, and it may have 92 different kinds of major expenses.

The categories that a company uses to keep track of particular types of assets, liabilities, or events are called *accounts*. A company might have numerous bank accounts, a separate liability account for every bank loan it has borrowed, and a variety of expense accounts, such as heating costs, salaries, payroll taxes, rent, etc. The number of accounts a company wants to use is a management choice. The purpose is to have enough distinct accounts to keep track of what is important to management.

The list of accounts a company uses is called a "chart of accounts."

The accounting record that includes information for all the accounts that comprise the accounting equation is called the general ledger.

In the days of manual bookkeeping, many companies had books where a page for an account would look like Table Appendix A.1:

This is called a "T account" because it is shaped like the letter T. The account name goes on the top. In this case, it is Cash. The page is divided in half by the vertical line in the letter T. There is a left side, and there is a right side. One side of the account is used for items that increase in the account balance, and the other side is used for things that decrease the account

Table Appendix A.1 T Account for Cash

Jan. 1 Starting balance	$100,000	Jan. 2 Rent expense paid	$12,000
Jan. 5 Loan proceeds received	$50,000	Jan. 15 Wages paid	$33,000
Jan. 12 Collections from customer	3,000		
Total	153,000	Total	$45,000

Net balance 153,000 – 45,000 = $108,000

balance. The trick to the system is that for different accounts, we use different sides of the account to record increases.

An entry to the *left* side of a T account is a *debit*. What you have to remember is that

Debits are on the left!

The word debit is used as a noun, a verb, and an adjective. An item on the left side of a T account is a debit. To "debit" an account is to make an entry to the left side of the account. (Sometimes an accountant will also "charge" an account, which also means to debit it.) The "debit side" of an account is the left side. In each of these cases,

Debits are on the left!

A "*credit*" is an entry to the right side of a T account. The word "credit" is also used as a noun, a verb, and an adjective. Note that the word "credit" has an "r" in it, and credits are on the right.[1]

The word "charge" is a synonym for debit.

In accounting, the words debit, credit, and charge have no implications of good or bad. They simply refer to the left and right sides of T accounts.

Relating the Accounting Equation to Debits and Credits

The clearest way to understand the relation of debits and credits to the fundamental accounting equation is with mathematical derivation. We start with the accounting equation as of the end of any given year.

1   Assets = liabilities + equity
     The equity is at the end of the year. We can relate it to the equity at the beginning of the year, based on the definitions of the other accounting elements.
2   Ending equity = beginning equity + capital contributions + revenues – expenses – dividends
     We use Equation 2 to substitute for equity in Equation 1. This gives us Equation 3.
3   Assets = liabilities + beginning equity + capital contributions + revenues – expenses – dividends
     This system was first developed before Europeans were comfortable with the idea of negative numbers. They preferred positive numbers. They rearranged the items to have all numbers stated positively, which gives us Equation 4.[2]
4   Assets + expenses + dividends = liabilities + beginning equity + capital contributions + revenues

We are done with the derivation. We now set three rules.

- All items on the left increase with debits.
- All items on the right increase with credits.
- We must always make the same dollar amount of debit entries as credit entries.

The items on the left, which increase with debits, are: assets, expenses, and dividends to owners.

The items on the right, which increase with credits, are liabilities: equity, owners' contributions, and revenues.

Decreasing an account is the opposite of increasing it, so you make entries on the opposite side of the T account.

So, if a company borrows $1 million, then there is an increase in an asset and an increase in a liability. It is clear how to record this using the accounting equation. Using the debit and credit system, we would say that cash is an asset, and assets are on the left side of Equation 4, so they increase with debits. Loans payable are liabilities, which are on the right side of Equation 4, so they increase with credits. Therefore, to record this event, we will need to record both a debit of $1 million to cash and a credit of $1 million to loans payable. We will have kept the equation in balance, by keeping the total debits equal to the total credits.

Other Ways of Remembering Which Accounts Increase With Debits

People use different ways of remembering which accounts increase with debits. My general advice is that you find a way that works for you, and stick with it. There are a number of old, and not very funny, accountant jokes in which the punchline is the method used to remember the system, such as "the debits are near the window."

The simplest memory trick is one created by my colleague, Linda Schain. She wrote on the board the listing of debit accounts:

Debits: Expenses   Assets   Dividends

She noticed that the first letter of each word spells out the word "Dead." This is simple: if you remember "dead" means that expenses, assets, and dividends *increase* with debits, then everything else falls into place. You can figure out how these three types of accounts must decrease, and how other accounts must increase and decrease.

A second method, that is almost as simple, is to remember that cash increases with debits. Just remember this one fact, and you can figure out everything else. Let's say you have forgotten what makes revenues increase. Just create a simple example for yourself, involving cash and revenues. So, assume your business made a $10 revenue transaction, and got cash. If you got cash, you must debit cash. The entry has to involve revenues, and it has to balance. This means you have to credit revenues. Revenues must increase with credits. And in fact that is correct.

A third method that can be helpful is more visual. The classical balance sheet is often shown in a form that looks like a T account, with the assets on the left side and the liabilities and equity on the right side. DEBITS ARE ON THE LEFT. The assets therefore must increase with debits. Equity is on the right side, and would increase with credits. Things that decrease equity are expenses and dividends. Since they *decrease* something on the right, they must be recorded with debits. Things that increase equity include revenues and owners' contributions, so they must be recorded with credits.

A fourth method was suggested by Yuji Ijiri (1982). He suggests the idea that the wealth of a company (which is its assets minus its liabilities) must equal the owners' claims on the assets. So, he focuses on the equation:

wealth = equity.

Debits are increases to wealth, and credits are increases to equity. Since liabilities are an offset to wealth, they also increase with credits. Revenues increase equity, so they increase with credits. Expenses and dividends decrease equity, so they increase with debits, not credits.

A fifth clue is that your liabilities are to your "creditors." Liabilities increase with credits.

The last method is to practice. This chapter will give you opportunities to practice the skill of expressing events in the form of debits and credits.

Box Appendix A.1 deals with one frequent source of confusion, which is the way the terms debit and credits are used on the bank and credit card statements you receive.

Recording Transactions and Posting to Ledgers

Recording in Journals

Under the traditional accounting method, when a transaction occurred, a bookkeeper would record it in a record called a journal by making a "journal entry." Journals are also called "books

---

Box Appendix A.1 "Why Don't My Bank and Credit Card Statements Follow Your Rules?"

Students are often confused about debits and credits because the rules taught in accounting class don't seem to match up with everyday experience. In class, students are taught that debit increase cash, and credits decrease cash. So, it seems like debits are good for cash, and credits are bad for cash. But, when students look at their own bank statements, they see the checks they wrote listed as debits, and the deposits listed as credits. Did the professor get things backwards? Is there a mistake here?

There is no mistake. However, your bank is *not doing your books*. They are showing you part of *their books*. Their position is the opposite of yours. To your bank, your checking account is a *liability*, not an asset. *They* owe *you* money. When you make a deposit, they owe you more money. They therefore credit their liability account that pertains to you. When you write a check, they gave you some of your own money back, and they have less of a liability. They debit their liability to reduce it. When you order new checks, they have earned some money from you, and they "charge" your account because they owe you less. "Charge" is a synonym for debit. When you use a "debit card," the result is a debit in their liability to you.

Visa and MasterCard don't do your books either. They send you statements of what their books show. To Visa, your credit card account is a receivable. You think of it as a liability, but they are in the opposite position from you. When you buy something using your card, they have an increased receivable from you. They "charge" your account. When you pay, they have less of an account receivable from you. To reduce their receivable, they have to credit it. So, on your Visa statement, "charges" increase their receivable, and "credits" reduce their receivable. From your point of view, which is the opposite of theirs, the charges they show on the statements increase the amount you owe them, and your payments to Visa show as credits on their statements.

The telephone companies, just like all the other people who send you bills, also don't do your books. They do their own. To them, the money you owe is a receivable. When you do something that increases what you owe them, they "charge" you. That's equivalent to debiting their receivable account from you. When you pay them, or do something else that means you owe them less, they "credit" your account.

---

of original entry" because they contained the first entry of a transaction.[3] The key functions of the journal entry are to:

- Record in the accounts that something has happened
- Classify the event into the relevant accounting elements
- Assign dollar amounts
- Use debit and credit markers to indicate whether accounts are increased or decreased
- Simultaneously record all parts of the transaction.

For example, let's assume that an accounting firm provided $3,000 of tax services to a customer, and the customer promised to pay in one month. The accounting records need to show that $3,000 of revenue has been earned, and that the accounts receivable has increased by $3,000. From the previous section, you know that asset accounts increase with debits. Accounts receivable is an asset account, so the company needs to debit it $3,000. Revenue accounts increase with credits, so the books need to show a $3,000 credit to services revenue. A typical journal entry to record this event would look like the following:

January 3, 2015   Dr. Accounts receivable $3,000
                           Cr. Revenue $3,000
Fees earned for Joe Smith's tax return preparation

This entry has the following elements. There is a date. There is an account that is debited, and an account that is credited. There is an amount. And there is an explanation.

By tradition and custom, the debits are listed first. Also, you will notice that I used indentations and tabs to make sure that the debits were on the left. The debit account is listed to the left, and the credit account is listed to the right. I used the abbreviations "dr." for debit and "cr." for credit.[4] The total debits equal the total credits.

Computerized accounting systems will typically not accept an entry when the total debits do not equal the total credits.

When the company receives Joe Smith's $3,000 payment, it would need to reduce accounts receivable by $3,000, and record the increase in cash. Since cash increases with debits, the company would debit cash, and it would credit accounts receivable because, now that Joe Smith has paid, the asset related to the amount he owes your company is reduced. The journal entry would look like the following:

January 28   Dr. Cash $3,000
                     Cr. Accounts receivable $3,000
Receipt of amount due from Joe Smith for invoice # 26

These are examples of entries in what is called a "general journal."

Most companies use various special journals, in addition to a general journal. The special journals you will see in practice include:

- Cash disbursements journals
- Cash receipts journals
- Purchases journals (typically used for inventory purchases on account)
- Sales journals
- Payroll journals

The special journals are each devoted to one type of transaction. There are several advantages to using them. One is to split work among several people. A second is to simplify training needs. The person handling the sales journal, for example, does not need to know the rules regarding payroll. A third is to simplify the recording process. Each item recorded in the sales journal is a sale. Therefore, there is no need to write the word "sale" every time. The reader understands this.

With modern technology, the function of journals can be performed electronically. For example, barcode scanners at checkout are effectively recording the receipt of cash and sales by scanning the barcodes of the products being bought. At the same time, the scanners are recording the reduction in inventory, and the cost of goods sold. While it is electronic, and does not use a traditional journal, the system is performing the key functions of a journal.

Summarizing Information by Account in the General Ledger

The journal is organized by the date something occurred. To organize information by the accounts involved, another record is needed. The *general ledger* is the collection of all the accounts that together make up the accounting equation for the company. Traditionally it was a book full of pages with T accounts, but modern ledgers are computer records.[5]

Each account in the ledger is meant to contain all the activity in that account for a period of time. The account starts with the beginning balance of that item for the year.

- For assets, liabilities, and equity, the beginning balance in any year = the ending balance of the previous year. These are sometimes called "real" or "permanent" accounts.
- Expenses, revenues, and dividends start each year at zero. These are sometimes called "temporal" or "nominal" accounts.

During the year, when things happen, information is first entered in the journal. Then it is copied into the appropriate accounts in the ledger. This process of copying information into ledger accounts is called "*posting.*"

In the previous section, there were two journal entries. During January, the information from each would have to be posted to the ledger. The first entry involved accounts receivable and revenue. The second involved both cash and accounts receivable. In the days of manual records, posting would usually happen at the end of the month. Now, it is often instantaneous when the journal entry is recorded.

Companies differ as to how they do posting. Some companies post every single transaction into the general ledger. Others use ways to summarize the data. For example, it is common for a company to only post to the ledger accounts receivable account the total collections for the month. Anyone looking for the details of what makes up the total could look at the cash receipts journal for the month.

The advantage of doing summary posting in a modern system is to have a less cluttered general ledger. In the days of manual records, posting on a summary basis also reduced manual work, and reduced the chance of copying errors.

Periodically, the figures in each ledger account should be totaled, and a new balance should be computed. In the days of manual records, this was typically done once per month. With computerized systems, the totals are usually updated automatically after every entry.

Subsidiary Ledgers

Most companies keep other records that provide more detail about particular assets or liabilities. These are called "subsidiary ledgers" or "subledgers." They fulfill a different purpose than the general ledger. The general ledger needs to contain the total balance of every account that is included in the fundamental accounting equation for the company. However, the general ledger need not have all the details of the transactions. For example, it is enough that the general ledger has all the collections of all the accounts receivable for the month of October. It does not need to have the details of which customer paid which day.

Subsidiary ledgers are used to keep track of the details about particular accounts that the company needs to run its business. For example, here are some subsidiary ledgers a company might keep:

Accounts receivable subledger—This keeps a separate record for each customer, with the details of all the transactions with that customer. Each new sale to the customer, each payment received, and all adjustments to the account, get recorded in the customer's account in the subledger. The accounts receivable subledger provides the information needed to generate bills, and to make decisions about a customer relationship.

Accounts payable subledger—This is a record of dealings with suppliers. It is used to track the amounts the company owes to particular suppliers. The account for each supplier is changed with new purchases, with payments the company makes for purchases, and for other adjustments to the account. It is used to make sure that the bills the suppliers send are correct.

Fixed asset subledger—This is a record of the particular fixed assets the company owns, the cost of each one, and the accumulated depreciation on those assets. It is used to keep track of the cost and related depreciation of particular assets. This information is needed to compute the gains or sales on the assets when they are sold.

Investment subledger—This is a record of the stocks and bonds the company owns.

Perpetual inventory records—This is a listing of inventory items. It would be updated for new purchases, and for items sold.[6]

Companies that use subsidiary ledgers need to update them each time they update their general ledgers.

A rule for correctness of subsidiary ledgers is that the total of the individual items in the subsidiary ledger should equal the total for the same account in the general ledger.

Recording Other Events Using Adjustments

The last section discussed recording transactions using journals, and posting the information to ledgers. This section deals with adjusting the accounts to reflect events that are not transactions, and to bring the accounts into compliance with the basic rules of accrual accounting.

At the end of each accounting period, the accountant must look at what's recorded in the books, and decide if the books need to be adjusted in order to reflect the revenue recognition and matching principles. Before adjustments, what are in the books are the opening balances and the effects of transactions recorded in accordance with the previous section of this appendix. The accountant asks three questions:

- What's now in each account?
- What should be in each account?
- What adjustment must I make to change the account from where it is to where it should be?

One concept that students often have trouble with is the distinction between the balance you want and the adjustment you need to make to get there. The books already have balances when the accountant starts the adjusting process. Those balances got there from the initial balances, and from all the transactions recorded during the period. The point of the adjusting process is to change the balances from what the books now show to what the books should show.

Example 1: Your friend John decides to join his college's football team. He now weighs 220 pounds. The coach suggests that he'd play better if he weighs 230. What adjustment does he need to make in order to "bulk up" to the right weight? If you say 10 pounds, you've got the idea. If you say he has to adjust his weight by 230 pounds, you're going to convince poor John to become a very flabby 450-pounder.

Example 2: The accountant prepares a trial balance, before making adjustments, and notices the balance in prepaid insurance is $1,200, representing 12 months' prepaid coverage at $100 per month. However, the accountant knows the policy will last only another 11 months. One month's coverage has been used up. What's the right balance in prepaid insurance, and what adjustment is needed to get the books to where they need to be? These are two different questions. The right *ending balance* is 11 months of prepaid insurance, or $1,100. The right *adjustment* to get from $1,200 of prepaid insurance to $1,100 of prepaid insurance is to reduce the prepaid insurance account by $100, and to increase insurance expense by $100. The journal entry would be:

Dr. Insurance expense $100
    Cr. Prepaid insurance $100
To reflect one month's usage of insurance

It would be very wrong to make an entry debiting prepaid insurance $1,100. This would result in adding $1,100 to the balance already in prepaid insurance, and ending up with $1,200 + $1,100 = $2,300 in the account.

Adjusting entries are a special type of journal entry. Adjusting entries are used to complete our understanding of what happened in the period. As you read through, you will see that the reason for the entries is that cash is moving in a different period than an expense or revenue should be recognized. Adjusting entries are needed to perform six functions:

1   *Record revenues which have been earned, but not yet received in cash.* For example, we may need to accrue interest receivable on a bank deposit. Such an entry would look something like the following (ignoring the date and explanation sections)

Dr. Cash in bank   1,243
    Cr. Interest earned   1,243

A landlord who has rented space to a tenant during the month, and has not yet been paid, would record:
Dr. Accrued rent receivable   6,000
    Cr. Rent revenue   6,000

2   *Record revenues when the cash was received in a prior period, but earned now.* For example, let's assume that a landlord was paid four months' rent in advance in October, to cover the rent for November, December, January, and February. When the landlord received the payment, it should have recorded a debit to cash and a credit to deferred revenue. Deferred revenue is a liability account. In each of the four months November through February, it needs to make a journal entry of the following type, for the amount of one month's rent.

Dr. Deferred revenue
    Cr. Rent revenue
To reflect earning rent previously received in October

3   *Avoid improperly treating cash received, but not earned, as revenue.* For example, a maga-zine publisher may treat all subscription checks as "revenue" when they come in. However, the revenue recognition principle precludes recognizing revenue for magazines before the pub-lisher earns the money by producing and mailing out the magazines. Therefore, an adjusting entry is needed to reclassify some of the revenue which was initially recorded to "unearned revenue", a liability account. The entry would be of the form:

Dr. Magazine subscription revenue
    Cr. Deferred magazine subscription revenue
To properly defer recognition of money received until earned.

4   *Record expenses, which have been incurred, but not yet paid in cash.* For example, a com-pany may incur expenses for taxes payable or utilities in one month, and pay them in the next. Adjusting entries are used to accrue these expenses and liabilities. For example, the entry to reflect the accrual of income taxes for a month might be of the form:

Dr. Income tax expense
    Cr. Income taxes payable

5   *Record expenses, when assets were acquired in a prior period but used up now.* This kind of entry is needed to reflect the consumption of valuable assets, and to avoid overstating their ending value. For example, a company may have bought supplies at the beginning of the month. Since it's not cost-effective to make journal entries each time supplies are used, the company's book would still show the supplies account at the original balance at the end of the month. An entry is needed to adjust the balance to the actual amount of supplies, which are unused, and to record a supplies expense for what was used up. The entry to reflect the usage of supplies would take the following form:

Dr. Supplies expense
   Cr. Supplies
To reflect the usage of supplies during the month

A second example would occur when a company had bought a property insurance policy covering a year. It would initially have debited prepaid insurance and credited cash. As each month goes by, it should make the following entry:

Dr. Insurance expense
   Cr. Prepaid insurance

A third example, that is handled a little differently, is depreciation of fixed assets. It is traditional to track the amount of depreciation used since a fixed asset was acquired in an account called "accumulated depreciation." This account is a modification of the fixed asset account itself. Such accounts are called "*contra accounts*." The accumulated depreciation account is a balance sheet account, and it increases with credits. Therefore, the typical entry made to record depreciation is:

Dr. Depreciation expense
   Cr. Accumulated depreciation

The reason for this special accumulated depreciation account is to provide extra information. For example, assume that a company has a brand new $20,000 car. No depreciation has been recorded on it yet. It also has a $200,000 sports car, with $180,000 of depreciation recorded. Each of them has a net debit balance of $20,000, but they are different cars. If you only saw the net balance, you would not see the difference.

6   *Avoid overstating expenses when costs incurred this period will benefit future periods.* For example, if a company pays for one year of auto insurance, and initially records the whole payment as an expense in the month it's paid, then an entry is needed to reduce the expense, and establish an asset for prepaid insurance. In this case, the necessary entry would be:

Dr. Prepaid auto insurance
   Cr. Auto insurance expense

The Accounting Cycle

General

Bookkeeping is a process that happens year after year. Typically, one speaks of various steps in an "accounting cycle" that starts with a set of beginning asset, liability and equity balances, and ends the year with financial statements and a set of new balances to start the new year with. The steps in the accounting cycle are as follows:

Step 1: Record transactions in journals as they occur.
Step 2: Post information from journals to the general ledger.
Step 3: Add the data in each general ledger account, and create an "*unadjusted trial balance*" of the ledger accounts.
Step 4: Prepare adjusting entries, post them to the ledgers, and add the general ledger data in each account.
Step 5: Prepare an adjusting trial balance.
Step 6: Prepare financial statements.
Step 7: Close the books, and prepare them for the next year.

We have already discussed steps 1, 2, and 4. The focus in this section is on the other steps.

Trial Balances—Steps 3 and 5

A "trial balance" is a listing of all the accounts in the general ledger, together with their balances. The name comes from the fact that this is used to perform a test, or trial, of the ledger. The test is to see if the total debits in the trial balance equal the total credits. If they don't, something is wrong!

With manual systems, it was common for the accountant's first attempt to make a trial balance to be incorrect. The accountant would need to check all the journal entries, all the postings, all the additions, and all of the copying from the ledger to the trial balance itself for errors. With properly programmed computerized systems, the trial balances will always balance.

The accountant should review the trial balance for the following to detect errors:

1   Equality of debits and credits. As noted, with computerized systems this will rarely be an issue.
2   Reasonableness of amounts. The accountant should usually have some idea of what normal balances are, and this review can catch obvious errors. For example, rent expense might have been accidentally entered twice, or forgotten altogether.
3   Accounts with the wrong type of balances. An expense should normally have a debit balance. When an expense account shows a credit balance on a trial balance, the credit balance is likely to indicate an error.

Certain types of errors will cause the trial balance to be out of balance. Let's assume that a journal entry was made to record the receipt of $110,000 of cash from a customer. The journal entry was:

Dr. Cash   110,000
      Cr. Accounts receivable   110,000

If it is posted and summarized properly, it will not cause problems with the trial balance. However, here are some things that could go wrong that will cause the trial balance to be unbalanced:

- Only the cash side of the entry is posted. The accountant forgets to post the receivables side. The impact would be to make the trial balance be off by $110,000, with more debits than credits. A simple omission causes an error in the trial balance of the amount of the omission.
- The accountant posts the cash side correctly, as a debit, but incorrectly posts a debit (not a credit) to accounts receivable of $110,000. The effect now is that the trial balance will be off by $220,000. A reversal of a single posting causes the trial balance to be out of balance by twice the amount of the item.
- The accountant posts the cash side correctly, but incorrectly posts the credit side, not as $110,000, but as $101,000. This is a transposition of digits. The trial balance will be out of balance by the difference between 110,000 and 101,000, or 9,000. The effect of a transposition is to create a difference that is evenly divisible by 9.[7]
- The accountant makes some other error in copying the amount of one side of the entry. The trial balance will be out of balance by the difference between the correct figure and the figure the accountant actually posted into the ledger.
- The accountant adds wrong in summarizing the activity in each ledger account.
- The accountant prepares the trial balance without remembering to include one of the general ledger accounts in the trial balance.

Unfortunately, there are many types of errors that can be made, and that will leave a trial balance in balance. These include:

- Not posting an entry at all, when one is needed
- Posting an entry twice by accident

- Posting an entry backwards—getting the debits and credits mixed up
- Posting an entry to a wrong account. If the accountant posted the $110,000 debit, not to cash, but to land, the trial balance would still balance. However, both the land and the cash accounts would be wrong
- Recording a transaction at the wrong amount. If the customer actually paid $80,000, not $110,000, the cash and accounts receivable accounts would be wrong, but the trial balance would still balance.

The only difference between an unadjusted and an adjusted trial balance is when they are prepared. The unadjusted trial balance is prepared before the adjusting entries that put the books on the accrual basis. The adjusted trial balance is prepared after those entries are made.

Step 6—*Preparing Financial Statements*

Chapter 3 describes the balance sheet, income statement, and statement of shareholders' equity. This step of the accounting cycle involves using information from the adjusted trial balance to prepare these statements.

With manual systems, the process of posting ledgers and creating trial balances was time-consuming, and statements were rarely prepared more often than monthly. With computerized systems, ledgers can be updated constantly, and statements can be prepared whenever needed.

Note that financial statements are typically more summarized than a trial balance. For example, a public company will present one figure for "cash," but it might have 300 bank accounts around the world. The general ledger and trial balance would list 300 different accounts. The process of summarizing the many detailed accounts into the smaller number of accounts shown on the financial statements is called "*grouping*."

The basic process is as follows:

1. The balances for revenues, expenses, gains, and losses from the adjusted trial balances are used to compute net income. Note that to do this computation, one should also compute income tax expense as one of the adjusting entries. The information from the many detailed revenue and expense accounts is summarized ("grouped") and presented in the form of an income statement.
2. The net income and information about owners' contributions, dividends, and beginning balances in retained earnings and other equity accounts are used to compute the ending equity account balances. This computation is summarized and presented in the form of a statement of owners' equity.
3. The information about asset and liability balances from the adjusted trial balance is summarized and presented in the form of the asset and liability section of the balance sheet. To prepare the equity section of the balance sheet, the accountant does *not* take the figures from the adjusted trial balance, but instead uses the ending figures from the statement of owner's equity prepared in step 2.
4. If the company is preparing a cash flow statement, it prepares it at this point using information from the ledger. The preparation of the cash flow statement is beyond the scope of this appendix.

Step 7—*Closing the Books and Preparing Them for Next Year*

The closing process happens once a year, at the end of the year, after financial statements have been prepared.

Note that during the year, we have done nothing to change the balance of retained earnings. When the company earned revenues, we credited revenue accounts. When it incurred expenses, we debited expense accounts. When it paid dividends, we debited a separate dividends account.

That means that the retained earnings figure on the adjusted trial balance does not reflect any of the activity for the year. That is why we don't use it in preparing the ending balance sheet.

So, at this point in the accounting cycle, at the end of business on December 31, we have balances in our revenue, expense, and dividend accounts that reflect the activity for the full year, but our retained earnings account does not reflect any of that activity. When the next year starts, on January 1, we want to start the year with the right balance in retained earnings, and with our revenue, expenses, and dividends accounts reset to zero. When the new year starts, we will have made no sales yet, and incurred no expenses yet. So, we have to change the books in two important ways:

- We need to reset the revenue, expense, and dividend accounts to zero
- We need to reflect all the year's income-related and dividend activity in the retained earnings ledger account.

These goals are achieved using "closing entries." One side of each closing entry is whatever it takes to bring a particular revenue, or expense, or dividend account balance to zero. The other side of the entry is to retained earnings. So, if a company's sales account had an ending credit balance of $12,345,800, the closing entry would be:

Dr. Sales   12,345,800
    Cr. Retained earnings   12,345,800
This brings the sales to zero, and moves the effect of the sales to retained earnings.

Closing entries do not involve judgment. They are very mechanical, and typically they are done by software automatically.

Historical Notes

While this chapter focuses on double-entry bookkeeping, it should be noted that civilizations around the world have had their own methods of bookkeeping for a long time. The earliest known treatise on accounting is by Kautilya, from India, around 300 before the Common Era (Mattessich 1998). China required merchants to keep records, which were to be reviewed monthly by government officials, in 1408. Korean kaesung accounting, developed by around 1400, had a day book, various journals and ledgers, and numerous other books. Similarly, Japan had a number of types of records and systematic ways of tracking business transactions (Huh 1979). In England, a method known as "charge and discharge" accounting was used. Here, a steward or manager was "charged" with responsibility for certain assets and had to show that he had properly "discharged" this responsibility (Jones 1994).

The double-entry method of bookkeeping began being used in Italy at some point around 1200. The first book describing it was written in 1458, by Bendetto Cotrugli, but his book was not published until the 1500s. In 1494, the Italian monk Luca Pacioli published a mathematical text titled *Summa de Arithmetica, Geometria, Proportioni et Proportionalita*. This text included a section that Pacioli said described a system of bookkeeping that was currently in use. He did not claim to be the inventor of this system. No one knows when it was first used. There have been claims made that double entry was used in ancient Rome, and in ancient India, but these claims are not generally accepted.[8]

His book was widely read, and the double-entry system spread. It was seen as having a variety of advantages over previous methods of accounting. The requirement that debits equal credits helped to detect errors, including the failure to consider all of a company's accounts. The system focused on measuring profit and owner's equity. It was also helped by the growth of the number of professional accountants, over time, who were trained in this method.[9] However, older methods of accounting remained in wide use in England until the Industrial Revolution.[10]

Box Appendix A.2 Excerpts from Chapter 36 of Pacioli's Summa de Arithmetica, Geometria, Proportioni et Proportionalita, published in 1494

Luca Pacioli, an Italian monk, published the first treatise on double-entry bookkeeping in 1494. He did not claim to invent this system. Instead, he said he was describing the methods used by successful businessmen in Venice. The excerpts below are from Chapter 36, *The Summary of Rules and Ways of Keeping a Ledger*. As you read them, consider to what extent they remain a valid description of double-entry bookkeeping.

1   All credits must be placed on the right-hand side of the Ledger, and all debits on the left-hand side.
2   All entries posted to the Ledger must consist of double entries, a debit and a credit.
3   Each debit and credit entry must contain three things: the date, the amount, and the reason for the entry. . . .
4   The credit posting shall be made on the same day as the debit posting.
5   A Trial Balance of the Ledger should be prepared by folding a sheet of paper lengthwise and recording the debit account balances on the left, and the credit account balances on the right. By summing, it is seen whether the debit balances equal the credit balances and whether the Ledger is in order.
6   The Trial Balance of the Ledger must be equal: The sum of the debits must be equal to the sum of the credits. Otherwise, there would be a mistake in the Ledger.
7   The Cash account should always have a debit balance or be equal. Otherwise, the account will be in error. . . .
8   No one should appear as a debtor in your Ledger without his permission and consent. If he did, the account would be considered false. . . .
9   The values in the Ledger must be recorded in one kind of money. . . .
10 When the Ledger is full or a new Ledger is to be opened, and you wish to transfer account balances into a new one, proceed as follows. . . . Take a trial balance of the old Ledger and see that it is equal and correct. Then copy into the new Ledger the debit and credit account balances in the order in which they appear in the trial balance. . . . In order to cancel the old Ledger, every open account shown on the trial balance must be closed. If an account in Ledger A has a credit balance (as the trial balance will indicate), it should be debited for the same amount. . . . The old Ledger is closed in this way, and the new Ledger opened.

As translated in Brown and Johnston (1963), pp. 102–104.

Box Appendix A.2 contains some of the rules in Pacioli's summary of double-entry bookkeeping. You will see that many of these rules are still used today.

Comments on the Future of Bookkeeping

The basic nature of double-entry bookkeeping has been stable from before Pacioli's book in 1494 to today. It is based on a basic algebraic equation, and the math will retain its usefulness. However, that does not mean that accounting will always be the same.

Mathematics has become much more sophisticated than in Pacioli's day. His system was based on elementary algebra, and tried to avoid the use of negative numbers. It is now possible to express the bookkeeping process in terms of linear algebra, and to bypass the cumbersome process of journals and ledgers and trial balances. For example, the beginning balances in the asset, liability, and equity accounts could be considered as a single mathematical vector. The events of the year can be represented as a matrix of data, and the ending balances are found by multiplying that matrix by the opening vector. Using the tools of linear algebra, it is possible to explore the relations of accounting to communications theory and to coding of information. See the lecture materials used by Dr. John Fellingham of Ohio State University[11] and his remarks to the American Accounting Association (Fellingham, 2007).

At least one Russian university teaches introductory accounting through the perspective of matrices and linear algebra. See Stoner and Vysotskaya (2012). The authors claim that:

> The use of the mathematical matrix modeling approach is significantly different (in both theoretic and practical senses) to the procedural nature of the traditional way of learning how to produce financial statements that is used in many conventional introductory accounting courses. In many such courses, even if the full nature of double-entry bookkeeping is not covered, the production of accounts is often learned alongside the procedures of creating accounts from, for example, a trial balance. In contrast, by using mathematical methods, matrix accounting can provide a verifiable process that leads to balanced accounts that reflect duality. . . . Further, the matrix method provides a very compact procedure that . . . delivers:
>
> 1   Compactness of representation of accounting data, as well as the required transformation of these data as appropriately formatted reports.
> 2   A way of eliminating the complex procedural steps of traditional bookkeeping.
> 3   Compactness and transparency of the logical reasoning and results. (p. 1028)

Another enormous change between Pacioli's day and today is the computerization of the book-keeping process. In his day, data was entered by clerks using quill pens and paper records. Now, much transaction data is entered by scanners or computers. Computers do the data entry when a company:

- Sells its goods through a website
- Sells retail goods using point of sale scanners
- Buys goods automatically through supplier websites
- Uses scanners to record incoming deliveries of new inventory
- Generates payroll transactions automatically using recurring payroll data
- Generates monthly adjusting entries based on past information
- Uses software to perform closing entries

Computerization has had several major impacts on bookkeeping so far:

- Fewer people are needed to do bookkeeping. Computers record data faster, and add it and copy it quickly and without errors.
- Data is available faster. Because it used to be very hard to add up all the data for a big company, it took a long time to create financial reports. Computerized systems allow information to be prepared quickly. Many major financial institutions track their trading positions worldwide on a daily basis.
- Reports are more reliable, as computerization reduces the number of recording and processing errors.
- More data can be accumulated, in more ways. In Pacioli's day, it was as much work as anyone wanted to do to note that a sale had occurred, its date, the customer, and the amount. Now, with scanners, computers, and databases, it is possible to add many tags to one event, and track information such as the time of day it was sold. Increasingly, companies are using data mining techniques to gain insights about "big data."

- Computerization makes the type of matrix manipulation discussed in the previous section feasible.
- Financial accounting systems are becoming integrated with broader enterprise resource planning systems that not only do bookkeeping, but simultaneously update systems related to production, marketing, and other related business areas. Instead of accountants keeping journals that are separate from the sales and production records, increasingly companies keep integrated data systems that can produce journals and ledgers as part of a broader set of reports.

There have also been attempts to extend the theory of double-entry bookkeeping to answer additional questions. For example, Yuji Ijiri (1982, 1986 and 1989) has proposed a system of triple-entry bookkeeping as an extension of the traditional system. He notes that in the traditional system, income explains the change in equity between two balance sheet dates. He has proposed a system that would also measure the rate at which income is being earned at various times during the year, which he calls momentum, and the factors ("forces") that explain changes in the rates at which income is being earned.[12] While his ideas have not been adopted, it is likely that accounting will continue to evolve over the years to come.

Questions and Problems

Comprehension Questions

C1. (Debits and credits) Indicate which accounts increase with debits.
C2. (Debits and credits) Indicate which accounts increase with credits.
C3. (Debits and credits) Is a "debit" a good thing for a business, a bad thing, or neither? Explain, and in your answer consider how debits affect assets and expenses.
C4. (Debits and credits) Is a "credit" a good thing for a business, a bad thing, or neither? Explain, and in your answer consider how credits affect revenues and liabilities.
C5. (Detecting errors) What are some types of errors in bookkeeping that will cause the trial balance to be out of balance?
C6. (Detecting errors) What are some types of errors in bookkeeping that will *not* cause the trial balance to be out of balance?

Application Questions

A1. (Debit and credit recognition) Which of the following accounts increase with debits?

    A. Cash
    B. Interest expense
    C. Interest revenue
    D. Land
    E. Accounts payable
    F. Retained earnings
    G. Sales
    H. Cost of goods sold
    I. Dividends
    J. Bank loans payable

A2. (Debit and credit recognition) Which of the following accounts increase with credits?

    A. Common stock (an equity account)
    B. Contributed capital in excess of par value

C.   Accounts receivable
D.   Prepaid expenses
E.   Revenue for services rendered
F.   Unearned revenues
G.   Accrued income taxes payable
H.   Insurance expense
I.   Prepaid insurance
J.   Intangible assets

A3. (Journal entries) For each of the following transactions, propose a journal entry, and also state how the transaction affected the fundamental accounting equation. Assume each one occurred June 1, 2015.

A.   The company issued stock of $2 million for cash.
B.   The company spent $200,000 to buy equipment.
C.   The company bought a 12-month insurance policy for $50,000.
D.   The company provided services to a customer and earned $10,000. The customer paid cash.
E.   The company paid a previously outstanding account payable, of $4,000, using cash.

A4. (Journal entries) For each of the following transactions, propose a journal entry, and also state how the transaction affected the fundamental accounting equation. Assume each one occurred May 1, 2015.

A.   The company made a sale of $30,000 for cash.
B.   In connection with the sale in part A, the company delivered inventory with a cost of $25,000 to the customer. (You need to record the reduction of inventory, and the cost of goods sold.)
C.   The company bought a car for $25,000 in cash.
D.   The company bought inventory from a supplier, for $30,000, on account. The company has 30 days to pay.
E.   A customer who had bought inventory in the previous month pays his bill of $2,400.

A5. (Accounting cycle) Indicate the order in which the following parts of the accounting cycle should occur. (They are presented in a scrambled order—your task is to sort them out.)

A.   Prepare financial statements
B.   Record transactions in journals
C.   Prepare closing entries
D.   Prepare an adjusted trial balance
E.   Prepare adjusting entries
F.   Prepare an unadjusted trial balance
G.   Post information from journals to ledgers

A6. (Adjusting entries) Make the appropriate adjusting entries in the situations below.

A.   The company has a machine with a cost of $60,000 which it bought in prior years. Depreciation expense should be $2,000 per month. No depreciation has been recorded yet this month.
B.   Four months ago, the company bought prepaid insurance for 24 months for a total price of $48,000. The company has been recognizing some insurance expense each month. An entry is needed this month to record the insurance expense.

C. The company loaned another company $100,000 at an interest rate of 6% per year. No interest is due to be paid this month, but an entry is needed to record the interest earned during this month.

D. The company has bonds payable of $12,000,000, with an effective interest rate of 4% per year. An entry is needed to accrue the interest expense and interest payable for this month.

A7. (Adjusting entries) Make the appropriate journal entries in the situations below.

A. The company has earned $1 million in income before taxes this month. The company's effective income tax rate is 30%. An entry is needed to record income tax expense and income tax payable.

B. The company previously received $200,000 in advance for two months of services to a customer. When it received the money, it credited "unearned revenues." This month, it has performed half of those services. An entry is needed to reduce the unearned revenues liability and record earned revenues.

C. The company had spent $30,000 on the first day of the month to create an inventory of supplies. When the supplies were bought, the company debited an asset, "supplies," for $30,000. At the end of the month, the company counts the supplies, and decides that $12,000 of supplies has been used. An entry is needed to record the supplies expense.

D. The situation is the same as in "C", but now assumes that when the supplies were bought, the company had debited $30,000 to supplies expense. What entry is now needed at the end of the month to recognize that not all the supplies have been used up?

A8. (Understanding entries) This question tests your ability to understand accounting entries. Each of the following is a typical journal entry, made either to record a transaction, or to adjust the books at the end of the month. Your task is to explain what the function of the entry is, and what event it is recording. For example, is it recording a sale for cash?

A.	Dr. Dividends	10,000	
	Cr. Cash		10,000
B.	Dr. Inventory	47,200	
	Cr. Accounts payable		47,200
C.	Dr. Accounts receivable	9,000	
	Dr. Cost of goods sold	6,000	
	Cr. Sales		9,000
	Cr. Inventory		6,000
D.	Dr. Prepaid rent	6,000	
	Cr. Cash		6,000
E.	Dr. Income tax expense	132,000	
	Cr. Income taxes payable		132,000
F.	Dr. Interest receivable	4,200	
	Cr. Interest revenue		4,200

A9. (Trial balance and financial statements) Table Appendix A.2 shows the Martin Company's adjusted trial balance as of the end of 2015.
Required: using the information given,

A. Create an income statement
B. Create a statement of changes in retained earnings
C. Create a year-end balance sheet. Remember, you need the ending retained earnings from part B for your ending balance sheet.

Table Appendix A.2 Trial Balance for Martin Company

Account	Debit	Credit
Cash	8,500	
Accounts receivable	4,500	
Supplies	900	
Prepaid insurance	4,230	
Equipment	62,000	
Accumulated depreciation		11,000
Accounts payable		8,000
Unearned revenue		3,100
Taxes payable		4,500
Common Stock		20,000
Retained earnings		28,220
Dividends	4,000	
Sales revenue—product 1		166,300
Sales revenue—product 2		52,700
Salaries expense—marketing	60,230	
Cost of goods sold	125,600	
Rent expense	8,400	
Advertising expense	6,500	
Insurance expense	5,560	
Depreciation expense	1,800	
Income tax expense	1,600	
Totals	293,820	293,820

Table Appendix A.3 Adjusted Trial Balance—Paul Company December 31, 2015

	Debit	Credit
Cash	9,500	
Accounts receivable	10,000	
Prepaid insurance	4,600	
Machinery and equipment	68,000	
Accumulated depreciation		11,000
Accounts payable		1,600
Income taxes payable		8,600
Common stock		29,000
Retained earnings		15,100
Services revenue		197,000
Other revenues		4,400
Salaries expense	140,800	
Rent expense	15,400	
Insurance expense	3,800	
Depreciation expense	6,000	
Income tax expense	8,600	
Totals	266,700	266,700

A10. (Closing process) Look at the information for the Martin Company in the previous question.

A.   Which accounts will need to be reset to zero in the year-end closing process?

B.   Why does the retained earnings account need to be adjusted in the closing process?

A11. (Trial balance and financial statements) Table Appendix A.3 shows the Paul Company's adjusted trial balance as of the end of 2015.

Required: using the information given,

A. Create an income statement
B. Create a statement of changes in retained earnings
C. Create a year-end balance sheet. Remember, you need the ending retained earnings from part B for your ending balance sheet.

A12 (Comprehensive question—lengthy to complete) The Northeast Company had the following balance sheet at the start of the year:

Northeast Company January 1, 20X1, Balance Sheet

Cash	20,000
Accounts receivable	100,000
Inventory (500 units at $20 each)	10,000
Equipment	9,000
Less: Accumulated depreciation	(2,000)
Total assets	137,000
Accounts payable	20,000
Long-term notes payable (5% interest, due in 10 years)	100,000
Capital stock	10,000
Retained earnings	7,000
	137,000

During the year, the following 10 events or transactions occurred:

1 The company collected $98,000 of the accounts receivable in cash.
2 The company paid $19,000 of its accounts payable in cash.
3 The company bought 900 units of inventory for $20 each in cash.
4 The company bought a one-year insurance policy for $2400 on October 1.
5 On Dec 31, the company prepaid rent for Jan. 20X2 for $1,500.
6 On Dec. 15, the company sold 1,300 units for $30 each. 1000 were sold for cash, and 300 on account. (Note—the cost of inventory did not change during this problem. Your entry needs to record the changes in sales; cash; accounts receivable; inventory; and cost of goods sold.)
7 The company recorded depreciation on the equipment. The equipment is one year old. It had a cost of $9,000, salvage value of $1,000, and an expected useful life of four years.
8 The company made the appropriate adjustment to reflect the fact the insurance policy only had nine more months left of effectiveness.
9 The company accrued the interest that had been built up on the long-term notes. The money had been borrowed on January 1, 20X1. No payments of interest were due until January 2 of 20X2.
10 On December 1, the company paid dividends of $1,000 to its shareholders.

Required:

A. Prepare journal entries for the 10 transactions or events.
B. Prepare a trial balance showing what the ending ledger balances would be after the ten journal entries have been posted to the ledger. Remember, you need to use the previous year's ending balances as beginning balances in this process.

C.   Prepare an income statement for the year.

D.   Prepare a statement of stockholders' equity for the year.

E.   Prepare a balance sheet at the end of the year. Remember to use the ending retained earnings from the statement of stockholders' equity for your ending balance sheet.

Notes

1 Debit and credit, in the accounting sense, have unclear etymologies. The Latin debitum means "debt," and the creditum means "thing entrusted to one." See Baladouni (1984). However, Sherman (1986) believes the terms are related to "debtor" and "creditor."

2 According to Yuji Ijiri (1982), while in India and China there was some use of negative numbers to represent debt, at the time Pacioli wrote the first widely read book describing double-entry bookkeeping, negative numbers were not generally accepted by mathematicians. Thomas Harriot (1560–1621) was the first mathematician to fully accept negative numbers. Thus, with credits and debits, negative numbers were used in accounting before being accepted fully in mathematics.

3 "Journal" comes from Middle and Old French "journee", meaning day. This comes from Latin "diurnalis", of the day. The English "diary" also comes from this Latin root. See Baladouni (1984).

4 W. Richard Sherman (1986) believes that these abbreviations started as abbreviations for "debtor" and "creditor." Debtors were those people who owed the company money, and the related accounts receivable were assets. Creditors had loaned the company money, resulting in accounts payable.

5 The word "ledger" came from Middle English "legger", meaning lying down. The idea is this book was lying in one place and open to inspection. See Baladouni (1984).

6 Some companies choose not to track inventory every time a sale is made. They use what is called the "periodic" inventory method. With the widespread use of scanners to record sales, this method is becoming less common.

7 This general effect of transpositions is not hard to show mathematically. Express some 5-digit number, for example, $a + b \times 10 + c \times 100 + d \times 1{,}000 + e \times 10{,}000$. Now transpose any two digits. Assume you transpose c and e. The new number is $a + b \times 10 + e \times 100 + d \times 1{,}000 + c \times 10{,}000$. When we subtract the new number from the old one, we get $c \times 100 - e \times 100 + e \times 10{,}000 - c \times 10{,}000$. This simplifies to $100 \times (c - e) + 10{,}000 \times (e - c)$ which $= 10{,}000\,(e - c) - 100(e - c)$. This equals $100 \times [(100 - 1)(e - c)]$. The number inside the brackets in the last equation includes $(100 - 1)$, which is 99. That is obviously divisible by nine. In general, whatever two places are transposed, the difference will include some power of 10 minus 1, resulting in a number divisible by 9.

8 See: Martinelli (1977), Nigam (1986) and Nobes (1987).

9 Martinelli (1977), Nigam (1986) and Nobes (1987).

10 See Bryer (2000) and Winjum (1972).

11 http://fisher.osu.edu/~fellingham.1/523/index.html (last accessed August 18, 2015).

12 For a critique of Ijiri's concepts, see Fraser (1993).

References

Baladouni, V. (1984). Etymological observations on some accounting terms. *The Accounting Historians Journal, 11(*2), 101–9.

Brown, R. G., & Johnston, K. S. (1963). *Paciolo on Accounting, a Translation*. New York: McGraw-Hill Book Company, Inc.

Bryer, R. A. (2000). The history of accounting and the transition to capitalism in England. Part one: Theory. *Accounting, Organizations, and Society, 25*, 131–62.

Fraser, I. A. (1993). Triple-entry bookkeeping: a critique. *Accounting and Business Research, 23*(90), 151–8.

Goethe, J. von. (1824). *Wilhelm Meister's Apprenticeship and Travels*. Book I, Vol. I. Trans. by T. Carlyle. London: Chapman and Hall.

Huh, J. H. (1979). The traditional accounting system in the oriental countries—Korea, China, Japan. Working Paper no. 22. In E. N. Coffman (Ed.), *The Academy of Accounting Historians Working Paper Series, Vol. 2 (Working Papers 21–40)*. Richmond, VA: Virginia Commonwealth University.

Fellingham, J. C. (2007). Is accounting an academic discipline? *Accounting Horizons, 21*(2), 159–63.

Ijiri, Y. (1982). *Triple-Entry Bookkeeping and Income Momentum*. Studies in Accounting Research # 18. Sarasota, FL: American Accounting Association.

Ijiri, Y. (1986). A framework for triple-entry bookkeeping. *Accounting Review, 61*(4) 745–59.

Ijiri, Y. (1989). *Momentum Accounting and Triple-Entry Bookkeeping: Exploring the Dynamic Structure of Accounting Measurements.* Studies in Accounting Research # 31. Sarasota, FL: American Accounting Association.

Jones, M. (1994). A forgotten casualty of Pacioli's system? *Management Accounting, 72*(5) 30–3.

Martinelli, A. (1977). Notes on the origin of double entry bookkeeping. *Abacus, 13*(1), 3–27.

Mattessich, R. (1998). Review and extension of Bhattacharyya's modern accounting concepts in Kautilya's Arthśāsastra. *Accounting, Business, and Financial History,* 8(2) 191–209.

Nigam, L. B. M. (1986). Bahi-Khata: The pre-Pacioli Indian double-entry system of bookkeeping. *Abacus, 22*(2), 148–61.

Nobes, C. (1987). The pre-Pacioli Indian double-entry system of bookkeeping: A comment. *Abacus, 23*(2), 182–4.

Sherman, W. R. (1986). Where's the "r" in debit? *The Accounting Historians Journal, 13*(2), 137–43.

Sombart, W. (1919). *Moderne Kapitalismus,* on double entry. Trans. in Most, K. S. (1979). Sombart on Accounting History. Working Paper No. 35. In E. N. Coffman (Ed.), *The Academy of Accounting Historians Working Paper Series, Vol. 2 (Working Papers 21–40).* Richmond, VA: Virginia Commonwealth University.

Stoner, G. N., & Vysotskaya, A. (2012). Introductory accounting, with matrices, at the Southern Federal University, Russia. *Issues in Accounting Education, 27*(4), 1019–44.

Winjum, J. O. (1972). *The Role of Accounting in the Economic Development of England: 1500–1750.* Champaign, IL: Center for Education and Research in Accounting, University of Illinois.

Appendix B   Present Value Concepts

This appendix deals with the time value of money. This is an extremely important concept in economics, finance, and accounting. Even though it is very important, it is treated in an appendix because many students in this course will already be familiar with it through previous course work. Readers wanting more detailed treatment can also see any standard intermediate accounting textbook.

Present value is used in accounting in various places. For example, there is a FASB rule that if payments or collections are scheduled more than one year away, and there is no stated interest rate, they must be accounted for using present value. A second example is that certain types of leases must be accounted for using the present value of the future lease payments.

Why do we need to compute present value? Very simply, we assume that people would prefer to have money today, rather than money in the future. A person would rather have $10,000 today than have the promise to receive $10,000 at the end of 10 years. In technical language:

"*Present value*" is the amount that some payment that is promised to us in the future is worth to us if we were to get it today.

"*Future value*" is the value that we would have if we took some amount of money today, and set it aside and invested it until some future data.

If we take some amount of money today, for example $1,000, and invest it for 10 years, what will our investment be worth at the end of 10 years? That depends on the interest rate. If we can invest if at 5%, our investment will grow as follows.

Year	Value (rounded)
1	1,050
2	1,103
3	1,158
4	1,216
5	1,276
6	1,340
7	1,407
8	1,477
9	1,551
10	1,629

Mathematically, where FV = future value, PV = present value, i = interest rate, and t = number of time periods away,

$$FV = PV \times (1 + i)^t$$

Present Value of Single Sums

We can turn this equation around, and solve for present value. That gives us:

$$PV = FV \div (1 + i)^t$$

This means that the present value of any future payment depends on: the amount of money we will receive in the future; how long we have to wait, and the interest rate. The amount we receive in the future is in the numerator, so, the higher the future payment, the larger the present value. The interest rate and the time we have to wait are in the denominator. If we have to wait longer, present value is lower. If the interest rate is higher, the present value is lower.

Another term you may hear for present value is "present discounted value." The present value is always lower, or "discounted" from the future value. You may also hear the interest rate referred to as the "discount rate."

Table Appendix B.1 shows the present value of $1 to be received in the future, at various interest rates. Note that you could compute every item in the table using the equation for present value. In fact, I created the table using the equation, and Excel, very quickly. Also, many "financial" calculators can compute present value. The table is a convenience, and is also helpful for teaching purposes.

Let's use Table Appendix B.1 to answer some questions:

1   What is the present value of a payment of $700 we expect to get in three years, if the interest rate is 4%? The table tells us that the present value of $1, in three years, at 4% = 0.889. Therefore, the present value of $700 should = 0.889 × 700 = $622.30.

2   At a 7% interest rate, how much would we have to receive in 20 years for this future payment to have a present value of $10,000? On Table B.1, the factor for 7% and 20 years is 0.258. This means that each dollar we receive 20 years from now has a current value of 25.8 cents. To put it another way, we need a future value that satisfies the equation FV × 0.258 = $10,000. When we solve this, we get an answer of $38,760 (rounded).

3   At what interest rate would a future payment of $10,000, received after 10 years, be worth about $5,000 today? To answer this, we divide the present value by the future value, and get $5,000/ $10,000, or 0.5. We now know that we are looking for an interest rate that, in the row of Table B.1 for 10 years, equals about 0.5. When we inspect the table, we see that the factor for 7% is 0.508, which is pretty close. The factor for 8% is 0.463. If we need a more precise answer, we have a couple of choices.

We could use trial and error with factors between 7% and 8%. This can be done quickly with Excel. We could also the mathematical technique of interpolation. The difference between 7% and 8% is, obviously, 1%. The difference in present value between the two numbers on the table is .508 −.463 = 0.045. One of the table figures is only 0.008 away from our target of 0.500. If the figures in the table behaved close to linearly, then we could solve for what fraction of the 1% distance between the table figures corresponds to the 0.008 difference from our target. We would see that 0.008/0.045 = 0.177. We would then expect a figure of 7.177% to give us a present value of the $10,000 equal to $5,000. And it does. By my computations, the result is $5,000.16.

Present Value of Multiple Future Payments.

Many business arrangements involve more than one future payment. Conceptually, this is no problem. We can just find the present value of each future payment separately, using the present value equation we already have, and add the values all up.

Table Appendix B.1 Table Showing Present Value of $1

Periods	1%	2%	3%	4%	5%	6%	7%	8%	9%	10%	15%
1	0.990	0.980	0.971	0.962	0.952	0.943	0.935	0.926	0.917	0.909	0.870
2	0.980	0.961	0.943	0.925	0.907	0.890	0.873	0.857	0.842	0.826	0.756
3	0.971	0.942	0.915	0.889	0.864	0.840	0.816	0.794	0.772	0.751	0.658
4	0.961	0.924	0.888	0.855	0.823	0.792	0.763	0.735	0.708	0.683	0.572
5	0.951	0.906	0.863	0.822	0.784	0.747	0.713	0.681	0.650	0.621	0.497
6	0.942	0.888	0.837	0.790	0.746	0.705	0.666	0.630	0.596	0.564	0.432
7	0.933	0.871	0.813	0.760	0.711	0.665	0.623	0.583	0.547	0.513	0.376
8	0.923	0.853	0.789	0.731	0.677	0.627	0.582	0.540	0.502	0.467	0.327
9	0.914	0.837	0.766	0.703	0.645	0.592	0.544	0.500	0.460	0.424	0.284
10	0.905	0.820	0.744	0.676	0.614	0.558	0.508	0.463	0.422	0.386	0.247
11	0.896	0.804	0.722	0.650	0.585	0.527	0.475	0.429	0.388	0.350	0.215
12	0.887	0.788	0.701	0.625	0.557	0.497	0.444	0.397	0.356	0.319	0.187
13	0.879	0.773	0.681	0.601	0.530	0.469	0.415	0.368	0.326	0.290	0.163
14	0.870	0.758	0.661	0.577	0.505	0.442	0.388	0.340	0.299	0.263	0.141
15	0.861	0.743	0.642	0.555	0.481	0.417	0.362	0.315	0.275	0.239	0.123
16	0.853	0.728	0.623	0.534	0.458	0.394	0.339	0.292	0.252	0.218	0.107
17	0.844	0.714	0.605	0.513	0.436	0.371	0.317	0.270	0.231	0.198	0.093
18	0.836	0.700	0.587	0.494	0.416	0.350	0.296	0.250	0.212	0.180	0.081
19	0.828	0.686	0.570	0.475	0.396	0.331	0.277	0.232	0.194	0.164	0.070
20	0.820	0.673	0.554	0.456	0.377	0.312	0.258	0.215	0.178	0.149	0.061
25	0.780	0.610	0.478	0.375	0.295	0.233	0.184	0.146	0.116	0.092	0.030
30	0.742	0.552	0.412	0.308	0.231	0.174	0.131	0.099	0.075	0.057	0.015

The equation that summarizes this is:

$$PV_0 = \sum_{t=0}^{t=\infty} \frac{FV_t}{(1+i)^t}$$

Here, each future payment to be received is identified by the subscript "t."

This formula is very general, and can be used for any problem involving multiple payments. Here are some implications:

1   Values that will be received in the very far future have present values that will become extremely small.
2   The higher the interest rate, the lower the present value.
3   The higher the expected future values, the higher the present values.

We can relate this formula to typical news stories about the stock market. We assume that investors use this equation to estimate the values of stocks.

When forecasts of company earnings increase, the stock market rises. This is because investors expect the higher earnings to turn into higher dividends in the future. This increases the numerator of the formula.

When interest rates rise, stock prices fall. This is because the interest rate is in the denominator of the formula, and higher interest rates lead to lower present values.

Present Values of "Ordinary" Annuities of Finite Numbers of Payments

An "ordinary" annuity is an arrangement where the same amount is paid at the end of each period. For example, a bond may pay fixed amounts of interest every six months for 15 years, starting six months after the date it was issued. This means that over its life, there are 30 payments. It would be cumbersome to use the equation 30 times to find 30 different present values, and then to add them up. Fortunately the mathematics can be simplified in this case, and also tables can be created to help the computation. Table Appendix B.2 is a table showing the present value of an ordinary annuity of $1, for various periods and interest rates.

For example, on Table Appendix B.2, the present value of an annuity of 10 payments, of $1 each, at a 3% interest rate, is $8.530. If the interest rate were 8%, the same 10 payments would have a present value of $6.710.

Tables like these are often used to help value the stream of payments from a bond. For example, assume a bond will make 20 interest payments of $500 each. The appropriate rate of interest for a year would be 6%, but the bonds pay interest every half year, so we will use half the interest rate, or 3%. The factor in Table B.2 for 3% and 20 payments is 14.877. If a $1 annuity is worth 14.877, the bond interest payments must be worth 14.877 × $500, or $7,439 (rounded).[1]

Present Values of Perpetual Ordinary Annuities

Mathematically, if there is an annuity that will go on forever, with a fixed payment, then the present value of this infinite stream of payments = (annual payment amount) ÷ (interest rate).

Questions and Problems

1   (Using Table B.1.) Find the present value of each of the following:

A. $700 to be received in 4 years when the interest rate = 9%
B. $700 to be received in 9 years when the interest rate = 4%
C. $900 to be received in 7 years when the interest rate = 5%

Table Appendix B.2 Table Showing Present Value of Ordinary Annuity of $1

Periods	1%	2%	3%	4%	5%	6%	7%	8%	9%	10%	15%
1	0.990	0.980	0.971	0.962	0.952	0.943	0.935	0.926	0.917	0.909	0.870
2	1.970	1.942	1.913	1.886	1.859	1.833	1.808	1.783	1.759	1.736	1.626
3	2.941	2.884	2.829	2.775	2.723	2.673	2.624	2.577	2.531	2.487	2.283
4	3.902	3.808	3.717	3.630	3.546	3.465	3.387	3.312	3.240	3.170	2.855
5	4.853	4.713	4.580	4.452	4.329	4.212	4.100	3.993	3.890	3.791	3.352
6	5.795	5.601	5.417	5.242	5.076	4.917	4.767	4.623	4.486	4.355	3.784
7	6.728	6.472	6.230	6.002	5.786	5.582	5.389	5.206	5.033	4.868	4.160
8	7.652	7.325	7.020	6.733	6.463	6.210	5.971	5.747	5.535	5.335	4.487
9	8.566	8.162	7.786	7.435	7.108	6.802	6.515	6.247	5.995	5.759	4.772
10	9.471	8.983	8.530	8.111	7.722	7.360	7.024	6.710	6.418	6.145	5.019
11	10.368	9.787	9.253	8.760	8.306	7.887	7.499	7.139	6.805	6.495	5.234
12	11.255	10.575	9.954	9.385	8.863	8.384	7.943	7.536	7.161	6.814	5.421
13	12.134	11.348	10.635	9.986	9.394	8.853	8.358	7.904	7.487	7.103	5.583
14	13.004	12.106	11.296	10.563	9.899	9.295	8.745	8.244	7.786	7.367	5.724
15	13.865	12.849	11.938	11.118	10.380	9.712	9.108	8.559	8.061	7.606	5.847
16	14.718	13.578	12.561	11.652	10.838	10.106	9.447	8.851	8.313	7.824	5.954
17	15.562	14.292	13.166	12.166	11.274	10.477	9.763	9.122	8.544	8.022	6.047
18	16.398	14.992	13.754	12.659	11.690	10.828	10.059	9.372	8.756	8.201	6.128
19	17.226	15.678	14.324	13.134	12.085	11.158	10.336	9.604	8.950	8.365	6.198
20	18.046	16.351	14.877	13.590	12.462	11.470	10.594	9.818	9.129	8.514	6.259
25	22.023	19.523	17.413	15.622	14.094	12.783	11.654	10.675	9.823	9.077	6.464
30	25.808	22.396	19.600	17.292	15.372	13.765	12.409	11.258	10.274	9.427	6.566

2   (Using Table B.1.) At what interest rate, approximately, would $1000 to be received in the future equal $700 today, in each of the following cases:

   A.   The payment will be received in 18 years
   B.   The payment will be received in 6 years
   C.   The payment will be received in 9 years

3   (Using Table B.1.) How much would you have to receive, in each case, to have a present value of $500 today?

   A.   After 6 years, with an interest rate of 4%
   B.   After 10 years, with an interest rate of 6%
   C.   After 20 years, with an interest rate of 1%

4   (Using Table B.2.) What is the value today of a $600 annuity of:

   A.   5 years, with a 3% interest rate?
   B.   10 years, with a 4% interest rate?
   C.   20 years, with a 4% interest rate?
   D.   30 years, with a 4% interest rate?

5   (Using Table B.2.) This is a pension problem. Assume that someone is planning retirement. They think they will be able to have savings equal to $1,000,000 at a retirement age of 65. They plan to take this money out, one payment at the end of each year, for some period of time. Your task is to figure out the amount of the yearly payment under each of the following assumptions:

   A.   They will live 15 years, and the interest rate is 6%
   B.   They will live 15 years, and the interest rate is 2%
   C.   They will live 25 years, and the interest rate is 6%
   D.   They will live 25 years, and the interest rate is 2%

   Comment on the effects of changed assumptions of both the life assumption and the interest rate assumption on the annual payments.

6   (Using Table B.2.) This is a somewhat different type of pension problem than the previous one. Companies need to value the amount of their pension obligations using present value. Assume that a company has made pension promises, which it believes will require it to make yearly annual payments of $10 million for each of the next 20 years. Compute the present value of this obligation under each of the following assumptions:

   A.   Interest rates are 2%
   B.   Interest rates are 4%
   C.   Interest rates are 6%
   D.   Interest rates are 8%

   Comment on the impact of changed interest rate assumptions on the size of the recorded liability.

Note

1   To find the total value of the bond, including the ending principal payment, we would also separately find the present value of the face value of the bond, using Table Appendix B.1. The total present value of the bond would equal the present value of the interest payments plus the present value of the ending principal payment.

Index

Page numbers in *italics* refer to tables.
Page numbers in **bold** font refer to boxes.